REA

SC

W9-CLD-361

Encyclopedia of American
religions, religious
American religious creeds

AMERICAN
RELIGIOUS

AMERICAN RELIGIOUS CREEDS

Volume I

Old Catholicism
Orthodoxy
Lutheranism
Reformed
Methodism
Twentieth-Century Holiness
—and many others

Volume II

Pentecostalism
Black Trinitarianism
German Mennonites
Primitive Baptists
Quakerism
Fundamentalism
British Israelism
—and many others

Volume III

Liberalism
Mail Order Churches
Mormonism
Christian Science
Spiritualism
Theosophy
Judaism
Islam
Hinduism
—and many others

AMERICAN RELIGIOUS CREEDS

VOLUME I

J. GORDON MELTON, EDITOR

Triumph™ Books
New York, New York

TRIUMPH BOOKS EDITION 1991
An Imprint of Gleneida Publishing Group, Inc.

This edition published by special arrangement with
Gale Research Inc.

Library of Congress Cataloging-in-Publication Data

Encyclopedia of American religions, religious creeds.
  American religious creeds : an essential compendium of more than
450 statements of belief and doctrine / J. Gordon Melton, editor.
    p.   cm.
  Reprint. Originally published: The Encyclopedia of American
religions, religious creeds. Detroit, Mich. : Gale Research Co.,
1988.
  Includes indexes.
  ISBN 0-8007-3014-3 (v. 1). — ISBN 0-8007-3015-1 (v. 2). — ISBN
0-8007-3016-X (v. 3)
  1. Creeds—Encyclopedias. 2. United States—Religion—1960—
Encyclopedias. I. Melton, J. Gordon. II. Title.
BL427.E52 1991
291.2′0973—dc20   90-47872
                                                                  CIP

Acknowledgments

Grateful acknowledgment is due to the
following publishers for use of their material.

"Account of Our Religion, Doctrine and Faith [Hutterite Brethren]." Reprinted from *Baptist Confessions of Faith*, edited by William L. Lumpkin, copyright © 1959 by Judson Press.

"Affirmations for Humanistic Jews [Sherwin T. Wine, Society for Humanistic Judaism]." Reprinted from *Judaism Beyond God: A Radical New Way to Be Jewish* by Sherwin T. Wine (copyright © 1985 by Sherwin T. Wine; reprinted by permission of the Society for Humanistic Judaism, 28611 W. Twelve Mile Rd., Farmington Hills, Mich. 48334), Society for Humanistic Judaism, 1985, p. 244.

Confessions [of the General Church of the New Jerusalem]. Reprinted from *Liturgy and Hymnal for the Use of the General Church of the New Jerusalem* (copyright 1916, 1921, 1939, and 1966 by the General Church of the New Jerusalem; reprinted by permission of the publisher), General Church of the New Jerusalem, 1966, pp. 217–20.

Creed of the Church of Scientology © 1954 L. Ron Hubbard. All Rights Reserved. Grateful acknowledgment is made to L. Ron Hubbard Library for permission to reprint a selection from the copyrighted works of L. Ron Hubbard.

"Dogma" and "Doctrine [Church of Seven Arrows]." Reprinted from *Shaman's Notes 2: Structure of Complete Belief-Systems* (copyright 1985 by Church of Seven Arrows; reprinted by permission of the publisher), Church of Seven Arrows, 1985, pp. 14–26.

"I Believe [Rabbi Joseph H. Gelberman, Little Synagogue]." Reprinted from *To Be . . . Fully Alive: A Collection of Essays for Life Enhancement on the Spiritual and Psychological Potential of Man* by Dr. Joseph H. Gelberman (copyright © 1983 by Dr. Joseph H. Gelberman; reprinted by permission of the publisher), Coleman Graphics, 1983, pp. xxiii-xxv.

"Our Message [Family of Love (Children of God)]." Reprinted from *The Basic Mo Letters* by Moses David (© Children of God, 1976), Children of God, 1976, pp. 27–31.

"Principles of Miracles." Reprinted from *A Course in Miracles* (copyright © 1975 by the Foundation for Inner Peace; reprinted by permission of the publisher), Foundation for Inner Peace, 1975, pp. 1–4.

"Statement of Principles" and "Affirmations of the Ethical Movement [American Ethical Union]." Reprinted from *Ethical Perspectives: Statements of the Ethical Culture Movement* (© 1972 New York Society for Ethical Culture; reprinted by permission of the publisher), New York Society for Ethical Culture, 1972.

"The Theological Declaration of Barmen." Reprinted from *The Church's Confession Under Hitler* by Arthur C. Cochrane, Westminster Press, 1962, pp. 237–42.

Contents

AMERICAN RELIGIOUS CREEDS—VOLUME I

Contents

ix

Introduction

The Encyclopedia of American Religions provided the first comprehensive study of religious and spiritual groups in the United States since the U.S. Census Bureau's last edition of *Religious Bodies* (1936), *American Religious Creeds* represents the first comprehensive compilation of the creeds, confessions, and statements of belief of America's religious groups in over a century. *American Religious Creeds* presents more than 450 creedal texts, covering not only Christian churches, but also the hundreds of Jewish, Islamic, Buddhist, Hindu, and other traditions possessing a following in the United States and Canada. In addition, historical notes and comments are provided to help researchers, librarians, students, and other information seekers understand the context in which creeds were written, revised, or discarded.

Authentic Text Used for All Creeds

The texts of the religious creeds presented in this volume are in their authentic form, although obvious typographical errors have been corrected. The authentic wording, grammar, and punctuation of each statement remains intact. In some cases, a creed's format was altered slightly for stylistic consistency and clarity. No attempt was made to introduce foreign material or explanatory notes into the body of the creed's text. Where alternate readings of a statement's text have been available, the editor chose an English language text currently in use by the church. Further, no attempt has been made to provide theological exposition, detailed textual analysis, or variant readings of a text, except in those few cases in which contemporary Christian churches disagree over the exact wording of the older creeds.

Types of Creeds and Statements Covered

Creeds are formal statements of belief to which members of a church are expected to give their intellectual assent. The writing of religious creeds is primarily an activity of Christian churches. At the same time, some other churches publish less rigid statements of belief reflecting a consensus of church teachings, while recognizing some variance of belief among members (and even leaders). A number of religious groups publish statements with an understanding that such beliefs are entirely secondary in the life of the group; emphasis is placed more upon piety, religious experience, liturgy, behavior (ethics), or membership in an ethnic group. On the other hand, some churches are strictly anti-creedal. Nevertheless, even the most anti-creedal and experience-oriented groups usually have a small body of assumed intellectual content (a system of beliefs that can be put into words) and, on occasion, official group statements are written for members' use. Such statements are considered to fall within the scope of this work.

Each creedal statement presented in this volume is acknowledged by at least one existing church or religious group described in the second edition of *The Encyclopedia of American Religions* (or its supplement). While the latter contains 1,550 entries, this work contains over 450. This difference is due to several factors. First, many creedal statements serve a variety of individual churches. For example, the Nicene Creed is the basic statement of faith for all Eastern Orthodox groups; divisions in this tradition have been based on nondoctrinal issues such as ethnicity, language, and political allegiances. Second, some groups simply have no summary statement of belief. The Plymouth Brethen groups, for example, are noncreedal, and many Hindu and Buddhist groups are centered more on experience than doctrine. Finally, some groups' statements are not listed because the editor, after repeated attempts, could not locate those creeds.

Contemporary Focus

Unlike previous collections, *American Religious Creeds* seeks to maintain a contemporary focus by presenting primarily creeds currently acknowledged by those religious groups operating in the United States and Canada. This volume makes no attempt to gather creedal statements from the various religious traditions, especially the older Christian families and, therefore, it is not intended to replace previously published works on Christian creeds, such as Philip Schaff's 1877 compilation, *The Creeds of Christendom* (Harper & Brothers, 1877); *Creeds of the Churches* (John H. Leith, editor; Doubleday, 1963); Arthur C. Cochrane's *Reformed Confessions of the 16th Century* (Westminster, 1966); Williston Walker's *Creeds and Platforms of Congregationalism* (Pilgrim, 1969); and William L. Lumpkin's *Baptist Confessions of Faith* (Judson, 1959).

Religious statements for *American Religious Creeds* were compiled from a variety of sources located in the files of the Institute for the Study of American Religion, including sources gathered over the years directly from the religious groups. Other material was obtained through mailings during the compilation of material for production of the most recent edition of *The Encyclopedia of American Religions*.

Contents and Arrangement

American Religious Creeds comprises 23 chapters organized into three volumes. The first chapter covers the four ancient Christian creeds (acknowledged and used by a majority of existing Christian groups and not associated with one in particular). The remaining chapters cover the statements of the individual churches, religious bodies, and spiritual groups that constitute the major religious families operating in the United States and Canada. Material within each chapter is arranged alphabetically by name of religious group or church, not by name of creed. Some material has been rearranged to highlight those creeds and confessions serving an entire religious family or group of churches. In addition, statements that partially define religious families or subfamilies are placed at the beginning of the appropriate chapter or subchapter. (See the detailed contents pages preceding this Introduction for an overview of the arrangement of each of the chapters in this volume.)

Creeds presented in *American Religious Creeds* contain the following elements:

Creed Title. The actual or descriptive title, followed by the name of the primary group related to the statement. (Where no formal title was given, a descriptive title was assigned.) Names of primary religious groups not contained in the creed's formal title are added parenthetically. (Other religious groups that acknowledge the particular statement are mentioned in the notes following the text.)

Text of Religious Creed. The full text of the creed in its authentic form.

Notes. These appear in italic type following the text of individual creeds. When applicable, these remarks provide data about the origin of the creed, call attention to particular ideas and emphases covered (or, in some cases, omitted) by the text, discuss variant readings of the text as used by different churches, and point out relationships to other religious statements. Also mentioned here are other religious groups that acknowledge the particular creed.

Name and Keyword Index Provided

To facilitate access to the material, *American Religious Creeds* contains a Creed/Organization Name and Keyword Index. This index lists, in a single alphabetic sequence, full titles of all the creeds presented in the volume as well as the names of all the religious traditions and individual churches mentioned in the text and notes. In addition, creed title and church name citations also appear in the index rotated by key word in title/name. Creed names appear in italic type to distinguish them from religious organizations. Citations refer users to the volume and page where the indexed creed or religious group appears.

Institute for the Study of American Religion

The Institute for the Study of American Religion was founded in 1969 for the purpose of researching and disseminating information about the numerous religious groups in the United States. More recently, the Institute's scope has been expanded to include religious groups in Canada, making it the only research facility of its kind to cover so broad a range of activity. After being located for many years in Evanston, Illinois, the Institute moved to Santa Barbara, California, in 1985. At that time, its collection of more than 25,000 books and its extensive files were donated to the Special Collections department of the library of the University of California—Santa Barbara.

Suggestions Are Welcome

Users of this volume with inquiries, additional information, corrections of inadvertent errors, or other suggestions for improvements are invited to write the Institute in care of its director. The Institute is particularly interested in obtaining copies of statements missing from this volume for inclusion in future editions.

Dr. J. Gordon Melton
Institute for the Study of American Religion
Box 90709
Santa Barbara, CA 93190-0709

AMERICAN RELIGIOUS CREEDS

VOLUME I

Chapter 1

Ancient Creeds of the Christian Church

THE APOSTLES' CREED

I believe in God the Father Almighty, Maker of heaven and earth. And in Jesus Christ His only Son, our Lord; Who was conceived by the Holy Ghost, Born of the Virgin Mary; Suffered under Pontius Pilate, Was crucified, dead, and buried; He descended into hell; The third day He rose again from the dead; He ascended into heaven, And sitteth on the right hand of God the Father Almighty; From thence He shall come to judge the quick and the dead.

I believe in the Holy Ghost; The holy Catholic Church, the Communion of Saints; The Forgiveness of sins; The Resurrection of the body; And the Life everlasting. Amen.

Notes: *The most widely accepted summary statement of the Christian faith is the Apostles' Creed. Derived from earlier statements, some dating from the beginning of the second century C.E., the present text was standardized by the eighth century. Some churches, most especially the Roman Catholic Church, have also formally and specifically named the Apostles' Creed as an official doctrinal statement, though almost all mainline Christian churches would adhere to its affirmations regardless of any formal denominational recognition. The creed commonly appears as an integral part of the standard orders of worship of many Protestant and Free Church denominations, and it is repeated weekly by worshippers much like the Lord's Prayer.*

Within the Protestant and Free Church liturgies, numerous variations of the text occur. Most reflect an attempt to counter any misunderstanding of the meaning of the phrase "holy Catholic Church." In order to underscore the belief that the Roman Catholic Church is not the object of belief, Protestants have substituted the phrase "holy Christian Church," (common to Lutherans) or "holy universal church" (used by many Free Churches). Occasionally, even where the original phrase is kept, an explanatory footnote is added.

Many of the church bodies that have emerged in the last two hundred years, particularly those growing out of the Methodist movement, have entirely dropped the phrase affirming that Christ "descended into hell." Such churches have found it confusing for members who do not understand

the difference between hell as "hades" (the abode of the dead in Hebrew thought) and hell as the place of final judgment and torment.

Finally, there is wide variation in the use of "Holy Spirit" as opposed to "Holy Ghost," even within denominational traditions. Confusion caused by the modern use of the term "ghost" to describe the shadowy apparitions of the dead has led to the adoption of a term felt to be more in keeping with the intent of the affirmation.

*   *   *.

THE NICENE CREED

I Believe in one God, the Father Almighty, Maker of heaven and earth, And of all things visible and invisible.

And in one Lord Jesus Christ, the Only-begotten Son of God, Begotten of His Father before all worlds, God of God, Light of Light, Very God of very God, Begotten, not made, Being of one substance with the Father, By Whom all things were made; Who, for us men, and for our salvation, came down from heaven, And was incarnate by the Holy Ghost of the Virgin Mary, And was made man; And was crucified also for us under Pontius Pilate. He suffered and was buried; and the third day He rose again, according to the Scriptures; And ascended into heaven, And sitteth on the right hand of the Father; And He shall come again with glory to judge both the quick and the dead; Whose kingdom shall have no end.

And I believe in the Holy Ghost, The Lord and Giver of Life, Who proceedeth from the Father and the Son, Who with the Father and the Son together is worshipped and glorified, Who spake by the Prophets. And I believe one holy Christian and Apostolic Church. I acknowledge one Baptism for the remission of sins; And I look for the Resurrection of the dead; And the Life of the world to come. Amen.

Notes: *During the fourth and fifth centuries, the Christian Church went through one of its most important eras theologically, and in the process hammered out what has become the standard orthodox position on the questions of God, Christ, and the nature of the Church. During this*

1

THE NICENE CREED (continued)

process, a variety of creeds were developed. The most important, because of its gaining almost universal acceptance among the major Christian groupings, was the Nicene Creed. It was first promulgated by the Council of Nicea in 325 C.E. and later expanded by the Council at Constantinople in 381. It became the standard creed of both the Eastern and Western Churches during the early middle ages and is integral to their liturgies. The creed is considered the unitive statement of faith by the organizationally separate Eastern Orthodox bodies. Like the Apostles' Creed, the Nicene Creed is formally recognized as a doctrinal standard by some Protestant bodies and informally recognized by most others. For example, it is printed as an optional confession of faith to be used in worship services in both the Hymnal *and the* Book of Worship *of the United Methodist Church.*

There is only one major variation in the text of the Nicene Creed. A theological difference between the Eastern and Western Churches at the time of the Great Schism of 1054 underlies the Roman Catholic Church's addition of the so-called "filioque clause," which affirmed that, within the mystery of the Godhead, the Holy Spirit proceeded from both the Father and the Son, not just the Father. Generally, churches deriving from the Roman Catholic Church have kept the clause in their reprinting of the creed. During the nineteenth century, the filioque (i.e., Latin for "and the Son") clause became a major item of discussion for the Old Catholics.

*   *   *

THE CHALCEDONIAN FORMULA

Following the holy fathers, we all unanimously teach that one and same Son, our Lord Jesus Christ, is to be confessed:

Perfect in Deity and perfect in Humanity,
Truly God and truly Man,
Of a *rational soul* and body,
Consubstantial with the Father according to his Deity,
Consubstantial with us according to his Humanity,
Like us in all respects, apart from sin;
Before the ages begotten of the Father according to his
   Deity,
And in these last days for us and for our salvation was
   born of the Virgin Mary, *the Mother of God
   [Theotokos]* according to his Humanity,
One and the same Christ, Son, Lord, only-begotten,
To be acknowledged in Two Natures
   without confusion or change
   without division or separation;
The difference of the Natures being by no means removed
   by the union,
but rather the property of each Nature being preserved
   and concurring in one Person and one Subsistence,
Not parted or divided into two Persons,
but one and the same Son and Only-begotten, God the
   Word, the Lord Jesus Christ;
According as at first the prophets, then the Lord Jesus
   Christ himself, taught us concerning him,
And as the Creed of the fathers has handed down to us.

Notes: *Largely confined to theological textbooks today, the Chalcedonian Formula promulgated in 451 C.E. represents the culmination of the major controversies that occupied the Christian Church leaders during the early centuries. It defined the orthodox solution to the problems of the Trinity, the dual nature of Jesus Christ, and the role of the Holy Spirit. The importance of its determinative theological role cannot be underestimated, though its popularity for liturgical use has never approached that of the Nicene Creed.*

Because the Chalcedonian Formula has not been utilized as a liturgical confession and the Greek words used in it continue to provoke theological discussions, no standard accepted English text exists, such as exist for the Apostles' and the Nicene Creeds. The formula's several translations vary from extremely literal to free flowing and interpretive. The text presented here tends toward the literal. Notice should be taken of the formula's affirmation of Mary as "theotokos" [mother of God], an implication of Jesus's divinity that had significant influence on the latter development of understanding the Virgin Mary in the life of the Church.

The Apostles' Creed, the Nicene Creed, and the Chalcedonian Formula were by no means the only creeds of the early church. They are the ones that continue to have the most direct effect upon contemporary church bodies by their use and theological impact.

*   *   *

THE CREED OF ATHANASIUS (*SYMBOLUM QUICUNQUE*)

1.   Whosoever will be saved, before all things it is necessary that he hold the Catholic [true Christian] faith,

2.   Which Faith except every one do keep whole and undefiled, without doubt he shall perish everlastingly.

3.   And the Catholic [true Christian] faith is this: that we worship one God in Trinity, and Trinity in Unity;

4.   Neither confounding the Persons; nor dividing the Substance.

5.   For there is one Person of the Father, another of the Son, and another of the Holy Ghost.

6.   But the Godhead of the Father, of the Son, and of the Holy Ghost, is all one: the Glory Equal, the Majesty Coeternal.

7.   Such as the Father is, such is the Son: and such is the Holy Ghost.

8.   The Father uncreate, the Son uncreate: and the Holy Ghost uncreate.

9.   The Father incomprehensible, the Son incomprehensible and the Holy Ghost incomprehensible.

10.   The Father eternal, the Son eternal: and the Holy Ghost eternal.

11.   And yet they are not three Eternals: but one Eternal.

12. As there are not three uncreated, nor three incomprehensibles: but one uncreated and one incomprehensible.

13. So likewise the Father is Almighty, the Son Almighty: and the Holy Ghost Almighty.

14. And yet they are not three Almighties: but one Almighty.

15. So the Father is God, the Son is God: and the Holy Ghost is God.

16. And yet they are not three Gods: but one God.

17. So likewise the Father is Lord, the Son Lord: and the Holy Ghost Lord.

18. And yet not three Lords: but one Lord.

19. For like as we are compelled by the Christian verity: to acknowledge every Person by himself to be God and Lord; So are we forbidden by the Catholic [Christian] Religion: to say, There be three Gods, or three Lords.

20. The Father is made of none: neither created nor begotten.

21. The Son is of the Father alone: not made, nor created, but begotten.

22. The Holy Ghost is of the Father, and of the Son; neither made, nor created, nor begotten, but proceeding.

23. So there is one Father, not three Fathers; one Son, not three Sons; one Holy Ghost, not three Holy Ghosts.

24. And in this Trinity none is before, or after other: none is greater, or less than another;

25. But the whole three Persons are coeternal together, and coequal: So that in all things, as is aforesaid: the Unity in Trinity, and the Trinity in Unity is to be worshipped.

26. He therefore that will be saved must thus think of the Trinity.

27. Furthermore, it is necessary to Everlasting Salvation; that he also believe rightly the Incarnation of our Lord Jesus Christ.

28. For the right Faith is, that we believe and confess: that our Lord Jesus Christ, the Son of God, is God and Man;

29. God, of the Substance of the Father begotten before the worlds: and Man of the Substance of his mother, born in the world;

30. Perfect God, and perfect Man: of a reasonable soul and human flesh subsisting.

31. Equal to the Father, as touching his Godhead: and inferior to the Father, as touching his Manhood.

32. Who although he be God and Man: yet he is not two, but one Christ;

33. One; not by conversion of the Godhead into flesh: but by taking the Manhood into God;

34. One altogether; not by confusion of Substance: but by Unity of Person.

35. For as the reasonable soul and flesh is one man: so God and Man is one Christ;

36. Who suffered for our salvation: descended into hell, rose again the third day from the dead.

37. He ascended into heaven; he sitteth on the right hand of the Father, God Almighty: from whence he shall come to judge the quick and the dead.

38. At whose coming all men shall rise again with their bodies: and shall give account for their own works.

39. And they that have done good shall go into life everlasting: and they that have done evil into everlasting fire.

40. This is the Catholic [true Christian] faith: which except a man believe faithfully, he cannot be saved.

Notes: *Although now thought to have been written sometime between the fourth and eighth centuries, this creed was for centuries ascribed to Athanasius (299?-373 C.E.), the fourth-century bishop who championed what became the orthodox Christian position on the nature of Christ. Even though the creed was never officially accepted by a church council (resulting in a variety of texts with different renderings, rather than one standard text), it became a widely accepted church document. Rendered into liturgical form, it was chanted in both the Roman Catholic Church and Church of England several times per year.*

The creed has lost popularity in the contemporary era, although it is still accepted and used in the Roman Catholic Church. The Lutherans included the creed in their doctrinal material as part of their broader case for catholic orthodoxy. The text reproduced here is taken from the Lutheran Book of Concord. The creed is also found in the official materials of other churches, such as the Psalter Hymnal of the Christian Reformed Church. The Protestant Episcopal Church deleted the creed from its prayer book in 1785.

The words in brackets have been inserted into the text by the Lutheran translators to explain their understanding of the word "catholic," which differs considerably from the common meaning of Roman Catholic.

Chapter 2
Western Liturgical Family

Roman Catholic Church

THE PROFESSION OF FAITH OF THE ROMAN CATHOLIC CHURCH

I, N., with firm faith believe and profess each and every article contained in the symbol of faith which the Holy Roman Church uses; namely: I believe in one God, the Father Almighty, maker of heaven and earth and of all things visible and invisible; and in one Lord Jesus Christ the only-begotten Son of God, born of the Father before all ages; God from God, light from light, true God from true God; begotten not made, of one substance with the Father; through whom all things were made; who for us men and for our salvation came down from heaven and was made incarnate by the Holy Spirit of the Virgin Mary and was made man. He was crucified also for us under Pontius Pilate, died and was buried; and he rose again the third day according to the Scriptures, and ascended into heaven; He sits at the right hand of the Father, and He will come again in glory to judge the living and the dead, and of His kingdom there will be no end. And I believe in the Holy Spirit, the Lord, and giver of life, who proceeds from the Father and the Son; who equally with the Father and the Son is adored and glorified; who spoke through the prophets. And I believe that there is one, holy, catholic, and apostolic Church. I confess one baptism for the remission of sins; and I hope for the resurrection of the dead, and the life of the world to come. Amen.

I resolutely accept and embrace the apostolic and ecclesiastical traditions and other practices and regulations of that same Church. In like manner I accept Sacred Scripture according to the meaning which has been held by the Holy Mother Church and which she now holds. It is her prerogative to pass judgment on the true meaning and interpretation of Sacred Scripture. And I will never accept or interpret it in a manner different from the unanimous agreement of the Fathers.

I also truly acknowledge that there are truly and properly seven sacraments of the New Law, instituted by Jesus Christ, our Lord, and that they are necessary for the salvation of the human race, although it is not necessary for each individual to receive them all. I acknowledge that the seven sacraments are: baptism, confirmation, Eucharist, penance, extreme unction, holy orders, and matrimony; and that they confer grace; and that of the seven, baptism, confirmation, and holy orders cannot be repeated without commiting a sacrilege. I also accept and acknowledge the customary and approved rites of the Catholic Church in the solemn administration of these sacraments. I accept and embrace each and every article on original sin and justification declared and defined in the most holy Council of Trent.

I likewise profess that in the Mass a true, proper, and propitiatory sacrifice is offered to God on behalf of the living and the dead, and that the Body and the Blood, together with the soul and the divinity, of our Lord Jesus Christ is truly, really, and substantially present in the most holy sacrament of the Eucharist, and that there is a change of the whole substance of the bread into the Body, and of the whole substance of the wine into Blood; and this change the Catholic Church calls transubstantiation. I also profess that the whole and entire Christ and a true sacrament is received under each separate species.

I firmly hold that there is a purgatory and that the souls detained there are helped by the prayers of the faithful. I likewise hold that the saints reigning together with Christ should be honored and invoked, that they offer prayers to God on our behalf, and that their relics should be venerated. I firmly assert that the images of Christ, of the Mother of God ever Virgin, and of the other saints should be owned and kept, and that due honor and veneration should be given to them. I affirm that the power of indulgences was left in the keeping of the Church by Christ, and that the use of indulgences is very beneficial to Christians.

I acknowledge the holy, catholic, and apostolic Roman Church as the Mother and teacher of all Churches; and I promise and swear true obedience to the Roman Pontiff, vicar of Christ, and the successor of Blessed Peter, Prince of the Apostles.

I unhesitatingly accept and profess all the doctrines (especially those concerning the primacy of the Roman Pontiff and his infallible teaching authority) handed down,

THE PROFESSION OF FAITH OF THE ROMAN CATHOLIC CHURCH (continued)

defined, and explained by the sacred canons and ecumenical councils, and especially those of this most holy Council of Trent (and by the ecumenical Vatican Council). At the same time, I condemn, reject, and anathematize everything that is contrary to those propositions, and all heresies without exception that have been condemned, rejected and anathematized by the Church. I, N., promise, vow, and swear that, with God's help, I shall most constantly hold and profess this true Catholic faith, outside which no one can be saved and which I now freely profess and truly hold. With the help of God I shall profess it whole and unblemished to my dying breath; and, to the best of my ability, I shall see to it that my subjects or those entrusted to me by virtue of my office, hold it, teach it and preach it. So help me God and His holy Gospel.

Notes: *The Roman Catholic Church accepts the four major ancient creeds as its doctrinal standard but has made a number of additional doctrinal commitments over the centuries. Possibly the most important statement made in the years since the standardization of the text of the Nicene Creed in the eleventh century was the Profession of Faith issued by Pope Paul IV in 1564. The profession summarized Catholic doctrine, and over the years its public confession has been required of converts and of members in the process of attaining certain high offices. The text has been modified on several occasions, most importantly in 1877 by Pope Pius IX to include the clause on papal infallibility. In the decades since Vatican II, use of the profession has diminished. New converts now go through a service receiving them into the church that includes the Nicene Creed. However, the profession remains a valid summary of Roman Catholic doctrinal distinctives.*

*   *   *

Old Catholicism

THE FOURTEEN THESES OF THE OLD CATHOLIC UNION CONFERENCE, BONN, GERMANY, 1874

I.   We agree that the apocryphal or deutero-canonical books of the Old Testament are not of the same canonicity as the books contained in the Hebrew Canon.

II.   We agree that no translation of Holy Scripture can claim an authority superior to that of the original text.

III. We agree that the reading of Holy Scripture in the vulgar tongue can not be lawfully forbidden.

IV.   We agree that, in general, it is more fitting, and in accordance with the spirit of the Church, that the Liturgy should be in the tongue understood by the people.

V.   We agree that Faith working by Love, not Faith without Love, is the means and condition of Man's justification before God.

VI.   Salvation cannot be merited by "merit of condignity," because there is no proportion between the infinite worth of salvation promised by God and the finite worth of man's works.

VII. We agree that the doctrine of "opera supererogationis" and of a "thesaurus meritorum sanctorum," i.e., that the overflowing merits of the Saints can be transferred to others, either by the rulers of the Church, or by the authors of the good works themselves, is untenable.

VIII. 1. We acknowledge that the number of sacraments was fixed at seven, first in the twelfth century, and then was received into the general teaching of the Church, not as a tradition coming down from the Apostles or from the earliest times, but as the result of theological speculation.

2. Catholic theologians acknowledge, and we acknowledge with them, that Baptism and the Eucharist are "principalia, praecipus, eximia salutis nostrae sacramenta."

IX.   1. The Holy Scriptures being recognized as the primary rule of Faith, we agree that the genuine tradition, i.e. the unbroken transmission partly oral, partly in writing of the doctrine delivered by Christ and the Apostles is an authoritative source of teaching for all successive generations of Christians. This tradition is partly to be found in the consensus of the great ecclesiastical bodies standing in historical continuity with the primitive Church, partly to be gathered by scientific method from the written documents of all centuries.

2. We acknowledge that the Church of England, and the Churches derived through her, have maintained unbroken the Episcopal succession.

X.   We reject the new Roman doctrine of the Immaculate Conception of the Blessed Virgin Mary, as being contrary to the tradition of the first thirteen centuries, according to which Christ alone is conceived without sin.

XI.   We agree that the practice of confession of sins before the congregation or a Priest, together with the exercise of the power of the keys, has come down to us from the primitive Church, and that, purged from abuses and free from constraint, it should be preserved in the Church.

XII. We agree that "indulgences" can only refer to penalties actually imposed by the Church herself.

XIII. We acknowledge that the practice of the commemoration of the faithful departed, i.e. the calling down of a richer outpouring of Christ's grace upon them, has come down to us from the primitive Church, and is to be preserved in the Church.

XIV. 1. The Eucharistic celebration in the Church is not a continuous repetition or renewal of the propitiatory sacrifice offered once for ever by Christ upon the cross; but its sacrificial character consists in this, that it is the permanent memorial of it, and a representation and presentation on earth of that one oblation of Christ for the salvation of redeemed mankind, which according to the Epistle to the Hebrews (9:11,12), is continuously presented in heaven by Christ, who now appears in the presence of God for us (9:24).

2. While this is the character of the Eucharist in reference to the sacrifice of Christ, it is also a sacred feast, wherein the faithful, receiving the Body and Blood of our Lord, have communion one with another (I Cor. 10:17).

Notes: *As a result of the Roman Catholic Church's adoption of the doctrine of papal infallibility as dogma at the First Vatican Council in 1870, many members in continental Europe left the Roman jurisdiction and formed the Old Catholic Church. They felt that the Roman Catholic Church had departed from traditional Catholic faith. The Old Catholic position was spelled out in a series of documents: the so-called Fourteen Theses issued by the Old Catholic Union Conference of 1874; the statement on the filioque clause in the Nicene Creed issued in 1875; and The Declaration of Utrecht [Holland], issued in 1889. An English translation of the latter was made in 1930 and printed that year in the Report of the Lambeth Conference (Anglican). The Old Catholic Church and the Anglican Communion have enjoyed many years of cordial relationship, disturbed only by the recent ordination of women by several of the Anglican church bodies.*

* * *

THE OLD CATHOLIC AGREEMENT ON THE FILIOQUE CONTROVERSY, 1875

1. We agree in accepting the ecumenical symbols and the decisions in matters of faith of the ancient undivided Church.

2. We agree in acknowledging that the addition *Filioque* to the symbol did not take place in an ecclesiastically regular manner.

3. We give our unanimous assent to the presentation of the doctrine of the Holy Spirit as taught by the Fathers of the undivided Church.

   (1) We accept the teachings of St. John of Damascus concerning the Holy Spirit, as it is expressed in the following paragraphs, in the sense of the doctrine of the ancient undivided Church.

   (a) The Holy Spirit proceeds from the Father as the beginning, the cause, the fountain of the Godhead.

   (b) The Holy Spirit proceeds not from the Son, because in the Godhead there is only one beginning one cause, by which all that is in the Godhead is produced.

   (c) The Holy Spirit proceeds from the Father through the Son.

   (d) The Holy Spirit is the image of the Son (as the Son is the image of the Father), proceeding from the Father, and resting in the Son as the power shining forth from him.

   (e) The Holy Spirit is the personal production out of the Father, belonging to the Son, but not out

of the mouth of the Godhead which pronounces the Word.

   (f) The Holy Spirit forms the mediation between the Father and the Son, and is, through the Son, united with the Father.

4. We reject every representation and every form of expression in which is contained the acceptance of two principles, or beginnings, or causes, in the Trinity.

* * *

THE DECLARATION OF UTRECHT, 1889

1. We adhere faithfully to the Rule of Faith laid down by St. Vincent of Lérins in these terms: "Id teneamus, quod ubique, quod semper, quod ab omnibus creditum est; hoc est etenim vere proprieque catholicum". For this reason we persevere in professing the faith of the primitive Church, as formulated in the ecumenical symbols and specified precisely by the unanimously accepted decisions of the Ecumenical Councils held in the undivided Church of the first thousand years.

2. We therefore reject the decrees of the so-called Council of the Vatican, which were promulgated July 18, 1870, concerning the infallibility and the universal episcopate of the Bishop of Rome—decrees which are in contradiction with the faith of the ancient Church and which destroy its ancient canonical constitution by attributing to the Pope all the plenitude of ecclesiastical powers over all dioceses and over all the faithful. By denial of his primatial jurisdiction we do not wish to deny the historic primacy which several ecumenical councils and the Fathers of the ancient Church have attributed to the Bishop of Rome by recognizing him as the *Primus inter pares.*

3. We also reject the dogma of the Immaculate Conception promulgated by Pope Pius IX in 1854 in defiance of the Holy Scriptures and in contradiction with the tradition of the first centuries.

4. As for encyclicals published by the Bishops of Rome in recent times, for example, the Bulls "Unigenitus" and "Auctorem fidei," and the Syllabus of 1864, we reject them on all such points as are in contradiction with the doctrine of the primitive Church, and we do not recognize them as binding on the consciences of the faithful. We also renew the ancient protests of the Catholic Church of Holland against the errors of the Roman Curia, and against its attacks upon the rights of national churches.

5. We refuse to accept the decrees of the Council of Trent in matters of discipline, and as for the dogmatic decisions of that Council we accept them only so far as they are in harmony with the teaching of the primitive Church.

6. Considering that the Holy Eucharist has always been the true central point of Catholic worship, we consider it our duty to declare that we maintain with

THE DECLARATION OF UTRECHT, 1889 (continued)

perfect fidelity the ancient Catholic doctrine concerning the Sacrament of the Altar, by believing that we receive the Body and the Blood of our Saviour Jesus Christ under the species of bread and wine. The Eucharistic celebration in the Church is neither a continual repetition nor a renewal of the expiatory sacrifice which Jesus offered once for all upon the Cross; but it is a sacrifice because it is the perpetual commemoration of the sacrifice offered upon the Cross, and it is the act by which we represent upon earth and appropriate to ourselves the one offering which Jesus Christ makes in Heaven, according to the Epistle to the Hebrews, 9.11-12, for the salvation of redeemed humanity, by appearing for us in the presence of God (Heb. 9. 24). The character of the Holy Eucharist being thus understood, it is, at the same time, a sacrificial feast, by means of which the faithful, in receiving the Body and Blood of our Saviour, enter into communion with one another (I Cor. I. 17).

7. We hope that Catholic theologians, in maintaining the faith of the undivided Church, will succeed in establishing an agreement upon questions which have been controverted ever since the divisions which have arisen between the churches. We exhort the priests under our jurisdiction to teach, both by preaching and by the instruction of the young, especially the essential Christian truths professed by all the Christian confessions, to avoid, in discussing controverted doctrines, any violation of truth or charity, and in word and deed to set an example to the members of our churches in accordance with the spirit of Jesus Christ our Saviour.

8. By maintaining and professing faithfully the doctrine of Jesus Christ, by refusing to admit those errors which by the fault of men have crept into the Catholic Church, by laying aside the abuses in ecclesiastical matters, together with the worldly tendencies of the hierarchy, we believe that we shall be able to combat efficaciously the great evils of our day, which are unbelief and indifference in matters of religion.

*   *   *

STATEMENT OF UNION, 1911

1. THE WAY OF SALVATION. Eternal Salvation is promised to mankind only through merits of our Saviour Jesus Christ, and upon condition of obedience to the teaching of the Gospel, which requires Faith, Hope, and Charity, and the due observance of the ordinances of the Orthodox and Catholic Religion.

2. FAITH, HOPE, AND CHARITY. Faith is a virtue infused by God, whereby man accepts, and believes without doubting, whatever God has revealed in the Church concerning true Religion.

Hope is a virtue infused by God, and following upon Faith; by it man puts his entire trust and confidence in the goodness and mercy of God, through Jesus Christ, and looks for the fulfillment of the Divine promises made to those who obey the Gospel.

Charity is a virtue infused by God, and likewise consequent upon Faith, whereby man, loving God above all things for His own sake, and his neighbor as himself for God's sake, yields up his will to a joyful obedience to the revealed will of God in the Church.

3. THE CHURCH. God has established the Holy Catholic Church upon earth to be the pillar and ground of the revealed Truth; and has committed to her the guardianship of the holy Scriptures and of holy Tradition, and the power of binding and loosing.

4. THE CREED. The Catholic Church has set forth the principal Doctrines of the Christian Faith in twelve articles as follows:

    I. I believe in one God the Father Almighty, Creator of heaven and earth, and of all things visible and invisible;

    II. And in one Lord Jesus Christ, the only-begotten Son of God, begotten of the Father before all Ages, God of God, Light of Light, Very God of Very God, begotten, not made of one substance with the Father, by Whom all things were made;

    III. Who for us men and for our salvation came down from heaven, and was Incarnate by the Holy Ghost of the Virgin Mary, and was made Man;

    IV. And was crucified also for us under Pontius Pilate, He suffered and was buried;

    V. And the third day He rose again, according to the Scriptures;

    VI. And ascended into heaven, and sitteth on the right hand of the Father;

    VII. And He shall come again, with glory, to judge the living and the dead; Whose kingdom shall have no end;

    VIII. And I believe in the Holy Ghost, the Lord, and Giver of Life, Who proceedeth from the Father, Who with the Father and the Son together is worshipped and glorified, Who spoke by the Prophets;

    IX. And in One, Holy, Catholic, and Apostolic Church;

    X. I acknowledge one Baptism for the remission of sins;

    XI. And I look for the Resurrection of the dead;

    XII. And the Life in the world to come. Amen.

5. THE SACRAMENTS. The fundamental ordinances of the Gospel, instituted by Jesus Christ as special means of conveying Divine grace and influence to the souls of men, which are commonly called

Mysteries or Sacraments, are Seven in number, namely Baptism, Confirmation, the holy Eucharist, holy Orders, Matrimony, Penance, and Unction.

THUS: Baptism is the first Sacrament of the Gospel, administered by threefold immersion in, or affusion with, water with the word, "I baptize thee in the Name of the Father, and of the Son, and of the Holy Ghost." It admits the recipient into the Church, bestows upon him the forgiveness of sins, original and actual, through the Blood of Christ, and causes in him spiritual change called Regeneration. Without valid Baptism no other Sacrament can be validly received.

Confirmation or Chrism is a Sacrament in which the baptised person, on being anointed with Chrism consecrated by the Bishops of the Church, with the imposition of hands, receives the sevenfold gifts of the Holy Ghost to strengthen him in the grace which he received at Baptism, making him a strong and perfect Christian and a good soldier of Christ.

The holy Eucharist is a Sacrament in which, under the appearances of bread and wine, the real and actual Body and Blood of Christ are given and received for the remission of sins, the increase of Divine grace, and the reward of everlasting Life. After the prayer of Invocation of the Holy Ghost in the Liturgy, the bread and wine are entirely converted into the living Body and Blood of Christ by an actual change of being, to which change the philosophical terms of Transubstantiation and Transmutation are rightly applied. The celebration of this Mystery or Sacrament, commonly called the Mass, constitutes the chief act of Christian worship, being a sacrificial Memorial or re-Presentation of our Lord's death. It is not a repetition of the Sacrifice offered once for all upon Calvary, but is a perpetuation of that Sacrifice by the Church on earth, as our Lord also perpetually offers it in heaven. It is a true and propitiatory Sacrifice, which is offered alike for the living and for the departed.

Holy Orders is a Sacrament in which the Holy Ghost, through the laying-on of hands of the Bishops, consecrates and ordains the pastors and ministers chosen to serve in the Church, and imparts to them special grace to administer the Sacraments, to forgive sins, and to feed the flock of Christ.

Matrimony is a Sacrament in which the voluntary union of husband and wife is sanctified to become an image of the union between Christ and His Church; and grace is imparted to them to fulfill the duties of their estate and its great responsibilities both of each other and to their children.

Penance is a Sacrament in which the Holy Ghost bestows the forgiveness of sins, by the ministry of the priest, upon those who, having sinned after Baptism, confess their sins with true repentance, and grace is given to amend their lives thereafter.

Unction is a Sacrament in which the priests of the Church anoint the sick with oil, for the healing of the infirmities of their souls, and if it should please God, those of their bodies also.

The efficiancy of the Sacraments depends upon the promise and appointment of God; howbeit they benefit only those who receive them worthily with faith, and with due preparation and disposition of mind.

6. HOLY SCRIPTURE. The Scriptures are writings inspired by God, and given to the Church for her instruction and edification. The Church is therefore the custodian and the only Divinely appointed interpreter of holy Scripture.

7. TRADITION. The Apostolic and Ecclesiastical Traditions received from the seven General Councils and the early Fathers of the Church may not be rejected; but are to be received and obeyed as being both agreeable to holy Scripture and to that Authority with which Christ endowed His Church. Matters of discipline and ceremony do not rank on the same level with matters of Faith or Morals, but may be altered from time to time and from place to place by the Authority of the Church, according as the welfare and greater devotions of the faithful may be furthered thereby.

8. THE COMMUNION OF SAINTS. There is a Communion of Saints in the Providence of God, wherein the souls of righteous men of all ages are united with Christ in the bond of faith and love. Wherefore it is pleasing to God, and profitable to men, to honour the Saints and to invoke them in prayer; and also to pray for the faithful departed.

9. RELIGIOUS SYMBOLS. The relics and representations of Saints are worthy of honour, as are also all other religious emblems; that our minds may be encouraged to devotion and to imitation of the deeds of the just. Honour shown to such objects is purely relative, and in no way implies a confusion of the symbol with the thing signified.

10. RITE AND CEREMONIES. It is the duty of all Christians to join in the worship of the Church, especially in the holy Sacrifice of the Mass, in accordance with our Lord's express command; and to conform to the ceremonies prescribed by holy Tradition for the greater dignity of that Sacrifice and for the edification of the faithful.

11. THE MORAL LAW. All Christians are bound to observe the Moral Law contained in the Ten Commandments of the Old Testament, developed with greater strictness in the New, founded upon the law of nature and charity, and defining our duty to God and to man. The laws of the Church are also to be obeyed, as proceeding from that Authority which Christ has committed to her for the instruction and salvation of His people.

12. THE MONASTIC ESTATE. The monastic life, duly regulated according to the laws of the Church, is a salutary institution in strict accord with the holy Scriptures; and is full of profit to them who, after

being carefully tried and examined, make full proof of their calling thereto.

ORGANIC ARTICLES

1. HEAD OF THE CHURCH. The Foundation Head and Supreme Pastor and Bishop of the Church is our Lord Jesus Christ Himself, from Whom all Bishops and Pastors derive their spiritual powers and jurisdiction.

2. OBEDIENCE. By the law and institution of our Lord Jesus Christ in the Gospel, all Christians owe obedience and submission in spiritual things to them who have rule and authority within the Church.

3. MINISTERIAL AUTHORITY. Our Lord Jesus Christ did not commit rule and authority within the Church to all the faithful indiscriminately, but only to the Apostles and to their lawful successors in due order.

4. APOSTOLIC SUCCESSION. The only lawful successors of the Apostles are the Orthodox and Catholic Bishops, united by profession of the self-same Belief, participation in the same Sacraments, and mutual recognition and Intercommunion. The Bishops of the Church, being true successors of the Apostles, are by Divine right and appointment the rulers of the Church.

In virtue of this appointment, each individual Bishop is supreme and independent in that part of the Church which has been committed to his care, so long as he remains in Faith and Communion with the united company of Catholic Bishops, who cannot exclude any from the Church save only them who stray from the path of virtue or err in Faith.

By virtue of this same Divine appointment, the supreme Authority over the whole Church on earth belongs to the collective Orthodox and Catholic Episcopate. They alone form the highest tribunal in spiritual matters, from whose united judgment there can be no appeal; so that it is unlawful for any single Bishop, or any smaller group of Bishops apart from them, or for any secular power or state to usurp this authority, or for any individual Christian to substitute his own private judgement for that interpretation of Scripture or Authority which is approved by the Church.

5. CHURCH AUTHORITY. The collective body of the Orthodox Catholic Episcopate, united by profession of the Faith, by the Sacraments, and by mutual recognition and actual Inter-communion, is the source and depository of all order, authority and jurisdiction in the Church, and is the center of visible Catholic Unity; so that no Pope, Patriarch or Bishop, or any number of Bishops separated from this united body can possess any authority or jurisdiction whatsoever.

The authority of this collective body is equally binding, however it may be expressed: whether by a General Council or by the regular and ordinary consultation and agreement of the bishops themselves.

It is an act of schism to appeal from the known judgement of the Orthodox and Catholic Episcopate, however it may have been ascertained; or to appeal from any dogmatic decree of any General Council even though such appeal be to a future Council. For the Episcopate, being a continuation of the Apostolate, is clearly a Divine institution, and its authority is founded in Divine right. But General Councils are not of themselves of direct Divine appointment; and so the Episcopate having clearly the Scriptural promise of Divine guidance into all Truth, cannot be hampered in the exercise of its authority by the necessity of assembling a General Council, which may obviously be rendered impossible through natural circumstances.

There have been seven General Councils only, which are recognized by the Whole of Catholic Christendom, held respectively in Nicaea (A.D. 325), Constantinople (381), Ephesus (431), Chalcedon (451), Constantinople (553), Constantinople (680), and Nicaea (787). At no other Councils was the entire body of the Orthodox and Catholic Episcopate representatively assembled; and the decrees and pronouncements of no others must of themselves be accepted as binding upon the conscience of the faithful.

The Authority of the Church can never be in abeyance, even though a General Council cannot be assembled. It is equally to be submitted to and obeyed in whatever way it may be exercised, and although it may be exercised only through the ordinary administration of their respective jurisdictions by individual Bishops.

6. HIERARCHY. All Patriarchs, Archbishops, and Metropolitans (that is to say, all Bishops who exercise any authority over other Bishops) owe that authority solely to the appointment or general consent of the Orthodox and Catholic Episcopate; nor can they ever cease from owing obedience to the collective body of the Episcopate in all matters concerning Faith and Morals.

7. THE FIVE PATRIARCHATES. There are five Patriarchates, which ought to be united and form the supreme authority in the administration and government of the Holy Catholic Church. These are Jerusalem, Antioch, Rome, Alexandria, and Constantinople. Unfortunately, owing to disputes and differences on the one hand, and to the lust for power and supremacy and domination on the other; the Patriarchs are not at present in Communion; and the welfare of Christendom is jeopardized by their disedifying quarrels, which, we pray, may soon have an end.

Notes: *In England, the Old Catholic Church was founded by Arnold Harris Mathew. In 1911, Mathew was able to work out a doctrinal statement that led to the reception into communion of his jurisdiction by the Antiochian Orthodox Church in Lebanon under Archbishop Gerassimos Messar-*

ra. The Statement of Union has joined the three nineteenth-century European Old Catholic documents as an authoritative doctrinal summary for many Old Catholic jurisdictions.

In the United States, Old Catholicism has splintered into many small church jurisdictions. Most of these Old Catholic bodies adhere to the Declaration of Utrecht, at least informally, and most would accept all four statements—the Fourteen Theses, statement on the filioque clause, Declaration of Utrecht, and Statement of Union. However, the majority of Old Catholic bodies have published no doctrinal statement beyond the Apostles' or Nicene Creeds that appear in the text of the liturgy of the mass.

*   *   *

STATEMENT OF FAITH OF THE ARCHDIOCESE OF THE OLD CATHOLIC CHURCH OF AMERICA

Article I. HOLY TRADITION OF THE TRUE FAITH.

Section 1. We hold that Holy Tradition (Scripture) is the true and living Word of God, and that its interpretation is to be found in the Nicene Creed, the teachings of the Seven Holy Synods of the Church and in the teachings of the Holy Fathers of the Christian Faith.

Section 2. We believe God inspired all the writers of Scripture with objective fact, free from error, for our instruction.

Section 3. The Faith as written and handed down to us through the Prophets, Apostles and the Fathers unaltered, we hold fast without additions or subtractions.

Section 4. God's truths do not rely on our acceptance or our feelings. Holy Tradition (Scripture), the Nicene Creed, the teachings of the Seven Holy Synods and the teachings of the Fathers are unchanging in our ever-changing world.

Article II. THE NICENE CREED, THE SEVEN SYNODS AND THE TEACHINGS OF THE FATHERS.

Section 1. We believe that the Nicene Creed, the teachings of the Seven Holy Synods of the Church and the teachings of the Fathers to be the true interpretation of Scriptures and the Holy Faith taught by the inspiration of the Holy Spirit.

Section 2. We hold that our salvation rests upon this Faith in Christ alone. Those of other views are of another spirit and we count them not as Christian in any sense of the word.

Section 3. We hold that traditions of men (customs), although valid expressions of Faith, are not necessarily part of the Orthodox Catholic Faith. We also hold that those who teach them as necessary are guilty of idol worship. Faith in Christ as taught by the Prophets, Apostles and the Fathers alone is necessary.

Article III. THE MYSTERIES OF THE ORTHODOX CATHOLIC FAITH (SACRAMENTS).

Section 1. We believe that Christ God did institute seven holy Mysteries as a means of sharing in the life of the Holy Spirit. They are (i) Baptism; (ii) Communion; (iii) the Keys (Absolution or Penance); (iv) Chrismation (Confirmation or the Imparting of the Holy Spirit); (v) Marriage; (vi) Ordination (Bishop, Presbyter and Deacon); and (vii) the Sacrament of the Sick (Unction).

Section 2. We believe Baptism to be valid when administered according to Christ's command, as found in the Scripture: That is, in the Name of the Holy Trinity with water.

Section 3. We believe that the true body and the true blood of Christ to be present in the Holy Eucharist as taught by Holy Scripture and all the Holy Fathers of the true Faith. In this definition we neither add nor subtract. Christ's own words suffice: "This is My Body"; "This is My Blood". Christ's words are sufficient for our faith. Additional definitions only tend to confuse and mislead; and, we hold them to be of man-made origin.

Section 4. We hold Chrismation (Confirmation) to be divinely instituted and recorded in the Epistle of I John 2: 20-27, "You have an unction from the Holy One, and You have received of Him abiding in you."

Section 5. Matrimony was instituted by God Himself in the Garden of Eden and this state was blessed and reaffirmed by Christ God at the Wedding of Cana. It has as its purpose the perpetuation of the human race, companionship, submission to God's moral law and the Christian upbringing of children. All sexual relations outside of Holy Matrimony we do hold as contrary to the Divine Law of God.

Section 6. We believe and hold the Orders of the Ministry (Bishop, Presbyter and Deacon) to be of divine origin as found in Holy Scripture and necessary to God's Holy Church. Holy Scripture and the teachings of the Fathers tell us that those who minister in the Church should be called to their station in life to teach the Word of God and administer the Sacraments according to divine institution, by laying on of hands by a bishop who is the representative of Christ and His Church. A proper ordination never takes place without the affirmation of both clergy and laity, the body of Christ.

Section 7. We believe and hold that the mystery of Holy Penance is of divine origin as found in Holy Scripture. The power of the "keys" was instituted by Christ God for the forgiveness of sin and the comfort of the penitent.

Section 8. The Sacrament of the Sick (Unction) we hold to be of Apostolic origin as found in the Epistle of St. James, for the health and consolation of the sick, by the working power of the Holy Spirit.

Article IV. THE MONASTIC STATE OF LIFE.

Section 1. We believe the monastic life to be a holy expression and witness to the Christian life, although we do not believe it to be necessary to the Church's life and we do not hold the monastic state as equal to a Sacrament.

Section 2. When monastic life is freely chosen by an individual for the honor and glory of God and in witness to the Faith, then it is a useful and holy thing in the Church. For, virginity is only preserved by the working and power of the Holy Spirit and is only of value to the Church when it is lived for God's own purposes.

Section 3. Those who claim that Matrimony is a lesser state than that of a monk and who claim Matrimony an alternative to the state of a monastic are but glory-seekers and know not the correct teachings of the Scriptures and the Fathers. Each state of life in the Christian Faith is a witness and confession of a divine call from God. God's will and purpose must be the aim of each person seeking to live a holy life.

Article V. FAITH AND GOOD WORKS.

Section 1. We believe and hold it true that salvation is a free gift of Faith in Christ Jesus.

Section 2. We believe that good works are a necessary witness of true faith in Christ Jesus.

Section 3. We hold it to be heresy to teach that any or all the saints together could merit the forgiveness of even one sin against God.

Section 4. It is through the sufferings and death of Christ our Lord that our Salvation has been granted to us.

Section 5. Faith and Salvation in Jesus Christ are free gifts from God without any merit on our part.

Section 6. The true faith is to be found in the Holy Scriptures and its true interpretation is found in the teachings of the Seven Holy Synods, the Nicene Creed and the teachings of the Fathers.

Article VI. THE VIRGIN MOTHER OF GOD AND THE SAINTS.

Section 1. We believe the Virgin Mary to be the virgin mother of Christ God, the Incarnate Word of God as taught in the Nicene Creed.

Section 2. We believe Mary to have been ever a Virgin as taught by the Scriptures indirectly and taught by history and the teachings of the Fathers directly.

Section 3. We believe in the communion of Saints, the just who have their Salvation in Faith in Christ Jesus our Lord.

Section 4. We believe that the Saints here on earth and those in heaven pray for us. Yet, we reject the teaching that the saints merit favors or salvation for us. For, they pray to God through the merits of Christ our High Priest and our only Mediator between God and Man. True veneration of the Saints is to follow their way of life and a practice of their example.

Section 5. We reject that to ask the prayers of others, living or dead, is against the teachings of the Christ God. Rather it is an affirmation of Faith in the true nature of the Church, the Body of Christ.

Article VII. THE VENERATION OF ICONS (IMAGES).

Section 1. We believe that respect, veneration and praying before icons is a good and helpful means of calling to mind Christ God and His Saints.

Section 2. Those who believe that icons are gods or alive are guilty of idol worship and those who believe we worship them as a god are guilty of the same sin for they attribute life to wood and paint and paper.

Section 3. The commandment of God forbids us to fall down and worship before any image as a god. It does not forbid us to cherish memories of the truths of our faith in the arts. Whoever says that Scripture forbids the right use of the arts denies the use of our God-given talents for God's honor and glory.

Article VIII. THE SECOND COMING OF CHRIST.

We believe that Christ will come again in the flesh as recorded in the Scripture and taught in the Nicene Creed.

Article IX. MORAL CODE.

Section 1. The moral code of the Christian life is to be found in Holy Scripture, the teachings of the Church and the Fathers.

Section 2. The Ten Commandments and the Two-fold Commandment of Jesus Christ are binding for all generations.

Article X. THE CHURCH.

Section 1. The Church is the Body of Christ, united in the true Faith handed down by the Apostles through the ages, with Christ as its head.

Section 2. We confess Christ to be the only true head of His Church and we accept no other.

Section 3. We believe the Church is guided by the Holy Spirit in all her teachings Holy Tradition (the Scriptures) and its interpretation from the Creed, the Seven Holy Synods and the teachings of the Fathers.

To these Articles of Faith we do confess of our own free will. In this faith we do live and desire to die, with the help of God.

* * *

SUMMARY OF BELIEF OF CHRIST CATHOLIC CHURCH

GOD. We believe that God is the Creator of heaven and earth. We believe that He seeks the fellowship of man that man might dwell in God and God in man.

Although God cannot be understood by the finite mind, He can be experienced. The human mind cannot grasp the significance of God, but it can come into His Presence.

At the Mass, we come to be with Jesus and to unite our hearts and minds with His, so that His Will becomes our will.

No catholic theologian would pretend that he could define God or describe His wonderous glory adequately.

The human mind is simply too small, and God is too great to be compressed or encompassed by any verbal definition.

JESUS CHRIST. We believe Jesus Christ is God and that He is living, true, and eternal. As Son of God, He is the inheritor of God's Heavenly Kingdom. He has come into this world to save us from sin and death and make us joint heirs with Him in His Heavenly Kingdom.

THE HOLY SPIRIT. We believe the Holy Spirit is God and that he dwells among men and seeks to guide and instruct men that they might direct their affairs heavenward.

THE CHURCH. We believe the Church is the Body of our Lord, Jesus Christ. It is the community of the faithful and is governed by our Lord Jesus Christ. It is made up of all those who profess the Christian faith and who faithfully and regularly participate in the celebration of the Mass and receive the blessed Sacrament. Jesus Christ is the one, infallible Head of the Church.

THE RIGHT OF PRIVATE JUDGMENT. We believe the Right of Private Judgment belongs to every member, both lay and clergy, in matters of doctrine. However, a clergyman found heterdox by the Presiding Bishop or the Holy Synod shall be deprived of faculties but shall retain all the rights and privileges of a lay member.

DOCTRINES OF THE CHURCH. The Church's doctrinal position in all matters of faith and practice shall be in accordance with the Holy Scriptures, the Ecumenical Creeds, the Seven Ecumenical Councils, and the Utrecht Confession. We further accept, because they shall conform to the above, the doctrines embodied in the official liturgy of the Church, the catechism, and the Constitution and Canons of this Holy Catholic Church.

*　　*　　*

THE LEIPSIC [LEIPZIG] INTERIM OF 1548 [EVANGELICAL ORTHODOX (CATHOLIC) CHURCH]

It is our judgment that obedience should be rendered the Roman Imperial Majesty, and such disposition should be shown that His Imperial Majesty and every one may note that we are all inclined to quiet, peace and unity. [In America, in view of complete separation of Church and State in matters dealing with spiritual authority and administration, all references to Imperial Majesty, princes and potentates have no authority upon us.] This we faithfully advise, and, as far as possible, will for ourselves always serve and admonish. For as some speak and write without cause, our mind and intention is directed to no dissension or unnecessary proceedings, but to all that already mentioned. This we testify before God himself, to whom all men's hearts are known, and this too our work shall and will prove.

Accordingly, we judge, first, that all that the ancient teachers have held in regard to *adiaphora*—i.e. matters of indifference, which may be observed without injury to the Divine Scriptures, and, on the other hand, are still in use— be henceforth observed, and that therein no burden or augmentation should be sought or applied, since this cannot occur without injury to a good conscience.

Secondly, so far as concerns the doctrine, first, of the state and nature of man before and after the fall, there is no controversy.

The Article of Justification is similar to that at Pegau. [Also they teach, that men cannot be Justified before God by their own strength, merits or works, but are freely justified for Christ's sake through faith, when they believe that they are received into favor and that their sins are forgiven for Christ's sake, who, by His death, hath made satisfaction for our sins. This faith God imputes for righteousness in his sight. Rom. 3 and 4.—AUGS. Conf.]

HOW MAN IS JUSTIFIED BEFORE GOD

As now it is said that out of God's wonderful, fathomless counsel his Son has been appointed Mediator and Saviour, and that for his sake the forgiveness of sins, the Holy Ghost, righteousness and eternal life are assuredly given, it should be known further how this exalted and great grace and blessings are received. Namely, thus:

Although God does not justify man by the merit of his own works which man does, but out of mercy, freely, without our merit, that the glory may not be ours, but Christ's, through whose merit alone we are redeemed from sins and justified, yet the merciful God does not work with man as with a block, but draws him, so that his will also co-operates if he be of understanding years. For such a man does not receive the benefits of Christ unless his will and heart be moved by prevenient grace, so that he is terrified before God's wrath and has dislike of sin. For since sin causes enmity between God and man, as Isaiah writes, no one can come to the throne of grace and mercy unless by true repentance he turn from his sins. Hence John when he prepared the way of the Lord, preached with great earnestness: "Repent, for the kingdom of heaven is at hand." And there is no doubt whatever that in conversion there must be pain and terror before God's wrath; and as long as security remains, which perseveres in sins against conscience, there is no conversion and no forgiveness. Isaiah therefore says: "With whom will God dwell? With him that is poor and of a contrite spirit, and trembleth at God's Word." Moses also says: "The Lord they God is a consuming fire"—i.e. he is truly and terribly incensed against all sin, and proclaimed his sentence shortly after the Fall by his Word and by punishments, and afterwards on this account have his law with authentic testimonials, and taught therein that death, ravages and other plagues are admonitions whereby we should recognize his wrath. Besides, he wishes that in his Church until its final redemption sin should be reproved in the heart by the Word and Holy Ghost, as it is written: "The Holy Ghost will reprove the world of sin" [John 16].

THE LEIPSIC [LEIPZIG] INTERIM OF 1548 [EVANGELICAL ORTHODOX (CATHOLIC) CHURCH] (continued)

But God has not only revealed his wrath, but has also given with it his gracious promise—viz. the Gospel of the Son of God—and it is his immutable will, confirmed by his oath and the blood of his Son and many miracles, that he will assuredly forgive sins, bestow on us the Holy Ghost, receive, renew and make us heirs of eternal blessedness, for his Son's sake, and not because of our merit or worth, if in this terror and pain we truly believe and trust that for the sake of the Mediator sins are assuredly forgiven us.

This true faith believes all the articles of faith. For every one must acknowledge God, and, together with other articles, believe also this: I believe the forgiveness of sins, that it is imparted to me, and not merely to others. For although many who live in an evil conscience, if they also confess the Christian doctrine, boast of their faith, yet it is not a living and justifying faith. For such a heart does not believe that the forgiveness of sins is given it individually, neither does it appropriate the promise, but flees from God, and both comfort in God and true invocation of him are absent. There is no doubt that the faith of the devil, who is grievously terrified before God's judgment, is a far different thing from this true faith, which appropriates the promise and gracious comfort, as Paul clearly testifies (Rom. 4), that he speaks of that faith which appropriates the promise, which is not merely knowledge, as in the devil or in men who live in evil conscience, but this faith, together with the other articles, believes the forgiveness of sins, appropriates the promise and is at heart a true trust upon the Son of God, which works consolation, invocation and other virtues; of which faith the words of Isaiah, which Paul quotes in Rom. 10, speak: "He that trusteth in him shall not be brought to confusion." And it is sure that there is no other way to God and to attain forgiveness of sins and grace than this alone through the Son of God, as it is written: "No one cometh to the Father, but by the Son." Therefore, the Holy Ghost is likewise given in our hearts if we thus grasp by faith the divine promises, and comfort and support ourselves therewith, as is clearly expressed in Gal. 3, that we receive the promise of the Holy Ghost by faith; and the Holy Ghost then works in the heart steadfast trust and life, and enkindles all necessary virtues, firm faith, invocation, fear of God, love, good intentions, hope and other virtues. And they who have thus received the forgiveness of sins and the Holy Ghost, and in whom the Holy Ghost begins faith and trust in the Son of God, love and hope, then become heirs of eternal salvation for the Saviour's sake, as Paul writes (Rom. 6): "Eternal life is a gift of God, through Jesus Christ our Lord."

And as God has always graciously continued to build and maintain a Church ever since he received again Adam and Eve, and gave them the promise of a future Saviour, he has continued also to maintain this understanding of forgiveness and faith, although indeed among many it was often obscured, who sought forgiveness by their own works, or remained fettered by doubts, as the heathen, among whom the remembrance of the promise no longer remains; yet God has clearly expressed this meaning in his Scriptures, and continues to declare it in his Church, in order that the knowledge and honor of his Son may not be effaced, and that he may continue to collect a Church and save many men.

But in the Christian Church all men should know both parts and truly believe. He who lives in sins against conscience should assuredly judge that he is in God's wrath, and that if he be not converted he will fall into eternal punishment; so again in true conversion it is God's earnest will and command that we accept his promise, and believe that not because of our worth, but because of the Redeemer and Mediator, God is gracious to us, will forgive our sins, and will accept and help us, etc.

But as some say that this is strange language, and that every one, nevertheless, experience that much doubt concerning God still inheres and remains in the heart, this is indeed true; much doubt, struggling and fleeing from God are and remain in all men. This weakness is the injury resulting from original sin. But God, on the other hand, has given us his promise to comfort and strengthen us, that we may overcome doubt and flee to God for refuge. And when St. Paul says: "I know nothing by myself; yet am I not thereby justified," he does not teach that we should doubt, but wishes us to assuredly hold both points—viz. that the conscience should stand erect, but that therewith still many faults remain in us, and therefore we should know that we are nevertheless righteous—i.e. pleasing to God, for his Son's sake; and that is correct which Augustine says: "The certainty of entire trust should be in the precious blood of Christ." And it is divine, immutable truth that in the heart which has received through faith the forgiveness of sins the Holy Ghost, prayer, love, hope and other virtues enter, and there must be therein a good intention and a good conscience, as Paul says, that faith and a good conscience must be together. John also says: "He that loveth not abideth in death."

This is all certainly true. And although, by the help of divine grace, they are able to live without vices and mortal sins, yet at the same time it must be known that in this weak life there is still much inclination against God's commandments, much ignorance, doubt and manifold irregularities, as St. Paul says to the Romans, chap. 7: "I see another law in my members, warring against the law of my mind." And the Psalmist says: "In thy sight shall no man living be justified." And Daniel says: "We do not present our supplications before thee for our righteousness, but for thy great mercies."

Although, therefore, a new obedience has been begun, yet we must not think that one has on this account forgiveness of sins, and is thus so pure that he needs no forgiveness of sins and no Mediator. The Son of God is, and continually remains, Mediator, and in God's secret counsel stands and prays for us that the grievous wrath of God against sin may not be poured out upon us. And it is not enough to say that God will not take account of the weakness that remains, and considers the person to be without sin, thus causing false confidence in one's own righteousness; but there must be in us both—viz. a good conscience and inchoate obedience; and besides this humility and faith—viz. that we confess that we still have sin, and that there is in us serious pain and displeasure at our sins; that we also confess that we have merited punishment, and are therein subject to God, as Daniel says: "O Lord, righteousness belongeth unto thee; but unto us shame and confusion of face." Besides, there must also be a necessary confidence that God will certainly receive persons, and, for his Son's sake, be gracious. This trust that thus contemplates the Mediator in God's judgment must always in this weak life overshadow the other virtues. When, therefore, Paul says: "Being justified by faith," this expression must not be understood in such sense as that faith alone is a preparation—viz. a confession—and procures other virtues because of which the person is truly justified; but his own honor should be accorded the Son of God, that he is and remains Mediator. We should also abide in this humility, that we confess we still have sins and need grace, and that God will certainly be thus gracious to us if, in this humility, we believe he is gracious to us for his Son's sake.

And that this consolation is necessary for all the godly every one experiences in his heart. In all anxiety and with intent invocation we all exclaim: "Alas, I am a poor sinner; I am not worthy that God should hear me." In such need we should not teach a man to imagine: "I have now many excellent virtues, and therefore I am pure;" but he should flee for refuge to the Son of God, and know that he should trust in the same because of the promise, as Daniel writes: "Not for our righteousness, but through mercy for the Lord's sake"—i.e. for the sake of the promised Saviour.

From all this it is clear both that it is true that in us a new obedience should begin, and yet that faith and trust in the Son of God must continue to abide, and receive the consolation that God is gracious to us for his Son's sake; and where this faith ceases there cannot be love and refuge to God and true prayer; but this faith works consolation, love and prayer, as it is said, and is not without love.

In those thus reconciled, virtues and good works should be called righteousness, yet not in the sense that the person on this account has forgiveness of sins or that the person is, in God's judgment, without sin, but that, for his Son's sake, God regards this weak, inchoate obedience of believers in this miserable, infirm, impure nature with pleasure; and of these works as righteousness John speaks when he says: "He that doeth righteousness is righteous." And it is true that where the works are contrary to God, there is contempt of God, and no conversion to God has occurred in the heart. As is the tree, so also are the fruits; as we have still further to say.

OF GOOD WORKS

We also have no doubt that our doctrine and interpretation of good works is in agreement with the Divine Scriptures and the understanding of the Catholic Church of all times; and since our writings on this subject have been published, there is no need of a long statement here. Yet, that there may be a definite rule, we declare that those works are good and necessary which God has commanded, according to the Ten Commandments and their explanation sufficiently set forth in the writings of the apostles. According to this rule, a distinction is to be made between a good and an evil conscience. And, as before said, it is God's serious command that we should live in good

conscience, and, as St. Paul writes, hold faith and a good conscience. He who perseveres in sins contrary to conscience is not converted to God, and is still God's enemy, and God's wrath abides upon him if he be not converted. This is precisely in accord with Gal. 5: "Of that which I tell you before, as I have told you in time past, that they which do such things shall not inherit the kingdom of God." God, too, has comprised both in an oath—viz. that this conversion is necessary, and that the forgiveness of sins should be believed: "As I live, I have no pleasure in the death of the wicked, but that the wicked turn from his way and live." Therefore, where there is no conversion there is no grace. This all intelligent persons know without a long explanation.

Further, if any one who has been in God's grace acts against God's command or his conscience, he grieves the Holy Ghost, loses grace and righteousness and falls beneath God's wrath; and if he be not again converted he falls into eternal punishment, as Saul and others. This is clearly expressed in Rom. 8: "We are debtors, not to the flesh, to live after the flesh; for if ye live after the flesh ye shall die"—i.e. if ye follow your wicked inclinations contrary to conscience, ye shall fall into eternal punishment. And such sins merit not only eternal punishment after this life, but also many grievous punishments in this life, whereby their perpetrators and many others with them are surprised; as David's adultery and murder were punished.

For these reasons, to speak briefly, it is readily understood that good works are necessary, for God has commanded them; and if the course of life be in opposition thereto, God's grace and the Holy Ghost are rejected, and such sins merit eternal condemnation. But virtues and good works please God thus, as we have said, in the reconciled, because, they believe that God receives their person for Christ's sake, and will be pleased with this imperfect obedience; and it is true that eternal life is given for the sake of the Lord Christ out of grace, and at the same time that all are heirs of eternal salvation who are converted to God and by faith receive forgiveness of sins and the Holy Ghost. Nevertheless, the new virtues and good works are so highly necessary that if they were not quickened in the heart there would be no reception of divine grace. Thus, there must be in us a reception of divine grace, and its consolation is not an indolent thought, but life and deliverance from great trouble, as King Hezekiah says, Isa. 38: "God, as a lion, did break all my bones; but he hath delivered my soul, and cast all my sins behind my back." Paul says: "We will be clothed upon, so that we shall not be found naked." And Rev. 2: "Be thou faithful unto death, and I will give thee a crown of life." In these passages two things are comprised: the first, that in this life the beginning must be made of eternal salvation; the second, that before our end we must not fall away therefrom.

Thus regeneration and eternal life are in themselves a new light, fear of God, love, joy in God and other virtues; as the passage says: "This is life eternal, to know thee the only true God, and me, Jesus Christ." As, now, this true knowledge must shine in us, it is certainly true that these virtues, faith, love, hope and others, must be in us, and are

THE LEIPSIC [LEIPZIG] INTERIM OF 1548 [EVANGELICAL
ORTHODOX (CATHOLIC) CHURCH] (continued)

necessary to salvation. All this is easy for the godly to understand who seek to experience consolation from God. And since the virtues and good works please God, as has been said, they merit also a reward in this life, both spiritual and temporal, according to God's counsel, and still more reward in eternal life, because of the divine promise.

But by this the error of the manks is in no way confirmed, that eternal salvation is merited by the worth of our works; also, that we can communicate our merit to others; but faith acknowledges our own weakness and flees for refuge to the Son of God, and receives this eternal consolation from his merit and treasure because of his gracious and exceeding abundant rich promise, and knows that we are always in conversion under obligation to believe God, who has there promised grace, and confirmed this promise with his oath, and regards despair as an affront against God, and thus the greatest sin.

Good works are adorned further in the Divine Scriptures with many temporal promises and great praise, whereof we have besides given Christian instruction at length in our writing, as we will continue always to do. For God wishes to be recognized and invoked also in temporal gifts, and that this invocation be made in faith and a good conscience.

What is to be said further of works which God has not commanded will be mentioned hereafter.

OF ECCLESIASTICAL POWER AND
AUTHORITY

What the true Christian Church, which is collected in the Holy Ghost, acknowledges determines and teaches in regard to matters of faith should be taught and preached, as it neither should nor can determine anything contrary to the Holy Scriptures.

OF ECCLESIASTICAL MINISTERS

That hereafter learned men should be presented and appointed to the prebendaryships in the bishoprics who have such understanding in the Divine Scriptures that they are competent to exercise the episcopal office, and for the care of the archdiaconate and the jurisdiction of the Church, and can rightly administer the same. And that by the statutes and customs which obtain in some bishoprics only qualified persons should be made canons—godly men who would be serviceable in the episcopal office, and would not be a hindrance; but since in the Papal ordinances and decrees they have been cashiered and dismissed, and it was found that the chapters were full of idle and unlearned men, learned pastors and ministers should be ordained who are capable and fit to teach the Word of God and in a Christian way to preside over the people.

And that all other ministers should be subject and obedient to the chief and other bishops who administer their episcopal office according to God's command, and use the same for edification and not for destruction; which ministers should be ordained also by such bishops upon presentation by the patrons. These ministers also when

they transgress, and especially the priests whose life is immoral or who urge impure doctrine, should be punished by the ordinary means, as by the deprivation of their office, and finally by excommunication.

OF BAPTISM

That infant baptism, together with exorcism, the assistance and confession of sponsors, and other ancient Christian ceremonies, should be taught and retained.

OF CONFIRMATION

That confirmation should be taught and retained, and especially that the youth when they have come to mature years should be examined as to their faith by their bishops or by persons to whom this is entrusted, that they confess it, and ratify the promises and renunciation of the devil made for them at baptism by their sponsors, and thus by the aid of divine grace be confirmed and established by the laying on of hands and Christian prayer and ceremonies.

OF REPENTENCE

That repentence, confession and absolution, and what pertains thereto, be diligently taught and preached, that the people confess to the priests, and receive of them absolution in God's stead, and be also diligently admonished and urged to prayer, fasting and almsgiving. Also, that no one to be admitted to the highly-venerable sacrament of the body and blood of Christ unless he have first confessed [to the priest] and received [of him] absolution. Besides, that the people be diligently taught and instructed that in this sacrament we are united with Jesus Christ our Saviour as the Head with the members of his body, so that by it we are nursed and nourished to all good. Also, that we grow in communion with the saints. For "we, being many, are one bread and one body," as St. Paul says.

That the people should be taught also that whoever partakes of this sacrament unworthily eats and drinks damnation to himself, and should therefore be urged to forsake his sinful life and to true repentance, prayer, alms, temperance and other Christian virtues. For whoever will receive and support life must avoid the cause of death, and must follow and obey the Physician who beckons us on and has gone before.

OF [EXTREME] UNCTION

Although in this country the unction has not been in use for many years, yet since it is written in Mark and James how the apostles used it, since James says: "Is any sick among you? Let him call for the elders of the Church, and let them pray over him, anointing him with oil in the name of the Lord; and the prayer of faith shall save the sick, and the Lord shall raise him up,"—such unction, according to the apostle, may be hereafter observed, and Christian prayer and words of consolation from the Holy Scriptures be spoken over the sick; and that the people should be instructed concerning this in such way as to reach the true understanding, and that all superstition and misunderstanding be removed and avoided.

ORDINATION OF MINISTERS

Also, that, as has been said, ministers should hereafter be ordained with Christian ceremonies, upon the presentation of patrons, by such bishops as administer their episcopal office, and that no one be allowed in the ministry unless, as has been said, he be presented by the patrons and have the permission of the bishops, so that no one may unbecomingly force himself or have himself appointed in a disorderly way. And that the sham examinations whereby many unlearned and unsuitable men have become pastors and church officers, to the grievous damage of conscience, be abolished; and that the bishops earnestly and diligently examine candidates for ordination, and especially those presented by patrons for ecclesiastical offices, in all ways themselves, and with the counsel, presence and co-operation of godly and learned men, in order that they may be found so qualified and suitable in doctrine, intelligence, life and walk as to be able aright to feed the flock of the Lord with God's Word, provide it with doctrine and example, and to administer their office.

OF MARRIAGE

That in all estates in this country marriage be observed according to God's institution.

OF THE MASS

That the mass be observed henceforth in this country, with ringing of bells, with lights and vessels, with chants, vestments and ceremonies. In places where there are sufficient persons the priests and ministrants should go in a becoming way before the altar in their regular church vestments and robes, speak in the beginning the *Confiteor*, and that the *Introit*, the *Kyrie eleison*, the *Gloria in excelsis Deo, et in terra*, etc., and the *Dominus vobiscum*, the Collects, the Epistle, and all that now current in Latin, be sung. And when the Epistle is sung, it should then be also read to the people in German; the *Gradual*, the *Hallelujah*, the *Sequence*, or a *Tractus* according to the occasion of the time or festival. The Gospel to be sung in Latin, and read to the people in German. The *Credo in unum Deum* according to the Creed throughout, as is customary in the chapters. In parishes where there is no chapter, for the *Gradual* the old German hymns may be sung: at Christmas, *Ein Kindelein so lobelich*; at Easter, *Christ ist erstanden*; at Whitsunday, *Nun bitten wirden heiligen Geist*, etc.; and instead of the Creed, *Wir glauben all an einen Gott, etc.* The sermon to be on the Gospel. The *Dominus vobiscum*, the *Oremus*, the *Offertorium*, the *Praefatio*, the *Sanctus*, the *Consecratio*, the Lord's Prayer in German, the *Agnus Dei*, the *Communio* and administration of the sacrament, the *Communicatio*, or partaking, Collects, the Benediction. Amended: The Liturgy remains the same—the language to be that commonly spoken and used by the local congregation: (German, French, Spanish, and English for British and American bodies.)

OF IMAGES

The images and pictures of the sufferings of Christ and of the saints may be also retained in the churches, and the people should be taught that they are there only as remembrances, and to these things no divine honor should be attached. To the images and pictures of the saints, however, no superstitious resort should occur or be encouraged.

OF SINGING IN THE CHURCHES

In the churches where they have been formerly observed the "canonical hours," the devout Psalms, should be sung in the chapters and towns at their times and on other high festivals, and also on Sundays. And therefore the usual ancient chants also be retained, according to the time and the chief festivals. There may be singing at and after burial, at the request of those who desire it, in memory of the dead and of our promise and sure resurrection.

OF HOLIDAYS

Sunday; our Lord's Birthday; St. Stephen's Day; St. John the Evangelist's Day; the Circumcision of the Lord; Day of the Three Holy Kings; Easter and the two days following; the Ascension of the Lord; Whitsunday, with the two days following; *Corpus Christi*; the Festivals of the Holy Virgin Mary; the days of the Holy Apostles; of St. John the Baptist; of St. Mary Magdalene; of St. Michael and some others, on which there should be only Church services, with preaching and mass and communion, as, of the Conversion of Paul; of the Beheading of John; Thursday, Friday and Saturday in Passion Week.

OF THE EATING OF MEAT

Likewise, that on Fridays and Saturdays, also in fasts, the eating of meat be abstained from, and that this be observed as an external ordinance [at the command of His Imperial Majesty]. Yet that those whom necessity excuses, as hard laborers, travellers, women with child and those in childbed, old weak persons, and children, be not bound hereby.

OF THE DEPORTMENT OF MINISTERS

And we regard it becoming and good that pastors and ministers, in their dress as well as otherwise, by propriety of deportment demean themselves in a clerical and creditable way, and that with the co-operation and advice of the bishops or consistories they make an arrangement with one another, and observe it, so that in their apparel a distinction may be observed between ministers and worldly persons, and proper reverence may be paid the priestly estate. And that every one should give due consideration to his pastor, preacher and minister also with respect to doctrine and deportment, and report whatever faults may be found to the bishop or consistory, who should remedy the wrong.

CONCLUSION

In other articles we are ready to diligently observe the Scriptures and the ancient teachers, and to show our friends and gracious lords the bishops our judgment, and in a friendly and submissive manner to confer with Their Beloved and Princely Graces, and to settle our differences in a Christian way.

Notes: *One of the least-heralded statements of the Reformation Era in Germany was the Leipsic [Leipzig] Interim of 1548. It was occasioned by the temporary rule of Catholic forces in Protestant territories in the middle of the sixteenth century. Written by a group of theologians under Philip Melancthon, it retained the major affirmation of Protestant thought, justification by grace through faith, while prescribing Roman ritual and practice. The necessity of the Interim was ended by the Peace of Augsburg in 1555.*

THE LEIPSIC [LEIPZIG] INTERIM OF 1548 [EVANGELICAL ORTHODOX (CATHOLIC) CHURCH] (continued)

The Evangelical Orthodox (Catholic) Church, which considers itself a non-papal Catholic body, adopted this all-but-forgotten document in 1941 as a "clearly written declaration of their position as Catholics in the true sense of the word."

* * *

TENETS OF FAITH (MARIAVITE OLD CATHOLIC CHURCH–PROVINCE OF NORTH AMERICA)

1. The Mariavite Old Catholic Churches bases itself upon the old Catholic tenets of faith and morals. These tenets are contained in the canonical books of the Holy Scripture of the Old and New Testament as well as in the early Tradition of the Universal Church and which were defined at the first seven Ecumenical Councils.

2. The Mariavite Old Catholic Church does not enact new dogmas and also does not admit dogmas, which individual Churches enacted after the separation of Christianity in the year 1054 into Roman Catholicism and Orthodoxy, since it observes, that only an Ecumenical Council (that is: representing all of Christianity) may enact a new dogma which obligates all Christians.

3. The Mariavite Old Catholic Church does not recognize the primacy of any Bishop in the Universal Church, as well as the infallability of an individual in matters of faith and morals.

4. In the Mariavite Old Catholic Church from 1924, there does not exist an obligatory clerical celibacy—consequently there are celibates and the married. All are obligated to maintain the Franciscan spirit.

5. The Mariavite Old Catholic Church believes, that God performs miracles in the soul of an individual, but it does not recognize so-called miraculous relics, pictures, and so forth; it does not however, reject the great respect which should surround pictures of religious content as well as relics and remembrances of the Saints.

6. Auricular (private) confession before the priest obliges children and youth to age 18. Adults (at their own request) may also profit from it, but what obliges them is the general confession before Christ with the absolution of the priest. (Until the year 1930, private confession obligated everyone.)

7. The Mariavite Old Catholic Church recognizes seven Holy Sacraments, namely: Baptism, Penance, Holy Eucharist, Confirmation, Holy Orders, Matrimony, and Extreme Unction.

8. Holy Communion is distributed to the faithful under both species (from the year 1922).

9. The Mariavite Old Catholic Church bases itself likewise on the Revelation of Divine Mercy, received by the Foundress of Mariavitism, the blessed Mother Maria Franciszka Kozlowska (the first revelation August 2nd, 1893), showing, that the salvation for the world threatened by its sins is in Christ present in the Most Blessed Sacrament, in Whom it is proper to believe and adore as well as in the invocation of the Perpetual Help of the Most Blessed Virgin Mary.

10. The spiritual purpose of the Mariavite Old Catholic Church is the furtherance of devotion for Jesus Christ concealed in the Most Blessed Sacrament and pointing out the need of invoking the perpetual help of the Most Blessed Mother, "because as there are perpetual efforts against God and the Church, thus is needed the Perpetual Help of Mary."

11. The worship of the Most Blessed Sacrament in the life of the faithful is expressed in the frequent and worthy reception of Holy Communion, accordingly to the words of Christ: "Unless you eat the body of the Son of Man and drink His blood, you have no life in yourselves" (John 6:53), as well as in the performance of the Adoration of Supplication. Each of the members has an obligation to perform an hourly Adoration of the Most Blessed Sacrament once in the week and in common, solemnly once in the month as well as the participation in the Holy Sacrifice of the Mass on Sundays and Holydays. The Clergy and Religious Sisters have the obligation to perform the Adoration daily.

12. The Clergy of the Mariavite Old Catholic Church remain under the protection of the Mother of God of Perpetual Help.

13. The Mariavite Old Catholic Church bears in its name the name of Mary, indicating the indispensability of imitating Her life: of solitude, of humility, spirit of prayer, great love for neighbor and readiness to fulfill the Will of God.

14. The Holy Sacrifice of the Mass and the entire liturgy (from Christmas Midnight Mass 1907) are celebrated exclusively in the language of the people. The use of the Latin language and the Polish language are also common in the Church of the Province of North America. The Mariavite Old Catholic Church does not recognize the need for liturgical reforms or innovations which water-down or often destroy Catholic belief, as is often witnessed in the state of affairs within the Roman Catholic Church since Vatican II. Rather, the Mariavite Old Catholic Church steadfastly preserves and maintains the old and traditional manner of celebrating the Holy Sacrifice of the Mass and performing rites and ceremonies as were common in the Roman Catholic Church before Vatican II and prior to the Holy Week reforms of Pope Pius XII in the early 1950's.

15. All religious ministrations are without cost, in agreement with the recommendation of Christ: "Freely you have received, freely give" (Mat. 10:8). It is however, permissable for the clergy to accept voluntary offerings for religious ministrations, but they cannot demand them.

16. The Mariavite Old Catholic Church received the Apostolic Succession from the Old Catholic Church of Holland. The Roman Catholic Church has always recognized as valid, the Holy Orders and Sacraments of the Old Catholic Church of Holland, and those of the Mariavite Old Catholic Church.

17. The Mariavite Old Catholic Church supports the ecumenical ideal, it cooperates with all Christian denominations; it is a member of the Polish Ecumenical Council and the World Council of Churches, it may belong to organizations with ecumenical or peace aims.

Notes: *The Mariavite Old Catholic Church is an independent jurisdiction that derives its beliefs from those of the Mariavite Old Catholic Church headquartered in Plock, Poland (with whom it has no official connection). The tenets make several specific references to the Mariavites, especially their devotion to the Virgin Mary, from which the church's name is derived. Article 17 is somewhat misleading, however. Although the Mariavite Old Catholic Church of Poland is a member of the Polish Ecumenical Council and the World Council of Churches, the Mariavite Old Catholic Church–Province of North America has no such connections.*

* * *

DOCTRINAL STATEMENT OF THE NORTH AMERICAN OLD ROMAN CATHOLIC CHURCH

Retaining as its goal a return to the ancient Catholicity of the Church of the first thousand years the North American Old Roman Catholic Church considers the Sacred Scriptures of both the Old and New Testaments, in which are found the record of the revelation of God himself to man through his people, Israel, and in his Son, Jesus Christ, the basic rule of the Christian Faith. In interpreting this scriptural revelation, the North American Old Roman Catholic Church accepts and seeks to apply the tradition of the Apostles and Fathers of the early Church. This tradition is received according to the Vincentian Canon, which dates from the fifth century:

> *In ipsa item Catholica Ecclesia magnopere curandum est, ut teneamus, quod ubique quod semper ab omnibus creditum est. Hoc est enim vere proprieque Catholicum—quod ipsa vis nominis ratioque declarat, quod omnia fere universaliter comprehendit. Sed hoc fiet si sequimur universalitatem, antiquitatem, consensionem.* (Vincent of Lérins, Commonitorium pro Catholicae fidei antiquitate et universalitate, capitalum III.)

Based on this canon, the North American Old Roman Catholic Church perseveres in professing the faith of the ancient Church as enfleshed in the Apostles' and Niceno-Constantinopolitan Creeds, and in the decisions of the Seven Ecumenical Councils of the Undivided Church. The North American Old Roman Catholic Church, retaining traceable unbroken succession of Orders from the undivided Church, adheres to the forms and formulae established by the early Roman Church in order to preserve the deposit of faith received through Roman Tradition.

True to the ancient heritage, the North American Old Roman Catholic Church holds the catholic doctrines of the Incarnation, honoring the Virgin Mary as the Mother of God and the ancient doctrine of the Virgin birth, of the Passion, Death, Resurrection and Ascension of the Lord Jesus Christ; and the personal union in him of two natures, one human, the other divine. If further adheres to the medieval doctrine of original sin, the eternal punishment of hell and the necessity of faith for salvation. The church teaches the doctrine of the real presence of Christ in the Eucharist and the spiritual efficacy of the Mass for both the living and the dead.

The North American Old Roman Catholic Church rejects those teachings of the Roman Church which have no warrant in Scripture or ancient tradition, such as the treasury of merits, indulgences, the novel doctrine of the Immaculate Conception and Papal Infallibility. Auricular confession is not obligatory; sins may be confessed before the congregation or a priest. Celibacy is optional. Women are not eligible for the priesthood.

In order to safeguard the validity of its sacramental ministrations, the North American Old Roman Catholic Church conforms strictly to the *Pontificale,* the *Missale* and *Rituale Romanum* of Pius V 1570. Each of the seven sacraments is administered according to the canons and prescriptions of the Western Rite. Liturgical vesture is also that of the Western Rite, while sacramentals and devotions of the Western Rite, as originating from the Roman Church, are utilized while avoiding the excesses that often lead to superstition.

The belief of the North American Old Roman Catholic Church, in accord with the historic faith of the undivided Church of the first thousand years is delineated by four documents. All of which follow hereafter.

The first document is the Statement of Union which served as the basis for the reception of the Old Roman Catholic Church of Great Britain (Western Orthodox Church) into Antiochene Orthodoxy by Archbishop Gerassimos Messerah of Beirut, on August 5, 1911. The second document is referred to as the Fourteen Theses. They resulted from the Old Catholic Union Conference of 1874, held at the University of Bonn. This conference, consisting of members of the Orthodox, Old Catholic and Anglican Churches, directed itself toward a confederation of the Churches on the basis of union in essentials and freedom in non-essentials. The Union Conference of the following year, also held in Bonn, produced the third document, an agreement resolving the time-worn Filioque controversy. The last document is the profession of faith, called the Declaration of Utrecht, which was formulated by the essembled Old Catholic Bishops at Utrecht on September 24, 1889.

The North American Old Roman Catholic Church, although not a member of the historic Old Catholic Churches of the Union of Utrecht, in the light of the above, thus considers itself an orthodox church, Catholic in its retension of the historic faith derived in unbroken line from the ancient church, without any doctrinal innovations, North American in its intended field of

DOCTRINAL STATEMENT OF THE NORTH AMERICAN
OLD ROMAN CATHOLIC CHURCH (continued)

mission, and Old Roman in the ancient tradition of the
apostolic see of Rome in the undivided Church.

* * *

PROFESSION OF FAITH (OLD CATHOLIC CHURCH IN AMERICA)

I, N.N., with a firm faith believe and profess all and every
one of those things which are contained in that creed
which the holy Catholic Church—that is, the Old Catholic
Church—makes use of. To wit: I BELIEVE in one God,
the Father almighty, maker of heaven and earth and of all
things visible and invisible. And in one Lord JESUS
Christ, the only-begotten Son of God. Born of the Father
before all ages. God of God, light of light, true God of true
God. Begotten not made, being of one substance with the
Father; by Whom all things were made. Who for us men,
and for our salvation, came down from heaven, and was
incarnate by the Holy Spirit of the Virgin Mary: and was
made Man. He was crucified also for us, suffered under
Pontius Pilate, and was buried. And the third day He rose
again according to the Scriptures. And ascended into
heaven. He sitteth at the right hand of the Father. And He
shall come again with glory to judge both the living and
the dead; of Whose kingdom there shall be no end. And in
the Holy Spirit, the Lord and giver of life: Who proceedeth
from the Father. Who together with the Father and the
Son is worshipped and glorified. Who spoke by the
prophets. And in one, holy, catholic and apostolic Church.
I confess one baptism for the remission of sins. And I look
for the resurrection of the dead. And the life of the age to
come. Amen.

I most steadfastly admit and embrace the apostolical and
ecclesiastical Traditions, and all other observances and
constitutions of the same Church.

I also admit the holy Scriptures, according to that sense
which our holy mother the Church has held and does hold,
to whom it belongs to judge of the true sense and
interpretation of the Scriptures; neither will I ever take and
interpret them otherwise than according to the consent of
the Fathers.

I also profess that there are truly and properly Seven
Sacraments of the new law, instituted by JESUS Christ our
Lord, and necessary for the salvation of mankind, though
not all for every one: to wit, Baptism, Confirmation, the
Eucharist, Penance, Extreme Unction, Holy Orders, and
Matrimony: and that they confer grace: and that of these
Baptism, Confirmation, and Holy Orders cannot be
repeated without sacrilege. I also receive and admit the
received and approved ceremonies of the Old Catholic
Church used in the solemn administration of the aforesaid
Sacraments.

I profess, likewise, that in the Mass there is offered to God
a true, proper, and propitiatory sacrifice for the living and
the dead. And that in the most holy sacrament of the
Eucharist there is truly, really and substantially the Body
and Blood, together with the soul and divinity, of our Lord
JESUS Christ; and that there is made a conversion of the
whole substance of the bread into the Body, and of the
whole substance of the wine into the Blood; which
Conversion the Old Catholic Church calls Transubstantiation.

I constantly hold that there is a Purgatory, and that the
souls therein detained are helped by the suffrages of the
faithful.

Likewise, that the Saints reigning together with Christ are
to be honored and invoked, and that they offer prayers to
God for us, and that their relics are to be had in
veneration.

I most firmly assert that the Images of Christ, of the Ever-
Virgin Mother of God, and also of other Saints, ought to
be had and retained and that due honor and veneration are
to be given them.

I acknowledge the Old Catholic Church to be truly the
One, Holy, Catholic and Apostolic Church; and I promise
true obedience to her bishops as the successors of the
Apostles and of JESUS Christ.

I likewise undoubtingly receive and profess all other things
delivered, defined, and declared by the sacred canons and
General Councils. And I reject all things contrary thereto,
and all heresies which the Church hath condemned,
rejected, and anathematized.

I, N.N., do at this present time freely profess and sincerely
hold this true, Catholic Faith, which I acknowledge to be
essential for my salvation: and I promise most constantly
to retain and confess the same entire and inviolate, by
God's assistance, to the end of my life.

Notes: *The Profession of Faith of the Old Catholic Church
in America is a variation of the profession of the Roman
Catholic Church.*

* * *

ARTICLES OF FAITH [CONGREGATION OF ST. PAUL, THE OLD CATHOLIC CHURCH (HAMEL)]

1. God is principal; his attributes manifest only through
   matter to the outer man. God is not a person, nor
   does he appear to the outer man in any form of cloud
   or glory. God is a spirit, and they who worship him
   must worship him in spirit and in truth.

2. The power and glory of God's dominion neither
   increases nor diminishes by man's belief or disbelief;
   and God does not set aside his laws to please
   mankind.

3. The ego in man is of God, and at one with God, and
   is consequently immortal and everlasting.

4. The forms of man and woman are manifestations of
   the truth of God, but God does not manifest himself
   in the form of man or woman as a being.

5. Man's body is the temple in which the soul resides,
   and from the windows of which we view God's
   creations and evolutions.

6. At the transition or separation of the soul and body, the soul enters that secret state where none of the conditions of the earth have any charms, but the soft breeze and great power of the Holy Ghost bring comfort and solace to the weary or the anxious who are awaiting future action. Those who fail, however, to exercise the blessings and gifts of God, and who follow the dictates of the tempter and of the false prophet and the ensnaring doctrines of the wicked, remain in the bosom of the earth until they are freed from the binding powers of materialism, purified and assigned to the secret kingdom.

7. To keep holy the one sacred day of the week, that the soul may commune in spirit and ascend to contact with God, resting from all labours, and discriminating in all actions.

8. To keep silent in disputes, to close the eyes before evil, and to stop the ears before the blasphemers.

9. To preserve the Sacred Doctrines from the profane, never to speak of them to those who are not ready or qualified to understand, and be prepared always to reveal to the world that knowledge which will enable man to rise to greater heights.

10. To remain steadfast in all friendships and all brotherly relations, even unto death; in all positions of trust never to abuse the power or privilege granted, and, in all human relationships to be kind and forgiving, even to the enemies of the Faith.

* * *

CREDO (PROFESSION OF FAITH) (POLISH NATIONAL CATHOLIC CHURCH OF AMERICA)

1. I believe in God, the Almighty, cause and reason of all existence; in the most perfect Being, whose Spirit permeates this universe, who is the source of all material and spiritual life and its development. God, in relation to man, reveals Himself by His omnipotence, His creative power, by His omniscience and with His divine providence molds the fate of every man, all nations, kingdoms, and all mankind. God, in His inimitable way, for He is the Spirit of true life, light, and good, influences chosen souls of all nations, who in epochs of the development of mankind are the creative factors in the edification of His kingdom, God's kingdom on earth. God does not limit exclusively His influence to any one nation, race, epoch, or era; but implies it for all nations and all times, giving life, nurturing its development and attainment of the highest degree of culture of each individual nation, country, and all mankind. This divine influence is the outflow or result of His godly powers over man, and fruits of His spiritual beneficence are reaped by all individuals, nations, countries, races, and mankind.

2. I believe in Jesus Christ, the Redeemer, Spiritual Regenerater and Guide of this earth. I believe that Christ, our Lord, was the Messenger of God, being of the substance with God, the Father, and was born of a poor woman, Mary; that this Master of Nazareth revealed His godly mission on earth, by His life of the most supreme of ideals of good, wisdom, and sacrifice for all mankind; especially, for those who have marred their souls with sin and for the disinherited hath He also given His life on the cross. I believe that by His labors, teachings, and martyrdom, He became the glowing ember of all true, new human life, taking His beginning, strength, and fullness in the comprehension and acknowledgment of God, the Father, by loving Him, and fulfilling His sacred will.

3. I believe in the Holy Spirit, that the spirit of God controls this universe in a natural and moral order, that all His laws in the universe, and those with which He governs the souls of individual man, as well as collective humanity, are the results flowing from His spirit of strong will-power, good, and justice.

4. From this Holy Spirit flows His grace, that is an invisible, internal, creative power, which infers that if man cooperates and coordinates with this Spirit, he will become a partisan of peace of mind and soul, until he finds himself in union with God, in eternal, sublime, good fortune.

5. I believe in the necessity of uniting all believers, confessors of the Christian faith, into one body, the church of God; that the Christian, Apostolic, Universal Church is the representation of God's congregation of mankind, so proclaimed by the Saviour for whose existence worked and labored all noble people, and for which yearns and longs the human soul, ever desiring truth, light, love, justice, and complete appeasement in God.

6. I believe the Christian church is the true teacher, preceptor of all mankind, that it is the steward of God's graces, leader and light of our temporal pilgrimage to God and salvation; inasmuch as the confessors and members of this church, both lay and clerical, are united with the Divine Founder through faith and life emanating from this sincere faith.

7. I believe that every righteous Christian should take an active part in the spiritual life of the church, and this by listening to God's Word, through worthy receiving of the holy sacraments, and through fulfilling the principles founded by Jesus Christ and His Apostles, which have been submitted to us by the Church of Christ.

8. I believe that all people, as children of one Father, our God, are equal; that privileges, flowing from a difference in the racial, sexual, and religious status, or caste, or from the possession of unlimited riches, are a great wrong and injury, they are a violation, a rupture of the principles and laws of man with which he is endowed by his Creator and a blot on the escutcheon of man's worthiness, bestowed by God: that these unmerited privileges are a detriment to man in attaining his aim in life.

CREDO (PROFESSION OF FAITH) (POLISH NATIONAL CATHOLIC CHURCH OF AMERICA) (continued)

9. I believe that all people have the same inalienable right to life, to happiness, and to those means and ways which lead to the preservation of existence, to the betterment and salvation of our souls; but I also believe that all people have sacred obligations, duties, tasks to God, themselves, their nation, government, and to all humanity.

10. I believe in the ultimate justice of God; in future eternal life, which will be a continuation of our mortal struggle and pilgrimage on this earth; as to the condition and degree of perfection and happiness, dependent as it is, upon our present life, and above all, upon the state of our soul in the last few moments of this life.

11. I believe in immortality and happiness in the life to come; in the union of people with God, all generations, and at all times; because I firmly believe in the omnipotence of God's love, mercy, justice, and nothing else do I desire, but that it might so be. Amen.

Notes: *The Polish National Catholic Church of America is the only American church in communion with the Old Catholic Church in Holland. Assent to the Profession of Faith must be given by individuals who join the church.*

*   *   *

Anglicanism

THE THIRTY-NINE ARTICLES OF RELIGION

I. OF FAITH IN THE HOLY TRINITY.

There is but one living and true God, everlasting, without body, parts, or passions; of infinite power, wisdom, and goodness; the Maker, and Preserver of all things both visible and invisible. And in unity of this Godhead there be three Persons, of one substance, power, and eternity; the Father, the Son, and the Holy Ghost.

II. OF THE WORD OR SON OF GOD, WHICH WAS MADE VERY MAN.

The Son, which is the Word of the Father, begotten from everlasting of the Father, the very and eternal God, and of one substance with the Father, took Man's nature in the womb of the blessed Virgin, of her substance: so that two whole and perfect Natures, that is to say, the Godhead and Manhood, were joined together in one Person, never to be divided, whereof is one Christ, very God, and very Man; who truly suffered, was crucified, dead, and buried, to reconcile his Father to us, and to be a sacrifice, not only for original guilt, but also for actual sins of men.

III. OF THE GOING DOWN OF CHRIST INTO HELL.

As Christ died for us, and was buried; so also is it to be believed, that he went down into Hell.

IV. OF THE RESURRECTION OF CHRIST.

Christ did truly rise again from death, and took again his body, with flesh, bones, and all things appertaining to the perfection of Man's nature; wherewith he ascended into Heaven, and there sitteth, until he return to judge all Men at the last day.

V. OF THE HOLY GHOST.

The Holy Ghost, proceeding from the Father and the Son, is of one substance, majesty, and glory, with the Father and the Son, very and eternal God.

VI. OF THE SUFFICIENCY OF THE HOLY SCRIPTURES FOR SALVATION.

Holy Scripture containeth all things necessary to salvation: so that whatsoever is not read therein, nor may be proved thereby, is not to be required of any man, that it should be believed as an article of the Faith, or be thought requisite or necessary to salvation. In the name of the Holy Scripture we do understand those canonical Books of the Old and New Testament, of whose authority was never any doubt in the Church.

OF THE NAMES AND NUMBER OF THE CANONICAL BOOKS.

> Genesis
> Exodus
> Leviticus
> Numbers
> Deuteronomy
> Joshua
> Judges
> Ruth
> The First Book of Samuel
> The Second Book of Samuel
> The First Book of Kings
> The Second Book of Kings
> The First Book of Chronicles
> The Second Book of Chronicles
> The First Book of Esdras
> The Second Book of Esdras
> The Book of Esther
> The Book of Job
> The Psalms
> The Proverbs
> Ecclesiastes or Preacher
> Cantica, or Songs of Solomon
> Four Prophets the greater
> Twelve Prophets the less

And the other Books (as Hierome saith) the Church doth read for example of life and instruction of manners; but yet doth it not apply them to establish any doctrine; such are these following:

> The Third Book of Esdras
> The Fourth Book of Esdras
> The Book of Tobias
> The Book of Judith
> The rest of the Book of Esther
> The Book of Wisdom
> Jesus the Son of Sirach
> Baruch the Prophet
> The Song of the Three Children

The Story of Susanna
Of Bel and the Dragon
The Prayer of Manasses
The First Book of Maccabees
The Second Book of Maccabees

All the Books of the New Testament, as they are commonly received, we do receive, and account them Canonical.

VII. OF THE OLD TESTAMENT.

The Old Testament is not contrary to the New: for both in the Old and New Testament everlasting life is offered to Mankind by Christ, who is the only Mediator between God and Man, being both God and Man Wherefore they are not to be heard, which feign that the old Fathers did look only for transitory promises. Although the Law given from God by Moses, as touching Ceremonies and Rites, do not bind Christian men, nor the Civil precepts thereof ought of necessity to be received in any commonwealth; yet notwithstanding, no Christian man whatsoever is free from the obedience of the Commandments which are called Moral.

VIII. OF THE CREEDS.

The Nicene Creed, and that which is commonly called the Apostles' Creed, ought thoroughly to be received and believed: for they may be proved by most certain warrants of Holy Scripture.

IX. OF ORIGINAL OR BIRTH-SIN.

Original sin standeth not in the following of Adam, (as the Pelagians do vainly talk;) but it is the fault and corruption of the Nature of every man, that naturally is engendered of the offspring of Adam; whereby man is very far gone from original righteousness, and is of his own nature inclined to evil, so that the flesh lusteth always contrary to the Spirit; and therefore in every person born into this world, it deserveth God's wrath and damnation. And this infection of nature doth remain, yea in them that are regenerated; whereby the lust of the flesh, called in Greek, φρονηυα σαρκοξ, (which some do expound the wisdom, some sensuality, some the affection, some the desire, of the flesh,) is not subject to the Law of God. And although there is no condemnation for them that believe and are baptized; yet the Apostle doth confess, that concupiscence and lust hath of itself the nature of sin.

X. OF FREE-WILL.

The condition of Man after the fall of Adam is such, that he cannot turn and prepare himself, by his own natural strength and good works, to faith, and calling upon God. Wherefore we have no power to do good works pleasant and acceptable to God, without the grace of God by Christ preventing us, that we may have a good will, and working with us, when we have that good will.

XI. OF THE JUSTIFICATION OF MAN.

We are accounted righteous before God, only for the merit of our Lord and Saviour Jesus Christ by Faith, and not for our own works or deservings. Wherefore, that we are justified by Faith only, is a most wholesome Doctrine, and very full of comfort, as more largely is expressed in the Homily of Justification.

XII. OF GOOD WORKS.

Albeit that Good Works, which are the fruits of Faith, and follow after Justification, cannot put away our sins, and endure the severity of God's judgment; yet are they pleasing and acceptable to God in Christ, and do spring out necessarily of a true and lively Faith; insomuch that by them a lively Faith may be as evidently known as a tree discerned by the fruit.

XIII. OF WORKS BEFORE JUSTIFICATION.

Works done before the grace of Christ, and the Inspiration of his Spirit, are not pleasant to God, forasmuch as they spring not of faith in Jesus Christ; neither do they make men meet to receive grace, or (as the School-authors say) deserve grace of congruity: yea rather, for that they are not done as God hath willed and commanded them to be done, we doubt not but they have the nature of sin.

XIV. OF WORKS OF SUPEREROGATION.

Voluntary Works besides, over and above, God's Commandments, which they call Works of Supererogation, cannot be taught without arrogancy and impiety: for by them men do declare, that they do not only render unto God as much as they are bound to do, but that they do more for his sake, than of bounden duty is required: whereas Christ saith plainly, When ye have done all that are commanded to you, say, We are unprofitable servants.

XV. OF CHRIST ALONE WITHOUT SIN.

Christ in the truth of our nature was made like unto us in all things, sin only except, from which he was clearly void, both in his flesh, and in his spirit. He came to be the Lamb without spot, who, by sacrifice of himself once made, should take away the sins of the world; and sin (as Saint John saith) was not in him. But all we the rest, although baptized, and born again in Christ, yet offend in many things; and if we say we have no sin, we deceive ourselves, and the truth is not in us.

XVI. OF SIN AFTER BAPTISM.

Not every deadly sin willingly committed after Baptism is sin against the Holy Ghost, and unpardonable. Wherefore the grant of repentance is not to be denied to such as fall into sin after Baptism. After we have received the Holy Ghost, we may depart from grace given, and fall into sin, and by the grace of God we may arise again, and amend our lives. And therefore they are to be condemned, which say, they can no more sin as long as they live here, or deny the place of forgiveness to such as truly repent.

XVII. OF PREDESTINATION AND ELECTION.

Predestination to Life is the everlasting purpose of God, whereby (before the foundations of the world were laid) he hath constantly decreed by his counsel secret to us, to deliver from curse and damnation those whom he hath chosen in Christ out of mankind, and to bring them by Christ to everlasting salvation, as vessels made to honour Wherefore, they which be endued with so excellent a benefit of God, be called according to God's purpose by his Spirit working in due season: they through Grace obey the calling: they be justified freely: they be made sons of God by adoption: they be made like the image of his only-begotten Son Jesus Christ: they walk religiously in good

THE THIRTY-NINE ARTICLES OF RELIGION (continued)

works, and at length, by God's mercy, they attain to everlasting felicity.

As the godly consideration of Predestination, and our Election in Christ, is full of sweet, pleasant, and unspeakable comfort to godly persons, and such as feel in themselves the working of the Spirit of Christ, mortifying the works of the flesh, and their earthly members, and drawing up their mind to high and heavenly things, as well because it doth greatly establish and confirm their faith of eternal Salvation to be enjoyed through Christ, as because it doth fervently kindle their love towards God: So, for curious and carnal persons, lacking the Spirit of Christ, to have continually before their eyes the sentence of God's Predestination, is a most dangerous downfall, whereby the Devil doth thrust them either into desperation, or into wretchlessness of most unclean living, no less perilous than desperation.

Furthermore, we must receive God's promises in such wise, as they be generally set forth to us in Holy Scripture: and, in our doings, that Will of God is to be followed, which we have expressly declared unto us in the Word of God.

XVIII. OF OBTAINING ETERNAL SALVATION ONLY BY THE NAME OF CHRIST.

They also are to be had accursed that presume to say, That every man shall be saved by the Law or Sect which he professeth, so that he be diligent to frame his life according to that Law, and the light of Nature. For Holy Scripture doth set out unto us only the Name of Jesus Christ, whereby men must be saved.

XIX. OF THE CHURCH.

The visible Church of Christ is a congregation of faithful men, in which the pure Word of God is preached, and the Sacraments be duly ministered according to Christ's ordinance, in all those things that of necessity are requisite to the same.

As the Church of Jerusalem, Alexandria, and Antioch, have erred; so also the Church of Rome hath erred, not only in their living and manner of Ceremonies, but also in matters of Faith.

XX. OF THE AUTHORITY OF THE CHURCH.

The Church hath power to decree Rites or Ceremonies, and authority in Controversies of Faith: and yet it is not lawful for the Church to ordain any thing that is contrary to God's Word written, neither may it so expound one place of Scripture, that it be repugnant to another. Wherefore, although the Church be a witness and a keeper of Holy Writ, yet, as it ought not to decree any thing against the same, so besides the same ought it not to enforce any thing to be believed for necessity of Salvation.

XXI. OF THE AUTHORITY OF GENERAL COUNCILS.

[The Twenty-first of the former Articles is omitted; because it is partly of a local and civil nature, and is provided for, as to the remaining parts of it, in other Articles.]

XXII. OF PURGATORY.

The Romish Doctrine concerning Purgatory, Pardons, Worshipping and Adoration, as well of Images as of Relics, and also Invocation of Saints, is a fond thing, vainly invented, and grounded upon no warranty of Scripture, but rather repugnant to the Word of God.

XXIII. OF MINISTERING IN THE CONGREGATION.

It is not lawful for any man to take upon him the office of public preaching, or ministering the Sacraments in the Congregation, before he be lawfully called, and sent to execute the same. And those we ought to judge lawfully called and sent, which be chosen and called to this work by men who have public authority given unto them in the Congregation, to call and send Ministers into the Lord's vineyard.

XXIV. OF SPEAKING IN THE CONGREGATION IN SUCH A TONGUE AS THE PEOPLE UNDERSTANDETH.

It is a thing plainly repugnant to the Word of God, and the custom of the Primitive Church, to have public Prayer in the Church, or to minister the Sacraments, in a tongue not understood of the people.

XXV. OF THE SACRAMENTS.

Sacraments ordained of Christ be not only badges or tokens of Christian men's profession, but rather they be certain sure witnesses, and effectual signs of grace, and God's good will towards us, by the which he doth work invisibly in us, and doth not only quicken, but also strengthen and confirm our Faith in him.

There are two Sacraments ordained of Christ our Lord in the Gospel, that is to say, Baptism, and the Supper of the Lord.

Those five commonly called Sacraments, that is to say, Confirmation, Penance, Orders, Matrimony, and Extreme Unction, are not to be counted for Sacraments of the Gospel, being such as have grown partly of the corrupt following of the Apostles, partly are states of life allowed in the Scriptures; but yet have not like nature of Sacraments with Baptism, and the Lord's Supper, for that they have not any visible sign or ceremony ordained of God.

The Sacraments were not ordained of Christ to be gazed upon, or to be carried about, but that we should duly use them. And in such only as worthily receive the same, they have a wholesome effect or operation: but they that receive them unworthily, purchase to themselves damnation, as Saint Paul saith.

XXVI. OF THE UNWORTHINESS OF THE MINISTERS, WHICH HINDERS NOT THE EFFECT OF THE SACRAMENTS.

Although in the visible Church the evil be ever mingled with the good, and sometimes the evil have chief authority in the Ministration of the Word and Sacraments, yet forasmuch as they do not the same in their own name, but in Christ's, and do minister by his commission and authority, we may use their Ministry, both in hearing the Word of God, and in receiving the Sacraments. Neither is the effect of Christ's ordinance taken away by their wickedness, nor the grace of God's gifts diminished from such as by faith, and rightly, do receive the Sacraments ministered unto them; which be effectual, because of Christ's institution and promise, although they be ministered by evil men.

Nevertheless, it appertaineth to the discipline of the Church, that inquiry be made of evil Ministers, and that they be accused by those that have knowledge of their offences; and finally, being found guilty, by just judgment be deposed.

XXVII. OF BAPTISM.

Baptism is not only a sign of profession, and mark of difference, whereby Christian men are discerned from others that be not christened, but it is also a sign of Regeneration or New-Birth, whereby, as by an instrument, they that receive Baptism rightly are grafted into the Church; the promises of the forgiveness of sin, and of our adoption to be the sons of God by the Holy Ghost, are visibly signed and sealed; Faith is confirmed, and Grace increased by virtue of prayer unto God.

The Baptism of young Children is in any wise to be retained in the Church, as most agreeable with the institution of Christ.

XXVIII. OF THE LORD'S SUPPER.

The Supper of the Lord is not only a sign of the love that Christians ought to have among themselves one to another; but rather it is a Sacrament of our Redemption by Christ's death: insomuch that to such as rightly, worthily, and with faith, receive the same, the Bread which we break is a partaking of the Body of Christ; and likewise the Cup of Blessing is a partaking of the Blood of Christ.

Transubstantiation (or the change of the substance of Bread and Wine) in the Supper of the Lord, cannot be proved by Holy Writ; but is repugnant to the plain words of Scripture, overthroweth the nature of a Sacrament, and hath given occasion to many superstitions.

The Body of Christ is given, taken, and eaten, in the Supper, only after an heavenly and spiritual manner. And the mean whereby the Body of Christ is received and eaten in the Supper, is Faith.

The Sacrament of the Lord's Supper was not by Christ's ordinance reserved, carried about, lifted up, or worshipped.

XXIX. OF THE WICKED, WHICH EAT NOT THE BODY OF CHRIST IN THE USE OF THE LORD'S SUPPER.

The Wicked, and such as be void of a lively faith, although they do carnally and visibly press with their teeth (as Saint Augustine saith) the Sacrament of the Body and Blood of Christ; yet in no wise are they partakers of Christ: but rather, to their condemnation, do eat and drink the sign or Sacrament of so great a thing.

XXX. OF BOTH KINDS.

The Cup of the Lord is not to be denied to the Lay-people: for both the parts of the Lord's Sacrament, by Christ's ordinance and commandment, ought to be ministered to all Christian men alike.

XXXI. OF THE ONE OBLATION OF CHRIST FINISHED UPON THE CROSS.

The Offering of Christ once made is that perfect redemption, propitiation, and satisfaction, for all the sins of the whole world, both original and actual; and there is none other satisfaction for sin, but that alone. Wherefore the sacrifices of Masses, in the which it was commonly said, that the Priest did offer Christ for the quick and the dead, to have remission of pain or guilt, were blasphemous fables, and dangerous deceits.

XXXII. OF THE MARRIAGE OF PRIESTS.

Bishops, Priests, and Deacons, are not commanded by God's Law, either to vow the estate of single life, or to abstain from marriage: therefore it is lawful for them, as for all other Christian men, to marry at their own discretion, as they shall judge the same to serve better to godliness.

XXXIII. OF EXCOMMUNICATE PERSONS, HOW THEY ARE TO BE AVOIDED.

That person which by open denunciation of the Church is rightly cut off from the unity of the Church, and excommunicated, ought to be taken of the whole multitude of the faithful, as an Heathen and Publican, until he be openly reconciled by penance, and received into the Church by a Judge that hath authority thereunto.

XXXIV. OF THE TRADITIONS OF THE CHURCH.

It is not necessary that Traditions and Ceremonies be in all places one, or utterly like; for at all times they have been divers, and may be changed according to the diversity of countries, times, and men's manners, so that nothing be ordained against God's Word. Whosoever, through his private judgment, willingly and purposely, doth openly break the Traditions and Ceremonies of the Church, which be not repugnant to the Word of God, and be ordained and approved by common authority, ought to be rebuked openly, (that others may fear to do the like,) as he that offendeth against the common order of the Church, and hurteth the authority of the Magistrate, and woundeth the consciences of the weak brethren.

Every particular or national Church hath authority to ordain, change, and abolish, Ceremonies or Rites of the Church ordained only by man's authority, so that all things be done to edifying.

XXXV. OF THE HOMILIES.

The Second Book of Homilies, the several titles whereof we have joined under this Article, doth contain a godly and wholesome Doctrine, and necessary for these times, as doth the former Book of Homilies, which were set forth in the time of Edward the Sixth; and therefore we judge them to be read in Churches by the Ministers, diligently and distinctly, that they may be understanded of the people.

OF THE NAMES OF THE HOMILIES.

1. Of the right Use of the Church.
2. Against Peril of Idolatry.
3. Of repairing and keeping clean of Churches.
4. Of good Works: first of Fasting.

THE THIRTY-NINE ARTICLES OF RELIGION (continued)

5. Against Gluttony and Drunkenness.

6. Against Excess of Apparel.

7. Of Prayer.

8. Of the Place and Time of Prayer.

9. That Common Prayers and Sacraments ought to be ministered in a known tongue.

10. Of the reverend Estimation of God's Word.

11. Of Alms-doing.

12. Of the Nativity of Christ.

13. Of the Passion of Christ.

14. Of the Resurrection of Christ.

15. Of the worthy receiving of the Sacrament of the Body and Blood of Christ.

16. Of the Gifts of the Holy Ghost.

17. For the Rogation-days.

18. Of the State of Matrimony.

19. Of Repentance.

20. Against Idleness.

21. Against Rebellion.

XXXVI. OF CONSECRATION OF BISHOPS AND MINISTERS.

The Book of Consecration of Bishops, and Ordering of Priests and Deacons, as set forth by the General Convention of this Church in 1792, doth contain all things necessary to such Consecration and Ordering; neither hath it any thing that, of itself, is superstitious and ungodly. And, therefore, whosoever are consecrated or ordered according to said Form, we decree all such to be rightly, orderly, and lawfully consecrated and ordered.

XXXVII. OF THE POWER OF THE CIVIL MAGISTRATES.

The Power of the Civil Magistrate extendeth to all men, as well Clergy as Laity, in all things temporal; but hath no authority in things purely spiritual. And we hold it to be the duty of all men who are professors of the Gospel, to pay respectful obedience to the Civil Authority, regularly and legitimately constituted.

XXXVIII. OF CHRISTIAN MEN'S GOODS, WHICH ARE NOT COMMON.

The Riches and Goods of Christians are not common, as touching the right, title, and possession of the same; as certain Anabaptists do falsely boast. Notwithstanding, every man ought, of such things as he possesseth, liberally to give alms to the poor, according to his ability.

XXXIX. OF A CHRISTIAN MAN'S OATH.

As we confess that vain and rash Swearing is forbidden Christian men by our Lord Jesus Christ, and James his Apostle, so we judge, that Christian Religion doth not prohibit, but that a man may swear when the Magistrate requireth, in a cause of faith and charity, so it be done according to the Prophet's teaching, in justice, judgment, and truth.

Notes: *One of the prime documents of the Elizabethan via-media settlement of the Protestant-Catholic polarity within the Church of England was a new doctrinal statement consisting of thirty-nine articles of religion. These articles, first published in 1563, have since been doctrinally definitive of the Anglican theological heritage and are printed in the back of the Prayer Book. As has been frequently noted, they are very brief in comparison with the Lutheran and Reformed confessions. Unlike the statements of the Continental Protestants, who were trying to give a lengthy summary of their full doctrinal position, the Thirty-nine Articles merely attempted a minimal doctrinal agreement for an otherwise diverse and inclusive national church. The articles do place the Anglicans in the Western Orthodox tradition while specifically rejecting some of the peculiarities of the Roman Catholic Church.*

The American Church made a few minor revisions to the text of the articles in 1801. The text reproduced here is from the 1928 Prayer Book. The Thirty-nine Articles of Religion is the doctrinal statement of the Protestant Episcopal Church in the U.S.A., the largest Anglican body in North America; its Canadian counterpart, the Anglican Church of Canada; and almost all of the smaller Anglican splinter groups.

*　　　*　　　*

THE AFFIRMATION OF ST. LOUIS (1976)

In the name of the Father and of the Son and of the Holy Ghost. Amen.

THE CONTINUATION OF ANGLICANISM. We affirm that the Church of our fathers, sustained by the most Holy Trinity, lives yet, and that we, being moved by the Holy Spirit to walk only in that way, are determined to continue in the Catholic Faith, Apostolic Order, Orthodox Worship and Evangelical Witness of the traditional Anglican Church, doing all things necessary for the continuance of the same. We are upheld and strengthened in this determination by the knowledge that many provinces and dioceses of the Anglican Communion have continued steadfast in the same Faith, Order, Worship and Witness, and that they continue to confine ordination to the priesthood and the episcopate to males. We rejoice in these facts and we affirm our solidarity with these provinces and dioceses.

THE DISSOLUTION OF ANGLICAN AND EPISCOPAL CHURCH STRUCTURE. We affirm that the Anglican Church of Canada and the Protestant Episcopal Church in the United States of America, by their unlawful attempts to alter Faith, Order and Morality (especially in their General Synod of 1975 and General Convention of 1976), have departed from Christ's One, Holy, Catholic and Apostolic Church.

THE NEED TO CONTINUE ORDER IN THE CHURCH. We affirm that all former ecclesiastical governments, being fundamentally impaired by the schismatic acts of lawless Councils, are of no effect among us, and that we must now reorder such godly discipline as will strengthen us in the continuation of our common life and witness.

THE INVALIDITY OF SCHISMATIC AUTHORITY. We affirm that the claim of any such schismatic person or body to act against any Church member, clerical or lay, for his witness to the whole Faith is with no authority of Christ's true Church, and any such inhibition, deposition or discipline is without effect and is absolutely null and void.

THE NEED FOR PRINCIPLES AND A CONSTITUTION. We affirm that fundamental principles (doctrinal, moral, and constitutional) are necessary for the present, and that a Constitution (redressing the defects and abuses of our former governments) should be adopted, whereby the Church may be soundly continued.

THE CONTINUATION OF COMMUNION WITH CANTERBURY. We affirm our continued relations of communion with the See of Canterbury and all faithful parts of the Anglican Communion.

WHEREFORE, with a firm trust in Divine Providence, and before Almighty God and all the company of heaven, we solemnly affirm, covenant and declare that we, lawful and faithful members of the Anglican and Episcopal Churches, shall now and hereafter continue and be the unified continuing Anglican Church in North America, in true and valid succession thereto.

FUNDAMENTAL PRINCIPLES. In order to carry out these declarations, we set forth these fundamental Principles for our continued life and witness.

PREFACE: In the firm conviction that "we shall be saved through the grace of the Lord Jesus Christ," and that "there is no other name under heaven given among men by which we must be saved," and acknowledging our duty to proclaim Christ's saving Truth to all peoples, nations and tongues, we declare our intention to hold fast the One, Holy, Catholic and Apostolic Faith of God.

We acknowledge that rule of faith laid down by St. Vincent of Lérins: "Let us hold that which has been believed everywhere, always and by all, for that is truly and properly Catholic."

I. PRINCIPLES OF DOCTRINE

1. THE NATURE OF THE CHURCH. We gather as people called by God to be faithful and obedient to Him. As the Royal Priestly People of God, the Church is called to be, in fact, the manifestation of Christ in and to the world. True religion is revealed to man by God. We cannot decide what is truth, but rather (in obedience) ought to receive, accept, cherish, defend and teach what God has given us. The Church is created by God, and is beyond the ultimate control of man.

   The Church is the Body of Christ at work in the world. She is the society of the baptized called out from the world: in it, but not of it. As Christ's faithful Bride, she is different from the world and must not be influenced by it.

2. THE ESSENTIALS OF TRUTH AND ORDER. We repudiate all deviation or departure from the Faith, in whole or in part, and bear witness to these essential principles of evangelical Truth and apostolic Order:

HOLY SCRIPTURES. The Holy Scriptures of the Old and New Testaments as the authentic record of God's revelation of Himself, His saving activity, and moral demands—a revelation valid for all men and all time.

THE CREEDS. The Nicene Creed as the authoritative summary of the chief articles of the Christian Faith, together with the Apostles' Creed, and that known as the Creed of St. Athanasius to be "thoroughly received and believed" in the sense they have had always in the Catholic Church.

TRADITION. The received Tradition of the Church and its teachings as set forth by "the ancient catholic bishops and doctors," and especially as defined by the Seven Ecumenical Councils of the undivided Church, to the exclusion of all errors, ancient and modern.

SACRAMENTS. The Sacraments of Baptism, Confirmation, the Holy Eucharist, Holy Matrimony, Holy Orders, Penance and Unction of the Sick, as objective and effective signs of the continued presence and saving activity of Christ our Lord among His people and as His covenanted means for conveying His grace. In particular, we affirm the necessity of Baptism and the Holy Eucharist (where they may be had)—Baptism as incorporating us into Christ (with its completion in Confirmation as the "seal of the Holy Spirit"), and the Eucharist as the sacrifice which unites us to the all-sufficient Sacrifice of Christ on the Cross and the Sacrament in which He feeds us with His Body and Blood.

HOLY ORDERS. The Holy Orders of bishops, priests and deacons as the perpetuation of Christ's gift of apostolic ministry to His Church, asserting the necessity of a bishop of apostolic succession (or a priest ordained by such) as the celebrant of the Eucharist—these Orders consisting exclusively of men in accordance with Christ's Will and institution (as evidenced by the Scriptures), and the universal practice of the Catholic Church.

DEACONESSES. The ancient office and ministry of Deaconesses as a lay vocation for women, affirming the need for proper encouragement of that office.

DUTY OF BISHOPS. Bishops as Apostles, Prophets, Evangelists, Shepherds and Teachers, as well as their duty (together with other clergy and the laity) to guard and defend the purity and integrity of the Church's Faith and Moral Teaching.

THE USE OF OTHER FORMULAE. In affirming these principles, we recognize that all Anglican statements of faith and liturgical formulae must be interpreted in accordance with them.

INCOMPETENCE OF CHURCH BODIES TO ALTER TRUTH. We disclaim any right or competence to suppress, alter or amend any of the ancient Ecumenical Creeds and definitions of Faith, to set aside or depart from Holy Scripture, or to alter or deviate from the essential prerequisites of any Sacrament.

THE AFFIRMATION OF ST. LOUIS (1976) (continued)

UNITY WITH OTHER BELIEVERS. We declare our firm intention to seek and achieve full sacramental communion and visible unity with other Christians who "worship the Trinity in Unity, and Unity in Trinity," and who hold the Catholic and Apostolic Faith in accordance with the foregoing principles.

II. PRINCIPLES OF MORALITY

The conscience, as the inherent knowledge of right and wrong, cannot stand alone as a sovereign arbiter of morals. Every Christian is obligated to form his conscience by the Divine Moral Law and the Mind of Christ as revealed in Holy Scriptures, and by the teachings and Tradition of the Church. We hold that when the Christian conscience is thus properly informed and ruled, it must affirm the following moral principles:

INDIVIDUAL RESPONSIBILITY. All people, individually and collectively, are responsible to their Creator for their acts, motives, thoughts and words, since "we must all appear before the judgment seat of Christ ..."

SANCTITY OF HUMAN LIFE. Every human being, from the time of his conception, is a creature and child of God, made in His image and likeness, an infinitely precious soul; and that the unjustifiable or inexcusable taking of life is always sinful.

MAN'S DUTY TO GOD. All people are bound by the dictates of the Natural Law and by the revealed Will of God, insofar as they can discern them.

FAMILY LIFE. The God-given sacramental bond in marriage between one man and one woman is God's loving provision for procreation and family life, and sexual activity is to be practiced only within the bonds of Holy Matrimony.

MAN AS SINNER. We recognize that man, as inheritor of original sin, is "very far gone from original righteousness," and as a rebel against God's authority is liable to His righteous judgment.

MAN AND GOD'S GRACE. We recognize, too, that God loves His children and particularly has shown it forth in the redemptive work of our Lord Jesus Christ, and that man cannot be saved by any effort of his own, but by the Grace of God, through repentance and acceptance of God's forgiveness.

CHRISTIAN'S DUTY TO BE MORAL. We believe, therefore, it is the duty of the Church and her members to bear witness to Christian Morality, to follow it in their lives, and to reject the false standards of the world.

III. CONSTITUTIONAL PRINCIPLES

In the constitutional revision which must be undertaken, we recommend, for the consideration of continuing Anglicans, the following:

RETAIN THE BEST OF BOTH PROVINCES. That the traditional and tested features of the Canadian and American ecclesiastical systems be retained and used in the administration of the continuing Church.

SELECTION OF BISHOPS. That a non-political means for selection of bishops be devised, adopted and used.

TRIPARTITE SYNOD. That the Church be generally governed by a Holy Synod of three branches (episcopal, clerical and lay), under the presidency of the Primate of the Church.

SCRIPTURAL STANDARDS FOR THE MINISTRY. That the apostolic and scriptural standards for the sacred Ministry be used for all orders of Ministers.

CONCURRENCE OF ALL ORDERS FOR DECISIONS. That the Constitution acknowledge the necessity of the concurrence of all branches of the Synod for decisions in all matters, and that extraordinary majorities by required for the favorable consideration of all matters of importance.

RE-ESTABLISHMENT OF DISCIPLINE. That the Church re-establish an effective permanent system of ecclesiastical courts for the defense of the Faith and the maintenance of discipline over all her members.

CONSTITUTIONAL ASSEMBLY TO BE CALLED. That our bishops shall call a Constitutional Assembly of lay and clerical representatives of dioceses and parishes to convene at the earliest appropriate time to draft a Constitution and Canons by which we may by unified and governed, with special reference to this Affirmation, and with due consideration to ancient Custom and the General Canon Law, and to the former law of our provinces.

INTERIM ACTION. In the meantime, trusting in the everlasting strength of God to carry us through all our trials, we commend all questions for decision to the proper authorities in each case: Episcopal, diocesan, and parochial, encouraging all the faithful to support our witness as subscribers to this Affirmation, and inviting all so doing to share our fellowship and the work of the Church.

IV. PRINCIPLES OF WORSHIP

PRAYER BOOK: THE STANDARD OF WORSHIP. In the continuing Anglican Church, the Book of Common Prayer is (and remains) one work in two editions: The Canadian Book of 1962 and the American Book of 1928. Each is fully and equally authoritative. No other standard for worship exists.

CERTAIN VARIANCES PERMITTED. For liturgical use, only the Book of Common Prayer and service books conforming to and incorporating it shall be used.

V. PRINCIPLES OF ACTION

INTERCOMMUNION WITH OTHER APOSTOLIC CHURCHES. The continuing Anglicans remain in full communion with the See of Canterbury and with all other faithful parts of the Anglican Communion, and should actively seek similar relations with all other Apostolic and Catholic Churches, provided that agreement in the essentials of Faith and Order first be reached.

NON-INVOLVEMENT WITH NON-APOSTOLIC GROUPS. We recognize that the World Council of Churches, and many national and other Councils adhering to the World Council, are non-Apostolic, humanist and secular in purpose and practice, and that under such circumstances, we cannot be members of any of them. We also recognize that the Consultation of Church Union (COCU) and all other such schemes, being non-Apostolic and non-Catholic in their present concept and form, are unacceptable to us, and that we cannot be associated with any of them.

NEED FOR SOUND THEOLOGICAL TRAINING. Re-establishment of spiritual, orthodox and scholarly theological education under episcopal supervision is imperative, and should be encouraged and promoted by all in authority; and learned and godly bishops, other clergy and lay people should undertake and carry on that work without delay.

FINANCIAL AFFAIRS. The right of congregations to control of their temporalities should be firmly and constitutionally recognized and protected.

ADMINISTRATIVE MATTERS. Administration should, we believe, be limited to the most simple and necessary acts, so that emphasis may be centered on worship, pastoral care, spiritual and moral soundness, personal good works, and missionary outreach, in response to God's love for us.

THE CHURCH AS WITNESS TO TRUTH. We recognize also that, as keepers of God's will and truth for man, we can and ought to witness to that will and truth against all manifest evils, remembering that we are as servants in the world, but God's servants first.

PENSIONS AND INSURANCE. We recognize our immediate responsibility to provide for the establishment of sound pension and insurance programs for the protection of the stipendiary clergy and other Church workers.

LEGAL DEFENSE. We recognize the immediate need to coordinate legal resources, financial and professional, for the defense of congregations imperiled by their stand for the Faith, and commend this need most earnestly to the diocesan and parochial authorities.

CONTINUATION, NOT INNOVATION. In this gathering witness of Anglicans and Episcopalians, we continue to be what we are. We do nothing new. We form no new body, but continue as Anglicans and Episcopalians.

NOW, THEREFORE, deeply aware of our duty to all who love and believe the Faith of our Fathers, of our duty to God, who alone shall judge what we do, we make this Affirmation.

Before God, we claim our Anglican/Episcopal inheritance, and proclaim the same to the whole Church, through Jesus Christ our Lord, to whom, with the Father and the Holy Ghost, be all honor and glory, world without end. Amen.

Notes: *In 1976, members and former members of the Protestant Episcopal Church in the U.S.A. and the Anglican Church of Canada gathered in St. Louis, Missouri, to protest changes within those jurisdictions. A lengthy statement was adopted by those in attendance and subsequently became a basis around which new jurisdictions, such as the Anglican Catholic Church, were formed. Although the affirmation describes and has influenced the position of many smaller Anglican bodies, most have not accepted the affirmation in any official manner.*

* * *

DECLARATION OF PRINCIPLES AND ARTICLES OF RELIGION (REFORMED EPISCOPAL CHURCH)

DECLARATION OF PRINCIPLES

I. The Reformed Episcopal Church, holding "the faith once delivered unto the saints," declares its belief in the Holy Scriptures of the Old and New Testaments as the Word of God, and the sole Rule of Faith and Practice; in the Creed "commonly called the Apostles' Creed;" in the Divine institution of the Sacraments of Baptism and the LORD'S Supper; and in the doctrines of grace substantially as they are set forth in the Thirty-nine Articles of Religion.

II. This Church recognizes and adheres to Episcopacy, not as of Divine right, but as a very ancient and desirable form of Church polity.

III. This Church, retaining a Liturgy which shall not be imperative or repressive of freedom in prayer, accepts The Book of Common Prayer, as it was revised, proposed, and recommended for use by the General Convention of the Protestant Episcopal Church, A. D. 1785, reserving full liberty to alter, abridge, enlarge, and amend the same, as may seem most conducive to the edification of the people, "provided that the substance of the faith be kept entire."

IV. This Church condemns and rejects the following erroneous and strange doctrines as contrary to God's Word:

First, That the Church of Christ exists only in one order or form of ecclesiastical polity:

Second, That Christian Ministers are "priests" in another sense than that in which all believers are "a royal priesthood:"

Third, That the LORD'S Table is an altar on which the oblation of the Body and Blood of Christ is offered anew to the Father:

Fourth, That the Presence of Christ in the LORD'S Supper is a presence in the elements of Bread and Wine:

Fifth, That Regeneration is inseparably connected with Baptism.

**DECLARATION OF PRINCIPLES AND ARTICLES OF
RELIGION (REFORMED EPISCOPAL CHURCH) (continued)**

ARTICLES OF RELIGION

Whereas, This Church has, in its Declaration of Principles, proclaimed its belief in the doctrines of grace substantially as they were set forth in the Thirty-nine Articles; therefore,

RESOLVED: As the sense of this Council, that the Articles reported by the Committee on Doctrine and Worship, and accepted at this Council, be and are hereby adopted, as containing substantially the great truths known as the "Doctrines of Grace."

RESOLVED: That the foregoing preamble and resolution be printed as a Prefatory Note to the Articles of Religion.

Article I. OF THE HOLY TRINITY

There is but one living and true God, who is a spirit, everlasting; of infinite power, wisdom, and goodness; the Maker and Preserver of all things, both visible and invisible. And in unity of this Godhead, there be three Persons, of one substance, power, and eternity; the Father, the Son, and the Holy Ghost.

Article II. OF THE WORD, OR SON OF GOD, WHICH WAS MADE VERY MAN

The Son, who is the Word of the Father, begotten from everlasting of the Father, the very and eternal God, of one substance with the Father, took man's nature in the womb of the blessed virgin, of her substance: so that two whole and perfect natures, that is to say, the Godhead and manhood, were joined together in one Person, never to be divided, whereof is one Christ, very God and very man; who truly suffered, was crucified, dead and buried, to satisfy Divine justice, and to reconcile us to his Father, and to be a sacrifice, not only for original sin, but also for actual sins of men.

Article III. OF THE RESURRECTION OF CHRIST, AND HIS SECOND COMING

Christ did truly rise from death, and took again his body, with flesh, bones, and all things appertaining to the perfection of man's nature, wherewith he ascended into heaven, and there sitteth, our High Priest and Advocate, at the right hand of the Father, whence he will return to judge the world in righteousness. This Second Coming is the blessed hope of the Church. The heavens have received him, till the times of the restitution of all things. To those who look for him he shall appear a second time without sin unto salvation. Then shall he change the body of our humiliation that it may be fashioned like unto his glorious body. He will take to himself his great power, and shall reign till he have put all enemies under his feet.

Article IV. OF THE HOLY GHOST

The Holy Ghost, proceeding from the Father and the Son, is of one substance, majesty, and glory, with the Father and the Son, very and eternal God.

It is the work of the Holy Ghost to reprove and convince the world of sin, and of righteousness, and of judgment; to take of the things of Christ and show them to men; to regenerate—making men willing, leading them to faith in Christ, and forming Christ in them the hope of glory; to strengthen them with might in their inner man, that Christ may dwell in their hearts by faith; and to secure in them that walking in the ways of God which is called the Fruit of the Spirit. The True Church is thus called out of the world, and is builded together for an habitation of God, through the Spirit.

Article V. OF THE SUFFICIENCY OF THE HOLY SCRIPTURES FOR SALVATION

All Scripture is given by inspiration of God. Holy men of God spake as they were moved by the Holy Ghost: Holy Scripture is therefore the Word of God; not only does it contain the Oracles of God, but it is itself the very Oracles of God. And hence it containeth all things necessary to salvation: so that whatsoever is not read therein, nor may be proved thereby, is not to be required of any man, that it should be believed as an article of faith, or be thought requisite or necessary to salvation. In the name of the Holy Scripture we do understand the canonical books of the Old and New Testament, viz.:

OF THE OLD TESTAMENT

Genesis	The Proverbs
Exodus	Ecclesiastes
Leviticus	Song of Solomon
Numbers	Isaiah
Deuteronomy	Jeremiah
Joshua	Lamentations of
Judges	Jeremiah
Ruth	Ezekiel
The 1st Book of Samuel	Daniel
The 2d Book of Samuel	Hosea
The 1st Book of Kings	Joel
The 2d Book of Kings	Amos
The 1st Book of Chronicles	Obadiah
	Jonah
The 2d Book of Chronicles	Micah
	Nahum
The Book of Ezra	Habakkuk
The Book of Nehemiah	Zephaniah
The Book of Esther	Haggai
The Book of Job	Zechariah
The Psalms	Malachi

OF THE NEW TESTAMENT

Matthew	1st Timothy
Mark	2d Timothy
Luke	Titus
John	Philemon
Acts of the Apostles	Hebrews
Romans	James
1st Corinthians	1st Peter
2d Corinthians	2d Peter
Galatians	1st John
Ephesians	2d John
Philippians	3d John
Colossians	Jude
1st Thessalonians	The Revelation
2d Thessalonians	

The Book commonly called "The Apocrypha" is not a portion of God's Word, and is not therefore to be read in churches, nor to be used in establishing any doctrine.

Article VI. OF THE OLD TESTAMENT

The Old Testament is not contrary to the New: for both in the Old and New Testament everlasting life is offered to Mankind by Christ, who is the only Mediator between God and Man, being both God and Man. Wherefore they are not to be heard, which feign that the old Fathers did look only for transitory promises; and although the Law given from God by Moses, as touching Ceremonies and Rites, does not bind Christian men, nor the Civil precepts thereof ought of necessity to be received in any commonwealth; yet notwithstanding, as a rule of right living, no Christian man whatsoever is free from the obedience of the Commandments which are called Moral.

Article VII. OF ORIGINAL OR BIRTH-SIN

Original sin standeth not in the following of Adam, as the Pelagians do vainly talk; but it is the fault and corruption of the nature of every man, that naturally is engendered of the offspring of Adam, whereby man is wholly gone from original righteousness, and is of his own nature inclined to evil, so that the flesh lusteth always contrary to the Spirit; and therefore in every person born into this world, it deserveth God's condemnation. Men are, as the Apostle speaks, "by nature the children of wrath." And this infection of nature doth remain, yea, in them that are regenerated. And although there is no condemnation for them that are in Christ Jesus, yet the Apostle doth confess, that concupiscence or lust in such hath of itself the nature of sin.

Article VIII. OF MAN'S CONDITION BY NATURE

The condition of man after the fall of Adam is such, that he cannot turn and prepare himself, by his own natural strength and good works, to faith, and calling upon God. Wherefore we have no power to do good works pleasant and acceptable to God, without the grace of God by Christ first inclining us, that we may have a good will, and working with us, when we have that good will.

Article IX. OF WORKS BEFORE JUSTIFICATION

Works commonly called good before the grace of Christ and the inspiration of his Spirit, have not the nature of obedience to God, forasmuch as they spring not of Faith in Jesus Christ, neither do they make men meet to deserve, or to receive grace.

Article X. OF REGENERATION, OR THE NEW BIRTH

Regeneration is the creative act of the Holy Ghost, whereby he imparts to the soul a new spiritual life.

And whosoever believeth in Christ is born again, for, saith the Scripture, "ye are all the children of God by faith in Christ Jesus."

Article XI. OF FAITH

The faith which brings justification is simply the reliance or dependence on Christ which accepts him as the sacrifice for our sins, and as our righteousness.

We may thus rely on Christ, either tremblingly or confidingly; but in either case it is saving faith. If, though tremblingly, we rely on him in his obedience for us unto death, instantly we come into union with him, and are justified. If, however, we confidingly rely on him, then have we the comfort of our justification. Simply by faith in Christ are we justified and saved.

Article XII. OF THE JUSTIFICATION OF MAN

We are pardoned and accounted righteous before God, only for the Merit of our LORD and Saviour Jesus Christ, by Faith; and not for our own Works or Deservings. He who knew no sin was made sin for us, that we might be made the righteousness of God in him. He bare our sins in his own body. It pleased our heavenly Father, of his infinite mercy, without any our desert or deserving, to provide for us the most precious sacrifice of Christ, whereby our ransom might be fully paid, the Law fulfilled, and his justice fully satisfied. So that Christ is himself the righteousness of all them that truly do believe in him. He for them paid their ransom, by his death. He for them fulfilled the Law, in his life. So that now in him, and by him, every true Christian man may be called a fulfiller of the Law. Wherefore, that we are justified by Faith only, is a most wholesome doctrine, and very full of comfort.

Article XIII. OF REPENTANCE

The Repentance required by Scripture, is a change of mind toward God, and is the effect of the conviction of sin, wrought by the Holy Ghost.

The unconverted man may have a sense of remorse, or of shame and self-reproach, and yet he may have neither a change of mind toward God, nor any true sorrow; but when he accepts Christ as his Saviour, therein he manifests a change of mind, and is in possession of repentance unto life. The sinner comes to Christ through no labored process of repenting and sorrowing; but he comes to Christ and repentance both at once, by means of simply believing. And ever afterwards his repentance is deep and genuine in proportion as his faith is simple and childlike.

Article XIV. OF THE SONSHIP OF BELIEVERS

Believers in Christ are born of God, through the regenerating power of his Spirit, and are partakers of the Divine nature; for if "that which is born of the flesh is flesh," so "that which is born of the Spirit is spirit."

And all who are thus born of God are sons of God, and joint heirs with Christ; and therefore, without distinction of name, brethren with Christ and with one another.

Article XV. OF GOOD WORKS

Good Works, which are the Fruits of Faith, and follow after justification, are pleasing and acceptable to God in Christ, and do spring out, necessarily, of a true and lively Faith; insomuch that by them a lively faith may be as evidently known, as a tree discerned by the fruit. They who truly believe will seek to do the will of God, and they who do not thus seek are not to be accounted true believers.

Article XVI. OF WORKS OF SUPEREROGATION

Voluntary Works, besides, over and above God's Commandments, which they call Works of Supererogation, cannot be taught without arrogancy and impiety. For by them men do declare, that they do not only render unto God as much as they are bound to do, but that they do more for his sake than of bounden duty is required:

Whereas Christ saith plainly, When ye have done all that
are commanded to you, say, We are unprofitable servants.

Article XVII. SALVATION ONLY IN CHRIST

Holy Scripture doth set out unto us the Name of Jesus
Christ only, whereby men must be saved. His was a
finished work, and completely sufficient. Without any
merit or deserving on our part, he has secured to believers
in him pardon, acceptance, sonship, sanctification, redemption, and eternal glory. Those who believe in him are
in him complete. They are even now justified and have a
present salvation; though they may not at all times have
the sense of its possession.

Article XVIII. OF ELECTION, PREDESTINATION, AND FREE WILL

While the Scriptures distinctly set forth the election,
predestination, and calling of the people of God unto
eternal life, as Christ saith: "All that the Father giveth me
shall come to me;" they no less positively affirm man's free
agency and responsibility, and that salvation is freely
offered to all through Christ.

This Church, accordingly, simply affirms these doctrines
as the Word of God sets them forth, and submits them to
the individual judgment of its members, as taught by the
Holy Spirit; strictly charging them that God commandeth
all men everywhere to repent, and that we can be saved
only by faith in Jesus Christ.

Article XIX. OF SIN AFTER CONVERSION

The grant of repentance is not to be denied to such as fall
into sin after conversion: that is to say, after, by the
quickening into life by the Holy Ghost, they have turned
to God by faith in Christ, and have been brought into that
change of mind which is repentance unto life. For after we
have received the Holy Ghost we may, through unbelief,
carelessness, and worldliness, fall into sin, and by the grace
of God we may arise again, and amend our lives; but every
such fall is a grievous dishonor to our LORD, and a sore
injury to ourselves.

Article XX. OF CHRIST, ALONE WITHOUT SIN

Christ, in the truth of our nature, was made like unto us in
all things, sin only excepted, from which he was clearly
void, both in his flesh, and in his spirit. He came to be the
Lamb without spot, who, by sacrifice of himself, made
once for ever, should take away the sin of the world; and
sin (as St. John saith) was not in him. But all we the rest,
although born again in Christ, yet offend in many things;
and if we say we have no sin, we deceive ourselves, and the
truth is not in us.

Article XXI. OF THE CHURCH

The souls dispersed in all the world, who adhere to Christ
by faith, who are partakers of the Holy Ghost, and
worship the Father in spirit and in truth, are the body of
Christ, the house of God, the flock of the Good Shepherd—the holy, universal Christian Church.

A visible Church of Christ is a congregation of believers in
which the pure Word of God is preached, and Baptism and
the LORD's Supper are duly ministered according to

Christ's ordinance, in all those things that of necessity are
requisite to the same. And those things are to be
considered requisite which the LORD himself did, he
himself commanded, and his apostles confirmed.

As the Church of Jerusalem, Alexandria, Antioch, and
Rome have erred: so also others have erred and may err,
not only in their living and manner of ceremonies, but also
in matters of Faith.

Article XXII. OF THE AUTHORITY OF A CHURCH

A church hath power to decree Ceremonies, and to
establish forms of worship, and laws for the government
and discipline of its members, and to declare its own faith;
yet it is not lawful for any Church to ordain or decide
anything that is contrary to God's Word written, neither
may it so expound one place of Scripture, that it be
repugnant to another. And as the Church ought not to
decree anything against the same, so besides the same
ought it not to enforce anything to be believed for necessity
of salvation. The Nicene Creed, as set forth in the Prayer-
book of this Church, and that which is commonly called
the Apostles' Creed, ought to be received and believed; for
they may be proved by Holy Scripture.

Article XXIII. OF THE AUTHORITY OF GENERAL COUNCILS

General Councils (forasmuch as they be an assembly of
men, whereof all be not governed with the Spirit and Word
of God), may err, and sometimes have erred, not only in
worldly matters, but also in things pertaining to God.
Wherefore things ordained by them as necessary to
salvation are not binding, as such, on a Christian man's
conscience, unless it may be proved that they be taken out
of Holy Scripture. No law or authority can override
individual responsibility, and therefore the right of private
judgment: For the individual Christian, as Christ distinctly
affirms, is to be judged by the Word. The only Rule of
Faith is God's Word written.

Article XXIV. OF MINISTERING IN THE CONGREGATION

Those who take upon themselves the office of public
preaching, or ministering the ordinances in the congregation, should be lawfully called thereunto, and sent to
execute the same. And those we ought to judge lawfully
called and sent, which be moved to this work by the Holy
Ghost, and are duly accredited by the LORD'S People.

That doctrine of "Apostolic Succession," by which it is
taught that the ministry of the Christian Church must be
derived through a series of uninterrupted ordinations,
whether by tactual succession or otherwise, and that
without the same there can be no valid ministry, no
Christian Church, and no due ministration of Baptism and
the LORD'S Supper, is wholly rejected as unscriptural,
and productive of great mischief.

This Church values its historic ministry, but recognizes
and honors as equally valid the ministry of other
Churches, even as God the Holy Ghost has accompanied
their work with demonstration and power.

Article XXV. OF THE SACRAMENTS

By the word Sacrament this Church is to be understood as meaning only a symbol or sign divinely appointed.

Our LORD Jesus Christ hath knit together his people in a visible company by sacraments, most few in number, most easy to be kept, most excellent in signification, viz.: Baptism and the LORD'S Supper.

Those five so-called Sacraments, that is to say, Confirmation, Penance, Orders, Matrimony, and Extreme Unction, are not to be counted for Sacraments of the Gospel, being such as have grown partly of the corrupt following of the Apostles, partly are states of life allowed by the Scriptures; but yet have not like nature of Sacraments with Baptism and the LORD'S Supper, for that they have not any visible sign or ceremony ordained of God.

And in such only as worthily receive Baptism and the LORD'S Supper are they of spiritual benefit, and yet not that of the work wrought (*ex opere operato*), as some men speak. Which word, as it is strange and unknown to Holy Scripture, so it gendereth no godly, but a very superstitious sense. In such as receive them rightly, faith is confirmed and grace increased by virtue of prayer to God. But they that receive them unworthily, purchase to themselves judgment, as St. Paul saith; while it is equally true that none, however conscious of unworthiness, are debarred from receiving them, if they are trusting in the LORD Jesus Christ alone for salvation.

Article XXVI. OF BAPTISM

Baptism represents the death of believers with Christ, and their rising with him to newness of life. It is a sign of profession, whereby they publicly declare their faith in him. It is intended as a sign of regeneration or new birth. They that are baptized are grafted into the visible Church: the promises of the forgiveness of sin and of adoption to be the sons of God by the Holy Ghost, are visibly set forth. The Baptism of young children is retained in this Church, as agreeable to ancient usage and not contrary to Holy Writ.

Article XXVII. OF THE LORD'S SUPPER

The Supper of the LORD is a memorial of our Redemption by Christ's death, for thereby we do show forth the LORD'S death till he come. It is also a symbol of the soul's feeding upon Christ. And it is a sign of the communion that we should have with one another.

Transubstantiation (or the change of the substance of bread and wine into the very body and blood of Christ) in the Supper of the LORD, cannot be proved by Holy Writ, is repugnant to the plain words of Scripture, overthroweth the nature of a Sacrament, and hath given occasion to many and idolatrous superstitions.

Consubstantiation (or the doctrine that Christ is veiled under the unchanged bread and wine, and that his very body and blood are present therein and separate the one from the other) is utterly without warrant of Scripture, is contradictory of the fact that Christ, being raised, dieth no more, and is productive, equally with transubstantiation, of idolatrous errors and practices.

We feed on Christ only through his Word, and only by faith and prayer; and we feed on him, whether at our private devotions, or in our meditations, or on any occasion of public worship, or in the memorial symbolism of the Supper.

The elements of the LORD'S Supper were not by Christ's ordinance designed to be reserved, carried about, lifted up, or worshipped.

Article XXVIII. OF BOTH KINDS

The Cup of the LORD is not to be denied to any of his people, for both the bread and the wine, by Christ's ordinance and commandment, ought to be ministered to all Christian men alike.

Article XXIX. OF UNWORTHY PERSONS MINISTERING IN THE CONGREGATION

Although in the visible Church the evil be ever mingled with the good, and sometimes the evil have chief authority in the ministration of the Word and ordinances: yet, forasmuch as they do not the same in their own name, but in Christ's, the believer is not deprived of the benefits of God's ordinances; because, though they be ministered by evil men, yet are they Christ's institution, and set forth his promise.

Nevertheless, it appertaineth to the discipline of the Church, that inquiry be made of evil ministers, and that they be accused by those that have knowledge of their offences: and finally, being found guilty, by just judgment, be deposed.

Article XXX. OF THE ONE OBLATION OF CHRIST FINISHED UPON THE CROSS

The Offering of Christ once made is that perfect redemption, propitiation, and satisfaction, for all the sins of the whole world, both original and actual; and there is none other satisfaction for sin, but that alone. And as there is only this one sacrifice in the Christian Church, once made, never to be repeated, so there is but the one Priest, even Jesus Christ, the Apostle and High Priest of our profession. Wherefore the sacrifices of Masses, in the which it is commonly said that the Priest offers Christ for the quick and the dead, for the remission of pain or guilt, or any representations of the LORD'S Supper as a sacrifice, are blasphemous fables and dangerous deceits.

Article XXXI. OF CERTAIN ERRONEOUS DOCTRINES AND PRACTICES

The Romish doctrines concerning purgatory, penance, and satisfaction, have no support from the Word of God, and are, besides, contradictory of the completeness and sufficiency of the redemption in Christ Jesus, of justification by faith, and of the sanctifying efficacy of God the Holy Ghost. Praying for the dead is man's tradition, vainly invented, and is in violation of the express warnings of Almighty God to the careless and unconverted. The adoration of relics and images, and the invocation of saints, besides that they are grounded upon no warranty of Scripture, are idolatrous practices, dishonoring to God, and compromising the mediatorship of Christ. It is also repugnant to the Word of God, to have public prayer in the Church, or to minister the ordinances, in a tongue not understood by the people.

DECLARATION OF PRINCIPLES AND ARTICLES OF
RELIGION (REFORMED EPISCOPAL CHURCH) (continued)

Article XXXII. OF CONFESSION AND ABSOLUTION

Private confession of sins to a priest, commonly known as Auricular Confession, has no foundation in the Word of God, and is a human invention. It makes the professed penitent a slave to mere human authority, entangles him in endless scruples and perplexities, and opens the way to many immoralities.

If one sin against his fellow-man, the Scripture requires him to make confession to the offended party; and so, if one sin, and bring scandal upon the Christian Society of which he is a member. And Christians may often, with manifest profit, confess to one another their sins against God, with a view solely to instruction, correction, guidance, and encouragement in righteousness. But in any and every case confession is still to be made to God; for all sins are committed against him, as well such as offend our fellow-man, as those that offend him alone.

Priestly absolution is a blasphemous usurpation of the sole prerogative of God. None can forgive sins as against God but God alone.

The blood of Jesus Christ only can cleanse us from our sins, and always we obtain forgiveness directly from God, whenever by faith in that blood we approach him with our confessions and prayers.

Article XXXIII. OF THE MARRIAGE OF MINISTERS

Christian Ministers are not commanded by God's Law either to vow the estate of single life, or to abstain from marriage; therefore it is lawful for them, as for all other Christian men, to marry at their own discretion.

Article XXXIV. OF THE POWER OF THE CIVIL AUTHORITY

The power of the Civil Magistrate extendeth to all men, as well Ministers as People, in all things temporal; but hath no authority in things purely spiritual. And we hold it to be the duty of all men who are professors of the Gospel, to pay respectful obedience to the civil authority, regularly and legitimately constituted.

Article XXXV. OF CHRISTIAN MEN'S GOODS

The riches and goods of Christian men are not common, but their own, to be controlled and used according to their Christian judgment. Every man ought, of such things as he possesseth, liberally to give alms to the poor, according to his ability; and as a steward of God, he should use his means and influence in promoting the cause of truth and righteousness, to the glory of God.

Notes: *The Reformed Episcopal Church's doctrinal statements were adopted in two stages, in 1873 and 1875. A brief Declaration of Principles professed substantial agreement with the Thirty-nine Articles of Religion of the Protestant Episcopal Church, and two years later, a text of thirty-five articles derived from these Thirty-nine Articles was adopted by the church's General Council. Both now appear at the very beginning of the Reformed Episcopal Church's Prayer Book.*

Chapter 3

Eastern Liturgical Family

Orthodoxy

DECLARATION OF FAITH OF THE AFRICAN ORTHODOX CHURCH

I. THE HOLY SCRIPTURES

The African Orthodox Church declares its belief in the Holy Scriptures of the Old and New Testaments as the Word of God and the only sufficient Rule of Faith and entreats all the faithful to read the same diligently, not only as their duty and privilege, but in obedience to Christ's command, "Search the Scriptures." For the moral instruction contained therein it accepts also the so called Apocryphal books.

II. THE CREEDS

The African Orthodox Church accepts the Nicene Creed without the "filioque" interpolation as the only one of universal obligation, but believes also the two symbols known as the Apostles' Creed and the Creed of S. Athanasius.

III. THE COUNCILS

The African Orthodox Church receives as Ecumenical the Seven General Councils whose dogmatic decrees are today accepted by all the Apostolic Churches of the East and West, Viz: (1) Nicea, 325; (2) Constantinople, 381; (3) Ephesus, 431; (4) Chalcedon, 451; (5) Constantinople, 553; (6) Constantinople, 680; (7) Nicea, 787.

IV. THE SACRAMENTS

The African Orthodox Church holds that a Sacrament is a sacred rite divinely instituted to convey grace, having a sensible or visible sign connected with prayer as the means by which the grace is conveyed. It receives as a part of the original deposit of the faith "once for all delivered to the saints" the Seven Gospel Sacraments.

i.   BAPTISM. It acknowledges Baptism as the Sacrament established by Christ to cleanse men from Original Sin and to make them members of the Christian Church. It is the Sacrament of Regeneration or the New Birth.

ii.   CONFIRMATION. It believes that Confirmation is the Sacrament in which the Holy Spirit is given with the fulness of His Gifts to the believer, and regards the Bishop as the ordinary minister of this Sacred Rite.

iii.   PENANCE. It believes that in the Sacrament of Penance, Jesus Christ Himself inwardly looses from their sins those who sincerely repent of them and outwardly make confession, and that every validly ordained priest has the power to pronounce Christ's pardon to penitent sinners confessing their sins. It allows both public and private confession, the mode being optional with the penitent.

iv.   THE EUCHARIST. It holds that the Eucharist is both a Sacrament and a Sacrifice offered for the living and the dead. It believes that in this most holy Sacrament of the Altar there is the Real Presence of the glorified spiritual Body and Blood of Christ under the forms of bread and wine, the mysterious transformation being effected by the Holy Spirit. Since this is a mystery it shuns all terms of definition and description. It maintains that the Chalice should not be denied the laity in holy communion; it believes that the Liturgy ought to be said in the language of the people; and it permits in connection with this Sacrament the use of the names Eucharist, Mass, or Divine Liturgy.

v.   UNCTION OF THE SICK. It believes Unction of the Sick to be a Sacrament of the New Dispensation, instituted for the spiritual and corporal solace of the sick, to be used for the benefit of the Christian when seriously ill, and not only when approaching death. Both the mode and the efficacy of this Sacrament are indicated in the fifth chapter of the Epistle of St. James.

vi.   SACRED ORDERS. It believes that Order is a Sacrament which confers upon those who validly receive it the power to exercise special ministerial function, Bishops alone being the ministers of this Sacrament. The greater, or Holy Orders, which are of divine institution, are the Episcopate, the Priesthood, and the Diaconate. The minor orders, which

DECLARATION OF FAITH OF THE AFRICAN ORTHODOX CHURCH (continued)

are of ecclesiastical origin, and may be regarded as steps to the greater are doorkeeper, reader, exorcist, acolyte and subdeacon. It believes the episcopate necessary for the life of the Church, that all bishops are equal in power and authority by divine right and that their prerogatives of honor and jurisdiction are derived from the Church and regulated by her canons.

vii. HOLY MATRIMONY. It believes marriage, when a man and woman are joined together according to the sacred rite of the Church, to be a Sacrament, and that the civil ceremony of marriage prescribed by law in certain countries, should always be blessed by the priest. There should be no dissolution of the bonds of marriage except for adultery and malicious desertion, and no priest of this Church is permitted to perform the marriage ceremony of any person who has a divorced husband or wife living, unless such person produces satisfactory evidence from court records that he or she is the innocent party in a divorce granted for the cause of adultery or malicious desertion. In all cases involving the marriage of a divorced person, the priest must submit the facts to, and receive the consent of his Bishop, before performing the rite.

V. THE SAINTS

The African Orthodox Church believes that the departed saints are not dead, but living, and that if the prayers of the righteous on earth avail much, the prayers of our glorified brethren nearer the throne of God must be more potent. Hence we consider it a good and useful practice to invoke the prayers of the saints for us, and to pray ourselves for the repose of the souls of the faithful departed.

VI. SACRED PICTURES AND IMAGES

The African Orthodox Church holds that pictures and images of Christ and the Saints may be reverenced as sacred things, though not adored. We do not deny to any Christian the use of this pious practice if it be an aid to his worship, but we caution against abuses thereof when the picture or image is given the adoration which belongs only to God, or its veneration considered necessary to salvation or justification.

Notes: *In comparison to the Western Churches, those out of the Eastern tradition have found little reason over the centuries to compose creedal statements. Almost universally, both orthodox and heterodox Eastern Churches accept the Apostles' and Nicene Creeds, differing in their acceptance of the post-Nicene creeds. The Orthodox accept the Athanasian Creed and the Chalcedonian Formula while the other churches do not accept any creeds after the Nicene. The Nicene Creed, without the filioque clause added by the Western Church, became an integral element in all of the Eastern liturgies. Most of the Eastern churches that have congregations in the United States use the liturgy of St. John Chrysostom.*

Several of the smaller independent Orthodox bodies, all formed during the twentieth century, have found it expe-

dient to author supplemental statements of faith. The African Orthodox Church adopted its Declaration of Faith in 1921. Its statement reflects an attempt to distinguish Orthodoxy from the position of the Protestant Episcopal Church (of which its founding archbishop had been a clergyman) and the Roman Catholic Church, both of which had built a following among black Americans.

*   *   *

DOGMATIC ARTICLES (AMERICAN CATHOLIC CHURCH, ARCHDIOCESE OF NEW YORK)

Eternal salvation is promised to mankind only through the merits of life, death, and resurrection of our Savior, Jesus Christ, upon the condition of obedience to the Gospel teachings, which require Faith, Hope and Charity, and true observance of the ordinances of the Catholic and Orthodox Church which He founded.

1. FAITH is a virtue infused into the soul at Baptism, whereby man accepts, without doubting, whatever God has revealed to the Church concerning His Church.

2. HOPE is a virtue infused into the soul by God, and following upon faith; by it man puts his entire trust and confidence in the goodness and mercy of God his Creator, through Jesus Christ, the Second Person of the Blessed Trinity, and looks for the fulfillment of the promises made to man to those who obey the Gospel.

3. CHARITY is a virtue infused into the soul by God, and likewise consequent upon faith, whereby man, loving God above all things for His Own sake, as his neighbor as himself for love of God, yields up his will to a joyful obedience to the revealed Will of Almighty God.

4. THE CHURCH. God has established the Holy Catholic Church upon earth to be the pillar and ground of the revealed truth; and has committed to her the guardianship of the Holy Scriptures and of Holy Tradition, and the power of binding and loosing.

5. THE SACRAMENTS. The fundamental ordinances of the Gospel, instituted by Jesus Christ as special means of conveying Divine grace and influence to the souls of men, which are commonly called Mysteries or Sacraments, are Seven in number, namely Baptism, Confirmation, the holy Eucharist, holy Orders, Matrimony, Penance, and Anointing of the Sick (Unction).

Baptism is the first Sacrament of the Gospel, administered by threefold immersion in, or affusion with, water with the words, "I baptise thee in the Name of the Father, and of the Son, and of the Holy Ghost." It admits the recipient into the Church, bestows upon him the forgiveness of sins, original and actual, through the Blood of Christ, and causes in him a spiritual change called Regeneration. Without valid Baptism no other Sacrament can be validly received.

Confirmation or Chrism is a Sacrament in which the baptised person, on being annointed with Chrism consecrated by the Bishops of the Church, with the imposition of hands, receives the seven-fold gifts of the Holy Ghost to strengthen him in the grace which he received at Baptism, making him a strong and perfect Christian and a good soldier of Christ.

The holy Eucharist is a Sacrament in which, under the appearances of bread and wine, the real and actual Body and Blood of Christ are given and received for the remission of sins, the increase of Divine grace, and the reward of everlasting Life. After the prayer of Invocation of the Holy Ghost in the Liturgy, the bread and wine are entirely converted into the living Body and Blood of Christ by an actual change of being, to which change the philosophical terms of Transubstantiation and Transmutation are rightly applied. The celebration of this Mystery or Sacrament, commonly called the Mass, constitutes the chief act of Christian worship, being a sacrificial Memorial or re-Presentation of our Lord's death. It is not a repetition of the Sacrifice offered once for all upon Calvary, but is a perpetuation of that Sacrifice by the Church on earth, as our Lord also perpetually offers it in heaven. It is a true and propitiatory Sacrifice, which is offered alike for the living and for the departed.

Holy Orders is a Sacrament in which the Holy Ghost, through the laying-on of hands of the Bishops, consecrates and ordains the pastors and ministers chosen to serve in the Church, and imparts to them special grace to administer the Sacraments, to forgive sins, and to feed the flock of Christ.

Matrimony is a Sacrament in which the voluntary union of husband and wife is sanctified to become an image of the union between Christ and His Church; and grace is imparted to them to fulfill the duties of their estate and its great responsibilities, both to each other and to their children.

Penance is a Sacrament in which the Holy Ghost bestows the forgiveness of sins, by the ministry of the priest, upon those who, having sinned after Baptism, confess their sins with true repentance, and grace is given to them to amend their lives thereafter.

Unction is a Sacrament in which the priests of the Church annoint the sick with oil, for the healing of the infirmities of their souls, and if it should please God, those of their bodies also.

The efficacy of the Sacraments depends upon the promise and appointment of God; howbeit they benefit only those who receive them worthily with faith, and with due preparation and disposition of mind.

6. HOLY SCRIPTURE. The Scriptures are writings inspired by God, and given to the Church for her instruction and edification. The Church is therefore the custodian and the only Divinely appointed interpreter of holy Scripture.

7. TRADITION. The Apostolic and Ecclesiastical Traditions received from the seven General Councils and the early Fathers of the Church may not be rejected; but are to be received and obeyed as being both agreeable to holy Scripture and to that Authority with which Christ endowed His Church. Matters of discipline and ceremonial do not rank on the same level with matters of Faith or Morals, but may be altered from time to time and from place to place by the Authority of the Church, according as the welfare and greater devotion of the faithful may be furthered thereby.

8. THE COMMUNION OF SAINTS. There is a Communion of Saints in the Providence of God, wherein the souls of righteous men of all ages are united with Christ in the bond of faith and love. Wherefore it is pleasing to God, and profitable to men, to honour the Saints and to invoke them in prayer; and also to pray for the faithful departed.

9. RELIGIOUS SYMBOLS. The relics and representations of Saints are worthy of honour, as are also all other religious emblems; that our minds may be encouraged to devotion and to imitation of the deeds of the just. Honour shown to such objects is purely relative, and in no way implies a confusion of the symbol with the thing signified.

10. RITES AND CEREMONIES. It is the duty of all Christians to join in the worship of the Church, especially in the holy Sacrifice of the Mass, in accordance with our Lord's express command; and to conform to the ceremonies prescribed by holy Tradition for the greater dignity of that Sacrifice and for the edification of the faithful.

11. THE MORAL LAW. All Christians are bound to observe the Moral Law contained in the Ten Commandments of the Old Testament, developed with greater strictness in the New, founded upon the law of nature and charity, and defining our duty to God and to man. The laws of the Church are also to be obeyed, as proceeding from that Authority which Christ has committed to her for the instruction and salvation of His people.

12. THE MONASTIC ESTATE. The monastic life, duly regulated according to the laws of the Church, is a salutary institution in strict accord with the holy Scriptures; and is full of profit to them who, after being carefully tried and examined, make full proof of their calling thereto.

Notes: *The small American Catholic Church, Archdiocese of New York, broke away from the African Orthodox Church and, like its parent, produced its own doctrinal statement.*

Non-Chalcedonian Orthodoxy

THE BELIEFS OF THE SYRO-CHALDEAN CHURCH OF NORTH AMERICA (NON-CHALCEDONIAN)

We believe that the Bible is the true Word of God. "All Scripture is inspired by God and profitable for teaching, for reproof, for correction, for training in righteousness." (II TIMOTHY 3:16)

We believe in the Trinity, God the Father, Jesus the Son, and the Holy Spirit, as specified throughout the Scriptures, the Nicene and the Apostles Creeds.

We believe in all the verities of the Faith of Jesus Christ— The Incarnation, His virginal conception, His Life and teachings, the atonement of the Cross and His Saving Blood, His mighty resurrection and victory over death, His ascension and pouring out of the Holy Spirit, His glorious coming again.

We believe in the sacramental aspect of the church. The sacraments are: Baptism and Confirmation, Holy Communion, Reconciliation, Annointing for Healing, Holy Matrimony and Holy Orders.

We believe that the major function of the church is to preach the Gospel to all of mankind and reach all with His love and message of salvation through Jesus Christ. "Go therefore and make disciples of all the nations, baptizing them in the name of the Father and the Son and the Holy Spirit, teaching them to observe all that I commanded you; and lo, I am with you always, even to the end of the age." (MATTHEW 28:19, 20)

We believe as a church we should stress the fruits of the Spirit is every Christian life. "But the fruit of the Spirit is love, joy, peace, patience, kindness, goodness, faithfulness, gentleness, self-control; against such things there is no law. If we live by the Spirit, let us also walk by the Spirit." (GALATIANS 5:22, 23, 25)

We believe God's power is still here today through the various gifts of the Spirit as were first experienced by the apostles and disciples in the upper room on Pentecost, (ACTS 2, I COR. 12) including God's power to heal in lives today—physically, spiritually, and emotionally. "Jesus Christ is the same yesterday and today, yes and forever." (HEBREWS 13:8)

Notes: *Claiming some relation to the Assyrian Church of the East, the Syro-Chaldean Church of North America has published a statement that manifests some influence of the modern Pentecostal movement in its reference to the "gifts of the spirit."*

Chapter 4
Lutheran Family

THE AUGSBURG CONFESSION (1530)

PREFACE.

Most Invincible Emperor, Cæsar Augustus, most Clement Lord:

Inasmuch as Your Imperial Majesty has summoned a Diet of the Empire here at Augsburg to deliberate concerning measures against the Turk, that most atrocious, hereditary and ancient enemy of the Christian name and religion, in what way effectually to withstand his furor and assaults by strong and lasting military provision; and then also concerning dissensions in the matter of our holy religion and Christian Faith, that in this matter of religion the opinions and judgments of parties might be heard in each other's presence, and considered and weighed among ourselves in charity, leniency and mutual kindness, to the end that the things in the Scriptures which on either side have been differently interpreted or misunderstood, being corrected and laid aside, these matters may be settled and brought back to one perfect truth and Christian concord, that for the future one pure and true religion may be embraced and maintained by us, that as we all serve and do battle under one Christ, so we may be able also to live in unity and concord in the one Christian Church. And inasmuch as we, the undersigned Electors and Princes, with others joined with us, have been called to the aforesaid Diet, the same as the other Electors, Princes and Estates, in obedient compliance with the Imperial mandate we have come to Augsburg, and, what we do not mean to say as boasting, we were among the first to be here.

Since then Your Imperial Majesty caused to be proposed to the Electors, Princes and other Estates of the Empire, also here at Augsburg at the very beginning of this Diet, among other things, that, by virtue of the Imperial Edict, the several Estates of the Empire should present their opinions and judgments in the German and Latin languages, after due deliberation, answer was given to Your Imperial Majesty, on the ensuing Wednesday, that on the next Friday the Articles of our Confession for our part would be presented.

Wherefore, in obedience to Your Imperial Majesty's wishes, we offer, in this matter of religion, the Confession of our preachers and of ourselves, showing what manner of doctrine from the Holy Scriptures and the pure Word of God has been up to this time set forth in our lands, dukedoms, dominions and cities, and taught in our churches. And if the other Electors, Princes and Estates of the Empire will present similar writings, to wit, in Latin and German, according to the said Imperial proposition, giving their opinions in this matter of religion, here before Your Imperial Majesty, our most clement Lord, we, with the Princes and friends aforesaid, are prepared to confer amicably concerning all possible ways and means, as far as may be honorably done, that we may come together, and, the matter between us on both sides being peacefully discussed without offensive strife, the dissension, by God's help, may be done away and brought back to one true accordant religion; for as we all serve and do battle under one Christ, we ought to confess the one Christ, and so, after the tenor of Your Imperial Majesty's Edict, everything be conducted according to the truth of God, which, with most fervent prayers, we entreat of God.

But, with regard to the other Electors, Princes and Estates, if they hold that this treatment of the matter of religion after the manner which Your Imperial Majesty has so wisely brought forward, namely, with such mutual presentation of writings and calm conferring together among ourselves, should not proceed, or be unfruitful in results; we, at least, leave behind the clear testimony that we decline or refuse nothing whatever, allowed of God and a good conscience, which may tend to bring about Christian concord; as also Your Imperial Majesty and the other Electors and Estates of the Empire, and all who are moved by sincere love and zeal for religion, and who will give an impartial hearing to this matter, will graciously perceive and more and more understand from this our Confession.

Your Imperial Majesty also, not only once but often, graciously signified to the Electors, Princes and Estates of the Empire, and at the Diet of Spires held A. D. 1526, according to the form of Your Imperial instruction and commission given and prescribed, caused it to be stated and publicly proclaimed, that Your Majesty, in dealing with this matter of religion, for certain reasons which were alleged in Your Majesty's name, was not willing to decide and could not determine anything, but that Your Majesty

THE AUGSBURG CONFESSION (1530) (continued)

would diligently use Your Majesty's office with the Roman Pontiff for the convening of a General Council, as the same was publicly set forth at greater length over a year ago at the last Diet which met at Spires. There Your Imperial Majesty, through his Highness Ferdinand, King of Bohemia and Hungary, our friend and clement Lord, as well as through the Orator and Imperial Commissioners, caused this, among other things, to be proclaimed: that Your Imperial Majesty had known of and pondered the resolution of Your Majesty's Representative in the Empire, and of the President and Imperial Counsellors, and the Legates from other Estates convened at Ratisbon, concerning the calling of a Council, and that this also was adjudged by Your Imperial Majesty to be of advantage; and because the matters to be adjusted between Your Imperial Majesty and the Roman Pontiff were nearing agreement and Christian reconciliation, Your Imperial Majesty did not doubt that the Roman Pontiff could be induced to hold a General Council; therefore Your Imperial Majesty himself signified that he would endeavor to secure the Chief Pontiff's consent together with Your Imperial Majesty to convene such General Council, and that letters to that effect would be publicly issued with all possible expedition.

In the event, therefore, that the differences between us and the other parties in the matter of religion cannot be amicably and in charity settled here before Your Imperial Majesty, we offer this in all obedience, abundantly prepared to join issue and to defend the cause in such a general, free, Christian Council, for the convening of which there has always been accordant action and agreement of votes in all the Imperial Diets held during Your Majesty's reign, on the part of the Electors, Princes and other Estates of the Empire. To this General Council, and at the same time to Your Imperial Majesty, we have made appeal in this greatest and gravest of matters even before this in due manner and form of law. To this appeal, both to Your Imperial Majesty and to a Council, we still adhere, neither do we intend, nor would it be possible for us, to relinquish it by this or any other document, unless the matter between us and the other side, according to the tenor of the latest Imperial citation, can be amicably and charitably settled and brought to Christian concord, of which this also is our solemn and public testimony.

I. CHIEF ARTICLES OF FAITH.

Article I.

Our Churches, with common consent, do teach, that the decree of the Council of Nicæa concerning the Unity of the Divine Essence and concerning the Three Persons, is true and to be believed without any doubting; that is to say, there is one Divine Essence which is called and which is God: eternal, without body, without parts, of infinite power, wisdom and goodness, the Maker and Preserver of all things, visible and invisible; and yet that there are three Persons, of the same essence and power, who also are co-eternal, the Father, the Son and the Holy Ghost. And the term "person" they use as the Fathers have used it, to signify, not a part or quality in another, but that which subsists of itself.

They condemn all heresies which have sprung up against this article, as the Manichæans who assumed two principles [gods], one Good, and the other Evil; also the Valentinians, Arians, Eunomians, Mohammedans, and all such. They condemn also the Samosatenes, old and new, who contending that there is but one Person, sophistically and impiously argue that the Word and the Holy Ghost are not distinct Persons, but that "Word" signifies a spoken word, and "Spirit" [Ghost] signifies motion created in things.

Article II.

Also they teach, that since the Fall of Adam, all men begotten according to nature, are born with sin, that is, without the fear of God, without trust in God, and with concupiscence; and that this disease, or vice of origin, is truly sin, even now condemning and bringing eternal death upon those not born again through baptism and the Holy Ghost.

They condemn the Pelagians and others, who deny that the vice of origin is sin, and who, to obscure the glory of Christ's merit and benefits, argue that man can be justified before God by his own strength and reason.

Article III.

Also they teach, that the Word, that is, the Son of God, did take man's nature in the womb of the blessed Virgin Mary, so that there are Two Natures, the divine and the human, inseparably conjoined in one Person, one Christ, true God and true man, who was born of the Virgin Mary, truly suffered, was crucified, dead and buried, that he might reconcile the Father unto us, and be a sacrifice, not only for original guilt, but for all actual sins of men. He also descended into hell, and truly rose again the third day; afterward he ascended into Heaven, that he might sit on the right hand of the Father, and forever reign, and have dominion over all creatures, and sanctify them that believe in Him, by sending the Holy Ghost into their hearts, to rule, comfort and quicken them, and to defend them against the devil and the power of sin. The same Christ shall openly come again to judge the quick and the dead, etc., according to the Apostles' Creed.

Article IV.

Also they teach, that men cannot be Justified before God by their own strength, merits or works, but are freely justified for Christ's sake through faith, when they believe that they are received into favor and that their sins are forgiven for Christ's sake, who, by His death, hath made satisfaction for our sins. This faith God imputes for righteousness in his sight. Rom. 3 and 4.

Article V.

That we may obtain this faith, the Office of Teaching the Gospel and administering the Sacraments was instituted. For through the Word and Sacraments as through instruments, the Holy Ghost is given, who worketh faith where and when it pleaseth God in them that hear the Gospel, to wit, that God, not for our own merits, but for Christ's sake, justified those who believe that they are received into favor for Christ's sake.

They condemn the Anabaptists and others, who think that the Holy Ghost cometh to men without the external Word, through their own preparations and works.

Article VI.

Also they teach, that this Faith is bound to bring forth Good Fruits, and that it is necessary to do good works commanded by God, because of God's will, but not that we should rely on those works to merit justification before God. For remission of sins and justification are apprehended by faith, as also the voice of Christ attests: "When ye shall have done all these things, say: We are unprofitable servants" [Luke 17:10]. The same is also taught by the Fathers. For Ambrose says: "It is ordained of God that he who believes in Christ, is saved; freely receiving remission of sins, without works, by faith alone."

Article VII.

Also they teach, that One holy Church is to continue forever. The Church is the congregation of saints, in which the Gospel is rightly taught and the Sacraments rightly administered. And to the true unity of the Church, it is enough to agree concerning the doctrine of the Gospel and the administration of the Sacraments. Nor is it necessary that human traditions, rites, or ceremonies, instituted by men, should be everywhere alike. As Paul says: "One faith, one baptism, one God and Father of all," etc. [Eph. 4:5, 6].

Article VIII.

Although the Church properly is the Congregation of Saints and true believers, nevertheless, since in this life, many hypocrites and evil persons are mingled therewith, it is lawful to use the Sacraments, which are administered by evil men; according to the saying of Christ: "The Scribes and the Pharisees sit in Moses' seat," etc. [Matt. 23:2]. Both the Sacraments and Word are effectual by reason of the institution and commandment of Christ, notwithstanding they be administered by evil men.

They condemn the Donatists, and such like, who denied it to be lawful to use the ministry of evil men in the Church, and who thought the ministry of evil men to be unprofitable and of none effect.

Article IX.

Of Baptism, they teach, that it is necessary to salvation, and that through Baptism is offered the grace of God; and that children are to be baptized, who, being offered to God through Baptism, are received into His grace.

They condemn the Anabaptists, who allow not the Baptism of children, and say that children are saved without Baptism.

Article X.

Of the Supper of the Lord, they teach, that the Body and Blood of Christ are truly present, and are distributed to those who eat in the Supper of the Lord; and they disapprove of those that teach otherwise.

Article XI.

Of Confession, they teach, that Private Absolution ought to be retained in the churches, although in confession an enumeration of all sins is not necessary. For it is impossible, according to the Psalm: "Who can understand his errors?" [Ps. 19: 12].

Article XII.

Of Repentance, they teach, that for those that have fallen after Baptism, there is remission of sins whenever they are converted; and that the Church ought to impart absolution to those thus returning to repentance.

Now repentance consists properly of these two parts: One is contrition, that is, terrors smiting the conscience through the knowledge of sin; the other is faith, which, born of the Gospel, or of absolution, believes that, for Christ's sake, sins are forgiven, comforts the conscience, and delivers it from terrors. Then good works are bound to follow, which are the fruits of repentance.

They condemn the Anabaptists, who deny that those once justified can lose the Holy Ghost. Also those who contend that some may attain to such perfection in this life that they cannot sin. The Novatians also are condemned, who would not absolve such as had fallen after Baptism, though they returned to repentance. They also are rejected who do not teach that remission of sins cometh through faith, but command us to merit grace through satisfactions of our own.

Article XIII.

Of the Use of the Sacraments, they teach, that the Sacraments were ordained, not only to be marks of profession among men, but rather to be signs and testimonies of the will of God toward us, instituted to awaken and confirm faith in those who use them. Wherefore we must so use the Sacraments that faith be added to believe the promises which are offered and set forth through the Sacraments.

They therefore condemn those who teach that the Sacraments justify by the outward act, and do not teach that, in the use of the Sacraments, faith which believes that sins are forgiven, is required.

Article XIV.

Of Ecclesiastical Order, they teach, that no one should publicly teach in the Church or administer the Sacraments, unless he be regularly called.

Article XV.

Of Rites and Usages in the Church, they teach, that those ought to be observed which may be observed without sin, and which are profitable unto tranquillity and good order in the Church, as particular holydays, festivals, and the like.

Nevertheless, concerning such things, let men be admonished that consciences are not to be burdened, as though such observance was necessary to salvation. They are admonished also that human traditions instituted to propitiate God, to merit grace and to make satisfaction for sins, are opposed to the Gospel and the doctrine of faith. Wherefore vows and traditions concerning meats and days, etc., instituted to merit grace and to make satisfaction for sins, are useless and contrary to the Gospel.

Article XVI.

Of Civil Affairs, they teach, that lawful civil ordinances are good works of God, and that it is right for Christians to bear civil office, to sit as judges, to determine matters by the Imperial and other existing laws, to award just punishments, to engage in just wars, to serve as soldiers, to make legal contracts, to hold property, to make oath when required by the magistrates, to marry, to be given in marriage.

They condemn the Anabaptists who forbid these civil offices to Christians. They condemn also those who do not place the perfection of the Gospel in the fear of God and in faith, but in forsaking civil offices; for the Gospel teaches an eternal righteousness of the heart. Meanwhile, it does not destroy the State or the family, but especially requires their preservation as ordinances of God, and in such ordinances the exercise of charity. Therefore, Christians are necessarily bound to obey their own magistrates and laws, save only when commanded to sin, for then they ought to obey God rather than men [Acts 5:29].

Article XVII.

Also they teach, that, at the Consummation of the World, Christ shall appear for judgment, and shall raise up all the dead; he shall give to the godly and elect eternal life and everlasting joys, but ungodly men and the devils he shall condemn to be tormented without end.

They condemn the Anabaptists who think that there will be an end to the punishments of condemned men and devils. They condemn also others, who are now spreading certain Jewish opinions that, before the resurrection of the dead, the godly shall take possession of the kingdom of the world, the ungodly being everywhere suppressed [exterminated].

Article XVIII.

Of the Freedom of the Will, they teach, that man's will has some liberty for the attainment of civil righteousness, and for the choice of things subject to reason. Nevertheless, it has no power, without the Holy Ghost, to work the righteousness of God, that is, spiritual righteousness; since the natural man receiveth not the things of the Spirit of God [1 Cor. 2:14]; but this righteousness is wrought in the heart when the Holy Ghost is received through the Word. These things are said in as many words by Augustine in his *Hypognosticon*, book iii.: "We grant that all men have a certain freedom of will in judging according to [natural] reason; not such freedom, however, whereby it is capable, without God, either to begin, or much less to complete aught in things pertaining to God, but only in works of this life, whether good or evil. 'Good,' I call those works which spring from the good in Nature, that is, to have a will to labor in the field, to eat and drink, to have a friend, to clothe oneself, to build a house, to marry, to keep cattle, to learn divers useful arts, or whatsoever good pertains to this life, none of which things are without dependence on the providence of God; yea, of Him and through Him they are and have their beginning. 'Evil,' I call such works as to have a will to worship an idol, to commit murder," etc.

They condemn the Pelagians and others who teach that, without the Holy Ghost, by the power of nature alone, we are able to love God above all things; also to do the commandments of God as touching "the substance of the act."

For, although nature is able in some sort to do the outward work (for it is able to keep the hands from theft and murder), yet it cannot work the inward motions, such as the fear of God, trust in God, chastity, patience, etc.

Article XIX.

Of the Cause of Sin, they teach, that although God doth create and preserve nature, yet the cause of sin is the will of the wicked, that is, of the devil and ungodly men; which will, unaided of God, turns itself from God, as Christ says [John 8:44]: "When he speaketh a lie, he speaketh of his own."

Article XX.

Our teachers are falsely accused of forbidding Good Works. For their published writings on the Ten Commandments, and others of like import, bear witness that they have taught to good purpose concerning all estates and duties of life, as to what estates of life and what works in every calling be pleasing to God. Concerning these things preachers heretofore taught but little, and urged only childish and needless works, as particular holydays, particular fasts, brotherhoods, pilgrimages, services in honor of saints, the use of rosaries, monasticism, and such like. Since our adversaries have been admonished of these things they are now unlearning them, and do not preach these unprofitable works as heretofore. Besides they begin to mention faith, of which there was heretofore marvellous silence. They teach that we are justified not by works only, but they conjoin faith and works, and say that we are justified by faith and works. This doctrine is more tolerable than the former one, and can afford more consolation than their old doctrine.

Forasmuch, therefore, as the doctrine concerning faith, which ought to be the chief one in the church, has lain so long unknown, as all must needs grant that there was the deepest silence in their sermons concerning the righteousness of faith, while only the doctrine of works was treated in the churches, our teachers have instructed the churches concerning faith as follows:

First, that our works cannot reconcile God or merit forgiveness of sins, grace and justification, but that we obtain this only by faith, when we believe that we are received into favor for Christ's sake, who alone has been set forth the Mediator and Propitiation [1 Tim. 2:5], in order that the Father may be reconciled through Him. Whoever, therefore, trusts that by works he merits grace, despises the merit and grace of Christ, and seeks a way to God without Christ, by human strength, although Christ has said of himself: "I am the Way, the Truth and the Life" [John 14:6].

This doctrine concerning faith is everywhere treated by Paul [Eph. 2:8]: "By grace are ye saved through faith; and that not of yourselves; it is the gift of God, not of works," etc.

And lest anyone should craftily say that a new interpretation of Paul has been devised by us, this entire matter is supported by the testimonies of the Fathers. For Augustine, in many volumes, defends grace and the righteousness of faith, over against the merits of works. And Ambrose, in his *De Vocatione Gentium*, and elsewhere, teaches to like effect. For in his *De Vocatione Gentium* he says as follows: "Redemption by the Blood of Christ would become of little value, neither would the pre-eminence of man's works be superseded by the mercy of God, if justification, which is wrought through grace, were due to the merits going before, so as to be, not the free gift of a donor, but the reward due to the laborer."

But, although this doctrine is despised by the inexperienced, nevertheless God-fearing and anxious consciences find by experience that it brings the greatest consolation, because consciences cannot be pacified through any works, but only by faith, when they are sure that, for Christ's sake, they have a gracious God. As Paul teaches [Rom. 5:1]: "Being justified by faith, we have peace with God." This whole doctrine is to be referred to that conflict of the terrified conscience; neither can it be understood apart from that conflict. Therefore inexperienced and profane men judge ill concerning this matter, who dream that Christian righteousness is nothing but the civil righteousness of natural reason.

Heretofore consciences were plagued with the doctrine of works, nor did they hear any consolation from the Gospel. Some persons were driven by conscience into the desert, into monasteries, hoping there to merit grace by a monastic life. Some also devised other works whereby to merit grace and make satisfaction for sins. There was very great need to treat of and renew this doctrine of faith in Christ, to the end that anxious consciences should not be without consolation, but that they might know that grace and forgiveness of sins and justification are apprehended by faith in Christ.

Men are also admonished that here the term "faith" doth not signify merely the knowledge of the history, such as is in the ungodly and in the devil, but signifieth a faith which believes, not merely the history, but also the effect of the history—namely, this article of the forgiveness of sins, to wit, that we have grace, righteousness, and forgiveness of sins, through Christ.

Now he that knoweth that he has a Father reconciled to him through Christ, since he truly knows God, knows also that God careth for him, and calls upon God; in a word, he is not without God, as the heathen. For devils and the ungodly are not able to believe this article of the forgiveness of sins. Hence, they hate God as an enemy; call not upon Him; and expect no good from Him. Augustine also admonishes his readers concerning the word "faith," and teaches that the term "faith" is accepted in the Scriptures, not for knowledge such as is in the ungodly, but for confidence which consoles and encourages the terrified mind.

Furthermore, it is taught on our part, that it is necessary to do good works, not that we should trust to merit grace by them, but because it is the will of God. It is only by faith that forgiveness of sins and grace are apprehended. And because through faith the Holy Ghost is received, hearts are renewed and endowed with new affections, so as to be able to bring forth good works. For Ambrose says: "Faith is the mother of a good will and right doing." For man's powers without the Holy Ghost are full of ungodly affections, and are too weak to do works which are good in

God's sight. Besides, they are in the power of the devil, who impels men to divers sins, to ungodly opinions, to open crimes. This we may see in the philosophers, who, although they endeavored to live an honest life, could not succeed, but were defiled with many open crimes. Such is the feebleness of man, when he is without faith and without the Holy Ghost, and governs himself only by human strength.

Hence it may be readily seen that this doctrine is not to be charged with prohibiting good works, but rather the more to be commended, because it shows how we are enabled to do good works. For without faith, human nature can in no wise do the works of the First or of the Second Commandment. Without faith, it does not call upon God, nor expect anything from Him, nor bear the cross; but seeks and trusts in man's help. And thus, when there is no faith and trust in God, all manner of lusts and human devices rule in the heart. Wherefore Christ said [John 15:5]: "Without me ye can do nothing," and the Church sings:

"Without Thy power divine
In man there nothing is,
Naught but what is harmful."

Article XXI.

Of the Worship of Saints, they teach, that the memory of saints may be set before us, that we may follow their faith and good works, according to our calling, as the Emperor may follow the example of David in making war to drive away the Turk from his country. For both are kings. But the Scripture teaches not the invocation of saints, or to ask help of saints, since it sets before us Christ, as the only Mediator, Propitiation, High-Priest and Intercessor. He is to be prayed to, and hath promised that He will hear our prayer; and this worship He approves above all, to wit, that in all afflictions He be called upon [1 John 2:1]: "If any man sin, we have an Advocate with the Father," etc.

This is about the Sum of our Doctrine, in which, as can be seen, there is nothing that varies from the Scriptures, or from the Church Catholic, or from the Church of Rome as known from its writers. This being the case, they judge harshly who insist that our teachers be regarded as heretics. The disagreement, however, is on certain Abuses, which have crept into the Church without rightful authority. And even in these, if there were some difference, there should be proper lenity on the part of bishops to bear with us by reason of the Confession which we have now drawn up; because even the Canons are not so severe as to demand the same rites everywhere, neither, at any time, have the rites of all churches been the same; although, among us, in large part, the ancient rites are diligently observed. For it is a false and malicious charge that all the ceremonies, all the things instituted of old, are abolished in our churches. But it has been a common complaint that some Abuses were connected with the ordinary rites. These, inasmuch as they could not be approved with a good conscience, have been to some extent corrected.

II. ARTICLES, IN WHICH ARE REVIEWED THE ABUSES WHICH HAVE BEEN CORRECTED.

Inasmuch then as our churches dissent in no article of the Faith from the Church Catholic, but omit some Abuses which are new, and which have been erroneously accepted by fault of the times, contrary to the intent of the Canons, we pray that Your Imperial Majesty would graciously hear both what has been changed, and also what were the reasons, in order that the people be not compelled to observe those abuses against their conscience. Nor should Your Imperial Majesty believe those, who, in order to excite the hatred of men against our part, disseminate strange slanders among our people. Having thus excited the minds of good men, they have first given occasion to this controversy, and now endeavor, by the same arts, to increase the discord. For Your Imperial Majesty will undoubtedly find that the form of doctrine and of ceremonies with us, is not so intolerable as these ungodly and malicious men represent. Furthermore, the truth cannot be gathered from common rumors, or the revilings of our enemies. But it can readily be judged that nothing would serve better to maintain the dignity of worship, and to nourish reverence and pious devotion among the people than that the ceremonies be rightly observed in the churches.

Article XXII.

To the laity are given Both Kinds in the Sacrament of the Lord's Supper, because this usage has the commandment of the Lord [in Matt. 26:27]: "Drink ye all of it"; where Christ has manifestly commanded concerning the cup that all should drink; and lest any man should craftily say that this refers only to priests, Paul [in 1 Cor. 11:27] recites an example from which it appears that the whole congregation did use both kinds. And this usage has long remained in the Church, nor is it known when, or by whose authority, it was changed; although Cardinal Cusanus mentions the time when it was approved. Cyprian in some places testifies that the Blood was given to the people. The same is testified by Jerome, who says: "The priests administer the Eucharist, and distribute the Blood of Christ to the people." Indeed, Pope Gelasius commands that the sacrament be not divided (*Dist. ii., De Consecratione, Cap. Comperimus*). Only custom, not so ancient, has it otherwise. But it is evident that any custom introduced against the commandments of God is not to be allowed, as the Canons witness (*Dist. iii., Cap. Veritate,* and the following chapters). But this custom has been received, not only against the Scripture but also against the old Canons and examples of the Church. Therefore if any preferred to use both kinds of the sacrament, they ought not to have been compelled with offence to their consciences to do otherwise.

And because the division of the sacrament does not agree with the ordinance of Christ, we are accustomed to omit the procession, which hitherto has been in use.

Article XXIII.

There has been common complaint concerning the Examples of Priests, who were not chaste. For that reason also, Pope Pius is reported to have said that there were certain reasons why marriage was taken away from priests, but that there were far weightier ones why it ought to be given back; for so Platina writes. Since, therefore, our priests were desirous to avoid these open scandals they married wives, and taught that it was lawful for them to contract matrimony. First, because Paul says [1 Cor. 7:2]: "To avoid fornication, let every man have his own wife." Also [9]: "It is better to marry than to burn." Secondly, Christ says [Matt. 19:11]: "All men cannot receive this saying," where he teaches that not all men are fit to lead a single life; for God created man for procreation [Gen. 1:28]. Nor is it in man's power, without a singular gift and work of God, to alter this creation. Therefore those that are not fit to lead a single life ought to contract matrimony. For no man's law, no vow, can annul the commandment and ordinance of God. For these reasons the priests teach that it is lawful for them to marry wives. It is also evident that in the ancient Church priests were married men. For Paul says [1 Tim. 3:2] that a bishop should be the husband of one wife. And in Germany, four hundred years ago for the first time, the priests were violently compelled to lead a single life, who indeed offered such resistance that the Archbishop of Mayence, when about to publish the Pope's decree concerning this matter, was almost killed in the tumult raised by the enraged priests. And so harsh was the dealing in the matter that not only were marriages forbidden for the time to come, but also existing marriages were torn asunder, contrary to all laws, divine and human, contrary even to the Canons themselves, made not only by the Popes but by most celebrated Councils.

Seeing also that, as the world is aging, man's nature is gradually growing weaker, it is well to guard that no more vices steal into Germany. Furthermore, God ordained marriage to be a help against human infirmity. The Canons themselves say that the old rigor ought now and then, in the latter times, to be relaxed because of the weakness of men; which it is to be devoutly wished were done also in this matter. And it is to be expected that the churches shall at length lack pastors, if marriage should be any longer forbidden.

But while the commandment of God is in force, while the custom of the Church is well known, while impure celibacy causes many scandals, adulteries, and other crimes deserving the punishments of just magistrates, yet it is a marvellous thing that in nothing is more cruelty exercised than against the marriage of priests. God has given commandment to honor marriage. By the laws of all well-ordered commonwealths, even among the heathen, marriage is most highly honored. But now men, and also priests, are cruelly put to death, contrary to the intent of the Canons, for no other cause than marriage. Paul [in 1 Tim. 4:3] calls that a doctrine of devils, which forbids marriage. This may now be readily understood when the law against marriage is maintained by such penalties.

But as no law of man can annul the commandment of God, so neither can it be done by any vow. Accordingly Cyprian also advises that women who do not keep the chastity they have promised should marry. His words are these [Book I., Epistle xi.]: "But if they be unwilling or unable to perserve, it is better for them to marry than to fall into the fire by their lusts; at least, they should give no offence to their brethren and sisters." And even the Canons show some leniency toward those who have taken vows before the proper age, as heretofore has generally been the case.

Article XXIV.

Falsely are our churches accused of Abolishing the Mass; for the Mass is retained on our part, and celebrated with the highest reverence. All the usual ceremonies are also preserved, save that the parts sung in Latin are interspersed here and there with German hymns, which have been added to teach the people. For ceremonies are needed to this end alone, that the unlearned be taught. And not only has Paul commanded to use in the Church a language understood by the people [1 Cor. 14:2, 9], but it has also been so ordained by man's law.

The people are accustomed to partake of the Sacrament together, if any be fit for it, and this also increases the reverence and devotion of public worship. For none are admitted except they be first proved. The people are also advised concerning the dignity and use of the Sacrament, how great consolation it brings anxious consciences, that they may learn to believe God, and to expect and ask of Him all that is good. This worship pleases God; such use of the Sacrament nourishes true devotion toward God. It does not, therefore, appear that the Mass is more devoutly celebrated among our adversaries, than among us.

But it is evident that for a long time, it has been the public and most grievous complaint of all good men, that Masses have been basely profaned and applied to purposes of lucre. For it is unknown how far this abuse obtains in all the churches, by what manner of men Masses are said only for fees or stipends, and how many celebrate them contrary to the Canons. But Paul severely threatens those who deal unworthily with the Eucharist, when he says [1 Cor. 11:27]: "Whosoever shall eat this bread, and drink this cup of the Lord unworthily, shall be guilty of the body and blood of the Lord." When, therefore, our priests were admonished concerning this sin, Private Masses were discontinued among us, as scarcely any Private Masses were celebrated except for lucre's sake.

Neither were the bishops ignorant of these abuses, and if they had corrected them in time, there would now be less dissension. Heretofore, by their own negligence, they suffered many corruptions to creep into the Church. Now, when it is too late, they begin to complain of the troubles of the Church, seeing that this disturbance has been occasioned simply by those abuses, which were so manifest that they could be borne no longer. Great dissensions have arisen concerning the Mass, concerning the Sacrament. Perhaps the world is being punished for such long-continued profanations of the Mass, as have been tolerated in the churches for so many centuries, by the very men who were both able and in duty bound to correct them. For, in the Ten Commandments, it is written (Exodus 20), "The Lord will not hold him guiltless that taketh His name in vain." But since the world began, nothing that God ever ordained seems to have been so abused for filthy lucre as the Mass.

There was also added the opinion which infinitely increased Private Masses, namely, that Christ, by His passion, had made satisfaction for original sin, and instituted the Mass wherein an offering should be made for daily sins, venial and mortal. From this has arisen the common opinion that the Mass taketh away the sins of the living and the dead, by the outward act. Then they began to dispute whether one Mass said for many were worth as much as special Masses for individuals, and this brought forth that infinite multitude of Masses. Concerning these opinions our teachers have given warning, that they depart from the Holy Scriptures and diminish the glory of the passion of Christ. For Christ's passion was an oblation and satisfaction, not for original guilt only, but also for all sins, as it is written to the Hebrews (10:10), "We are sanctified through the offering of Jesus Christ, once for all." Also, 10:14: "By one offering he hath perfected forever them that are sanctified." Scripture also teaches that we are justified before God through faith in Christ, when we believe that our sins are forgiven for Christ's sake. Now if the Mass take away the sins of the living and the dead by the outward act, justification comes of the work of Masses, and not of faith, which Scripture does not allow.

But Christ commands us [Luke 22:19], "This do in remembrance of me;" therefore the Mass was instituted that the faith of those who use the Sacrament should remember what benefits it receives through Christ, and cheer and comfort the anxious conscience. For, to remember Christ, is to remember his benefits, and to realize that they are truly offered unto us. Nor is it enough only to remember the history, for this the Jew and the ungodly also can remember. Wherefore the Mass is to be used to this end, that there the Sacrament [Communion] may be administered to them that have need of consolation; as Ambrose says: "Because I always sin, I am always bound to take the medicine."

Now forasmuch as the Mass is such a giving of the Sacrament, we hold one communion every holyday, and also other days, when any desire the Sacrament it is given to such as ask for it. And this custom is not new in the Church; for the Fathers before Gregory make no mention of any private Mass, but of the common Mass [the Communion] they speak very much. Chrysostom says that the priest stands daily at the altar, inviting some to the Communion and keeping back others. And it appears from the ancient Canons, that some one celebrated the Mass from whom all the other presbyters and deacons received the Body of the Lord; for thus the words of the Nicene Canon say: "Let the deacons, according to their order, receive the Holy Communion after the presbyters, from the bishop or from a presbyter." And Paul [1 Cor. 11:33] commands concerning the Communion: "Tarry one for another," so that there may be a common participation.

Forasmuch, therefore, as the Mass with us has the example of the Church, taken from the Scripture and the Fathers, we are confident that it cannot be disapproved, especially since the public ceremonies are retained for the most part, like those hitherto in use; only the number of Masses differs, which, because of very great and manifest abuses, doubtless might be profitably reduced. For in olden times, even in churches, most frequented, the Mass was not celebrated every day, as the Tripartite History (Book 9, chapt. 33) testifies: "Again in Alexandria, every Wednesday and Friday, the Scriptures are read, and the doctors expound them, and all things are done, except only the celebration of the Eucharist."

THE AUGSBURG CONFESSION (1530) (continued)

Article XXV.

Confession in our churches is not abolished; for it is not usual to give the Body of the Lord, except to them that have been previously examined and absolved. And the people are most carefully taught concerning the faith and assurance of absolution, about which, before this time, there was profound silence. Our people are taught that they should highly prize the absolution, as being the voice of God, and pronounced by His command. The power of the Keys is commended, and we show what great consolation it brings to anxious consciences; that God requires faith to believe such absolution as a voice sounding from Heaven, and that such faith in Christ truly obtains and receives the forgiveness of sins.

Aforetime, satisfactions were immoderately extolled; of faith and the merit of Christ, and the righteousness of faith, no mention was made; wherefore, on this point, our churches are by no means to be blamed. For this even our adversaries must needs concede to us, that the doctrine concerning repentance has been most diligently treated and laid open by our teachers.

But of Confession, they teach, that an enumeration of sins is not necessary, and that consciences be not burdened with anxiety to enumerate all sins, for it is impossible to recount all sins, as the Psalm testifies [19:13]: "Who can understand his errors?" Also Jeremiah [17:9]: "The heart is deceitful, who can know it?" But if no sins were forgiven, except those that are recounted, consciences could never find peace; for very many sins they neither see, nor can remember.

The ancient writers also testify that an enumeration is not necessary. For, in the Decrees, Chrysostom is quoted, who thus says: "I say not to thee, that thou shouldest disclose thyself in public, nor that thou accuse thyself before others, but I would have thee obey the prophet who says: 'Disclose thy way before God.' Therefore confess thy sins before God, the true Judge, with prayer. Tell thine errors, not with the tongue, but with the memory of thine conscience." And the Gloss ("Of Repentance," *Distinct. v, Cap. Consideret*) admits that Confession of human right only. Nevertheless, on account of the great benefit of absolution, and because it is otherwise useful to the conscience, Confession is retained among us.

Article XXVI.

It has been the general persuasion, not of the people alone, but also of such as teach in the churches, that making Distinctions of Meats, and like traditions of men, are works profitable to merit grace, and able to make satisfactions for sins. And that the world so thought, appears from this, that new ceremonies, new orders, new holydays, and new fastings were daily instituted, and the teachers in the churches did exact these works as a service necessary to merit grace, and did greatly terrify men's consciences, if they should omit any of these things. From this persuasion concerning traditions, much detriment has resulted in the Church.

First, the doctrine of grace and of the righteousness of faith has been obscured by it, which is the chief part of the Gospel, and ought to stand out, as the most prominent in the Church, that the merit of Christ may be well known, and that faith, which believes that sins are forgiven for Christ's sake may be exalted far above works. Wherefore Paul also lays the greatest stress on this article, putting aside the law and human traditions, in order to show that the righteousness of the Christian is another than such works, to wit, the faith which believes that sins are freely forgiven for Christ's sake. But this doctrine of Paul has been almost wholly smothered by traditions, which have produced an opinion that, by making distinctions in meats and like services, we must merit grace and righteousness. In treating of repentance, there was no mention made of faith; all that was done was to set forth those works of satisfaction, and in these all repentance seemed to consist.

Secondly, these traditions have obscured the commandments of God; because traditions were placed far above the commandments of God. Christianity was thought to consist wholly in the observance of certain holydays, fasts and vestures. These observances had won for themselves the exalted title of being the spiritual life and the perfect life. Meanwhile the commandments of God, according to each one's calling, were without honor, namely, that the father brought up his family, that the mother bore children, that the Prince governed the Commonwealth,— these were accounted works that were worldly and imperfect, and far below those glittering observances. And this error greatly tormented devout consciences, which grieved that they were bound by an imperfect state of life, as in marriage, in the office of magistrate, or in other civil ministrations; on the other hand, they admired the monks and such like, and falsely imagined that the observances of such men were more acceptable to God.

Thirdly, traditions brought great danger to consciences; for it was impossible to keep all traditions, and yet men judged these observances to be necessary acts of worship. Gerson writes that many fell into despair, and that some even took their own lives, because they felt that they were not able to satisfy the traditions; and meanwhile, they heard not the consolation of the righteousness of faith and grace.

We see that the summists and theologians gather the traditions together, and seek mitigations whereby to ease consciences, and yet they do not succeed in releasing them, but sometimes entangle consciences even more. And with the gathering of these traditions, the schools and sermons have been so much occupied that they have had no leisure to touch upon Scripture, and to seek the more profitable doctrine of faith, of the cross, of hope, of the dignity of civil affairs, of consolation of sorely tried consciences. Hence Gerson, and some other theologians, have grievously complained, that by these strivings concerning traditions, they were prevented from giving attention to a better kind of doctrine. Augustine also forbids that men's consciences should be burdened with such observances, and prudently advises Januarius, that he must know that they are to be observed as things indifferent; for these are his words.

Wherefore our teachers must not be looked upon as having taken up this matter rashly, or from hatred of the bishops, as some falsely suspect. There was great need to warn the churches of these errors, which had arisen from misunderstanding the traditions. For the Gospel compels us to insist in the churches upon the doctrine of grace, and of the righteousness of faith; which, however, cannot be understood, if men think that they merit grace by observances of their own choice.

Thus, therefore, they have taught, that by the observance of human traditions we cannot merit grace, or be justified; and hence we must not think such observances necessary acts of worship.

They add hereunto testimonies of Scripture. Christ [Matt. 15:3] defends the Apostles who had not observed the usual tradition, which however, seemed to pertain to a matter not unlawful, but indifferent, and to have a certain affinity with the purifications of the law, and says [9]: "In vain do they worship me with the commandments of men." He, therefore, does not exact an unprofitable service. Shortly after, he adds [11]: "Not that which goeth into the mouth, defileth a man." So also Paul [Rom. 14:17]: "The Kingdom of God is not meat and drink." [Col. 2:16]: "Let no man therefore judge you in meat, or in drink, or in respect of an holyday, or of the Sabbath day;" also [v. 20, sq.]: "If ye be dead with Christ from the rudiments of the world, why, as though living in the world, are ye subject to ordinances, touch not, taste not, handle not?" And Peter says [Acts 15:10]: "Why tempt ye God, to put a yoke upon the neck of the disciples, which neither our fathers, nor we were able to bear; but we believe that through the grace of the Lord Jesus Christ, we shall be saved, even as they." Here Peter forbids to burden the consciences with many rites, either of Moses, or of others.

And in 1 Tim. [4:1, 3], Paul calls the prohibition of meats a doctrine of devils; for it is against the Gospel to institute or to do such works that by them we may merit grace, or as though Christianity could not exist without such service of God.

Here our adversaries cast up that our teachers are opposed to discipline and mortification of the flesh, as Jovinian. But the contrary may be learned from the writings of our teachers. For they have always taught concerning the cross, that it behooves Christians to bear afflictions. This is the true, earnest and unfeigned mortification, to wit, to be exercised with divers afflictions, and to be crucified with Christ.

Moreover, they teach, that every Christian ought to exercise and subdue himself with bodily restraints and labors, that neither plenty nor slothfulness tempt him to sin, but not that we may merit grace or make satisfaction for sins by such exercises. And such external discipline ought to be urged at all times, not only on a few and set days. So Christ commands [Luke 21:34]: "Take heed, lest your hearts be overcharged with surfeiting;" also [Matt. 17:21]: "This kind goeth not out but by prayer and fasting." Paul also says [1 Cor. 9:27]: "I keep under my body and bring it into subjection." Here he clearly shows that he was keeping under his body, not to merit forgiveness of sins by that discipline, but to have his body in subjection and fitted for spiritual things, and for the discharge of duty according to his calling. Therefore, we do not condemn fasting, but the traditions which prescribe certain days and certain meats, with peril of conscience, as though works of such kinds were a necessary service.

Nevertheless, very many traditions are kept on our part, which conduce to good order in the Church, as the Order of Lessons in the Mass, and the chief holydays. But, at the same time, men are warned that such observances do not justify before God, and that, in such things, it should not be made sin, if they be omitted without scandal. Such liberty in human rites was not unknown to the Fathers. For in the East they kept Easter at another time than at Rome, and when, on account of this diversity, the Romans accused the Eastern Church of schism, they were admonished by others that such usages need not be alike everywhere. And Irenæus says: "Diversity concerning fasting does not destroy the harmony of faith." As also Pope Gregory intimates in *Dist.* xii., that such diversity does not violate the unity of the Church. And in the Tripartite History, Book 9, many examples of dissimilar rites are gathered, and the following statement is made: "It was not the mind of the Apostles to enact rules concerning holydays, but to preach godliness and a holy life."

Article XXVII.

What is taught, on our part, concerning Monastic Vows, will be better understood, if it be remembered what has been the state of the monasteries, and how many things were daily done in those very monasteries, contrary to the Canons. In Augustine's time, they were free associations. Afterward, when discipline was corrupted, vows were everywhere added for the purpose of restoring discipline, as in a carefully planned prison. Gradually, many other observances were added besides vows. And these fetters were laid upon many before the lawful age, contrary to the Canons. Many also entered into this kind of life through ignorance, being unable to judge their own strength, though they were of sufficient age. Being thus ensnared, they were compelled to remain, even though some could have been freed by the provision of the Canons. And this was more the case in convents of women than of monks, although more consideration should have been shown the weaker sex. This rigor displeased many good men before this time, who saw that young men and maidens were thrown into convents for a living, and what unfortunate results came of this procedure, and what scandals were created, what snares were cast upon consciences! They were grieved that the authority of the Canons in so momentous a matter was utterly despised and set aside.

To these evils, was added an opinion concerning vows, which, it is well known, in former times, displeased even those monks who were more thoughtful. They taught that vows were equal to Baptism; they taught that, by this kind of life, they merited forgiveness of sins and justification before God. Yea, they added that the monastic life not only merited righteousness before God, but even greater things, because it kept not only the precepts, but also the so-called "evangelical counsels."

Thus they made men believe that the profession of monasticism was far better than Baptism, and that the monastic life was more meritorious than that of magistrates, than the life of pastors and such like, who serve

THE AUGSBURG CONFESSION (1530) (continued)

their calling in accordance with God's commands, without any man-made services. None of these things can be denied; for they appear in their own books.

What then came to pass in the monasteries? Aforetime, they were schools of Theology and other branches, profitable to the Church; and thence pastors and bishops were obtained. Now it is another thing. It is needless to rehearse what is known to all. Aforetime they came together to learn; now they feign that it is a kind of life instituted to merit grace and righteousness; yea, they preach that it is a state of perfection, and they put it far above all other kinds of life ordained of God.

These things we have rehearsed without odious exaggeration, to the end that the doctrine of our teachers, on this point, might be better understood. First, concerning such as contract matrimony, they teach, on our part, that it is lawful for all men who are not fitted for single life to contract matrimony, because vows cannot annual the ordinance and commandment of God. But the commandment of God is [1 Cor. 7:2]: "To avoid fornication, let every man have his own wife." Nor is it the commandment only, but also the creation and ordinance of God, which forces those to marry who are not excepted by a singular work of God, according to the text [Gen. 2:18]: "It is not good that the man should be alone." Therefore they do not sin who obey this commandment and ordinance of God. What objection can be raised to this? Let men extol the obligation of a vow as much as they list, yet shall they not bring to pass that the vow annuls the commandment of God. The Canons teach that the right of the superior is excepted in every vow; much less, therefore, are these vows of force which are against the commandments of God.

Now if the obligation of vows could not be changed for any cause whatever, the Roman Pontiffs could never have given dispensation; for it is not lawful for man to annul an obligation which is altogether divine. But the Roman Pontiffs have prudently judged that leniency is to be observed in this obligation, and therefore we read that many times they have dispensed from vows. The case of the King of Aragon who was called back from the monastery is well known, and there are also examples in our own times.

In the second place, Why do our adversaries exaggerate the obligation or effect of a vow, when, at the same time, they have not a word to say of the nature of the vow itself, that it ought to be in a thing possible, free, and chosen spontaneously and deliberately. But it is not known to what extent perpetual chastity is in the power of man. And how few are there who have taken the vow spontaneously and deliberately! Young men and maidens, before they are able to judge, are persuaded, and sometimes even compelled, to take the vow. Wherefore it is not fair to insist so rigorously on the obligation, since it is granted by all that it is against the nature of a vow to take it without spontaneous and deliberate action.

Many canonical laws rescind vows made before the age of fifteen; for before that age, there does not seem sufficient judgment in a person to decide concerning a perpetual life.

Another Canon, granting even more liberty to the weakness of man, adds a few years, and forbids a vow to be made before the age of eighteen. But whether we followed the one or the other, the most part have an excuse for leaving the monasteries, because most of them have taken the vows before they reached these ages.

But, finally, even though the violation of a vow might be rebuked, yet it seems not forthwith to follow that the marriages of such persons ought to be dissolved. For Augustine denies that they ought to be dissolved (xxvii. Quæst. I., Cap, *Nuptiarum*); and his authority is not lightly to be esteemed, although other men afterwards thought otherwise.

But although it appears that God's command concerning marriage delivers many from their vows, yet our teachers introduce also another argument concerning vows, to show that they are void. For every service of God, ordained and chosen of men without the commandment of God to merit justification and grace, is wicked; as Christ says [Matt. 15:9]: "In vain do they worship me with the commandments of men." And Paul teaches everywhere that righteousness is not to be sought by our own observances and acts of worship, devised by men, but that it comes by faith to those who believe that they are received by God into grace for Christ's sake.

But it is evident that monks have taught that services of man's making satisfy for sins and merit grace and justification. What else is this but to detract from the glory of Christ and to obscure and deny the righteousness of faith? It follows, therefore, that the vows thus commonly taken, have been wicked services, and, consequently, are void. For a wicked vow, taken against the commandment of God, is not valid; for (as the Canon says) no vow ought to bind men to wickedness.

Paul says [Gal. 5:4]: "Christ is become of no effect unto you, whosoever of you are justified by the law; ye are fallen from grace." They, therefore, who want to be justified by their vows, are made void of Christ and fall from grace. For such as ascribe justification to vows, ascribe to their own works that which properly belongs to the glory of Christ. But it is undeniable that the monks have taught that, by their vows and observances, they were justified, and merited forgiveness of sins, yea, they invented still greater absurdities, saying that they could give others a share in their works. If any one should be inclined to enlarge on these things with evil intent, how many things could he bring together, whereof even the monks are now ashamed! Over and above this, they persuaded men that services of man's making were a state of Christian perfection. And is not this assigning justification to works? It is no light offence in the Church to set forth to the people a service devised by men, without the commandment of God, and to teach that such service justifies men. For the righteousness of faith in Christ, which chiefly ought to be in the Church, is obscured, when this wonderful worshipping of angels, with its show of poverty, humility and chastity, is cast before the eyes of men.

Furthermore, the precepts of God and the true service of God are obscured when men hear that only monks are in a state of perfection. For Christian perfection is to fear God from the heart, again to conceive great faith, and to trust that, for Christ's sake, we have a gracious God, to ask of God, and assuredly to expect his aid in all things that, according to our calling, are to be borne; and meanwhile, to be diligent in outward good works, and to serve our calling. In these things consist the true perfection and the true service of God. It does not consist in the unmarried life, or in begging, or in vile apparel. But the people conceive many pernicious opinions from the false commendations of monastic life. They hear unmarried life praised above measure; therefore they lead their married life with offence to their consciences. They hear that only beggars are perfect; therefore they keep their possessions and do business with offence to their consciences. They hear that it is an evangelical counsel not to avenge; therefore some in private life are not afraid to take revenge, for they hear that it is but a counsel, and not a commandment; while others judge that the Christian cannot properly hold a civil office, or be a magistrate.

There are on record examples of men who, forsaking marriage and the administration of the Commonwealth, have hid themselves in monasteries. This they called fleeing from the world, and seeking a kind of life which should be more pleasing to God. Neither did they see that God ought to be served in those commandments which he himself has given, and not in commandments devised by men. A good and perfect kind of life is that which has for it the commandment of God. It is necessary to admonish men of these things. And before these times, Gerson rebuked this error concerning perfection, and testified that, in his day, it was a new saying that the monastic life is a state of perfection.

So many wicked opinions are inherent in the vows, such as that they justify, that they constitute Christian perfection, that they keep the counsels and commandments, that they have works of supererogation. All these things, since they are false and empty, make vows null and void.

Article XXVIII.

There has been great controversy concerning the Power of Bishops, in which some have awkwardly confounded the power of the Church and the power of the sword. And from this confusion very great wars and tumults have resulted, while the Pontiffs, emboldened by the power of the Keys, not only have instituted new services and burdened consciences with reservation of cases, but have also undertaken to transfer the kingdoms of this world, and to take the Empire from the Emperor. These wrongs have long since been rebuked in the Church by learned and godly men. Therefore, our teachers, for the comforting of men's consciences, were constrained to show the difference between the power of the Church and the power of the sword, and taught that both of them, because of God's commandment, are to be held in reverence and honor, as among the chief blessings of God on earth.

But this is their opinion, that the power of the Keys, or the power of the bishops, according to the Gospel, is a power or commandment of God, to preach the Gospel, to remit and retain sins, and to administer sacraments. For with that commandment, Christ sends forth his Apostles [John 20:21 sqq.]: "As my Father has sent me, even so send I you. Receive ye the Holy Ghost. Whosesoever sins ye remit, they are remitted unto them; and whosesoever sins ye retain, they are retained." [Mark 16:15]: "Go, preach the Gospel to every creature."

This power is exercised only by teaching or preaching the Gospel and administering the sacraments, according to the calling, either to many or to individuals. For thereby are granted, not bodily, but eternal things, as eternal righteousness, the Holy Ghost, eternal life. These things cannot come but by the ministry of the Word and the sacraments. As Paul says [Rom. 1:16]: "The Gospel is the power of God unto salvation to every one that believeth." Therefore, since the power of the Church grants eternal things, and is exercised only by the ministry of the Word, it does not interfere with civil government; no more than the art of singing interferes with civil government. For civil government deals with other things than does the Gospel; the civil rulers defend not souls, but bodies and bodily things against manifest injuries, and restrain men with the sword and bodily punishments in order to preserve civil justice and peace.

Therefore the power of the Church and the civil power must not be confounded. The power of the Church has its own commission, to teach the Gospel and to administer the sacraments. Let it not break into the office of another; let it not transfer the kingdoms of this world; let it not abrogate the laws of civil rulers; let it not abolish lawful obedience; let it not interfere with judgments concerning civil ordinances or contracts; let it not prescribe laws to civil rulers concerning the form of the Commonwealth. As Christ says [John 18:36]: "My kingdom is not of this world"; also [Luke 12:14]: "Who made me a judge or a divider over you?" Paul also says [Phil. 3:20]: "Our citizenship is in Heaven"; [2 Cor. 10:4]: "The weapons of our warfare are not carnal; but mighty through God to the casting down of imaginations." After this manner, our teachers discriminate between the duties of both these powers, and command that both be honored and acknowledged as gifts and blessings of God.

If bishops have any power of the sword, that power they have, not as bishops, by the commission of the Gospel, but by human law, having received it of Kings and Emperors, for the civil administration of what is theirs. This, however, is another office than the ministry of the Gospel.

When, therefore, a question arises concerning the jurisdiction of bishops, civil authority must be distinguished from ecclesiastical jurisdiction. Again, according to the Gospel, or, as they say, according to Divine Law, to the bishops as bishops, that is, to those to whom has been committed the ministry of the Word and the sacraments, no jurisdiction belongs, except to forgive sins, to discern doctrine, to reject doctrines contrary to the Gospel, and to exclude from the communion of the Church wicked men, whose wickedness is known, and this without human force, simply by the Word. Herein the congregations are bound by Divine Law to obey them, according to Luke 10:16: "He that heareth you, heareth me."

But when they teach or ordain anything against the Gospel, then the congregations have a commandment of God prohibiting obedience [Matt. 7:15]: "Beware of false

THE AUGSBURG CONFESSION (1530) (continued)

prophets"; [Gal. 1:8]: "Though an angel from heaven preach any other Gospel let him be accursed"; [2 Cor. 13:8]: "We can do nothing against the truth; but for the truth." Also [v. 10]: "The power which the Lord hath given me to edification, and not to destruction." So, also, the Canonical Laws command (II. Q. vii. Cap., *Sacerdotes* and Cap. *Oves*). And Augustine (*Contra Petiliani Epistolam*): "Not even to Catholic bishops must we submit, if they chance to err, or hold anything contrary to the Canonical Scriptures of God."

If they have any other power or jurisdiction, in hearing and judging certain cases, as of matrimony or of tithes, they have it by human law. But where the ordinaries fail, princes are bound, even against their will, to dispense justice to their subjects, for the maintenance of peace.

Moreover, it is disputed whether bishops or pastors have the right to introduce ceremonies in the Church, and to make laws concerning meats, holydays and degrees, that is, orders of ministers, etc. They that claim this right for the bishops, refer to this testimony [John 16:12, 13]: "I have yet many things to say unto you, but ye cannot bear them now. Howbeit when he, the Spirit of truth is come, he will guide you into all truth." They also refer to the example of the Apostles, who commanded to abstain from blood and from things strangled [Acts 15:29]. They refer to the Sabbath Day, as having been changed into the Lord's Day, contrary to the Decalogue, as it seems. Neither is there any example whereof they make more than concerning the changing of the Sabbath Day. Great, say they, is the power of the Church, since it has dispensed with one of the Ten Commandments!

But, concerning this question, it is taught on our part (as has been shown above), that bishops have no power to decree anything against the Gospel. The Canonical laws teach the same thing (*Dist.* ix.). Now it is against Scripture to establish or require the observance of any traditions, to the end that, by such observance, we may make satisfaction for sins, or merit grace and righteousness. For the glory of Christ's merit is dishonored when, by such observances, we undertake to merit justification. But it is manifest that, by such belief, traditions have almost infinitely multiplied in the Church, the doctrine concerning faith and the righteousness of faith being meanwhile suppressed. For gradually more holydays were made, fasts appointed, new ceremonies and services in honor of saints instituted; because the authors of such things thought that, by these works, they were meriting grace. Thus, in times past, the Penitential Canons increased, whereof we still see some traces in the satisfactions.

Again, the authors of traditions do contrary to the command of God when they find matters of sin in foods, in days, and like things, and burden the Church with bondage of the law, as if there ought to be among Christians, in order to merit justification, a service like the Levitical, the arrangement of which God has committed to the Apostles and bishops. For thus some of them write; and the Pontiffs in some measure seem to be misled by the example of the law of Moses. Hence are such burdens, as that they make it mortal sin, even without offence to others, to do manual labor on holydays, to omit the Canonical Hours, that certain foods defile the conscience, that fastings are works which appease God, that sin in a reserved case cannot be forgiven but by the authority of him who reserved it; whereas the Canons themselves speak only of the reserving of the ecclesiastical penalty, and not of the reserving of the guilt.

Whence have the bishops the right to lay these traditions upon the Church for the ensnaring of consciences, when Peter [Acts 15:10] forbids to put a yoke upon the neck of the disciples, and Paul says [2 Cor. 13:10] that the power given him was to edification, not to destruction? Why, therefore, do they increase sins by these traditions?

But there are clear testimonies which prohibit the making of such traditions, as though they merited grace or were necessary to salvation. Paul says [Col. 2:16]: "Let no man judge you in meat, or in drink, or in respect of a holyday, or of the new moon, or of the Sabbath days"; [v. 20, 23]: "If ye be dead with Christ from the rudiments of the world, why, as though living in the world, are ye subject to ordinances (touch not; taste not; handle not, which all are to perish with the using); after the commandments and doctrines of men? which things have indeed a show of wisdom." Also in Tit. [1:14] he openly forbids traditions: "Not giving heed to Jewish fables and commandments of men that turn from the truth." And Christ [Matt. 15:14] says of those who require traditions: "Let them alone; they be blind leaders of the blind"; and he rebukes such services [v. 13]: "Every plant which my Heavenly Father hath not planted, shall be plucked up."

If bishops have the right to burden churches with infinite traditions, and to ensnare consciences, why does Scripture so often prohibit to make and to listen to traditions? Why does it call them "doctrines of devils"? [1 Tim. 4:1]. Did the Holy Ghost in vain forewarn of these things?

Since, therefore, ordinances instituted as things necessary, or with an opinion of meriting grace, are contrary to the Gospel, it follows that it is not lawful for any bishop to institute or exact such services. For it is necessary that the doctrine of Christian liberty be preserved in the churches, namely, that the bondage of the Law is not necessary to justification, as it is written in the Epistle to the Galatians [5:1]: "Be not entangled again with the yoke of bondage." It is necessary that the chief article of the Gospel be preserved, to wit, that we obtain grace freely by faith in Christ, and not for certain observances or acts of worship devised by men.

What, then, are we to think of the Sunday and like rites in the house of God? To this we answer, that it is lawful for bishops or pastors to make ordinances that things be done orderly in the Church, not that thereby we should merit grace or make satisfaction for sins, or that consciences be bound to judge them necessary services, and to think that it is a sin to break them without offence to others. So Paul ordains [1 Cor. 11:5], that women should cover their heads in the congregation [1 Cor. 14:30], that interpreters of Scripture be heard in order in the church, etc.

It is proper that the churches should keep such ordinances for the sake of charity and tranquility, so far that one do not offend another, that all things be done in the churches in order, and without confusion; but so that consciences be not burdened to think that they be necessary to salvation, or to judge that they sin when they break them without offence to others; as no one will say that a woman sins who goes out in public with her head uncovered, provided only that no offence be given.

Of this kind, is the observance of the Lord's Day, Easter, Pentecost, and like holydays and rites. For those who judge that, by the authority of the Church, the observance of the Lord's Day instead of the Sabbath Day was ordained as a thing necessary, do greatly err. Scripture has abrogated the Sabbath Day; for it teaches that, since the Gospel has been revealed, all the ceremonies of Moses can be omitted. And yet, because it was necessary to appoint a certain day, that the people might know when they ought to come together, it appears that the Church [the Apostles] designated the Lord's Day for this purpose; and this day seems to have been chosen all the more for this additional reason, that men might have an example of Christian liberty, and might know that the keeping neither of the Sabbath, nor of any other day, is necessary.

There are monstrous disputations concerning the changing of the law, the ceremonies of the new law, the changing of the Sabbath Day, which all have sprung from the false belief that there must needs be in the Church a service like to the Levitical, and that Christ had given commission to the Apostles and bishops to devise new ceremonies as necessary to salvation. These errors crept into the Church when the righteousness of faith was not clearly enough taught. Some dispute that the keeping of the Lord's Day is not indeed of divine right; but in a manner so. They prescribe concerning holydays, how far it is lawful to work. What else are such disputations but snares of consciences? For although they endeavor to modify the traditions, yet the equity can never be perceived as long as the opinion remains that they are necessary, which must needs remain where the righteousness of faith and Christian liberty are disregarded.

The Apostles commanded to abstain from blood. Who doth now observe it? And yet they that do it not, sin not; for not even the Apostles themselves wanted to burden consciences with such bondage; but they forbade it for a time, to avoid offense. For, in any decree, we must perpetually consider what is the aim of the Gospel. Scarcely any Canons are kept with exactness, and, from day to day, many go out of use even with those who are the most zealous advocates of traditions. Neither can due regard be paid to consciences unless this equity be observed, that we know that the Canons are kept without holding them to be necessary, and that no harm is done consciences, even though traditions go out of use.

But the bishops might easily retain the lawful obedience of the people, if they would not insist upon the observance of such traditions as cannot be kept with a good conscience. Now they command celibacy; they admit none, unless they swear that they will not teach the pure doctrine of the Gospel. The churches do not ask that the bishops should restore concord at the expense of their honor; which, nevertheless, it would be proper for good pastors to do. They ask only that they would release unjust burdens

which are new and have been received contrary to the custom of the Church Catholic. It may be that there were plausible reasons for some of these ordinances; and yet they are not adapted to later times. It is also evident that some were adopted through erroneous conceptions. Therefore, it would be befitting the clemency of the Pontiffs to mitigate them now; because such a modification does not shake the unity of the Church. For many human traditions have been changed in process of time, as the Canons themselves show. But if it be impossible to obtain a mitigation of such observances as cannot be kept without sin, we are bound to follow the Apostolic rule [Acts 5:29], which commands us to obey God rather than men. Peter [1 Pet. 5:3] forbids bishops to be lords, and to rule over the churches. Now it is not our design to wrest the government from the bishops, but this one thing is asked, namely, that they allow the Gospel to be purely taught, and that they relax some few observances which cannot be kept without sin. But if they make no concession, it is for them to see how they shall give account to God for having, by their obstinacy, caused a schism.

CONCLUSION.

These are the Chief Articles which seem to be in controversy. For although we might have spoken of more Abuses, yet to avoid undue length, we have set forth the chief points, from which the rest may be readily judged. There have been great complaints concerning indulgences, pilgrimages, and the abuses of excommunications. The parishes have been vexed in many ways by the dealers in indulgences. There were endless contentions between the pastors and the monks concerning the parochial rites, confessions, burials, sermons on extraordinary occasions, and innumerable other things. Things of this sort we have passed over, so that the chief points in this matter, having been briefly set forth, might be the most readily understood. Nor has anything been here said or adduced to the reproach of any one. Only those things have been recounted, whereof we thought that it was necessary to speak, so that it might be understood that, in doctrine and ceremonies, nothing has been received on our part, against Scripture or the Church Catholic, since it is manifest that we have taken most diligent care that no new and ungodly doctrine should creep into our churches.

The above articles we desire to present in accordance with the edict of Your Imperial Majesty, so that our Confession should therein be exhibited, and a summary of the doctrine of our teachers might be discerned. If anything further be desired, we are ready, God willing, to present ampler information according to the Scriptures.

JOHN, Duke of Saxony, Elector.
GEORGE, Margrave of Brandenburg.
ERNEST, Duke of Lüneburg.
PHILIP, Landgrave of Hesse.
JOHN FREDERICK, Duke of Saxony.
FRANCIS, Duke of Lüneburg.
WOLFGANG, Prince of Anhalt.
SENATE and MAGISTRACY of Nuremburg.
SENATE of Reutlingen.

Notes: *When the Western Church was disrupted in the sixteenth century, those church bodies separating from*

THE AUGSBURG CONFESSION (1530) (continued)

Roman Catholic jurisdiction began to generate statements "confessing" their position on the ancient symbols (creeds) by which Christianity had defined itself for centuries and on newer issues that had led to their rejection of Rome. Thus, in the decades after Luther nailed the 95 Theses to the church door at Wittenburg, a variety of confessional statements came forth from Lutheran, Reformed-Presbyterian, Brethren-Mennonite, and Anglican leaders and representative bodies. Frequently joining the confessional statements were catechisms that became major tools for training the younger generation in the faith.

For the Lutherans, the single most definitive confession was the first one, the Augsburg Confession, produced in 1530 in response to the demand of Emperor Charles V for an explicit statement of Lutheran belief. Philip Melancthon is generally given credit as the major author, though he received the assistance and counsel of others. The original texts were in German and Latin.

Eventually, the Augsburg Confession was gathered with a selection of three ancient creeds (Apostles', Nicene, Athanasian) and several sixteenth century documents (an addenda or Apology to the Augsburg Confession produced in 1531, Luther's Smaller and Larger Catechisms, The Smalcald Articles, and the Formula of Concord) into The Book of Concord. *The Book of Concord, a sizable volume of six to seven hundred pages (depending upon which edition is consulted), has remained the common standard of Lutheran doctrine despite the organizational splintering that has occurred over the centuries since the book's original publication in 1580. In addition to the items mentioned above, various editions of* The Book of Concord *have contained the Treatise on the Power and Primacy of the Pope (a document written by Melancthon in 1537), Luther's Order of Baptism, Luther's Marriage Booklet, the Catalog of Testimonies, and the Christian Visitation Articles.*

The Augsburg Confession is generally considered the best attempt of the Lutherans to present their central teachings in terms of the core of the orthodox Western tradition. It affirms the theology of the ecumenical councils, specifically condemning the classical heretics (including the Donatists and Pelegians). It makes a point of Luther's stance on salvation by grace through faith. The majority of the confession deals with specifics of the reforms in the Roman Catholic Church sought by the Lutherans. The Augsburg Confession stands in sharp contrast to the lengthier Formula of Concord (1577), which deals in depth with many Lutheran theological distinctives.

All Lutherans would accept the Augsburg Confession. Different churches vary in the strictness with which conformity to the confession is demanded of members and leaders, as well as the relative weight given to it and the other statements in The Book of Concord.

SMALCALD ARTICLES (1537)

PREFACE OF DR. MARTIN LUTHER

When Pope Paul III. convoked a Council last year to assemble at Mantua about Whitsuntide, and afterwards transferred it from Mantua, so that it is not yet clear where he will or can fix it; and we on our part had reason to expect that we would either be summoned also to the Council or be condemned unsummoned; I was directed to compose and collect the articles of our doctrine, in case there should be any deliberation as to what and how far we could yield to the Papists, and upon what we intended finally to persevere and abide.

I have accordingly collected these articles and presented them to our side. They have also been accepted and unanimously confessed by those with us, and it has been resolved that in case the Pope with his adherents should ever be so bold as seriously and in good faith, without lying and cheating, to hold a truly free Christian Council (as indeed he would be in duty bound to do), they be publicly presented, and express the Confession of our faith.

But since the Romish court is so dreadfully afraid of a free Christian Council, and shuns the light so shamefully, that it has removed, even from those who are on its side, the hope that it will permit a free Council, and much less itself hold it, whereat, as is just, they are greatly offended and have on that account no little trouble, since they notice thereby that the Pope prefers to see all Christendom lost, and all souls damned, rather than that either he or his adherents be reformed even a little, and permit a limit to be fixed to their tyranny; I have, nevertheless, determined to bring these articles to light through the public press, so that should I die before there would be a Council (as I fully expect and hope, because the knaves by fleeing the light and shunning the day take such wretched pains to delay and hinder the Council), they who live and remain after me may thereby have my testimony and confession to produce, concerning the Confession which I had before published, whereby up to this time I still abide, and, by God's grace, will abide.

For what shall I say? How shall I complain? I am still in life, am writing, preaching and lecturing daily; and yet there are spiteful men, not only among the adversaries, but also false brethren that profess to be on our side, who attempt to represent my writings and doctrine directly contrary to myself, and compel me to hear and see it, although they know well that I teach otherwise, and who wish to adorn their venom with my labor, and under my name to mislead the poor people. How will such occurrences continually increase after my death!

Yea, it is but just that I should reply to everything while I am still living. But, on the other hand, how can I alone stop all the mouths of the devil? Especially of those (as they all are embittered) who will not hear or notice what we write, but solely exercise themselves with all diligence how they may most shamefully pervert and corrupt our word in every letter. These I let the devil answer, or at last God's wrath, as they deserve. I often think of the good person, who doubts whether anything good should be published. If it be not done, many souls are neglected who could be delivered; but if it be done, the devil is there, with malignant, villainous tongues without number which envenom and pervert everything, so that the fruit is still prevented. Yet what they gain thereby is manifest. For seeing that they have lied so shamefully against us, and by means of lies wish to retain the people, God has constantly advanced his work, and been ever making their assembly less and ours greater, and by their lies they have been and still continue to be brought to shame.

I must tell a story. There was a doctor sent here to Wittenberg from France, who said publicly before us that his king was sure, and more than sure, that among us there is no Church, no magistrate, no marriage, but all live promiscuously as cattle, and each one does as he will. Say now, how will those who by their writings have represented such gross lies to the king and to other countries as the pure truth, look at us on that day before the judgment-seat of Christ? Christ, the Lord and Judge of us all, knows well that they lie and have lied, whose sentence they must again hear; that I know certainly. God convert those who can be converted to repentance! To the rest it will be said, Woe, and, alas! eternally.

But to return to the subject. I sincerely desire to see a truly Christian Council, whereby yet many matters and persons would be helped. Not that we need it, for our churches are now, through God's grace, so illumined and cared for by the pure Word and right use of the sacraments, by knowledge of the various callings and of right works, that we on our part ask for no Council, and on such points have nothing better to hope or expect from a Council; but because we see in the bishoprics everywhere so many parishes vacant and desolate that one's heart would break. And yet neither the bishops nor canons care how the poor people live or die, for whom nevertheless Christ has died, and who cannot hear him speaking with them as the true Shepherd with his sheep. This causes me to shudder and fear that at some time he may send a council of angels upon Germany that may utterly destroy us, as Sodom and Gomorrah, because we so presumptuously mock him concerning this Council.

Besides such necessary ecclesiastical affairs, there would be also in the political estate innumerable matters of great importance to improve. There is the disagreement between the princes and the states; usury and avarice have burst in like a flood, and have the semblance of right; wantonness, lewdness, pride in dress, gluttony, gambling, idle display, with all kinds of bad habits and wickedness, insubordination of subjects, domestics and laborers of every trade, also the exactions of the peasants (and who can enumerate all?) have so increased that they cannot be rectified by ten Councils and twenty Diets. If such chief matters of the spiritual and worldly estates as are contrary to God would be considered in the Council, they would render all hands so full that the child's play and absurdity of long gowns, large tonsures [wax tapers], broad cinctures, bishops' or cardinals' hats or maces, and like jugglery would be all the while forgotten. If we first had performed God's command and order in the spiritual and worldly estate, we would find time enough to reform food, clothing, tonsures and surplices. But if we swallow such camels, and instead strain out gnats, let the beams stand and judge the motes, we might indeed be satisfied with the Council.

Therefore I have presented a few articles; for we have without this so many commands of God to observe in the Church, the state, and the family, that we can never fulfil them. What then is the use? or wherefore does it profit that many decrees and statutes thereon are made in the Council, especially when these chief matters commanded of God are neither observed nor maintained? Just as though he were to be entertained by our jugglery while we tread his solemn commandments under foot. But our sins weigh upon us and cause God not to be gracious to us; for we do not repent, and besides wish to defend every abomination.

O Lord Jesus Christ, do thou thyself convoke a Council, and deliver thy servants by thy glorious advent. The Pope and his adherents are lost; they wish thee not. So do thou help us, poor and needy, who sigh to thee, and beg thee earnestly, according to the grace which thou hast given us, through the Holy Ghost, who liveth and reigneth with thee and the Father, blessed for ever. Amen.

PART FIRST. OF THE CHIEF ARTICLES CONCERNING THE DIVINE MAJESTY, as:

I. That Father, Son and Holy Ghost, three distinct persons in one divine essence and nature, are one God, who has created heaven and earth.

II. That the Father is begotten of no one; the Son of the Father; the Holy Ghost proceeds from Father and Son.

III. That not the Father, not the Holy Ghost, but the Son became man.

IV. That the Son became man thus: that he was conceived, without the co-operation of man, by the Holy Ghost, and was born of the pure, holy [and always] Virgin Mary. Afterwards he suffered, died, was buried, descended to hell, rose from the dead, ascended to heaven, sits at the right hand of God, will come to judge the quick and the dead, etc., as the Creed of the Apostles, as well as that of St. Athanasius, and the Catechism in common use for children, teach.

Concerning these articles there is no contention or dispute, since we on both sides confess them. Wherefore it is not necessary to treat further of them.

PART SECOND IS CONCERNING THE ARTICLES WHICH REFER TO THE OFFICE AND WORK OF JESUS CHRIST, OR OUR REDEMPTION.

I. OF THE MERIT OF CHRIST, AND THE RIGHTEOUSNESS OF FAITH.

The first and chief article is this, that Jesus Christ, our God and Lord, died for our sins, and was raised again for our justification, Rom. 4:25.

And he alone is the Lamb of God, which taketh away the sins of the world, John 1:29; and God has laid upon him the iniquities of us all, Isa. 53:6.

Likewise: All have sinned and are justified without merit [freely, and without their own works or merits] by his grace, through the redemption that is in Christ Jesus, in his blood, Rom. 3:23 sq.

Since it is necessary to believe this, and it can be acquired or apprehended otherwise by no work, law or merit, it is clear and certain that this faith alone justifies us, as St. Paul says (Rom. 3:28): "For we conclude that a man is justified by faith without the deeds of the Law." Likewise (v. 26): "That he might be just, and the justifier of him which believeth in Christ."

Of this article nothing can be yielded or surrendered, even though heaven and earth and all things should sink to ruin. "For there is none other name under heaven, given among men, whereby we must be saved," says Peter, Acts 4:12. "And with his stripes we are healed," Isa. 53:5. And upon this article all things depend, which, against the Pope, the devil and the whole world, we teach and practise. Therefore, we must be sure concerning this doctrine, and not doubt; for otherwise all is lost, and the Pope and devil and all things against us gain the victory and suit.

II. ARTICLE OF THE MASS.

That the Mass in the Papacy must be the greatest and most horrible abomination, as it directly and powerfully conflicts with this chief article, and yet above all other popish idolatries it is the chief and most specious. For it is held that this sacrifice or work of the Mass, even though it be rendered by a wicked and abandoned scoundrel, frees men from sins, not only in this life, but also in purgatory, although only the Lamb of God frees us, as has been said above. Of this article nothing is to be surrendered or conceded; because the former article does not allow this.

With the more reasonable Papists we might speak thus in a friendly way: First, why do they so rigidly uphold the Mass? since it is only an invention of men, and has not been commanded by God; and every invention of man we may discard, as Christ declares (Matt. 15:9): "In vain do they worship me, teaching for doctrines the commandments of men."

Secondly. It is an unnecessary thing, which can be omitted without sin and danger.

Thirdly. The sacrament can be received in a better and more blessed way [more acceptable to God], (yea, the only blessed way), according to the institution of Christ. Why, therefore, on account of fictitious, unnecessary matters, do they drive the world to extreme misery, when even otherwise it can be well and more blessed?

Let care be taken that it be publicly preached to the people that the Mass as a toy [commentitious affair or human figment] can, without sin, be done away with, and that no one will be condemned who does not observe it, but that men can be saved in a better way without the Mass. Thus it will come to pass that the Mass will perish of its own accord, not only among the rude common people, but also in the minds of all pious, Christian, reasonable, God-fearing hearts; and this much the more when they have heard that the Mass is a very dangerous thing, fabricated and invented without the will and Word of God.

Fourthly. Since such innumerable and unspeakable abuses have arisen in the whole world from the buying and selling of masses, the Mass should by right be relinquished for no other purpose than to prevent abuses, even though in itself it had something advantageous and good. But how much more, since it is altogether unnecessary, useless and dangerous, and without the Mass all things can be held with greater necessity, profit and certainty, ought we to relinquish it, so as to escape for ever these horrible abuses?

Fifthly. But since the Mass is nothing else, and can be nothing else (as the Canon and all books declare), than a work of men (even of wicked scoundrels), by which one attempts to reconcile to God himself and others with himself, and to obtain and merit the remission of sins and grace (for thus the Mass is regarded when it is esteemed at the very best; otherwise what would it profit?); for this very reason it must and should be condemned and rejected. For this directly conflicts with the chief article, which says that it is not a wicked or a godly celebrant of the Mass with his own work, but the Lamb of God and the Son of God, that taketh away our sins.

But if any one should advance the pretext that for the sake of devotion he wishes to administer the communion to himself, this is not in earnest. For if he would commune in sincerity, the sacrament would be administered in the surest and best way according to Christ's institution. But that one commune by himself is a human persuasion, uncertain, unnecessary, yea even prohibited. For he does not know what he does, while without the Word of God he obeys a false human opinion and invention. So too it is not right (even though the matter were otherwise plain) for one to use the public sacrament of the Church for his own private devotion, and without God's Word and apart from the communion of the Church to trifle therewith.

The Council will especially labor and be occupied with this article concerning the Mass. For although it would be possible for them to concede to us all the other articles, yet they could not concede this. As Campegius said at Augsburg that he would be torn to pieces before he would relinquish the Mass, so, by the help of God, I too would suffer my body to be reduced to ashes before I would allow a celebrant of the Mass, be he good or bad, to be made equal to Christ Jesus, my Lord and Saviour, or to be exalted above him. Thus we are and remain eternally separated and opposed to one another. They think indeed with entire correctness, that when the Mass falls the Papacy lies in ruins. Before they would permit this to occur, they would put us all to death if they could.

Beyond all things, this dragon's tail (I mean the Mass) has produced manifold abominations and idolatries.

First, purgatory. For by masses for souls, and vigils, and weekly, monthly and yearly celebrations of obsequies, and finally by the Common Week and All Souls' Day, by lustrations for purgatory, they have been so occupied that the Mass is used almost alone for the dead, although Christ has instituted the sacrament alone for the living. Wherefore purgatory, and every solemnity, rite and profit connected with it, is to be regarded nothing but a spectre of the devil. For it conflicts with the first article, which teaches that only Christ, and not the works of men, can help souls. Besides also nothing has been divinely commanded or enjoined upon us concerning the dead. Therefore all this can be safely omitted, even though there were no error and idolatry in it.

The Papists quote here Augustine and some of the Fathers who have written concerning purgatory, and they think that we do not understand for what purpose and to what end they thus spake. Augustine does not write that there is a purgatory, neither does he have a testimony of Scripture to constrain him thereto, but leaves the question as to its existence in doubt, and says that his mother asked him that she should be remembered at the altar or sacrament. Now all this is indeed nothing but the devotion of men, and that too of individuals, and does not establish an article of faith, which is a work belonging to God alone.

Our Papists, however, cite those opinions of men, in order that faith may be had in their horrible, blasphemous and cursed traffic in masses for souls in purgatory [or in sacrifices for the dead and oblations]. But they will never prove these things from Augustine. And when they have abolished the traffic in masses for purgatory, of which Augustine never dreamt, we will then discuss with them as to whether the expressions of Augustine, being without the warrant of the Word, are to be admitted, and whether the dead should be remembered at the Eucharist. For it is of no consequence that articles of faith are framed from the works or words of the holy Fathers; otherwise their mode of life, style of garments, of house, etc., would become an article of faith, just as they have trifled with the relics of the saints. We have, however, another rule, viz. that the Word of God should frame articles of faith; otherwise no one, not even an angel.

Secondly. From this it has followed that evil spirits have exercised much wickedness, and appeared as the souls of the departed, and with horrible lies and tricks demanded masses, vigils, pilgrimages, and other alms. All of which we had to receive as articles of faith, and to live accordingly; and the Pope confirmed these things, as also the Mass and all other abominations. Here there is no yielding or surrendering.

Thirdly. Hence arose pilgrimages. Instead of these, masses, the remission of sins and the grace of God were demanded; for the Mass controlled everything. But it is very certain that such pilgrimages, without the Word of God, have not been commanded us, neither are they necessary, since the soul can be cared for in a better way, and these pilgrimages can be omitted without all sin and danger. Why do they leave at home their pastors, the Word of God, wives, children, etc., attention to whom is necesary and has been commanded, and run after unnecessary, uncertain, pernicious *ignes fatui* of the devil? Besides the devil was in the Pope when he praised and established these, whereby the people, in a great number, revolted from Christ to their own works, and became idolaters; which is worst of all, for the reason that it is neither necessary nor commanded, but is senseless and doubtful, and besides harmful. Wherefore to yield or concede anything here is not permitted, etc. And it should be taught in preaching that such pilgrimages are not necessary, but dangerous; and then see what will become of the pilgrimages. [For thus they will perish of their own accord.]

Fourthly. Fraternities [or societies], in which cloisters, chapters, and associations of vicars have bound themselves in writing, and by a definite contract and confirmed sale have made common property of all masses and good works, etc., both for the living and the dead. This is not only altogether a human bauble, without the Word of God, entirely unnecessary and not commanded, but also is contrary to the chief article, Of Redemption. Wherefore it is in no way to be tolerated.

Fifthly. The relics of the saints, about which there are so many falsehoods, trifles and absurdities concerning the bones of dogs and horses, that at such rascality even the devil has laughed, ought long ago to have been condemned, even though there were some good in them: and so much the more in that, without the Word of God, they are an entirely unneceasary and useless thing. But the worst is that they have imagined that these relies work the indulgence and forgiveness of sins [and have revered them] as a good work and service of God, as the Mass, etc.

Sixthly. Here belong the precious indulgences granted (but only for money) to the living and the dead, by which the miserable Judas or pope has sold the merit of Christ, together with the superfluous merits of all saints and of the entire Church, etc. All of which is not to be borne, because it is without the Word of God, and without necessity, and is not commanded; but conflicts with the chief article. For the merit of Christ is [apprehended and] obtained not by our works or pence, but from grace through faith, without money and merit; and is offered [and presented] not through the power of the Pope, but through the preaching of God's Word.

OF THE INVOCATION OF SAINTS.

The invocation of saints is also one of the abuses of Antichrist, which conflicts with the chief article, and destroys the knowledge of Christ. It is also neither commanded nor advised, has no example [or testimony] in Scripture, and in Christ we have everything a thousand-fold better, even though it were a precious thing, as it is not.

And although the angels in heaven pray for us (as even Christ also does), as also do the saints on earth, and perhaps also in heaven; yet it does not follow thence that we should invoke and adore the angels and saints, and for them fast, hold festivals, celebrate Mass, make offerings, and establish churches, altars, divine worship, and in still other ways serve them, and regard them as helpers in need, and divide among them all kinds of help, and ascribe to each one a particular form of assistance, as the Papists teach and do. For this is idolatry, and such honor belongs alone to God.

For as a Christian and saint upon earth, you can pray for me, not only in one, but in many necessities. But, for this reason, I ought not to adore and invoke you, and celebrate festivals, fasts, oblations, masses for your honor [and worship], and put my faith in you for my salvation. I can in other ways indeed honor, love and thank you in Christ. If now such idolatrous honor were withdrawn from angels and deceased saints, the remaining honor would be

SMALCALD ARTICLES (1537) (continued)

without danger, and would quickly be forgotten. For where advantage and assistance, both bodily and spiritual, are no more to be expected, there the worship of the saints will depart in peace, whether they be in their graves or in heaven. For without a purpose, or out of pure love, no one will much remember, or esteem, or honor them [bestow on them divine honor].

In short: Whatever the [Papal] Mass is, and whatever proceeds from it and clings to it, we cannot [in general] tolerate, but we are compelled to condemn, in order that we may retain the holy sacrament pure and certain, according to the institution of Christ, employed and received through faith.

ARTICLE III. OF CHAPTERS AND CLOISTERS.

That chapters and cloisters were formerly founded with the good intention to educate learned men and chaste and modest women, and ought again to be turned to such use, in order that pastors, preachers, and other ministers of the Churches may be had, and likewise other necessary persons for the administration of the government [or for the state] in cities and governments, and well-educated maidens for mothers and housekeepers, etc.

If they will not serve this purpose, it is better that they should be abandoned or altogether destroyed, rather than continued with their blasphemous services invented by men as something better than the ordinary Christian life and the offices and callings appointed by God. For all this also is contrary to the first chief article concerning the redemption made through Jesus Christ. In addition, that they also (as all other human inventions) have not been commanded, are needless and useless, and besides afford occasion for dangerous and vain labor [dangerous annoyances and fruitless worship], such services as the prophets call *Aven, i.e.* pain and labor.

ARTICLE IV. OF THE PAPACY.

That the Pope is not, according to divine law or according to the Word of God, the head of all Christendom (for this name belongs to Jesus Christ solely and alone), but is only the bishop and pastor of the Church at Rome, and of those who voluntarily [and of their own accord] or through a human creature (that is a political magistrate) attach themselves to him, not to be under him as a lord, but with him as brethren [colleagues] and associates, as Christians; as the ancient councils and the age of St. Cyprian show.

But to-day none of the bishops venture to address the Pope as brother [as was done in the age of Cyprian]; but they must call him most gracious lord, even though they be kings or emperors. Such arrogance we neither will, can, nor ought with a good conscience to approve. Let him, however, who will do it, do so without us.

Hence it follows that all things which the Pope, from a power so false, mischievous, blasphemous and arrogant, has undertaken and done, have been and still are purely diabolical affairs and transactions (with the exception of the administration of his civil power, where God often blesses a people, even though a tyrant and faithless scoundrel) for the ruin of the entire holy [Catholic or] Christian Church (so far as it is in his power), and for the destruction of the first and chief article concerning the redemption made through Jesus Christ.

For all his bulls and books are extant, in which he roars like a lion (as the angel in Rev. 12 indicates), crying out that no Christian can be saved unless he obey him and be subject to him in all things that he wishes, that he says and that he does. All of which is nothing else than though it were said, that although you believe in Christ, and have in him everything that is necessary to salvation, yet nothing profits you unless you regard me your god, and be subject and obedient to me; although, it is nevertheless manifest that there was a holy Church without the Pope for at least more than five hundred years, and that even to the present day the churches of the Greeks and of many other languages neither have been nor are still under the Pope. Thus it is, as has often been said, a human figment which is not commanded, and is unnecessary and useless. For the holy Christian [or Catholic] Church can exist very well without such a head, and it would certainly have remained better [purer], and its career would have been more prosperous] if such a head had not been raised up by the devil. And the Papacy is also of no use in the Church, because it exercises no ecclesiastical office; and therefore it is necessary for the Church to remain and continue to exist without the Pope.

But supposing that the Pope acknowledge that he is supreme, not by divine right or from God's command, but that for the purpose of preserving the unity of Christians against sects and heretics they should have a head to whom all the rest should adhere; and that such a head should be chosen by men, and that it also be placed within the choice and power of men to change or remove this head, just as the Council of Constance almost in this very way treated the popes, deposing three and electing a fourth; supposing (I say), that the Pope and See at Rome would yield and accept this (which, nevertheless, is impossible; for thus he would suffer his entire realm and estate to be overthrown and destroyed, with all his rights and books, a thing which, to speak in few words, he cannot do); nevertheless, even in this way Christianity would not be helped, but many more sects would arise than before.

For since obedience would be rendered this head not from God's command, but from man's free will, it would easily and in a short time be despised, and at last retain no member; neither would it be necessary that it be confined to Rome or any other place, but be wherever and in whatever church God would grant a man fit for the office. Oh, the indefiniteness and confusion that would result!

Wherefore the Church can never be governed and preserved better than if we all live under one head, Christ, and all the bishops, equal in office (although they be unequal in gifts), be diligently joined in unity of doctrine, faith, sacraments, prayer and works of love, etc., just as St. Jerome writes that the priests at Alexandria together and in common governed the churches, as did also the apostles, and afterwards all bishops throughout all Christendom, until the Pope raised his head above all. This article clearly shows that the Pope is the very Antichrist, who has exalted and opposed himself against Christ, because he does not wish Christians to be saved without his power, which nevertheless is nothing, and is neither established nor commanded by God. This is, properly speaking, to "exalt himself above all that is called God," as Paul says, 2 Thess. 2:4. This indeed neither the Turks nor the Tartars do, although they are great enemies of Christians, but they allow whoever wishes to believe in Christ, and they receive [outward or] bodily tribute and obedience from Christians.

The Pope, however, prohibits this faith, saying that if any one wish to be saved he must obey. This we are unwilling to do, even though on this account we must die in God's name. This all proceeds from the fact that the Pope has wished to be considered the supreme head of the Christian Church according to divine law. Accordingly he has made himself equal to and above Christ, and has caused himself to be proclaimed the head, and then the lord of the Church, and finally of the whole world, and simply God on earth, until he has attempted to issue commands even to the angels in heaven. And when a distinction is made between a dogma of the Pope and Holy Scripture, and a comparison of the two is made, it is found that the dogma of the Pope, even the best, has been taken from [civil] imperial and heathen law, and treats of political matters and decisions or rights, as the Decretals show; afterwards, it teaches of ceremonies concerning churches, garments, food, persons and like shows, masks and comical things above measure, but in all these things nothing at all of Christ, faith and the commandments of God; and lastly is nothing else than the devil himself, while over and against God he urges [and disseminates] his falsehoods concerning masses, purgatory, a monastic life, one's own works and [fictitious] divine worship (for this is the true Papacy, upon each of which the Papacy is altogether founded and is standing), and condemns, murders and tortures all Christians who do not exalt and honor these abominations of the Pope above all things. Wherefore just as we cannot adore the devil himself as Lord and God, so we cannot endure his apostle, the Pope or Antichrist, in his rule as head or lord. For to lie and to kill, and to destroy body and soul eternally, is a prerogative of the Papal government, as I have very clearly shown in many books.

In these four articles they will have enough to condemn in the Council. For they will not concede us even the least point in these articles. Of this we should be certain, and keep the hope in mind, that Christ our Lord has attacked his adversary, whom he will pursue and destroy, both by his Spirit and coming. Amen.

For in the Council we will stand not before the Emperor or the political magistrate, as at Augsburg (where the Emperor published a most gracious edict, and caused matters to be heard kindly and dispassionately), but we will appear before the Pope and devil himself, who intends to hear nothing, but merely [when the case has been publicly announced] to condemn, to murder and to force to idolatry. Wherefore we ought not here to kiss his feet, or to say: "Thou art my gracious lord," but as the angel in Zechariah 3:2 said to Satan: "The Lord rebuke thee, O Satan."

PART THIRD.

Concerning the following articles we will be able to treat with learned and reasonable men, or even among our-

selves. The Pope and the Papal government do not care much about these. For with them conscience is nothing, but money, glory, honors, power are to them everything.

I. OF SIN.

Here we must confess, as Paul says in Rom. 5:11, that sin originated [and entered the world] from one man Adam, by whose disobedience all men were made sinners, and subject to death and the devil. This is called original or capital sin.

The fruits of this sin are afterwards the evil deeds which are forbidden in the Ten Commandments, such as [distrust] unbelief, false faith, idolatry, to be without the fear of God, arrogance, blindness, and, to speak briefly, not to know or regard God; secondly, to lie, to swear by [to abuse] God's name [to swear falsely], not to pray, not to call upon God, not to regard God's Word, to be disobedient to parents, to murder, to be unchaste, to steal, to deceive, etc.

This hereditary sin is so deep [and horrible] a corruption of nature, that no reason can understand it, but it must be [learned and] believed from the revelation of Scriptures, Ps. 51:5; Rom. 5:12 sqq.; Ex. 33:3; Gen. 3:7 sqq. Wherefore the dogmas of the scholastic doctors are pure errors and obscurations contrary to this article, for by them it is taught:

That since the fall of Adam the natural powers of man have remained entire and incorrupt, and that man by nature has right reason and a good will, as the philosophers teach.

And that man has a free will to do good and omit evil, and, again, to omit good and do evil.

Also that man by his natural powers can observe and do all the commands of God.

And that, by his natural powers, he can love God above all things, and his neighbor as himself.

Also if a man do as much as is in him, God certainly grants to him his grace.

And if he wish to come to the sacrament, there is no need of a good intention to do good, but it is sufficient if he have not a wicked purpose to commit sin; so entirely good is his nature and so efficacious the sacrament.

Also that it is not founded upon Scripture that, for a good work, the Holy Ghost with his grace is necessary.

Such and many similar things have arisen from want of understanding and learning concerning both sins and Christ our Saviour, and they are truly heathen dogmas which we cannot endure. For if these dogmas would be right, Christ has died in vain, since there is in man no sin and misery for which he should have died; or he would have died only for the body, not for the soul, inasmuch as the soul is entirely sound, and the body only is subject to death.

II. OF THE LAW.

Here we hold that the Law was given by God, first to restrain in by threats and the dread of punishment, and by the promise and offer of grace and favor. But all these miscarried, on account of the wickedness which sin has wrought in man. For thereby a part were rendered worse, who are hostile to the Law, because it forbids those things which they do willingly, and enjoins those things which they do unwillingly. Therefore, if they were not restrained by punishment, they would do more against the Law than before. For these are rude and wicked [unbridled and secure] men, who do evil wherever they have the opportunity.

The rest are blind and arrogant, and think that they observe and can observe the Law by their own powers, as has been said above concerning the scholastic theologians; thence come the hypocrites and false saints.

But the chief office or power of the Law is that it reveal original sin with all its fruits, and show man how very low his nature has fallen, and that it has become utterly corrupted; as the Law must tell that man neither has nor cares for God, and adores other gods, a matter which before and without the Law would not have been believed. In this way he becomes terrified, is humbled, desponds, despairs and anxiously desires aid; neither does he know whither to flee; he begins to be enraged at God, and to murmur, etc. This is what Paul says (Rom. 4:15): "The Law worketh wrath." And Rom. 5:20: "Sin is increased by the Law." [The Law entered that the offence might abound."]

III. OF REPENTANCE.

This office [of the Law] the New Testament retains and exercises, as St. Paul (Rom. 1:18) does, saying: "The wrath of God is revealed from heaven against all ungodliness and unrighteousness of men." And 3:19: "All the world is guilty before God." "No man is righteous before him." And Christ (John 16:8) says: "The Holy Ghost will reprove the world of sin."

This therefore is a thunderbolt of God, by which he strikes manifest sinners and hypocrites in one mass, and declares no one righteous, but forces them all together to terror and despair. This is the hammer, as Jeremiah says (23:29): "Is not my Word like a hammer that breaketh the rock in pieces?" This is not *activa contritio,* or manufactured repentance, but *passiva contritio* [torture of conscience], true sorrow of heart, suffering and sense of death.

For that is the beginning of true repentance; and here man must hear such a sentence as this: "You are all of no account, whether you be manifest sinners or saints [in your own opinion]; you all must become different and do otherwise than you now are and are doing, be you great, wise, powerful and holy as you may. Here no one is [righteous, holy], godly," etc.

But to this office the New Testament immediately adds the consolatory promise of grace through the Gospel, which must be believed, as Christ declares (Mark 1:15): "Repent and believe the Gospel," *i.e.* become different and do otherwise, and believe my promise. And before him John is named a preacher of repentance, but "for the remission of sins," *i.e.* John was to accuse all, and prove that they were sinners, that they might know what they were before God, and might acknowledge that they were lost men, and might thus be prepared for the Lord, to receive grace, and to expect and accept from him the remission of sins. Thus

Christ also (Luke 24:47) himself says: "That repentance and remission of sins should be preached in his name among all nations."

But when the Law alone, without the co-operation of the Gospel, exercises this, its office is death and hell, and man must despair, as Saul and Judas; just as St. Paul (Rom. 7:10) says that through sin the Law killeth. On the contrary, the Gospel brings consolation and remission, not only in one way, but through the Word and sacraments and the like, as we will hear afterward that "with the Lord is plenteous redemption," as Ps. 130:7 says, against the dreadful captivity of sin.

We will next contrast the false repentance of the sophists with true repentance, in order that both may be the better understood.

OF THE FALSE REPENTANCE OF THE PAPISTS.

It was impossible that they should teach correctly concerning repentance, since they did not rightly know what sins are. For, as has been shown above, they do not believe aright concerning original sin, but say that the natural powers of man have remained unimpaired and incorrupt; that reason can teach aright, and the will can accordingly do aright [those things which are taught], that God certainly gives his grace when a man does only as much as is in him, according to his free will.

From this dogma it follows that they must repent only for actual sins, such as wicked thoughts that are acquiesced in (for wicked emotion [concupiscence, vicious feelings and inclinations], lust and improper dispositions [according to them] are not sins), and for wicked words and deeds, which the free will could readily have omitted. And to such repentance they fix three parts, contrition, confession and satisfaction, with this consolation and promise added: If man truly repent, confess, render satisfaction, he thereby merits forgiveness, and settles for his sins with God. Thus in repentance men were instructed to repose confidence in their own works. Hence the expression originated, which was employed in the pulpit when public absolution was announced to the people: "Prolong, O God, my life, until I shall make satisfaction for my sins and amend my life."

Here neither Christ nor faith was mentioned; but they hoped, by their own works, to overcome and efface sins before God. And with this intention we became priests and monks, that we might array ourselves against sin.

As to contrition, the state of the case was this: Since no one could retain all his sins in memory (especially as committed through an entire year), they inserted this provision, viz. that if the remembrance of a concealed sin should perhaps return, this also should be repented of and confessed, etc. Meanwhile they were commended to the grace of God.

Since also no one could know how great the contrition ought to be which would be sufficient before God, they gave this consolation: He who could not have contrition, at least ought to have attrition, which I may call a half or beginning of contrition. Both these terms every one of them has understood, and now knows, as little as I. Such attrition is reckoned as contrition to those going to confession.

And when any one said that he could not have contrition, or could not lament his sins (as might have occurred in illicit love or the desire for revenge, etc.), they asked whether he did not wish or desire to lament. When one would reply Yes (for who, save the devil himself, would here say No?), they accepted this as contrition, and forgave him his sins on account of this good work of his [which they adorned with the name of contrition]. Here they cite the example of Bernard, etc.

Here we see how blind reason, in matters pertaining to God, gropes about, and, according to its own imagination, seeks for consolation in its own works, and cannot think of Christ and faith. But if it be considered in the light, this contrition is a manufactured and fictitious thought [or imagination], derived from man's own powers, without faith and without the knowledge of Christ. And in it, sometimes the poor sinner, when he reflected upon his own lust and desire for revenge, would have laughed, rather than wept, except one who either has been struck by [the lightning of] the Law, or has been vainly vexed by the devil with a sorrowful spirit. Such contrition is certainly mere hypocrisy, and has not mortified the lust for sins [flames of lust]; for they must grieve, even though, if it had been free to them, they would have preferred to sin.

With confession it stood thus: Every one must enumerate all his sins (which is an impossible thing). This was a great torment. But if any one had forgotten some sins, he would be absolved on the condition that if they would occur to him he must still confess them. Thereby he could never know whether he had confessed sufficiently, or when the confession would ever have an end. Yet they were pointed to their own works, and comforted thus: The more perfectly one confesses, and the more he is ashamed of himself and blames himself to the priest, the sooner and better he renders satisfaction for his sins; for such humility certainly earns grace before God.

Here there was no faith or Christ, and the virtue of the absolution was not declared to him, but upon the enumeration of sins and the shame depended the consolation. What torture, rascality and idolatry such confession has produced cannot be enumerated.

But the satisfaction is most indefinite [involved] of all. For no man could know how much to render for a single sin, to say nothing for all. Here they have resorted to the device of a small satisfaction, which could indeed be rendered, as five Paternosters, a day's fast, etc.; for the rest of the repentance they point to purgatory.

Here also there was extreme misery. For some thought that they would get out of purgatory, because, according to the old canons, seven years' repentance belongs to a single mortal sin. Nevertheless confidence was placed upon our work of satisfaction, and if the satisfaction could have been perfect, confidence would have been placed in it entirely, and neither faith nor Christ would have been of use. But this was impossible. If any one had repented in that way for a hundred years, he would still not have known whether he had repented enough. This is always to repent and never to come to repentance.

Here now the holy See at Rome came to the aid of the poor Church, and invented indulgences, whereby it remitted and waived [expiation or] satisfaction, first, for a single year, for seven years, for a hundred years, and distributed them among the cardinals and bishops, so that one could grant indulgence for a hundred years, and another for a hundred days. But it reserved to itself alone the power to waive all the satisfaction.

Since now this began to yield money, and the traffic in bulls was profitable, it devised a golden jubilee year [a truly gold bearing year], and fixed it at Rome. It called this the remission of all punishment and guilt. Thither the people ran, because every one wished to be freed from a grievous, insupportable burden. This was to find and raise the treasures of the earth.

Immediately the Pope pressed still further, and multiplied the golden years one upon another. But the more he devoured money, the wider did his jaws open. Therefore by his legates these years were published [everywhere] in the countries, until all churches and houses were full of the jubilee. At length he resorted to purgatory among the dead, first by establishing masses and vigils, afterwards by indulgences and a golden year, and finally souls became so cheap that he released one for a farthing.

Nevertheless even this is not half. For although the Pope taught men to depend upon, and trust in, these indulgences for salvation, yet he rendered the whole matter again uncertain. For in his bulls he puts it thus: He who wishes to become participant in the indulgences of a year of jubilee, ought to be contrite, and to have confessed, and to pay money. Moreover we have heard above that this contrition and confession are with them uncertain and hypocrisy. Likewise also no one knew what soul was in purgatory, and if some were therein, no one knew who had repented and confessed aright. Therefore he took the coveted money, and comforted them meanwhile with his power and indulgence, and pointed them again to their uncertain work.

If now there were some who did not regard themselves guilty of such actual sins in thoughts, words and works (as I and my like, in monasteries and chapters, wished to be monks and priests, and by fasting, watching, praying, saying Mass, harsh clothing and hard beds to protect ourselves from evil spirits, and with heart and soul to be holy), yet the hereditary, inborn evil sometimes in sleep did that (as also St. Augustine and Jerome among others confess) which is its nature. Nevertheless each one was regarded by the others as so holy, as we taught, without sin and full of good works, that we could communicate and sell our good works to others, as being superfluous to us for heaven. This is indeed true, and seals, letters and illustrations are at hand.

Such as these did not need repentance. For of what would they repent, as they had not acquiesced in the wicked thoughts? What would they confess [concerning words not uttered], as they had avoided the expression? For what should they render satisfaction, as they were so guiltless of any deed that they could even sell their superfluous righteousness to other poor sinners? Such saints were also the Pharisees and Scribes in the time of Christ.

SMALCALD ARTICLES (1537) (continued)

Here comes the fiery angel, St. John, the true preacher of repentance, and strikes with one bolt all of both classes [those selling and those buying works] in one mass, and says: "Repent" (Matt. 3:2). Thus the former imagine: We nevertheless have repented. The latter: We need no repentance. John says: Repent ye all, for ye are false penitents; so are these false saints, and all of both classes need the forgiveness of sins, because ye all still know not what true sin is, to be silent as to your obligation to repent and escape from it. For no one of you is good; you are full of unbelief, stupidity and ignorance of God and God's will. For here he is present: "Of whose fulness have all we received, and grace for grace" (John 1:16), and without him no man can be just before God. Wherefore if you wish to repent, repent aright; your repentance is nothing. And you hypocrites, who do not need repentance, you generation of vipers, who has warned you to flee from the wrath to come? etc. (Matt. 3:7; Luke 3:7).

In the same way Paul also preaches (Rom. 3:10-12): "There is none righteous, there is none that understandeth, there is none that seeketh after God, there is none that doeth good, no not one; they are all gone out of the way; they are together become unprofitable." And Acts 17:30: "God now commandeth all men everywhere to repent." "All men," he says; no one excepted who is a man. This repentance teaches us to discern sin, viz. that we are altogether lost, and that with us, both within and without, there is nothing good, and that we ought absolutely to become other and new men.

This repentance is not partial and beggarly [incomplete], such as is that for actual sins, nor is it even as uncertain as that. For it does not dispute as to whether there is or is not sin, but it overthrows everything in a mass, and affirms that with respect to us, all is nothing but sin. For why do we wish longer to investigate, to divide or distinguish? Therefore, this contrition also is not uncertain. For nothing remains there by which we can think of any good thing to pay for sin, but we only despair concerning all things that we are, that we think, that we speak and do, etc.

Likewise the confession also cannot be false, uncertain or partial. For he who confesses that all in him is nothing but sin, comprehends all sins, excludes none, forgets none. So also the satisfaction cannot be uncertain, because it is not an uncertain, sinful work of ours, but it is the suffering and blood of the innocent Lamb of God who taketh away the sin of the world.

Of this repentance John preaches; and afterwards Christ in the Gospel, and we also. By this preaching of repentance we dash to the ground the Pope and everything that is built upon our good works. For all are built upon a rotten and vain foundation, which is called a good work or law, even though no good work be there, but only wicked works, and no one does the Law (as Christ, John 7:19, says), but all transgress it. Therefore the building is nothing but falsehood and hypocrisy, even [in the part] where it is most holy and beautiful.

This repentance in Christians continues until death, because, through the entire life, it contends with sin remaining in the flesh, as Paul (Rom. 7:14-25) shows, that he wars with the law in his members, etc.; and this not by his own powers, but by the gift of the Holy Ghost that follows the remission of sins. This gift daily cleanses and purges the remaining sins, and works so as to render man pure and holy. Hereof the Pope, the theologians, the jurists, and every other man know nothing [from their own reason], but it is a doctrine from heaven revealed through the Gospel, and is proclaimed as heresy by the godless saints.

But if certain sectarists would arise, some of whom are perhaps already present, and in the time of the insurrection of the peasants came to my view, holding that all those who have once received the Spirit or the forgiveness of sins, or have become believers, even though they would afterwards sin, would still remain in the faith, and sin would not injure them, and cry thus: "Do whatever you please; if you believe, it is all nothing; faith blots out all sins," etc.—They say, besides, that if any one sins after he has received faith and the Spirit, he never truly had the Spirit and faith. I have seen and heard of many men so insane, and I fear that such a devil is still remaining in some.—

If, therefore, I say, such persons would hereafter also arise, it is necessary to know and teach that if saints who still have and feel original sin, and also daily repent, and strive with it, fall in some way into manifest sins, as David into adultery, murder and blasphemy, faith and the Holy Ghost are then absent from them [they cast out faith and the Holy Ghost]. For the Holy Ghost does not permit sin to have dominion, to gain the upper hand so as to be completed, but represses and restrains it so that it must not do what it wishes. But if it do what it wishes, the Holy Ghost and faith are not there present. For St. John says (1 Ep. 3:9): "Whosoever is born of God doth not commit sin, . . . and he cannot sin." And yet that is also the truth which the same St. John says (1 Ep. 1:8): "If we say that we have no sin, we deceive ourselves and the truth is not in us."

IV. OF THE GOSPEL.

We will now return to the Gospel, which not merely in one way gives us counsel and aid against sin; for God is superabundantly rich in his grace. First, through the spoken Word by which the forgiveness of sins is preached in the whole world; which is the peculiar office of the Gospel. Secondly, through baptism. Thirdly, through the holy sacrament of the altar. Fourthly, through the power of the keys, and also through the mutual conversation and consolation of brethren, Matt. 18:20: "Where two or three are gathered together," etc.

V. OF BAPTISM.

Baptism is nothing else than the Word of God [with mersion] in the water, commanded by his institution, or as Paul says: "A washing in the Word;" just as Augustine also says: "The Word comes to the element, and it becomes a sacrament." Therefore, we do not hold with Thomas and the monastic preachers or Dominicans, who forget the Word (God's institution) and say that God has imparted to the water a spiritual power, which, through the water, washes away sin. Nor do we agree with Scotus and the Barefooted monks [Minorites or Franciscan monks], who teach that, by the assistance of the divine will, baptism washes away sins, and that this ablution occurs only through the will of God, and by no means through the Word and water.

Of the baptism of children, we hold that children ought to be baptized. For they belong to the promised redemption made through Christ, and the Church should administer it to them.

VI. OF THE SACRAMENT OF THE ALTAR.

Of the sacrament of the altar we hold that bread and wine in the Supper are the true body and blood of Christ, and are given and received not only by the godly, but also by wicked Christians.

And that not only one form is to be given. For we do not need that high art which teaches us that under the one form there is as much as under both, as the sophists and Council of Constance teach.

For although it may perhaps be true that there is as much under one as under both, yet the one form is not the entire ordinance and institution established and commanded by Christ. And we especially condemn, and in God's name execrate, those who not only omit both forms, but also tyrannically prohibit, condemn and blaspheme them as heresy, and so exalt themselves against and above Christ, our Lord and God, etc.

We care nothing about the sophistical subtlety concerning transubstantiation, by which they teach that bread and wine leave or lose their own natural substance, and remain only the appearance and color of bread, and not true bread. For it agrees best with Holy Scripture that the bread be and remain there, as Paul himself calls it (1 Cor. 10:16): "The bread which we break." And (1 Cor. 11:28): "Let him so eat of that bread."

VII. OF THE KEYS.

The keys are an office and power given by Christ to the Church for binding and loosing sins, not only such as are gross and well known, but also such as are subtle, hidden, and known only to God, as it is written in Ps. 19:13: "Who can understand his errors?" And in Rom. 7:25, St. Paul complains that with the flesh he serves the law of sin. For it is not in our power, but belongs to God alone, to judge what, how great and how many are sins, as it is written in Ps. 144 (143:2): "Enter not into judgment with thy servant; for in thy sight shall no man living be justified." And Paul (1 Cor. 4:4) says: "For I know nothing by myself; yet am I not hereby justified?"

VIII. OF CONFESSION.

Since absolution or the power of the keys is also a consolation and aid against sin and a bad conscience, appointed by Christ himself in the Gospel, Confession or absolution ought by no means to be abolished in the Church, especially on account of [tender and] timid consciences and uncultivated youth, in order that they may be heard, and instructed in Christian doctrine.

But the enumeration of sins ought to be free to every one, as to what he wishes to enumerate or not to enumerate. For as long as we are in the flesh, we will not lie when we say: "I am a poor man, full of sins." Rom. 7:23: "I see another law in my members," etc. For since private absolution arises from the office of the keys, it should not be neglected, but must be esteemed of the greatest worth, just as all other offices also of the Christian Church.

And in those things which concern the spoken, outward Word, we must firmly hold that God grants his Spirit or grace to no one, except through or with the preceding outward Word. Thereby we are protected against enthusiasts, *i.e.* spirits who boast that they have the Spirit without and before the Word, and accordingly judge Scripture or the spoken Word, and explain and stretch it at their pleasure, as Münzer did, and many still do at the present day; they wish to be acute judges between the Spirit and the letter, and yet know not what they say or propose. Because the Papacy also is nothing but enthusiasm, by which the Pope boasts that all laws exist in the shrine of his heart, and whatever he decides and commands in his churches is spirit and law, even though it be above and contrary to Scripture and the spoken Word.

All this is the old devil and old serpent, who also converted Adam and Eve into enthusiasts, and led them from the outward Word of God to spiritualism and self-conceit, and nevertheless he effected this through other outward words. Just so our enthusiasts [at the present day] condemn the outward Word, and nevertheless they themselves are not silent, but they fill the world with their pratings and writings, as though indeed the Spirit were unable to come through the writings and spoken word of apostles, but he must come through their writings and words. Why therefore do not they also omit their own sermons and writings, until the Spirit himself come to men, without their writings and before them, as they boast that they have received the Spirit without the preaching of the Scriptures? But of these matters there is not time now to dispute at greater length; we have heretofore paid sufficient attention to this subject.

For even those who believe before baptism, or become believing in baptism, believe through the outward Word that precedes, as the adults, who have come to reason, must first have heard: "He that believeth and is baptized, shall be saved," even though they are at first unbelieving, and receive the Spirit and baptism ten years afterwards. Cornelius (Acts 10:1 sqq.) had heard long before among the Jews of the coming Messiah, through whom he was righteous before God, and in such faith his prayers and alms were acceptable to God (as Luke calls him devout and fearing God), and without such preceding Word and hearing could not have believed or been righteous. But St. Peter had to reveal to him that the Messiah (in whom, as one that was to come, he had hitherto believed) had already come, and his faith in the coming Messiah did not hold him captive among the hardened and unbelieving Jews, but he knew that he was now to be saved by a present Messiah, and he neither denied nor persecuted him, as did the Jews.

In a word, enthusiasm inheres in Adam and his children from the beginning to the end of the world; its poison has

SMALCALD ARTICLES (1537) (continued)

been implanted and infused into them by the old dragon, and is the origin, power and strength of all heresy, especially of that of the Papacy and Mahomet. Therefore in regard to this we ought and must constantly maintain that God does not wish to deal with us otherwise than through the spoken Word and the sacraments, and that whatever without the Word and sacraments is extolled as spirit is the devil himself. For God also wished to appear to Moses through the burning bush and spoken Word; and no prophet, neither Elijah nor Elisha, received the Spirit without the Ten Commandments or spoken Word. Neither was John the Baptist conceived without the preceding word of Gabriel, nor did he leap in his mother's womb without the voice of Mary. And Peter says (2 Ep. 1:21): "The prophecy came not by the will of man; but holy men of God spake as they were moved by the Holy Ghost." Without the outward Word they were not holy, neither as unholy did the Holy Ghost move them to speak; but they were holy Peter says, when the Holy Ghost spake through them.

IX. OF EXCOMMUNICATION.

The greater excommunication, as the Pope calls it, we regard only as a civil penalty, and not pertaining to us ministers of the Church. But the less is true Christian excommunication, which prohibits manifest and obstinate sinners from the sacrament and other communion of the Church until they are reformed and avoid sin. And ministers ought not to confound this ecclesiastical punishment or excommunication with civil penalties.

X. OF ORDINATION AND THE CALL.

If the bishops were true bishops, and would devote themselves to the Church and the Gospel, they might be allowed, for the sake of love and unity, and not from necessity, to ordain and confirm us and our preachers; nevertheless, under the condition that all masks and phantoms [deceptions, absurdities and appearances] of unchristian nature and display be laid aside. Yet because they neither are nor wish to be true bishops, but worldly lords and princes, who will neither preach, nor teach, nor baptize, nor administer the Lord's Supper, nor perform any work or office of the Church, but persecute and condemn those who being called discharge this duty; for their sake the Church ought not to remain without ministers.

Therefore, as the ancient examples of the Church and the Fathers teach us, we ourselves will and ought to ordain suitable persons to this office; and (even according to their own laws) they have not the right to forbid or prevent us. For their laws say that those ordained even by heretics should be regarded and remain as ordained, as St. Jerome writes of the Church at Alexandria, that at first it was governed in common by the bishops through the priests and preachers.

XI. OF THE MARRIAGE OF PRIESTS.

In prohibiting marriage, and burdening the divine order of priests with perpetual celibacy, they have neither reason nor right, but have treated it as antichristian, tyrannical, sceptical scoundrels, and have afforded occasion for all kinds of horrible, abominable sins of impurity, in which they still wallow. But just as the power has been given neither to us nor to them to make a woman out of a man, or man out of a woman, or to annihilate both, so also it has not been given them; so also power has not been given them to sunder and separate such creatures of God, or to forbid them from living honorably in marriage with one another. Therefore we are unwilling to assent to their abominable celibacy, nor will we even tolerate it, but we wish to have marriage free as God has instituted and appointed it, and we wish neither to rescind nor hinder his work; for Paul says that this prohibition of marriage is a doctrine of devils (1 Tim. 4:1 sqq.).

XII. OF THE CHURCH.

We do not acknowledge them as the Church, and they are not [because in truth they are not the Church]; we also will not listen to those things which, under the name of Church, they either enjoin or forbid. For, thank God, to-day a child seven years old knows what the Church is, viz. saints, believers and lambs who hear the voice of their Shepherd. For the children repeat: "I believe in one holy [Catholic or] Christian Church." This holiness does not consist in an alb, a tonsure, a long gown and other of their ceremonies devised by them beyond Holy Scripture, but consists in the Word of God and true faith.

XIII. HOW MAN IS JUSTIFIED BEFORE GOD, AND OF GOOD WORKS.

What I have hitherto and constantly taught concerning this I cannot in the least change, viz. that by faith (as St. Peter says) we acquire a new and clean heart, and God accounts, and will account us righteous, for the sake of Christ, our Mediator. And although sin in the flesh has not been altogether removed and become dead, yet he will not punish or regard this.

For good works follow this faith, renewal and forgiveness of sins. And that in them which is still sinful and imperfect is not accounted as sin and defect, even for Christ's sake; but the entire man, both as to his person and his works, is and is called just and holy, from pure grace and mercy, shed upon us [unfolded] and displayed in Christ. Wherefore we cannot boast of our many merits and works, if they be viewed apart from grace and mercy, but as it is written, (1 Cor. 1:31): "He that glorieth, let him glory in the Lord," viz. that he has a gracious God. For thus all is well. We say besides that if good works do not follow, faith is false and not true.

XIV. OF MONASTIC VOWS.

As monastic vows directly conflict with the first chief article, they ought to be absolutely abolished. For it is of them that Christ says (Matt. 24:5, 23 sqq.): "I am Christ," etc. For he who makes a vow to live in a monastery believes that he will enter upon a mode of life holier than the ordinary Christians, and by his own works wishes to earn heaven not only for himself, but also for others; this is to deny Christ. And they boast from their St. Thomas that a monastic vow is on an equality with baptism. This is blasphemy against God.

XV. OF HUMAN TRADITIONS.

The declaration of the Papists that human traditions serve for the remission of sins, or merit salvation, is altogether unchristian and condemned, as Christ says (Matt. 15:9): "In vain they do worship me, teaching for doctrines the commandments of men." And Tit. 1:14: "That turn from the truth." Also their declaration that it is a mortal sin if one do not observe these statutes, is not right.

These are the articles on which I must stand; and if God so will I shall stand even to my death. And I do not know how to change or to concede anything in them. If any one else will concede anything, he will do it at the expense of his conscience.

Lastly, the Pope's bundle of impostures still remains, concerning foolish and childish articles, as the dedication of churches, the baptism of bells, the baptism of the altar-stone, with its godfathers to pray and offer gifts. Such baptism is administered to the reproach and mockery of holy baptism, and should not be tolerated. Afterwards, concerning the consecration of wax tapers, palm-branches, cakes, spices, oats, etc., which nevertheless cannot be called consecrations, but are nothing but mockery and fraud. There are infinite other such deceptions, which we commit to their god, and which may be adored by them, until they are weary of them. We will not be confused by [ought to have nothing to do with] them.

DR. MARTIN LUTHER subscribed.
DR. JUSTUS JONAS, Rector, subscribed.
DR. JOHN BUGENHAGEN, POMERANUS subscribed.
DR. CASPAR CREUTZIGER subscribed.
NICLAS AMSDORF of Magdeburg subscribed.
GEORGE SPALATINE of Altenburg subscribed.
I, PHILIP MELANCHTHON, approve the above articles as right and Christian. But of the Pope, I hold that if he would allow the Gospel, for the sake of the peace and general unity of Christians, who are now under him, and may be under him hereafter, the superiority over bishops which he has in other respects could be allowed to him, according to human right, also by us.
JOHN AGRICOLA of Eisleben subscribed.
GABRIEL DIDYMUS subscribed.
I, DR. URBAN RHEGIUS, Superintendent of the churches in the Duchy of Lüneburg, subscribe my name and the names of my brethren, and of the Church of Hanover.
I, STEPHEN AGRICOLA, Minister at Hof, subscribe.
Also I, JOHN DRACONITES, Professor and Minister at Marburg.
I, CONRAD FIGENBOTZ, for the glory of God subscribe that I have thus believed, and am still preaching and firmly believing as above.
I, ANDREW OSIANDER of Nürnberg, subscribe.
I, M. VEIT DIETERICH, Minister at Nürnberg, subscribe.
I, ERHARD SCHNEPF, Preacher at Stuttgart, subscribe.
CONRAD OETINGER, Preacher of Duke Ulrich at Pforzheim.
SIMON SCHNEEWEIS, Pastor of the Church at Crailsheim.

I, JOHN SCHLAINHAUFFEN, Pastor of the Church at Koethen, subscribe.
M. GEORGE HELT of Forchheim.
M. ADAM of Fulda,
M. ANTHONY CORVINUS, Preachers in Hesse.
I, JOHN BUGENHAGEN, POMERANUS, Doctor, again subscribe in the name of M. JOHN BRENTZ, as on departing from Smalcald he directed me orally and by a letter which I have shown to these breathen who have subscribed.
I, DIONYSIUS MELANDER, subscribe to the Confession, the Apology, and the Concordia on the subject of the Eucharist.
PAUL RHODIUS, Superintendent of Stettin.
GERARD OENIKEN, Superintendent of the Church at Minden.
I, BRIXIUS NORTHANUS, Minister of the Church of Christ which is at Soest, subscribe to the Articles of the reverend Father, Martin Luther, and confess that hitherto I have thus believed and taught, and by the Spirit I will continue thus to believe and teach.
MICHAEL COELIUS, Preacher at Mansfeldt, subscribed.
M. PETER GELTNER, Preacher at Frankfort, subscribed.
WENDAL FABER, Pastor of Seeburg in Mansfeldt.
I, John AEPINUS, subscribe.
Likewise, I, JOHN AMSTERDAM of Bremen.
I, FREDERICK MYCONIUS, Pastor of the Church at Gotha in Thuringia, subscribe in my own name, and in that of JUSTUS MENIUS of Eisenach.
I, JOHN LANG, D., and Preacher of the Church at Erfurt, in my own name, and in that of my other co-workers in the Gospel, viz.:
Licentiate LUDWIG PLATZ of Melsungen.
M. SIGISMUND KIRCHNER.
M. WOLFGANG KISMETTER.
M. MELCHIOR WEITMAN.
M. JOHN TALL.
M. JOHN KILLIAN.
M. NICHOLAS FABER.
M. ANDREW MENSER, I subscribe with my hand.
And I, EGIDIUS MECHLER, have subscribed with my hand.

APPENDIX. OF THE POWER AND PRIMACY OF THE POPE. (Treatise Written by Theologians assembled at Smalcald, in the year MDXXXVII.)

The Roman pontiff claims for himself that by divine right he is above all bishops and pastors [in all Christendom].

Secondly, he adds also that by divine right he has both swords, *i.e.* the right of bestowing and transferring kingdoms.

And thirdly, he says that to believe this is necessary for salvation. And for these reasons the Roman bishop calls himself the vicar of Christ on earth.

These three articles we hold to be false, godless, tyrannical and pernicious to the Church.

In order, moreover, that our affirmation may be understood, we will first define what they call to be above all by

SMALCALD ARTICLES (1537) (continued)

divine right. For they mean that he is universal, or as they say oecumenical bishop, *i.e.* from whom all bishops and pastors throughout the entire world ought to seek ordination and confirmation, who has the right of electing, ordaining, confirming, deposing all bishops [and pastors]. Besides this, he claims for himself the authority to frame laws concerning services, concerning changing the sacraments and concerning doctrine, and wishes his articles, his decrees, his laws to be regarded equal to the divine laws, *i.e.* he holds that, by the Papal laws, the consciences of men are so bound that those who neglect them, even without public offence, sin mortally [that they cannot be discontinued without sin. For he wishes to found this power upon divine right and the Holy Scriptures; yea, he wishes that they be preferred to the Holy Scriptures and God's commands]. And it is still more horrible that he adds that belief in all these things belongs to the necessity of salvation.

I. OF THE FIRST ARTICLE.

A. FROM THE GOSPEL.

First, therefore, we will show from the Gospel that the Roman bishop is not by divine right above other bishops and pastors.

Luke 22:25. Christ expressly prohibits lordship among the apostles [that any should have the pre-eminence over the rest]. For this was the very question which they were disputing when Christ spake of his passion, viz. who should command, and be as it were the vicar of the absent Christ. There Christ reproves this error of the apostles, and teaches that there shall not be lordship or superiority among them, but that the apostles would be sent forth as equals to the common ministry of the Gospel. Accordingly, he says: "The kings of the Gentiles exercise lordship over them; and they that exercise authority upon them are called benefactors, but ye shall not be so; but he that is greatest among you, let him be as the younger; and he that is chief, as he that doth serve." The antithesis here shows that lordship is disapproved.

The same is taught by the parable when Christ in the same dispute concerning the kingdom (Matt. 18:2) sets a little child in the midst, signifying that among ministers there is not to be sovereignty, just as a child neither takes nor seeks sovereignty for himself.

John 20:21. Christ sends forth his disciples on an equality without any distinction when he says: "As my Father hath sent me, even so send I you." He says that he sends individuals in the same manner as he himself was sent; and hence grants a prerogative or lordship to no one above the rest.

Gal. 2:7 sq. Paul manifestly affirms that he was neither ordained nor confirmed by Peter, nor does he acknowledge Peter to be one from whom confirmation should be sought. And he expressly contends from this circumstance that his call does not depend upon the authority of Peter. But he ought to have acknowledged Peter as a superior if by divine right

Peter was superior. Paul accordingly says that he had at once preached the Gospel without consulting Peter. Also: "Of those who seemed to be somewhat (whatsoever they were, it maketh no matter to me; God accepteth no man's person)." And: "They who seemed to be somewhat in conference added nothing to me." Since Paul therefore clearly testifies that he did not even wish to seek for the confirmation of Peter, even when he had come to him, he teaches that the authority of the ministry depends upon the Word of God, and that Peter was not superior to the other apostles, and that ordination or confirmation was not to be sought from Peter alone [that the office of the ministry proceeds from the general call of the apostles, and that it is not necessary for all to have the call or confirmation of this person alone].

In 1 Cor. 3:6, Paul makes ministers equal, and teaches that the Church is above the ministers. Hence superiority or lordship over the Church or the rest of the ministers is not ascribed to Peter. For he says thus: "All things are yours; whether Paul, or Apollos, or Cephas," *i.e.* Let not other ministers or Peter assume for themselves lordship or superiority to the Church; let them not burden the Church with traditions; let not the authority of any avail more than the Word [of God]; let not the authority of Cephas be opposed to the authority of the other apostles, as they reasoned at that time: "Cephas, who is an apostle of higher rank, observes this; therefore, Paul and the rest ought to observe this." Paul removes this pretext from Peter, and denies that his authority is to be preferred to the rest or to the Church.

B. FROM HISTORY.

The Council of Nice resolved that the bishop of Alexandria should administer the churches in the East, and the Roman bishop the suburban, *i.e.* those which were in the Roman provinces in the West. Hence it was first by human law, *i.e.* the resolution of the Council, that the authority of the Roman bishop arose. If already by divine law the Roman bishop would have had the superiority, it would not have been lawful for the Council to have removed any right from him and to have transferred it to the bishop of Alexandria; yea all the bishops of the East ought perpetually to have sought ordination and confirmation from the bishop of Rome. The Council of Nice determined also that bishops should be elected by their own churches, in the presence of a neighboring bishop or of several. The same was observed also in the West and in the Latin churches, as Cyprian and Augustine testify. For Cyprian says in his fourth letter to Cornelius: "For which reason you must diligently observe and keep the divine observance and apostolic practice, as it is also observed among us and in almost all the provinces, that for celebrating properly ordinances all the neighboring bishops of the same province should assemble; and the bishop should be chosen in the presence of the people, who have most fully known the life of each one, which we also see was done among us in the ordination of our colleague, Sabinus; so that by the suffrage of the entire brotherhood, and by the judgment of the bishops who had assembled in their presence, the episcopate was conferred and hands imposed upon him."

Cyprian calls this custom a divine tradition and an apostolic observance, and affirms that it was observed in almost all the provinces. Since therefore neither ordination nor confirmation was sought from a bishop of Rome in the greater part of the world in the Latin and Greek churches, it is sufficiently apparent that the churches did not then ascribe superiority and domination to the bishop of Rome.

Such superiority is impossible. For it is impossible for one bishop to be the inspector of the churches of the whole world, or for churches situated in the most remote lands [all the ministers] to seek ordination from one. For it is manifest that the kingdom of Christ has been dispersed through the whole world; and to-day there are many churches in the East which do not seek ordination or confirmation from the Roman bishop [which have ministers ordained neither by the Pope nor his bishops]. Therefore since such superiority [which the Pope, contrary to all Scripture, arrogates to himself] is impossible, and the churches in the greater part of the world have not acknowledged it, it is sufficiently apparent that it was not established [by Christ, and does not spring from divine law].

Many ancient Synods have been proclaimed and held in which the bishop of Rome did not preside; as that of Nice and very many others. This also testifies that the Church did not then acknowledge the primacy or superiority of the bishop of Rome.

Jerome says: "If authority is sought, the world is greater than the city. Wherever there has been a bishop, whether at Rome, or Eugubium, or Constantinople, or Rhegium, or Alexandria, he is of the same merit and priesthood."

Gregory, writing to the patriarch at Alexandria, forbids himself to be called universal bishop. And in the "Register" he says that in the Council of Chalcedon the primacy was offered to the bishop of Rome, and was not accepted.

Lastly, how can the Pope be by divine right over the entire Church, when the Church has the election, and the custom gradually prevailed that bishops of Rome should be confirmed by emperors?

Also, since there had been for a long time contests concerning the primacy between the bishops of Rome and Constantinople, the emperor Phocas at length determined that the primacy should be assigned to the bishop of Rome. But if the ancient Church had acknowledged the primacy of the Roman pontiff, this contention would not have occurred, neither would there have been need of a decree of the emperor.

C.   ARGUMENTS OF THE ADVERSARIES.

But they cite against us certain passages, viz. (Matt. 16:18 sq.): "Thou art Peter, and upon this rock I will build my Church." Also: "I will give unto thee the keys." Also (John 21:15): "Feed my sheep," and some others. But since this entire controversy has been fully and accurately treated of elsewhere in the books of our theologians, and all things cannot be reviewed in this place, we refer to those writings, and wish them to be regarded as repeated. Yet we will briefly reply concerning the interpretation of the passages quoted.

In all these passages Peter is the representative of the entire assembly of apostles, as appears from the text itself. For Christ asks not Peter alone, but says: "Whom do ye say that I am?" And what is here said in the singular number: "I will give unto thee the keys; and whatsoever thou shalt bind," etc., is elsewhere expressed in the plural (Matt. 18:18): "Whatsoever ye shall bind," etc. And in John 20:23: "Whatsoever sins ye remit," etc. These words testify that the keys are given alike to all the apostles, and that all the apostles are alike sent forth.

In addition to this, it is necessary to confess that the keys pertain not to the person of a particular man, but to the Church, as many most clear and firm arguments testify. For Christ, speaking concerning the keys (Matt. 18:19), adds: "If two of you shall agree on earth," etc. Therefore he ascribes the keys to the Church principally and immediately; just as also for this reason the Church has principally the right of calling. [For just as the promise of the Gospel belongs certainly and immediately to the entire Church, so the keys belong immediately to the entire Church, because the keys are nothing else than the office whereby this promise is communicated to every one who desires it, just as it is actually manifest that the Church has the power to ordain ministers of the Church. And Christ speaks in these words: "Whatsoever ye shall bind," etc., and means that to which he has given the keys, namely, the Church: "Where two or three are gathered together in my name" (Matt. 18:20). Likewise Christ gives supreme and final jurisdiction to the Church, when he says: "Tell it to the Church."]

Therefore it is necessary in these passages that Peter be the representative of the entire assembly of the apostles, and for this reason they do not ascribe any prerogative, or superiority, or lordship to Peter.

As to the declaration: "Upon this rock I will build my Church," certainly the Church has not been built upon the authority of man, but upon the ministry of the confession which Peter made, in which he proclaims that Jesus is the Christ, the Son of God. He accordingly addresses him as a minister: "Upon this rock," i.e. upon this ministry. [Therefore he addresses him as a minister of such an office as is to be pervaded by this confession and doctrine, and says: "Upon this rock," i.e. this declaration and ministry.]

Furthermore, the ministry of the New Testament is not bound to persons and places, as the Levitical ministry, but it is dispersed throughout the whole world, and is there where God gives his gifts, apostles, prophets, pastors, teachers; neither does this ministry avail on account of the authority of any person, but on account of the Word given by Christ.

And in this way most of the holy Fathers, as Origen, Cyprian, Augustine, Hilary and Bede, interpret this passage (Upon this rock). Chrysostom says thus: "'Upon this rock,' not upon Peter. For he built his Church not upon man, but upon the faith of Peter. But what was his faith? 'Thou art the Christ, the Son of the living God.'" And Hilary says: "To Peter the Father revealed that he should say, 'Thou art the Son of the living God.' Therefore the building of the Church is upon this rock of confession; this faith is the foundation of the Church," etc.

And as to that which is said (John 21:15 sqq.): "Feed my sheep," and "Lovest thou me more than these?" it does not as yet follow hence that a peculiar superiority was given Peter. He bids him "feed," *i.e.* teach the Word, or rule the Church with the Word, which Peter has in common with the other apostles.

II. OF THE SECOND ARTICLE.

The second article is still clearer, because Christ gave to the apostles only spiritual power, *i.e.* the command to teach the Gospel, to announce the forgiveness of sins, to administer the sacraments, to excommunicate the godless without temporal force; and he did not give the power of the sword or the right to establish, occupy or confer kingdoms of the world. For Christ says (Matt. 28:20): "Go ye, teaching them to observe all things whatsoever I have commanded you." Also (John 20:21): "As my Father hath sent me, even so send I you." But it is manifest that Christ was not sent to bear the sword or possess a worldly kingdom, as he himself says (John 18:36): "My kingdom is not of this world." And Paul says (2 Cor. 1:24): "Not for that we have dominion over your faith." And (2 Cor. 10:4): "The weapons of our warfare are not carnal," etc.

As, therefore, Christ in his passion is crowned with thorns, and led forth to be derided in royal purple, it was thereby signified that his spiritual kingdom being despised, *i.e.* the Gospel being suppressed, another kingdom of the world would be established with the pretext of ecclesiastical power. Wherefore the constitution of Boniface VIII. and the chapter *Omnes*, Dist. 22, and similar opinions which contend that the Pope is by divine right the ruler of the kingdoms of the world, are false and godless. From this persuasion horrible darkness has overspread the Church, and also great commotions have arisen in Europe. For the ministry of the Gospel was neglected, and the knowledge of faith and a spiritual kingdom became extinct; Christian righteousness was supposed to be that external government which the Pope had established. Then the popes began to seize upon kingdoms for themselves, they transferred kingdoms, they vexed with unjust excommunications and wars the kings of almost all nations in Europe, but especially the German emperors; so that they sometimes occupied the cities of Italy, and at other times reduced to subjection the bishops of Germany, and wrested from the emperors the conferring of episcopates. Yea in the Clementines it is even written: That when the empire is vacant, the Pope is the legitimate successor. Thus the Pope has not only usurped dominion, contrary to Christ's command, but has also tyrannically exalted himself above all kings. Neither in this matter is the deed itself so much to be reprehended as it is to be detested, that he assigns as a pretext the authority of Christ; that he transfers the keys to a worldly government; that he binds salvation to these godless and execrable opinions, when he says that it belongs to necessity for salvation that men believe that this dominion is in accordance with divine right. Since such errors as these obscure faith and the kingdom of Christ, they are in no way to be disguised. For the result shows that they have been great pests to the Church.

III. OF THE THIRD ARTICLE.

In the third place, this must be added: Even though the bishop of Rome would have, by divine right, the primacy and superiority, nevertheless obedience is not due those pontiffs who defend godless services, idolatry and doctrine conflicting with the Gospel; yea such pontiffs and such a government ought to be regarded as a curse, as Paul clearly teaches (Gal. 1:8): "Though an angel from heaven preach any other Gospel unto you than that which we have preached unto you, let him be accursed." And in Acts (5:29): "We ought to obey God, rather than men." Likewise the canons also clearly teach that we should not obey an heretical Pope.

The Levitical priest was high priest by divine right, and yet godless priests were not to be obeyed, as Jeremiah and other prophets dissented from the priests. So the apostles dissented from Caiaphas, and were under no obligations to obey them.

It is, however, manifest that the Roman pontiffs, with their adherents, defend godless doctrines and godless services. And the marks of Antichrist plainly agree with the kingdom of the Pope and his adherents. For Paul (2 Ep. 2:3), in describing to the Thessalonians Antichrist, calls him an adversary of Christ, "who opposeth and exalteth himself above all that is called God, or that is worshipped, so that he as God sitteth in the temple of God." He speaks therefore of one ruling in the Church, not of heathen kings, and he calls this one the adversary of Christ, because he will devise doctrine conflicting with the Gospel, and will assume to himself divine authority.

Moreover, it is manifest, in the first place, that the Pope rules in the Church, and by the pretext of ecclesiastical authority and of the ministry has established for himself this kingdom. For he assigns as a pretext these words: "I will give to thee the keys." Secondly, the doctrine of the Pope conflicts in many ways [in all ways] with the Gospel, and the Pope assumes to himself divine authority in a threefold manner: First, because he takes to himself the right to change the doctrine of Christ and services instituted by God, and wishes his own doctrine and his own services to be observed as divine. Secondly, because he takes to himself the power not only of binding and loosing in this life, but also the right concerning souls after this life. Thirdly, because the Pope does not wish to be judged by the Church or by any one, and prefers his own authority to the decision of Councils and the entire Church. But to be unwilling to be judged by the Church or by any one is to make one's self God. Lastly, these errors so horrible, and this impiety, he defends with the greatest cruelty, and puts to death those dissenting.

This being the case, all Christians ought to beware of becoming partakers of the godless doctrine, blasphemies and unjust cruelties of the Pope. On this account they ought to desert and execrate the Pope with his adherents, as the kingdom of Antichrist; just as Christ has command-ed (Matt. 7:15): "Beware of false prophets." And Paul commands that godless teachers should be avoided and execrated as cursed (Gal. 1:8; Tit. 3:10). And (2 Cor. 6:14) says: "Be ye not unequally yoked together with unbeliev-ers; for what communion hath light with darkness?"

To dissent from the agreement of so many nations and to be called schismatics is a serious matter. But divine authority commands all not to be allies and defenders of impiety and unjust cruelty.

On this account our consciences are sufficiently excused; for the errors of the kingdom of the Pope are manifest. And Scripture with its entire voice exclaims that these errors are a doctrine of demons and of Antichrist. The idolatry in the profanation of the masses is manifest, which, besides other faults, are shamelessly applied to most base gain. The doctrine of repentance has been utterly corrupted by the Pope and his adherents. For they teach that sins are remitted because of the worth of our works. Then they bid us doubt whether the remission occur. They nowhere teach that sins are remitted freely for Christ's sake, and that by this faith we obtain remission of sins. Thus they obscure the glory of Christ, and deprive consciences of firm consolation, and abolish true divine services, viz. the exercises of faith struggling with [unbelief and] despair [concerning the promise of the Gospel].

They have obscured the doctrine concerning sin, and have framed a tradition concerning the enumeration of offences, producing many errors and despair. They have devised in addition satisfactions, whereby they have also obscured the benefit of Christ.

From these, indulgences have been born, which are pure falsehoods, fabricated for the sake of gain.

Then how many abuses, and what horrible idolatry, the invocation of saints has produced!

What shameful acts have arisen from the tradition concerning celibacy!

What darkness the doctrine concerning vows has spread over the Gospel! They have there feigned that vows are righteousness before God, and merit the remission of sins. Thus they have transferred the benefit of Christ to human traditions, and have altogether extinguished the doctrine concerning faith. They have feigned that the most trifling traditions are services of God and perfection, and they have preferred these to the works of callings which God requires and has ordained. Neither are these errors to be regarded light; for they detract from the glory of Christ

and bring destruction to souls, neither can they be passed by unnoticed.

Then to these errors two great sins are added: The first, that he defends these errors by unjust cruelty and punishments. The second, that he appropriates the deci-sion of the Church, and does not permit ecclesiastical controversies [such matters of religion] to be judged according to the prescribed mode; yea, he contends that he is above the Council, and that the decrees of Councils can be rescinded, just as the canons sometimes impudently speak. But the examples testify that this was done with much more impudence by the pontiffs.

Quest. 9, canon 3, says: "No one shall judge the first seat; for the judge is judged neither by the emperor, nor by all the clergy, nor by the kings, nor by the people."

The Pope exercises a twofold tyranny; he defends his errors by force and by murders, and forbids judicial examination. The latter does even more injury than any punishments. Because when the true judgment of the Church is removed, godless dogmas and godless services cannot be removed, and for many ages are destroying infinite souls.

Therefore let the godly consider the great errors of the kingdom of the Pope and his tyranny, and let them ponder first that the errors must be rejected and the true doctrine embraced, for the glory of God and to the salvation of souls. Then let them ponder also how great a crime it is to aid unjust cruelty in killing saints, whose blood God will undoubtedly avenge.

But especially the chief members of the Church, kings and princes, ought to guard the interests of the Church, and to see to it that errors be removed and consciences be healed [rightly instructed], as God expressly exhorts kings (Ps. 2:10): "Be wise, now, therefore, O ye kings; be instructed, ye judges of the earth." For it should be the first care of kings [and great lords] to advance the glory of God. Wherefore it is very shameful for them to exercise their influence and power to confirm idolatry and infinite other crimes, and to slaughter saints.

And in case the Pope should hold Synods [a Council], how can the Church be healed if the Pope suffer nothing to be decreed contrary to his will, if he allow no one to express his opinion except his adherents, whom by dreadful oaths and curses he has bound, without any exception concern-ing God's Word, to the defence of his tyranny and wickedness?

But since the decisions of Synods are the decisions of the Church, and not of the Popes, it is especially incumbent on kings to check the license of the popes [not allow such roguery], and to so act that the power of judging and decreeing from the Word of God be not wrested from the Church. And as other Christians ought to censure the remaining errors of the Pope, so they ought also to rebuke the Pope when he evades and impedes the true knowledge and true decision of the Church.

Therefore even though the bishop of Rome would have the primacy by divine right, yet since he defends godless services and doctrine conflicting with the Gospel, obedi-ence is not due him, yea it is necessary to resist him as

SMALCALD ARTICLES (1537) (continued)

Antichrist. The errors of the Pope are manifest and not trifling.

Manifest also is the cruelty [against godly Christians] which he exercises. And it is clear that it is God's command that we flee from idolatry, godless doctrine and unjust cruelty. On this account all the godly have great, manifest and necessary reasons for not obeying the Pope. And these necessary reasons comfort the godly against all the reproaches which are usually cast against them concerning offences, schism and discord.

But those who agree with the Pope and defend his doctrine and [false] services, defile themselves with idolatry and blasphemous opinions, became guilty of the blood of the godly, whom the Pope [and his adherents] persecutes, detract from the glory of God, and hinder the welfare of the Church, because they strengthen errors and crimes [for injury to all the world and] to all posterity.

PART II. OF THE POWER AND JURISDICTION OF BISHOPS.

[In our Confession and the Apology we have in general narrated what we have had to say concerning ecclesiastical power. For, etc.] The Gospel has assigned to those who preside over churches the command to teach the Gospel, to remit sins, to administer the sacraments, and besides jurisdiction, viz. the command to excommunicate those whose crimes are known, and again of absolving the repenting.

And by the confession of all, even of the adversaries, it is clear that this power by divine right is common to all who preside over churches, whether they be called pastors, or elders, or bishops. And accordingly Jerome openly teaches in the apostolic letters that all who preside over churches are both bishops and elders, and cites from Titus (Tit. 1:5 sq.): "For this cause left I thee in Crete, that thou shouldest ordain elders in every city." Then he adds: "A bishop must be the husband of one wife." Likewise Peter and John call themselves elders (1 Pet. 5:1; 2 John 1). And he then adds: "But that afterwards one was chosen to be placed over the rest," occurred as a remedy for schism, lest each one by attracting to himself might rend the Church of Christ. For at Alexandria, from Mark the evangelist to the bishops Heracles and Dionysius, the elders always elected one from themselves, and placed him in a higher station, whom they called bishop; just as an army would make a commander for itself. The deacons, moreover, may elect from themselves one whom they know to be active, and name him archdeacon. For with the exception of ordination, what does the bishop that the elder does not?

Jerome therefore teaches that it is by human authority that the grades of bishop and elder or pastor are distinct. And the subject itself declares this, because the power [the office and command] is the same, as he has said above. But one matter afterwards made a distinction between bishops and pastors, viz. ordination, because it was so arranged that one bishop might ordain ministers in a number of churches.

But since by divine authority the grades of bishop and pastor are not diverse, it is manifest that ordination by a pastor in his own church has been appointed by divine law [if a pastor in his own church ordain certain suitable persons to the ministry, such ordination is, according to divine law, undoubtedly effective and right].

Therefore when the regular bishops become enemies of the Church, or are unwilling to administer ordination, the churches retain their own right. [Because the regular bishops persecute the Gospel and refuse to ordain suitable persons, every church has in this case full authority to ordain its own ministers.]

For wherever the Church is, there is the authority [command] to administer the Gospel. Wherefore it is necessary for the Church to retain the authority to call, elect and ordain ministers. And this authority is a gift exclusively given to the Church, which no human power can wrest from the Church, as Paul also testifies to the Ephesians (4:8) when he says: "He ascended, he gave gifts to men." And he enumerates among the gifts specially belonging to the Church "pastors and teachers," and adds that such are given "for the ministry, for the edifying the body of Christ." Where there is therefore a true church, the right to elect and ordain ministers necessarily exists. Just as in a case of necessity even a layman absolves, and becomes the minister and pastor of another; as Augustine narrates the story of two Christians in a ship, one of whom baptized the catechumen, who after baptism then absolved the baptizer.

Here belong the words of Christ which testify that the keys have been given to the Church, and not merely to certain persons (Matt. 18:20): "Where two or three are gathered together in my name," etc.

Lastly, the declaration of Peter also confirms this (1 Ep. 2:9): "Ye are a royal priesthood." These words pertain to the true Church, which, since it alone has the priesthood, certainly has the right to elect and ordain ministers.

And this also a most common custom of the Church testifies. For formerly the people elected pastors and bishops. Then a bishop was added, either of that church or a neighboring one, who confirmed the one elected by the laying on of hands; neither was ordination anything else than such a ratification. Afterwards, new ceremonies were added, many of which Dionysius describes. But he is a recent and fictitious author [this book of Dionysius is a new fiction under a false title], just as the writings of Clement also are supposititious. Then the moderns added: "I give thee the power to sacrifice for the living and the dead." But not even this is in Dionysius. From all these things it is clear that the Church retains the right to elect and ordain ministers. And the wickedness and tyranny of bishops afford cause for schism and discord [therefore, if the bishops either are heretics or will not ordain suitable persons, the churches are in duty bound before God, according to divine law, to ordain for themselves pastors and ministers. Even though this be now called an irregularity or schism, it should be known that the godless doctrine and tyranny of the bishops is chargeable with it], because Paul (Gal. 1:7 sq.) enjoins that bishops who teach and defend a godless doctrine and godless services should be regarded accursed.

We have spoken of ordination, which alone, as Jerome says, distinguished bishops from other elders. Therefore there is need of no discussion concerning the other duties of bishops. Nor is it indeed necessary to speak of confirmation, nor of the consecration of bells, which are almost the only things which they have retained. Something must be said concerning jurisdiction.

It is manifest that the common jurisdiction of excommunicating those guilty of manifest crimes belongs to all pastors. This they have tyrannically transferred to themselves alone, and have applied it to the acquisition of gain. For it is manifest that the officials, as they are called, employed a license not to be tolerated, and either on account of avarice or because of other wanton desires tormented men and excommunicated them without any due process of law. But what tyranny is it for the officials in the states to have arbitrary power to condemn and excommunicate men without due process of law! And with respect to what did they abuse this power? Clearly not in punishing true offences, but in regard to the violation of fasts or festivals, or like trifles? Only they sometimes punished adulteries; and in this matter they often vexed [abused and defamed] innocent and honorable men.

Since, therefore, bishops have tyrannically transferred this jurisdiction to themselves alone, and have basely abused it, there is no need, because of this jurisdiction, to obey bishops. But since the reasons why we do not obey are just, it is right also to restore this jurisdiction to godly pastors [to whom, by Christ's command, it belongs], and to see to it that it be legitimately exercised for the reformation of life and the glory of God.

Jurisdiction remains in those cases which, according to canonical law, pertain to the ecclesiastical court, as they say, and especially in cases of matrimony. It is only by human right that the bishops have this also; and indeed the ancient bishops did not have it, as it appears from the *Codex* and *Novelli* of Justinian that decisions concerning marriage at that time belonged to the magistrates. And by divine law worldly magistrates are compelled to make these decisions if the bishops [judge unjustly or] be negligent. The canons also concede the same. Wherefore also on account of this jurisdiction it is not necessary to obey bishops. And indeed since they have framed certain unjust laws concerning marriages, and observe them in their courts, also for this reason there is need to establish other courts. For the traditions concerning spiritual relationship [the prohibition of marriage between sponsors] are unjust. Unjust also is the tradition which forbids an innocent person to marry after divorce. Unjust also is the law which in general approves all clandestine and underhanded betrothals in violation of the right of parents. Unjust also is the law concerning the celibacy of priests. There are also other spares of consciences in their laws, to recite all of which is of no profit. It is sufficient to have recited this, that there are many unjust laws of the Pope concerning matrimonial subjects on account of which the magistrates ought to establish other courts.

Since therefore the bishops, who are devoted to the Pope, defend godless doctrine and godless services, and do not ordain godly teachers, yea aid the cruelty of the Pope, and besides have wrested the jurisdiction from pastors, and exercise this only tyrannically [for their own profit]; and lastly, since in matrimonial cases they observe many unjust laws; the reasons why the churches do not recognize these as bishops are sufficiently numerous and necessary.

But they themselves should remember that riches have been given to bishops as alms for the administration and advantage of the churches [that they may serve the Church, and perform their office the more efficiently], just as the rule says: "The benefice is given because of the office." Wherefore they cannot with a good conscience possess these alms, and meanwhile defraud the Church, which has need of these means for supporting ministers, and aiding studies [educating learned men], and caring for the poor, and establishing courts, especially matrimonial. For so great is the variety and extent of matrimonial controversies, that there is need of a special tribunal for these, and for establishing this there is need of the means of the Church. Peter predicted (2 Ep. 2:13) that there would be godless bishops, who would abuse the alms of the Church for luxury and neglect the ministry. Therefore let those who defraud know that they will pay God the penalty for this crime.

Notes: *These articles, written by Martin Luther primarily for the Holy Roman Emperor, clarified some issues that were a matter of intense controversy between the Reformers and the Roman Catholic Church. The tone is less conciliatory than that of the Augsburg Confession, attacking the pope in the opening paragraphs and presenting a number of Lutheran distinctives in forceful language.*

In 1580, the articles were placed alongside the Augsburg Confession and the Formula of Concord in The Book of Concord, *the main collection of Lutheran doctrinal materials. Today the Smalcald Articles are accepted fully as a doctrinal standard by the Lutheran Church-Missouri Synod and the Wisconsin Evangelical Lutheran Synod, but not accorded an equal status with the Augsburg Confession by either the Lutheran Church in America or the American Lutheran Church.*

*   *   *

THE FORMULA OF CONCORD (1580)

PART FIRST.

EPITOME. OF THE ARTICLES IN CONTROVERSY AMONG THE THELOGIANS OF THE AUGSBURG CONFESSION, SET FORTH AND RECONCILED IN A CHRISTIAN WAY, ACCORDING TO GOD'S WORD, IN THE FOLLOWING RECAPITULATION.

INTRODUCTION. OF THE COMPREHENSIVE SUMMARY, RULE AND STANDARD ACCORDING TO WHICH ALL DOGMAS SHOULD BE JUDGED, AND THE CONTROVERSIES THAT HAVE OCCURRED SHOULD, IN A CHRISTIAN WAY, BE DECIDED AND SET FORTH.

I.   We believe, teach and confess that the only rule and standard according to which at once all dogmas and teachers should be esteemed and judged are nothing else than the prophetic and apostolic Scriptures of

THE FORMULA OF CONCORD (1580) (continued)

the Old and of the New Testament, as it is written (Ps. 119:105): "Thy Word is a lamp unto my feet, and a light unto my path." And St. Paul (Gal. 1:8): "Though an angel from heaven preach any other Gospel unto you, let him be accursed."

Other writings, of ancient or modern teachers, whatever reputation they may have, should not be regarded as of equal authority with the Holy Scriptures, but should altogether be subordinated to them, and should not be received other or further than as witnesses, in what manner and at what places, since the time of the apostles, the [purer] doctrine of the prophets and apostles was preserved.

II. And because directly after the times of the apostles, and even in their lives, false teachers and heretics arose, and against them, in the early Church, symbols, *i.e.* brief, plain confessions, were composed, which were regarded as the unanimous, universal Christian faith, and confession of the orthodox and true Church, namely, THE APOSTLES' CREED, THE NICENE CREED, and the ATHANASIAN CREED; we confess them as binding upon us, and hereby reject all heresies and dogmas which, contrary to them, have been introduced into the Church of God.

III. Moreover as to the schism in matters of faith which has occurred in our time, we regard the unanimous consensus and declaration of our Christian faith and confession, especially against the Papacy and its false worship, idolatry, superstition, and against other sects, as the symbol of our time, viz. THE FIRST UNALTERED AUGSBURG CONFESSION, delivered to the Emperor Charles V. at Augsburg in the year 1530, in the great Diet, together with its APOLOGY, and the ARTICLES composed at SMALCALD in the year 1537, and subscribed by the chief theologians of that time.

And because such matters pertain also to the laity and the salvation of their souls, we confessionally acknowledge the SMALL and LARGE CATECHISMS of Dr. Luther, as they are included in Luther's works, as the Bible of the laity, wherein everything is comprised which is treated at greater length in Holy Scripture, and is necessary that a Christian man know for his salvation.

In accordance with this direction, as above announced, all doctrines should be adjusted, and that which is contrary thereto should be rejected and condemned, as opposed to the unanimous declaration of our faith.

In this way the distinction between the Holy Scriptures of the Old and of the New Testament and all other writings is preserved, and the Holy Scriptures alone remain the only judge, rule, and standard, according to which, as the only test-stone, all dogmas should and must be discerned and judged, as to whether they be good or evil, right or wrong.

But the other symbols and writings cited are not judges, as are the Holy Scriptures, but only a witness and declaration of the faith, as to how at any time the Holy Scriptures have been understood and explained in the articles in controversy in the Church of God by those who then lived, and how the opposite dogma was rejected and condemned [by what arguments the dogmas conflicting with the Holy Scripture were rejected and condemned].

CHAPTER I. OF ORIGINAL SIN.

STATEMENT OF THE CONTROVERSY.

Whether Original Sin be properly and without any distinction man's corrupt nature, substance and essence, or indeed the principal and best part of his essence [substance], namely, the rational soul itself in its highest state and powers? Or whether, even since the fall, there be a distinction between man's substance, nature, essence, body, soul, and Original Sin, so that the nature is one thing, and Original Sin, which inheres in the corrupt nature and corrupts the nature, is another?

AFFIRMATIVE.

The pure doctrine, faith and confession according to the above standard and comprehensive declaration:

1. We believe, teach and confess that there is a distinction between man's nature, not only as he was originally created by God, pure and holy, and without sin, but also as we have it [that nature] now, since the fall, namely, between the nature itself, which ever since the fall is and remains a creature of God, and Original Sin, and that this distinction is as great as the distinction between a work of God and a work of the devil.

2. We believe, teach and confess also that this distinction should be maintained with the greatest care, because the dogma that no distinction is to be made between our corrupt human nature and original sin conflicts with the chief articles of our Christian faith, concerning Creation, Redemption, Sanctification and the resurrection of our body, and cannot coexist therewith.

For God created not only the body and soul of Adam and Eve before the fall, but also our bodies and souls since the fall, notwithstanding that they are corrupt, which God also still acknowledges as his work, as it is written (Job 10:8): "Thine hands have made me and fashioned me together round about." Deut. 32:18; Isa. 45:9 sqq.; 54:5; 64:8; Acts 17:28; Job 10:8; Ps. 100:3; 139:14; Eccl. 12:1.

This human nature, nevertheless without sin, and, therefore, not of other's but our own flesh, the Son of God has assumed into the unity of his person, and according to it become our true brother. Heb. 2:14: "Forasmuch then as the children were partakers of flesh and blood, He also himself likewise took part of the same." Again, v. 16; 4:15: "He took not on him the nature of angels, but he took on him the seed of Abraham. Wherefore in all things it behoved him to be made like unto his brethren," "yet without sin." Therefore Christ has redeemed it, as his work, sanctifies it as his work, raises it from the dead and gloriously adorns it as his work. But Original Sin he has not created, assumed, redeemed, sanctified; he also will not raise it, or with the elect adorn or save it, but in the [blessed] resurrection it will be entirely destroyed.

Hence the distinction between the corrupt nature and the corruption which infects the nature and by which the nature became corrupt, can easily be discerned.

3. But, on the other hand, we believe, teach and confess that Original Sin is not a slight, but so deep a corruption of human nature, that nothing healthy or uncorrupt in man's body or soul, in inner or outward powers, remains, but, as the Church sings:

"Through Adam's fall is all corrupt,
Nature and essence human."

This unspeakable injury cannot be discerned by the reason, but only from God's Word. And [we affirm] that the nature and this corruption of nature no one but God alone can ever separate from one another; and yet this fully comes to pass, through death, in the resurrection, where our nature which we now bear will rise and live eternally, without original sin, and separated and sundered from it, as it is written (Job 19:26): "I shall be compassed again with this my skin, and in my flesh shall I see God, whom I shall see for myself, and mine eyes shall behold."

NEGATIVE. *Rejection of the false opposite dogmas.*

Therefore we reject and condemn the dogma that Original Sin is only a *reatus* or debt, on account of what has been committed by another [diverted to us] without any corruption of our nature.

2. Also that evil lusts are not sin, but concreated, essential properties of the nature, as though the above-mentioned defect and evil were not true sin, because of which man without Christ [not ingrafted into Christ] is to be a child of wrath.

3. We likewise reject the error of the Pelagians, by which it is alleged that man's nature, even since the fall, is incorrupt, and, especially with respect to spiritual things, in *naturalibus, i.e.* in its natural powers, it has remained entirely good and pure.

4. Also that Original Sin is only external, a slight, insignificant spot, sprinkle, or stain dashed upon the nature, beneath which [nevertheless] the nature has retained its powers unimpaired even in spiritual things.

5. Also that Original Sin is only an external impediment to unimpaired spiritual powers, and not a despoliation or want of the same, as when a magnet is smeared with garlic-juice its natural power is not thereby removed, but only impeded; or that this stain can be easily washed away, as a spot from the face or pigment from the wall.

6. Also, that in man the human nature and essence are not entirely corrupt, but that man still has something good in him, even in spiritual things, namely, piety, skill, aptness or ability in spiritual things to begin to work, or to co-work for something [good].

7. On the other hand, we also reject the false dogma of the Manichaeans, when it is taught that Original Sin, as something essential and self-subsisting, has been infused by Satan into the nature, and intermingled with it, as poison and wine are mixed.

8. Also that not the natural man, but something else and extraneous to man, sins, and, on this account, not the nature, but only Original Sin in the nature, is accused.

9. We reject and condemn also as a Manichaean error the doctrine that Original Sin is properly, and without any distinction, the substance, nature and essence itself of the corrupt man, so that no distinction between the corrupt nature, considered by itself, since the fall, and Original Sin, can be conceived of, nor can they be distinguished from one another even in thought.

10. Moreover this Original Sin is called by Dr. Luther natural sin, personal sin, essential sin (Natursünde, Personsünde, Wesentlichle Sünde); not that the nature, person or essence of the man is, without any distinction, itself Original Sin, but that, by such words, the distinction might be indicated between Original Sin which inheres in human nature, and other sins which are called actual sins.

11. For Original Sin is not a sin which is committed, but it inheres in the nature, substance and essence of man, so that though no wicked thought ever should arise in the heart of corrupt man, nor idle word be spoken, nor wicked deed be done, yet the nature is nevertheless corrupt through Original Sin, which is born in us by reason of the sinful seed, and is a fountain-head of all other actual sins, as wicked thoughts, words and works, as it is written (Matt. 15:19): "Out of the heart proceed evil thoughts." Also (Gen. 6:5; 8:21): "The imagination of man's heart is evil from his youth."

12. Thus it also well to note the diverse signification of the word "nature," whereby the Manichaeans cover their error and lead astray many simple men. For sometimes it means the essence [the very substance] of man, as when it is said: God created human nature. But at other times it means the disposition and the vicious quality [disposition, condition, defect or vice] of a thing, which inheres in the nature or essence, as when it is said: The nature of the serpent is to bite, and the nature and disposition of man is to sin, and is sin; here the word *nature* does not mean the substance of man, but something that inheres in the nature or substance.

13. But as to the Latin terms "substance" and "accident," because they are not words of Holy Scripture, and besides unknown to the ordinary man, they should not be used in sermons before ordinary, uninstructed people, but simple people should be excused from this [in this matter regard should rightly be had to the simple and uneducated]. But in

the schools, among the learned, these words are rightly retained in disputations concerning Original Sin, because they are well known and used without any misunderstanding, to distinguish exactly between the essence of a thing and what is attached to it in an accidental way.

For the distinction between God's work and that of the devil is thereby designated in the clearest way, because the devil can create no substance, but can only, in an accidental way, from God's decree [God permitting] corrupt a substance created by God.

CHAPTER II. OF THE FREE WILL.

STATEMENT OF THE CONTROVERSY.

Since the will of man is found in four dissimilar states, namely: 1. Before the fall; 2. Since the fall; 3. After regeneration; 4. After resurrection of the body, the chief question is only concerning the will and ability of man in the second state, namely, what powers, in spiritual things, he has, from himself, since the fall of our first parents, and before regeneration, and whether, from his own powers, before he has been born again by God's Spirit, he be able to dispose and prepare himself for God's grace, and to accept [and apprehend] or not, the grace offered through the Holy Ghost in the Word and holy [divinely-instituted] sacraments.

AFFIRMATIVE. *The pure doctrine concerning this article, according to God's Word.*

1. Concerning this subject, our doctrine, faith and confession is, that, in spiritual things, the understanding and reason of man are [altogether] blind, and, from their own powers, understand nothing, as it is written (1 Cor. 2:14): "The natural man receiveth not the things of the Spirit of God; for they are foolishness to him; neither can he know them, because he is examined concerning spiritual things."

2. Likewise we believe, teach and confess that the will of unregenerate man is not only turned away from God, but also has become an enemy of God, so that it has inclination and desire for that which is evil and contrary to God, as it is written (Gen. 8:21): "The imagination of man's heart is evil from his youth." Also (Rom. 8:7): "The carnal mind is enmity against God; for it is not subject to the Law of God, neither indeed can be." Yea, as unable as a dead body is to quicken and restore itself to bodily, earthly life, just so unable is man, who by sin is spiritually dead, to raise himself to spiritual life, as it is written (Eph. 2:5): "Even when we were dead in sins, he hath quickened us together with Christ;" (2 Cor. 3:5): "Not that we are sufficient of ourselves to think anything good, as of ourselves, but that we are sufficient is of God."

3. Yet God the Holy Ghost effects conversion, not without means; but uses for this purpose the preaching and hearing of God's Word, as it is written (Rom. 1:16): "The Gospel is the power of God unto salvation to every one that believeth." Also (Rom. 10:17): "Faith cometh by hearing of the Word of

God." And it is God's will that his Word should be heard, and that man's ears should not be closed. With this Word the Holy Ghost is present, and opens hearts, so that they, as Lydia, in Acts 16, are attentive to it, and are thus converted through the grace and power of the Holy Ghost, whose work alone the conversion of man is. For, without his grace, and if he do not grant the increase, our willing and running, our planting, sowing and watering, all are nothing, as Christ says (John 15:5): "Without me, ye can do nothing." In these short words he denies to the free will all power, and ascribes everything to God's grace, in order that no one may boast before God: 1 Cor. 1:29 [2 Cor. 12:5; Jer. 9:23].

NEGATIVE. *Contrary false doctrine.*

We therefore reject and condemn all the following errors, as contrary to the standard of God's Word:

1. The host [insane dogma] of philosophers who are called Stoics, as also of the Manichaeans, who taught that everything that happens must have happened so, and could not have happened otherwise, and that everything that man does, even in outward things, he does by necessity, and that he is coerced to evil works and deeds, as inchastity, robbery, murder, theft and the like.

2. We reject also the gross error of the Pelagians, who taught that man by his own powers, without the grace of the Holy Ghost, can turn himself to God, believe the Gospel, be obedient in heart to God's Law, and thus merit the forgiveness of sins and eternal life.

3. We reject also the error of the Semi-Pelagians, who teach that man, by his own powers, can make a beginning of his conversion, but without the grace of the Holy Ghost cannot complete it.

4. Also when it is taught that, although man by his free will before regeneration, is too weak to make a beginning, and, by his own powers, to turn himself to God, and in heart to be obedient to God; yet, if the Holy Ghost, by the preaching of the Word, have made a beginning, and offered therein his grace, then the will of man, from its own natural powers, to a certain extent, although feebly, can add, help and cooperate therewith, can qualify and prepare itself for grace, and embrace and accept it, and believe the Gospel.

5. Also that man, after he has been born again, can perfectly observe and completely fulfil God's Law, and that this fulfilling is our righteousness before God, by which we merit eternal life.

6. Also that we condemn the error of the Enthusiasts,* who imagine that God, without means, without the hearing of God's Word, also without the use of the holy sacraments, draws men to himself, and enlightens, justifies and saves them.

* Enthusiasts are those who expect the illumination of the Spirit [celestial revelation] without the preaching of God's Word.

7. Also that in conversion and regeneration God entirely exterminates the substance and essence of the old Adam, and especially the rational soul, and, in this conversion and regeneration, creates a new soul out of nothing.

8. Also, when the following expressions are employed with out explanation, viz. that the will of man, before, in, and after conversion, resists the Holy Ghost, and that the Holy Ghost is given to those who resist him intentionally and persistently; "for," as Augustine says, "in conversion God changes the unwilling into willing, and dwells in the willing."

As to the expressions of ancient and modern church teachers, when it is said: *Deus trahit, sed volentem trahit, i.e.* "God draws, but he draws the willing," and *Hominis voluntas in conversione non est otiosa sed agit aliquid, i.e.* "In conversion the will of man is not idle, but effects something," we maintain that, inasmuch as these expressions have been introduced for confirming the false opinion concerning the powers of the natural free will in man's conversion, against the doctrine concerning God's grace, they are not in harmony with the form of sound doctrine, and therefore, when we speak of conversion to God, should be avoided.

But, on the other hand, it is correctly said that, in conversion God, through the drawing of the Holy Ghost, changes stubborn and unwilling into willing men, and that after such conversion, in the daily exercise of repentance, the regenerate will of man is not idle, but also co-operates in all the deeds of the Holy Ghost, which he works through us.

9. Also what Dr. Luther has written, viz. that man's will is in his conversion purely passive, *i.e.* it does nothing whatever, is to be understood in respect of divine grace in kindling new motions, i.e. when God's Spirit, through the heard Word or the use of the holy sacrament, lays hold upon man's will, and works [in man] the new birth and conversion. For if [after] the Holy Ghost has wrought and accomplished this, and man's will has been changed and renewed alone by his divine power and working, then the new will of man is an instrument and organ of God the Holy Ghost, so that he not only accepts grace, but also, in the works which follow, co-operates with the Holy Ghost.

Therefore, before the conversion of man, there are only two efficient causes, namely, the Holy Ghost and the Word of God, as the instrument of the Holy Ghost, whereby he works conversion. To this Word man ought to listen, nevertheless it is not from his own powers, but only through the grace and working of the Holy Ghost, that he can believe and accept it.

CHAPTER III. OF THE RIGHTEOUSNESS OF FAITH BEFORE GOD.

STATEMENT OF THE CONTROVERSY.

Since it is unanimously confessed in our churches, upon the authority of God's Word and according to the sense of the Augsburg Confession, that we poor sinners are justified before God, and saved alone by faith in Christ, and thus Christ alone is our righteousness, who is true God and man, because in him the divine and human natures are personally united with one another (Jer. 23:6; 1 Cor. 1:30; 2 Cor. 5:21), the question has arisen: "According to which nature is Christ our righteousness?" and thus two contrary errors have arisen in some churches.

For the one side has held that Christ alone, according to his divinity, is our righteousness, if he dwell in us by faith; contrasted with which divinity, dwelling in men by faith, all the sins of men should be regarded as a drop of water to the great ocean. On the contrary, others have held that Christ is our righteousness before God, alone according to the human nature.

AFFIRMATIVE. *Pure Doctrine of the Christian Churches against both errors just mentioned.*

1. Against both the errors just recounted, we unanimously believe, teach and confess that Christ is our righteousness, neither according to the divine nature alone, nor according to the human nature alone, but the entire Christ according to both natures, alone in his obedience, which as God and man he rendered the Father even to death, and thereby merited for us the forgiveness of sins and eternal life, as it is written: "As by one man's disobedience, many were made sinners, so by the obedience of one, shall many be made righteous" (Rom. 5:19).

2. Therefore we believe, teach and confess that our righteousness before God is, that God forgives us our sins out of pure grace, without any work, merit or worthiness of ours preceding, attending or following, for he presents and imputes to us the righteousness of Christ's obedience, on account of which righteousness we are received into grace by God, and regarded righteous.

3. We believe, teach and confess that faith alone is the means and instrument whereby we lay hold of Christ, and thus in Christ of that righteousness which avails before God, for the sake of which this faith is imputed to us for righteousness (Rom. 4:5).

4. We believe, teach and confess that this faith is not a bare knowledge of the history of Christ, but such a great gift of God that thereby we come to the right knowledge of Christ as our Redeemer in the Word of the Gospel, and trust in him that alone for the sake of his obedience, out of grace, we have the forgiveness of sins, and are regarded holy and righteous before God the Father, and eternally saved.

5. We believe, teach and confess that, according to the usage of Holy Scripture, the word justify means in this article, "to absolve," that is, to declare free from sins. Prov. 17:15: 'He that justifieth the wicked, and he that condemneth the righteous, even they both are abomination to the Lord." Also (Rom. 8:33): "Who shall lay anything to the charge of God's elect? It is God that justifieth."

And when in place of this, the words regeneration and vivification are employed, as in the Apology, this is done in the same sense; for by these terms, in other places, the renewal of man is understood, and [which] is distinguished from justification by faith.

6. We believe, teach and confess also that although many weaknesses and defects cling to the rightly believing and truly regenerate, even to the grave, yet they have reason to doubt neither of the righteousness which is imputed to them by faith, nor of the salvation of their souls, but should regard it certain that for Christ's sake, according to the promise and [immovable] Word of the holy Gospel, they have a gracious God.

7. We believe, teach and confess that, for the maintenance of the pure doctrine concerning the righteousness of faith before God, it is necessary that the exclusive particles, *i.e.*, the following words of the holy apostle Paul, whereby the merit of Christ is entirely separated from our works, and the honor given to Christ alone, be retained with especial care, as when the holy apostle Paul writes: "Of grace," "without merit," "without law," "without works," "not of works." All these words, taken together, mean that "we are justified and saved alone by faith in Christ" (Eph. 2:8; Rom. 1:17; 3:24; 4:3 sqq.; Gal. 3:11; Heb. 11).

8. We believe, teach and confess that although the contrition that precedes, and the good works that follow, do not belong to the article of justification before God, yet such a faith should not be imagined as can coexist with a wicked intention to sin and to act against conscience. But after man is justified by faith, then a true living faith worketh by love (Gal. 5:6). Thus good works always follow justifying faith, and are surely found with it, if it be true and living; for it never is alone, but always has with it love and hope.

ANTITHESIS OR NEGATIVE. *Contrary Doctrine Rejected.*

Therefore we reject and condemn all the following errors:

1. That Christ is our righteousness alone according to his divine nature.

2. That Christ is our righteousness alone according to his human nature.

3. That in the expressions of the prophets and apostles, when the righteousness of faith is spoken of, the words "justify" and "be justified" do not signify to declare or be declared free from sins, and obtain the forgiveness of sins, but actually to be made righteous before God, because of love infused by the Holy Ghost, virtues and the works following them.

4. That faith looks not only to the obedience of Christ, but to his divine nature, as it dwells and works in us, and that by this indwelling our sins are covered.

5. That faith is such a trust in the obedience of Christ as can exist and remain in a man who has no genuine repentance, in whom also no love follows, but he persists in sins against conscience.

6. That not God himself, but only the gifts of God, dwell in the believer.

7. That faith saves, on this account, viz. because by faith the renewal, which consists in love to God and one's neighbor, is begun in us.

8. That faith has the first place in justification, although also renewal and love belong to our righteousness before God, in such a manner that they [renewal and love] are not the chief cause of our righteousness, but, nevertheless, our righteousness before God is, without this love and renewal, not entire or complete.

9. That believers are justified before God, and saved partly by the imputed righteousness of Christ, and by the beginning of new obedience, or in part by the imputation of Christ's righteousness, but in part also by the beginning of new obedience.

10. That the promise of grace is imputed to us by faith in the heart, and by the confession which is made with the mouth, and by other virtues.

11. That faith without good works does not justify, and therefore that good works are necessarily required for righteousness, and without their presence man cannot be justified.

CHAPTER IV. OF GOOD WORKS.

STATEMENT OF THE CONTROVERSY.

Concerning the doctrine of good works two divisions have arisen in some churches:

1. First, some theologians have differed with reference to the following expressions, where the one side wrote: "Good works are necessary for salvation." "It is impossible to be saved without good works." Also: "No one has ever been saved without good works." But the other side, on the contrary, wrote: "Good works are injurious to salvation."

2. Afterwards a schism arose also between some theologians with respect to the two words, "necessary" and "free," since the one side contended that the word "necessary" should not be employed concerning the new obedience, which does not proceed from necessity and coercion, but from the free will. The other side has retained the word "necessary," because this obedience is not at our option, but regenerate men are bound to render this obedience.

From this disputation concerning the terms a controversy concerning the subject itself afterwards occurred. For the one side contended that among Christians the law should not at all be urged, but men should be exhorted to good works alone from the Holy Gospel. The other side contradicted this.

AFFIRMATIVE. *Pure Doctrine of the Christian Churches concerning this Controversy.*

For the thorough statement and decision of this controversy, our doctrine, faith and confession is:

1. That good works certainly and without doubt follow true faith, if it be not a dead, but a living faith, as the fruit of a good tree.

2. We believe, teach and confess also that good works should be entirely excluded, as well when the question at issue is concerning salvation, as in the article of justification before God, as the apostle testifies with clear words, where it is written: "Even as David also describeth the blessedness of the man unto whom God imputeth righteousness without works, saying, . . . Blessed is the man to whom the Lord will not impute sin," etc. (Rom. 4:6 sqq.). And elsewhere: "By grace are ye saved through faith; and that not of yourselves, it is the gift of God; not of works, lest any man should boast" (Eph. 2:8, 9).

3. We believe, teach and confess also that all men, but those especially who are born again and renewed by the Holy Ghost, are bound to do good works.

4. In this sense the words "necessary," "should" and "must" are employed correctly and in a Christian manner, also with respect to the regenerate, and in no way are contrary to the form and language of sound words.

5. Nevertheless by the words mentioned, "necessity" and "necessary," if they be employed concerning the regenerate, not coercion, but only due obedience is understood, which the truly believing, so far as they are regenerate, render not from coercion or the impulse of the Law, but from the free will; because they are no more under the Law, but under grace (Rom. 6:14; 7:6; 8:14).

6. Therefore we also believe, teach and confess that when it is said: The regenerate do good works from the free will; this should not be understood as though it were at the option of the regenerate man to do or to forbear doing good when he wished, and nevertheless could retain faith when he intentionally persevered in sins.

7. Yet this should not be understood otherwise than as the Lord Christ and his apostles themselves declare, namely, that the liberated spirit does not do this from fear of punishment, as a slave, but from love of righteousness, as children (Rom. 8:15).

8. Although this free will in the elect children of God is not complete, but is burdened with great weakness, as St. Paul complains concerning himself (Rom. 7:14-25; Gal. 5:17).

9. Nevertheless, for the sake of the Lord Christ, the Lord does not impute this weakness to his elect, as it is written: "There is therefore now no condemnation to them which are in Christ Jesus" (Rom. 8:1).

10. We believe, teach and confess also, that not works, but alone the Spirit of God, through faith, maintains faith and salvation in us, of whose presence and indwelling good works are evidences.

NEGATIVE. *False Contrary Doctrine.*

1. We reject and condemn the following modes of speaking, viz. when it is taught and written that good works are necessary to salvation. Also, that no one ever has been saved without good works. Also, that it is impossible without good works to be saved.

2. We reject and condemn the unqualified expression: Good works are injurious to salvation, as offensive and detrimental to Christian discipline.

For, especially in these last times, it is no less needful to admonish men to Christian discipline [to the way of living aright and godly] and good works, and instruct them how necessary it is that they exercise themselves in good works as a declaration of their faith and gratitude to God, than that the works be not mingled in the article of justification; because men may be damned by an epicurean delusion concerning faith, as well as by Papistic and Pharisaic confidence in their own works and merits.

3. We also reject and condemn the dogma that faith and the indwelling of the Holy Ghost are not lost by wilful sin, but that the saints and elect retain the Holy Ghost, even though they fall into adultery and other sins, and persist therein.

CHAPTER V. OF THE LAW AND THE GOSPEL.

STATEMENT OF THE CONTROVERSY.

Whether the preaching of the Holy Gospel be properly not only a preaching of grace, which announces the forgiveness of sins, but also a preaching of repentance and censure, rebuking unbelief, which is rebuked not in the Law, but alone through the Gospel.

AFFIRMATIVE. *Pure Doctrine of God's Word.*

1. We believe, teach and confess that the distinction between the Law and the Gospel is to be maintained in the Church as an especially brilliant light, whereby, according to the admonition of St. Paul, the Word of God may be rightly divided.

2. We believe, teach and confess that the Law is properly a divine doctrine, which teaches what is right and pleasing to God, and reproves everything that is sin and contrary to God's will.

3. Therefore everything that reproves sin is and belongs to the preaching of the Law.

4. But the Gospel is properly such a doctrine as teaches what man who has not observed the Law, and therefore is condemned by it, should believe, viz. that Christ has expiated and made satisfaction for all sins, and, without any merit of theirs [no merit of the sinner intervening], has obtained and acquired forgiveness of sins, righteousness that avails before God, and eternal life.

5. But since the term Gospel is not used in one and the same sense in the Holy Scriptures, on account of which this dissension originally arose, we believe, teach and confess that if by the term Gospel the entire doctrine of Christ be understood, which he proposed in his ministry, as also did his apostles (in which sense it is employed, Mark 1:15; Acts 20:21), it is correctly said and written that the Gospel is a preaching of repentance and of the forgiveness of sins.

6. But if the Law and the Gospel be contrasted with one another, as Moses himself is called a teacher of the Law, and Christ a preacher of the Gospel, we

believe, teach and confess that the Gospel is not a preaching of repentance or reproof, but properly nothing else than a preaching of consolation, and a joyful message which does not reprove or terrify, but against the terrors of the Law consoles consciences, points alone to the merit of Christ, and again comforts them by the precious preaching of the grace and favor of God, obtained through Christ's merit.

7. As to the revelation of sin, because the veil of Moses hangs before the eyes of all men as long as they hear the bare preaching of the Law, and nothing concerning Christ, and therefore do not learn from the Law to perceive their sins aright, but either become presumptuous hypocrites [who swell with the opinion of their own righteousness] as the Pharisees, or despair as did Judas; Christ takes the Law into his hands, and explains it spiritually (Matt. 5:21 sqq.; Rom. 7:14). And thus the wrath of God is revealed from heaven against all sinners (Rom. 1:18), how great it is; by this means they are instructed in the Law, and then from it first learn to know aright their sins—a knowledge to which Moses never could coerce them.

Therefore, although the preaching of the suffering and death of Christ, the Son of God, is an earnest and terrible proclamation and declaration of God's wrath, whereby men are for the first time led aright to the Law, after the veil of Moses has been removed from them, so that they first know aright how great things God in his Law requires of us, nothing of which we can observe, and therefore should seek all our righteousness in Christ—

8. Yet as long as all this (namely, Christ's suffering and death) proclaims God's wrath and terrifies man, it is still not properly the preaching of the Gospel, but the preaching of Moses and the Law, and therefore a "strange work" of Christ, whereby he attains his proper office, *i.e.* to preach grace, console and quicken, which is properly the preaching of the Gospel.

NEGATIVE. *Contrary Doctrine which is Rejected.*

Therefore we reject and regard incorrect and injurious the dogma that the Gospel is properly a preaching of repentance or reproof, and not alone a preaching of grace. For thereby the Gospel is again converted into a law, the merit of Christ and the Holy Scriptures obscured, Christians robbed of true consolation, and the door opened again to [the errors and superstitions of] the Papacy.

CHAPTER VI. OF THE THIRD USE OF THE LAW.

STATEMENT OF THE CONTROVERSY.

Since the Law was given to men for three reasons: *first,* that thereby outward discipline might be maintained against wild, disobedient men [and that wild and intractable men might be restrained, as though by certain bars]; *secondly,* that men thereby may be led to the knowledge of their sins; *thirdly,* that after they are regenerate and [much of] the flesh notwithstanding cleaves to them, they may

have, on this account, a fixed rule, according to which they should regulate and direct their whole life; a dissension has occurred between some few theologians, concerning the third use of the Law, viz. whether it is to be urged or not upon regenerate Christians. The one side has said, Yea; the other, Nay.

AFFIRMATIVE. *The true Christian Doctrine Concerning this Controversy.*

1. We believe, teach and confess that although men rightly believing [in Christ] and truly converted to God have been freed and exempted from the curse and coercion of the Law, they nevertheless are not on this account without Law, but have been redeemed by the Son of God, in order that they should exercise themselves in it day and night [that they should meditate upon God's Law day and night, and constantly exercise themselves in its observance (Ps. 1:2)], (Ps. 119). For even our first parents before the fall did not live without Law, which Law of God was also written upon their hearts, because they were created in the image of God (Gen. 1:26 sq.; 2:16 sqq.; 3:3).

2. We believe, teach and confess that the preaching of the Law is to be urged with diligence, not only upon the unbelieving and impenitent, but also upon the rightly believing, truly converted, regenerate, and justified by faith.

3. For although they are regenerate and renewed in the spirit of their mind, yet, in the present life, this regeneration and renewal are not complete, but are only begun, and believers are, in the spirit of their mind, in a constant struggle against the flesh, *i.e.* against the corrupt nature and disposition which cleaves to us unto death. On account of this old Adam, which still inheres in the understanding, will and all the powers of man, it is needful that the Law of the Lord always shine upon the way before him, in order that he may do nothing from self-imposed human devotion [that he may frame nothing in a matter of religion from the desire of private devotion, and may not choose divine services not instituted by God's Word]; likewise, that the old Adam also may not employ his own will, but may be subdued against his will, not only by the admonition and threatening of the Law, but also by punishments and blows, so that he may follow and surrender himself captive to the Spirit (1 Cor. 9:27; Rom. 6:12; Gal. 6:14; Ps. 119:1 sqq.; Heb. 13:21 [Heb. 12:1]).

4. Then as to the distinction between the works of the Law and the fruits of the Spirit, we believe, teach and confess that the works which are done according to the Law, as long as they are and are called works of the Law, are only extorted from man by the force of punishment and the threatening of God's wrath.

5. But the fruits of the Spirit are the works which the Spirit of God who dwells in believers works through the regenerate, and are done by believers so far as they are regenerate [spontaneously and freely], as though they knew of no command, threat or reward; for in this manner the children of God live in the

Law and walk according to the Law of God, a manner which St. Paul, in his Epistles, calls the Law of Christ and the Law of the mind [Rom. 7:25; 8:7 [Rom. 8:2; 2; Gal. 6:2]).

6. Thus the Law is and remains both to the penitent and impenitent, both to regenerate and unregenerate men, one and the same Law, namely, the immutable will of God; and the distinction, so far as it concerns obedience, is alone in the men, inasmuch as one who is not yet regenerate does what is required him by the Law out of constraint and unwillingly (as also the regenerate do according to the flesh); but the believer, so far as he is regenerate, without constraint and with a willing spirit, does that which no threatening [however severe] of the Law could ever extort from him.

NEGATIVE. *False Contrary Doctrine.*

Therefore we reject as a dogma and error injurious and conflicting with Christian discipline and true piety that the Law in the above-mentioned way and degree should not be urged upon Christians and those truly believing, but only upon unbelievers and those not Christian, and upon the impenitent.

CHAPTER VII. OF THE LORD'S SUPPER.

Although the Zwinglian teachers are not to be reckoned among the theologians who acknowledge and profess the Augsburg Confession, as they separated from them when this Confession was presented, nevertheless since they are intruding themselves [with their assembly], and are attempting, under the name of this Christian Confession, to introduce their error, we have wished also to make such a report as is needful [we have judged that the Church of Christ should be instructed also] concerning this controversy.

STATEMENT OF THE CONTROVERSY. *Chief Controversy between our Doctrine and that of the Sacramentarians upon this article.*

Whether in the Holy Supper the true body and blood of our Lord Jesus Christ are truly and essentially present, are distributed with the bread and wine, and received with the mouth by all those who use this sacrament, whether they be worthy or unworthy, godly or ungodly, believing or unbelieving; by the believing, for consolation and life; by the unbelieving, for judgment [so that the believing receive from the Lord's Supper consolation and life, but the unbelieving take it for their judgment]? The Sacramentarians say, No; we say, Yea.

For the explanation of this controversy it is to be noted in the beginning that there are two kinds of Sacramentarians. Some are gross Sacramentarians, who declare in clear [*deutschen*] words what they believe in their hearts, viz. that in the Holy Supper nothing but bread and wine is present, and distributed and received with the mouth. Others, however, are subtle Sacramentarians, and the most injurious of all, who partly speak very speciously in our own words, and assert that they also believe in a true presence of the true, essential, living body and blood of Christ in the Holy Supper, yet that this occurs spiritually through faith. Nevertheless beneath these specious words,

precisely the former gross opinion is contained, viz. that in the Holy Supper nothing is present and received with the mouth except bread and wine. For with them the word *spiritually* means nothing else than the Spirit of Christ, or the power of the absent body of Christ, and his merit, which are present; but the body of Christ is in no mode or way present, except only above in the highest heaven, to which in heaven we should elevate ourselves by the thoughts of our faith, and there, and not at all in the bread and wine of the Holy Supper, should seek this body and blood [of Christ].

AFFIRMATIVE. *Confession of the Pure Doctrine concerning the Holy Supper against the Sacramentarians.*

1. We believe, teach and confess that, in the Holy Supper the body and blood of Christ are truly and essentially present, and are truly distributed and received with the bread and wine.

2. We believe, teach and confess that the words of the testament of Christ are not to be understood otherwise than as they sound, according to the letters; so that the bread does not signify the absent body, and the wine the absent blood of Christ, but that, on account of the sacramental union, they [the bread and wine] are truly the body and blood of Christ.

3. As to the consecration, we believe, teach and confess that no work of man or declaration of the minister [of the church] produces this presence of the body and blood of Christ in the Holy Supper, but that this should be ascribed only and alone to the almighty power of our Lord Jesus Christ.

4. But at the same time we also unanimously believe, teach and confess that in the use of the Holy Supper the words of the institution of Christ should in no way be omitted, but should be publicly recited, as it is written (1 Cor. 10:16): "The cup of blessing, which we bless, is it not the communion of the blood of Christ?" etc. This blessing occurs through the recitation of the Word of Christ.

5. Moreover the foundations upon which we stand against the Sacramentarians in this matter are those which Dr. Luther has laid down in his Large Confession concerning the Lord's Supper.

The first is this article of our Christian faith: Jesus Christ is true, essential, natural, perfect God and man in one person, undivided and inseparable.

The second: That God's right hand is everywhere; at which Christ is in deed and in truth placed according to his human nature, [and therefore] being present rules, and has in his hands and beneath his feet everything that is in heaven and on earth [as Scripture says (Eph. 1:22)]: There [at this right hand of God] no man else, or angel, but only the Son of Mary, is placed; whence he can effect this [those things which we have said].

The third: That God's Word is not false, and does not deceive.

The fourth: That God has and knows of many modes of being in a place, and not only the one [is not

THE FORMULA OF CONCORD (1580) (continued)

bound to the one] which philosophers call local [or circumscribed].

6. We believe, teach and confess that the body and blood of Christ are received with the bread and wine, not only spiritually by faith, but also orally; yet not in a Capernaitic, but in a supernatural, heavenly mode, because of the sacramental union; as the words of Christ clearly show, where Christ directs to take, eat and drink, as was then done by the apostles, for it is written (Mark 14:23): "And they all drank of it." St. Paul likewise says (1 Cor. 10:16): "The bread which we break is it not the communion of the body of Christ?" *i.e.* he who eats this bread, eats the body of Christ, which also the chief ancient teachers of the Church, Chrysostom, Cyprian, Leo I., Gregory, Ambrose, Augustine, unanimously testify.

7. We believe, teach and confess that not only the truly believing [in Christ] and worthy, but also the unworthy and unbelieving, receive the true body and blood of Christ; yet not for life and consolation, but for judgment and condemnation, if they are not converted and do not repent (1 Cor. 11:27,29).

For although they repel Christ from themselves as a Saviour, yet they must admit him even against their will as a strict Judge, who is present also to exercise and render judgment upon impenitent guests, as well as to work life and consolation in the hearts of the truly believing and worthy.

8. We believe, teach and confess also that there is only one kind of unworthy guests, viz. those who do not believe; concerning whom it is written (John 3:18): "He that believeth not is condemned already." By the unworthy use of the Holy Supper this judgment is augmented, increased, and aggravated (1 Cor. 11:29).

9. We believe, teach and confess that no true believer, as long as he retain living faith, however weak he may be, receives the Holy Supper to his judgment, which was instituted especially for Christians weak in faith, and yet penitent, for the consolation and strengthening of their weak faith (Matt. 9:12; 11:5, 28).

10. We believe, teach and confess that all the worthiness of the guests of this heavenly feast is and consists alone in the most holy obedience and absolute merit of Christ, which we appropriate to ourselves by true faith, and of it [this merit] we are assured by the sacrament. This worthiness does not at all depend upon our virtues or inner and outward preparations.

NEGATIVE. *Contrary condemned Doctrines of the Sacramentarians.*

On the other hand, we unanimously reject and condemn all the following erroneous articles, which are opposed and contrary to the above-presented doctrine, simple [simplicity of] faith, and the [pure] confession concerning the Lord's Supper:

1. The Papistic transubstantiation, where it is taught in the Papacy that in the Holy Supper the bread and wine lose their substance and natural essence, and are thus annihilated; that they are changed into the body of Christ, and the outward form alone remains.

2. The Papistic sacrifice of the mass for the sins of the living and the dead.

3. That [the sacrilege whereby] to laymen only one form of the sacrament is given, and the cup is withheld from them, against the plain words of the testament of Christ, and they are [thus] deprived of his blood.

4. When it is taught that the words of the testament of Christ should not be understood or believed simply as they sound, but that they are obscure expressions, whose meaning must be sought first in other passages of Scripture.

5. That in the Holy Supper the body of Christ is not received orally with the bread; but that with the mouth only bread and wine are received, and the body of Christ only spiritually by faith.

6. That the bread and wine in the Holy Supper are nothing more than [symbols or] tokens, whereby Christians recognize one another.

7. That the bread and wine are only figures, similitudes and representations of the far, absent body of Christ.

8. That the bread and wine are no more than a memorial, seal and pledge, through which we are assured, when faith elevates itself to heaven, that it there becomes participant of the body and blood of Christ as truly as, in the Supper, we eat bread and drink wine.

9. That the assurance and confirmation of our faith [concerning salvation] occur in the Holy Supper alone through the external signs of bread and wine, and not through the truly present true body and blood of Christ.

10. That in the Holy Supper only the power, efficacy and merit of the far absent body and blood of Christ are distributed.

11. That the body of Christ is so enclosed in heaven that it can in no way be at one and the same time in many or all places upon earth where his Holy Supper is celebrated.

12. That Christ has not promised, neither can afford, the essential presence of his body and blood in the Holy Supper, because the nature and property of his assumed human nature cannot suffer or permit it.

13. That God, according to [even by] his omnipotence (which is dreadful to hear), is not able to render his body essentially present in more than one place at one time.

14. That not the omnipotent Word of Christ's testament, but faith, produces and makes [is the cause of] the presence of the body and blood of Christ in the Holy Supper.

15. That believers should not seek the body [and blood] of Christ in the bread and wine of the Holy Supper,

but from the bread should raise their eyes to heaven, and there seek the body of Christ.

16. That unbelieving, impenitent Christians in the Holy Supper do not receive the true body and blood of Christ, but only bread and wine.

17. That the worthiness of the guests in this heavenly meal consists not alone in true faith in Christ, but also in the external preparation of men.

18. That even the truly believing, who have and retain a true, living, pure faith in Christ, can receive this sacrament to their judgment, because they are still imperfect in their outward life.

19. That the external visible elements in the Holy Sacrament should be adored.

20. Likewise, we consign also to the just judgment of God all presumptuous, ironical, blasphemous questions (which out of regard to decency are not to be mentioned), and other expressions, which very blasphemously and with great offence [to the Church] are proposed by the Sacramentarians in a gross, carnal, Capernaitic way concerning the supernatural, heavenly mysteries of this sacrament.

21. As, then, we hereby utterly [reject and] condemn the Capernaitic eating [manducation] of the body of Christ, which the Sacramentarians, against the testimony of their conscience, after all our frequent protests, wilfully force upon us, and in this way make our doctrine odious to their hearers, as though [we taught that] his flesh were rent with the teeth, and digested as other food; on the contrary, we maintain and believe, according to the simple words of the testament of Christ, in the true, yet supernatural eating of the body of Christ, as also in the drinking of his blood, a doctrine which man's sense and reason does not comprehend, but, as in all other articles of faith, our reason is brought into captivity to the obedience of Christ, and this mystery is not embraced otherwise than by faith alone, and is not revealed elsewhere than in the Word alone.

CHAPTER VIII. OF THE PERSON OF CHRIST.

From the controversy concerning the Holy Supper a disagreement has arisen between the pure theologians of the Augsburg Confession and the Calvinists, who also have confused some other theologians, concerning the person of Christ and the two natures in Christ and their properties.

STATEMENT OF THE CONTROVERSY. *Chief Controversy in this Dissension.*

The chief question, however, has been whether, because of the personal union, the divine and human natures, as also their properties, have really, that is, in deed and truth, a communion with one another in the person of Christ, and how far this communion extends?

The Sacramentarians have asserted that the divine and human natures in Christ are united personally in such a way that neither has really, that is, in deed and truth, in common with the other that which is peculiar to either nature, but that they have in common nothing more than the names alone. For "union," they plainly say, "makes common names," *i.e.* the personal union makes nothing more than the names common, namely, that God is called man, and man God, yet in such a way that God has nothing really, that is, in deed and truth, in common with humanity, and humanity nothing in common with divinity, as to its majesty and properties. Dr. Luther, and those who hold with him, have, against the Sacramentarians, contended for the contrary.

AFFIRMATIVE. *Pure Doctrine of the Christian Church concerning the Person of Christ.*

To explain this controversy, and settle it according to the guidance [analogy] of our Christian faith, our doctrine, faith and confession is as follows:

1. That the divine and human natures in Christ are personally united, so that there are not two Christs, one the Son of God, the other the Son of man, but that one and the same is the Son of God and Son of man (Luke 1:35; Rom. 9:5).

2. We believe, teach and confess that the divine and human natures are not mingled into one substance, nor the one changed into the other, but each retains its own essential properties, which can never become the properties of the other nature.

3. The properties of the divine nature are: to be almighty, eternal, infinite, and, according to the property of its nature and its natural essence, to be, of itself, everywhere present, to know everything, etc.; which never become properties of the human nature.

4. The properties of the human nature are: to be a corporeal creature, to be flesh and blood, to be finite and circumscribed, to suffer, to die, to ascend and descend, to move from one place to another, to suffer hunger, thirst, cold, heat, and the like; which never become properties of the divine nature.

5. As the two natures are united personally, *i.e.* in one person, we believe, teach and confess that this union is not such a combination and connection that neither nature should have anything in common with the other, personally, *i.e.* because of the personal union, as when two boards are glued together, where neither gives anything to the other, or takes anything from the other. But here is the highest communion, which God has truly with [assumed] man, from which personal union and the highest and ineffable communion that follows therefrom, all results that is said and believed of the human concerning God, and of the divine concerning the man Christ; as the ancient teachers of the Church explained this union and communion of the natures by the illustration of iron glowing with fire, and also by the union of body and soul in man.

6. Hence we believe, teach and confess that God is man and man is God, which could not be if the divine and human natures had, in deed and truth, absolutely no communion with one another.

For how could a man, the son of Mary, in truth be called or be God, the Son of the Highest, if his humanity were not personally united with the Son of

THE FORMULA OF CONCORD (1580) (continued)

God, and he thus had really, *i.e.* in deed and truth nothing in common with him, except only the name of God?

7. Hence we believe, teach and confess that Mary conceived and bore not a mere man, and no more, but the true Son of God; therefore she is also rightly called and is the mother of God.

8. Hence we also believe, teach and confess that it was not a mere man who, for us, suffered, died, was buried, descended to hell, arose from the dead, ascended into heaven, and was raised to the majesty and almighty power of God, but a man whose human nature has such a profound, ineffable union and communion with the Son of God that it is [was made] one person with him.

9. Therefore the Son of God truly suffered for us, nevertheless according to the property of the human nature, which he assumed into the unity of his divine person, and made it his own, so that he might suffer and be our high priest for our reconciliation with God, as it is written (1 Cor. 2:8): "They have crucified the Lord of glory." And (Acts 20:28): "We are purchased with God's blood."

10. Hence we believe, teach and confess that the Son of man is really, that is, in deed and truth, exalted, according to his human nature, to the right hand of the almighty majesty and power of God, because he [that man] was assumed into God when he was conceived of the Holy Ghost in his mother's womb, and his human nature was personally united with the Son of the Highest.

11. This majesty, according to the personal union, he [Christ] always had, and yet, in the state of his humiliation, he abstained from it, and, on this account, truly grew in all wisdom and favor with God and men; therefore he exercised this majesty, not always, but when [as often as] it pleased him, until, after his resurrection, he entirely laid aside the form of a servant, and not the nature, and was established in the full use, manifestation and declaration of the divine majesty, and thus entered into his glory (Phil. 2:6 sqq.), so that now not only as God, but also as man, he knows all things, can do all things, is present with all creatures, and has, under his feet and in his hands, everything that is in heaven, and on earth, and under the earth, as he himself testifies (Matt. 28:18; John 13:3): "All power is given unto me in heaven and in earth." And St. Paul says (Eph. 4:10): "He ascended up far above all heavens, that he might fill all things." Everywhere present, he can exercise this his power, and to him everything is possible and everything known.

12. Hence, being present, he also is able, and to him it is very easy, to impart his true body and blood in the Holy Supper, not according to the mode or property of the human nature, but according to the mode and property of the right hand of God, as Dr. Luther says in our Christian Faith for Children [according to the analogy of our Christian faith comprised in his Catechism]; which presence [of Christ in the Holy Supper] is not [physical or] earthly, or Capernaitic; nevertheless it is true and substantial, as the words of his testament sound: "This is, *is,* IS my body," etc.

By this our doctrine, faith and confession the person of Christ is not divided, as it was by Nestorius, who denied the *communicatio idiomatum, i.e.* the true communion of the properties of both natures in Christ, and thus separated the person, as Luther has explained in his book concerning the Councils. Neither are the natures, together with their properties, confounded with one another [or mingled] into one essence, as Eutyches erred; neither is the human nature in the person of Christ denied, or extinguished, nor is either creature changed into the other; but Christ is and remains, for all eternity, God and man in one undivided person, which, next to the Holy Trinity, is the highest mystery, as the Apostle testifies (1 Tim. 3:16), upon which our only consolation, life and salvation depend.

NEGATIVE. *Contrary False Doctrines concerning the Person of Christ.*

Therefore we reject and condemn, as contrary to God's Word and our simple [pure] Christian faith, all the following erroneous articles, when it is taught:

1. That God and man in Christ are not one person, but that the one is the Son of God, and the other the Son of man, as Nestorius raved.

2. That the divine and human natures have been mingled with one another into one essence, and the human nature has been changed into Deity, as Eutyches fanatically asserted.

3. That Christ is not true, natural and eternal God, as Arius held [blasphemed].

4. That Christ did not have a true human nature [consisting] of body and soul, as Marcion imagined.

5. That the personal union renders only the names and titles common.

6. That it is only a phrase and mode of speaking when it is said: God is man, man is God; for that the divinity has nothing in common with the humanity, as also the humanity has nothing really, that is, in deed and truth, common with the divinity [Deity].

7. That the communication is only verbal when it is said: "The Son of God died for the sins of the world;" "The Son of man has become almighty."

8. That the human nature in Christ has become an infinite essence in the same manner as the divinity, and from this, essential power and property, imparted and effused upon the human nature, and separated from God, is everywhere present in the same manner as the divine nature.

9. That the human nature has become equal to, and like the divine nature, in its substance and essence, or in its essential properties.

10. That the human nature of Christ is locally extended in all places of heaven and earth, which should not be ascribed even to the divine nature.

11. That, because of the property of his human nature, it is impossible for Christ to be able to be at the same time in more than one place, much less to be everywhere with his body.

12. That only the mere humanity has suffered for us and redeemed us, and that the Son of God in suffering had actually no participation with the humanity, as though it did not pertain to him.

13. That Christ is present with us on earth in the Word, the sacraments and all our troubles, only according to his divinity, and this presence does not at all pertain to his human nature, according to which he has also nothing more whatever to do with us even upon earth, since he redeemed us by his suffering and death.

14. That the Son of God, who assumed human nature, since he has laid aside the form of a servant does not perform all the works of his omnipotence in, through and with his human nature, but only some, and those too only in the place where his human nature is locally.

15. That, according to his human nature, he is not at all capable of omnipotence and other attributes of the divine nature against the express declaration of Christ (Matt. 28:18): "All power is given unto me in heaven and in earth." And [they contradict] St. Paul [who says] (Col. 2:9): "In him dwelleth all the fulness of the Godhead bodily."

16. That to him [to Christ according to his humanity] great power is given in heaven and upon earth, namely, greater and more than to all angels and other creatures, but that he has no participation in the omnipotence of God, and that this also has not been given him. Hence they devise an *intermediate power*, that is, such power between the almighty power of God and the power of other creatures, given to Christ, according to his humanity, by the exaltation, as is less than God's almighty power, and greater than that of other creatures.

17. That Christ, according to his human spirit, has a certain limit as to how much he should know, and that he knows no more than is becoming and needful for him to know for [the execution of] his office as judge.

18. That not even yet does Christ have a perfect knowledge of God and all his works; of whom, nevertheless, it is written (Col. 2:3): "In whom are hid all the treasures of wisdom and knowledge."

19. That it is impossible for Christ, according to his human mind, to know what has been from eternity, what at the present time is everywhere occurring, and will be yet to [all] eternity.

20. When it is taught, and the passage (Matt. 28:18): "All power is given unto me," etc., is thus interpreted and blasphemously perverted, viz. that to Christ according to the divine nature, at the resurrection and his ascension to heaven, was restored, *i.e.* delivered again all power in heaven and on earth; as though, in his state of humiliation, he had also, according to his divinity, divested himself of this and abandoned it. By this doctrine, not only are the words of the testament of Christ perverted, but also the way is prepared for the accursed Arian heresy, so that finally the eternal divinity of Christ is denied, and thus Christ, and with him our salvation, are entirely lost where this false doctrine is not [constantly] contradicted from the firm foundation of God's Word and our simple Christian [Catholic] faith.

CHAPTER IX. OF THE DESCENT OF CHRIST TO HELL.

STATEMENT OF THE CONTROVERSY. *Chief Controversy concerning this Article.*

There has also been a controversy among some theologians, who have subscribed to the Augsburg Confession concerning the following article: When, and in what manner, the Lord Christ, according to our simple Christian faith, descended to hell, whether this was done before or after his death? Also, whether it occurred according to the soul alone, or according to the divinity alone, or in body and soul, spiritually or bodily? Also, whether this article belongs to the passion or to the glorious victory and triumph of Christ?

But since this article, as also the preceding, cannot be comprehended by the senses or by the reason, but must be grasped alone by faith, it is our unanimous advice that there should be no disputation concerning it, but that it should be believed and taught only in the simplest manner; according as Dr. Luther of blessed memory, in his sermon at Torgau in the year 1533, has, in a very Christian manner, explained this article, separated from it all useless, unnecessary questions, and admonished all godly Christians to Christian simplicity of faith.

For it is sufficient that we know that Christ descended to hell, destroyed hell for all believers, and delivered them from the power of death and of the devil, from eternal condemnation [and even] from the jaws of hell. But how this occurred, we should [not curiously investigate, but] reserve until the other world, where not only this point [mystery], but also still others, will be revealed which we here simply believe, and cannot comprehend with our blind reason.

CHAPTER X. OF CHURCH RITES WHICH ARE [COMMONLY] CALLED ADIAPHORA OR MATTERS OF INDIFFERENCE.

Concerning ceremonies or church rites which are neither commanded nor forbidden in God's Word, but have been introduced into the Church for the sake of good order and propriety, a dissension has also occurred among the theologians of the Augsburg Confession.

STATEMENT OF THE CONTROVERSY.

The chief question has been, whether, in time of persecution and in case of confession, even if the enemies of the Gospel do not agree with us in doctrine, yet some abrogated ceremonies, which in themselves are matters of

THE FORMULA OF CONCORD (1580) (continued)

indifference and are neither commanded nor forbidden by God, may without violence to conscience be re-established in compliance with the pressure and demand of the adversaries, and thus in such ceremonies and adiaphora we may [rightly] have conformity with them? The one side says, Yea; the other says, Nay, thereto.

AFFIRMATIVE. *The Pure and True Doctrine and Confession concerning this Article.*

1. For settling also this controversy we unanimously believe, teach and confess that the ceremonies or church rites which are neither commanded nor forbidden in God's Word, but have been instituted alone for the sake of propriety and good order, are in and of themselves no service, nor are even a part of the service of God. Matt. 15:9: "In vain they do worship me, teaching for doctrines the commandments of men."

2. We believe, teach and confess that the Church of God of every place and every time has the power, according to its circumstances, to change such ceremonies, in such manner as may be most useful and edifying to the Church of God.

3. Nevertheless, that herein all inconsiderateness and offence should be avoided, and especial care should be taken to exercise forbearance to the weak in faith (1 Cor. 8:9; Rom. 14:13).

4. We believe, teach and confess that in time of persecution, when a bold [and steadfast] confession is required of us, we should not yield to the enemies in regard to such adiaphora, as the apostle has written (Gal. 5:1): "Stand fast, therefore, in the liberty wherewith Christ hath made us free, and be not entangled again in the yoke of bondage." Also (2 Cor. 6:14): "Be not unequally yoked together with unbelievers," etc. "For what concord hath light with darkness?" Also (Gal. 2:5): "To whom we gave place, no, not for an hour, that the truth of the Gospel might remain with you." For in such a case it is no longer a question concerning adiaphora, but concerning the truth of the Gospel, concerning [preserving] Christian liberty, and concerning sanctioning open idolatry, as also concerning the prevention of offence to the weak in the faith [how care should be taken lest idolatry be openly sanctioned and the weak in faith be offended]; in which we have nothing to concede, but should boldly confess and suffer what God sends, and what he allows the enemies of his Word to inflict upon us.

5. We believe, teach and confess also that no Church should condemn another because one has less or more external ceremonies not commanded by God than the other, if otherwise there is agreement among them in doctrine and all its articles, as also in the right use of the holy sacraments, according to the well-known saying: "Disagreement in fasting does not destroy agreement in faith."

NEGATIVE. *False Doctrines concerning this Article.*

Therefore we reject and condemn as wrong, and contrary to God's Word, when it is taught:

1. That human ordinances and institutions should be regarded in the churches as in themselves a service or part of the service of God.

2. When such ceremonies, ordinances and institutions are violently forced upon the Church of God, contrary to the Christian liberty which it has in external things.

3. Also, that in the time of persecution and public confession [when a clear confession is required] we may comply with the enemies of the Gospel in the observance of such adiaphora and ceremonies, or may come to an agreement with them,—which causes injury to the truth.

4. Also, when these external ceremonies and adiaphora are abrogated in such a manner as though it were not free to the Church of God to employ one or more [this or that] in Christian liberty, according to its circumstances, as may be most useful at any time to the Church [for edification].

CHAPTER XI. OF GOD'S ETERNAL FOREKNOWLEDGE [PREDESTINATION] AND ELECTION.

Concerning this article no public dissension has occurred among the theologians of the Augsburg Confession. But since it is a consolatory article, if treated properly, and by this means the introduction in the future of a controversy likely to cause offence may be avoided, it is also explained in this writing.

AFFIRMATIVE. *The Pure and True Doctrine concerning this Article.*

1. First of all, the distinction between foreknowledge and predestination, that is, between God's foreknowledge and his eternal election, ought to be accurately observed.

2. For the foreknowledge of God is nothing else than that God knows all things before they happen, as it is written (Dan. 2:28): "There is a God in heaven that revealeth secrets and maketh known to the king Nebuchadnezzar what shall be in the latter days."

3. This foreknowledge is occupied alike with the godly and the wicked; but it is not the cause of evil or of sin, so that men do what is wrong (which originally arises from the devil and the wicked, perverse will of man); nor the cause of their ruin [that men perish], for which they themselves are responsible [which they ought to ascribe to themselves]; but only regulates it, and fixes to it a limit [how far it should progress and] how long it should last, and that everything, notwithstanding that in itself it is evil, should serve his elect for their salvation.

4. The predestination or eternal election of God, however, is occupied only with the godly, beloved children of God, and this is a cause of their salvation, which he also provides as well as disposes what belongs thereto. Upon this [predestination of God]

our salvation is founded so firmly that the gates of hell cannot overcome it (John 10:28; Matt. 16:18).

5. This is not to be investigated in the secret counsel of God, but to be sought in the Word of God, where it is also revealed.

6. But the Word of God leads us to Christ, who is the Book of Life, in whom all are written and elected that are to be saved, as it is written (Eph. 1:4): "He hath chosen us in him" [Christ] "before the foundation of the world."

7. Thus Christ calls to himself all sinners, and promises them rest, and he is anxious that all men should come to him and permit him to help them. To them he offers himself in his Word, and wishes them to hear it, and not to stop their ears or [neglect and] despise the Word. He promises besides the power and efficiency of the Holy Ghost, and divine assistance for perseverance and eternal salvation [that we may remain steadfast in the faith and attain eternal salvation].

8. Therefore we should judge concerning this our election to eternal life neither from reason nor from the Law of God, which would lead either into a dissipated, dissolute epicurean life, or into despair, and would excite in the heart of men pernicious thoughts (and such thoughts cannot be effectually guarded against as long as they follow their own reason), so that they think to themselves: "If God has elected me to salvation, I cannot be condemned, although I do whatever I will." And again: "If I am not elected to eternal life, it matters not what good I do; for my efforts are nevertheless all in vain."

9. But the true judgment concerning predestination must be learned alone from the Holy Gospel concerning Christ, in which it is clearly testified that "God hath concluded them all in unbelief, that he might have mercy upon all," and that "he is not willing that any should perish, but that all should come to repentance" (Rom. 11:32; Ez. 18:23; 33:11; 2 Pet. 3:9; 1 John 2:2).

10. To him, therefore, who is really concerned about the revealed will of God, and proceeds according to the order which St. Paul has observed in the Epistle to the Romans, who first directs men to repentance, knowledge of sins, to faith in Christ, to divine obedience, before he speaks of the mystery of the eternal election of God, this doctrine [concerning God's predestination] is useful and consolatory.

11. That, however, "many are called, few are chosen," does not mean that God is unwilling that all should be saved, but the reason is that they either do not at all hear God's Word, but wilfully despise it, close their ears and harden their hearts, and in this manner foreclose the ordinary way to the Holy Ghost, so that he cannot effect his work in them, or, when it is heard, they consider it of no account, and do not heed it. For this [that they perish] not God or his election, but their wickedness, is responsible (2 Pet. 2:1 sqq.; Luke 11:49, 52; Heb. 12:25 sq.).

12. Moreover, a Christian should apply himself [in meditation] to the article concerning the eternal election of God, so far as it has been revealed in God's Word, which presents Christ to us as the Book of Life, which, by the preaching of the holy Gospel, he opens and spreads out to us, as it is written (Rom. 8:30): "Whom he did predestinate, them he also called." In him, therefore, we should seek the eternal election of the Father, who, in his eternal divine counsel, determined that he would save no one except those who acknowledge his Son, Christ, and truly believe on him. Other thoughts are to be entirely banished [from the minds of the godly], as they proceed not from God, but from the suggestion of Satan, whereby he attempts to weaken or to entirely remove from us the glorious consolation which we have in this salutary doctrine, viz. that we know [assuredly] that out of pure grace, without any merit of our own, we have been elected in Christ to eternal life, and that no one can pluck us out of his hand; as he has promised this gracious election not only with mere words, but has also certified it with an oath, and sealed it with the holy sacraments, which we can [ought to] call to mind in our most severe temptations, and from them comfort ourselves, and thereby quench the fiery darts of the devil.

13. Besides, we should endeavor with the greatest pains to live according to the will of God, and, as St. Peter admonishes (2 Ep. 1:10), "make our calling sure," and especially adhere to [not recede a finger's breadth from] the revealed Word, that can and will not fail us.

14. By this brief explanation of the eternal election of God his glory is entirely and fully given to God, that alone, out of pure mercy, without all merit of ours, he saves us, according to the purpose of his will; besides, also, no cause is given any one for despondency or an abandoned, dissolute life [no opportunity is afforded either for those more severe agitations of mind and faintheartedness or for epicureanism].

ANTITHESIS OR NEGATIVE. *False Doctrine concerning this Article.*

Therefore we believe and hold: When the doctrine concerning the gracious election of God to eternal life is so presented that troubled Christians cannot comfort themselves therewith, but thereby despondency or despair is occasioned, or the impenitent are strengthened in their wantonness, that such doctrine is treated [wickedly and erroneously] not according to the Word and will of God, but according to reason and the instigation of Satan. "For," as the apostle testifies (Rom. 15:4), "whatsoever things were written aforetime were written for our learning, that we, through patience and comfort of the Scriptures, might have hope." Therefore we reject the following errors:

1. As when it is taught that God is unwilling that all men repent and believe the Gospel.

2. Also, that when God calls us to himself he is not in earnest that all men should come to him.

THE FORMULA OF CONCORD (1580) (continued)

3. Also, that God does not wish every one to be saved, but, without regard to their sins, alone from the counsel, purpose and will of God, some are appointed to condemnation, so that they cannot be saved.

4. Also, that not only the mercy of God and the most holy merit of Christ, but also in us is a cause of God's election, on account of which God has elected us to everlasting life.

All these erroneous doctrines are blasphemous and dreadful, whereby there is removed from Christians all the comfort which they have in the holy Gospel and the use of the holy sacraments, and therefore should not be tolerated in the Church of God.

This is a brief and simple explanation of the controverted articles, which for a time have been discussed and taught with conflicting opinions among the theologians of the Augsburg Confession. Hence every simple Christian, according to the guidance of God's Word and his simple Catechism, can distinguish what is right or wrong, where not only the pure doctrine is stated, but also the erroneous contrary doctrine is repudiated and rejected, and thus the controversies, full of causes of offence, that have occurred, are thoroughly settled and decided.

May Almighty God, the Father of our Lord Jesus, grant the grace of his Holy Ghost, that we all may be one in him, and constantly abide in this Christian unity, which is well pleasing to him! Amen.

CHAPTER XII. OF OTHER FACTIONS [HERESIES] AND SECTS, WHICH NEVER EMBRACED THE AUGSBURG CONFESSION.

In order that such [heresies and sects] may not silently be ascribed to us, because, in the preceding explanation, no mention of them has been made, we wish at the end [of this writing] simply to enumerate the mere articles wherein they [the heretics of our time] err and teach what is contrary to our Christian faith and confession above presented.

ERRONEOUS ARTICLES OF THE ANABAPTISTS.

The Anabaptists are divided into many sects, as one contends for more, another for less error; nevertheless, they all in common propound [profess] such doctrine as is neither to be tolerated nor allowed in the Church, the commonwealth and worldly government or domestic life.

ARTICLES THAT CANNOT BE TOLERATED IN THE CHURCH.

1. That Christ did not assume his body and blood of the Virgin Mary, but brought them with him from heaven.

2. That Christ is not true God, but only [is superior to other saints, because he] has more gifts of the Holy Ghost than any other holy man.

3. That our righteousness before God consists not only in the sole merit of Christ, but in renewal, and thus in our own godliness [uprightness] in which we walk. This is based in great part upon one's own special, self-chosen [and humanly-devised] spirituality [holi-

ness], and in fact is nothing else than a new sort of monkery.

4. That children who are not baptized are not sinners before God, but righteous and innocent, who, in their innocency, because they have not yet attained their reason [the use of reason], will be saved without baptism (which, according to their assertion, they do not need). Therefore they reject the entire doctrine concerning original sin, and what belongs to it.

5. That children should not be baptized until they have attained their reason [the use of reason], and can themselves confess their faith.

6. That the children of Christians, because they have been born of Christian and believing parents, are holy and the children of God, even without and before baptism. For this reason also they neither attach much importance to the baptism of children, nor encourage it, contrary to the express words of God's promise, which pertains only to those *who keep God's covenant and do not despise it* (Gen. 17:7 sqq.).

7. That there is no true Christian congregation [church] wherein sinners are still found.

8. That no sermon should be heard or attended in those churches in which the Papal masses have previously been observed and said.

9. That no one [godly man] should have anything to do with those ministers of the Church who preach the Gospel according to the Augsburg Confession, and censure the sermons and errors of the Anabaptists; also, that no one should serve or in any way labor for them, but should flee from and shun them as perverters of God's Word.

ARTICLES THAT CANNOT BE TOLERATED IN THE GOVERNMENT.

1. That, under the New Testament, the magistracy is not an estate pleasing to God.

2. That a Christian cannot, with a good, inviolate conscience, hold or exercise the office of magistrate.

3. That a Christian cannot, without injury to conscience, use the office of the magistracy against the wicked in matters as they occur [matters so requiring], nor may subjects invoke for their protection and screening the power which the magistrates possess and have received from God.

4. That a Christian cannot, with a good conscience, take an oath, neither can he by an oath do homage [promise fidelity] to his prince or sovereign.

5. That, under the New Testament, magistrates cannot, without injury to conscience, inflict capital punishment upon transgressors.

ARTICLES THAT CANNOT BE TOLERATED IN DOMESTIC LIFE.

1. That a Christian cannot [with an inviolate conscience] hold or possess property, but is in duty bound to devote it to the church.

2. That a Christian cannot, with a good conscience, be a landlord, merchant, or cutler [maker of arms].

3. That on account of diverse faith married persons may be divorced and abandon one another, and be married to another person of the same faith.

ERRONEOUS ARTICLES OF THE SCHWENCKFELDIANS.

1. That all who regard Christ according to the flesh as a creature have no true knowledge of Christ as reigning King of heaven.

2. That, by his exaltation, the flesh of Christ has so assumed all divine properties that Christ as man is in might, power, majesty and glory equal to the Father and to the Word, everywhere as to degree and condition of essence, so that now there is only one essence, property, will and glory of both natures in Christ, and that the flesh of Christ belongs to the essence of the Holy Trinity.

3. That the Church service [ministry of the Word], the Word preached and heard, is not a means whereby God the Holy Ghost teaches men, and works in them saving knowledge of Christ, conversion, repentance, faith and new obedience.

4. That the water of baptism is not a means whereby God the Lord seals adoption and works regeneration.

5. That bread and wine in the Holy Supper are not means through and by which Christ distributes his body and blood.

6. That a Christian who is truly regenerated by God's Spirit can, in this life, observe and fulfil the Law of God perfectly.

7. That there is no true Christian congregation [church] where no public excommunication [and some formal mode of excommunication] or no regular process of the ban [as it is commonly called] is observed.

8. That the minister of the church who is not on his part truly renewed, regenerate, righteous and godly cannot teach other men with profit or distribute true sacraments.

ERROR OF THE NEW ARIANS.

That Christ is not true, essential, natural God, of one eternal, divine essence with God the Father and the Holy Ghost, but is only adorned with divine majesty beneath and beside God the Father [is so adorned with divine majesty, with the Father, that he is inferior to the Father].

ERROR OF THE ANTI-TRINITARIANS.

This is an entirely new sect, not heard of before in Christendom, composed of those who believe, teach and confess that there is not only one, eternal, divine essence of the Father, Son and Holy Ghost, but as God the Father, Son and Holy Ghost are three distinct persons, so each person has its essence distinct and separate from the other persons of the Godhead; and nevertheless [some of them think] that all three, just as in another respect three men distinct and separate from one another are of equal power, wisdom, majesty and glory, or [others think that these three persons and essences] are unequal with one another

in essence and properties, so that the Father alone is properly and truly God.

These and like errors, one and all, with whatever other errors depend upon and follow from them, we reject and condemn as wrong, false, heretical, contrary to the Word of God, the three Creeds, the Augsburg Confession and Apology, the Smalcald Articles and Luther's Catechisms, against which all godly Christians, of both high and low station, should be on their guard as they love the welfare and salvation of their souls.

That this is the doctrine, faith and confession of us all, for which we will answer, at the last day, before the just Judge, our Lord Jesus Christ, and that against this we will neither secretly nor publicly speak or write, but that we intend, by the grace of God, to persevere therein, we have, after mature deliberation, testified, in the true fear of God and invocation of his name, by signing with our own hands this Epitome.

Bergen, May 29th, 1577.

PART SECOND.

SOLID, PLAIN AND CLEAR REPETITION AND DECLARATION. OF CERTAIN ARTICLES OF THE AUGSBURG CONFESSION, CONCERNING WHICH, FOR SOME TIME, THERE HAS BEEN CONTROVERSY AMONG SOME THEOLOGIANS WHO SUBSCRIBE THERETO, STATED AND SETTLED ACCORDING TO THE ANALOGY OF GOD'S WORD AND THE SUMMARY CONTENTS OF OUR CHRISTIAN DOCTRINE.

PREFACE.

By the inestimable goodness and mercy of the Almighty, the doctrine concerning the chief articles of our Christian religion, which under the Papacy was horribly obscured by human opinions and traditions, has been explained and corrected, in accordance with God's Word, by Dr. Martin Luther of holy and blessed memory, and the Papistic errors, abuses and idolatry have been rebuked. This pure reformation, however, has been regarded by its opponents as introducing new doctrine; it has been violently and falsely charged with being directly contrary to God's Word and Christian ordinances, and has to bear the burden of numberless other calumnies and accusations. On this account the electors, princes and estates that have embraced the pure doctrine of the Holy Gospel, and have reformed their churches in a Christian manner according to God's Word, at the great Diet of Augsburg in the year 1530 had a Christian Confession prepared from God's Word, which they delivered to the Emperor Charles V. In this they clearly and plainly made a Christian Confession as to what was held and taught in the Christian evangelical churches concerning the chief articles, and those especially in controversy between them and the Papists. This Confession was received by their opponents with disfavor, but, thank God, remains to this day without refutation or invalidation. From our inmost hearts we herewith once again confess this Christian Augsburg Confession, which is so thoroughly grounded in God's Word. We abide by the simple, clear and plain meaning of the same that its words

THE FORMULA OF CONCORD (1580) (continued)

convey, and regard it in all respects as a Christian symbol, which at the present time true Christians should receive next to God's Word; just as in former times, when great controversies arose in the Church of God, symbols and confessions were composed, which pure teachers and hearers confessed with heart and mouth. We intend also, by the grace of the Almighty, to faithfully abide until our end by this Christian Confession, as it was delivered in the year 1530 to the Emperor Charles V.; and it is our purpose, neither in this nor in any other writing, to recede in the least from that Confession or to compose another or new confession.

Although the Christian doctrine of this Confession has, in great part, remained unchallenged, save among the Papists, yet it cannot be denied that some theologians have departed from some of its principal and most important articles, and that they either have not learned the true meaning of these articles, or have not continued steadfastly therein, but that some have even undertaken to attach to it an extraneous meaning, while at the same time professing to adhere to the Augsburg Confession, and availing themselves of this boast as a pretext. From this, grievous and injurious dissensions have arisen in the pure evangelical churches; just as during the lives of the holy apostles, among those who wished to be called Christians and boasted of Christ's doctrine, horrible error arose. For some sought to be justified and saved by the Law (Acts 15: 1-29); others denied the resurrection of the dead (1 Cor. 15:12); and still others did not believe that Christ was true and eternal God. These the holy apostles in their sermons and writings earnestly opposed, although such pernicious errors and severe controversy could not occur without offence, both to believers and to those weak in the faith; just as at present our opponents, the Papists, rejoice at the dissensions among us, in the unchristian and vain hope that these discords will finally cause the suppression of the pure doctrine. Because of them, those that are weak in faith are also greatly offended, and some doubt whether, amid such dissensions, the pure doctrine be with us, while others know not with whom to side with respect to the articles in controversy. For these controversies are not mere misunderstandings or disputes concerning words, as are apt to occur where one side has not sufficiently understood the meaning of the other, and thus the dispute is confined to a few words, whereon nothing of much moment depends. But here the subjects of controversy are great and important, and of such a nature that the opinion of the party in error cannot be tolerated in the Church of God, much less be excused or defended.

Necessity, therefore, requires us to explain these controverted articles according to God's Word and approved writings; so that every one who has Christian understanding can notice what opinion concerning the matters in controversy accords with God's Word, and what disagrees therewith. Thus the errors and corruptions that have arisen may be shunned and avoided by sincere Christians who prize the truth aright.

OF THE COMPREHENSIVE SUMMARY, FOUNDATION, RULE AND STANDARD WHEREBY, ACCORDING TO GOD'S WORD, ALL DOGMAS SHOULD BE JUDGED, AND THE CONTROVERSIES THAT HAVE OCCURRED SHOULD, IN A CHRISTIAN MANNER, BE EXPLAINED AND DECIDED.

Because, for thorough, permanent unity in the Church, it is before all things necessary that we have a comprehensive, unanimously approved summary and form, wherein are brought together from God's Word the common doctrines, reduced to a brief compass, which the churches that are of the true Christian religion acknowledge as confessional (just as the ancient Church always had for this use its fixed symbols); and this authority should not be attached to private writings, but to such books as have been composed, approved and received in the name of the churches which confessionally bind themselves to one doctrine and religion; we have declared to one another, with heart and mouth, that we will neither make nor receive any separate or new confession of our faith, but acknowledge as confessional the public common writings which always and everywhere were received in all the churches of the Augsburg Confession, as such symbols or public confessions, before the dissensions arose among those who accept the Augsburg Confession, and as long as, in all articles, there was, on all sides, a unanimous adherence to, and maintenance and use of, the pure doctrine of God's Word, as the late Dr. Luther explained it.

1. First, we receive and embrace the Prophetic and Apostolic Scriptures of the Old and New Testaments as the pure, clear fountains of Israel, which are the only true standard whereby to judge all teachers and doctrines.

2. And because, of old, the true Christian doctrine, in a pure, sound sense, was collected from God's Word into brief articles or sections against the corruption of heretics, we accept as confessional the three Ecumenical Creeds, namely, the Apostles', the Nicene and the Athanasian, as glorious confessions of the faith, brief, devout and founded upon God's Word, wherein all the heresies which at that time had arisen in the Christian Church are clearly and unanswerably refuted.

3. Thirdly, because, in these last times, God, out of especial grace, from the darkness of the Papacy has brought his truth again to light, through the faithful service of the precious man of God, Dr. Luther, and against the corruptions of the Papacy and also of other sects has collected the same doctrine, from and according to God's Word, into the articles and sections of the Augsburg Confession; we confessionally accept also the first unaltered Augsburg Confession (not because it was composed by our theologians, but because it has been derived from God's Word, and is founded firmly and well therein, precisely in the form in which it was committed to writing in the year 1530, and presented to the Emperor Charles V. by some electors, princes and deputies of the Roman Empire as a common confession of the reformed churches at Augsburg) as

the symbol of our time, whereby our Reformed churches are distinguished from the Papists and other repudiated and condemned sects and heresies, after the custom and usage of the early Church, whereby succeeding councils, Christian bishops and teachers appealed to the Nicene Creed, and confessed it [publicly declared that they embraced it].

4. Fourthly, in order that the proper and true sense of the often-quoted Augsburg Confession might be more fully set forth and guarded against the Papists, and that under the name of the Augsburg Confession condemned errors might not steal into the Church of God after the Confession was delivered, a fuller Apology was composed, and published in the year 1531. We unanimously accept this also as confessional, because in it the said Augsburg Confession is not only sufficiently elucidated and guarded, but also confirmed by clear, irrefutable testimonies of Holy Scripture.

5. Fifthly, the Articles composed, approved and received at Smalcald in the large assembly of theologians in the year 1537 we confessionally accept, in the form in which they were first framed and printed in order to be delivered in the council at Mantua, or wherever it would be held, in the name of the electors, princes and deputies, as an explanation of the above-mentioned Augsburg Confession, wherein by God's grace they determined to abide. In them the doctrine of the Augsburg Confession is repeated, and some articles are stated at greater length from God's Word, and besides the cause and foundation why we have abandoned the papistical errors and idolatries, and can have no fellowship with them, and also why we have not determined or even thought of coming to any agreement with the Pope concerning them, are sufficiently indicated.

6. Lastly, because these highly important matters belong also to the common people and laity, who, for their salvation, must distinguish between pure and false doctrine, we accept as confessional also the Large and the Small Catechisms of Dr. Luther, as they were written by him and incorporated in his works, because they have been unanimously approved and received by all churches adhering to the Augsburg Confession, and publicly used in churches, schools and [privately in] families, and because also in them the Christian doctrine from God's Word is comprised in the most correct and simple way, and, in like manner, is sufficiently explained for simple laymen.

These public common writings have been always regarded in the pure churches and schools as the sum and type of the doctrine which the late Dr. Luther has admirably deduced against the Papacy and other sects from God's Word, and firmly established; to whose full explanations in his doctrinal and polemical writings we appeal in the manner and to the extent indicated by Dr. Luther himself in the necessary and Christian admonition concerning his writings, made in the Latin preface to his published works, wherein he has expressly drawn this distinction, viz. that God's Word alone is and should remain the only standard and rule, to which the writings of no man should be regarded equal, but to it everything should be subordinated.

But hereby other good, useful, pure books, expositions of the Holy Scriptures, refutations of errors, explanations of doctrinal articles (which, as far as consistent with the above-mentioned type of doctrine, are regarded as useful expositions and explanations, and can be used with advantage) are not rejected. But by what has thus far been said concerning the summary of our Christian doctrine we have only meant that we have a unanimously received, definite, common form of doctrine, which our Evangelical churches together and in common confess; from and according to which, because it has been derived from God's Word, all other writings should be judged and adjusted as to how far they are to be approved and accepted.

For that we have embodied the above-mentioned writings, viz. the Augsburg Confession, Apology, Smalcald Articles, Luther's Large and Small Catechisms, as the sum of our Christian doctrine, has occurred for the reason that these have been always and everywhere regarded as containing the common, unanimously received understanding of our churches, since the chief and most enlightened theologians of that time subscribed them, and all evangelical churches and schools have cordially received them. As they also, as before mentioned, were all written and sent forth before the divisions among the theologians of the Augsburg Confession arose, and then because they were held as impartial, and neither can nor should be rejected by any part of those who have entered into controversy, and no one who is true to the Augsburg Confession will complain of these writings, but will cheerfully accept and tolerate them as witnesses [of the truth]; no one, therefore, can blame us that we derive from them an explanation and decision of the articles in controversy, and that, as we lay God's Word, the eternal truth, as the foundation, so also we introduce and quote these writings as a witness of the truth, and a presentation of the unanimously received correct understanding of our predecessors who have steadfastly held to the pure doctrine.

OF THE ARTICLES IN CONTROVERSY WITH RESPECT TO THE ANTITHESIS, OR OPPOSITE DOCTRINE.

For the maintenance of pure doctrine, and for thorough, permanent, godly unity in the Church, it is necessary not only that pure, wholesome doctrine be rightly presented, but also that the opponents who teach otherwise be reproved (1 Tim. 3 [2 Tim. 3:16]; Tit. 1:9). For faithful shepherds, as Luther says, should do both, viz. feed or nourish the lambs and defend from the wolves, so that they may flee from strange voices (John 10:12) and may separate the precious from the vile (Jer. 15:19).

THE FORMULA OF CONCORD (1580) (continued)

Therefore concerning this, we have thoroughly and clearly declared to one another as follows: that a distinction in every way should and must be observed between, on the one hand, unnecessary and useless wrangling, whereby, since it scatters more than it builds up, the Church ought not to be disturbed, and, on the other hand, necessary controversy, as when such a controversy occurs as involves the articles of faith or the chief heads of the Christian doctrine, where for the defence of the truth the false opposite doctrine must be reproved.

Although the aforesaid writings afford the Christian reader, who has pleasure and love for the divine truth, a clear and correct answer concerning each and every controverted article of our Christian religion, as to what, according to God's Word of the Prophetic and Apostolic Scriptures, he should regard and receive as right and true, and what he should reject, shun and avoid as false and wrong; yet, in order that the truth may be preserved the more distinctly and clearly, and be separated from all errors, and be not hidden and concealed under rather general words, we have clearly and expressly made a declaration to one another concerning the chief and highly important articles, taken one by one, which at the present time have come into controversy; so that there might be a public, definite testimony, not only for those now living, but also for our posterity, as to what is and should remain the unanimously received understanding and judgment of our churches in reference to the articles in controversy, namely:

1. First, that we reject and condemn all heresies and errors which, in the primitive, ancient, orthodox Church, were rejected and condemned, upon the true, firm ground of the holy divine Scriptures.

2. Secondly, we reject and condemn all sects and heresies which are rejected in the writings, just mentioned, of the comprehensive summary of the Confession of our churches.

3. Thirdly, because within thirty years, on account of the Interim and otherwise, some divisions arose among some theologians of the Augsburg Confession, we have wished plainly, distinctly and clearly to state and declare our faith and confession concerning each and every one of these taken in thesis and antithesis, *i.e.* the true doctrine and its opposite, for the purpose in all articles of rendering the foundation of divine truth manifest, and censuring all unlawful, doubtful, suspicious and condemned doctrines (wherever and in whatever books they may be found, and whoever may have written them or even now may be disposed to defend them); so that every one may be faithfully warned to avoid the errors, diffused on all sides, in the writings of some theologians, and no one be misled herein by the reputation of any man. If the Christian reader will carefully examine this declaration in every emergency, and compare it with the writings enumerated above, he will find that what was in the beginning confessed concerning every article in the comprehensive summary of our religion and faith, and what was afterward restated at various times, and is repeated by us in this document, is in no way contradictory, but the simple, immutable, permanent truth, and that we, therefore, do not change from one doctrine to another, as our adversaries falsely assert, but earnestly desire to retain the once-delivered Augsburg Confession, and its unanimously received Christian sense, and through God's grace to abide thereby firmly and constantly, in opposition to all corruptions which have entered.

CHAPTER I. OF ORIGINAL SIN.

First, a controversy concerning Original Sin has occurred among some theologians of the Augsburg Confession with respect to what it properly is. For one side contended that, because, through the fall of Adam, man's nature and essence are entirely corrupt now since the fall, the nature, substance and essence of the corrupt man, or indeed the principal, highest part of his being, namely, the rational soul in its highest state and principal powers, is Original Sin itself. This is called "natural" or "personal sin," for the reason that it is not a thought, word or work, but the nature itself, whence, as from a root, all other sins proceed, and on this account there is now since the fall, because the nature is corrupt through sin, no distinction whatever between the nature and essence of man and Original Sin.

But the other side taught, in opposition, that Original Sin is not properly the nature, substance or essence of man, *i.e.* man's body or soul, which even now since the fall are and remain the creatures and works of God in us, but it is something in the nature, body and soul of man, and in all his powers, namely, a horrible, deep, inexpressible corruption of the same, so that man is destitute of the righteousness wherein he was originally created, and in spiritual things is dead to good and perverted to all evil; and that, because of this corruption and inborn sin, which inheres in the nature, all actual sins flow forth from the heart; and that a distinction must, therefore, be observed between, on the one hand, the nature and essence of the corrupt man, or his body and soul, which as the creatures of God pertain to us even since the fall, and Original Sin, on the other, which is a work of the devil, whereby the nature has become corrupt.

Now this controversy concerning Original Sin is not unnecessary wrangling, but if this doctrine be rightly presented from and according to God's Word, and be separated from all Pelagian and Manichaean errors, then (as the Apology says, the benefits of Christ and his precious merit, and the gracious efficacy of the Holy Ghost, will be the better known and the more extolled; the honor which belongs to him will also be ascribed to God, if his work and creation in men be rightly distinguished from the work of the devil, whereby the nature has been corrupted. In order, therefore, to explain this controversy in the Christian way and according to God's Word, and to maintain the correct, pure doctrine, we will collect from the above-mentioned writings the thesis and antithesis, that is, the correct doctrine and its opposite, into brief paragraphs:

1. And first it is true that Christians should not only regard and recognize as sins the actual transgression

of God's commands; but also that the horrible, dreadful hereditary malady whereby the entire nature is corrupted, should above all things be regarded and recognized as sin, yea, as the chief sin, which is a root and fountain-head of all actual sins. This is called by Luther a "natural" or "personal sin," in order to declare that even though man would think, speak or do nothing evil (which, nevertheless, since the fall of our first parents, is impossible in this life), yet that his nature and person are sinful, *i.e.* by Original Sin, as a spiritual leprosy, he is thoroughly and utterly infected and corrupted before God; and on account of this corruption, and because of the fall of the first man, the nature or person is accused or condemned by God's Law, so that we are by nature the children of wrath, death and damnation, unless delivered therefrom by the merit of Christ.

2. It is also clear and true, as the Nineteenth Article of the Augsburg Confession teaches, that God is not a creator, author or cause of sin, but from the instigation of the devil, through one man, sin (which is a work of the devil) has entered the world (Rom. 5:12; 1 John 3:7). And even at the present day, in this connection of sin and nature [in this corruption of nature], God does not create and make sin in us, but with the nature which God at the present day still creates and makes in men, Original Sin is propagated from sinful seed, through carnal conception and birth of father and mother.

3. Thirdly, what [and how great] this hereditary evil is, no reason knows and understands, but, as the Smalcald Articles say, it must be learned and believed from the revelation contained in Scripture. And in the Apology this is briefly comprehended in the following paragraphs:

1. That this hereditary evil is the cause of our all being, by reason of the disobedience of Adam and Eve, in God's displeasure, and by nature children of wrath, as the apostle shows (Rom. 5:12 sqq.; Eph. 2:3).

2. Secondly, that there is an entire want or lack of the con-created original righteousness, or of God's image, according to which man was originally created in truth, holiness and righteousness; and likewise an inability and unfitness for all the things of God, or, as the Latin words read: Descriptio peccati originalis detrahit naturae non renovatae, et dona, et vim, seu facultatem et actus inchoandi et efficiendi spiritualia. That is: The definition of original sin takes away from the unrenewed nature the gifts, the power, and all activity for beginning and effecting anything in spiritual things.

3. That Original Sin (in human nature) is not only such an entire absence of all good in spiritual, divine things, but that it is at the same time also, instead of the lost image of God in man, a deep, wicked, horrible, fathomless, inscrutable and unspeakable corruption of the entire nature and all its powers, especially of the highest, principal powers of the soul in understanding, heart and will; that now, since the fall, man receives by inheritance *an inborn wicked disposition, an inward impurity of heart, wicked lusts and propensities;* that we all have by nature inherited from Adam such a heart, feeling and thoughts as, according to their highest powers and the light of reason, are naturally inclined and disposed directly contrary to God and his chief commands, yea, they are at enmity with God, especially as to what concerns divine and spiritual things. For, in other respects, as regards natural, external things which are subject to the reason, man still has, to a certain degree, understanding, power and ability, although very much weakened, all of which, nevertheless, has been so infected and contaminated by Original Sin that before God it is of no use.

4. The penalties of Original Sin, which God has imposed upon the children of Adam and upon Original Sin, are death, eternal damnation, and also other bodily and spiritual, temporal and eternal miseries, and the tyranny and dominion of the devil, so that human nature is subject to the kingdom of the devil, and has been surrendered to the power of the devil, and is held captive under his sway, who stupefies [fascinates] and leads astray many great, learned men in the world by means of dreadful error, heresy and other blindness, and otherwise delivers men to all sorts of crime.

5. Fifthly, this hereditary evil is so great and horrible that it can be covered and forgiven before God only for Christ's sake, and in the baptized and believing. Human nature also, which is deranged and corrupted thereby, must and can be healed only by the regeneration and renewal of the Holy Ghost, which, nevertheless, is only begun in this life, but will at length be fully completed in the life to come.

These points, which have been quoted here only in a summary way, are set forth more fully in the above-mentioned writings of the common confession of our Christian doctrine.

But this doctrine must now be so maintained and guarded that it may not incline either to the Pelagian or the Manichaean side. Therefore the contrary doctrine concerning this article, which is censured and rejected in our churches, should also be briefly reported.

1. And first, in opposition to the old and the new Pelagians, the following false opinions and dogmas are censured and rejected, namely, that Original Sin is only a *reatus* or debt, on account of what has been committed by another without any corruption of our nature.

2. Also that sinful, evil lusts are not sins, but conditions, or concreated and essential properties of the nature.

3. Or as though the above-mentioned defect and evil were not before God properly and truly sin, on

account of which man without Christ [unless he be grafted into Christ and be delivered through him] must be a child of wrath and damnation, and also be beneath the power and in the kingdom of Satan.

4. The following Pelagian errors and the like are also censured and rejected, namely: that nature, ever since the fall, is incorrupt, and that especially with respect to spiritual things it is entirely good and pure, and *in naturalibus, i.e.,* in its natural powers, it is perfect.

5. Or that Original Sin is only external, a slight, insignificant spot sprinkled or stain dashed upon the nature of man, or *corruptio tantum accidentium aut qualitatum, i.e.* a corruption only of some accidental things, along with and beneath which the nature, nevertheless, possesses and retains its integrity and power even in spiritual things.

6. Or that Original Sin is not a despoliation or deficiency, but only an external impediment to these spiritual good powers, as when a magnet is smeared with garlic-juice, whereby its natural power is not removed, but only impeded; or that this stain can be easily washed away, as a spot from the face or pigment from the wall.

7. They likewise are rebuked and rejected who teach that the nature has indeed been greatly weakened and corrupted through the fall, but that, nevertheless, it has not entirely lost all good with respect to divine, spiritual things, and that what is sung in our churches, "Through Adam's fall is all corrupt, Nature and essence human," is not true, but from natural birth we still have something good (small, little and inconsiderable though it be), namely: capacity, skill, aptness or ability in spiritual things to begin to work or co-work for something. For concerning external temporal, worldly things and transactions, which are subject to reason, there will be an explanation in the succeeding article.

These and doctrines of like kind, contrary to the truth, are censured and rejected for the reason that God's Word teaches that the corrupt nature, of and by itself, has no power for anything good in spiritual things, not even for the least, as good thoughts, but that, of and by itself, it can do nothing but sin. Gen. 6:5; 8:21.

Therefore [But] this doctrine must also be guarded, on the other side, from Manichaean errors. Accordingly, the following erroneous doctrines and the like are rejected, namely: that now, since the fall, human nature is in the beginning created pure and good, and that afterwards Original Sin from without is infused and mingled by Satan (as something essential) in the nature, as poison is mingled with wine [that in the beginning human nature was created by God pure and good, but that now, since the fall, Original Sin, etc.].

For although in Adam and Eve the nature was originally created pure, good and holy, nevertheless sin has not entered nature through the fall in the way fanatically taught by the Manichaeans, as though Satan had created or made something essentially evil, and mingled it with their nature. But since, from the seduction of Satan, through the fall, according to God's judgment and sentence, man, as a punishment, has lost his concreated original righteousness, human nature, as has been said above, is perverted and corrupt by this deprivation or deficiency, want and injury, which has been caused by Satan; so that at present the nature of all men, who in a natural way are conceived and born, is transmitted by inheritance with the same want and corruption. For since the fall human nature is not at first created pure and good, and only afterward corrupted by Original Sin, but in the first moment of our conception the seed whence man is formed is sinful and corrupt. Thus also Original Sin is not something existing of itself in or apart from the nature of the corrupt man, as it is also not the peculiar essence, body or soul of the corrupt man, or the man himself.

Original Sin, and the nature of man corrupted thereby, cannot and should not, therefore, be so distinguished, as though the nature before God were pure, good, holy, but Original Sin alone which dwells therein were evil.

Also, as Augustine writes of the Manichaeans, as though it were not the corrupt man himself who sins by reason of inborn Original Sin, but something different and foreign in man, and therefore that God, by the Law, accuses and condemns not the nature as corrupt by sin, but only the Original Sin therein. For, as stated above in the thesis, *i.e.* the explanation of the pure doctrine concerning Original Sin, the entire nature of man, which is born in the natural way of father and mother, is entirely and to the farthest extent corrupted and perverted by Original Sin, in body and soul, in all its powers that pertain and belong to the goodness, truth, holiness and righteousness concreated with it in Paradise. Nevertheless, the nature is not entirely exterminated or changed into another substance [diverse in genus or species], which, according to its essence, is not like our nature, and therefore cannot be one essence with us.

Because of this corruption the entire corrupt nature of man would be accused and condemned by the Law, if sin were not, for Christ's sake, forgiven.

But the Law accuses and condemns nature, not because we have been created men by God, but because we are sinful and wicked; not because and so far as nature and its essence, ever since the fall, is a work and creature of God in us, but because and so far as it has been poisoned and corrupted by sin.

But although Original Sin, like a spiritual poison or leprosy (as Luther says), has poisoned and corrupted all human nature, so that we cannot clearly show and point out the nature apart by itself, and Original Sin apart by itself; nevertheless, *the corrupt nature,* or essence of the corrupt man, body and soul, or the man himself whom God has created (and within whom dwells the Original Sin that also corrupts the nature, essence or the entire man), and *Original Sin,* which dwells in man's nature or essence, and corrupts it, are not one thing; as also in external leprosy the body which is leprous, and the leprosy on or in the body, are not, properly speaking, one thing. A distinction must be observed also between our nature, as created and preserved by God, and Original Sin, which dwells in the nature. These two must and also can be considered, taught and believed with their distinctions according to Holy Scripture.

The chief articles also of our Christian faith urge and compel us to preserve this distinction.

For, *first,* in the article of Creation, Scripture shows that not only has God before the fall created human nature, but also that, since the fall, it is a creature and work of God (Deut 32:6; Isa. 45:11; 54:5; 64:8; Acts 17:25; Rev. 4:11).

"Thine hands," says Job (10:8-12), "have made me and fashioned me together round about; yet thou dost destroy me. Remember, I beseech thee, that thou hast made me as the clay; and wilt thou bring me into dust again? Hast thou not poured me out as milk, and curdled me as cheese? Thou hast clothed me with skin and flesh, and fenced me with bones and sinews. Thou hast granted me life and favor, and thy visitation hath preserved my spirit."

"I will praise thee," says David (Ps. 139:14-16), "for I am fearfully and wonderfully made; marvellous are thy works; and that my soul knoweth right well. My substance was not hid from thee when I was made in secret, and curiously wrought in the lowest parts of the earth. Thine eyes did see my substance yet being unperfect; and in thy book all my members were written, which in continuance were fashioned, when as yet there was none of them."

In the Ecclesiastes of Solomon it is written [12:7]: "Then shall the dust return to the earth as it was, and the spirit to God who gave it."

These passages clearly testify that God ever since the fall is the Creator of man, and creates his body and soul. Therefore the corrupt man cannot be, without any distinction, sin itself, for otherwise God would be a creator of sins; as also our Small Catechism, in the explanation of the First Article, confesses: "I believe that God has created me with all that exists, that he has given and still preserves to me my body and soul, with all my limbs and senses, my reason and all the faculties of my mind." Likewise in the Large Catechism it is thus written: "I believe and mean to say that I am a creature of God, *i.e.* that he has given and constantly preserves to me my body, soul and life, members great and small, and all my senses." Although the same creature and work of God is lamentably corrupted by sin; for the mass (*massa*), from which God now forms and makes man was in Adam corrupted and perverted, and is thus transmitted by inheritance to us.

And here pious Christian hearts ought to consider the unspeakable goodness of God that God did not immediately cast from himself into hell-fire this corrupt, perverted, sinful mass, but from it forms and makes human nature of the present day, which is lamentably corrupted by sin, in order that by his dear Son he may cleanse it from all sin, sanctify and save it.

From this article now the distinction is indisputable and clear. For Original Sin does not originate with God. God is not a creator or author of sin. Original Sin also is not a creature or work of God, but a work of the devil.

If, now, there would be no difference whatever between the nature or essence of our body and soul, which is corrupted by Original Sin, and Original Sin, by which the nature is corrupted, it would follow either that God, because he is the creator of this our nature, also created and made Original Sin, which would also be his work and creature; or, because sin is a work of the devil, that Satan would be the creator of this our nature, soul and body, which must also be a work or creation of Satan if, without any distinction, our corrupt nature should be regarded as sin itself; both of which are contrary to the article of our Christian faith. Wherefore, in order that God's creation and work in man may be distinguished from the work of the devil, we say that it is God's creation that man has body and soul. Also that it is God's work that man can think, speak, do and work anything; for "in him we live, and move, and have our being." But that the nature is corrupt, that its thoughts, words and works are wicked, is originally a work of Satan, who, through sin, thus corrupted God's work in Adam, which from him is transmitted by inheritance to us.

Secondly, in the article of Redemption, the Scriptures testify forcibly that God's Son assumed our human nature without sin, so that he was, in all things, sin excepted, made like us, his brethren, Heb. 2:14. Hence all the old orthodox teachers have maintained that Christ, according to his assumed humanity, is, of one essence with us, his brethren; for he has assumed a human nature, which in all respects (sin alone excepted) is like our human nature in its essence and all essential attributes, and they have condemned the contrary doctrine as manifest heresy.

If, now, there were no distinction between the nature or essence of corrupt man and Original Sin, it must follow that either Christ did not assume our nature, because he did not assume sin; or that because he assumed our nature he also assumed sin; both of which are contrary to the Scriptures. But inasmuch as the Son of God assumed our nature, and not Original Sin, it is hence clear that human nature, ever since the fall, and Original Sin, are not one thing, but must be distinguished.

Thirdly, in the article of Sanctification, Scripture testifies that God cleanses, washes and sanctifies men from sin (1 John 1:7), and that Christ saves his people from their sins (Matt. 1:21). Sin, therefore, cannot be man himself; for God, for Christ's sake, receives man into grace, but he remains hostile to sin to eternity. Wherefore that Original Sin is baptized in the name of the Holy Trinity, sanctified and saved, and other such expressions, whereby we will not offend simple-minded people, that are found in the writings of the recent Manichaeans, are unchristian and dreadful to hear.

Fourthly, in the article of the Resurrection, Scripture testifies that it is precisely the substance of this our flesh, but without sin, which will rise again, and that in eternal life we will have and retain precisely this soul, but without sin.

If, now, there were no difference whatever between our corrupt body and soul, and Original Sin, it would follow, contrary to this article of the Christian faith, that either this our flesh will not rise again at the last day, and that in eternal life we will not have body and soul of the present essence, but another substance (or another soul), because

THE FORMULA OF CONCORD (1580) (continued)

then we will be without sin, or that [at the last day] sin also will rise again, and, in eternal life, will be and remain in the elect.

Hence it is clear that we must reject this doctrine [of the Manichaeans] (with all that depends upon it and follows from it), which asserts and teaches that Original Sin is the nature, substance, essence, body or soul itself or corrupt man, so that between our corrupt nature, substance and essence, and Original Sin, there is no distinction whatever. For the chief articles of our Christian faith forcibly and emphatically testify why a distinction should and must be maintained between man's nature or substance, which is corrupted by sin, and sin, whereby man is corrupted. For a simple statement of the doctrine and its opposite, with respect to the main point involved in this controversy, this is sufficient in this place, where the subject is not argued at length, but only the principal points are treated, article by article.

But with respect to terms and expressions, it is best and surest to use and retain the form of sound words employed concerning this article in the Holy Scriptures and the above-mentioned books.

Also to avoid strife about words, equivocal terms, *i.e.* words and expressions, which may be understood and used in several senses, should be carefully and distinctly explained, as when it is said: God creates the nature of men, where by the term "nature" the essence, body and soul of men are understood. But often the disposition or vicious quality is called its nature, as: "It is the nature of the serpent to bite and poison." Thus Luther says that sin and to sin are the disposition and nature of the corrupt man.

Therefore Original Sin properly signifies the deep corruption of our nature, as it is described in the Smalcald Articles. But sometimes we thereby understand the concrete or the subject, *i.e.* man himself with body and soul, wherein sin is and inheres, on account of which man is corrupted, infected with poison and sinful, as when Luther says: "Thy birth, thy nature, thy entire essence is sin", *i.e.* sinful and unclean.

Luther himself declares that by "natural sin," "personal sin," "essential sin," he means that not only words, thoughts and works are sin, but that the entire nature, person and essence of man is entirely corrupted [and is altogether depraved] by Original Sin.

Moreover, as to the Latin terms "substance" and "accident," we are of the opinion that, in sermons to congregations of plain people, they should be avoided, because such terms are unknown to ordinary men. But when learned men, in treating this subject, employ them among themselves or with others to whom this word is not unknown, as Eusebius, Ambrose and especially Augustine, and also still other eminent church-teachers, from the necessity of explaining this doctrine in opposition to the heretics, they regard them as constituting an "immediate division," *i.e.* a division between which there is no mean, so that everything which there is must be either "substance," *i.e.* an independent essence, or "accident," *i.e.* an incidental

matter which does not exist by itself essentially, but in another independent essence, and can be distinguished therefrom; which division Cyril and Basil also use.

And because, among others, it is also an indubitable, indisputable axiom in theology that every substance or self-existing essence, so far as it is a substance, is either God himself or a work and creation of God; Augustine, in many writings against the Manichaeans, in common with all true teachers, has, after due consideration and with earnestness, rejected and condemned the expression: *Peccatum originis est substantia vel natura, i.e.* Original Sin is man's nature or substance. In conformity with him, all the learned and intelligent also have always maintained that what does not exist by itself, neither is a part of another self-existing essence, but exists, subject to change, in another thing, is not a substance, *i.e.* something self-existing, but an accident, *i.e.* something incidental. Thus Augustine is accustomed to speak constantly in this way: Original Sin is not the nature itself, but an *accidens vitium in natura, i.e.* an incidental defect and damage in the nature. In this way also, in our schools and churches, previous to this controversy, [learned] men spoke, according to the rules of logic, freely and without any suspicion [of heresy], and, on this account, were never censured either by Dr. Luther or any orthodox teacher of our pure, evangelical Church.

For since it is the indisputable truth that everything that there is, is either a substance or an accident, *i.e.* either a self-existing essence or something incidental in it, as has been just shown and proved by the testimony of the church-teachers, and no truly intelligent man has ever doubted concerning this; if the question be asked whether Original Sin be a substance, *i.e.* such a thing as exists of itself, and not in another, or an accident, *i.e.* such a thing as does not exist by itself, but in another, and cannot exist or be by itself, necessity constrains us, and no one can evade it, to confess directly and candidly that Original Sin is no substance, but an accident.

Hence also the permanent peace of the Church of God with respect to this controversy will never be promoted, but the dissension will rather be strengthened and maintained, if the ministers of the Church remain in doubt as to whether Original Sin be a substance or accident, and whether it be thus rightly and properly named.

Hence if the churches and schools are to be relieved of this scandalous and very mischievous controversy, it is necessary that each and every one be properly instructed concerning this matter.

But if it be further asked as to what kind of an accident Original Sin is, it is another question, and one to which no philosopher, no Papist, no sophist, yea, no human reason, however acute it may be, can give the right explanation, but all understanding and every explanation of it must be derived solely from the Holy Scriptures, which testify that Original Sin is an unspeakable evil, and such an entire corruption of human nature that in it and all its internal and extenal powers nothing pure or good remains, but everything is entirely corrupt, so that, on account of Original Sin, man is in God's sight truly, spiritually dead, and, with all his powers, has died to that which is good.

In this way, then, by the word "accident," Original Sin is not extenuated [namely] when it is explained according to [the analogy of] God's Word, after the manner in which Dr. Luther, in his Latin exposition of the third chapter of Genesis, has written with great earnestness against the extenuation of Original Sin; but this word is employed only to designate the distinction between the work of God (which is our nature, notwithstanding that it is corrupt) and the work of the devil (which is sin), that inheres in God's work, and is a most profound and indescribable corruption of it.

Therefore Luther also has employed in his treatment of this subject the term "accident," as also the term "quality," and has not rejected them; but likewise, with especial earnestness and great zeal, he has taken the greatest pains to explain and to represent to each and every one what a horrible quality and accident it is, whereby human nature is not merely polluted, but is so deeply corrupted that nothing pure or uncorrupt remains in it, as his words on Ps. 90 run: Sive igitur peccatum originis *qualitatem* sive *morbum* vocavermus, profecto extremum malum est non solum pati aeternam iram et mortem, sed ne agnoscere quidem, quae pateris. That is: Whether we call Original Sin a *quality* or a *disease,* it is indeed the utmost evil not only to suffer the eternal wrath of God and eternal death, but also not to understand what we suffer. And again on Gen. 3: Qui isto veneno peccati originis a planta pedis usque ad verticem infecti sumus, siquidem in natura adhuc integra accidere. That is: We are infected by the poison of Original Sin from the sole of the foot to the crown of the head, inasmuch as this happened to us in a nature still perfect.

CHAPTER II. OF THE FREE WILL, OR HUMAN POWERS.

Since a dissent has occurred not only between the Papists and us, but also even among some theologians of the Augsburg Confession, concerning the free will, we will first of all exactly show the points of the controversy.

For since man, with respect to his free will, can be found and considered in four distinct, dissimilar states, the question at present is not concerning his condition with regard to the same *before the fall,* or his ability *since the fall,* and before his conversion, *in external things* which pertain to this temporal life; also not concerning his ability in spiritual things after he has been *regenerated* and is controlled by God's Spirit; or the sort of a free will he will have when he rises *from the dead.* But the principal question is only and alone as to the ability of the understanding and will of the *unregenerate* man in his *conversion* and regeneration from his own *powers surviving* since the fall: Whether when the Word of God is preached, and the grace of God is offered, he can prepare himself for grace, accept the same, and assent thereto? This is the question upon which now for quite a number of years there has been a controversy among some theologians in the churches of the Augsburg Confession.

For the one side has held and taught that although man, from his own powers, cannot fulfil God's command, or truly trust, fear and love God, without the grace of the Holy Ghost; nevertheless, before regeneration sufficient natural powers survive for him to prepare himself to a certain extent for grace, and to assent, although feebly; yet, if the grace of the Holy Ghost were not added thereto, he could by this accomplish nothing, but must be vanquished in the struggle.

On the other side, the ancient and modern enthusiasts have taught that God, through his Spirit, converts men and leads them to the saving knowledge of Christ, without any means and instrument of the creature, *i.e.* without the external preaching and hearing of God's Word.

Against both these parties the pure teachers of the Augsburg Confession have taught and contended that by the fall of our first parents man was so corrupted that, in divine things pertaining to our conversion and the salvation of our souls, he is by nature blind when the Word of God is preached, and neither does nor can understand it, but regards it foolishness, and also does not of himself draw nigh to God, but is and remains an enemy of God, until by the power of the Holy Ghost, through the preached and heard Word, out of pure grace, without any co-operation of his own, he is converted, made believing [presented with faith], regenerated and renewed.

In order to explain this controversy in a Christian manner, according to the guidance of God's Word, and by his grace to decide it, our doctrine, faith and confession are as follows:

Namely, that in spiritual and divine things the intellect, heart and will of the unregenerate man cannot, in any way, by their own natural powers, understand, believe, accept, think, will, begin, effect, do, work or concur in working anything, but they are entirely dead to good, and corrupt; so that in man's nature, since the fall, there is, before regeneration, not the least spark of spiritual power remaining still present, by which, of himself, he can prepare himself for God's grace, or accept the offered grace, or, for and of himself, be capable of it, or apply or accommodate himself thereto, or, by his own powers, be able of himself, as of himself, to aid, do, work or concur in working anything for his conversion, either entirely, or in half, or in even the least or most inconsiderable part, but he is the servant [and slave] of sin (John 8:34; Eph. 2:2; 2 Tim. 2:26). Hence the natural free will, according to its perverted disposition and nature, is strong and active only with respect to what is displeasing and contrary to God.

This declaration and general reply to the chief question and statement of the controversy presented in the introduction to this article, the following arguments from God's Word confirm and strengthen, and although they are contrary to proud reason and philosophy, yet we know that the wisdom of this perverted world is only foolishness before God, and that articles of faith should be judged only 'from God's Word.

For, first, although man's reason or natural understanding has still indeed a dim spark of the knowledge that there is a God, as also (Rom. 1:19 sqq.) of the doctrine of the Law; yet it is so ignorant, blind and perverted that when even the most able and learned men upon earth read or hear the Gospel of the Son of God and the promise of eternal salvation, they cannot, from their own powers, perceive, apprehend, understand or believe and regard it true, but

THE FORMULA OF CONCORD (1580) (continued)

the more diligence and earnestness they employ in order to comprehend, with their reason, these spiritual things, the less they understand or believe, and, before they become enlightened or taught of the Holy Ghost, they regard all this only as foolishness or fictions. (1 Cor. 2:14): "The natural man receiveth not the things of the Spirit of God; for they are foolishness to him." (1 Cor. 1:21): "For after that, in the wisdom of God, the world by wisdom knew not God, it pleased God, by the foolishness of preaching, to save them that believe." (Eph. 4:17 sq.): "They" (*i.e.* those not born again of God's Spirit) "walk in the vanity of their mind, having the understanding darkened, being alienated from the life of God, through the ignorance that is in them, because of the blindness of their heart." (Matt. 13:11 sqq. [Luke 8:18]): "They seeing, see not, and hearing, they hear not, neither do they understand; but it is given unto you to know the mysteries of the kingdom of heaven." (Rom. 3:11, 12): "There is none that understandeth, there is none that seeketh after God. They are all gone out of the way, they are all together become unprofitable; there is none that doeth good, no, not one."

So, too, the Scriptures expressly call natural men, in spiritual and divine things, darkness. (Eph. 5:8; Acts 26:18; John 1:5): "The light shineth in darkness" (*i.e.* in the dark, blind world, which does not know or regard God), "and the darkness comprehendeth it not." Also the Scriptures teach that man in sins is not only weak and sick, but also entirely dead (Eph. 2:1, 5; Col. 2:13).

As now a man who is physically dead cannot, of his own powers, prepare or adapt himself to obtain again temporal life; so the man who is spiritually dead in sins cannot, of his own strength, adapt or apply himself to the acquisition of spiritual and heavenly righteousness and life, unless he be delivered and quickened by the Son of God from the death of sin.

Therefore the Scriptures deny to the understanding, heart and will of the natural man all aptness, skill, capacity and ability in spiritual things, to think, to understand, begin, will, undertake, do, work or concur in working anything good and right, as of himself. (2 Cor. 3:5): "Not that we are sufficient of ourselves, to think anything, as of ourselves; but our sufficiency is of God." (Rom. 3:12): "They are altogether unprofitable." (John 8:7): "My Word hath no place in you." (John 1:5): "The darkness comprehendeth" (or receiveth) "not the light." (1 Cor. 2:14): "The natural man perceiveth not" (or, as the Greek word properly signifies, taketh not, comprehendeth not, receiveth not) "the things of the Spirit," *i.e.* he is not capable of spiritual things; "for they are foolishness unto him; neither can he know them." Much less can he truly believe the Gospel, or assent thereto and regard it as truth. (Rom. 8:7): "The carnal mind," or that of the natural man, "is enmity against God; for it is not subject to the Law of God, neither indeed can be." And, in a word, that remains eternally true which the Son of God says (John 15:5): "Without me ye can do nothing." And Paul (Phil. 2:13): "It is God which worketh in you, both to will and to do of his good pleasure." This precious passage is very comforting to all godly Christians, who feel and experience in their hearts a small spark or earnest longing for divine grace and eternal salvation; for they know that God has kindled in their hearts this beginning of true godliness, and that he will further strengthen and help them in their great weakness to persevere in true faith unto the end.

To this also all the prayers of the saints relate, in which they pray that they may be taught, enlightened and sanctified of God, and thereby declare that those things which they ask of God they cannot have from their own natural powers; as in Ps. 119, alone, David prays more than ten times that God may impart to him understanding, that he may rightly receive and learn the divine doctrine. [Very many] similar prayers are in the writings of Paul (Eph. 1:17; Col. 1:9; Phil. 1:9). These prayers and the testimonies concerning our ignorance and inability have been written, not for the purpose of rendering us idle and remiss in reading, hearing and meditating upon God's Word, but first that from the heart we should thank God that, through his Son, he has delivered us from the darkness of ignorance and the captivity of sin and death, and, through baptism and the Holy Ghost, has regenerated and illumined us.

And after God, through the Holy Ghost in baptism, has kindled and made a beginning of the true knowledge of God and faith, we should pray him without intermission that, through the same Spirit and his grace, by means of the daily exercise of reading, and applying to practice, God's Word, he may preserve in us faith and his heavenly gifts, strengthen us from day to day, and support us to the end. For unless God himself be our school-teacher, we can study and learn nothing that is acceptable to him and that is salutary to ourselves and others.

Secondly, God's Word testifies that the understanding, heart and will of the natural, unregenerate man in divine things are not only turned entirely from God, but also turned and perverted against God to every evil. Also, that he is not only weak, feeble, impotent and dead to good, but also through Original Sin is so lamentably perverted, infected and corrupted that, by his disposition and nature, he is entirely evil, perverse and hostile to God, and that, with respect to everything that is displeasing and contrary to God, he is strong, alive and active. (Gen. 8:22): "The imagination of man's heart is evil from his youth." (Jer. 17:9): "The heart of man is defiant and despairing," or perverted and full of misery, "so that it is unfathomable." This passage St. Paul explains (Rom. 8): "The carnal mind is enmity against God." (Gal. 5:17): "The flesh lusteth against the spirit; . . . and these are contrary the one to the other." (Rom. 7:14): "We know that the Law is spiritual; but I am carnal, sold under sin." And soon afterward (18, 23): "I know that in me, that is, in my flesh, dwelleth no good thing. For I delight in the Law of God, after the inward man," which, through the Holy Ghost, is regenerate; "but I see another law in my members, warring against the law of my mind, and bringing me into captivity to the law of sin."

If, now, in St. Paul and in other regenerate men the natural or carnal free will, even after regeneration, strives against God's Law, much more perverse and hostile to God's Law and will, will it be before regeneration. Hence it is manifest (as in the article concerning Original Sin it is further declared, to which, for the sake of brevity, we now refer) that the free will, from its own natural powers, not only cannot work or co-work as to anything for its own conversion, righteousness and salvation, or follow, believe or assent to the Holy Ghost, who through the Gospel offers him grace and salvation, but rather from its innate, wicked, perverse nature it hostilely resists God and his will, unless it be enlightened and controlled by God's Spirit.

On this account, also, the Holy Scriptures compare the heart of the unregenerate man to a hard stone, which does not yield to the one who touches it, but resists, and to a rough block, and to a wild, unmanageable beast; not that man, since the fall, is no longer a rational creature, or is converted to God without hearing and meditating upon God's Word, or in external, worldly things cannot understand, or do or abstain from doing, anything of his free will, good or evil.

For, as Doctor Luther says upon Ps. 90: "In worldly and external affairs, which pertain to the livelihood and maintenance of the body, man is intelligent, reasonable and very active, but in spiritual and divine things, which pertain to the salvation of the soul, man is like a pillar of salt, like Lot's wife, yea, like a log and a stone, like a lifeless statue, which uses neither eyes nor mouth, neither sense nor heart. For man neither sees nor perceives the fierce and terrible wrath of God on account of sin and death [resulting from it], but he continues even knowingly and willingly in his security, and thereby falls into a thousand dangers, and finally into eternal death and damnation; and no prayers, no supplications, no admonitions, yea, also no threats, no reprimands are of any avail; yea, all teaching and preaching are lost upon him, until he is enlightened, converted and regenerated by the Holy Ghost. For this [renewal of the Holy Ghost] no stone or block, but man alone, was created. And although God, according to his just, strict sentence, eternally casts away the fallen evil spirits, he has nevertheless, out of pure mercy, willed that poor fallen human nature might again become capable and participant of conversion, the grace of God and eternal life; not from its own natural [active or] effective skill, aptness or capacity (for the nature of man is perverse enmity against God), but from pure grace, through the gracious efficacious working of the Holy Ghost." And this Dr. Luther calls capacity (not active, but passive) which he thus explains: Quando patres liberum arbitrium defendunt, capacitatem libertatis ejus praedicant, quod scilicet verti potest ad bonum per gratiam Dei et fieri revera liberum, ad quod creatum est. That is: When the Fathers defend the free will, they say of it that it is capable of freedom in so far that, through God's grace, it can be turned to good, and become truly free, for which it was created. Tom. 1, p. 236.

(Augustine also has written to like effect, lib. 2. *Contra Julianum.* Dr. Luther on Hosea 6; also in the Church-Postils on the Epistle for Good Friday; also on the Gospel for the third Sunday after Epiphany.)

But before man is enlightened, converted, regenerated, renewed and led by the Holy Ghost, he can of himself and of his own natural powers begin, work or co-operate as to anything in spiritual things, and in his own conversion or regeneration, as little as a stone or a block or clay. For although he can control the outward members and hear the Gospel, and to a certain extent meditate upon it and discourse concerning it, as is to be seen in the Pharisees and hypocrites; nevertheless he regards it foolishness, and cannot believe it, and also in this case he is worse than a block, in that he is rebellious and hostile to God's will, if the Holy Ghost be not efficacious in him, and do not kindle and work in him faith and other virtues pleasing to God, and obedience.

Thirdly, for the Holy Scriptures, besides, refer conversion, faith in Christ, regeneration, renewal, and all that belongs to their efficacious beginning and completion, not to the human powers of the natural free will, either entirely, or half, or the least or most inconsiderable part; but ascribe them *in solidum, i.e.* entirely, alone to the divine working and the Holy Ghost, as also the Apology teaches.

The reason and free will have the power, to a certain extent, to live an outwardly decent life; but to be born anew, and to obtain inwardly another heart, sense and disposition, this only the Holy Ghost effects. He opens the understanding and heart to understand the Scriptures and to give heed to the Word, as it is written (Luke 24:45): "Then opened he their understanding, that they might understand the Scriptures." Also (Acts 16:11): "Lydia heard us; whose heart the Lord opened, that she attended unto the things which were spoken of Paul." "He worketh in us, both to will and to do of his own good pleasure" (Phil. 2:13). He gives repentance (Acts 5:31; 2 Tim. 2:25). He works faith (Phil. 1:29): "For unto you it is given, in behalf of Christ, not only to believe on him." (Eph. 2:8): "It is the gift of God." (John 6:29): "This is the work of God, that ye believe on Him whom he hath sent." He gives an understanding heart, seeing eyes, and hearing ears (Deut. 29:4; Matt. 13:15). The Holy Ghost is a spirit of regeneration and renewal (Tit. 3:5, 6). He takes away the hard heart of stone, and gives a new tender heart of flesh, that we may walk in his commands (Ez. 11:19; Deut. 30:6; Ps. 51:10). He creates us in Christ Jesus to good works (Eph 2:10), and makes us new creatures (2 Cor. 5:17; Gal. 6:15). And, in short, every good gift is of God (James 1:17). No one can come to Christ unless the Father draw him (John 6:44). No one knoweth the Father, save him to whom the Son will reveal him (Matt. 11:27). No one can call Christ Lord, but by the Holy Ghost (1 Cor. 12:3). "Without me," says Christ, "ye can do nothing" (John 15:5). All "our sufficiency is of God" (2 Cor. 3:5). "What hast thou which thou didst not receive? Now, if thou didst receive it, why dost thou glory as if thou hadst not received it?" (1 Cor. 4:7). And indeed St. Augustine writes particularly of this passage, that by it he was constrained to lay aside the former erroneous opinion which he had held concerning this subject. *De Proedestinatione,* cap. 3: Gratiam Dei in eo tantum consistere, quod in praeconis veritatis Dei voluntas nobis revelaretur; ut autem praedicato nobis evangelio consentiremus, nostrum esse proprium, et ex nobis esse. Item erravi (inquit), eum dicerem, nostrum esse credere et velle; Dei autem, dare credentibus et volentibus facultatem operandi. That is: "I erred in this,

THE FORMULA OF CONCORD (1580) (continued)

that I held that the grace of God consists alone in that God, in the preaching of the truth, reveals his will; but that we consent to the preached Gospel is our own work, and stands within our own powers." For St. Augustine also writes further: "I erred when I said that it stands within our own power to believe the Gospel and to will; but it is God's work to give to them that believe and will the power of working."

This doctrine is founded upon God's Word, and conformable to the Augsburg Confession and other writings above mentioned, as the following testimonies prove.

In Article XX, the Confession says as follows: "Because through faith the Holy Ghost is given, the heart thus becomes qualified for the doing of good works. For before, because it is without the Holy Ghost, it is too weak, and besides is in the devil's power, who drives poor human nature into many sins." And a little afterward: "For without faith and Christ human nature and ability is much too weak to do good works."

These passages clearly testify that the Augsburg Confession pronounces the will of man in spiritual things as anything else than free, but says that he is the devil's captive; how, then, from his own powers, is he to be able to turn himself to the Gospel or Christ?

The Apology teaches of the free will thus: "We also say that reason has, to a certain extent, a free will; for in the things which are to be comprehended by the reason we have a free will." And a little after: "For such hearts as are without the Holy Ghost are without the fear of God, without faith. Without trust towards God they do not believe that God listens to them, that he forgives their sins, and helps them in necessities; therefore they are godless. Now, 'a corrupt tree cannot bring forth good fruit,' and 'without faith it is impossible to please God.' Therefore, although we concede that it is within our ability to perform such an outward work, nevertheless, we say that, in spiritual things, the free will and reason have no ability," etc. Here it is clearly seen that the Apology ascribes no ability to the will of man, either for beginning good or for itself co-operating.

In the Smalcald Articles the following errors concerning the free will are also rejected: "That man has a free will to do good and omit evil," etc. And shortly afterward the error is also rejected: "That it is not founded upon Scripture, that, for a good work, the Holy Ghost, with his grace, is necessary."

It is further maintained in the Smalcald Articles as follows: "And this repentance, in Christians, continues until death, because through the entire life it contends with sin remaining in the flesh, as Paul (Rom. 7:23) shows that he wars with the Law in his members, etc.; and this, not by his own powers, but by the gift of the Holy Ghost, that follows the remission of sins. This gift daily cleanses and purges the remaining sins, and works so as to render man pure and holy." These words say nothing whatever of our will, or that it also of itself works in regenerate men, but ascribe it to the gift of the Holy Ghost, which cleanses man

and makes him daily more godly and holy, and thus our own powers are entirely excluded therefrom.

In the Large Catechism of Dr. Luther it is written thus: "And I also am a part and member of the same, a participant and joint owner of all the good it possesses, brought to it and incorporated into it by the Holy Ghost, in that I have heard and continue to hear the Word of God, which is the means of entrance. For formerly, before we had attained to this, we were of the devil, knowing nothing of God and of Christ. Thus, until the last day, the Holy Ghost abides with the holy congregation or Christian people. By means of this congregation he brings us to Christ and teaches, and preaches to us the Word, whereby he works and promotes sanctification, causing [this community] daily to grow and become strong in the faith and the fruits of the Spirit, which he produces."

In these words the Catechism mentions not a word concerning our free will or co-operation, but refers everything to the Holy Ghost, viz. that, through the office of the ministry, he brings us into the Church of God, wherein he sanctifies us, and so provides that we daily grow in faith and good works.

And although the regenerate, even in this life, advance so far that they will what is good, and love it, and even do good and grow in it, nevertheless this (as above quoted) is not of our will and ability, but the Holy Ghost, as Paul himself speaks concerning this, works "to will and to do" (Phil. 2:13). As also in Eph. 2:10 he ascribes this work to God alone, when he says: "For we are his workmanship, created in Christ Jesus unto good works, which God hath before ordained that we should walk therein."

In the Small Catechism of Dr. Luther it is thus written: "I believe that I cannot by my own reason or strength believe in Jesus Christ, my Lord, or come to him; but the Holy Ghost has called me through the Gospel, enlightened me by his gifts, and sanctified and preserved me in the true faith; in like manner as he calls, gathers, enlightens and sanctifies the whole Christian Church on earth, and preserves it in union with Jesus Christ in the true faith," etc.

And in the explanation of the second petition of the Lord's Prayer the following words occur: "When is this effected? When our Heavenly Father gives us his Holy Spirit, so that by his grace we believe his holy Word and live a godly life," etc.

These passages declare that, from our own powers, we cannot come to Christ, but God must give us his Holy Ghost, by whom we are enlightened, sanctified, and thus brought to Christ through faith, and upheld in him; and no mention is made of our will or co-operation.

To this we will add a passage in which Dr. Luther expresses himself, together with a solemn declaration added thereto, that he intends to persevere in this doctrine unto the end, in his Large Confession concerning the Holy Supper: "Hereby I reject and condemn, as nothing but error all dogmas which extol our free will; as they directly conflict with this help and grace of our Saviour, Jesus Christ. For since, out of Christ, death and sin are our lords, and the devil our god and prince, there can be no power or might, no wisdom or understanding, in us, whereby we can qualify ourselves for, or strive after righteousness and life; but we are evidently the blinded and imprisoned ones of sin and the devil, to do and to think what pleases him and is contrary to God and his commandments."

In these words Dr. Luther of godly and holy memory ascribes no power whatever to our free will to qualify itself for righteousness or strive after it, but says that man is blinded and held captive, to do only the devil's will and that which is contrary to God the Lord. Therefore here there is no co-operation of our will in the conversion of man, and man must be drawn and be born anew of God; otherwise the thought of turning one's self to the Holy Gospel for the purpose of accepting it cannot arise in our hearts. Of this matter Dr. Luther also wrote in his book *De Servo Arbitrio, i.e.* Of the Captive Will of Man, in opposition to Erasmus, and well and thoroughly elucidated and supported this position, and afterward in his magnificent exposition of the book of Genesis, especially of chapter 26, he repeated and explained it. He has there also in the best and most careful way guarded against all misunderstanding and perversion, his opinion and understanding of some other peculiar disputations introduced incidentally by Erasmus, as Of Absolute Necessity, etc.; to which we also hereby appeal, and we recommend it to others.

On this account the doctrine is incorrect by which it is asserted that the unregenerate man has still sufficient power to desire to receive the Gospel and to be comforted by it, and that thus the natural human will co-operates in a manner in conversion. For such an erroneous opinion is contrary to the holy, divine Scriptures, the Christian Augsburg Confession, its Apology, the Smalcald Articles, the Large and the Small Catechisms of Luther, and other writings of this excellent highly [divinely] illumined theologian.

This doctrine concerning the inability and wickedness of our natural free will, and concerning our conversion and regeneration, viz. that it is a work of God alone and not of our powers, is impiously abused both by enthusiasts and by Epicureans; and by their speeches many persons have become disorderly and irregular, and in all the Christian exercises of prayer, reading and devout meditation have become idle and indolent, as they say that, because from their own natural powers they are unable to convert themselves to God, they will always strive with all their might against god, or wait until God violently convert them against their will; or because they can do nothing in these spiritual things, but everything is of the operation alone of God the Holy Ghost, they will neither hear nor read the Word nor use the sacrament, but wait until God, without means, infuses from heaven his gifts, so that they can truly, in themselves, feel and perceive that God has converted them.

Other desponding hearts [our godly doctrine concerning the free will not being rightly understood] might perhaps fall into hard thoughts and perilous doubt as whether God have elected them, and through the Holy Ghost will work also in them his gifts, especially when they are sensible of

no strong, them his gifts, especially when they are sensible of no strong, burning faith and sincere obedience, but only weakness, fear and misery.

For this reason we will now relate still further from God's Word how man is converted to God, how and through what means (namely, through the oral Word and the holy Sacraments) the Holy Ghost is efficacious in us, and is willing to work and bestow, in our hearts, true repentance, faith and new spiritual power and ability for good, and how we should act ourselves towards these means, and [how] use them.

It is not God's will that any one should perish, but that all men should be converted to him and be saved eternally. (Ez. 33:11): "As I live, I have no pleasure in the death of the wicked; but that the wicked turn from his way and live." (John 3:16): "For God so loved the world that he gave his only-begotten Son, that whosoever believeth in him should not perish, but have everlasting life."

Therefore God, out of his immense goodness and mercy, causes his divine eternal Law and his wonderful plan concerning our redemption, namely, the holy, only saving Gospel of his dear Son, our only Saviour and Redeemer, to be publicly proclaimed; and by this [preaching] collects for himself from the human race an eternal Church, and works in the hearts of men true repentance and knowledge of sins, and true faith in the Son of God, Jesus Christ. And by this means, and in no other way, namely, through his holy Word, when it is heard as preached or is read, and the holy Sacraments when they are used according to the Word, God desires to call men to eternal salvation, to draw them to himself, and to convert, regenerate and sanctify them. (1 Cor. 1:21): "For after that, in the wisdom of God, the world by wisdom knew not God, it pleased God, by the foolishness of preaching, to save them that believe." (Acts 10:5, 6): Peter "shall tell thee what thou oughtest to do." (Rom. 10:17): "Faith cometh by hearing, and hearing by the Word of God." (John 17:17, 20): "Sanctify them by thy truth; thy Word is truth," etc. "Neither pray I for these alone; but for them also which shall believe on me through their word." Therefore the eternal Father calls down from heaven, concerning his dear Son, and concerning all who, in his name, preach repentance and forgiveness of sins: "Hear ye him" (Matt. 17:5).

This preaching [of God's Word] all who wish to be saved ought to hear. For the preaching and hearing of God's Word are instruments of the Holy Ghost, by, with and through which he desires to work efficaciously, and to convert men to God, and to work in them both to will and to do.

This Word man can externally hear and read, even though he be not yet converted to God and regenerate; for in these external things, as above said, man, even since the fall, has, to a certain extent, a free will, so that he can go to church and hear or not hear the sermon.

Through this means, namely, the preaching and hearing of his Word, God works, and breaks our hearts, and draws man, so that through the preaching of the Law he sees his sins and God's wrath, and experiences in his heart true terrors, repentance and sorrow [contrition], and, through

THE FORMULA OF CONCORD (1580) (continued)

the preaching and consideration of the holy Gospel concerning the gracious forgiveness of sins in Christ, a spark of faith is kindled in him, which accepts the forgiveness of sins for Christ's sake, and comforts itself with the promise of the Gospel, and thus the Holy Ghost (who works all this) is given to the heart (Gal. 4:6).

Although now both, viz. the planting and watering of the preacher, and the running and willing of the hearer, would be to no purpose, and no conversion would follow, if the power and efficacy of the Holy Ghost were not added thereto, who, through the Word preached and heard, enlightens and converts the hearts, so that men believe this Word, and assent thereto; nevertheless neither preacher nor hearer should doubt this grace and efficacy of the Holy Ghost, but should be certain, if the Word of God is preached purely and clearly, according to the command and will of God, and men listen attentively and earnestly, and meditate upon it, that God is certainly present with his grace, and grants, as has been said, what man can otherwise from his own powers neither accept nor give. For concerning the presence, operation and gifts of the Holy Ghost we should not and cannot always judge from sense, *i.e.* as to how and when they are experienced in the heart; but because they are often covered and occur in great weakness, we should be certain, from and according to the promise, that preaching and hearing the Word of God is [truly] an office and work of the Holy Ghost, whereby he is certainly efficacious and works in our hearts (2 Cor. 2:14 sqq.) [3:5 sqq.].

But if a man will not hear preaching or read God's Word, but despises the Word and Church of God, and thus dies and perishes in his sins, he neither can console himself with God's eternal election nor obtain his mercy; for Christ, in whom we are chosen, offers to all men his grace in Word and holy sacraments, and wishes earnestly that the Word he heard, and has promised that where two or three are gathered together in his name, and are occupied with his holy Word, he will be in their midst.

But where such a man despises the instrument of the Holy Ghost, and will not hear, no injustice befalls him if the Holy Ghost do not enlighten him, but he be allowed to remain in the darkness of his unbelief, and to perish; for of this it is written (Matt. 23:37): "How often would I have gathered thy children together, even as a hen gathereth her chickens under her wings, and ye would not!"

And in this respect it might well be said that man is not a stone or block. For a stone or block does not resist that which moves it, and does not understand and is not sensible of what is being done with it, as a man, as long as he is not converted, with his will resists God the Lord. And it is nevertheless true that a man before his conversion is still a rational creature, having an understanding and will, yet not an understanding with respect to divine things, or a will to will something good and salutary. Yet he can do nothing whatever for his conversion (as has also been said [frequently] above), and is in this respect much worse than a stone and block; for he resists the Word and will of God, until God awakens him from the death of sin, enlightens and renews him.

And although God does not force man to become godly (for those who always resist the Holy Ghost and persistently oppose the known truth, as Stephen says of the hardened Jews (Acts 7:51), will not be converted), yet God the Lord draws the man whom he wishes to convert, and draws him, too, in such a way that his understanding, in place of darkened, becomes enlightened, and his will, in place of perverse, becomes obedient. And the Scriptures call this "creating a new heart" (Ps. 51:10).

For this reason it cannot be correctly said that man, before his conversion, has a certain *modus agendi,* namely, a way of working in divine things something good and salutary. For inasmuch as man, before his conversion, is dead in sins (Eph. 2:5), there can be in him no power to work anything good in divine things, and therefore he has also no *modus agendi,* or way of working in divine things. But when a declaration is made concerning this matter as to how God works in man, God has nevertheless a *modus agendi,* or way of working in a man, as in a rational creature, quite different from his way of working in another creature that is irrational, or in a stone and block. Nevertheless to man, before his conversion, a *modus agendi,* or any way of working something good in spiritual things, cannot be ascribed.

But when man is converted, and is thus enlightened, and his will is renewed, man (so far as he is regenerate or is a new man) wills what is good, and "delights in the Law of God after the inward man" (Rom. 7:22), and henceforth does good to such an extent and as long as he is impelled by God's Spirit, as Paul says (Rom. 8:14): "For as many as are led by the Spirit of God, they are the sons of God." And this impulse of the Holy Ghost is not a *coactio* or coercion, but the converted man does good spontaneously, as David says (Ps. 110:4): "Thy people shall be willing in the day of thy power." And nevertheless that [the strife of the flesh and spirit] also remains in the regenerate, of which St. Paul wrote (Rom. 7:22 sq.): "For I delight in the Law of God after the inward man: but I see another law in my members, warring against the law of my mind, and bringing me into captivity to the law of sin which is in my members." Also (v. 25): "So then with my mind I myself serve the Law of God; but with the flesh the law of sin." Also (Gal. 5:17): "For the flesh lusteth against the spirit, and the spirit against the flesh; and these are contrary the one to the other; so that ye cannot do the things that ye would."

From this, then, it follows that as soon as the Holy Ghost, as has been said, through the Word and holy Sacraments, has begun in us this his work of regeneration and renewal, it is certain that, through the power of the Holy Ghost, we can and should co-operate, although still in great weakness. But this does not occur from our fleshly natural powers, but from the new powers and gifts which the Holy Ghost has begun in us in conversion, as St. Paul expressly and earnestly exhorts that "as workers together" we "receive not the grace of God in vain" (2 Cor. 6:1). This, then, is nothing else, and should thus be understood, than that the converted man does good to such an extent and so long as God, by his Holy Spirit, rules, guides and leads him, and that as soon as God would withdraw from him his gracious hand, he could not continue for a moment in obedience to God. But if this would be understood thus [if any one would take the expression of St. Paul in this sense], that the converted man co-works with the Holy Ghost, in the manner that two horses together draw a wagon, this can in no way be conceded without prejudice to the divine truth.

[(2 Cor. 6:1): We who are servants or co-workers with God beseech you who are "God's husbandry" and "God's building" (1 Cor. 3:9) to imitate our example, that the grace of God may not be among you in vain (1 Cor. 15:10), but that ye may be the temple of God, living and dwelling in you (2 Cor. 6:16)].

Therefore there is a great difference between baptized and unbaptized men. For since, according to the doctrine of St. Paul (Gal. 3:27), all who have been baptized have put on Christ, and thus are truly regenerate, they have now a liberated will, i.e. as Christ says they have been made free again (John 8:36); for this reason they afterward not only hear the Word, but also, although in great weakness, are able to assent to it and accept it.

For since we, in this life, receive only the first-fruits of the Spirit, and the new birth is not complete, but only begun in us, the combat and struggle of the flesh against the spirit remains even in the elect and truly regenerate man, in which there is a great difference perceptible not only among Christians, in that one is weak and another strong in the spirit, but also every Christian experiences in himself that at one time he is joyful in spirit, and at another fearful and alarmed; at one time ardent in love, strong in faith and hope, and at another cold and weak.

But when the baptized have acted against conscience, allowed sin to prevail in them, and thus have grieved and lost the Holy Ghost in them, they need not be rebaptized, but must again be converted, as has been sufficiently said before.

For it is once for all true that in genuine conversion a change, new emotion [renewal] and movement in understanding, will and heart must occur, namely, that the heart perceive sin, dread God's wrath, turn itself from sin, perceive and accept the promise of grace in Christ, have good spiritual thoughts, a Christian purpose and diligence, and strive against the flesh. For where none of these occurs or is present there is also no true conversion. But since the question is concerning the efficient cause, i.e. who works this in us, and whence man has this, and how he attains it, this doctrine is thus stated: Because the natural powers of man cannot act or help thereto (1 Cor. 2:14; 2 Cor. 3:5), God, out of his infinite goodness and mercy, comes first to us, and causes his holy Gospel to be preached, whereby the Holy Ghost desires to work and accomplish in us this conversion and renewal, and through preaching and meditation upon his Word kindles in us faith and other divine virtues, so that they are gifts and operations of the Holy Ghost alone. This doctrine also directs us to the means whereby the Holy Ghost desires to begin and work this [which we have mentioned], instructs us how those gifts are preserved, strengthened and increased, and admonishes us that we should not receive this grace of God in vain, but diligently ponder how grievous a sin it is to hinder and resist such operations of the Holy Ghost.

From this thorough explanation of the entire doctrine concerning the free will we can now judge also with respect to the last of the questions upon which, for quite a number of years, there has been controversy in the churches of the Augsburg Confession: (Whether man before, in or after his conversion resists the Holy Ghost, or does nothing whatever, but only suffers what God works in him [or is purely passive]? Whether in conversion man is like a block? Whether the Holy Ghost is given to those who resist him? Whether conversion occur by coercion, so that God coerces men to conversion against their wills?), and the opposite dogmas and errors are seen, exposed, censured and rejected, namely:

1. First, the folly of the Stoics and Manichaeans, [who asserted] that everything that happens must so happen, and that man does everything from coercion, and that even in outward things the will of man has no freedom or ability to afford to a certain extent external righteousness and respectable deportment, and to avoid external sins and vices, or that the will of man is coerced to external wicked deeds, inchastity, robbery and murder, etc.

2. Secondly, the gross error of the Pelagians, that the free will, from its own natural powers and without the Holy Ghost, can turn itself to God, believe the Gospel, and be obedient in heart to God's Law, and by this, its voluntary obedience, can merit the forgiveness of sins and eternal life.

3. Thirdly, the error of the Papists and scholastics, who have presented it in a somewhat more subtile form, and have taught that man from his own natural powers can make a beginning of doing good and of his own conversion, and that then the Holy Ghost, because man is too weak to bring it to completion, comes to the aid of the good that has been begun from his own natural powers.

4. Fourthly, the doctrine of the Synergists, who pretend that man is not absolutely dead to good in spiritual things, but is badly wounded and half dead. Therefore, although the free will is too weak to make a beginning, and by its own powers to convert itself to God, and to be obedient in heart to God's Law; nevertheless when the Holy Ghost makes a beginning, and calls us through the Gospel, and offers his grace, the forgiveness of sins and eternal salvation, that then the free will, from its own natural powers, meets God, and to a certain extent, although feebly, can act, help and co-operate thereto, can qualify itself for, and apply itself to grace, and embrace and accept it, and believe the Gospel, and also, in the progress and support of this work, it can co-operate, by its own powers, with the Holy Ghost.

But, on the contrary, it has above been shown at length that such power, namely, the *facultas applicandi se ad gratiam, i.e.* to qualify one's self from nature for grace, does not proceed from our own natural powers, but alone from the operation of the Holy Ghost.

5. Also the following doctrine of the popes and monks, that, since regeneration, man, in this life, can

completely fulfil the Law of God, and through the fulfilment of the Law be righteous before God and merit eternal life.

6. On the other hand, the enthusiasts should be rebuked with great severity and zeal, and should in no way be tolerated in the Church of God, who fabricate that God, without any means, without the hearing of the divine Word, and without the use of the holy Sacraments, draws man to himself, and enlightens, justifies and saves him.

7. Also those who fabricate that in conversion and regeneration God so creates a new heart and new man that the substance and essence of the old Adam, and especially the rational soul, are altogether annihilated, and a new essence of the soul is created out of nothing. This error St. Augustine expressly rebukes on Psalm 25, where he quotes the passage from Paul (Eph. 4:22): "Put off the old man," etc., and explains it in the following words: "That no one may think that some substance is to be laid aside, he has explained what it is to lay aside the old man, and to put on the new, when he says in the succeeding words: 'Putting away lying, speak the truth.' So that is to put off the old man and to put on the new."

8. Also if the following expressions be used without being explained, viz. that the will of man, before, in, and after conversion, resists the Holy Ghost, and that the Holy Ghost is given to those who resist him.

For from the preceding explanation it is manifest that where no change whatever occurs through the Holy Ghost to that which is good in understanding, heart and will, and man does not at all believe the promise, and is not rendered fit by God for grace, but entirely resists the Word, there no conversion has occurred or can exist. For conversion is such a change through the operation of the Holy Ghost, in the understanding, will and heart of man, that, by this operation of the Holy Ghost, man can receive the offered grace. And indeed all those who obstinately and persistently resist the operations and movements of the Holy Ghost, which take place through the Word, do not receive, but grieve and lose the Holy Ghost.

There remains, nevertheless, also in the regenerate a refractoriness of which the Scriptures speak, namely, that "the flesh lusteth against the spirit" (Gal. 5:17), that "fleshly lusts war against the soul" (1 Pet. 2:11), and that "the law in the members wars against the law of the mind" (Rom. 7:23).

Therefore the man who is not regenerate wholly resists God, and is altogether a servant of sin (John 8:34; Rom. 6:16). But the regenerate delights in the Law of God after the inward man, but nevertheless sees in his members the law of sin, which wars against the law of the mind; on this account, with his mind, he serves the Law of God, but, with the flesh, the law of sin (Rom. 7:25). In this way the correct opinion can and should be thoroughly, clearly and discreetly explained and taught.

As to the expressions of Chrysostom and Basil: *Trahit Deus, sed volentem trahit; tantum velis, et Deus praeoccur-*

rit, and also the expression of the scholastics [and Papists], *Hominis voluntas in conversione non est otiosa, sed agit aliquid, i.e.* "God draws, but he draws the willing," and "In conversion the will of man is not idle, but effects something," (expressions which have been introduced for confirming the natural free will in man's conversion, against the doctrine concerning God's grace), from the explanation heretofore presented it is manifest that they are not in harmony with the form of sound doctrine, but are contrary to it, and therefore when we speak of conversion to God should be avoided.

For the conversion of our corrupt will, which is nothing else than a resuscitation of it from spiritual death, is only and alone a work of God, just as also the resuscitation in the resurrection of the body should be ascribed to God alone, as has been above fully set forth and proved by manifest testimonies of Holy Scripture.

But how in conversion, through the drawing of the Holy Ghost, God changes stubborn and unwilling into willing men, and that after such conversion, in the daily exercise of repentance, the regenerate will of man is not idle, but also co-operates in all the deeds of the Holy Ghost, which he works through us, has already been sufficiently explained above.

So also when Luther says that with respect to his conversion man is purely passive, *i.e.* does nothing whatever thereto, but only suffers what God works in him, his meaning is not that conversion occurs without the preaching and hearing of God's Word; his meaning also is not that in conversion no new emotion is awakened in us by the Holy Ghost, and no spiritual operation begun; but he means that man of himself, or from his natural powers, cannot contribute anything or help to his conversion, and that conversion is not only in part, but altogether an operation, gift and present and work of the Holy Ghost alone, who accomplishes and effects it, by his virtue and power, through the Word, in the understanding, will and heart of man, *tanquam in subjecto patiente, i.e.* where man does or works nothing, but only suffers. Not as a statue is cut in a stone or a seal impressed into wax, which knows nothing of it, and also perceives and wills nothing of it, but in the way which is above narrated and explained.

Because also the youth in the schools have been greatly perplexed by the doctrine of the three efficient causes concurring in the conversion to God of the unregenerate man, as to the manner in which they, namely, the Word of God preached and heard, the Holy Ghost and the will of man concur; it is again manifest from the explanation above presented that conversion to God is a work of God the Holy Ghost alone, who is the true master-workman that alone works this in us, for which he uses the preaching and hearing of his Holy Word as his ordinary [and lawful] means and instrument. But the understanding and will of the unregenerate man are nothing else than the *subjectum convertendum, i.e.* that which is to be converted, as the understanding and will of a spiritually dead man, in whom the Holy Ghost works conversion and renewal, for which work the will of the man who is to be converted does nothing, but only lets God work in him, until he is regenerate; and then also by the Holy Ghost he works [co-operates] in other succeeding good works that which is pleasing to God, in the way and to the extent fully set forth above.

CHAPTER III. OF THE RIGHTEOUSNESS OF FAITH BEFORE GOD.

The third dissent has arisen among some theologians of the Augsburg Confession concerning the righteousness of Christ or of faith, which, out of grace, is imputed by God, through faith, to poor sinners for righteousness.

For one side has contended that the righteousness of faith, which the apostle calls the righteousness of God, is God's essential righteousness, which is Christ himself as the true, natural and essential Son of God, who, by faith, dwells in the elect and impels them to do right, and who thus is their righteousness, compared with which righteousness the sins of all men are as a drop of water compared with the great ocean.

On the contrary, others have held and taught that Christ is our righteousness, alone according to his human nature.

In opposition to both these sides, it is unanimously taught by the other teachers of the Augsburg Confession that Christ is our righteousness, not alone according to his divine nature, nor also alone according to his human nature, but according to both natures, who as God and man has, through his complete obedience, redeemed, justified and saved us from our sins; that therefore the righteousness of faith is the forgiveness of sins, reconciliation with God, and our acceptance as God's children on account of the obedience only of Christ, which alone through faith, out of pure grace, is imputed for righteousness to all true believers, and on account of it they are absolved from all their unrighteousness.

Besides this [controversy] there are on account of the Interim [by occasion of the formula of the Interim or of Inter-religion], and otherwise, still other disputes caused and excited concerning the article Of Justification, which will hereafter be explained in the antithesis, i.e. in the enumeration of those errors which are contrary to the pure doctrine in this article.

This article concerning Justification by Faith (as the Apology says) is the chief in the entire Christian doctrine, without which no poor conscience has any firm consolation, or can know aright the riches of the grace of Christ, as Dr. Luther also has written: "If only this article remain in view pure, the Christian Church also remains pure, and is harmonious and without all sects; but if it do not remain pure, it is not possible to resist any error or fanatical spirit" (Tom. 5, Jena Ed., p. 159). And concerning this article Paul especially says that "a little leaven leaveneth the whole lump." Therefore, in this article he emphasizes with so much zeal and earnestness the exclusive particles, or the words whereby the works of men are excluded (namely, "without Law," "without works," "out of grace" ["freely," Rom. 3:28; 4:5; Eph. 2:8, 9]), in order to indicate how highly necessary it is that in this article, by the side of the presentation of the pure doctrine, the antithesis, i.e. all contrary dogmas, by this means be separated, exposed and rejected.

Therefore, in order that this dissent may be explained in a Christian way according to God's Word, and, by his grace, be settled, our doctrine, faith and confession are as follows:

Concerning the righteousness of faith before God we unanimously believe, teach and confess, according to the comprehensive summary of our faith and confession above presented, viz. that a poor sinful man is justified before God, i.e. absolved and declared free and exempt from all his sins, and from the sentence of well-deserved condemnation, and adopted into sonship and heirship of eternal life, without any merit or worth of his own, also without all preceding, present or subsequent works, out of pure grace, alone because of the sole merit, complete obedience, bitter suffering, death and resurrection of our Lord Christ, whose obedience is reckoned to us for righteousness.

These treasures are offered us by the Holy Ghost in the promise of the holy Gospel; and faith alone is the only means whereby we lay hold upon, accept and apply and appropriate them to ourselves. This faith is a gift of God, whereby we apprehend aright Christ our Redeemer in the Word of the Gospel, and trust in him, that for the sake of his obedience alone, out of grace, we have the forgiveness of sins, and before God the Father are regarded godly and righteous, and are eternally saved. Therefore the expressions of Paul, that we are "justified by faith" (Rom. 3:28), or that "faith is counted for righteousness" (Rom. 4:5), and that we are "made righteous by the obedience of one" (Rom. 5:19), or that "by the righteousness of one justification of faith came to all men" (Rom. 5:18), are regarded and received as equivalents. For faith justifies, not because it is so good a work and so fair a virtue, but because, in the promise of the Gospel, it lays hold of and accepts the merit of Christ; for if we are to be justified thereby, this must be applied and appropriated by faith. Therefore the righteousness which, out of pure grace, is imputed to faith or the believer, is the obedience, suffering and resurrection of Christ, by which he has made satisfaction for us to the Law, and paid the price of our sins. For since Christ is not alone man, but God and man in one undivided person, he was as little subject to the Law, because he is the Lord of the Law, as, in his own person, to suffering and death. Therefore his obedience not only in suffering and dying, but also that he in our stead was voluntarily subject to the Law, and fulfilled it by his obedience, is imputed to us for righteousness, so that, on account of this complete obedience, which by deed and by suffering, in life and in death, he rendered his heavenly Father for us, God forgives our sins, regards us godly and righteous, and eternally saves us. This righteousness is offered us by the Holy Ghost through the Gospel and in the sacraments, and is applied, appropriated and received through faith, whence believers have reconciliation with God, forgiveness of sins, the grace of God, sonship and heirship of eternal life.

Accordingly, the word justify here means to declare righteous and free from sins, and, for the sake of Christ's righteousness, which is imputed by God to faith (Phil. 3:9), to absolve one from their eternal punishment. For this use and understanding of this word is common in the Holy Scriptures of the Old and the New Testament. (Prov. 17:15): "He that justifieth the wicked, and he that condemneth the just, even they both are abomination to the Lord." (Isa. 5:23): "Woe unto them which justify the wicked for reward, and take away the righteousness of the righteous from him!" (Rom. 8:33): "Who shall lay anything to the charge of God's elect? It is God that justifieth,"*i.e.* absolves from sins, and declares exempt.

But because sometimes the word "regeneration" is employed for the word "justification," it is necessary that this word be properly explained, in order that the renewal which follows the justification of faith may not be confounded with the justification of faith, but they may be properly distinguished from one another.

For, in the first place, the word "regeneration" is employed so as to comprise at the same time the forgiveness of sins alone for Christ's sake, and the succeeding renewal which the Holy Ghost works in those who are justified by faith. Again, it is restricted to the remission of sins and adoption as sons of God. And in this latter sense the word is much and often used in the Apology, where it is written: "Justification is regeneration," although St. Paul has fixed a distinction between these words (Tit. 3:5): "He saved us by the washing of regeneration and renewal of the Holy Ghost." As also the word "vivification" has sometimes been used in a like sense. For if a man is justified through faith (which the Holy Ghost alone works), this is truly a regeneration, because from a child of wrath he becomes a child of God, and thus is transferred from death to life, and it is written (Eph. 2:5): "When we were dead in sins, he hath quickened us together with Christ." Also: "The just shall live by faith" (Rom. 1:17 [Heb. 2:4]). In this sense the word is much and often used in the Apology.

But again, it is often taken for sanctification and renewal, which succeed the righteousness of faith, as Dr. Luther has thus used it in his book concerning the Church and the Councils, and elsewhere.

But when we teach that through the operation of the Holy Ghost we are born anew and justified, the sense is not that after regeneration no unrighteousness clings any more, in being and life, to the justified and regenerate, but that Christ, with his complete obedience, covers all their sins, which still in this life inhere in their nature. But without regard to this, through faith and for the sake of Christ's obedience (which Christ rendered the Father for us from his birth to his most ignominious death upon the cross), they are declared and regarded godly and righteous, although, on account of their corrupt nature, they are still sinners, and so remain to the grave [while they bear about this mortal body]. But, on the other hand, the meaning is not that we dare or should, without repentance, conversion and renewal, obey sins, and remain and continue in them.

For true [and not feigned] contrition must precede; and to those who thus, as has been said, out of pure grace, for the sake of Christ the only Mediator, without all works and merit, are righteous before God, *i.e.* are received into grace, the Holy Ghost is also given, who renews and sanctifies them, and works in them love to God and to their neighbor. But since the incipient renewal is in this life

imperfect, and sins still dwell in the flesh, even in the regenerate, the righteousness of faith before God consists in the gracious imputation of the righteousness of Christ, without the addition of our works, so that our sins are forgiven us, and covered and not imputed (Rom. 4:6 sqq.).

But here with special diligence the greatest attention must afterwards be given, if the article of justification is to remain pure, that not that which precedes faith and that which succeeds it be mingled together or inserted as necessary and belonging to it, because to speak of conversion and to speak of justification are not one and the same thing.

For not everything that belongs to conversion belongs likewise to the article of justification, in and to which only the following belong and are necessary: the grace of God, the merit of Christ, and faith which receives this in the promise of the Gospel, whereby the righteousness of Christ is imputed to us, whence we receive and have forgiveness of sins, reconciliation with God, sonship and heirship of eternal life.

Therefore true, saving faith is not in those who are without contrition and sorrow, and who have a wicked purpose to remain and persevere in sins; but true contrition precedes, and genuine faith is in or with true repentance [justifying faith is in those who repent truly, not feignedly].

Love is also a fruit which surely and necessarily follows true faith. For that one does not love is a sure indication that he is not justified, but is still in death, or has lost again the righteousness of faith, as John says (1 John 3:14). But when Paul says (Rom. 3:28): "We are justified by faith without works," he indicates thereby that neither the contrition that precedes nor the works that follow belong to the article or transaction of justification by faith. For good works do not precede justification, but follow it, and the person must be justified before he can do a good work.

In like manner also, although the renewal or sanctification is also a benefit of Christ the Mediator and a work of the Holy Ghost, it does not belong to the article or transaction of justification before God, but follows the same, since, on account of our corrupt flesh, it is not, in this life, entirely perfect and complete, as Dr. Luther has written well concerning this in his excellent and extended exposition of the Epistle to the Galatians, in which he says as follows: "We concede indeed that instruction should be given also concerning love and good works, yet in such a way that this be done when and where it is necessary, as, namely, when we have to do with works over and beyond this matter of justification. But here the chief point with which we have to do is this, that the question is not whether we should also do and love good works, but by what means we may be justified before God, and saved. And here we answer with St. Paul: that we are justified alone by faith in Christ, and not by the deeds of the Law or love. Not that we hereby entirely reject works and love, as the adversaries falsely defame and accuse us, but that we dare not allow ourselves to be led away, as Satan would desire, from the chief point with which we have here to do, to another and foreign transaction which does not belong whatever to this question. Therefore, whereas, and as long as, we have to do with this article of justification we reject and condemn works, since this article can admit of no disputation or treatment whatever of the subject of works; therefore in this matter we absolutely sever all Law and works of the Law." So far Luther.

In order, therefore, that troubled hearts may have a firm, sure consolation, and also that due honor be accorded the merit of Christ and the grace of God, the Scriptures teach that the righteousness of faith before God consists alone in the gracious [gratuitous] reconciliation or the forgiveness of sins, which is presented to us out of pure grace, for the sake of the merit alone of Christ as Mediator, and is received alone through faith in the promise of the Gospel. Therefore, in justification before God, faith relies neither upon contrition nor upon love or other virtues, but alone upon Christ, and in him upon his complete obedience, whereby for us he has fulfilled the Law, which [obedience] is imputed to believers for righteousness.

It is also neither contrition nor love or any other virtue, but faith alone, which is the sole means and instrument whereby we can receive and accept the grace of God, the merit of Christ, and the forgiveness of sins, which are offered us in the promise of the Gospel.

It is also correctly said that believers who through faith in Christ are justified, in this life have first the imputed righteousness of faith, and afterwards also the incipient righteousness of the new obedience or good works. But these two must not be confounded or inserted at the same time into the article of justification by faith before God. For since this incipient righteousness or renewal is incomplete and imperfect in us in this life because of the flesh, the person cannot stand therewith and thereby before God's tribunal, but before God's tribunal only the righteousness of the obedience, suffering and death of Christ, which is imputed to faith, can stand, namely, that only for the sake of this obedience the person (even after his renewal, when he has already many good works and is in the best life) is pleasing and acceptable to God, and is received into adoption and heirship of eternal life.

Here belongs also what St. Paul writes (Rom. 4:3), that Abraham was justified before God alone through faith, for the sake of the Mediator, without the co-operation of his works, not only when he was first converted from idolatry and had no good works, but also when he was afterwards renewed by the Holy Ghost, and adorned with many excellent good works (Gen. 15:6; Heb. 11:8). And Paul puts the following question (Rom. 4:1 sqq.): In what, then, did the righteousness, for everlasting life, of Abraham before God, whereby God was gracious to him, and he was pleasing and acceptable to God, consist?

Thereupon he answers: "To him who worketh not, but believeth on him that justifieth the ungodly, his faith is counted for righteousness;" as David also (Ps. 32:1) speaks of the blessedness of the man to whom God imputes righteousness without works.

Therefore, even though the converted and believing have incipient renewal, sanctification, love, virtue and good works, yet these neither can nor should be introduced into or confounded with the article of justification before God, in order that that honor which belongs to him may remain with Christ the Redeemer, and since our new obedience is incomplete and imperfect, tempted consciences may have sure consolation.

And this is the intention of the apostle Paul when in this article he so diligently and earnestly emphasizes the exclusive particles, *i.e.* the words whereby works are excluded from the article of justification: *absque operibus, sine lege, gratis, non ex operibus, i.e.* "of grace," "without merit," "without works," "not of works." These exclusive particles are all comprised in the expression: "By faith alone in Christ we are justified before God and saved." For thereby works are excluded, not in the sense that a true faith can exist without contrition, or that good works should, must and dare not follow true faith as sure and indubitable fruits, or that believers neither dare nor must do anything good; but that good works are excluded from the article of justification before God, so that in the transaction of the justification of the poor sinner before God they should not be introduced, inserted, or intermingled as necessary or belonging thereto. The true sense of the exclusive particles in the article of justification is this, which should, with all diligence and earnestness, be urged in this article:

1. That thereby [through these particles] all our own works, merit, worth, glory and confidence in all our works in the article of justification be entirely excluded, so that our works be neither constituted nor regarded, either entirely or in half or in the least part, as the cause or merit of justification, upon which God in this article and transaction looks, or we could or should rely.

2. That this office and property abides with faith alone, that it alone, and nothing else whatever, is the means or instrument by and through which God's grace and the merit of Christ are, in the promise of the Gospel, received, apprehended, accepted, applied to us, and appropriated; and that from this office and property of such application or appropriation, love and all other virtues or works are excluded.

3. That neither renewal, sanctification, virtues nor good works be constituted and appointed *tanquam forma aut pars aut causa justificationis, i.e.* our righteousness before God, or a part or cause of our righteousness, or should otherwise be intermingled under any pretext, title or name whatever in the article of justification as necessary and belonging thereto; but that the righteousness of faith consists alone in the forgiveness of sins out of pure grace, alone for the sake of Christ's merit; which blessings are offered us in the promise of the Gospel, and are received, accepted, applied and appropriated alone by faith.

Therefore the true order between faith and good works, and also between justification and renewal or sanctification, must abide and be maintained.

For good works do not precede faith, neither does sanctification precede justification. But in conversion, first faith is kindled in us by the Holy Ghost from the hearing of the Gospel. It lays hold of God's grace in Christ, whereby the person is justified. Then, when the person is justified, he is renewed and sanctified by the Holy Ghost,

THE FORMULA OF CONCORD (1580) (continued)

from which renewal and sanctification the fruits of good works then follow. This should not be understood as though justification and renewal were sundered from one another, in such a manner that a genuine faith sometimes could exist and continue for a long time, together with a wicked intention, but hereby only the order [of causes and effects, of antecedents and consequents] is indicated, as to how one precedes or succeeds the other. For that nevertheless remains true which Luther has correctly said: "Faith and good works [well] agree and fit [are inseparably connected]; but it is faith alone, without works, which lays hold of the blessing; and yet it is never and at no time alone." This has been set forth above.

Many disputations also are usefully and well explained by means of this true distinction, of which the Apology treats in reference to the passage (James 2:20). For when the subject is concerning how faith justifies, the doctrine of St. Paul is that faith alone, without works, justifies (Rom. 3:28), since, as has been said, it applies and appropriates the merit of Christ. But if the question be: Wherein and whereby a Christian can perceive and distinguish, either in himself or in another, a true living faith from a feigned and dead faith, since many idle, secure Christians imagine for themselves a delusion in place of faith, while they nevertheless have no true faith? the Apology gives this answer: "James calls that dead faith where every kind of good works and fruits of the Spirit do not follow." And to this effect the Latin edition of the Apology says: "James is right in denying that we are justified by such faith as is without works, *i.e.* which is dead."

But James speaks, as the Apology says, concerning the works of those who, through Christ, have already been justified, reconciled with God, and obtained forgiveness of sins. But if the question be asked, Whereby and whence faith has this, and what appertains to its justifying and saving? it is false and incorrect to say: that faith cannot justify without works; or that faith justifies or makes righteous, so far as it has love with it, for the sake of which love this is ascribed to faith [it has love with it, by which it is formed]; or that the presence of works with faith is necessary if man is to be justified thereby before God; or that the presence of good works in the article of justification, or for justification, is needful; likewise that the good works are a cause without which man cannot be justified, and that they are not excluded from the article of justification by the exclusive particles, as when St. Paul says: "Without works," etc. For faith makes righteous alone in that, as a means and instrument, it lays hold of and accepts, in the promise of the Gospel, the grace of God and the merit of Christ.

Let this suffice, according to the plan of this document, as a compendious setting forth of the doctrine of justification by faith, which is treated more at length in the above-mentioned writings. From these, the antitheses also, i.e. the false contrary dogmas, are easily understood, namely, that in addition to the errors recounted above, the following and the like, which conflict with the explanation now published, must be censured, exposed and rejected, as when it is taught:

1. That our love or good works are merit or cause, either entirely or even in part, of justification before God.

2. Or that by good works man must render himself worthy and fit that the merit of Christ be imparted to him.

3. Or that our formal righteousness before God is our inherent newness or love, i.e. that our real righteousness before God is the love or renewal which the Holy Ghost works in us and is in us.

4. Or that the righteousness of faith before God consists of two parts, namely, the gracious forgiveness of sins, and then, secondly, also renewal or sanctification.

5. That faith justifies only initially, or partially, or primarily, and that our newness or love justifies even before God, either completively or secondarily.

6. Also that believers are justified before God, or are righteous before God, at the same time both by imputation and by beginning, or partly by the imputation of Christ's righteousness, and partly by the beginning of new obedience.

7. Also that the application of the promise of grace occurs both by faith of the heart and confession of the mouth, and by other virtues. That is: Faith alone makes righteous, for the reason that righteousness by faith is begun in us, or that in justification faith has the pre-eminence; nevertheless, the renewal and love belong also to our righteousness before God, yet in such a way that it is not the chief cause of our righteousness, but that our righteousness before God is not entire and complete without such love and renewal. Also that believers are justified and righteous before God, at the same time, by the imputed righteousness of Christ and the incipient new obedience, or in part by the imputation of Christ's righteousness and in part by the incipient new obedience. Also that the promise of grace is appropriated by us, by faith in the heart, and confession which is made with the mouth, and by other virtues.

It is also incorrect to teach that man must be saved in some other way, or through something else, than as he is justified before God; so that while we are justified before God by faith alone, without works, yet without works it is impossible to be saved or obtain salvation.

This is false, for the reason that it is directly contrary to the declaration of Paul (Rom. 4:6): "The blessedness of the man unto whom God imputeth righteousness without works." And the basis of Paul's argument is that we obtain salvation just in the same way as righteousness; yea, that precisely by this means, when we are justified by faith, we receive adoption and heirship of eternal life and salvation; and, on this account, Paul employs and emphasizes the exclusive particles, i.e. those words whereby works and our own merits are entirely excluded, namely, "out of grace," "without works," as forcibly in the article concerning salvation as in the article concerning righteousness.

Likewise also the disputation concerning the indwelling in us of the essential righteousness of God must be correctly explained. For although, by faith, in the elect, who are justified by Christ and reconciled with God, God the Father, Son and Holy Ghost, who is eternal and essential righteousness, dwells (for all Christians are temples of God the Father, Son and Holy Ghost, who also impels them to do right); yet this indwelling of God is not the righteousness of faith, of which St. Paul treats and which he calls the righteousness of God, for the sake of which we are declared righteous before God; but it follows the preceding righteousness of faith, which is nothing else than the forgiveness of sins and the gracious acceptance of the poor sinner, alone for the sake of Christ's obedience and merit.

Therefore, since in our churches it is acknowledged [established beyond controversy] among the theologians of the Augsburg Confession that all our righteousness is to be sought outside of ourselves and the merits, works, virtues and worthiness of all men, and rests alone upon Christ the Lord; yet it is well to consider in what respect Christ is called, in this matter of justification, our righteousness, namely, that our righteousness rests not upon one or the other nature, but upon the entire person of Christ, who as God and man is our righteousness in his sole, entire and complete obedience.

For even though Christ had been conceived without sin by the Holy Ghost, and thus been born, and in his human nature alone would have fulfilled all righteousness, and yet would have not been true and eternal God, this obedience and suffering of his human nature could not have been imputed to us for righteousness. As also, if the Son of God had not become man the divine nature alone could not have been our righteousness. Therefore we believe, teach and confess that the entire obedience of the entire person of Christ, which he has rendered the Father for us, even to his most ignominious death upon the cross, is imputed for righteousness. For the human nature alone, without the divine, could neither by obedience nor suffering render satisfaction to eternal almighty God for the sins of all the world; and the divinity alone without the humanity could not mediate between God and us.

But because, as above mentioned, the obedience is [not only of one nature, but] of the entire person, it is a complete satisfaction and expiation for the human race, whereby the eternal, immutable righteousness of God, revealed in the Law, is satisfied, and is thus our righteousness, which avails before God and is revealed in the Gospel, and upon which faith before God relies, which God imputes to faith, as it is written (Rom. 5:19): "For as by one man's disobedience many were made sinners, so by the obedience of one shall many be made righteous." (1 John 1:7): "The blood of Jesus Christ, the Son of God, cleanseth us from all sins." Also: "The just shall live by his faith" (Hab. 2:4 [Rom. 1:17]).

Thus neither the divine nor the human nature of Christ is of itself imputed for righteousness, but only the obedience of the person who is at the same time God and man. And faith thus regards the person of Christ, who was made subject to the Law for us, bore our sins, and in his going to the Father offered to his Heavenly Father for us poor sinners his entire, complete obedience, from his holy birth even unto death, and who has thereby covered all our

disobedience which inheres in our nature, and its thoughts, words and works, so that it is not imputed to us for condemnation, but out of pure grace, alone for Christ's sake, is pardoned and forgiven.

Therefore we reject and unanimously condemn, besides the above-mentioned, also the following and all similar errors, as contrary to God's Word, the doctrine of the prophets and apostles, and our Christian faith:

1. When it is taught that Christ is our righteousness before God, alone according to his divine nature.

2. That Christ is our righteousness, alone according to his human nature.

3. That in the expressions of the prophets and apostles, when the righteousness of faith is spoken of, the words "justify" and "be justified" do not signify to declare free from sins and obtain the forgiveness of sins, but in deed and truth to be made righteous, because of love infused by the Holy Ghost, virtues and the works following thence.

4. That faith looks not only to the obedience of Christ, but to his divine nature, as it dwells and works in us, and that by this indwelling our sins are covered before God.

5. That faith is such a trust in the obedience of Christ as can be and remain in a man who has no genuine repentance, in whom also no love follows, but he persists in sins against conscience.

6. That not God, but only the gifts of God, dwell in the believer.

These errors and the like, one and all, we unanimously reject as contrary to the clear Word of God, and, by God's grace, we abide firmly and constantly in the doctrine of the righteousness of faith before God, as in the Augsburg Confession and the Apology which follows it is presented, developed and proved from God's Word.

Concerning what besides is needful for the real explanation of this sublime and chief article of justification before God, upon which rests the salvation of our souls, we will direct every one to the excellent and magnificent exposition by Dr. Luther of the Epistle of St. Paul to the Galatians, and for the sake of brevity to it we hereby refer.

CHAPTER IV. OF GOOD WORKS.

A disagreement has occurred among the theologians of the Augsburg Confession also concerning good works. For a part are accustomed to speak in the following words and manner: "Good works are necessary for salvation;" "It is impossible to be saved without good works;" "No one can be saved without good works;" because by the rightly believing good works are required as fruits of faith, and faith without love is dead, although such love is no cause of salvation.

But the other side, on the contrary, have contended that good works are indeed necessary; not for salvation, but for other reasons; and that, on this account, the preceding propositions or expressions used (as they are not in accord with the form of sound doctrine and with the Word, and have been always and are still set over against our Christian faith by the Papists, in which we confess "that

THE FORMULA OF CONCORD (1580) (continued)

faith alone justifies and saves") are not to be tolerated in the Church, in order that the merit of Christ our Saviour be not diminished, and the promise of salvation may be and remain firm and certain to believers.

In this controversy also the following controverted proposition or expression was introduced by some few, viz. "that good works are injurious to salvation." It has also been disputed by some that good works are not "necessary," but are "voluntary" [free and spontaneous], because they are not extorted by fear and the penalty of the Law, but are to be done from a voluntary spirit and a joyful heart. On the contrary, the other side contend "that good works are necessary."

This latter controversy was originally introduced with respect to the words "necessity" and "liberty," because especially the word "necessity" signifies not only the eternal, immutable order according to which all men are indebted and obliged to obey God, but also sometimes a coercion, whereby the Law forces men to good works.

But afterwards there was a disputation not alone concerning the words, but, in the most violent manner, the doctrine itself was called into question, and it was contended that the new obedience in the regenerate, in accordance with the above-mentioned divine order, is not necessary.

In order to explain this disagreement in a Christian way and according to the guidance of God's Word, our doctrine, faith and confession are as follows:

First, there is no controversy among our theologians concerning the following points in this article, namely: that it is God's will, regulation and command that believers should walk in good works; and that truly good works are not those which every one, with a good intention, himself contrives, or which are done according to human ordinances, but those which God himself has prescribed and commanded in his Word. Also, that truly good works are done, not from our own natural powers, but when by faith the person is reconciled with God and renewed by the Holy Ghost, or (as Paul says) "created anew in Christ Jesus to good works" (Eph. 2:10).

There is also no controversy as to how and for what reason the good works of believers, although, in this flesh, they are impure and incomplete, please God and are acceptable, namely, for the sake of the Lord Christ, by faith, because the person is acceptable to God. For the works which pertain to the maintenance of external discipline, which are done also by the unbelieving and unconverted, and required of them, although commendable before the world, and besides rewarded by God in this world with temporal possessions; yet, because they do not proceed from true faith, are in God's sight sins, *i.e.* stained with sin, and are regarded by God as sins and impure on account of the corrupt nature and because the person is not reconciled with God. For "a corrupt tree cannot bring forth good fruit" (Matt. 7:18), as also it is written (Rom. 14:23): "For whatsoever is not of faith is sin." For the person must first be accepted of God, and that alone for the sake of Christ, if the works of that person are to please him.

Therefore, of works that are truly good and well pleasing to God, which God will reward in this world and the world to come, faith must be the mother and source; and on this account they are correctly called by St. Paul "fruits of faith," as also "of the Spirit." For, as Luther writes in the introduction of St. Paul's Epistle to the Romans: "Thus faith is a divine work in us, that changes us, of God regenerates us, and puts to death the old Adam, makes us entirely different men in heart, spirit, mind and all powers, and confers the Holy Ghost. Oh, it is a living, efficacious, active thing that we have in faith, so that it is impossible for it not to do good without intermission. It also does not ask whether good works are to be done; but before the question is asked it has wrought them, and is always busy. But he who does not produce such works is a faithless man, and gropes and looks about after faith and good works, and knows neither what faith nor what good works are, yet meanwhile babbles and prates, in many words, concerning faith and good works. Justifying faith is a living, firm trust in God's grace, so certain that a man would die a thousand times for it [rather than suffer this trust to be wrested from him]. And this trust and knowledge of divine grace renders him joyful, fearless and cheerful with respect to God and all creatures, which joy and cheerfulness the Holy Ghost works though faith; and on account of this, man becomes ready and cheerful to do good to every one and to suffer everything for love and praise to God, who has conferred this grace. Therefore it is impossible to separate works from faith, yea, just as impossible as for heat and light to be separated from fire."

But since there is no controversy on this point among our theologians, we will not treat it here at greater length, but only make a simple and plain statement of the controverted points.

And first as to the necessity or voluntariness of good works, it is manifest that in the Augsburg Confession and its Apology the following expressions are often used and repeated: that good works are necessary, which also should necessarily follow faith and reconciliation, also, that we necessarily should do and must do the good works which God has commanded. Thus also in the Holy Scriptures themselves the words "necessity," "needful" and "necessary," also "should" and "must," are used concerning what we are bound to do, because of God's arrangement, command and will, as Rom. 13:5; 1 Cor. 9:9; Acts 5:29; John 15:12; 1 John 4:21.

Therefore it is wrong to censure and reject the expressions or propositions mentioned in this Christian and proper sense, as has been done by some. For it is right to employ them for the purpose of censuring and rejecting the secure, Epicurean delusion, by which many fabricate for themselves a dead faith or vain persuasion which is without repentance and without good works, as though there could be at the same time in a heart true faith and the wicked intention to persevere and continue in sins—an impossibility; or, as though any one, indeed, could have and retain true faith, righteousness and salvation, even though he be and remain a corrupt and unfruitful tree, whence no good fruits whatever come; yea, even though he persist in sins against conscience, or wilfully relapse into these sins—all of which is incorrect and false.

But here also mention must be made of the following distinction, viz. that necessity of Christ's arrangement, command and will, and of our debt, be understood; but not necessity of coercion. That is: When the word "needful" is employed, it should be understood not of coercion, but alone of the arrangement made by God's immutable will, to which we are debtor; for his commandment also shows that the creature should be obedient to its Creator. For in other places, as 2 Cor. 9:7, and in the Epistle of St. Paul to Philemon (v. 14), also 1 Pet. 5:2, the term "of necessity" is used for that to which any one is forced against his will or otherwise, so that he acts externally for appearance, but nevertheless without and against his will. For such hypocritical works God will not have [does not approve], but wishes the people of the New Testament to be a "willing people" (Ps. 110:3), and "sacrifice freely" (Ps. 54:7), "not grudgingly or of necessity, but to be obedient from the heart" (2 Cor. 9:7; Rom. 6:17). "For God loveth a cheerful giver" (2 Cor. 9:7). In this understanding, and in such sense, it is correctly said and taught that truly good works should be done freely or from a voluntary spirit by those whom the Son of God has liberated; as the disputation concerning the voluntariness of good works has been introduced especially with this intention.

But here, again, it is also well to note the distinction of which St. Paul says (Rom. 7:22 sq.) "I delight in the Law of God" [I am ready to do good] "after the inward man. But I see another law in my members," that is not only unwilling or disinclined, but also "warring against the law of my mind." And concerning the unwilling and rebellious flesh Paul says (1 Cor. 9:27): "I keep under my body, and bring it into subjection," and (Gal. 5:24; Rom. 8:13): "They that are Christ's have crucified," yea, slain, "the flesh with its affections and lusts." But the opinion is false, and must be censured, when it is asserted and taught that good works are so free to believers that it is optional with them to do or to omit them, or that they can act contrary thereto, and none the less are able to retain faith and God's favor and grace.

Secondly, when it is taught that good works are needful, the statement must also be made wherefore and for what reasons they are needful, as these causes are enumerated in the Augsburg Confession and Apology.

But here we must be well on our guard lest into the article of Justification and Salvation works may be introduced, and confused with it. Therefore the propositions are justly rejected, "that to believers good works are needful for salvation, so that it is impossible without good works to be saved." For they are directly contrary to the doctrine concerning the exclusive particles in the article of Justification and Salvation, i.e. they directly conflict with the words by which St. Paul entirely excludes our works and merit from the article of Justification and Salvation, and ascribes everything alone to the grace of God and merit of Christ, as explained in the preceding article. Again they [these propositions concerning the necessity of good works for salvation] take from tempted, troubled consciences the comfort of the Gospel, give occasion for doubt, are in many ways dangerous, strengthen presumption in one's own righteousness and confidence in one's own works; besides are accepted by the Papists, and quoted in their interest, against the pure doctrine of salvation by faith alone. Thus they are contrary also to the form of sound words, where it is written that blessedness is only "of the man unto whom God imputeth righteousness without works" (Rom. 4:6). Also in the sixth article of the Augsburg Confession it is written that "we are saved without works, by faith alone." Thus Luther also has rejected and condemned these propositions:

1. In the false prophets among the Galatians [who led the Galatians into error].

2. In the Papists, in very many places.

3. In the Anabaptists, when they presented this interpretation: "We should not indeed rest faith upon the merit of works, but we should nevertheless regard them as things needful to salvation."

4. Also in some among his contemporaries, who wished to interpret the proposition thus: "Although we require works as needful to salvation, yet we do not teach to place trust in works." On Gen. 22.

Accordingly, and for the reasons now enumerated, it should, in accordance with what is right, be settled in our churches that the aforesaid modes of speech should not be taught, defended or excused, but be rejected from our churches and repudiated as false and incorrect, and as expressions which, being renewed by the Interim, originated in times of persecution, when there was especial need of a clear, correct confession against all sorts of corruptions and adulterations of the article of Justification, and were drawn [again] into disputation.

Thirdly, since also it is disputed whether good works preserve salvation, or whether they be needful for preserving faith, righteousness and salvation, and upon this much that is of great importance depends; for "he that shall endure unto the end, the same shall be saved" (Matt. 24:13); also (Heb. 3:6, 14): "We are made partakers of Christ, if we hold fast the beginning of our confidence steadfast unto the end;" we must declare precisely how righteousness and salvation are to be maintained in us, lest it be again lost.

And therefore the false Epicurean delusion is to be earnestly censured and rejected, by which some imagine that faith and the righteousness and salvation received can be lost through no sins or wicked deeds, even though wilful and intentional, but that even if a Christian without fear and shame indulge his wicked lusts, resist the Holy Ghost, and intentionally acquiesce in sins against conscience, yet that he none the less retains faith, God's grace, righteousness and salvation.

Against this pernicious delusion the following true, immutable, divine threats and severe punishments and admonitions to Christians who are justified by faith should be often repeated and impressed. (1 Cor. 6:9): "Be not deceived: neither fornicators, nor idolaters, nor adulterers, etc., shall inherit the kingdom of God." (Gal. 5:21; Eph. 5:5): "They which do such things shall not inherit the kingdom of God." (Rom. 8:13): "If ye live after the flesh, ye shall die." (Col. 3:6): "For which thing's sake the wrath of God cometh upon the children of disobedience."

THE FORMULA OF CONCORD (1580) (continued)

But when and in what way, from this foundation, the exhortations to good works can be earnestly urged without an obscuration of the doctrine of faith and of the article of Justification, the Apology affords an excellent model, where in Article xx., on the passage (2 Pet. 1:10): "Give diligence to make your calling and election sure," it says as follows: "Peter teaches why good works should be done, viz. that we may make our calling sure, *i.e.* that we may not fall from our calling if we again sin. 'Do good works,' he says, 'that you may persevere in your heavenly calling, that you may not fall away again, and lose the Spirit and the gifts, which have fallen to you, not on account of works that follow, but of grace, through Christ, and are now retained by faith. But faith does not remain in those who lead a sinful life, lose the Holy Ghost and reject repentance." Thus far the Apology.

But, on the other hand, the sense is not that faith only in the beginning lays hold of righteousness and salvation, and afterwards resigns its office to works that they may in the future sustain faith, the righteousness received and salvation; but in order that the promise, not only of receiving, but also of retaining righteousness and salvation, may be firm and sure to us; St. Paul (Rom. 5:2) ascribes to faith not only the entrance to grace, but also that we stand in grace and boast of future glory, *i.e.* he ascribes the beginning, middle and end, all to faith alone. Also (Rom. 11:20): "Because of unbelief, they were broken off, and thou standest by faith." (Col. 1:22): "He will present you holy and unblamable and unreprovable in his sight, if ye continue in the faith." (1 Pet. 1:5, 9): "By the power of God we are kept through faith, unto salvation." "Receiving the end of your faith, even the salvation of your souls."

Since, therefore, from God's Word it is manifest that faith is the proper and only means whereby righteousness and salvation are not only received, but also preserved by God, the decree of the Council of Trent, and whatever elsewhere is set forth in the same sense, should by right be rejected, viz. that our good works support salvation, or that the righteousness of faith received, or even faith itself, is either entirely or in part supported and preserved by our works.

For although before this controversy some few pure teachers employed such expressions and the like, in the exposition of the Holy Scriptures, yet thereby it was in no way intended to establish the above-mentioned error of the Papists; nevertheless, because afterwards controversy arose concerning such expressions, from which all sorts of offensive amplifications [debates, offences and dissensions] followed, it is safest of all, according to the admonition of St. Paul (2 Tim. 1:13), to hold fast to the form of sound words, as the pure doctrine itself, whereby much unnecessary wrangling may be avoided and the Church be preserved from many scandals.

Fourthly, as to the proposition that good works are injurious to salvation, we explain ourselves clearly, as follows: If any one should wish to introduce good works into the article of Justification, or rest his righteousness or trust for salvation thereon, in order to merit God's grace and thereby be saved, to this we say nothing, but St. Paul himself declares, and repeats it three times (Phil. 3:7 sqq.),

that to such a man his works are not only useless and a hindrance, but also "injurious." But the fault is not in the good works themselves, but in the false confidence placed upon the works, contrary to the express Word of God.

Nevertheless, it by no means follows thence that we should say simply and barely: "Good works are injurious to believers or to their salvation;" for in believers good works are indications of salvation when they occur from proper causes and for true ends, *i.e.* as God requires them of the regenerate (Phil. 1:20). Since it is God's will and express command that believers should do good works, which the Holy Ghost works in believers, and with which, for Christ's sake, God is pleased, and to which he promises a glorious reward in this life and the life to come.

For this reason, also, this proposition is censured and rejected in our churches, viz. because it is stated in so absolutely false and offensive a manner, whereby discipline and decency are impaired, and a barbarous, savage, secure, Epicurean life is introduced and strengthened. For what is injurious to his salvation a person should with the greatest diligence avoid.

Since, however, Christians should not be deterred from good works, but should be admonished and urged thereto most diligently, this bare proposition cannot and should not be tolerated, borne or defended in the churches.

CHAPTER V. OF THE LAW AND THE GOSPEL.

As the distinction between the Law and the Gospel is a very brilliant light, which is of service in rightly dividing God's Word, and properly explaining and understanding the Scriptures of the holy prophets and apostles, we must with especial care observe it, in order that these two doctrines may not be mingled with one another, or out of the Gospel a law be made whereby the merit of Christ is obscured and troubled consciences robbed of their comfort, which they otherwise have in the holy Gospel when it is preached in its purity, and by which also they can support themselves in their most grievous temptations against the terrors of the Law.

But here, likewise, there has occurred a dissent among some which rebukes the greatest sin, viz. unbelief. But the other side held and contended that the Gospel is not properly a preaching of repentance or of reproof [preaching of repentance, convicting sin], as it properly belongs to God's Law to reprove all sins, and therefore unbelief also; but that the Gospel is properly a preaching of the grace and favor of God for Christ's sake, through which the unbelief of the converted, which previously inhered in them and which the Law of God reproved, is pardoned and forgiven.

When we now consider aright this dissent, it is especially caused by this, viz. that the term "Gospel" is not always employed and understood in one and the same sense, but in two ways, in the Holy Scriptures, as also by ancient and modern church-teachers. For sometimes it is employed so that thereby is understood the entire doctrine of Christ our Lord, which he inculcated in his ministry upon earth, and commanded to be inculcated in the New Testament, and thus comprised the explanation of the Law and the proclamation of the favor and grace of God, his heavenly

Father, as it is written (Mark 1:1): "The beginning of the Gospel of Jesus Christ, the Son of God." And shortly afterwards the chief heads are stated: "Repentance and forgiveness of sins." Therefore when Christ, after his resurrection, commanded the apostles to preach the Gospel in all the world (Mark 16:15), he compressed the sum of this doctrine into a few words, when he said (Luke 24:46, 47): "Thus it is written, and thus it behoved Christ to suffer, and to rise from the dead the third day; and that repentance and remission of sins should be preached in his name among all nations." So, too, Paul (Acts 20:21) calls his entire doctrine the Gospel, but he embraces the sum of this doctrine under the two heads: "Repentance toward God, and faith toward our Lord Jesus Christ." And in this sense the general definition, *i.e.* the description of the word "Gospel," when employed in a wide sense, and without the peculiar distinction between the Law and the Gospel, is correct, when it is said that the Gospel is a preaching of repentance and remission of sins. For John, Christ and the apostles began their preaching with repentance, and explained and urged not only the gracious promise of the forgiveness of sins, but also the Law of God. Afterwards the term "Gospel" is employed in another, namely, in its peculiar sense, by which it comprises not the preaching of repentance, but only the preaching of the grace of God, as follows directly afterwards (Mark 1:15), where Christ says: "Repent and believe the Gospel."

But also the term "repentance" is not employed in the Holy Scriptures in one and the same sense. For in some passages of Holy Scripture it is employed and understood with reference to the entire conversion of man, as Luke 13:5: "Except ye repent, ye shall all likewise perish." And in chap. 15:7: "Likewise joy shall be in heaven over one sinner that repenteth." But in Mark 1:15, as also elsewhere, where a distinction is made between repentance and faith in Christ (Acts 20:21) or between repentance and remission of sins (Luke 24:46, 47), repentance means to do nothing else than to truly acknowledge sins, from the heart to regret them, and to abstain therefrom. This knowledge proceeds from the Law, but does not suffice for saving conversion to God, if faith in Christ be not added, whose merits the consolatory preaching of the holy Gospel offers to all penitent sinners who are terrified by the preaching of the Law. For the Gospel proclaims the forgiveness of sins, not to coarse and secure hearts, but to the bruised or penitent (Luke 4:18). And that from repentance or the terrors of the Law despair may not result, the preaching of the Gospel must be added, that it may be repentance to salvation (2 Cor. 7:10).

For since the mere preaching of the Law, without Christ, either makes men presumptuous, who imagine that by outward works they can fulfil the Law, or forces them utterly to despair, Christ takes the Law into his hands, and explains it spiritually, from Matt. 5:21 sqq.; Rom. 7:14 and 1:18, and thus reveals his wrath from heaven upon all sinners, and shows how great it is; whereby they are instructed in the Law, and from it first learn aright to know their sins—a knowledge to which Moses never could coerce them. For as the apostle testifies (2 Cor. 3:14 sq.), even though Moses be read, yet nevertheless the veil which hangs before the face always remains unremoved, so that

they cannot perceive that the Law is spiritual and how great things it requires of us, and how severely it curses and condemns us because we cannot observe or fulfil it. "Nevertheless, when it shall turn to the Lord, the veil shall be taken away" (2 Cor. 3:16).

Therefore the Spirit of Christ must not only comfort, but also, through the office of the Law, reprove the world of sin, and thus do in the New Testament what the prophet calls "a strange work" (viz. reprove), in order that he may do his own work, which is to comfort and preach of grace. For on this account, through Christ, he was obtained [from the Father] and sent to us, and for this reason also is called the Comforter, as Dr. Luther has explained in his exposition of the Gospel for the Fifth Sunday after Trinity, in the following words:

"That is all a preaching of the Law which holds forth our sins and God's wrath, let it be done how or when it will. Again, the Gospel is such a preaching as shows and gives nothing else than grace and forgiveness in Christ, although it is true and right that the apostles and preachers of the Gospel (as Christ himself also did) sanction the preaching of the Law, and begin it with those who do not yet acknowledge their sins nor are terrified before [by the sense of] God's wrath; as he says (John 16:8): 'The Holy Ghost will reprove the world of sin, because they believe not on me.' Yea, what more forcible and more terrible declaration and preaching of God's wrath against sin is there than the suffering and death of Christ his Son? But as long as this all preaches God's wrath and terrifies men, it is still properly the preaching neither of the Gospel nor of Christ, but of Moses and the Law, against the impenitent. For the Gospel and Christ were never provided and given to us in order to terrify and condemn, but to comfort and cheer those who are terrified and timid." And again, "Christ says (John 16:8): 'The Holy Ghost will reprove the world of sin;' which cannot happen except through the explanation of the Law" (Jena Ed., vol. ii., p. 455).

So, too, the Smalcald Articles say: "The New Testament maintains and urges the office of the Law, which reveals sins and God's wrath; but to this office it immediately adds the promise of grace through the Gospel."

And the Apology says: "To a true and salutary repentance the preaching of the Law is not sufficient, *but the Gospel should be added thereto.*" Therefore the two doctrines belong together, and should also be urged by the side of each other, but in a definite order and with a proper distinction; and the Antinomians or assailants of the Law are justly condemned, who abolish the preaching of the Law from the Church, and wish sins to be reproved, and repentance and sorrow to be taught, not from the Law, but from the Gospel.

But in order that every one may see that in the dissent of which we are treating we conceal nothing, but present the matter to the eyes of the Christian reader plainly and clearly:

We unanimously believe, teach and confess that the Law is properly a divine doctrine, wherein the true, immutable will of God is revealed as to how man ought to be, in his nature, thoughts, words and works, in order to be pleasing and acceptable to God; and it threatens its transgressors

THE FORMULA OF CONCORD (1580) (continued)

with God's wrath and temporal and eternal punishment. For as Luther writes against the Antinomians: "Everything that reproves sin is and belongs to the Law, whose peculiar office it is to reprove sin and to lead to the knowledge of sins (Rom. 3:20; 7:7);" and as unbelief is the root and spring of all reprehensible sins, the Law reproves unbelief also.

But it is likewise true that the Law with its doctrine is illustrated and explained by the Gospel; and nevertheless it remains the peculiar office of the Law to reprove sins and teach concerning good works.

In this manner the Law reproves unbelief if the Word of God be not believed. Since now the Gospel, which alone peculiarly teaches and commands to believe in Christ, is God's Word, the Holy Ghost, through the office of the Law, also reproves unbelief, *i.e.* that sinners do not believe in Christ, although it is the Gospel alone which peculiarly teaches concerning saving faith in Christ.

But the Gospel is properly a doctrine which teaches (as man does not observe the Law of God, but transgresses it, and his corrupt nature, thoughts, words and works conflict therewith, and for this reason he is subject to God's wrath, death, all temporal calamities and the punishment of hell-fire) what man should *believe*, that with God he may obtain forgiveness of sins, viz. that the Son of God, our Lord Christ, has taken upon himself and borne the curse of the Law, has expiated and settled for all our sins, through whom alone we again enter into favor with God, obtain by faith forgiveness of sins, are exempted from death and all the punishments of sins, and are eternally saved.

For everything that comforts, that offers the favor and grace of God to transgressors of the Law, is and is properly said to be the Gospel, a good and joyful message that God does not will to punish sins, but, for Christ's sake, to forgive them.

Therefore every penitent sinner ought to believe, *i.e.* place his confidence alone, in the Lord Christ, that "he was delivered for our offences, and was raised again for our justification" (Rom. 4:25), who was "made sin for us who knew no sin, that we might be made the righteousness of God in him" (2 Cor. 5:21), "who of God is made unto us wisdom and righteousness and sanctification and redemption" (1 Cor. 1:30), whose obedience is reckoned for us before God's strict tribunal as righteousness, so that the *Law*, as above set forth, is a ministration that kills through the letter and preaches condemnation (2 Cor. 3:7), but the Gospel "is the power of God unto salvation to every one that believeth" (Rom. 1:16), that preaches righteousness and gives the Spirit (1 Cor. 1:18; Gal. 3:2). Dr. Luther has urged this distinction with especial diligence in nearly all his writings, and has properly shown that the knowledge of God derived from the Gospel is far different from that which is taught and learned from the Law, because even the heathen had to a certain extent, from the natural law, a knowledge of God, although they neither knew him aright nor glorified him (Rom. 1:20 sq.).

These two proclamations [kinds of doctrines] from the beginning of the world have been always inculcated alongside of each other in the Church of God, with a proper distinction. For the successors of the venerated patriarchs, as also the patriarchs themselves, not only constantly called to mind how man was in the beginning created by God righteous and holy, and through the fraud of the serpent transgressed God's command, became a sinner, and corrupted and precipitated himself, with all his posterity, into death and eternal condemnation; but also, on the other hand, encouraged and comforted themselves by the preaching concerning the Seed of the woman, who would bruise the serpent's head (Gen. 3:15). Also, concerning the Seed of Abraham, in whom all the nations of the earth shall be blessed (Gen. 22:18). Also, concerning David's Son, who should restore again the kingdom of Israel and be a light to the heathen (Ps. 110:1; Isa. 49:6; Luke 2:32), who "was wounded for our transgressions, and bruised for our iniquities," by whose "stripes we are healed." Isa. 53:5.

These two doctrines we believe and confess, viz. that even to the end of the world they should be diligently inculcated in the Church of God, although with proper distinction, in order that, through the preaching of the *Law* and its threats in the ministry of the New Testament, the hearts of impenitent men may be terrified, and be brought to a knowledge of their sins and to repentance; but not in such a way that they inwardly despair and doubt, but that (since "the Law is a schoolmaster unto Christ, that we might be justified by faith" (Gal. 3:24), and thus points and leads us not from Christ, but to Christ, who "is the end of the Law," Rom. 10:4), they be on the other hand comforted and strengthened by the preaching of the holy *Gospel* concerning Christ our Lord, viz. that to those who believe the Gospel, God, through Christ, forgives all their sins, adopts them for his sake as children, and out of pure grace, without any merit on their part, justifies and saves them, but nevertheless not in such a way that they abuse and sin against the grace of God. Paul (2 Cor. 3:7 sqq.) thoroughly and forcibly shows this distinction between the Law and the Gospel.

Therefore, in order that the two doctrines, viz. that of the Law and that of the Gospel, be not mingled and confounded with one another, and to the one that be ascribed which belongs to the other, whereby the merit and benefits of Christ are obscured and the Gospel made again a doctrine of the Law, as has occurred in the Papacy, and thus Christians be deprived of the true comfort which in the Gospel they have against the terrors of the Law, and the door be again opened in the Church of God to the Papacy; the true and proper distinction between the Law and the Gospel must with all diligence be inculcated and preserved, and whatever gives occasion for confusion between the Law and the Gospel, *i.e.* whereby the two doctrines, Law and Gospel, may be confounded and mingled into one doctrine, should be diligently avoided. It is on this account dangerous and wrong to convert the Gospel, properly so called as distinguished from the Law, into a preaching of repentance or reproof [a preaching of repentance, reproving sin]. For otherwise, if understood in a general sense of the whole doctrine, as the Apology also sometimes says, the Gospel is a preaching of repentance and forgiveness of sins. But close by the Apology also shows that the Gospel is properly the promise of the forgiveness of sins, and of justification through Christ; but that the Law is a doctrine which reproves sins and condemns.

CHAPTER VI. OF THE THIRD USE OF THE DIVINE LAW.

Since the Law of God is useful, not only that thereby, external discipline and decency be maintained against wild, disobedient men; 2, likewise, that through it men be brought to a knowledge of their sins; 3, but even when they have been born anew by the Spirit of God and converted to the Lord, and thus the veil of Moses has been removed from them, they live and walk in the Law; a dissension has occurred between some few theologians concerning this last use of the Law. For the one side taught and maintained that the regenerate should not learn the new obedience, or in what good works they ought to walk, from the Law; neither is this doctrine to be urged thence, because they have been liberated by the Son of God, have become the temples of his Spirit, and therefore are free, so that, just as the sun of itself without any constraint fulfils its course, so also they of themselves, by the prompting and impulse of the Holy Ghost, do what God requires of them. The other side taught, on the contrary: Although the truly believing are really moved by God's Spirit, and thus, according to the inner man, do God's will from a free spirit; yet the Holy Ghost uses with them the written law for instruction, whereby even the truly believing may learn to serve God, not according to their own thoughts, but according to his written Law and Word, which are a sure rule and standard of a godly life and walk, directed according to the eternal and immutable will of God.

For the explanation and final settlement of this dissent we unanimously believe, teach and confess that although the truly believing and truly converted to God and justified Christians are liberated and made free from the curse of the Law; yet that they should daily exercise themselves in the Law of the Lord, as it is written (Ps. 1:2; 119:1): "Blessed is the man whose delight is in the Law of the Lord; and in his Law doth he meditate day and night." For the Law is a mirror, in which the will of God and what pleases him are exactly represented, so that it should be constantly held forth to believers and be diligently urged upon them without intermission.

For although "the Law is not made for a righteous man," as the apostle testifies (1 Tim. 1:9), "but for the unrighteous," yet this is not to be understood so absolutely as that the justified should live without law. For the Law of God is written in their heart, and to the first man immediately after his creation a law also was given, according to which he should have acted. But the meaning of St. Paul is that the Law cannot burden with its curse those who through Christ are reconciled to God, and need not vex with its coercion the regenerate, because, after the inner man, they have pleasure in God's Law.

And indeed, if the believing and elect children of God would be completely renewed by the indwelling Spirit in this life, so that in their nature and all its powers they would be entirely free from sin, they would need no law, and so also no impeller, but what they are in duty bound to do according to God's will they would do of themselves, and altogether voluntarily, without any instruction, admonition, solicitation or urging of the Law; just as the sun, the moon and all the constellations of heaven have of themselves, unobstructed, their regular course, without admonition, solicitation, urging, force or necessity, according to the arrangement of God which God once gave them, yea, just as the holy angels render an entirely voluntary obedience.

But since in this life believers have not been renewed perfectly or completely, *completive vel consummative* [as the ancients say], (for although their sins are covered by the perfect obedience of Christ, so that they are not imputed to believers for condemnation, and also, through the Holy Ghost, the mortification of the old Adam and the renewal in the spirit of their mind is begun), nevertheless the old Adam always clings to them in their nature and all its internal and external powers. Of this the apostle has written (Rom. 7:18 sqq.): "I know that in me [that is, in my flesh] dwelleth no good thing." And again: "For that which I do, I allow not; for what I would, that do I not; but what I hate, that do I." Again: "I see another law in my members, warring against the law of my mind, and bringing me into captivity to the law of sin." Also (Gal. 5:17): "The flesh lusteth against the spirit, and the spirit against the flesh; and these are contrary the one to the other: so that ye cannot do the things that ye would."

Therefore, because of these lusts of the flesh, the truly believing, elect and regenerate children of God require not only the daily instruction and admonition, warning and threatening of the Law, but also frequently reproofs, whereby they are roused [the old man is shaken from them] and follow the Spirit of God, as it is written (Ps. 119:71): "It is good for me that I have been afflicted, that I might learn thy statutes." And again (1 Cor. 9:27): "I keep under my body and bring it into subjection; lest that, by any means, when I have preached to others, I myself should be a castaway." And again (Heb. 12:8): "But if ye be without chastisement, whereof all are partakers, then are ye bastards and not sons;" as Dr. Luther in more words has fully explained in the summer part of the Church Postils, on the Epistle for the Nineteenth Sunday after Trinity.

But we must also separately explain what with respect to the new obedience of believers the Gospel does, affords and works, and what herein, so far as concerns the good works of believers, is the office of the Law.

For the Law says indeed that it is God's will and command that we should walk in a new life, but it does not give the power and faculty so that we can begin and do it; but the Holy Ghost, who is given and received, not through the Law, but through the preaching of the Gospel (Gal. 3:14), renews the heart. Afterwards the Holy Ghost employs the Law, so that from it he teaches the regenerate, and in the Ten Commandments points out and shows them "what is the good and acceptable will of God" (Rom. 12:2), in what good works "God hath before ordained that they should walk" (Eph. 2:10). He exhorts them thereto, and when, because of the flesh in them, they are idle, negligent and rebellious, he reproves them on that account through the Law, so that he carries on both offices together; he slays and makes alive, he leads to hell and brings up again. For his office is not only to *console,* but also to *reprove,* as is written: "When the Holy Ghost is come, he will reprove the world" (under which also is the old Adam) "of sin, and of righteousness and of judgment." But sin is everything that is contrary to God's Law. And St. Paul says: "All Scripture given by inspiration of God is profitable for doctrine, for reproof," etc., and to reprove is the peculiar office of the Law. Therefore as often as believers stumble they are reproved by the Holy Ghost from the Law, and by the same Spirit are again comforted and consoled with the preaching of the Holy Gospel.

But in order that, so far as possible, all misunderstanding may be avoided, and the distinction between the works of the Law and those of the Spirit be properly taught and preserved, it is to be noted with especial diligence that when the subject of good works which are in accordance with God's Law (for otherwise they are not good works) is treated, the word "Law" has only one sense, viz. the immutable will of God, according to which men should conduct themselves in their lives.

But there is a distinction in the works, because of the distinction with respect to the men who strive to live according to this Law and will of God. For as long as man is not regenerate, and conducts himself according to the Law, and does the works because they are thus command-ed, from fear of punishment or desire for reward, he is still under the Law, and his works are properly called by St. Paul works of the Law, for they are extorted by the Law, as those of slaves; and they are saints after the order of Cain [that is, hyprocrites].

But when man is born anew by the Spirit of God, and liberated from the Law, *i.e.* made exempt from this coercion, and is led by the Spirit of Christ, he lives according to the immutable will of God, comprised in the Law, and does everything, so far as he is born anew, out of a free, cheerful spirit; and this is called not properly a work of the Law, but a work and fruit of the Spirit, or as St. Paul names it "the law of the mind" and "the Law of Christ." For such men are no more under the Law, but under grace, as St. Paul says (Rom. 8 [Rom. 7:23; 8:2; 1 Cor. 9:21]).

But since believers are not, in this world, completely renewed, but the old Adam clings to them even to the grave, there also remains in them a struggle between the spirit and the flesh. Therefore they have indeed pleasure in God's Law according to the inner man, but the law in their members struggles against the law in their mind to such an extent that they are never without law, and nevertheless are not under, but in the Law, and live and walk in the Law of the Lord, and yet do nothing from *constraint* of the Law.

But so far as concerns the old Adam, which still clings to them, it must be urged on not only with the Law, but also with punishments; nevertheless it does everything against its will and under coercion, no less than the godless are

urged on and held in obedience by the threats of the Law (1 Cor. 9:27; Rom. 7:18, 19).

So, too, this doctrine of the Law is needful for believers, in order that they may not depend upon their own holiness and devotion, and under the pretext of the Spirit of God establish a self-chosen form of divine worship, without God's Word and command, as it is written (Deut. 12:8, 28, 32): "Ye shall not do . . . every man whatsoever is right in his own eyes" etc., but "observe and hear all these words which I command thee." "Thou shalt not add thereto, nor diminish therefrom."

So, too, the doctrine of the Law, in and with good works of believers, is needful for this reason, for otherwise man can easily imagine that his work and life are entirely pure and perfect. But the Law of God prescribes to believers good works in this way, that, at the same time, it shows and indicates, as in a mirror, that in this life they are still imperfect and impure in us, so that we must say with the apostle (1 Cor. 4:4): "I know nothing by myself; yet am I not hereby justified." Therefore, when Paul exhorts the regenerate to good works, he presents to them expressly the Ten Commandments (Rom. 13:9), and that his good works are imperfect and impure he recognizes from the Law (Rom. 7:7 sqq.); and David declares (Ps. 119:35): "I have run the way of thy commandments," but "enter not into judgment with thy servant; for in thy sight shall no man living be justified" (Ps. 143:2).

But how and why the good works of believers, although in this life, because of sin in the flesh, they are imperfect and impure, nevertheless are acceptable and well pleasing to God, the Law does not teach, as it requires an entire, perfect, pure obedience if it is to please God. But the Gospel teaches that our spiritual offerings are acceptable to God, through faith, for Christ's sake (1 Pet. 2:5; Heb. 11:4 sqq.). In this way Christians are not under the Law, but under grace, because by faith in Christ the persons [of the godly] are freed from the curse and condemnation of the Law; and because their good works, although they are still imperfect and impure, are acceptable, through Christ, to God, because they do, not by coercion of the Law, but by renewing of the Holy Ghost, voluntarily and spontane-ously from their hearts, what is pleasing to God, so far as they have been born anew according to the inner man; although nevertheless they maintain a constant struggle against the old Adam.

For the old Adam, as an intractable, pugnacious ass, is still a part of them, which is to be coerced to the obedience of Christ, not only by the doctrine, admonition, force and threatening of the Law, but also oftentimes by the club of punishments and troubles, until the sinful flesh is entirely put off, and man is perfectly renewed in the resurrection, where he needs no longer either the preaching of the Law or its threatenings and reproofs, as also no longer the Gospel; as these belong to this [mortal and] imperfect life. But as they will behold God face to face, so, through the power of the indwelling Spirit of God, will they do the will of God [the heavenly Father] with unmingled joy, volun-tarily, unconstrained, without any hindrance, with entire purity and perfection, and will eternally rejoice in him.

Accordingly, we reject and condemn as an error pernicious and prejudicial to Christian discipline, as also to true piety, the teaching that the Law, in the above-mentioned way and degree, should not be urged upon Christians and those truly believing, but only upon the unbelieving, not Christian, and impenitent.

CHAPTER VII. OF THE HOLY SUPPER.

Although perhaps, according to the opinion of some, the exposition of this article should not be inserted into this document, wherein it has been our intention to explain the articles which have been drawn into controversy among the theologians of the Augsburg Confession (from which the Sacramentarians almost in the beginning, when the Confession was first composed and presented to the Emperor at Augsburg in 1530, entirely withdrew and separated, and presented their own Confession), yet, alas! as we have still some theologians and others who glory in the Augsburg Confession, who in the last few years no longer secretly, but partly publicly, have given their assent in this article to the Sacramentarians, and against their own conscience have wished violently to cite and pervert the Augsburg Confession as in entire harmony in this article with the doctrine of the Sacramentarians; we neither can nor should forbear in this document to give testimony in accordance with our confession of divine truth, and to repeat the true sense and proper understanding, with reference to this article, of the Word of Christ and of the Augsburg Confession, and [for we recognize it to be our duty] so far as in us lies, by God's help, to preserve it [this pure doctrine] also to posterity, and to faithfully warn our hearers, together with other godly Christians, against this pernicious error, which is entirely contrary to the divine Word and the Augsburg Confession, and has been frequently condemned.

STATEMENT OF THE CONTROVERSY. *The Chief Conflict between our Doctrine and that of the Sacramentarians in this Article.*

Although some Sacramentarians strive to speak and to employ words the very nearest the Augsburg Confession and the form and mode of these churches, and confess that in the Holy Supper the body of Christ is truly received by believers, yet if they be forced to declare their meaning properly, sincerely and clearly, they all unanimously explain themselves thus, viz. that the true essential body and blood of Christ is as far from the consecrated bread and wine in the Holy Supper as the highest heaven is distant from the earth. For their own words run thus: Abesse Christi corpus ct sanguinem a signis tanto intervallo dicimus, quanto abest terra ab altissimis coelis. That is: "We say that the body and blood of Christ are as far from the signs as the earth is distant from the highest heaven." Therefore, they understand this presence of the body of Christ not as here upon earth, but only with respect to faith [when they speak of the presence of the body and blood of Christ in the Supper, they do not mean that they are present upon earth, except with respect to faith], *i.e.* that our faith, reminded and excited by the visible signs, as by the preached Word, elevates itself and rises up above all heavens, and there receives and enjoys the body of Christ, which is present there in heaven, yea, Christ himself,

together with all his benefits, in a true and essential, but nevertheless *only spiritual,* manner. For [they think that] as the bread and wine are here upon earth and not in heaven, so the body of Christ is now in heaven and not upon earth, and on this account nothing else is received by the mouth in the Holy Supper but bread and wine.

In the first place, they have alleged that the Lord's Supper is only an external sign, whereby Christians may be known, and that therein nothing else is offered but mere bread and wine (which are bare signs [symbols] of the absent body of Christ). Since this would not stand the test, they have confessed that the Lord Christ is truly present in his Supper, namely by the *communicatio idiomatum, i.e.* alone according to his divine nature, but not with his body and blood.

Afterwards, when they were forced by Christ's words to confess that the body of Christ is present in the Supper, they still understood and declared it in no other way than spiritually, that is, through faith to partake of his power, efficacy and benefits [than that they believed the presence only spiritual, *i.e.* that Christ only makes us partakers of his power, efficacy and benefits], because [they say] through the Spirit of Christ, who is everywhere, our bodies, in which the Spirit of Christ dwells here upon earth, are united with the body of Christ, which is in heaven.

Thus through these grand, plausible words many great men were deceived when they proclaimed and boasted that they were of no other opinion than that the Lord Christ is present in his Holy Supper truly, essentially, and as one alive; but they understand this alone according to his divine nature, and not of his body and blood, which are now in heaven, and nowhere else [for they think concerning these that they are only in heaven, etc.], and that he gives us with the bread and wine his true body and blood to eat, that we may partake of them spiritually through faith, but not bodily with the mouth.

For they understand the words of the Supper: "Eat, this is my body," not properly, as they sound, according to the letter, but as figurative expressions; thus, that "eating" the body of Christ means nothing else than "believing," and that "body" is equivalent to "symbol," *i.e.* a sign or figure of the body of Christ, which is not in the Supper on earth, but alone in heaven. The word *is* they interpret sacramentally, or in a significative manner, in order that no one may regard the thing so joined with the signs, that the flesh also of Christ is now present on earth in an invisible and incomprehensible manner. That is: "The body of Christ is united with the bread sacramentally, or significatively, so that believing, godly Christians as surely partake spiritually of the body of Christ, which is above in heaven, as with the mouth they eat the bread." But that the body of Christ is present here upon earth in the Supper essentially although invisibly and incomprehensibly, and is received orally, with the consecrated bread, even by hypocrites or those who are Christians only in appearance [by name], this they are accustomed to execrate and condemn as a horrible blasphemy.

On the other hand, it is taught in the Augsburg Confession from God's Word concerning the Lord's Supper, thus:

THE FORMULA OF CONCORD (1580) (continued)

"That the true body and blood of Christ are truly present in the Holy Supper under the form of bread and wine, and are there communicated and received, and the contrary doctrine is rejected" (namely, that of the Sacramentarians, who at the same time at Augsburg presented their own Confession, that the body of Christ, because he has ascended to heaven, is not truly and essentially present here upon earth in the sacrament [which denied the true and substantial presence of the body and blood of Christ in the sacrament of the Supper administered on earth, on this account, viz. because Christ had ascended into heaven]. For this opinion is clearly expressed in Luther's Small Catechism in the following words: "The sacrament of the altar is the true body and blood of our Lord Jesus Christ under the bread and wine, given unto us Christians to eat and to drink, as it was instituted by Christ himself." Still more clearly in the Apology is this not only declared, but also established by the passage from Paul (1 Cor. 10:16), and by the testimony of Cyril, in the following words: "The tenth article has been received [approved], in which we confess that in the Lord's Supper the body and blood of Christ are truly and substantially present, and are truly offered with the visible elements, bread and wine, to those who receive the sacrament. For since Paul says: 'The bread which we break is the communion of the body of Christ,' etc., it would follow, if the body of Christ were not, but only the Holy Ghost were truly present, that the bread is not a communion of the body, but of the Spirit of Christ. Thus we know that not only the Romish, but also the Greek Church, has taught the bodily presence of Christ in the Holy Supper." And testimony is also produced from Cyril that Christ also dwells bodily in us in the Holy Supper by the communication of his flesh.

Afterwards, when those who at Augsburg delivered their Confession concerning this article seemed to be willing to approve the Confession of our churches, the following *Formula Concordia, i.e.* articles of Christian agreement between the Saxon theologians and those of Upper Germany, was composed and signed at Wittenberg in the year 1536, by Dr. Martin Luther and other theologians on both sides:

"We have heard how Mr. Martin Bucer explained his own opinion, and that of other preachers who came with him from the cities, concerning the holy sacrament of the body and blood of Christ, viz. as follows:

"They confess, according to the words of Irenaeus, that in this sacrament there are two things, a heavenly and an earthly. Therefore they hold and teach that, with the bread and wine, the body and blood of Christ are truly and essentially present, offered and received. And although they believe in no trans-substantiation, *i.e.* an essential transformation of the bread and wine into the body and blood of Christ, and also do not hold that the body and blood of Christ are included locally, *i.e.* with respect to space, in the bread, or are otherwise permanently united therewith apart from the use of the sacrament; yet they concede that through the sacramental union the bread is the body of Christ, etc. [that when the bread is offered the body of Christ is at the same time present, and is truly

tendered]. For apart from use, if the bread be laid by and preserved in a pyx, or be carried about and exhibited in processions, as occurs in the Papacy, they do not hold that the body of Christ is present.

"Secondly, they hold that the institution of this sacrament made by Christ is efficacious in Christendom [the Church], and that it does not depend upon the worthiness or unworthiness of the minister who offers the sacrament or of the one who receives it. Therefore, as St. Paul says, that even the unworthy partake of the sacrament, they hold that also to the unworthy the body and blood of Christ are truly offered, and the unworthy truly receive them, where the institution and command of the Lord Christ are observed. But such persons receive them to condemnation, as St. Paul says; for they abuse the holy sacrament, because they receive it without true repentance and without faith. For it was instituted for this purpose, viz. that it might testify that to them the grace and benefits of Christ are there applied, and that they are incorporated into Christ and are washed by his blood, who there truly repent and comfort themselves by faith in Christ."

In the following year, when the chief theologians of the Augsburg Confession assembled from all Germany at Smalcald, and deliberated as to what to present in the Council concerning this doctrine of the Church, by common consent the Smalcald Articles were composed by Dr. Luther, and were signed by all the theologians, collectively and individually, in which the true and proper opinion is clearly expressed in short, plain words, which agree most accurately with the words of Christ, and every door and mode of escape for the Sacramentarians was closed. For they had interpreted to their advantage [perverted] the Formula of Concord, *i.e.* the above-mentioned articles of union, framed the preceding year, so that it should be understood that the body of Christ is offered with the bread in no other way than as it is offered, together with all his benefits, by the Word of the Gospel, and that by the sacramental union nothing else than the spiritual presence of the Lord Christ by faith is meant. These articles, therefore, declare: "The bread and wine in the Holy Supper are the true body and blood of Jesus Christ, which are tendered and received, not only by the godly, but also by godless Christians" [those who have nothing Christian except the name].

Dr. Luther has also more amply expounded and confirmed this opinion from God's Word in the Large Catechism, where it is written:

"What is therefore the Sacrament of the Altar? Answer: It is the true body and blood of our Lord Jesus Christ, in and under the bread and wine, which we Christians are commanded by the Word of Christ to eat and to drink." And shortly after: "It is the Word, I say, which makes and distinguishes this sacrament, so that it is not mere bread and wine, but is, and is properly called the body and blood of Christ." Again: "With this Word you can strengthen your conscience and say: If a hundred thousand devils, together with all fanatics, raise the objection, How can bread and wine be the body and blood of Christ? I know that all spirits and scholars together are not as wise as is the Divine Majesty in his little finger. For here stands the

Word of Christ: 'Take, eat; this is my body. Drink ye all of this; this is the new testament in my blood,' etc. Here we abide, and would like to see those who will constitute themselves his masters, and make it different from what he has spoken. It is true, indeed, that if you take away the Word, or regard it without the Word, you have nothing but mere bread and wine. But if the Word be added thereto, as it must be, then in virtue of the same it is truly the body and blood of Christ. For as the lips of Christ have spoken, so it is, as he can never lie or deceive.

"Hence it is easy to reply to all manner of questions about which at the present time men are anxious, as, for instance: Whether a wicked priest can administer and distribute the sacrament? and such like other points. For here conclude and reply: Even though a knave take or distribute the sacrament, he receives the true sacrament, *i.e.* the true body and blood of Christ, just as truly as he who receives or administers it in the most worthy manner. For it is not founded upon the holiness of men, but upon the Word of God. And as no saint upon earth, yea, no angel in heaven, can change bread and wine into the body and blood of Christ, so also can no one change or alter it, even though it be abused.

"For the Word, by which it became a sacrament and was instituted, does not become false because of the person or his unbelief. For he does not say: If you believe or are worthy you will receive my body and blood, but: 'Take, eat and drink; this is my body and blood.' Likewise: 'Do this' (viz. what I now do, institute, give and bid you take). That is as much as to say, No matter whether you be worthy or unworthy, you have here his body and blood, by virtue of these words which are added to the bread and wine. This mark and observe well; for upon these words rest all our foundation, protection and defence against all error and temptation that have ever come or may yet come."

Thus far the Large Catechism, in which the true presence of the body and blood of Christ in the Holy Supper is established from God's Word; and the same is understood not only of the believing and worthy, but also of the unbelieving and unworthy.

But inasmuch as this highly-illumined man [Dr. Luther, the hero illumined with unparalleled and most excellent gifts of the Holy Ghost] foresaw that after his death some would suspect that he had receded from the above-mentioned doctrine and other Christian articles, he has appended the following protest to his Large Confession:

"Because I see the longer the time the greater the number of sects and errors, and that there is no end to the rage and fury of Satan, in order that henceforth during my life, and after my death, some of them may not, in future, support themselves by me, and in order to strengthen their error falsely quote my writings, as the Sacramentarians and Anabaptists begin to do; I will in this writing, before God and all the world, confess my faith, point by point [concerning all the articles of our religion]. In this I intend to abide until my death, and therein (and may God help me as to this!) to depart from this world and to appear before the judgment-seat of Jesus Christ; and if after my death any one will say: If Dr. Luther were now living he would teach and hold this or that article differently, for he

did not sufficiently consider it, against this I say now as then, and then as now, that, by God's grace, I have most diligently considered all these articles by means of the Scriptures [have examined them, not once, but very often, according to the standard of Holy Scripture], and often have gone over them, and will contend as confidently for them as I am now contending for the Sacrament of the Altar. I am not drunk or inconsiderate; I know what I say; I also am sensible of the account which I will render at the coming of the Lord Christ at the final judgment. Therefore no one should interpret this as jest or mere idle talk; to me it is serious; for by God's grace I know Satan in great part; if he can pervert or confuse God's Word, what will he not do with my words or those of another?"

After this protest, Dr. Luther, of holy memory, presents among other articles this also: "In the same manner I also speak and confess" (he says) "concerning the Sacrament of the Altar, that there the body and blood of Christ are in truth orally eaten and drunken in the bread and wine, even though the priests [ministers] who administer it [the Lord's Supper], or those who receive it, do not believe or otherwise abuse it. For it does not depend upon the faith or unbelief of men, but upon God's Word and ordinance, unless they first change God's Word and ordinance and interpret it otherwise, as the enemies of the sacrament do at the present day, who, of course, have nothing but bread and wine; for they also do not have the Word and appointed ordinance of God, but have perverted and changed it according to their own caprice."

Dr. Luther (who certainly, above others, understood the true and proper meaning of the Augsburg Confession, and who constantly, even to his end, remained steadfast thereto, and defended it) shortly before his death, with great zeal, repeated in his last Confession his faith concerning this article, where he writes thus: "I reckon all in one mass as Sacramentarians and fanatics, as they also are who will not believe that the bread in the Lord's Supper is his true natural body, which the godless as Judas himself received with the mouth, as well as did St. Peter, and all [other] saints; he who will not believe this (I say) should let me alone, and not hope for any fellowship with me; there is no alternative [thus my opinion stands, which I am not going to change]."

From these explanations, and especially from that of Dr. Luther as the chief teacher of the Augsburg Confession, every ir˙elligent man, if he be desirous of the truth and of peace, can undoubtedly perceive what has always been the proper sense and understanding of the Augsburg Confession in regard to this article.

For the reason that in addition to the expressions of Christ and St. Paul (viz. that the bread in the Supper "is the body of Christ" or "the communion of the body of Christ"), also the forms: "under the bread," "with the bread," "in the bread" ["the body of Christ is present and offered"], are employed, is that hereby the Papistical transubstantiation may be rejected, and the sacramental union of the unchanged essence of the bread and of the body of Christ may be indicated; just as the expression, "the Word was made flesh" (John 1:14), is repeated and explained by the equivalent expressions: "The Word dwelt among us;" (Col.

THE FORMULA OF CONCORD (1580) (continued)

2:9): "In him dwelleth all the fulness of the Godhead bodily;" also (Acts 10:38): "God was with him;" also (2 Cor. 5:19): "God was in Christ," and the like; namely, that the divine essence is not changed into the human nature, but the two natures unchanged are personally united. [These phrases repeat the expression of John above-mentioned, and declare that, by the incarnation, the divine essence is not changed into the human nature, but that the two natures without confusion are personally united.]

And indeed many eminent ancient teachers, Justin, Cyprian, Augustine, Leo, Gelasius, Chrysostom and others, use this simile concerning the words of Christ's testament: "This is my body," viz. that just as in Christ two distinct, unchanged natures are inseparably united, so in the Holy Supper the two substances, the natural bread and the true natural body of Christ, are present here together upon earth in the appointed administration of the sacrament. Although this union of the body and blood of Christ with the bread and wine is not a personal union, as that of the two natures in Christ, but a sacramental union, as Dr. Luther and our theologians, in the frequently-mentioned Articles of Agreement [Formula of Concord] in the year 1536 and in other places, call it; in order to declare that although they also employ the forms, "in the bread," "under the bread," "with the bread," yet the words of Christ they receive properly and as they sound, and understand the proposition, *i.e.* the words of Christ's testament: "This is my body," not as a figurative, but as an unusual expression. For Justin says: "This we receive not as common bread and common drink, but as Jesus Christ, our Saviour, through the Word of God became flesh, and on account of our salvation also had flesh and blood, so we believe that, by the Word and prayer, the food blessed by him is the body and blood of our Lord Jesus Christ." Dr. Luther also in his Large and especially in his last Confession, concerning the Lord's Supper, with great earnestness and zeal defends the very form of expression which Christ used at the first Supper.

For since Dr. Luther is to be regarded the most distinguished teacher of the churches which confess the Augsburg Confession, whose entire doctrine as to sum and substance was comprised in the articles of the frequently-mentioned Augsburg Confession, and was presented to the Emperor Charles V.; the proper understanding and sense of the said Augsburg Confession can and should be derived from no other source more properly and correctly than from the doctrinal and polemical writings of Dr. Luther.

And indeed this very opinion, just cited, is founded upon the only firm, immovable and indubitable rock of truth, from the words of institution in the holy, divine Word, and was thus understood, taught and propagated by the holy evangelists and apostles and their disciples.

For since our Lord and Saviour, Jesus Christ, concerning whom, as our only Teacher, this solemn command: "Hear ye him," has been given from heaven to all men, who is not a mere man or angel, and also not only true, wise and mighty, but the eternal truth and wisdom itself and Almighty God, who knows very well what and how he should speak, and who also can powerfully effect and execute everything that he speaks and promises, as he says (Luke 21:33): "Heaven and earth shall pass away; but my words shall not pass away;" also (Matt. 28:18): "All power is given unto me in heaven and in earth,"—

Since now this true, almighty Lord, our Creator and Redeemer, Jesus Christ, after the Last Supper, when he is just beginning his bitter suffering and death for our sins, on that last sad time, with great consideration and solemnity, in the institution of this most venerable sacrament (which was to be used until the end of the world with great reverence and obedience [and humility], and was to be an abiding memorial of his bitter suffering and death and all his benefits, a sealing [and confirmation] of the New Testament, a consolation of all distressed hearts and a firm bond and means of union of Christians with Christ their head and with one another), in the founding and institution of the Holy Supper spake these words concerning the bread which he blessed and gave [to his disciples]: "Take, eat; this is my body, which is given for you," and concerning the cup or wine: "This is my blood of the new testament, which is shed for many for the remission of sins;"—

We are in duty bound not to interpret and explain these words of the eternal, true and almighty Son of God, our Lord, Creator and Redeemer, Jesus Christ, as allegorical, metaphorical, tropical expressions, as may appear to be in conformity with our reason, but with simple faith and due obedience to receive the words as they sound, in their proper and plain sense, and allow ourselves to be diverted therefrom [from this express testament of Christ] by no objections or human contradictions spun from human reason, however charming they may appear to the reason.

As when Abraham heard God's Word concerning offering his son, although indeed he had cause enough for disputing as to whether the words should be understood according to the letter or with a moderate or mild interpretation, since they conflicted not only with all reason and with divine and natural law, but also with the chief article of faith concerning the promised Seed, Christ, who was to be born of Isaac; and yet, as before, when the promise of the blessed Seed from Isaac was given him (although it appeared to his reason impossible), he gave God the honor of truth, and most confidently concluded and believed that God could do what he promised; so also here faith understands and believes God's Word and command plainly and simply, as they sound, according to the letter, and resigns the entire matter to the divine omnipotence and wisdom, which it knows has many more modes and ways to fulfil the promise of the Seed from Isaac than man with his blind reason can comprehend.

Thus, with all humility and obedience we too should simply believe the plain, firm, clear and solemn word and command of our Creator and Redeemer, without any doubt and disputation as to how it may agree with our reason or be possible. For these words THE LORD, who is infinite wisdom and truth itself, has spoken, and everything which he promises he also can execute and accomplish.

Now, all the circumstances of the institution of the Holy Supper testify that these words of our Lord and Saviour,

Jesus Christ, which in themselves are simple, plain, clear, firm and indubitable, cannot and should not be understood otherwise than in their usual, proper and common signification. For since Christ gave this command [concerning eating his body, etc.] at his table and at the Supper, there is indeed no doubt that he speaks of real, natural bread and of natural wine, also of oral eating and drinking, so that there can be no metaphor, *i.e.* an alteration of meaning, in the word "bread," as though the body of Christ were a spiritual bread or a spiritual food of souls. So also Christ himself carefully shows that there is no metonymy, *i.e.* that there is no alteration of meaning in the same way, in the word "body," and that he does not speak concerning a sign of his body, or concerning a symbol or figurative body, or concerning the virtue of his body and the benefits which he has earned by the sacrifice of his body [for us], but of his true, essential body, which he delivered for us to death, and of his true, essential blood, which he shed for us on the tree [altar] of the cross, for the remission of sins.

Now, indeed, there is no interpreter of the Word of Jesus Christ so faithful and sure as the Lord Christ himself, who understands best his words and his heart and opinion, and who is the wisest and most knowing in expounding them; who here, as in the making of his last will and testament and of his ever-abiding covenant and union, as elsewhere in [presenting and confirming] all articles of faith, and in the institution of all other signs of the covenant and of grace or sacraments, as [for example] circumcision, the various offerings in the Old Testament and holy baptism, has employed not allegorical, but entirely proper, simple, indubitable and clear words; and in order that no misunderstanding could occur with the words: "given for you," "shed for you," he has made a clear explanation. He also allowed his disciples to rest in the simple, proper sense, and commanded them that they should teach all nations to observe what he had commanded them, the apostles.

Therefore, also, all three evangelists (Matt. 26:26; Mark 14:22; Luke 22:19) and St. Paul, who received it [the institution of the Lord's Supper] after the ascension of Christ [from Christ himself], (1 Cor. 11:24), unanimously and with one and the same words and syllables, concerning the consecrated and distributed bread repeat these distinct, clear, firm and true words of Christ: "This is my body," altogether in one way, without any explanation [trope, figure] and variation. Therefore there is no doubt that also concerning the other part of the sacrament these words of Luke and Paul: "This cup is the new testament in my blood," can have no other meaning than that which St. Matthew and St. Mark give: "This" (namely, that which you orally drink out of the cup) "is my blood of the new testament," whereby I establish, seal and confirm with you men my testament and the new covenant, viz. the forgiveness of sins.

So also that repetition, confirmation and explanation of the Word of Christ which St. Paul makes (1 Cor. 10:16), as an especially clear testimony of the true, essential presence and distribution of the body and blood of Christ in the Supper, is to be considered with all diligence and solemnity [accurately], where he writes as follows: "The cup of blessing which we bless, is it not the communion of the blood of Christ? The bread which we break, is it not the communion of the body of Christ?" From this we clearly learn that not only the cup which Christ consecrated at the first Supper, and not only the bread which Christ broke and distributed, but also that which *we* break and bless, is the communion of the body and blood of Christ, so that all who eat this bread and drink of this cup truly receive and are partakers of the true body and blood of Christ. For if the body of Christ were present and partaken of, not truly and essentially, but only according to its power and efficacy, the bread would not be a communion of the body, but must be called a communion of the Spirit, power and benefits of Christ, as the Apology argues and concludes. And if Paul speaks only of the spiritual communion of the body of Christ through faith, as the Sacramentarians pervert this passage, he would not say that the bread, but that the spirit or faith, was the communion of the body of Christ. But as he says that the bread is the communion of the body of Christ, viz. that all who partake of the consecrated bread also become participants of the body of Christ, he must speak indeed not of a spiritual, but of a sacramental or oral participation of the body of Christ, which is common to godly and godless Christians [Christians only in name].

As also the causes and circumstances of this entire declaration of St. Paul show that he deters and warns those who ate of offerings to idols and had fellowship with heathen demonolatry, and nevertheless went also to the table of the Lord and became partakers of the body and blood of Christ, that they should not receive the body and blood of Christ for judgment and condemnation to themselves. For since all those who were partakers of the consecrated and broken bread in the Supper have communion also with the body of Christ, St. Paul cannot speak indeed of spiritual communion with Christ, which no man can abuse, and from which also no one should be warned.

Therefore, also, our dear fathers and predecessors, as Luther and other pure teachers of the Augsburg Confession, explain this expression of Paul with such words that it accords most fully with the words of Christ when they write thus: The bread which we break is the distributed body of *Christ,* or the common [communicated] body of Christ, distributed to those who receive the broken bread.

By this simple, well-founded exposition of this glorious testimony (1 Cor. 10) we unanimously abide, and we justly are astonished that some are so bold as to venture to cite this passage, which they themselves had previously opposed to the Sacramentarians, as now a foundation for their error, that in the Supper the body of Christ is only spiritually partaken of. [For thus they speak]: "The bread is the communion of the body of Christ, *i.e.* that by which there is fellowship with the body of Christ (which is the Church), or is the means by which we believers are united with Christ, just as the Word of the Gospel is the means, apprehended by faith, through which we are spiritually united to Christ and inserted into the body of Christ, which is the Church."

For that not only the godly, pious and believing Christians, but also unworthy, godless hypocrites, as Judas and his

THE FORMULA OF CONCORD (1580) (continued)

companions, who have no spiritual communion with Christ, and go to the table of the Lord without true repentance and conversion to God, also receive orally in the sacrament the true body and [true] blood of Christ, and by their unworthy eating and drinking grievously sin against the body and blood of Christ, St. Paul teaches expressly. For he says (1 Cor. 11:27): "Whosoever shall eat this bread, and drink this cup of the Lord, unworthily," sins not merely against the bread and wine, not merely against the signs or symbols and representation of the body and blood, but "shall be guilty of the body and blood of the Lord," which, present there [in the Holy Supper], he dishonors, abuses and disgraces, as the Jews who in very deed violated the body of Christ and killed him; just as the ancient Christian Fathers and church-teachers unanimously have understood and explained this passage.

There is, therefore, a twofold eating of the flesh of Christ, one "spiritual," of which Christ especially treats (John 6:54), which occurs in no other way than with the Spirit and faith, in the preaching and consideration of the Gospel, as well as in the Lord's Supper, and by itself is useful and salutary, and necessary at all times for salvation to all Christians; without which spiritual participation also the sacramental or oral eating in the Supper is not only not salutary, but even injurious and a cause of condemnation.

But this spiritual eating is nothing else than *faith,* namely, to hearken to God's Word (wherein Christ, true God and man, is presented, together with all his benefits which he has purchased for us by his flesh given for us to death, and by his blood shed for us, namely, God's grace, the forgiveness of sins, righteousness and eternal life), to receive it with faith and appropriate it to ourselves, and in the consolation that we have a gracious God, and eternal salvation on account of the Lord Jesus Christ, with sure confidence and trust, to firmly rely and abide in all troubles and temptations. [He who hears these things related from the Word of God, and in faith receives and applies them to himself, and relies entirely upon this consolation (that we have God reconciled and life eternal on account of the Mediator, Jesus Christ),—he, I say, who with true confidence rests in the Word of the Gospel in all troubles and temptations, spiritually eats the body of Christ and drinks his blood.]

The other eating of the body of Christ is *oral* or *sacramental,* where, in the Holy Supper, the true, essential body and blood of Christ are received and partaken of by all who eat and drink in the Supper the consecrated bread and wine—by the believing as an infallible pledge and assurance that their sins are surely forgiven them, and Christ dwells and is efficacious in them, but by the unbelieving for their judgment and condemnation. This the words of the institution by Christ expressly teach, when at the table and during the Supper he offers his disciples natural bread and natural wine, which he calls his true body and true blood, and in addition says: "Eat and drink." Such a command, in view of the circumstances, cannot indeed be understood otherwise than of oral eating and drinking, not in a gross, carnal, Capernaitic, yet in a supernatural, incomprehensible way; to which the other command adds still another and spiritual eating, when the Lord Christ says further: "This do in remembrance of me," where he requires faith (which is the spiritual partaking of Christ's body).

Therefore all the ancient Christian teachers expressly, and in full accord with the entire holy Christian Church, teach, according to these words of the institution of Christ and the explanation of St. Paul, that the body of Christ is not only received spiritually by faith, which occurs also without the use of the sacrament, but also orally, not only by believing and godly, but also by unworthy, unbelieving, false and wicked Christians. As this is too long to be narrated here, we will have to refer the Christian reader, for the sake of brevity, to the more ample writings of our theologians.

Hence it is manifest how unjustly and maliciously the Sacramentarian fanatics deride the Lord Christ, St. Paul and the entire Church in calling this oral partaking, and that of the unworthy, *duos pilos caudae equinae et commentum, cujus vel ipsum Satanam pudeat,* as also the doctrine concerning the majesty of Christ, *excrementum Satanae, quo diabolus sibi ipsi et hominibus illudat, i.e.* they speak so dreadfully thereof that a godly Christian man should be ashamed to translate it.

But it must also be carefully stated who are the unworthy guests of this Supper—namely, those who go to this sacrament without true repentance and sorrow for their sins, and without true faith and the good intention to improve their lives, and by their unworthy eating of the body of Christ incur temporal and eternal punishments and are guilty of the body and blood of Christ.

For Christians of weak faith, diffident and troubled, who, because of the greatness and number of their sins, are terrified, and think that, in this their great impurity, they are not worthy of this precious treasure and the benefits of Christ, and who feel and lament their weakness of faith, and from their hearts desire that they may serve God with stronger, more joyful faith and pure obedience, are the truly worthy guests for whom this highly venerable sacrament [and sacred feast] has been especially instituted and appointed; as Christ says (Matt. 11:28): "Come unto me, all ye that labor and are heavy laden, and I will give you rest." Also (Matt. 9:12): "They that be whole need not a physician, but they that be sick." Also (2 Cor. 12:9): "God's strength is made perfect in weakness." Also (Rom. 14:1): "Him that is weak in the faith receive ye" (v.3), "for God hath received him." "For whosoever believeth in the Son of God," be it with a strong or with a weak faith, "has eternal life" (John 3:15 sq.).

And the worthiness does not depend upon great or small weakness or strength of faith, but upon the merit of Christ, which the distressed father of little faith (Mark 9:24) enjoyed as well as Abraham, Paul and others, who had a joyful and strong faith.

Thus far we have spoken of the true presence and two-fold participation of the body and blood of Christ, which occurs either by faith spiritually or also orally, both by worthy and unworthy [which latter is common to worthy and unworthy].

Since also concerning the consecration and the common rule, that "nothing is a sacrament without the appointed use" [or divinely-instituted act], a misunderstanding and dissension has occurred between some teachers of the Augsburg Confession, we have also, concerning this matter, made a fraternal and unanimous declaration to one another to the following purport, viz. that not the word or work of any man produces the true presence of the body and blood of Christ in the Supper, whether it be the merit or declaration of the minister, or the eating and drinking or faith of the communicants; but all this should be ascribed alone to the power of Almighty God and the institution and ordination of our Lord Jesus Christ. [But all that which we have present in the Supper of Christ is to be ascribed absolutely and altogether to the power and Word of Almighty God and the institution, etc.]

For the true and almighty words of Jesus Christ, which he spake at the first institution, were efficacious not only at the first Supper, but they endure, have authority, operate and are still efficacious [their force, power and efficacy endure and avail even to the present]; so that in all places where the Supper is celebrated according to the institution of Christ, and his words are used, from the power and efficacy of the words which Christ spake at the first Supper the body and blood of Christ are truly present, distributed and received. For where his institution is observed and his words concerning the bread and cup [wine] are spoken, and the consecrated bread and cup [wine] are distributed, Christ himself, through the spoken words, is still efficacious *by virtue of the first institution,* through his Word which he wishes to be there repeated. As Chrysostom says in his sermon concerning the passion: "Christ himself prepares this table and blesses it; for no man makes the bread and wine set before us the body and blood of Christ, but Christ himself who was crucified for us. The words are spoken by the mouth of the priest, but, by God's power and grace, the elements presented are consecrated in the Supper by the Word, where he speaks: 'This is my body.' And just as the declaration (Gen. 1:28): 'Be fruitful, and multiply, and replenish the earth,' was spoken only once, but is ever efficacious in nature, so that it is fruitful and multiplies; so also this declaration [This is my body; this is my blood] was once spoken, but even to this day and to his advent it is efficacious, and works so that in the Supper of the churches his true body and blood are present."

Luther also [writes concerning this very subject in the same manner], (vol. vi., Jena Ed., p. 99): "This his command and institution are able and effect it that we administer and receive not mere bread and wine, but his body and blood, as his words run: 'This is my body,' etc.; 'This is my blood,' etc. It is not our work or declaration, but the command and ordination of Christ, that makes the bread the body, and the wine the blood, from the beginning of the first Supper even to the end of the world, and that through our service and office they are daily distributed."

Also (vol. iii., Jena, p. 446): "Thus here also, even though I should pronounce over all bread the words: 'This is Christ's body,' it would of course not follow thence, but if we say, according to his institution and command, in the administration of the Holy Supper: 'This is my body,' it is

his body, not on account of our declaration or demonstration [because these words when uttered have this efficacy], but because of his command—that he has commanded us thus to speak and to do, and has united his command and act with our declaration."

And indeed, in the administration of the Holy Supper the words of institution should be publicly [before the church] spoken or sung, distinctly and clearly, and should in no way be omitted [and this for very many and the most important reasons. First,] in order that obedience may be rendered to the command of Christ: "This do" [that therefore should not be omitted which Christ himself did in the Holy Supper], and [secondly] that the faith of the hearers concerning the nature and fruit of this sacrament (concerning the presence of the body and blood of Christ, concerning the forgiveness of sins and all benefits which have been purchased by the death and shedding of blood of Christ, and are bestowed upon us in Christ's testament) may be excited, strengthened and confirmed by Christ's Word, and [besides that the elements of bread and wine may be consecrated or blessed for this holy use], in order that the body and blood of Christ may therewith be administered to be eaten and to be drunk [that with them the body of Christ may be offered us to be eaten and his blood to be drunk], as Paul declares (1 Cor. 10:16): "The cup of blessing which we bless," which indeed occurs in no other way than through the repetition and recitation of the words of institution.

Nevertheless, this blessing, or the narration of the words of institution of Christ, does not alone make a sacrament if the entire action of the Supper, as it was instituted by Christ, be not observed, as [for example] when the consecrated bread is not distributed, received and partaken of, but is enclosed, sacrificed or carried about. But the command of Christ, "This do," which embraces the entire action or transaction in this sacrament, viz. that in an assembly of Christians bread and wine are taken, consecrated, distributed, received, *i.e.* eaten and drunk, and the Lord's death is thereby shown forth, should be observed unseparated and inviolate, as also St. Paul presents before our eyes the entire action of the breaking of bread or of distribution and reception (1 Cor. 10:16).

[Let us now come also to the second point, of which mention was made a little before.] To preserve the true Christian doctrine concerning the Holy Supper, and to avoid and obliterate various idolatrous abuses and perversions of this testament, the following useful rule and standard has been derived from the words of institution: "Nothing has the nature of a sacrament apart from the use instituted by Christ," or "apart from the action divinely instituted." That is: "If the institution of Christ be not observed as he appointed it, there is no sacrament." This is by no means to be rejected, but with profit can and should be urged and maintained in the churches of God. And the use or action here is not chiefly the faith, also not only the oral participation, but the entire, external, visible action of the Lord's Supper instituted by Christ. [To this indeed is required], the *consecration,* or words of institution, and the *distribution* and *reception,* or oral partaking [manducation] of the consecrated bread and wine, likewise the partaking of the body and blood of Christ. And apart from this use,

THE FORMULA OF CONCORD (1580) (continued)

when, in the Papistic mass, the bread is not distributed, but offered up or enclosed and borne about, and presented for adoration, it is to be regarded as no sacrament; just as the water of baptism, if used to consecrate bells or to cure leprosy, or otherwise presented for worship, would be no sacrament or baptism. For from the beginning [of the reviving Gospel] this rule has been opposed to these Papistic abuses, and is explained by Dr. Luther himself (vol. iv., Jena Edition).

But we must besides observe also this, viz. that the Sacramentarians artfully and wickedly pervert this useful and necessary rule, in order to deny the true, essential presence and oral partaking of the body of Christ, which occurs here upon earth alike by the worthy and the unworthy; and who interpret it as referring to the use by faith, *i.e.* the spiritual and inner use of faith, as though with the unworthy there were no sacrament, and the partaking of the body occurred only spiritually through faith, or as though faith made the body of Christ present in the Holy Supper, and therefore unworthy, unbelieving hypocrites do not actually receive the body of Christ.

Now, it is not our faith that makes the sacrament, but only the true word and institution of our Almighty God and Saviour, Jesus Christ, which always is and remains efficacious in the Christian Church, and neither by the worthiness or unworthiness of the minister nor the unbelief of the one who receives it is it as anything invalidated or rendered inefficacious. Just as the Gospel, even though godless hearers do not believe it, yet is and remains none the less the true Gospel, but does not work in the unbelieving to salvation; so, whether those who receive the sacrament believe or do not believe, Christ remains none the less true in his words when he says: "Take, eat: this is my body," and effects this [his presence] not by our faith, but by his omnipotence.

But it is a pernicious, shameless error that some from cunning perversion of this familiar rule ascribe more to our faith, which [in their opinion] alone renders present and partakes of the body of Christ, than to the omnipotence of our Lord and Saviour, Jesus Christ.

Concerning what pertains to the various imaginary reasons and futile counter-arguments of the Sacramentarians with respect to the essential and natural attributes of a human body, the ascension of Christ, his departure from this world, etc., inasmuch as these have one and all been considered thoroughly and in detail, from God's Word, by Dr. Luther in his controversial writings: "Against the Heavenly Prophets," "That these words, 'This is my body,' still stand firm;" likewise in his "Large" and his "Small Confession concerning the Holy Supper," [published some years afterwards], and other of his writings, and inasmuch as since his death nothing new has been advanced by the factious spirits, for the sake of brevity we will refer and appeal thereto.

For that we neither will, nor can, nor should allow ourselves to be led away by thoughts of human wisdom, whatever authority or outward appearance they may have, from the simple, distinct and clear sense of the Word and testament of Christ to a strange opinion, other than the words sound, but that, in accordance with what is above stated, we understand and believe them simply; our reasons upon which we rest in this matter, ever since the controversy concerning this article arose, are those which Dr. Luther himself, in the very beginning, presented against the Sacramentarians in the following words: "The reasons upon which I rest in this matter are the following:

"1. The first is this article of our faith: Jesus Christ is essential, natural, true, perfect God and man in one person, undivided and inseparable.

"2. The second, that God's right hand is everywhere.

"3. The third, that God's Word is not false and does not deceive.

"4. The fourth, that God has and knows of many modes of being in any place, and not only the single one concerning which fanatics talk flippantly and which philosophers call local."

Also: "The one body of Christ [says Luther] has a three-fold mode or three modes of being anywhere.

"First, the comprehensible, bodily mode, as he went about in the body upon earth, when, according to his size, he made and occupied room [was circumscribed by fixed places]. It is mode he can still use whenever he will, as he did after the resurrection, and will use at the last day, as Paul says (1 Tim. 6:15): "Which in his times He shall show who is the blessed and only Potentate, the King of kings and Lord of lords." And to the Colossians (3:4) he says: "When Christ who is our life shall appear." In this manner he is not in God or with the Father, neither in heaven, as the wild spirits dream; for God is not a bodily space or place. And to this effect are the passages of Scripture which the fanatical spirits cite, how Christ left the world and went to the Father.

"Secondly, the incomprehensible, spiritual mode, according to which he neither occupies nor makes room, but penetrates all creatures according to his [most free] will, as, to make an imperfect comparison, my sight penetrates air, light or water, and does not occupy or make room; as a sound or tone penetrates air or water or board and wall, and is in them, and also does not occupy or make room; likewise, as light and heat penetrate air, water, glass, crystal, and the like, and is in them, and also does not make or occupy room; and much more of the like [many comparisons of this matter could be adduced]. This mode he used when he rose from the closed [and sealed] sepulchre; and passed through the closed door [to his disciples], and in the bread and wine in the Holy Supper, and, as it is believed, when he was born of his mother [the most holy Virgin Mary].

"Thirdly, the divine, heavenly mode, since he is one person with God, according to which, of course, all creatures must be far more penetrable and present to him than they are according to the second mode. For if, according to that second mode, he can be so in and with creatures that they do not feel, touch, circumscribe or comprehend him, how much more wonderfully is he in all creatures according to this sublime third mode, so that they neither circumscribe nor comprehend him, but rather that he has them present before himself, and circumscribes and comprehends them! For you must place this mode of the presence of Christ, as he is one person with God, as far beyond creatures as God is beyond them; and again as deep and near to all creatures as God is in, and near them. For he is one inseparable person with God; where God is there must he also be, or our faith is false. But who will say or think how this occurs? We know indeed that it is so that he is in God beyond all creatures, and is one person with God, but how it occurs we do not know; this [mystery] is above nature and reason, even above the reason of all the angels in heaven; it is understood only by God. Because, therefore, it is unknown to us, and yet is true, we should not deny his words before we know how to prove to a certainty that the body of Christ can by no means be where God is, and that this mode of being [presence] is false. This the fanatics ought to prove; but we challenge them to do so.

"That God indeed has and knows still more modes in which Christ's body is anywhere, I will not herewith deny; but I would indicate what awkward and stupid men our fanatics are, that they concede to the body of Christ no more than the first, comprehensible way; although they can not even prove the same, that it conflicts with our meaning. For I in no way will deny that the power of God is able to effect so much as that a body should at the same time be in a number of places, even in a bodily, comprehensible way. For who will prove that this is impossible with God? Who has seen an end to his power? The fanatics think indeed that God cannot effect it, but who will believe their thoughts? Whereby will they confirm such thoughts?"

From these words of Dr. Luther it is also clear in what sense the word *spiritual* is employed in our churches with reference to this matter. For to the Sacramentarians this word *(spiritual)* means nothing else than the spiritual communion, when through faith those truly believing are in the spirit incorporated into Christ, the Lord, and become true spiritual members of his body.

But when this word *spiritual* is employed in regard to this matter by Dr. Luther or us, we understand thereby the spiritual, supernatural, heavenly mode, according to which Christ is present in the Holy Supper, and not only works trust and life in the believing, but also condemnation in the unbelieving; whereby we reject the Capernaitic thoughts of the gross [and] carnal presence which is ascribed to and forced upon our churches, against our manifold public testimonies, by the Sacramentarians. In this sense we also say [wish the word *spiritually* to be understood when we say] that in the Holy Supper the body and blood of Christ are spiritually received, eaten and drunken; although this participation occurs with the mouth, yet the mode is spiritual.

Therefore our faith in this article, concerning the true presence of the body and blood of Christ in the Holy Supper, is based upon the *truth* and *omnipotence* of the true, almighty God, our Lord and Saviour Jesus Christ. These foundations are sufficiently strong and firm to strengthen and establish our faith in all temptations concerning this article, and to subvert and refute all the counter-arguments and objections of the Sacramentarians,

however agreeable and plausible they may always be to the reason; and upon them a Christian heart also can firmly and securely rest and rely.

Accordingly, with heart and mouth we reject and condemn as false, erroneous and misleading, all errors which are discordant, contrary and opposed to the doctrines above mentioned and founded upon God's Word, as,

1. The Papistic transubstantiation, where it is taught that the consecrated or blessed bread and wine in the Holy Supper lose entirely their substance and essence, and are changed into the substance of the body and blood of Christ, in such a way that only the mere form of bread and wine is left, or the accidents without the object; under which form of the bread, which is no more bread, but according to their assertion has lost its natural essence, the body of Christ is present, even apart from the administration of the Holy Supper, when the bread is enclosed in the pyx or is presented for display and adoration. For nothing can be a sacrament without God's command and the appointed use for which it is instituted in God's Word, as is shown above.

2. We likewise reject and condemn all other Papistic abuses of this sacrament, as the abomination of the sacrifice of the mass for the living and dead.

3. Also, that contrary to the public command and institution of Christ, to the laity only one form of the sacrament is administered; as the same Papistic abuses are thoroughly refuted by means of God's Word and the testimonies of the ancient churches, in the common confession of our churches, and the Apology, the Smalcald Articles, and other writings of our theologians.

But because in this document we have undertaken especially to present our Confession and explanation only concerning the true presence of the body and blood of Christ against the Sacramentarians, some of whom, under the name of the Augsburg Confession, have shamelessly insinuated themselves into our churches; we will also present and enumerate especially here the errors of the Sacramentarians, in order to warn our hearers to [detect and] be on their guard against them.

Accordingly, with heart and mouth we reject and condemn as false, erroneous and misleading all Sacramentarian opinions and doctrines which are discordant, contrary and opposed to the doctrines above presented and founded upon God's Word:

1. As when they assert that the words of institution are not to be understood simply in their proper signification, as they sound, of the true, essential presence of the body and blood of Christ in the Holy Supper, but should be wrested, by means of tropes or figurative interpretations, to another new, strange sense. We hereby reject all such Sacramentarian opinions and self-contradictory notions [of which some even conflict with each other], however various and manifold they may be.

2. Also, that the oral participation of the body and blood of Christ in the Holy Supper is denied [by the

THE FORMULA OF CONCORD (1580) (continued)

Sacramentarians], and it is taught, on the contrary, that the body of Christ in the Holy Supper is partaken of only spiritually by faith, so that in the Holy Supper our mouth receives only bread and wine.

3. Likewise, also, when it is taught that bread and wine in the Lord's Supper should be regarded as nothing more than tokens, whereby Christians are to recognize one another; or,

4. That they are only figures, similitudes and representations [symbols, types] of the far-absent body of Christ, in such a manner that just as bread and wine are the outward food of our body, so also the absent body of Christ, with its merit, is the spiritual food of our souls.

5. Or that they are no more than tokens and memorials of the absent body of Christ, by which signs, as an external pledge, we should be assured that the faith which turns from the Holy Supper and ascends above all heavens becomes there as truly participant of the body and blood of Christ as in the Supper we truly receive with the mouth the external signs; and that thus the assurance and confirmation of our faith occur in the Holy Supper only through the external signs, and not through the true, present body and blood of Christ offered to us.

6. Or that in the Lord's Supper the power, efficacy and merit of the far-*absent* body of Christ are distributed only to *faith*, and we thus become partakers of his absent body; and that, in this just-mentioned way, the sacramental union is to be understood, viz. with respect to the analogy of the sign and that which is signified, *i.e.* as the bread and wine have a resemblance to the body and blood of Christ.

7. Or that the body and blood of Christ cannot be received and partaken otherwise than only spiritually by faith.

8. Likewise, when it is taught that, because of his ascension into heaven with his body, Christ is so enclosed and circumscribed in a definite place in heaven that with the same [his body] he cannot or will not be truly present with us in the Holy Supper, which is celebrated according to the institution of Christ upon earth, but that he is as remote therefrom as heaven and earth are from one another, as some Sacramentarians have wilfully and wickedly falsified the text (Acts 3:21): "Who must occupy heaven," for the confirmation of their error, and instead therefore have rendered it: "Who must be received by heaven" or "in heaven," or be circumscribed and contained, so that in his human nature he could or would be in no way with us upon earth.

9. Likewise, that Christ has not promised the true, essential presence of his body and blood in his Supper, and that he neither can nor will afford it, because the nature and property of his assumed human nature cannot suffer or permit it.

10. Likewise, when it is taught that not only the Word and omnipotence of Christ, but faith, renders the body of Christ present in the Holy Supper; on this account the words of institution in the administration of the Holy Supper are omitted by some. For although the Papistic consecration, in which efficacy is ascribed to the speaking as the work of the priest, as though it constitutes a sacrament, is justly rebuked and rejected, yet the words of institution can or should in no way be omitted, as is shown in the preceding declaration.

11. Likewise, that believers do not seek the body of Christ, according to the words of Christ's institution, with the bread and wine of the Supper, but are sent with their faith from the bread of the Holy Supper to heaven, the place where the Lord Christ is with his body, that they should become partakers of it there.

12. We reject also the doctrine that unbelieving and impenitent, godless Christians, who only bear the name of Christ, but do not have right, true, living and saving faith, receive in the Lord's Supper not the body and blood of Christ, but only bread and wine. And since there are only two kinds of guests found at this heavenly meal, the worthy and the unworthy, we reject also the distinction made [by some] among the unworthy, viz. that the godless Epicureans and deriders of God's Word, who are in the external fellowship of the Church in the use of the Holy Supper, do not receive the body and blood of Christ for condemnation, but only bread and wine.

13. So too the doctrine that worthiness consists not only in true faith, but in man's own preparation.

14. Likewise, the doctrine that even the truly believing, who have and retain a right, true, living faith, and yet are without the above-mentioned sufficient preparation of their own, can, just as the unworthy guests, receive this sacrament to condemnation.

15. Likewise, when it is taught that the elements or the visible form of the consecrated bread and wine ought to be adored. But no one unless he be an Arian heretic can deny that Christ himself, true God and man, who is truly and essentially present in the Supper in the true use of the same, should be adored in spirit and in truth, as also in all other places, especially where his congregation is assembled.

16. We reject and condemn also all presumptuous, derisive, blasphemous questions and expressions which are presented with respect to the supernatural, heavenly mysteries of this Supper in a gross, carnal, Capernaitic way.

Other and additional antitheses, or rejected contrary doctrines, are reproved and rejected in the preceding declaration, which, for the sake of brevity, we will not repeat here. The condemnable or erroneous opinions that still remain, can be easily understood and named from the preceding declaration; for we reject and condemn everything that is discordant, contrary and opposed to the doctrine which is above mentioned and is thoroughly grounded in God's Word.

CHAPTER VIII. OF THE PERSON OF CHRIST.

A controversy has also occurred among the theologians of the Augsburg Confession concerning *the Person of Christ,* which nevertheless did not first arise among them, but was originally introduced by the Sacramentarians.

For since Dr. Luther, in opposition to the Sacramentarians, maintained, with firm foundations from the words of institution, the true, essential presence of the body and blood of Christ in the Holy Supper; the objection was urged against him by the Zwinglians that, if the body of Christ were present at the same time in heaven and on earth in the Holy Supper, it could be no real, true human body; for of such majesty as is peculiar to God, the body of Christ is not capable.

But as Dr. Luther contradicted and effectually refuted this Holy Supper show, which, as well as his doctrinal writings, we hereby publicly confess [approve and wish it to be publicly attested]; some theologians of the Augsburg Confession, since his death, although they have not yet been willing publicly and expressly to confess themselves with the Sacramentarians concerning the Lord's Supper, have introduced and employed precisely the same foundations concerning the person of Christ whereby the Sacramentarians attempted to remove the true, essential presence of the body and blood of Christ from his Supper, viz. that nothing should be ascribed to the human nature in the person of Christ which is above or contrary to its natural, essential property; and in regard to this have burdened the doctrine of Dr. Luther, and all those who have embraced it as in conformity with God's Word, with the charge of almost all the ancient monstrous heresies.

To explain this controversy in a Christian way, in conformity with God's Word, according to the guidance [analogy] of our simple Christian faith, and by God's grace entirely settle it, our unanimous doctrine, faith and confession are as follows:

We believe, teach and confess, although the Son of God has been from eternity a particular, distinct, entire divine person, and thus, with the Father and the Holy Ghost, true, essential, perfect God, nevertheless that, in the fulness of time, he also assumed human nature into the unity of his person, not in such a way that there now are two persons or two Christs, but that Christ Jesus is now in one person, at the same time true, eternal God, born of the Father from eternity, and a true man, born of the blessed Virgin Mary, as it is written (Rom. 9:5): "Of whom, as concerning the flesh, Christ came, who is over all, God blessed for ever."

We believe, teach and confess, that now, in this one undivided person, there are two distinct natures, the divine, which is from eternity, and the human, which in time was assumed into the unity of the person of the Son of God; which two natures in the person of Christ are never either mingled or separated from one another or changed the one into the other, but each abides in its nature and essence in the person of Christ to all eternity.

We believe, teach and confess also, that, as both natures mentioned abide unmingled and destroyed, each retains also its natural, essential properties, and for all eternity

does not lay them aside, neither do the essential properties of the one nature ever become the essential properties of the other nature.

Accordingly we believe, teach and confess, that to be almighty, eternal, infinite, to be of itself everywhere present at the same time naturally, that is, according to the property of its nature and its natural essence, and to know all things, are essential attributes of the divine nature, which never to eternity become essential properties of the human nature.

On the other hand, to be a corporeal creature, to be flesh and blood, to be finite and circumscribed, to suffer, to die, to ascend and descend, to move from one place to another, to suffer hunger, cold, thirst, heat and the like, are properties of the human nature, which never become properties of the divine nature.

We believe, teach and confess also, that now, since the incarnation, each nature in Christ does not so subsist of itself that each is or constitutes a separate person, but that they are so united that they constitute only one person, in which, at the same time, both the divine and the assumed human nature are and subsist, so that now, since the incarnation, to the entire person of Christ belongs not only his divine nature, but also his assumed human nature; and that, as without his divinity, so also without his humanity, the person of Christ or of the incarnate Son of God, *i.e.* the Son of God who has assumed flesh and become man, is not entire. Hence Christ is not two distinct persons, but is only one person, notwithstanding that two distinct natures are found in him, unconfused in their natural essence and properties.

We believe, teach and confess also, that the assumed human nature in Christ not only has and retains its natural, essential properties, but that, besides, through the personal union with divinity, and afterwards through glorification, it has been exalted to the right hand of majesty, power and might, over everything that can be named, not only in this world, but also in that which is to come (Eph. 1:21).

With respect now to this majesty, to which Christ has been exalted according to his humanity, he did not first receive it when he arose from the dead and ascended into heaven, but when, in his mother's womb, he was conceived and became man and the divine and human natures were personally united with one another. Nevertheless, this personal union is not to be understood, as some incorrectly explain it, as though the two natures, the divine and the human, were united with one another, as two boards are glued together, so that they really, *i.e.* in deed and truth, have no communication whatever with one another. For this was the error and heresy of Nestorius and Samosatenus, who, as Suidas and Theodore, presbyter of Raithu, testify, taught and held: δύο ψύσεις ἀχοινωνήτούς πρὸς ξαυτὰς παντάπασιν, *i.e.* the two natures have no communication whatever with one another. Thereby the two natures are separated from one another, and thus two Christs are constituted, so that the one is Christ, and the other God the Word, who dwells in Christ.

For thus Theodore the Presbyter wrote: "At the same time in which the heretic Manes lived, one by the name of Paul,

THE FORMULA OF CONCORD (1580) (continued)

who by birth was indeed of Samosata, but was a bishop at Antioch in Syria, wickedly taught that the Lord Christ was nothing but a man in whom God the Word dwelt, just as in each of the prophets; therefore he also held that the divine and human natures are apart and separate, and that in Christ they have no communion whatever with one another, as though the one were Christ, and the other God the Word, who dwells in him."

Against this condemned heresy the Christian Church has always and everywhere simply believed and held that the divine and human natures in the person of Christ are so united that they have a true communion with one another; whereby the natures [do not meet and] are not mingled in one essence, but, as Dr. Luther writes, in one person. Accordingly, on account of this personal union and communion, the ancient teachers of the Church, before and after the Council of Chalcedon, frequently employed the word *mixture* in a good sense and with [true] discrimination. For this purpose [the sake of confirming this matter] many testimonies of the Fathers (if needful) could be adduced, which also are to be found frequently in the writings of our divines, and explain the personal union and communion by the illustration of the soul and body, and of glowing iron. For the body and soul, as also fire and iron, have communion with each other, not by a phrase or mode of speaking, or in mere words, but truly and really, *i.e.* in deed and truth; and, nevertheless, no confusion or equalizing of the natures is thereby introduced, as when from honey and water hydromel is made, which is no more pure water or pure honey, but is a mixed drink. For in the union of the divine and human natures in the person of Christ it is far different. For it is a far different, more sublime, and [altogether] ineffable communion and union between the divine and human natures in the person of Christ, on account of which union and communion God is man and man is God. Nevertheless, thereby neither the natures nor their properties are intermingled, but each nature retains its own essence and properties.

On account of this personal union (without which such a true communion of the natures would not be thought of, neither could exist) not the mere human nature, whose property it is to suffer and die, has suffered for the sins of the world, but the Son of God himself truly suffered (nevertheless, according to the assumed human nature), and in accordance with our simple Christian faith [as our Apostles' Creed testifies] truly died, although the divine nature can neither suffer nor die. This Dr. Luther has fully explained in his Large Confession concerning the Holy Supper in opposition to the blasphemous *alloeosis* of Zwingli, as he taught that one nature should be taken and understood for the other, which Dr. Luther committed, as a mark of the devil, to the abyss of hell.

For this reason the ancient teachers of the Church combined both words, χοινυνία and ἐνιυσιξ, *i.e. communion* and *union,* in the explanation of this mystery, and have explained the one by the other. (Irenaeus, Book iv., ch. 37; Athanasius, in the Letter to Epietetus; Hilary, concerning the Trinity, Book 9; Basil and Gregory of Nyssa, in Theodoret; Damascenus, Book 3, ch. 19.)

On account of this personal union and communion of the divine and human natures in Christ we believe, teach and confess also, according to our simple Christian faith, all that is said concerning the majesty of Christ according to his humanity, [by which he sits] at the right hand of the almighty power of God, and what follows therefrom; all of which would not be, and could not occur, if this personal union and communion of the natures in the person of Christ did not exist really, *i.e.* in deed and truth.

On account of this personal union and communion of the natures, Mary, the blessed Virgin, bore not a mere man, but such a man as is truly the Son of the Most High God, as the angel [Gabriel] testifies; who showed his divine majesty even in his mother's womb, that he was born of a virgin, with her virginity uninjured. Therefore she is truly the mother of God, and nevertheless truly remained a virgin.

Because of this he also wrought all his miracles, and manifested this his divine Majesty, according to his pleasure, when and as he willed, and therefore not only after his resurrection and ascension, but also in his state of humiliation. For example, at the wedding at Cana of Galilee; also when he was twelve years old among the learned; also, in the garden, where with a word he cast his enemies to the ground; likewise in death, where he died not merely as any other man, but in and with his death conquered sin, death, hell, and eternal damnation; which his human nature alone would not have been able to do if it had not been thus personally united and did not have communion with the divine nature.

Hence also the human nature had, after the resurrection from the dead, its exaltation above all creatures in heaven and on earth; which is nothing else than that he entirely laid aside the form of a servant, and nevertheless did not lay aside his human nature, but retains it to eternity, and according to his assumed human nature is put in the full possession and use of the divine majesty. This majesty he nevertheless had already in his conception, even in his mother's womb; but as the apostle testifies (Phil. 2:7): "He humbled himself," and, as Dr. Luther explains, in the state of his humiliation he concealed it, and did not employ it except when he wished.

But now, since not merely as any other saint he has ascended to heaven, but, as the apostle testifies (Eph. 4:10), "above all heavens," and also truly fills all things, and is everywhere present not only as God, but also as man [has dominion and] rules from sea to sea and to the ends of the earth; as the prophets predict (Ps. 8:1, 6; 93:1 sq.; Zach. 9:10) and the apostles testify (Mark 16:20) that he everywhere wrought with them and confirmed the word with signs following. Yet this occurred not in an earthly way, but, as Dr. Luther explains, according to the manner of the right hand of God, which is no fixed place in heaven, as the Sacramentarians assert without any ground in the Holy Scriptures, but is nothing else than the almighty power of God, which fills heaven and earth, in [possession of] which Christ is placed according to his humanity, really, *i.e.* in deed and truth, without confusion and equalizing of the two natures in their essence and essential properties. From this communicated [divine] power, according to the words of his testament, he can be and is truly present with his body and blood in the Holy Supper, to which he directs us by his Word. This is possible to no man besides, because no man is in such a way united with the divine nature, and placed in this divine almighty majesty and power through and in the personal union of the two natures in Christ, as Jesus, the Son of Mary. For in him the divine and human natures are personally united with one another, so that in Christ "dwelleth all the fulness of the Godhead bodily" (Col. 2:9), and in this personal union have such a sublime, inner, ineffable communion that even the angels are astonished at it, and, as St. Peter testifies, look into these things with delight and joy (1 Pet. 1:12); all of which will shortly be explained in order and more fully.

From this foundation, of which mention has now been made, and which the personal union declares, *i.e.* from the manner in which the divine and human natures in the person of Christ are united with one another, so that they have not only the names in common, but have communion with one another, without any commingling or equalizing of the same in their essence, proceeds also the doctrine concerning the *Communicatio Idiomatum, i.e.* concerning the true communion of the properties of the natures, of which more will be said hereafter.

For since this is true, viz. that "properties do not leave their subjects," *i.e.* that each nature retains its essential properties, and these are not separated from one nature and transferred to another, as water is poured from one vessel into another; so also no communion of properties could be or subsist if the above-mentioned personal union or communion of the natures in the person of Christ were not true. This, next to the article of the Holy Trinity, is the greatest mystery in heaven and on earth, as Paul says (1 Tim. 3:16): "Without controversy, great is the mystery of godliness, that God was manifest in the flesh." For since the apostle Peter in clear words testifies (2 Ep. 1:4) that we also in whom Christ dwells only by grace, on account of that sublime mystery, are in Christ, "partakers of the divine nature," what then must be the nature of the communion of the divine nature, of which the apostle says that "in Christ dwelt all the fulness of the Godhead bodily," so that God and man are one person?

But since it is highly important that this doctrine of the *Communicatio Idiomatum, i.e.* of the communion of the properties of both natures, be treated and explained with proper discrimination (for the propositions or assertions, *i.e.* expressions, concerning the person of Christ, and his natures and properties, are not all of one kind and mode, and when they are employed without proper discrimination the doctrine becomes erroneous and the simple reader is readily led astray), the following statement should be carefully noted, which, for the purpose of making it plainer and simple, may be presented under three heads:

First, since in Christ two distinct natures exist and remain unchanged and unconfused in their natural essence and properties, and moreover there is only one person of both natures, that which is an attribute of only one nature is ascribed not to that nature apart, as though separate, but to the entire person, which is at the same time God and man, whether called God or man.

But in this genus, *i.e.* this mode of speaking, it does not follow that what is ascribed to the person is at the same time a property of both natures, but a discriminative declaration is made as to what nature it is according to which anything is ascribed to the entire person. Thus the Son of God was "born of the seed of David according to the flesh" (Rom. 1:3). Also: Christ was put to death according to the flesh, and hath suffered according to the flesh (1 Pet. 3:18; 4:1).

But since, when it is said that that is ascribed to the entire person which is peculiar to one nature, beneath the words secret and open Sacramentarians conceal their pernicious error, by naming indeed the entire person, but nevertheless understanding thereby only the one nature, and entirely excluding the other nature—as though merely the human nature had suffered for us—inasmuch as Dr. Luther has written concerning the alloeosis of Zwingli in his Large Confession concerning the Holy Supper, we will here present Luther's own words, in order that the Church of God may be guarded in the best way against this error. His words are as follows:

"Zwingli calls that an *alloeosis* when anything is ascribed to the divinity of Christ which nevertheless belongs to the humanity or the reverse. As Luke 24:26: 'Ought not Christ to have suffered these things, and to enter into his glory?' Here Zwingli triflingly declares that [the word] Christ is understood with respect to the human nature. Beware, beware, I say, of the alloeosis; for it is a mask of the devil, as it at last forms such a Christ after which I certainly would not be a Christian. For its design is that henceforth Christ should be no more, and do no more with his sufferings and life, than another mere saint. For if I believe [permit myself to be persuaded] that only the human nature has suffered for me, Christ is to me a Saviour of little worth, since he indeed himself stands in need of a Saviour. In a word, what the devil seeks by the alloeosis is inexpressible."

And shortly afterwards: "If the old sorceress, Dame Reason, the grandmother of the alloeosis, should say, Yea, divinity can neither suffer nor die; you should reply, That is true; yet, because in Christ divinity and humanity are one person, Scripture, on account of this personal union, ascribes also to divinity everything that occurs to the humanity, and the reverse. And thus, indeed, it is in truth. For this must certainly be said [acknowledged], viz. the person (he refers to Christ) suffers and dies. Now the person is true God; therefore, it is rightly said: The Son of God suffers. For although the one part (so to say), viz. the divinity, does not suffer, yet the person, which is God, suffers in the other part, viz. in his humanity; for in truth God's Son has been crucified for us, *i.e.* the person which is God. For the person, the person, I say, was crucified according to the humanity."

And again shortly afterwards: "If the alloeosis exist, as Zwingli proposes, it will be necessary for Christ to have two persons, one divine and one human, because Zwingli applies the passages concerning suffering, alone to the human nature, and of course diverts them from the

THE FORMULA OF CONCORD (1580) (continued)

divinity. For if the works be parted and disunited, the person must also be divided, since all the works or sufferings, are ascribed not to the natures, but to the person. For it is the person that does and suffers everything, one thing according to one nature, and another according to the other nature, all of which the learned know well. Therefore we consider our Lord Christ as God and man in one person, so that we neither confound the natures nor divide the person."

Dr. Luther says also in his book, "Of the Councils and the Church:" "We Christians must know that if God were not in the [one] balance, and gave it weight, we would sink to the ground with our scale of the balance. By this I mean: If it were not said [if these things were not true], 'God has died for us,' but only a man, we are lost. But if the death of God, and that God died, lie in the scale of the balance, he sinks down, and we rise up as a light, empty scale. But he also can indeed rise again or spring from the scale; yet he could not have descended into the scale unless he had first become a man like us, so that it could be said: 'God died,' 'God's passion,' 'God's blood,' 'God's death.' For in his nature God cannot die; but now God and man are united in one person, so that the expression 'God's death' is correct, when the man dies who is one thing or one person with God." Thus far Luther.

Hence it is manifest that it is incorrect to say or write that the above-mentioned expressions ("God suffered," "God died") are only verbal assertions, that is, mere words, and that it is not so in fact. For our simple Christian faith proves that the Son of God, who became man, suffered for us, died for us, and redeemed us with his blood.

Secondly, as to the execution of the office of Christ, the person does not act and work in, with, through, or according to only one nature, but in, according to, with and through both natures, or, as the Council of Chalcedon declares, one nature operates, with the communion of the other, in that which is a property of either. Therefore Christ is our Mediator, Redeemer, King, High Priest, Head, Shepherd, etc., not only according to one nature, whether it be the divine or the human, but according to both natures, as this doctrine is in other places more fully treated.

Thirdly, but it is still a much different thing when the subject of the question, or declaration, or discussion concerning this is, whether then the natures in the personal union in Christ have nothing else or nothing more than only their natural, essential properties; for that they have and retain these, is mentioned above.

Therefore, as to the divine nature in Christ, since in God there is no change (James 1:17) by the incarnation, his divine nature, in its essence and properties, is not abated or advanced; is thereby, in or by itself, neither diminished nor increased.

But as to the assumed human nature in the person of Christ, there have indeed been some who have wished to contend that this also, in the personal union with divinity, has nothing more than only the natural, essential properties according to which it is in all things like its brethren;

and that, on this account, nothing should or could be ascribed to the human nature in Christ which is beyond or contrary to its natural properties, even though the testimony of Scripture is to this effect. But that this opinion is false and incorrect is so clear from God's Word that even their own comrades censure and reject such error. For the Holy Scriptures, and the ancient Fathers from the Scriptures, very plainly testify that the human nature in Christ, inasmuch as it has been personally united with the divine nature in Christ (because, since the form of a servant and humiliation has been laid aside, it is glorified and exalted to the right hand of the majesty and power of God), has received, over and beyond its natural, essential, permanent properties, also special, high, great, supernatural, inscrutable, ineffable, heavenly prerogatives and excellences in majesty, glory, power and might above everything that can be named, not only in this world, but also in that which is to come (Eph. 1:21). So that the human nature in Christ, in its measure and mode, is employed at the same time in the execution of the office of Christ, and has also its efficacy, *i.e.* power and force, not only from, and according to, its natural, essential attributes, or only so far as its ability extends, but chiefly from and according to the majesty, glory, power and might which it has received through the personal union, glorification and exaltation. And even now the adversaries can or dare scarcely deny this, except that they dispute and contend that those are only created gifts or finite qualities, as in the saints, with which the human nature is endowed and furnished; and that, according to their [artful] thoughts or from their own [silly] argumentations or [fictitious] proofs, they wish to measure and calculate of what the human nature in Christ, without annihilation, is capable or incapable.

But the best, most certain and sure way in this controversy is this, viz. that what Christ has received, according to his assumed nature, through the personal union, glorification or exaltation, and of what his assumed human nature is capable beyond the natural properties, without annihilation, no one can know better or more thoroughly than the Lord Christ himself; and he has revealed in his Word as much thereof as it is needful for us to know. Of this, so far as pertains to the present matter, we have in the Scriptures clear, certain testimonies that we should simply believe, and in no way dispute to the contrary, as though the human nature in Christ were not capable of the same.

Now that is indeed correct and true which has been said concerning the created gifts which have been given and imparted to the human nature in Christ, viz. that it possesses them in or of itself. But these do not sufficiently explain the majesty which the Scriptures, and the ancient Fathers from Scripture, ascribe to the assumed human nature in Christ.

For to quicken, to have all judgment and power in heaven and on earth, to have all things in his hands, to have all things in subjection beneath his feet, to cleanse from sin, etc., are not created gifts, but divine, infinite properties, which, nevertheless, according to the declaration of Scripture, are given and communicated to the man Christ (John 5:27; 6:39; Matt. 28:18; Dan. 7:14; John 3:35; 13:3; Matt. 11:27; Eph. 1:22; Heb. 2:8; 1 Cor. 15:27; John 1:3).

And that this communication is to be understood, not as a phrase or mode of speaking, *i.e.* only in words with respect to the person, and only according to the divine nature, but according to the assumed human nature, the three following strong, irrefutable arguments and reasons show:

1. First, there is a unanimously-received rule of the entire ancient orthodox Church that what Holy Scripture testifies that Christ received in time he received not according to the divine nature (according to which he has everything from eternity), but the person has received it in time, by reason of, and with respect to, the assumed human nature.

2. Secondly, the Scriptures testify clearly (John 5:21 sq.; 6:39 sq.) that the power to quicken and to exercise judgment has been given to Christ because he is the Son of man and as he has flesh and blood.

3. Thirdly, the Scriptures speak not merely in general of the Son of man, but also expressly indicate his assumed human nature (1 John 1:7): "The blood of Jesus Christ, his Son, cleanseth us from all sin," not only according to the merit [of the blood of Christ] which was one attained on the cross; but in this place John speaks thereof, that in the work or act of justification not only the divine nature in Christ, but also his blood, by mode of efficacy, *i.e.* actually, cleanses us from all sins. Therefore, in John 6 [48-58], the flesh of Christ is a quickening food; as the Council of Ephesus also declared that the flesh of Christ has power to quicken; while concerning this article many other glorious testimonies of the ancient orthodox Church are elsewhere cited.

That Christ, therefore, according to his human nature, has received this, and that it has been given and communicated to the assumed human nature in Christ, we should and must believe according to the Scriptures. But, as above said, because the two natures in Christ are so united that they are not mingled with one another or changed one into the other, and each retains its natural, essential property, so that the properties of one nature never become properties of the other nature; this doctrine must also be rightly explained and be diligently preserved against all heresies.

While we, then, invent nothing new from ourselves, but receive and repeat the explanations which the ancient orthodox Church has given hereof from the good foundation of Holy Scripture, viz. that this divine power, light, might, majesty and glory was not given the assumed *human* nature in Christ it such a way as the Father, from eternity, has communicated to the Son, according to the divine nature, his essence and all divine attributes, whence he is of one nature with the Father and is equal to God. For Christ is only according to the divine nature equal to the Father, but according to the assumed human nature he is beneath God; hence it is manifest that we make no confusion, equalization or abolition of natures in Christ. So, too, the power to quicken is not in the flesh of Christ as in his divine nature, viz. as an essential property.

Moreover, this communication or impartation has not occurred through an essential or natural infusion of the properties of the divine nature into the human, as though the humanity of Christ had these by itself and apart from the divine essence, or as though the human nature in Christ had thereby [by this communication] entirely laid aside its natural, essential properties, and were now either transformed into divinity, or in and by itself, with such communicated properties, had become equal to the same, or that now the natural, essential properties of both natures are of one kind, or indeed equal. For these and similar erroneous doctrines were justly rejected and condemned in ancient approved councils from the foundation of Holy Scripture. "For in no way is either conversion, confusion or equalization of the natures in Christ, or the essential properties, to be either made or admitted."

We indeed never understand the words *"real communication"* or *"communes really"* *(i.e.* the impartation or communion which occurs in deed and truth) of any physical communication or essential transfusion, *i.e.* of any essential, natural communion or effusion, whereby the natures would be confused in their essence, and their essential properties (as, against their own conscience, some have craftily and wickedly made perversions, in order to make the pure doctrine suspected); but only have opposed them to *"verbal communication,"* *i.e.* the doctrine when such persons assert that it is only a phrase and mode of speaking, or nothing more than mere words, titles and names, upon which they have also laid so much stress that they are not willing to know of any other communion. Therefore, for the true explanation of the majesty of Christ we have used the terms, "Of the Real Communion," and wish thereby to show that this communion has occurred in deed and truth, nevertheless without any confusion of natures and their essential properties.

Therefore we hold and teach, with the ancient orthodox Church, as it explained this doctrine from the Scriptures, that the human nature in Christ has received this majesty according to the manner of the personal union, viz. because the entire fulness of the divinity dwells in Christ, not as in other holy men or angels, but bodily, as *in its own body*, so that with all its majesty, power, glory and efficacy in the assumed human nature, voluntarily when and as he [Christ] wills, it shines forth, and in, with, and through the same manifests, exercises, and executes its divine power, glory and efficacy, as the sould does in the body and fire in glowing iron. For by this illustration, as is also mentioned above, the entire ancient Church explained this doctrine. At the time of the humiliation this majesty was concealed and withheld [for the greater part]; but now since the form of a servant [or *exinanitio*] has been laid aside, it fully, powerfully and publicly is exercised in heaven and on earth before all saints, and in the life to come we will also behold this his glory face to face (John 17:24).

Therefore in Christ there is and remains only one divine omnipotence, power, majesty and glory, which is peculiar alone to the divine nature; but it shines, manifests and exercises itself fully, yet voluntarily, in, with and through the assumed, exalted human nature in Christ. Just as in glowing iron there are not two kinds of power to shine and burn [(as though the fire had a peculiar, and the iron also a peculiar and separate power of shining and burning)], but the power to shine and to burn is a property of the fire; yet because the fire is united with the iron it manifests and

THE FORMULA OF CONCORD (1580) (continued)

exercises this its power to shine and to burn in, with and through the glowing iron, so that the glowing iron has thence from this union the power to shine and to burn without conversion of the essence and of the natural properties of fire and iron.

On this account we understand such testimonies of Scripture as speak of the majesty to which the human nature in Christ is exalted, not so that the divine majesty which is peculiar to the divine nature of the Son of God should be ascribed in the person of the Son of man [to Christ] only according to his divine nature, or that this majesty in the human nature of Christ should be only of such a kind that his human nature should have only the mere title and name by a phrase and mode of speaking, *i.e.* only in words, but in deed and truth should have no communion whatever with it. For, since God is a spiritual, undivided essence, and therefore is present everywhere and in all creatures, and in whom he is (but he dwells especially in believers and saints), there he has with him his majesty, it might also with truth be said that in all creatures in whom God is, but especially in believers and saints, in whom he dwells, all the fulness of the Godhead dwells bodily, all treasures of wisdom and knowledge are hid, all power in heaven and earth is given, because the Holy Ghost, who has all power, is given them. For in this way there is no distinction made between Christ according to his human nature and other holy men, and thus Christ is deprived of his majesty, which he has received above all creatures, as a man or according to his human nature. For no other creature, neither man nor angel, can or should say: "All power is given unto me in heaven and in earth;" since although God is in the saints with all the fulness of his Godhead, which he has everywhere with himself; yet in them he does not dwell bodily, or with them is not personally united, as in Christ. For from such personal union it follows that Christ says, even according to his human nature (Matt. 28:18): "All power is given unto me in heaven and in earth." Also (John 13:3): "Jesus knowing that the Father had given all things into his hands." Also (Col. 2:9): "In him dwelleth all the fulness of the Godhead bodily." Also: "Thou crownedst him with glory and honor, and didst set him over the works of thy hands; thou hast put all things in subjection under his feet. For in that he put all in subjection under him, he left nothing that is not put under him" (Heb. 2:7 sq.; Ps. 8:6). "He is excepted which did put all things under him" (1 Cor. 15:27).

Moreover we believe, teach and confess that there is in no way such an infusion of the majesty of God, and of all his properties, into the human nature of Christ, whereby the divine nature is weakened [anything of the divine nature departs], or anything of its own is surrendered to another, that [in this manner] it does not retain for itself, or that the human nature has received in its substance and essence, equal majesty separate or diverse from the nature and essence of the Son of God, as when water, wine or oil is poured from one vessel into another. For the human nature, as also no other creature, either in heaven or on earth, is capable of the omnipotence of God in such a manner that it would be in itself an almighty essence, or

have in and by itself almighty properties; for thereby the human nature in Christ would be denied, and would be entirely converted into divinity, which is contrary to our Christian faith, as also to the doctrine of all the apostles and prophets.

But we believe, teach and confess that God the Father has so given his Spirit to Christ his beloved Son, according to the assumed humanity (for on this account he is called also *Messias, i.e.* the Anointed), that he has received the gifts of the Spirit, not, as other saints, in measure. For upon Christ the Lord, according to his assumed human nature (since according to his divinity he is of one essence with the Holy Ghost), there rests "the Spirit of wisdom and understanding, the Spirit of counsel and might, the Spirit of knowledge and of the fear of the Lord" (Col. 2:3; Isa. 11:2; 61:1). This occurs not in such a way that, on this account, as a man he knew and had ability only with regard to some things, as other saints know and are able by the grace of God, which works in them only created gifts. But since Christ, according to his divinity, is the second person in the Holy Trinity, and from him, as also from the Father, the Holy Ghost proceeds, and is and remains his Spirit and that of the Father for all eternity, not separated from the Son of God; the entire fulness of the Spirit (as the Fathers say) has been communicated by the personal union to Christ according to the flesh, which is personally united with the Son of God. This voluntarily manifests and exercises itself, with all its power therein, therewith and thereby [in, with and through the human nature of Christ], not so that he [Christ according to his human nature] not only knows some things and is ignorant of others, has ability with respect to some and is without ability with respect to others, but [according to the assumed human nature] knows and has ability with respect to all things. For upon him the Father poured without measure the Spirit of wisdom and power, so that, as man in deed and truth, he has received through this personal union all knowledge and all power. And thus all the treasures of wisdom are hidden in him, thus all power is given to him, and he is seated at the right hand of the majesty and power of God. From history it is also manifest that at the time of the Emperor Valens there was among the Arians a peculiar sect which was called the Agnoetae, because they imagined that the Son, the Word of the Father, knew indeed all things, but that his assumed human nature is ignorant of many things; against whom Gregory the Great also wrote.

On account of this personal union, and the communion following therefrom, which the divine and human natures have with one another in deed and truth in the person of Christ, there is ascribed to Christ, according to the flesh, that which his flesh, according to its nature and essence, cannot be of itself, and, apart from this union, cannot have, viz. that his flesh is a true quickening food, and his blood a true quickening blood; as the two hundred Fathers of the Council of Ephesus have testified, that "the flesh of Christ is quickening or a quickener." Hence also this man only, and no man besides, either in heaven or on earth, can say with truth (Matt. 18:20): "Where two or three are gathered together in my name, there am I in the midst of them." Also (Matt. 28:20): "Lo, I am with you always, even unto the end of the world."

These testimonies we also do not understand, as though with us in the Christian Church and congregation only the divinity of Christ were present, and such presence in no way whatever pertained to Christ according to his humanity; for in like manner Peter, Paul and all the saints in heaven would also be with us on earth, since divinity, which is everywhere present, dwells in them. This the Holy Scriptures testify only of Christ, and of no other man besides. But we hold that by these words [the passages of Scripture above] the majesty of the man Christ is declared, which Christ has received, according to his humanity, at the right hand of the majesty and power of God, viz. that he also, according to his assumed human nature and with the same, can be and is present where he will, and especially that in his Church and congregation on earth, as Mediator, Head, King and High Priest, he is not half present or there is only the half [one part of him] present, but the entire person of Christ is present, to which two natures belong, the divine and the human: not only according to his divinity, but also according to and with his assumed human nature, by which he is our brother and we are flesh of his flesh and bone of his bone. For the certain assurance and confirmation of this he has instituted his Holy Supper, that also according to our nature, by which he has flesh and blood, he will be with us, and in us dwell, work and be efficacious.

Upon this firm foundation Dr. Luther, of holy memory, has also written [faithfully and clearly] concerning the majesty of Christ according to his human nature.

In the Large Confession concerning the Lord's Supper he writes thus concerning the person of Christ: "Since Christ is such a man as is supernaturally one person with God, and apart from this man there is no God, it must follow that also, according to the third supernatural mode, he is and can be everywhere that God is, and all things are entirely full of Christ, even according to humanity, not according to the first corporeal, comprehensible mode, but according to the supernatural, divine mode."

"For here you must stand [confess] and say: 'Wherever Christ is according to the divinity, there he is a natural, divine person, and he is also there naturally and personally, as his conception in his mother's womb well shows. For if he were God's Son, he must naturally and personally be in his mother's womb and become man. But if, wherever he is, he is naturally and personally, he must also be in the same place as man. For there are not [in Christ] two separate persons, but only one person. Wherever it is, there the person is only one and undivided; and wherever you can say: 'Here is God,' there you must also say: 'Therefore Christ the man is also there.' And if you would show a place where God would be, and not the man, the person would be already divided, because I could then say with truth: 'Here is God who is not man, and who never as yet has become man.'

"Far be it from me that I should acknowledge or worship such a God. For it would follow hence that space and place separated the two natures from one another, and divided the person, which, nevertheless, death and all devils could not divide or rend from one another. And there would remain to me a poor sort of Christ [a Christ of

how much value, pray?], who would be no more than a divine and human person at the same time in only one place, and in all other places he must be only a mere separate God and divine person without humanity. No, friend, wherever you place God for me, there you must also place with him for me humanity; they do not allow themselves to be separated or divided from one another. They became one person, which [as Son of God] does not separate from itself [the assumed humanity]."

In the little book concerning the Last Words of David, which Dr. Luther wrote shortly before his death, he says as follows: "According to the other, the temporal, human birth, the eternal power of God has also been given him, yet in time, and not from eternity. For the humanity of Christ has not been from eternity, as the divinity; but as we reckon and write Jesus, the Son of Mary, is this year 1543 years old. But from the instant when divinity and humanity were united in one person, the man, the Son of Mary, is and is called almighty, eternal God, has eternal might, and has created and sustains, by the *communicatio idiomatum*, all things, because he is one person with divinity, and is also true God. Of this he speaks (Matt. 11:27): 'All things are delivered unto me of my Father;' and (Matt. 28:18): 'All power is given unto me in heaven and in earth.' To what me? To me, Jesus of Nazareth, the Son of Mary, and born man. From eternity I had it of the Father, before I became man. But when I became man I received it in time, according to humanity, and kept it concealed until my resurrection and ascension; then it was to be manifested and declared, as St. Paul says (Rom. 1:4): 'He is declared and proved to be a Son of God with power.' John (17:10) calls it 'glorified.'"

Similar testimonies are found in Dr. Luther's writings, but especially in the book: "That these Words still stand Firm," and in the "Large Confession concerning the Holy Supper;" to which writings, as well-grounded explanations of the majesty of Christ at the right hand of God, and of his testament, we refer, for the sake of brevity, in this article, as well as in the Holy Supper, as has been heretofore mentioned.

Therefore we regard it a pernicious error when to Christ, according to his humanity, such majesty is denied. For thereby there is removed from Christians the very great consolation which they have from the presence and dwelling with them of their Head, King and High Priest, who has promised them that not only his mere divinity should be with them, which to us poor sinners is as a consuming fire to dry stubble, but that very man who has spoken with us, who has experienced all troubles in his assumed human nature, who can therefore have with us, as with men and brethren, sympathy, will be with us in all our troubles also according to the nature in which he is our brother and we are flesh of his flesh.

Therefore we unanimously reject and condemn, with mouth and heart, all errors not in accordance with the doctrine presented, as contrary to the Prophetic and Apostolic Scriptures, the pure [received and approved] symbols, and our Christian Augsburg Confession:

THE FORMULA OF CONCORD (1580) (continued)

1. As when it is believed or taught by any one that, on account of the personal union, the human nature is mingled with the divine or is changed into it.

2. Also, that the human nature in Christ, in the same mode as the divinity, is everywhere present, as an infinite essence, from essential power, likewise from a property of its nature.

3. Also, that the human nature in Christ has become equal to and like the divine nature in its substance and essence or in its essential properties.

4. Also, that the humanity of Christ is locally extended in all places of heaven and earth; which should not be ascribed even to the divinity. But that Christ, by his divine omnipotence, can be present with his body, which he has placed at the right hand of the majesty and power of God, wherever he will; especially where, as in the Holy Supper, he has, in his Word, promised this his presence, this his omnipotence and wisdom can well accomplish without change or abolition of his true human nature.

5. Also, that merely the human nature of Christ has suffered for us and redeemed us, with which the Son of God had no communion whatever in suffering.

6. Also, that Christ is present with us on earth, only according to his divinity, in the preached Word and right use of the sacraments; and this presence of Christ does not in any way pertain to his assumed human nature.

7. Also, that the assumed human nature in Christ has in deed and truth no communion whatever with the divine power, might, wisdom, majesty and glory, but has in common only the mere title and name.

These errors, and all that are contrary and opposed to the [godly and pure] doctrine presented above, we reject and condemn, as contrary to the pure Word of God, the Scriptures of the holy prophets and apostles, and our Christian faith and confession. And we admonish all Christians, since in the Holy Scriptures Christ is called a mystery, upon which all heretics dash their heads, not in a presumptuous manner to indulge in subtile inquiries with their reason concerning such mysteries, but with the venerated apostles simply to believe, to close the eyes of their reason, and bring into captivity their understanding to the obedience of Christ (2 Cor. 10:5), and thence console themselves [seek most delightful and sure consolation]; and thus rejoice without ceasing that our flesh and blood are placed so high at the right hand of the majesty and almighty power of God. Thus will we assuredly find constant consolation in every adversity, and remain well guarded from pernicious error.

CHAPTER IX. OF THE DESCENT OF CHRIST TO HELL.

And because, even in the ancient Christian teachers of the Church, as well as in some among us, dissimilar explanations of the article concerning the Descent to Hell are found, we, in like manner, abide by the simplicity of our Christian faith [comprised in the Creed], to which Dr.

Luther in his sermon in the castle at Torgau in 1533, "Concerning the Descent to Hell," has referred, where we confess: "I believe in Jesus Christ, His only Son, our Lord, . . . dead and buried. He descended into hell." For in this Confession the burial and descent of Christ to hell are distinguished as different articles; and we simply believe that the entire person, God and man, after the burial descended into hell, conquered the devil, destroyed the power of hell, and took from the devil all his might. We should not, however, trouble ourselves with sublime and acute thoughts as to how this occurred; for this article can be comprehended by the reason and the five senses as little as the preceding, as to how Christ is placed at the right hand of the almighty power and majesty of God; but [in such mysteries of faith] we have only to believe and adhere to the Word. Thus we retain the substance [sound doctrine] and [true] consolation that neither hell nor devil can take captive or injure us and all who believe in Christ.

CHAPTER X. OF CHURCH RITES WHICH ARE [COMMONLY] CALLED ADIA PHORA, OR MATTERS OF INDIFFERENCE.

Concerning Ceremonies and Church Rites which are neither commanded nor forbidden in God's Word, but have been introduced into the Church with a good intention, for the sake of good order and propriety, or otherwise to maintain Christian discipline, a dissension has in like manner arisen among some theologians of the Augsburg Confession. Since the one side held that also in time of persecution and in case of confession [when confession of faith is to be made], even though the enemies of the Gospel do not agree with us in doctrine, yet some [long-since] abrogated ceremonies, which in themselves are adiaphora, and neither commanded nor forbidden by God, may, without violence to conscience, be re-established in compliance with the pressure and demand of the adversaries, and thus in such [things of themselves] adiaphora, or matters of indifference [we may indeed have conformity with them. But the other side contended that in case of confession in time of persecution, especially when thereby the adversaries design through force and compulsion, or in an insidious manner, to suppress the pure doctrine, and gradually to introduce again into our churches their false doctrine, this which has been said can in no way occur without violence to conscience and prejudice to the divine truth.

To explain this controversy, and by God's grace at last to settle it, we present to the Christian reader the following simple statement [in conformity with the Word of God]: Namely, when, under the title and pretext of external adiaphora, such things are proposed as (although painted another color) are in fact contrary to God's Word, these are not to be regarded adiaphora, but should be avoided as things prohibited by God. In like manner, also, among the genuine adiaphora such ceremonies should not be reckoned which have the appearance, or to avoid thereby persecution, feign the appearance, as though our religion and that of the Papists were not far apart, or as though the latter were not highly offensive to us; or when such ceremonies are designed for the purpose, and therefore are required and received, as though by and through them two contrary religions were reconciled and became one body;

or, again, when an advance towards the Papacy and a departure from the pure doctrine of the Gospel and true religion should occur or gradually follow therefrom [when there is danger lest we seem to have advanced towards the Papacy, and to have departed, or to be on the point of departing gradually, from the pure doctrine of the Gospel].

For in this case what Paul writes (2 Cor. 6:14, 17) must have weight: "Be ye not unequally yoked together with unbelievers; what communion hath light with darkness? Wherefore, Come out from among them, and be ye separate, saith the Lord."

Likewise, when there are useless, foolish spectacles, that are profitable neither for good order, nor Christian discipline, nor evangelical propriety in the Church, these also are not genuine adiaphora, or matters of indifference.

But concerning those things which are genuine adiaphora, or matters of indifference (as before explained), we believe, teach and confess that such ceremonies, in and of themselves, are no worship of God, also no part of the worship of God, but should be properly distinguished from this, as it stands written: "In vain they do worship me, teaching for doctrines the commandments of men" (Matt. 15:9).

Therefore we believe, teach and confess that the Church of God of every place and every time has, according to its circumstances, the authority, power and right [in matters truly adiaphora] to change, to diminish and to increase them, without thoughtlessness and offence, in an orderly and becoming way, as at any time it may be regarded most profitable, most beneficial and the best for [preserving] good order [maintaining], Christian discipline [and for ευταξία worthy of the profession of the Gospel], and the edification of the Church. How even to the weak in faith we can yield and give way with a good conscience in such external adiaphora Paul teaches (Rom. 14), and proves it by his example (Acts 16:3; 21:26; 1 Cor. 9:19).

We believe, teach and confess also that at the time [in which a confession of the heavenly truth is required] of confession, when the enemies of God's Word desire to suppress the pure doctrine of the holy Gospel, the entire Church of God, yea, every Christian, but especially the ministers of the Word, as the presidents of the congregation of God [as those whom God has appointed to rule his Church], are bound, according to God's Word, to confess the [godly] doctrine, and what belongs to the whole of [pure] religion, freely and openly, not only in words, but also in works and with deeds; and that then, in this case, even in such [things truly and of themselves] adiaphora, they must not yield to the adversaries, or permit these adiaphora to be forced upon them by their enemies, whether by violence or cunning, to the detriment of the true worship of God and the introduction and sanction of idolatry. For it is written (Gal. 5:1): "Stand fast, therefore, in the liberty wherewith Christ has made us free, and be not again entangled in the yoke of bondage." Also (Gal. 2:4 sq.): "And that because of false brethren unawares brought in, who came in privily to spy out our liberty which we have in Christ Jesus, that they might bring us into bondage; to whom we gave place by subjection, no,

not for an hour; that the truth of the Gospel might continue with you."

And [it is manifest that] Paul speaks in the same place concerning circumcision, which at the time was an adiaphoron (1 Cor. 7:18 sq.), and was used by Paul at other places [nevertheless] with [Christian and] spiritual freedom (Acts 16:3). But when the false apostles demanded and abused circumcision for confirming their false doctrine, as though the works of the Law were needful for righteousness and salvation, Paul says that he would yield not for an hour, in order that the truth of the Gospel might continue [unimpaired].

Thus Paul yields and gives way to the weak in [the observance of] food and times or days (Rom. 14:6). But to the false apostles who wished to impose these upon the conscience as *necessary things* he will yield not even in those things which in themselves are adiaphora (Col. 2:16): "Let no man therefore judge you in meat, or in drink, or in respect of an holy day." And when Peter and Barnabas yielded to a certain extent [more than they ought], Paul openly reproves them as those who have not walked aright, according to the truth of the Gospel (Gal. 2:11 sqq.)

For here it is no longer a question concerning adiaphora, which, in their nature and essence are and remain of themselves free, and accordingly can admit of no command or prohibition that they be employed or be intermitted; but it is a question, in the first place, concerning the sacred article of our Christian faith, as the apostle testifies, "in order that the truth of the Gospel might continue," which is obscured and perverted by such compulsion and command, because such adiaphora are either publicly required for the sanction of false doctrine, superstition and idolatry, and for the suppression of pure doctrine and Christian liberty, or at least are abused for this purpose by the adversaries, and are thus received [or certainly are thus received by them, and are believed to be restored for this abuse and wicked end].

Likewise, the article concerning Christian liberty is also here at stake, to preserve which the Holy Ghost so earnestly charged his Church through the mouth of the holy apostle, as heard above. For as soon as this is weakened and the ordinances of men [human traditions] are urged with compulsion upon the Church, as though they were necessary and their omission were wrong and sinful, the way is already prepared for idolatry, whereby the ordinances of men [human traditions] are gradually multiplied and regarded as a service of God, not only equal to the ordinances of God, but are even placed above them.

So also by such [untimely] yielding and conformity in external things, where there has not been previously Christian union in doctrine, idolaters are confirmed in their idolatry; on the other hand, the truly believing are distressed, offended and weakened in their faith [their faith is grievously shaken, and made to totter as though by a battering-ram]; both of which every Christian for the sake of his soul's welfare and salvation is bound to avoid, as it is written: "Woe unto the world because of offences!" Also: "Whoso shall offend one of these little ones which believe in me, it were better for him that a millstone were hanged

THE FORMULA OF CONCORD (1580) (continued)

about his neck and that he were drowned in the depth of the sea" (Matt. 18:6, 7.)

But especially is that to be remembered which Christ says: "Whosoever therefore shall confess me before men, him will I confess also before my Father which is in heaven."

Moreover, that this has been always and everywhere the faith and confession concerning such adiaphora, of the chief teachers of the Augsburg Confession, into whose footsteps we have entered, and intend by God's grace to persevere, in this their Confession, the following testimonies drawn from the Smalcald Articles, which was composed and subscribed in the year 1537 [most clearly], show:

TESTIMONIES DERIVED FROM THE SMALCALD ARTICLES, WRITTEN IN THE YEAR 1537.

The Smalcald Articles say concerning this as follows: "We do not acknowledge them as the Church, and also they are not; we also will not listen to those things which, under the name of Church, they either enjoin or forbid. For, thank God, today a child seven years old knows what the Church is, namely, saints, believers and lambs, who hear the voice of their Shepherd."

And shortly before: "If the bishops were true bishops, and would devote themselves to the Church and the Gospel, they might be allowed, for the sake of love and unity, and not from necessity, to ordain and confirm us and our preachers; nevertheless, under the condition that all masks and phantoms of an unchristian nature and display be laid aside. Yet because they neither are nor wish to be true bishops, but worldly lords and princes, who will neither preach, nor teach, nor baptize, nor administer the Lord's Supper, nor perform any work or office of the Church, but persecute and condemn those who, being called, discharge their duty; for their sake, the Church ought not to remain without ministers."

And in the article, "Of the Primacy of the Pope," the Smalcald Articles say: "Wherefore, just as we cannot adore the devil himself as Lord and God, so we cannot endure his apostle, the Pope or Antichrist, in his rule as head or lord. For to lie and to kill and to destroy body and soul eternally is a prerogative of the Papal government."

And in the treatise "Concerning the Power and Primacy of the Pope," which is appended to the Smaleald Articles, and was also subscribed by the theologians then present with their own hands, stand these words: "No one should burden the Church with his own traditions, but here it should be enjoined that the power or influence of no one should avail more than the Word of God."

And shortly afterwards: "This being the case, all Christians ought most diligently to beware of becoming partakers of the godless doctrine, blasphemies and unjust cruelties of the Pope; but ought to desert and execrate the Pope with his members as the kingdom of Antichrist, just as Christ has commanded (Matt. 7:15): 'Beware of false prophets.' And Paul commands us to avoid false teachers and execrate them as an abomination. And in (2 Cor. 6:14), he says: 'Be ye not unequally yoked together with unbelievers, for what communion hath light with darkness?'

"It is difficult to separate one's self from so many lands and nations, and to be willing to maintain this doctrine; but here stands God's command, that every one should beware and not agree with those who maintain false doctrine or who think of supporting it by means of cruelty."

So, too, Dr. Luther has amply instructed the Church of God in an especial treatise concerning what should be thought of ceremonies in general, and especially of adiaphora, vol. iii., Jena ed., p. 523; likewise also in 1530, in German, vol. v., Jena ed.

From this explanation every one can understand what it is proper for every Christian congregation and every Christian man, especially in time of confession [when a confession of faith should be made], and most of all preachers, to do or to leave undone, without injury to conscience, with respect to adiaphora, in order that God may not be incensed [provoked to just indignation], love may not be injured, the enemies of God's Word be not strengthened, and the weak in the faith be not offended.

1. Therefore, we reject and condemn as wrong when the ordinances of men in themselves are regarded as a service or part of the service of God.

2. We reject and condemn also as wrong when these ordinances are urged by force upon the congregation of God as necessary.

3. We reject and condemn also as wrong the opinion of those who hold that at a time of persecution we may comply with the enemies of the holy Gospel in [restoring] such adiaphora, or may come to an agreement with them, which causes injury to the truth.

4. We likewise regard it a sin worthy of punishment when, in the time of persecution, on account of the enemies of the Gospel, anything either in adiaphora or in doctrine, and what otherwise pertains to religion, is done in word and act contrary and opposed to the Christian confession.

5. We reject and condemn also when these adiaphora are abrogated [the madness of those who abrogate] in such a manner as though it were not free to the Church of God at any time and place to employ one or more in Christian liberty, according to its circumstances, as may be most useful to the Church.

According to this doctrine the churches will not condemn one another because of dissimilarity of ceremonies when, in Christian liberty, one has less or more of them, provided they otherwise are in unity with one another in doctrine and all its articles, and also in the right use of the holy sacraments, according to the well-known saying: "Disagreement in fasting does not destroy agreement in the faith."

CHAPTER XI. OF GOD'S ETERNAL FOREKNOWLEDGE [PREDESTINATION] AND ELECTION.

Although among the theologians of the Augsburg Confession no public dissension whatever, causing offence, and that is widespread, has as yet occurred concerning the eternal election of the children of God; yet since in other places this article has been brought into very painful controversy, and even among our theologians there was some agitation concerning it, and similar expressions were not always employed concerning it by the theologians; in order by the aid of divine grace to prevent disagreement and separation in the future among our successors, as well as among us, we have desired here also to present an explanation of the same, so that every one may know what is our unanimous doctrine, faith and confession concerning this article also. For the doctrine concerning this article, if presented from and according to the pattern of the divine Word [and analogy of God's Word and of faith], neither can nor should be regarded as useless or unnecessary, much less as causing offence or injury, because the Holy Scriptures not only in but one place and incidentally, but in many places, thoroughly discuss and urge [explain] the same. Therefore, on account of abuse or misunderstanding we should not neglect or reject the doctrine of the divine Word, but precisely on that account, in order to avert all abuse and misunderstanding, the true meaning should and must be explained from the foundation of the Scriptures. According to this the plain sum and substance [of the heavenly doctrine] concerning this article consists in the following points:

First, the distinction between the *eternal foreknowledge of God,* and the *eternal election of his children to eternal salvation,* is to be accurately observed. For foreknowledge or prevision, *i.e.* that God sees and knows everything before it happens, which is called *God's foreknowledge [prescience],* extends to all creatures, good and bad; namely, that he foresees and foreknows everything that is or will be, that is occurring or will occur, whether it be good or bad, since before God all things, whether they be past or future, are manifest and present. Thus it is written (Matt. 10:29): "Are not two sparrows sold for a farthing, and one of them shall not fall on the ground without your Father." And (Ps. 139:16): "Thine eyes did see my substance, yet being imperfect; and in they book all my members were written, which in continuance were fashioned, when as yet there were none of them." Also (Isa. 37:28): "I know thy abode, and they going out, and thy coming in, and thy rage against me."

But the *eternal election of God*, or predestination, *i.e. God's appointment to salvation,* pertains not at the same time to the godly and the wicked, but only to the children of God, who were elected and appointed to eternal life before the foundation of the world was laid, as Paul says (Eph. 1:4, 5): "He hath chosen us in him, having predestinated us unto the adoption of children by Jesus Christ."

The foreknowledge of God (prescience) foresees and foreknows also that which is evil, but not in such a manner as though it were God's gracious will that evil should happen. But all that the perverse, wicked will of the devil and of men purposes and desires to do, and will do, God sees and knows before; and his prescience, *i.e.* foreknowledge, so observes its order also, even in wicked acts or works, that to the evil which God does not will its limit and measure are fixed by God, how far it should go and how long it should last, when and how he would hinder and punish it; yet all this God the Lord so rules that it must redound to the glory of the divine name and to the salvation of his elect; and the godless, on that account, must be put to confusion.

Moreover, the beginning and cause of the evil is not God's; foreknowledge (for God does not procure and effect or work that which is evil, neither does he help or promote it); but the wicked, perverse will of the devil and of men [is the cause of the evil], as it is written (Hos. 13:9): "O Israel, thou hast destroyed thyself; but in me is thy help." Also (Ps. 5:4): "Thou art not a God that hath pleasure in wickedness."

But the eternal election of God not only foresees and foreknows the salvation of the elect, but is also, from the gracious will and pleasure of God in Christ Jesus, a cause which procures, works, helps and promotes what pertains thereto; upon this [divine predestination] also our salvation is so founded that "the gates of hell cannot prevail against it" (Matt. 16:18). For it is written (John 10:28): "Neither shall any man pluck my sheep out of my hand." And again (Acts 13:48): "And as many as were ordained to eternal life, believed."

This eternal election or appointment of God to eternal life is also not to be considered merely in God's secret, inscrutable counsel in such a manner as though it comprised in itself nothing further, or nothing more belonged thereto, and nothing more were to be considered therein, than that God foresaw who and how many would be saved, and who and how many would be damned, or that he only held a review, and would say thus: "This one shall be saved, that one shall be damned; this one shall remain steadfast [in faith to the end], that one shall not remain steadfast."

For from this many derive and adopt strange, dangerous and pernicious thoughts, which occasion and strengthen either security and impenitence or despondency and despair, so that they fall into troublesome thoughts and [for thus some think, with peril to themselves, nay, even sometimes] speak thus: Since "before the foundation of the world was laid" (Eph. 1:4) "God has foreknown [predestinated] his elect for salvation, and God's foreknowledge cannot err or be injured or changed by any one" (Isa. 14:27; Rom. 9:19), "if I, then, am foreknown [elected] for salvation, nothing can injure me with respect to it, even though, without repentance, I practise all sorts of sin and shame, do not regard the Word and sacraments, concern myself neither with repentance, faith, prayer nor godliness. But I nevertheless will and must be saved; because God's foreknowledge [election] must come to pass. If, however, I am not foreknown [predestinated], it nevertheless helps me nothing, even though I would observe the Word, repent, believe, etc.; for I cannot hinder or change God's foreknowledge [predestination]."

THE FORMULA OF CONCORD (1580) (continued)

And such thoughts occur indeed even to godly hearts, although, by God's grace, they have repentance, faith and a good purpose [of living in a godly manner], so that they think: "If you are not foreknown [predestinated or elected] from eternity for salvation, everything [your every effort and entire labor] is of no avail." This especially occurs when they regard their weakness and the examples of those who have not persevered [in faith to the end], but have fallen away again [from true godliness to ungodliness, and have become apostates].

Against this false delusion and such dangerous thoughts we should establish the following firm foundation, which is sure and cannot fail, namely: Since all Scripture has been given by God, not for [cherishing] security and impenitence, but should serve "for reproof, for correction, for instruction in righteousness" (2 Tim. 3:16); also, since everything in God's Word has been prescribed to us, not that we should thereby be driven to despair, but "that we, through patience and comfort of the Scriptures, might have hope" (Rom. 15:4); it is without doubt in no way the sound sense or right use of the doctrine concerning the eternal foreknowledge of God that thereby either impenitence or despair should be occasioned or strengthened. Therefore the Scriptures present to us this doctrine in no other way than to direct us thereby to the [revealed] Word (Eph. 1:13; 1 Cor. 1:7), exhort to repentance (2 Tim. 3:16), urge to godliness (Eph. 1:14; John 15:3), strengthen faith and assure us of our salvation (Eph. 1:13; John 10:27 sq.; 2 Thess. 2:13 sq.).

Therefore, if we wish to think or speak correctly and profitably concerning eternal election, or the predestination and foreordination of the children of God to eternal life, we should accustom ourselves not to speculate concerning the mere, secret, concealed, inscrutable foreknowledge of God, but how the counsel, purpose and ordination of God in Christ Jesus, who is the true book of life, has been revealed to us through the Word, viz. that the entire doctrine concerning the purpose, counsel, will and ordination of God pertaining to our redemption, call, righteousness and salvation should be taken together; as Paul has treated and explained this article (Rom. 8:29 sq.; Eph. 1:4 sq.), as also Christ in the parable (Matt. 22:1 sqq.), namely, that God in his purpose and counsel decreed:

1. That the human race should be truly redeemed and reconciled with God through Christ, who, by his faultless [innocency] obedience, suffering and death, has merited for us righteousness which avails before God, and eternal life.

2. That such merit and benefits of Christ should be offered, presented and distributed to us through his Word and sacraments.

3. That he would be efficacious and active in us by his Holy Ghost, through the Word, when it is preached, heard and pondered, to convert hearts to true repentance and preserve them in the true faith.

4. That all those who, in true repentance, receive Christ by a true faith he would justify and receive into grace, adoption and inheritance of eternal life.

5. That those also who are thus justified he would sanctify in love, as St. Paul (Eph. 1:4) says.

6. That, in their great weakness, he also would defend them against the devil, the world, and the flesh, and would rule and lead them in his ways, and when they stumble would raise them again [place his hand beneath them], and under the cross and in temptation would comfort and preserve them [for life].

7. That the good work which he has begun in them he would strengthen, increase and support to the end, if they observe God's Word, pray diligently, abide in God's goodness [grace] and faithfully use the gifts received.

8. That those whom he has elected, called and justified, he would eternally save and glorify in life eternal.

And that in his counsel, purpose and ordination he prepared salvation not only in general, but in grace considered and chose to salvation each and every person of the elect, who shall be saved through Christ, and ordained that in the way just mentioned he would by his grace, gifts and efficacy bring them thereto [make them participants of eternal salvation], and aid, promote, strengthen and preserve them.

All this, according to the Scriptures, is comprised in the doctrine concerning the eternal election of God to adoption and eternal salvation, and should be comprised with it, and not omitted, when we speak of God's purpose, predestination, election and ordination to salvation. And when, according to the Scriptures, thoughts concerning this article are thus formed, we can, by God's grace, simply [and correctly] adapt ourselves to it [and advantageously treat of it].

This also belongs to the further explanation and salutary use of the doctrine concerning God's predestination to salvation, viz.: Since only the elect, whose names are written in the book of life, are saved, how can we know whence, and whereby can we decide, who are the elect and those by whom this doctrine can and should be received for comfort?

And of this we should not judge according to our reason, also not according to the Law or from any external appearance. Neither should we attempt to investigate the secret, concealed abyss of divine predestination, but should give heed to the revealed will of God. For he has "made known unto us the mystery of his will," and made it manifest through Christ that it might be preached (Eph. 1:9 sqq; 2 Tim. 1:9 sq.).

But this is revealed to us thus, as St. Paul says (Rom. 8:29 sq.): "Whom God predestinated, elected and foreordained, be also called." Now, God calls not without means, but through the Word, as he has commanded "repentance and remission of sins to be preached in his name" (Luke 24:47). St. Paul also testifies to like effect when he writes (2 Cor. 5:20): "We are ambassadors for Christ, as though God did beseech you by us; we pray you in Christ's stead, Be ye reconciled to God." And the guests whom the King will have at the wedding of his Son he calls through his ministers sent forth (Matt. 22:2 sqq.)—some at the first and some at the second, third, sixth, ninth, and even at the eleventh hour (Matt. 20:3 sqq.).

Therefore, if we wish with profit to consider our eternal election to salvation, we must in every way hold rigidly and firmly to this, viz. that as the preaching of repentance so also the promise of the Gospel is universal, i.e. it pertains to all men (Luke 24). Therefore Christ has commanded "that repentance and remission of sins should be preached in his name among all nations." For God loved the world and gave his Son (John 3:16). Christ bore the sins of the world (John 1:29), gave his flesh for the life of the world (John 6:51); his blood is the propitiation for the sins of the whole world (1 John 1:7; 2:2). Christ says: "Come unto me, all ye that labor and are heavy laden, and I will give you rest" (Matt. 11:28). "God hath concluded them all in unbelief, that he might have mercy upon all" (Rom. 11:32). "The Lord is not willing that any should perish, but that all should come to repentance" (2 Pet. 3:9). "The same Lord over all is rich unto all that call upon him." (Rom. 10:12). "The righteousness of God, which is by faith of Jesus Christ, unto all and upon all them that believe" (Rom. 3:22). "This is the will of Him that sent me, that every one that seeth the Son and believeth on him may have everlasting life." Therefore it is Christ's command that to all in common to whom repentance is preached this promise of the Gospel also should be offered (Luke 24:47; Mark 16:15).

And this call of God, which is made through the preaching of the Word, we should regard as no delusion, but know that thereby God reveals his will, viz. that in those whom he thus calls he will work through the World, that they may be enlightened, converted and saved. For the Word, whereby we are called, is "a ministration of the Spirit," that gives the Spirit, or whereby the Spirit is given (2 Cor. 3:8), and "a power of God unto salvation" (Rom. 1:16). And since the Holy Ghost wishes to be efficacious through the Word, and to strengthen and give power and ability, it is God's will that we should receive the Word, believe and obey it.

For this reason the elect are described thus: "My sheep hear my voice, and I know them, and they follow me, and I give unto them eternal life" (John 10:27 sq.) And (Eph. 1:11, 13): Who according to the purpose are predestinated to an inheritance, who hear the Gospel, believe in Christ, pray and give thanks, are sanctified in love, have hope, patience and comfort under the cross (Rom. 8:25); and although in them all this is very weak, yet they hunger and thirst for righteousness (Matt. 5:6).

Thus the Spirit of God gives to the elect the testimony that they are children of God, and when they do not know for what they should pray as they ought, he intercedes with groanings that cannot be uttered (Rom. 8:16, 26).

Thus, also, Holy Scripture shows that God, who has called us, is so faithful when he has begun a good work in us that he also will preserve and continue it to the end, if we do not turn ourselves from him, but retain firmly to the end the work begun, for retaining which he has promised his grace (1 Cor. 1:9; Phil. 1:6; [1 Pet. 5:10]; 2 Pet. 3:9; Heb. 3:2).

With this revealed will of God we should concern ourselves, and should follow and study it, because the Holy Ghost, through the Word whereby he calls us, bestows, to this end, grace, power and ability, and we should not attempt to scrutinize the abyss of God's hidden predestination, as it is written in Luke 13:24, where to one who asks: "Lord, are there few that be saved?" Christ answers: "Strive to enter in at the strait gate." Accordingly, Luther says [in the Preface to the Epistle to the Romans]: "Follow the Epistle to the Romans in its order, concern yourself first with Christ and his Gospel, that you may recognize your sins and his grace. Afterwards contend with sin, as Paul teaches from the first to the eighth chapter. Then when in the eighth chapter you will come into temptation under the cross and afflictions, the ninth, tenth and eleventh chapters will teach you how consolatory is predestination."

But that many are called and few are chosen is not owing to the fact that the meaning of the call of God, made through the Word, is as though God were to say: "Outwardly, through the Word, I indeed call to my kingdom all of you to whom I give my Word, yet in my heart I intend it not for all, but only for a few; for it is my will that the greatest part of those whom I call through the Word should not be enlightened or converted, but be and remain lost, although, through the Word in the call, I declare myself to them otherwise." For this would be to asign to God contradictory wills. That is, in such a manner it would be taught that God, who is, however, eternal truth, would be contrary to himself; and yet God also punishes the fault when one thing is declared, and another is thought and meant in the heart (Ps. 5:9 and 12:2 sq.). Thereby, also, the necessary consolatory foundation is rendered altogether uncertain and of no value, as we are daily reminded and admonished, that only from God's Word, whereby he treats with us and calls us, should we learn and conclude what his will to us is, and that that, to which he gives his Word and which he promises, we should certainly believe and not doubt.

Therefore Christ causes the promise of the Gospel to be offered not only in general, but through the sacraments, which he attaches as seals of the promise, he seals and thereby especially confirms it [the certainty of the promise of the Gospel] to every believer.

For that reason we also retain, as the Ausburg Confession, Art. xi. says, Private Absolution, and teach that it is God's command that we believe such absolution, and regard it as sure, when we believe the word of absolution, that we are as truly reconciled to God as though we had heard a voice from heaven; as the Apology explains this article. This consolation would be entirely taken from us if we are not to infer the will of God towards us from the call which is made through the Word and through the sacraments.

There would also be overthrown and taken from us the foundation that the Holy Ghost wills to be certainly present with the Word preached, heard, considered, and thereby to be efficacious and to work. Therefore the opinion should in no way be entertained of which mention has heretofore been made, that these would be the elect, even though they despise the Word of God, reject, calumniate and persecute it (Matt. 22:6; Acts 13:46), or, when they hear it, harden their hearts (Heb. 4:2, 7), resist the Holy Ghost (Acts 7:51), without repentance persevere in sins (Luke 14:18), do not truly believe in Christ (Mark 16:16), only present [godliness in] an outward appearance (Matt. 7:22; 22:12), or seek other ways for righteousness and holiness apart from Christ (Rom. 9:31). But as God has ordained in his [eternal] counsel that the Holy Ghost should call, enlighten and convert the elect through the Word, and that all those who, through true faith, receive Christ he will justify and save; he has also determined in his counsel that he will harden, reprobate and condemn those who are called through the Word if they reject the Word and resist the Holy Ghost, who wishes to be efficacious and to work in them through the Word. And for this reason "many are called, but few are chosen."

For few receive the Word and follow it; the greatest number despise the Word, and will not come to the wedding (Matt. 22: 3sqq). The cause for this contempt for the Word is not God's knowledge [or predestination], but the perverse will of man, which rejects or perverts the means and instrument of the Holy Ghost, which God offers him through the call, and resists the Holy Ghost, who wishes to be efficacious, and works through the Word, as Christ says (Matt. 23:37): "How often would I have gathered thee together, and ye would not."

Therefore many receive the Word with joy, but afterwards fall away again (Luke 8:13). But the cause is not as though God were unwilling to grant grace for perseverance to those in whom he has begun the good work, for this is contrary to St. Paul (Phil. 1:6); but the cause is that they wilfully turn away again from the holy commandment [of God], grieve and exasperate the Holy Ghost, implicate themselves again in the filth of the world and garnish again the habitation of the heart for the devil; with them the last state is worse than the first (2 Pet. 2:10, 20; Eph. 4:30; Heb. 10:26; Luke 11:25).

Thus far is the mystery of predestination revealed to us in God's Word, and if we abide thereby and cleave thereto, it is a very useful, salutary, consolatory doctrine; for it establishes very effectually the article that we are justified and saved without all works and merits of ours, purely out of grace, alone for Christ's sake. For before the ages of the world, before we were born, yea, before the foundation of the world was laid, when we indeed could do nothing good, we were according to God's purpose chosen out of grace in Christ to salvation (Rom. 9:11; 2 Tim. 1:9). All opinions and erroneous doctrines concerning the powers of our natural will are thereby overthrown, because God in his counsel, before the ages of the world, decided and ordained that he himself, by the power of his Holy Ghost, would produce and work in us, through the Word, everything that pertains to our conversion.

Therefore this doctrine affords also the excellent, glorious consolation that God was so solicitous concerning the conversion, righteousness and salvation of every Christian, and so faithfully provided therefor, that before the

foundation of the world was laid he deliberated concerning it, and in his [secret] purpose ordained how he would bring me thereto [call and lead me to salvation] and preserve me therein. Also, that he wished to secure my salvation so well and certainly that since, through the weakness and wickedness of our flesh, it could easily be lost from our hands, or through craft and might of the devil and the world be torn or removed therefrom, in his eternal purpose, which cannot fail or be overthrown, he ordained it, and placed it for preservation in the almighty hand of our Saviour Jesus Christ, from which no one can pluck us (John 10:28). Hence Paul also says (Rom. 8:28, 39): "Because we have been called according to the purpose of God, who will separate us from the love of God in Christ?" [Paul builds the certainty of our blessedness upon the foundation of the divine purpose, when, from our being called according to the purpose of God, he infers that no one can separate us, etc.]

Under the cross also and amid temptations this doctrine affords glorious consolation, namely, that God in his counsel, before the time of the world, determined and decreed that he would assist us in all distresses [anxieties and perplexities], grant patience [under the cross], give consolation, excite [nourish and encourage] hope, and produce such a result as would contribute to our salvation. Also, as Paul in a very consolatory way treats this (Rom. 8:28, 29, 35, 38, 39), that God in his purpose has ordained before the time of the world by what crosses and sufferings he will conform his elect to the image of his Son, and that to every one his cross should and must serve for the best, because called according to the purpose, whence Paul concludes that it is certain and indubitable that "neither tribulation nor distress," "nor death nor life," etc., "shall be able to separate us from the love of God, which is in Christ Jesus our Lord."

This article also affords a glorious testimony that the Church of God will abide against all the gates of hell, and likewise teaches what is the true Church of God, so that we may not be offended by the great authority [and majestic appearance] of the false Church (Rom. 9:24, 25).

From this article also powerful admonitions and warnings are derived, as (Luke 7:30): "They rejected the counsel of God against themselves." (Luke 14:24): "I say unto you that none of those men which were bidden shall taste of my supper." Also (Matt. 20:16): "Many be called, but few chosen." Also (Luke 8:8, 18): "He that hath ears to hear, let him hear," and: "Take heed how ye hear." Thus the doctrine concerning this article can be employed with profit for consolation, and so as to contribute to salvation [and can be transferred in many ways to our use].

But with especial care the distinction must be observed between that which is expressly revealed concerning this in God's Word and what is not revealed. For, in addition to that hitherto mentioned which has been revealed in Christ concerning this, God has still kept secret and concealed much concerning this mystery, and reserved it alone for his wisdom and knowledge. Concerning this we should not investigate, nor indulge our thoughts, nor reach conclusions, nor inquire curiously, but should adhere [entirely] to the revealed Word of God. This admonition is in the highest degree necessary.

For our curiosity has always much more pleasure in concerning itself therewith [with investigating those things which ere hidden and abstruse] than with what God has revealed to us concerning this in his Word, since we cannot harmonize them, which we also have not been commanded to do [since certain things occur in this mystery so intricate and involved that we are not able by the penetration of our natural ability to harmonize them, but this has not been demanded of us by God]:

Thus there is no doubt that God most exactly and certainly saw before the time of the world, and still knows, who of those who are called will believe or will not believe; also who of the converted will persevere [in faith] and who will not; who after a fall [into grievous sins] will return, and who will fall into obduracy [will perish in their sins]. So, too, the number, how many there are of these on both sides, is beyond all doubt perfectly known to God. Yet since God has reserved this mystery for his wisdom, and in his Word revealed nothing to us concerning it, much less commanded us to investigate it with our thoughts, but has earnestly discouraged us therefrom (Rom. 11:33 sqq.), we should not indulge our thoughts, reach conclusions nor inquire curiously therein, but should adhere to his revealed Word, to which he points us.

Thus without any doubt God also knows and has determined for every one the time and hour of his call and conversion [and when he will raise again one who has lapsed]. Yet since this is not revealed, we have the command always to adhere to the Word, but to entrust the time and hour [of conversion] to God (Acts 1:7).

Likewise, when we see that God gives his Word at one place [to one kingdom or realm], but not at another [to another nation]; removes it from one place [people], and allows it to remain at another; also, that one is hardened, blinded, given over to a reprobate mind, while another, who is indeed in the same guilt, is again converted, etc.; in these and similar questions Paul (Rom. 11:22 sqq.) fixes before us a certain limit as to how far we should go, viz. that, in the one part we should recognize God's judgement [for he commands us to consider in those who perish the just judgment of God and the penalties of sins]. For they are richly-deserved penalties of sins when God so punishes a land or nation for despising his Word that the punishment extends also to their posterity, as is to be seen in the Jews. Thereby God shows to those that are his, his severity in some lands and persons, in order to indicate what we all have richly deserved, since we have acted wickedly in opposition to God's Word [are ungrateful for the revealed Word, and live unworthily of the Gospel] and often have sorely grieved the Holy Ghost; so that we may live in God's fear, and acknowledge and praise God's goodness, in and with us, without and contrary to our merit, to whom he gives and grants his Word, and whom he does not harden and reject.

For inasmuch as our nature has been corrupted by sin, and is worthy of, and under obligation to, God's wrath and condemnation, God owes to us neither Word, Spirit, nor grace, and when, out of grace, he bestows these gifts, we

often repel them from us, and judge ourselves unworthy of everlasting life (Acts 13:46). Therefore this his righteous, richly-deserved judgment he displays in some countries, nations and persons, in order that when we are considered with respect to them, and compared with them, we may learn the more attentively to recognize and praise God's pure [immense], unmerited grace in the vessels of mercy.

For no injustice is done those who are punished and receive the wages of their sins; but in the rest, to whom God gives and preserves his Word, and thereby enlightens, converts and preserves men, God commends his pure [immense] grace and mercy, without their merit.

When we proceed thus far in this article we remain upon the right [safe and royal] way, as it is written (Hos. 13:9): "O Israel, thou hast destroyed thyself; but in me is thy help."

But with respect to that in this disputation which will proceed too high and beyond these limits, we should, with Paul, place the finger upon our lips, and remember and say (Rom. 9:20): "O man, who art thou that repliest against God?"

For that in this article we neither can nor should inquire after and investigate everything, the great apostle Paul declares [by his own example]. For when, after having argued much concerning this article from the revealed Word of God, he comes to where he points out what, concerning this mystery, God has reserved for his hidden wisdom, he suppresses and cuts off the discussion with the following words (Rom. 11:33 sq.): "Oh the depth of the riches both of the wisdom and knowledge of God! How unsearchable are his judgments, and his ways past finding out! For who hath known the mind of the Lord?" i.e. in addition to and beyond that which he has revealed in his Word.

Therefore this eternal election of God is to be considered in Christ, and not beyond or without Christ. For "in Christ," testifies the apostle Paul (Eph. 1:4 sq.), "he hath chosen us before the foundation of the world;" as it is written: "He hath made us accepted in the Beloved." But this election is revealed from heaven through the preached Word when the Father says (Matt. 17:5): "This is my beloved Son, in whom I am well pleased; hear ye him." And Christ says (Matt. 11:28): "Come unto me, all ye that labor and are heavy laden, and I will give you rest." And concerning the Holy Ghost Christ says (John 16:14): "He shall glorify me; for he shall receive of mine, and shall show it unto you." Therefore the entire Holy Trinity, Father, Son and Holy Ghost, direct all men to Christ, as to the Book of Life, in which they should seek the eternal election of the Father. For it has been decided by the Father from eternity that whom he would save he would save through Christ (John 14:6): "No man cometh unto the Father but by me." And again (John 10:9): "I am the door; by me, if any man enter in, he shall be saved."

But Christ as the only-begotten Son of God, who is in the bosom of the Father, has published to us the will of the Father, and thus also our eternal election to eternal life, viz. when he says (Mark 1:15): "Repent ye, and believe the Gospel; the kingdom of God is at hand." He also says (John 6:40): "This is the will of Him that sent me, that every one which seeth the Son and believeth on him may have everlasting life." And again (John 3:16): "God so loved the world that he gave his only-begotten Son, that whosoever believeth in him should not perish, but have everlasting life."

This proclamation the Father wishes that all men should hear, and that they should come to Christ. Those who come Christ does not repel from himself, as it is written (John 6:37): "Him that cometh to me I will in no wise cast out."

And in order that we may come to Christ, the Holy Ghost works, through the hearing of the Word, true faith, as the apostle testifies when he says (Rom. 10:17): "Faith cometh by hearing, and hearing by the Word of God," viz. when it is preached in its purity and without adulteration.

Therefore no one who would be saved should trouble or harass himself with thoughts concerning the secret counsel of God, as to whether he also is elected and ordained to eternal life; for with these miserable Satan is accustomed to attack and annoy godly hearts. But they should hear Christ [and in him look upon the Book of Life in which is written the eternal election], who is the Book of Life and of God's eternal election of all God's children to eternal life; who testifies to all men without distinction that it is God's will that all men who labor and are heavy laden with sin should come to him, in order that he may give them rest and save them (Matt. 11:28).

According to this doctrine of Christ, they should abstain from their sins, repent, believe his promise, and entirely entrust themselves to him; and since this we cannot do by ourselves of our own powers, the Holy Ghost desires to work repentance and faith in us through the Word and sacraments. And in order that we may attain this, and persevere and remain steadfast, we should implore God for his grace, which he promised us in holy baptism, and not doubt he will impart it to us according to his promise, as he has said (Luke 11:11 sqq.); "If a son shall ask bread of any of you that is a father, will he give him a stone? or if he ask a fish, will he for a fish give him a serpent? or if he shall ask an egg, will he offer him a scorpion? If ye then, being evil, know how to give good gifts unto your children, how much more shall your heavenly Father give the Holy Spirit to them that ask him?"

And since the Holy Ghost dwells in the elect, who become believing, as in his temple, and is not inactive in them, but impels the children of God to obedience to God's commands; believers, in like manner, should not be inactive, and much less resist the impulse of God's Spirit, but should exercise themselves in all Christian virtue, in all godliness, modesty, temperance, patience, brotherly love, and give all diligence to make their calling and election sure, in order that the more they experience the power and strength of the Spirit within them they may doubt the less concerning it. For the Spirit bears witness to the elect that they are God's children (Rom. 8:16). And although they sometimes fall into temptation so grievous that they think that they perceive no more power of the indwelling Spirit of God, and say with David (Ps. 31:22): "I said in my haste, I am cut off from before thine eyes," yet they should again [be encouraged and] say with David, without regard to what they experience in themselves: "Nevertheless thou heardest the voice of my supplications when I cried unto thee."

And since our election to eternal life is founded not upon our godliness or virtue, but alone upon the merit of Christ and the gracious will of his Father, who, because he is unchangeable in will and essence, cannot deny himself; on this account, when his children depart from obedience and stumble, he calls them again through the Word to repentance, and the Holy Ghost will thereby to be efficacious in them for conversion; and when in true repentance by a right faith they turn again to him, he will always manifest his old paternal heart to all those who tremble at his Word and from their heart turn again to him, as it is written (Jer. 3:1): "If a man put away his wife, and she go from him and become another man's, shall he return unto her again? shall not that land be greatly polluted? but thou hast played the harlot with many lovers; yet return again to me, saith the Lord."

Moreover, the declaration (John 6:44) that no one can come to Christ except the Father draw him is right and true. But the Father will not do this without means, and has ordained for this purpose his Word and sacraments as ordinary means and instruments; and it is the will neither of the Father nor of the Son that a man should not hear or should despise the preaching of his Word, and without the Word and sacraments should expect the drawing of the Father. For the Father draws indeed by the power of his Holy Ghost, but, nevertheless, according to his usual order [the order decreed and instituted by himself], by the hearing of his holy, divine Word, as with a net, whereby the elect are delivered from the jaws of the devil. Every poor sinner should therefore repair thereto [to holy preaching], hear it attentively, and should not doubt the drawing of the Father. For the Holy Ghost will be with his Word in his power, and thereby work; and this is the drawing of the Father.

But the reason that not all who hear it believe, and some are therefore condemned the more deeply [eternally to severer punishments], is not that God has not desired their salvation; but it is their own fault, as they have heard the Word in such a manner as not to learn, but only to despise, traduce and disgrace it, and have resisted the Holy Ghost, who through the Word wishes to work in them. There was one form of this at the time of Christ in the Pharisees and their adherents. Therefore the apostle distinguishes with especial care the work of God, who alone makes vessels of honor, and the work of the devil and of man, who by the instigation of the devil, and not of God, has made himself a vessel of dishonor. For thus it is written (Rom. 9:22 sq.): "God endured with much long-suffering the vessels of wrath fitted to destruction, that he might make known the riches of his glory on the vessels of mercy, which he had afore prepared unto glory."

For here the apostle clearly says: "God endured with much long-suffering the vessels of wrath," but does not say that he made them vessels of wrath; for if this had been his will, he would not have required for it any great long-suffering. The fault, however, that they are fitted for destruction belongs to the devil and to men themselves, and not to God.

For all preparation for condemnation is by the devil and man, through sin, and in no respect by God, who does not wish that any man be damned; how then should he prepare any man for condemnation? For as God is not a cause of sins, so too he is no cause of the punishment, *i.e.* the condemnation; but the only cause of the condemnation is sin, for "the wages of sin is death" (Rom. 6:23). And as God does not wish sin, and has no pleasure in sin, he also does not wish the death of the sinner (Ez. 33:11), and has no pleasure in his condemnation. For he is not "willing that any should perish, but that all should come to repentance" (2 Pet. 3:9). So too it is written (in Ez. 18:23; 33:11): "As I live, saith the Lord God, I have no pleasure in the death of the wicked; but that the wicked turn from his way and live." And St. Paul testifies in clear words that from vessels of dishonor vessels of honor may be made by God's power and working, as he writes (2 Tim. 2:21) thus: "If a man, therefore, purge himself from these, he shall be a vessel unto honor, sanctified and meet for the Master's use, and prepared unto every good work." For he who is to purge himself must first have been unclean, and therefore a vessel of dishonor. But concerning the vessels of mercy he says clearly that the Lord himself has prepared them for glory, which he does not say concerning the condemned, who themselves, and not God, have prepared themselves as vessels of condemnation.

It is also to be attentively considered, when God punishes sin with sins, *i.e.* afterwards punishes those who have been converted with obduracy and blindness, because of their subsequent security, impenitence and wilful sins, that it should not be inferred hence that it never was God's good pleasure that such persons should come to the knowledge of the truth and be saved. For it is God's revealed will, both:

First, that God will receive into grace all who repent and believe in Christ.

Secondly, that those who wilfully turn away from the holy commandment, and are again entangled in the pollutions of the world (2 Pet. 2:20), and garnish their hearts for Satan (Luke 11:25 sq.), and do despite unto the Spirit of God (Heb. 10:29), he will punish, and when they persist therein they shall be hardened, blinded and eternally condemned.

Therefore, even Pharaoh (of whom it is written (Ex. 9:16; Rom. 9:17): "In very deed for this cause have I raised thee up, for to show in thee my power; and that my name may be declared throughout all the earth") was lost, not because God did not desire his salvation, or because it was his good pleasure that Pharaoh should be condemned and lost. For God "is not willing that any should perish" (2 Pet. 3:9); he also has "no pleasure in the death of the wicked, but that the wicked turn from his way and live" (Ez. 33:11).

But that God hardened Pharaoh's heart, viz. that Pharaoh still continued to sin, and the more he was admonished the more obdurate he became, were punishments of his preceding sins and horrible tyranny, which, in many and manifold ways, he exercised towards the children of Israel inhumanly and against the accusations of his conscience. And since God caused his Word to be preached and his will to be proclaimed, and Pharaoh wilfully resisted it in direct contradiction of all admonitions and warnings, God withdrew his hand from him, and thus his heart was hardened, and God executed his judgment upon him; for he deserved nothing else than hellfire. And indeed the holy apostle introduces the example of Pharaoh for no other reason than hereby to prove the justice of God, which he exercises towards the impenitent and despisers of his Word. Yet in no way is it there to be thought or understood that God did not desire his salvation, or that there is any man whose salvation he did not desire, but that he was so ordained to eternal damnation in God's secret counsel that he neither should, could, nor might be saved.

Through this doctrine and explanation of the eternal and saving choice of the elect children of God his own glory is entirely and fully given to God, that in Christ he saves us out of pure [and free] mercy, without any merits or good works of ours, according to the purpose of his will, as it is written (Eph. 1:5 sq.): "Having predestinated us unto the adoption of children by Jesus Christ to himself, according to the good pleasure of his will, to the praise of the glory of his grace, wherein he hath made us accepted in the Beloved." Therefore it is false and wrong [conflicts with the Word of God] when it is taught that not alone the mercy of God and the most holy merit of Christ, but also that there is in us a cause of God's election, on account of which God has chosen us to eternal life. For not only before we did anything good, but also before we were born, yea, even before the foundations of the world were laid, he elected us in Christ; and "that the purpose of God according to election might stand, not of works, but of Him that calleth, it was said unto her, The elder shall serve the younger, as it is written, Jacob have I loved, but Esau have I hated" (Rom. 9:11 sqq.; Gen. 25:23; Mal. 1:2 sq.).

Moreover, no occasion is afforded either for despondency or for a shameless, dissolute life by this doctrine, viz. when men are taught that they should seek eternal election in Christ and his holy Gospel, as in the Book of Life, which excludes no penitent sinner, but allures and calls all the poor, heavy-laden, and troubled [with the sense of God's wrath], and promises the Holy Ghost for purification and renewal. This article correctly explained thus gives the most permanent consolation to all troubled, tempted men, viz. that they know that their salvation is not placed in their own hands (for otherwise it would be much more easily lost, as was the case with Adam and Eve in Paradise—ay, it would be lost every hour and moment), but in the gracious election of God, which he has revealed to us in Christ, from whose hand no man shall pluck us (John 10:28; 2 Tim. 2:19).

Wherefore, if any one should so present the doctrine concerning the gracious election of God in such a manner that troubled Christians cannot console themselves therewith, but thereby occasion is afforded for despair, or the impenitent are confirmed in their wickedness; it is undoubtedly sure and true that such a doctrine is put forth, not according to the Word and will of God, but according to [the blind judgment of human] reason and the instigation of the devil.

For, as the apostle testifies (Rom. 15:4): "Whatsoever things were written aforetime were written for our learning, that we through patience and comfort of the Scriptures might have hope." But when by the Scriptures this consolation and hope are weakened or entirely removed, it is certain that they are understood and explained contrary to the will and meaning of the Holy Ghost.

By this simple, correct [clear], useful explanation, which has firm ground in God's revealed will, we abide; we flee from and shun all lofty, acute questions and disputations [useless for edifying]; and reject and condemn that which is contrary to this simple, useful explanation.

So much concerning the controverted articles which have been discussed among the theologians of the Augsburg Confession for many years already, since in reference to them some have erred and severe controversies have arisen.

From this our explanation, friends and enemies, and therefore every one, will clearly infer that we have not thought of yielding aught of the eternal, immutable truth of God for the sake of temporary peace, tranquillity and unity (as to do this is also not in our power). Such peace and unity, since devised against the truth and for its suppression, would have no permanency. Much less are we inclined to adorn and conceal a corruption of the pure doctrine and manifest, condemned errors. But for that unity we entertain heartfelt pleasure and love, and this, on our part, we are sincerely inclined and anxious to advance according to our utmost power, by which his glory remains to God uninjured, nothing of the divine truth of the Holy Gospel is surrendered, no place is admitted for the least error, poor sinners are brought to true, genuine repentance, encouraged by faith, confirmed in new obedience, and thus justified and eternally saved alone through the sole merit of Christ.

CHAPTER XII. OF OTHER FACTIONS [HERETICS] AND SECTS, WHICH NEVER EMBRACED THE AUGSBURG CONFESSION.

The sects and factions [sectarists and heretics] which never embraced the Augsburg Confession, and of which, in this our explanation, express mention has not been made, such as are the Anabaptists, Schwenekfeldians, New Arians and Anti-trinitarians, whose errors are unanimously condemned by all churches of the Augsburg Confession, we have not wished to notice particularly and especially in this explanation; for the reason that at the present time only this has been sought [that we might above all refute the charges of our adversaries the Papists].

Since our opponents, with shameless mouths, alleged and proclaimed, throughout all the world, of our churches and their teachers, that not two preachers are found who in each and every article of the Augsburg Confession agree, but that they are rent asunder and separated from one another to such an extent that not even they themselves any longer know what is the Augsburg Confession and its proper [true, genuine and germane] sense; we have wished to make a common confession, not only in mere, brief words or names, but to make a clear, luminous, distinct declaration concerning all the articles which have been discussed and controverted only among the theologians of the Augsburg Confession, in order that every one may see that we do not wish in a cunning manner to screen or cover up all this, or to come to an agreement only in appearance; but to remedy the matter thoroughly, and so to set forth our opinion, that even our adversaries themselves must confess that in all this we abide by the true, simple, natural and only sense of the Augsburg Confession, in which we desire, through God's grace, to persevere constantly even to our end, and, so far as it is placed at our service, we will not connive at or be silent, so that anything contrary to the same [the genuine and sacred sense of the Augsburg Confession] be introduced into our churches and schools, in which the Almighty God and Father of our Lord Jesus Christ has appointed us teachers and pastors.

But in order that the condemned errors of the above enumerated factions and sects may not be silently ascribed to us—since for the most part they have secretly stolen into localities, and especially, as is the nature of such spirits, at the time when no place or space was allowed to the pure Word of the holy Gospel, but all its orthodox teachers and confessors were persecuted, and the deep darkness of the Papacy still prevailed, and poor simple men who were compelled to feel the manifest idolatry and false faith of the Papacy embraced, alas! in their simplicity, whatever was said to be according to the Gospel, and was not Papistic—we cannot forbear testifying also against them publicly, before all Christendom, that we have neither part nor fellowship with these errors, but reject and condemn them, one and all, as wrong and heretical, and contrary to the Scriptures of the prophets and apostles, as well as to our well-grounded Augsburg Confession.

ERRONEOUS ARTICLES OF THE ANABAPTISTS.

Namely, the erroneous, heretical doctrines of the Anabaptists, which are to be tolerated and allowed neither in the Church, nor in the commonwealth, nor in domestic life, since they teach:

1. That our righteousness before God consists not only in the sole obedience and merit of Christ, but in our renewal and our own piety, in which we walk before God; which they, for the most part, base upon their own peculiar observances and self-chosen spirituality, as upon a new sort of monkery.

2. That children who are not baptized are not sinners before God, but are righteous and innocent, and thus are saved in their innocency without baptism, which they do not need. And in this way they deny and reject the entire doctrine concerning Original Sin and what belongs to it.

3. That children should not be baptized until they have attained the use of reason and can themselves confess their faith.

4. That the children of Christians, because they have been born of Christian and believing parents, are

holy and the children of God even without and before baptism. For this reason also they neither attach much importance to the baptism of children nor encourage it, contrary to the express words of the promise, which pertains only to those who keep God's covenant and do not despise it (Gen. 17:9).

5. That there is no true Christian assembly or congregation [church] in which sinners are still found.

6. That no sermon should be heard or attended in those churches in which the Papal masses have previously been said.

7. That no one should have anything to do with those ministers of the Church who preach the holy Gospel according to the Augsburg Confession, and censure the errors of the Anabaptists; also that no one should serve or in any way labor for them, but should flee from and shun them as perverters of God's Word.

8. That under the New Testament the magistracy is not a godly estate.

9. That a Christian cannot, with a good, inviolate conscience, hold the office of magistrate.

10. That a Christian cannot, without injury to conscience, use the office of the magistracy in carnal matters against the wicked, neither can subjects appeal to the power of magistrates.

11. That a Christian cannot, with a good conscience, take an oath before a court, neither can he by an oath do homage to his prince or sovereign.

12. That without injury to conscience magistrates cannot inflict upon evil-doers capital punishment.

13. That a Christian cannot, with a good conscience, hold or possess any property, but that he is in duty bound to devote it to the community.

14. That a Christian cannot, with a good conscience, be a landlord, merchant or cutler.

15. That on account of faith [diversity of religion] married persons may be divorced, abandon one another, and be married to another of the same faith.

16. That Christ did not assume his flesh and blood of the Virgin Mary, but brought them with him from heaven.

17. That he also is not true, essential God, but only has more and higher gifts than other men.

And still more articles of like kind; for they are divided into many bands [sects], and one has more and another fewer erros, and thus their entire sect is in reality nothing but a new kind of monkery.

ERRONEOUS ARTICLES OF THE SCHWENCKFELDIANS.

As, when the Schwenckfeldians assert:

1. That all those have no knowledge of Christ as the reigning King of heaven who regard Christ, according to the flesh or his assumed humanity, as a creature; that the flesh of Christ has by exaltation so assumed all divine properties that in might, power, majesty and glory he is everywhere, in degree and place of essence equal to the Father and the eternal Word, so that there is the same essence, properties, will and glory of both natures in Christ, and that the flesh of Christ belongs to the essence of the Holy Trinity.

2. That church service, i.e. the Word preached and heard, is not a means whereby God the Holy Ghost teaches men, and works in them saving knowledge of Christ, conversion, repentance, faith and new obedience.

3. That the water of baptism is not a means whereby God the Lord seals adoption and works regeneration.

4. That bread and wine in the Holy Supper are not means whereby Christ distributes his body and blood.

5. That a Christian man who is truly regenerated by God's Spirit can in this life observe and fulfil the Law of God perfectly.

6. That there is no true Christian congregation [church] in which no public excommunication nor regular process of the ban is observed.

7. That the minister of the Church who is not on his part truly renewed, righteous and godly cannot teach other men with profit or administer true sacraments.

ERRONEOUS ARTICLES OF THE NEW ARIANS.

Also, when the New Arians teach that Christ is not a true, essential, natural God, of one eternal divine essence with God the Father, but is only adorned with divine majesty beneath and beside God the Father.

ERRONEOUS ARTICLES OF THE ANTI-TRINITARIANS.

1. Also, when some Anti-trinitarians reject and condemn the ancient approved creeds, the Nicene and Athanasian, both as to their sense and words, and teach that there is not only one eternal divine essence of the Father, Son and Holy Ghost, but as there are three distinct persons, God the Father, Son and Holy Ghost, so each person has also its essence distinct and separate from the other persons; yet that all three, as three men otherwise distinct and separate in their essence, are either [some imagine] of the same power, wisdom, majesty and glory, or [others think] in essence and properties are not equal.

2. That the Father alone is true God.

These and like articles, one and all, with what pertains to them and follows from them, we reject and condemn as wrong, false, heretical, and contrary to the Word of God, the three Creeds, the Augsburg Confession, the Smalcald Articles and the Catechisms of Luther. Of these articles all godly Christians will and should beware, as the welfare and salvation of their souls is dear to them.

Therefore in the sight of God and of all Christendom [the entire Church of Christ], to those now living and those who shall come after us, we wish to testify that the above declaration, concerning all the controverted articles presented and explained, and no other, is our faith, doctrine and confession, in which we also will appear, by God's grace, with unterrified hearts before the judgment-seat of

THE FORMULA OF CONCORD (1580) (continued)

Jesus Christ, and for it will give an account. We also will neither speak nor write, privately or publicly, anything contrary to this declaration, but, by the help of God's grace, intend to abide thereby. After mature deliberation we have, in God's fear and with the invocation of his name, attached our signatures with our own hands.

Notes: *The Formula of Concord was issued on the fiftieth anniversary of the Augsburg Confession. Its purpose was to unite the several factions that had arisen in the Lutheran Church since the death of Martin Luther. While the Augsburg Confession detailed the Lutheran Church's solid standing within the traditional faith of the Christian Church, the Formula of Concord dealt with those issues of most concern to Lutherans and those which distinguished them from both the Roman Catholic Church and the Reformed Church. At the time of its completion, the Formula was placed beside the other Lutheran symbolic books in* The Book of Concord *(1580).*

While the Augsburg Confession finds universal agreement among contemporary Lutherans, the Formula of Concord has not attained that status. Like the Smalcald Articles, the Formula is not accepted as a standard of doctrine to which subscription is required by the American Lutheran Church. The Lutheran Church in America acknowledges the Formula as a valid interpretation of the Augsburg Confession. Both the Lutheran Church-Missouri Synod and the Wisconsin Evangelical Lutheran Synod accept the Formula equally with the Augsburg Confession.

*   *   *

CONFESSION OF FAITH (AMERICAN LUTHERAN CHURCH)

401. The American Lutheran Church accepts all the canonical books of the Old and New Testaments as a whole and in all their parts as the divinely inspired, revealed, and inerrant Word of God, and submits to this as the only infallible authority in all matters of faith and life.

402. As brief and true statements of the doctrines of the Word of God, the Church accepts and confesses the following Symbols, subscription to which shall be required of all its members, both congregations and individuals:

402.1 The ancient ecumenical Creeds: the Apostolic, the Nicene, and the Athanasian;

402.2 The unaltered Augsburg Confession and Luther's Small Catechism.

403. As further elaboration of and in accord with these Lutheran Symbols, the Church also receives the other documents in the Book of Concord of 1580: the Apology, Luther's Large Catechism, the Smalcald Articles, and the Formula of Concord; and recognizes them as normative for its theology.

404. The American Lutheran Church accepts without reservation the symbolical books of the evangelical Lutheran Church, not insofar as but because they are

the presentation and explanation of the pure doctrine of the Word of God and a summary of the faith of the evangelical Lutheran Church.

Notes: *As part of its constitution, the American Lutheran Church has included a brief confessional statement that is the enumeration of both documents to which all members subscribe and those the church accepts as "normative" for its theology. The Lutheran Church-Missouri Synod and the Lutheran Church in America have similar statements.*

*   *   *

A BRIEF STATEMENT OF THE PRINCIPLES AND DOCTRINE OF THE APOSTOLIC LUTHERAN CHURCH OF AMERICA

There can be found no better or more direct instructions in reference to the principles and doctrine of Christ than the Bible: the Holy Word of God, as is recorded in Hebrews 6:1, and 2:

> "Therefore, leaving the principles of the doctrine of Christ, let us go on unto perfection; not laying again the foundation of repentance from dead works, and of faith toward God. Of the doctrine of baptisms, and of the laying on of hands, and of resurrection of the dead, and of eternal judgment."

CONVERSION AND JUSTIFICATION

An unbeliever is brought to grace through repentance and faith in the Gospel. The baptized person who has fallen from grace has the same condition of heart as an unbeliever, and can be restored to grace only by repentance and faith in the Gospel. Conversion is the work of God in sinful man who in himself is entirely helpless. This person first must be awakened by the righteous and holy Law of God: the Ten Commandments, to see the horror of sin and know that he is condemned under the curse of the Law.

This applies to a careless sinner as well as to a self-righteous person. He is under the curse of the Law and cannot find peace for his soul. Thus, this person is awakened to seek a means of reconciliation. He is now awakened from his dead condition. "And you hath he quickened, who were dead in trespasses and sins." (Ephesians 2:1)

Now the gospel of Christ will lead him to the cross of Calvary where the pains of the newbirth begin, as he beholds that he has nailed the Son of God to the cross with his sins. "My little children, of whom I travail in birth again until Christ be formed in you." (Galatians 4:19)

"And as Moses lifted up the serpent in the wilderness, even so must the Son of man be lifted up: that whosoever believeth in Him should not perish, but have eternal life." (John 3:14, 15)

"A woman when she is in travail hath sorrow, because her hour is come: but as soon as she is delivered of the child, she remembereth no more the anguish, for joy that a man is born into the world. And ye now therefore have sorrow: but I will see you again, and your heart shall rejoice, and your joy no man taketh from you." (John 16:21, 22)

At the cross he will hear the cry of Jesus, "It is finished." The righteous Law has now received all that it demanded by the suffering and death of Jesus.

We believe that the Ten Commandments, or the moral Law, has been given so that unruly men may be governed by it and punishment meted out to those that break it. We also believe that the Law convicts a person of his sins and his corrupt nature, as St. Paul states in Romans 3:20: "For by the law is the knowledge of sin." This Law of God was given "that every mouth may be stopped, and all the world may become guilty before God." (Romans 3:19) But St. Paul also states in 1 Timothy 1:9: "Knowing this, that the law is not made for the righteous man, but for the lawless and disobedient, for the ungodly and for sinners, for unholy and profane," etc. Therefore he concludes: "Wherefore the Law was our schoolmaster to bring us to Christ, that we might be justified by faith. But after that faith is come, we are no longer under a schoolmaster." (Galatians 3:24, 25)

Now the Holy Ghost becomes the Teacher and begins to lead this person into all truth. He takes up his bed of sin and walks; that is, he makes restitution of the wrongs he has done in the past, as Jesus says: "But he that doeth truth cometh to the light, that his deeds may be made manifest, that they are wrought in God." (John 3:21) This person has now come to the narrow road of life and the Holy Spirit is his Guide. He has entered inside the living church of Jesus, Christ being the cornerstone of that building which is not made with hands.

THE DOCTRINE OF THE CHURCH

We believe in the inspired Word of God, as Peter says: "Knowing this first, that no prophecy of the scripture is of private interpretation. For the prophecy came not in old time by the will of man: but holy men of God spake as they were moved by the Holy Ghost." (2 Peter 1:20, 21) And Paul says: "All scripture is given by inspiration of God, and is profitable for doctrine, for reproof, for correction, for instruction in righteousness." (2 Timothy 3:16)

We believe in the unity and trinity of God the Father, the Son and the Holy Ghost. "For there are three that bear record in heaven, the Father, the Word, and the Holy Ghost: and these three are one." (1 John 5:7)

We believe in the forgiveness of sins in Jesus' Name and blood as the means of redemption and reconciliation with God, through repentance and faith, as the Bible records: "The time is fulfilled, and the kingdom of God is at hand: repent ye, and believe the gospel." (Mark 1:15) And in Colossians 1:14: "In whom we have redemption through His blood, even the forgiveness of sins." Then in Hebrews 9:14: "How much more shall the blood of Christ, who through the eternal Spirit offered Himself without spot to God, purge your conscience from dead works to serve the living God?" And in 1 Peter 1:19: "But with the precious blood of Christ, as of a lamb without blemish and without spot." Also in Luke 24:47: "And that repentance and remission of sins should be preached in His name among all nations, beginning at Jerusalem." And in John 20:23: "Whose soever sins ye remit, they are remitted unto them; and whose soever sins ye retain, they are retained."

The fruits of living faith will now appear. "For the kingdom of God is not meat and drink; but righteousness, and peace, and joy in the Holy Ghost." (Romans 14:17) This will lead a person to follow Jesus in doctrine and life and in suffering, as Jesus says: "If any man will come after Me, let him deny himself, and take up his cross, and follow me." (Matthew 16:24) and St. Paul says: "Now thanks be unto God, which always causeth us to triumph in Christ, and maketh manifest the savour of His knowledge by us in every place." (2 Corinthians 2:14)

We believe that a person asks when in need. He seeks when he wants to find and he knocks when he wants to come in, as Jesus says: "Ask, and it shall be given; seek, and ye shall find; knock, and it shall be opened unto you: For every one that asketh receiveth; and he that seeketh findeth; and to him that knocketh it shall be opened." (Matthew 7:7, 8)

BAPTISMS

WATER BAPTISM. *We believe* in the Doctrine of Baptisms. (Hebrews 6:2)

Water baptism, which was instituted by God, is a means of grace. Even though God changed the outward token of grace from circumcision to baptism, we do not believe that He changed the Covenant. The essence of the Covenant that God made with Abraham of old was this: "And I will establish my covenant between me and thee and thy seed after thee in their generations for an everlasting covenant, to be a God unto thee and to thy seed after thee." (Genesis 17:7)

This Covenant, being everlasting, remains the same even though God Who ended the Old Testament and began the New, in place of circumcision, instituted baptism, and in the place of the Passover Lamb instituted the Lord's Supper. Thus the same wording is needed: "I will be to them a God, and they shall be to me a people." (Hebrews 8:10; Ezekiel 37:27)

The requirement of the Old Covenant commanded those who were circumcised to keep, or fulfill, the Law of God. This they were unable to do, "because they continued not in my covenant, and I regarded them not, saith the Lord." (Hebrews 8:9)

The New Covenant also has its own requirements, for the Lord says: "He that believeth and is baptized shall be saved; but he that believeth not shall be damned." (Mark 16:16) Thus, "Without faith it is impossible to please God" (Hebrews 11:6) no matter what else we may do.

We believe that infants have capacity for faith, for it is God who instills faith in the heart. God-given faith is not a faith of the mind but of the heart. "For with the heart man believeth unto righteousness." (Romans 10:10) They who insist that an infant's mind is not sufficiently developed to believe, ignore the Words of our Saviour Who said: "Except ye be converted, and become as little children, ye shall not enter into the kingdom of heaven. But whoso shall offend one of these little ones *which believe on Me*, it were better for him that a millstone were hanged

A BRIEF STATEMENT OF THE PRINCIPLES AND DOCTRINE OF THE APOSTOLIC LUTHERAN CHURCH OF AMERICA (continued)

about his neck, and that he were drowned in the depth of the sea." (Matthew 18:3-6)

If Jesus, the All-Knowing, says they believe on Him, who are we to argue against Him? We believe that Jesus meant infants also, for in Luke 18:15, 16, we read: "And they brought unto Him also infants that He should touch them: but when His disciples saw it, they rebuked them. But Jesus called them unto Him, and said, Suffer little children to come unto me and forbid them not: *for of such* is the kingdom of God."

We believe that God has not instituted a single sacrament for unbelievers, neither has He made a covenant with them. His sacraments and covenants are for believers only. The argument that He made His covenants with adults only does not prove that children were to be excluded, for it is written: "and to thy seed after thee." (Genesis 17:7) "Therefore infants, at the age of eight days were circumcised." (Genesis 17:12)

OF THE HOLY SPIRIT. *We believe* in the baptism of the Holy Ghost and of Fire, as John the Baptist witnesses of Jesus, saying: "He shall baptize you with the Holy Ghost and with fire." (Matthew 3:11)

We believe that Jesus refers to this Baptism as He said: "I am come to send fire on the earth; and what will I, if it be already kindled?" (Luke 12:49) We believe that St. Paul also refers to the Baptism of the Holy Ghost and of fire, as he writes: "And hope maketh not ashamed; because the love of God is shed abroad in our hearts by the Holy Ghost which is given unto us." (Romans 5:5) Likewise St. John writes: "and every one that loveth Him that begat loveth him also that is begotten of Him." (1 John 5:1)

We believe that this divine love binds the children of God together by the Holy Spirit which is in them. This "is the bond of perfectness," (Col. 3:14) and that all who are born of the Holy Spirit are the children of God. "The Spirit itself beareth witness with our spirit that we are the children of God." (Romans 8:16)

THE BAPTISM OF BLOOD. *We believe* this to be the Baptism that Jesus refers to as He states: "But I have a baptism to be baptized with; and how am I straitened till it be accomplished." (Luke 12:50) And again: "Are ye able to drink of the cup that I shall drink of, and to be baptized with the baptism that I am baptized with? (Matt. 20:22)

We believe that those persons who are following Jesus "in the way of regeneration" (Matthew 19:28) are not regenerated until they have experienced this which Jesus states: "Ye shall drink indeed of my cup and be baptized with the baptism that I am baptized with . . . " (Matthew 20:23)

Men who have sinned must taste the bitterness of their sin and the cleansing power of the blood of Jesus in order that they be regenerated. Then they have drunk of the cup that Jesus drank of and are baptized with His baptism. They then have experienced "godly sorrow which worketh repentance to salvation not to be repented of." (2 Corinthians 7:10) And "the blood of sprinkling, that speaketh better things than that of Abel" (Hebrews 12:24) occurs in the spoken words of the forgiveness of sins in the Name of Jesus and His atoning blood.

THE LAYING ON OF HANDS

We believe in the laying on of hands as Ananias did to Paul (Acts 9:12): "And hath seen in a vision a man named Ananias coming in, and putting his hand on him, that he might receive his sight."

And as Peter and John did to the Samaritans, (Acts 8:17): "Then laid they their hands on them, and they received the Holy Ghost."

As Paul did to the disciples at Ephesus, (Acts 19:6): "And when Paul laid his hands upon them, the Holy Ghost came on them; and they spake with tongues, and prophesied."

And as Christ did to the children. Laying on of hands belongs to the principles of the doctrine of Christ.

We also believe that if a Christian falls into sin after he has been blessed with the forgiveness of sins, receiving peace and joy in his heart, the Holy Spirit will guide him, and urge him to put away that sin and ask for the forgiveness of his sin, that the gospel of forgiveness will be extended to him in Jesus' Name and blood. Thus he regains the peace of heart and soul. But if this person continues in sin and does not obey the guidance of the Spirit, the Holy Spirit will flee from him. "And the Lord said, My spirit shall not always strive with man, for that he also is flesh:" (Genesis 6:3) Then he falls again under the condemnation of the Law.

THE DOCTRINE OF CONFESSION

We believe as stated in the Small Catechism that we should confess before God that we are guilty of all kinds of sins, even of those which we do not know. But to the confessor we should confess those sins which we know and feel in our heart, and which burden our consciences. The confession of sins to a trusted Christian brother (confessor) is a good gift of God and a privilege which every Christian should use according to his needs and the demands of his conscience.

Confession should never be taught in an exacting spirit, as if it were a command; neither should it be taught as a condition for salvation, for the only condition for salvation is Scriptural faith in Jesus. Jesus says: "He that believeth on me, as the scripture hath said, out of his belly shall flow rivers of living water." (John 7:38) "Verily, verily, I say unto you, He that believeth on Me hath everlasting life." (John 6:48)

If a believer is burdened in his conscience with some sins which he has committed and which he has never confessed to anybody except God, and these sins are a hindrance to his faith and he feels an inner need and urge to confess them to a trusted Christian brother, this is the voice of the

Holy Spirit to which he should be obedient. Confession of sins to a confessor is no meritorious work and the believer is not justified by that, for he is already righteous in Christ. He confesses his sins in order to restore peace of conscience through absolution, and in order that he may be able to appropriate the Gospel, he is not to think that only those sins which he confessed are forgiven, (for absolution means that all his sins are forgiven, even the sins which he does not know).

If such sins which he already has confessed and which are forgiven, again begin to trouble him, or if doubt assails him as to whether his sins were truly forgiven through the absolution, then that voice is his own corruption and the voice of the devil, which he should reject. He should remember the promise of Christ that his sins which are forgiven by a Christian brother on earth are truly forgiven before God in heaven.

"DEEPENING" IN FAITH, "CIRCUMCISION OF HEART"

Every Christian admits and knows that he has not as yet reached perfection in faith and the knowledge of Christ, or in righteousness, peace, joy, or in sanctification. Therefore, every Christian continues to pray that God will increase in him the grace and light of the Holy Spirit in order that he may know Christ and His redemptive sacrifice better and also grow in love and in the fruits of faith.

"That I may know Him, and the power of his resurrection, and the fellowship of His sufferings, being made conformable unto His death; Not as though I had already attained, either were already perfect: but I follow after, if that I may apprehend that for which also I am apprehended of Christ Jesus." (Philippians 3:10, 12)

Such a deepening and growth do not justify a Christian, for through faith he is already justified before God through Christ and His merits, and is wholly His own without spot or blemish. But he wants to grow in the knowledge of this redemption and justification through the Holy Spirit and the Word of God. This growth and deepening do not, however, mean that the Christian himself feels that he is becoming better and better, but only that he realizes more and more his sinfulness, and at the same time, wholly relies on the grace of God in Christ. Thus he himself decreases, but Christ increases in him.

All this is not an achievement of his own but the work and gift of God, as the Apostle says: "Work out your own salvation with fear and trembling; for it is God which worketh in you both to will and to work, for His good pleasure." (Philippians 2:12, 13)

This is what the Apostle means when he says: "Let us go on to perfection." We are to leave the principles of the doctrine of Christ alone. We are not to change them, to add or to detract from them. Therefore we are warned in Revelation 22:18, 19: "If any man shall add unto these things, God shall add unto him the plagues that are written in this book: And if any man shall take away from the words of the book of this prophecy, God shall take away his part out of the book of life, and out of the holy city, and from the things which are written in this book."

If the repentance or conversion of a person has been only an "outward repentance," that is, if he has confessed his sinfulness and accepted forgiveness, without any real change of heart or comprehension of the redemptive work of Christ within his heart, it is necessary that he experience a real awakening of his conscience and that he comes to know in a personal way, in his heart, the redemptive grace and pardon of God, which is "the circumcision of the heart in the Spirit."

All Christians have received the Holy Spirit to dwell in their hearts when they were converted, and born again, and have become believers. But not all Christians are "filled with the Spirit" in the same measure; that is, not all are fully controlled by the Spirit. A Christian who once was "fervent in Spirit" may grow cold in his faith and spiritual life, losing the living knowledge of Christ and the power to bear witness for Him. Such may and should pray for a new blessing or "filling" of the Holy Spirit (Ephesians 5:18), in order that he may grasp, in a living way, the significance of the redemptive grace of God and the forgiveness of sins, in Jesus' Name and blood, that he may be able to live for Christ with his whole heart and be His witness. It is not the will of God that any of His children should be lukewarm. (Revelation 3:16)

The Apostolic Lutheran Christians, in general, yearn and pray for "new showers of blessings" from God, a new pouring out of His Spirit, a "latter rain." They crave for this in order that they may be refreshed and quickened in their faith and be endued with power from on high. This "latter rain" is also prayed for in order that the children of Christian parents and other unbelievers would again, in multitudes, be awakened, both at home and in foreign lands, and return from the ways of the world to the kingdom of God.

Notes: *Growing out of the institutional expression of an evangelical pietist movement within Finnish Lutheranism, the position of the Apostolic Lutherans is unique in both the content and tone of its doctrinal presentation. It is a much warmer, more personal statement centered upon the Christian's relationship to God. Of all like statements used by American Lutheran bodies, this one alone neglects mention of* The Book of Concord, *though it makes passing reference to Luther's Smaller Catechism. Other Lutherans would possibly have trouble with the doctrines of baptisms and the emphasis upon the "latter rain."*

* * *

DECLARATION OF FAITH (ASSOCIATION OF FREE LUTHERAN CONGREGATIONS)

Having a common purpose and seeking one goal, we join together as free congregations for Christian fellowship, mutual edification, the salvation of souls and whatever work may be necessary that the Kingdom of God may come among us and our fellow men. No bonds of compulsion bind us save those which the Holy Spirit lays upon us.

No man fully understands the times and the situations in which he lives. At best we see through a glass darkly. Nevertheless, each Christian must decide in the light of

God's Word and the evidence which he has what course of
action he should take and to what causes his life should be
given. It is the same for the Christian congregation.
Imperfect as it is, it must decide in what fellowship of
other congregations it can best live out its purpose for
being. Out of considerable soul-searching and prayer we
have come to choose to continue as Lutheran free
churches.

As we stand at this particular moment of time we give
thanks for the heritage of the past. We recognize and
confess our indebtness to many noble souls of the faith,
both the relatively unknown who are faithful in their
places and the ones on whom God placed the mantle of
leadership. Even as it is true that before the Cross of Christ
there are no self-made men, so it is true that we have
shared in blessings from many and are debtors.

It seems good to us as we joi   ther for common work
and fellowship to state our beliefs in regard to the
following matters.

I. DOCTRINE

1. We accept and believe in the Holy Bible as the
   complete written Word of God given and preserved
   to us by the Holy Spirit for our salvation and
   instruction.

2. We endorse the statement on the Word as found in
   the United Testimony on Faith and Life and would
   quote here the following. "We bear witness that the
   Bible is our only authentic and infallible source of
   God's revelation to us and all men, and that it is the
   only inerrant and completely adequate source and
   norm of Christian doctrine and life. We hold that the
   Bible, as a whole and in all its parts, is the Word of
   God under all circumstances regardless of man's
   attitude toward it."

3. We accept the ancient ecumenical symbols, namely,
   the Apostles', the Nicene, and the Athanasian
   Creeds; Luther's Small Catechism and the Unaltered
   Augsburg Confession as the true expression of the
   Christian faith and life.

4. We reject any affiliations or associations which do
   not accept the Bible alone as definitive for the life
   and practice of man and the Church.

5. We submit all religious teaching to the test of II John
   7-11.

6. We endorse no one version or revision of the Bible to
   the exclusion of others. We recommend all which are
   reverent and true translations.

II. CHRISTIAN UNITY

1. He who believes in and accepts the sufficient work of
   Jesus for his salvation and is baptized is a child of
   God.

2. The Christian is united by the strongest bonds to
   those who share this faith with him whether they
   come from his own denomination or another.

3. We believe that Jesus in His High Priestly Prayer
   prayed that those who believe in Him might find and
   accept each other.

4. In some situations and in some times it is possible
   that unions of groups of congregations may be
   desirable.

5. We recommend that our congregations cooperate
   wherever possible with like-minded Lutheran
   congregations and movements in programs of evangelism and witness.

6. We envision opportunities for our congregations to
   cooperate with other Protestant churches in the
   areas of evangelism and witness to their communi-
   ties. However, care must be taken not to compromise
   the Lutheran understanding of the Scriptures.

III. CHURCH POLITY

1. We believe that final human authority in the
   churches is vested in the local congregation, subject
   to the Word of God and the Holy Spirit.

2. Scripture does not command or forbid any particular
   organization for fellowship of congregations. In the
   absence of this we believe it is most safe to operate in
   a democratic way.

3. Conferences of the congregations of our fellowship
   do not enact law for the congregations, but simply
   recommend actions and practices to them.

4. In a free association of congregations such as this,
   neither its officers or conferences can negotiate the
   union of any or all of the congregations with another
   fellowship of congregations. This is an individual
   matter for the congregation.

5. We accept the Guiding Principles of the Lutheran
   Free Church as a true statement of our belief in
   regard to church polity.

6. The Holy Christian Church consists of those who in
   their hearts truly believe in Jesus Christ as Lord and
   Saviour.

7. A free congregation selects and calls its own pastor,
   conducts its own program of worship, fellowship and
   service, and owns and maintains its own property.

IV. PRACTICAL LIFE

1. The Christian seeks to refrain from those acts,
   thoughts and words which are against a stated law of
   God.

2. Where actions and practices are neither forbidden
   nor encouraged in Scripture by name, the earnest
   believer will search in the Scriptures for principles to
   guide his decisions and conduct.

3. He is aware that there is a separation which is
   necessary between the Christian and the world.

4. Ultimately every Christian makes his own decisions
   as to life and practice in the presence of His God.
   But he welcomes the sincere counsel of fellow
   believers.

5. Every Christian is responsible for his witness by life
   to others and will govern himself, with the Lord's
   help, accordingly.

6. The Christian will refrain from belonging to organizations which practice a religion without Christ as the only Saviour. Belonging to such a group places the believer in a hopelessly compromised position and destroys his witness for Christ.

V. CHURCH LIFE

1. We make no recommendation as to the use of liturgy and vestments except that we encourage simplicity in worship.

2. We believe the earliest Christians were extremely simple in their order of service. Whatever is added to the service carries the danger of becoming only form.

3. Even the simple parts of the service may become only form.

4. The preaching of the Word of God must be the central part of the service.

5. True Gospel preaching endeavors to meet the needs of all who hear: the believer who desires to grow in his life with God, the seeking and uncertain souls who want to see Him, the hypocrite who must be awakened from his self-righteousness, and the hardened sinner who must still be called to saving faith.

6. The Sacraments must always be met by the response of faith in the heart of the recipient to be efficacious.

7. Hymn books should be such as will give honor to the Word of God and the Sacraments.

8. Congregations will cherish opportunities for Bible study and prayer fellowship.

9. Congregations are encouraged to have fellowship with one another in various activities.

10. The Lord has given talents and gifts to Christian lay people as well as pastors, and opportunity should be given for the practice of these gifts in the life of the congregations, also in meetings of fellowship outside the congregation, and in service to a needy world.

Notes: *This declaration adopted in 1962 outlines the documents that are accepted as theologically authoritative, but it proceeds to dedicate the body of the text to outlining a position on those issues that occasioned the creation of the association. The separation from those whose doctrinal standards are lax is of prime importance.*

*   *   *

CONFESSION (CHURCH OF THE LUTHERAN CONFESSION)

The doctrinal position of this body is defined by the following statements:

A. We accept without reservation the canonical Scriptures of the Old and the New Testaments as the verbally inspired Word of God ("verbally"—I Corinthians 2:13; "inspired"—II Timothy 3:16; cf. also II Peter 1:21) and therefore as the sole and only infallible rule of doctrine and life.

B. We confess the Apostolic, Nicene, and Athanasian Creeds and the Particular Symbols of the Lutheran Church as published in the Book of Concord of 1580,

because they are a true exposition of the Word of God.

C. We also subscribe to the Brief Statement of 1932.

D. Because of differences that have arisen within the Synodical Conference we have found it necessary to define our position in a particular statement entitled *Concerning Church Fellowship* as well as in *Theses on the Relation of Synod and Local Congregation to the Holy Christian Church and Theses on the Ministry of the Keys and the Public Ministry.*

Notes: *Even more conservative than the Wisconsin Synod, the Church of the Lutheran Confession has rejected relations with any church less conservative than itself. Along with adherence to* The Book of Concord, *the church additionally demands adherence to the Brief Statement adopted by the Missouri Synod in 1932. This confession comes from the church's constitution.*

*   *   *

CONFESSION (FEDERATION FOR AUTHENTIC LUTHERANISM)

FAL, and every member of FAL, accepts without reservation:

1. The Holy Scripture, both the Old and New Testament, as the very Word of God. His infallible revelation given by inspiration of the Holy Spirit, in all parts and words recorded without error in the original manuscripts by the Prophets, Apostles and Evangelists at the only rule and norm of faith and practice:

2. All the Symbolical Books of the Evangelical Lutheran Church as a true and Unadulterated statement and exposition of the Word of God (and subscribe to these symbols because *(quia)* they are a proper exposition of God's Word), to wit: the three Ecumenical Creeds (the Apostles' Creed, the Nicene Creed, the Athanasian Creed), the Unaltered Augsburg Confession, the Apology of the Augsburg Confession, the Smalcald Articles, the Large Catechism of Luther, the Small Catechism of Luther, and the Formula of Concord:

3. The Brief Statement of the Doctrinal Position of the Missouri Synod adopted in 1932. We recognize the need for the development of additional confessional statements dealing with the theological problems and concerns of each age. Therefore, additional confessional statements may be added to this confessional base as the need arises. All confessional statements which are added must be in total agreement with the existing confessional standard.

Notes: *Withdrawing from the Lutheran Church-Missouri Synod in the 1970s, the Federation for Authentic Lutheranism represented theologically the most conservative wing of the synod, a position reflected in its confession.*

CONFESSION OF FAITH (LUTHERAN CHURCH IN AMERICA)

Section 1. This church confesses Jesus Christ as Lord of the Church. The Holy Spirit creates and sustains the Church through the Gospel and thereby unites believers with their Lord and with one another in the fellowship of faith.

Section 2. This church holds that the Gospel is the revelation of God's sovereign will and saving grace in Jesus Christ. In Him, the Word Incarnate, God imparts Himself to men.

Section 3. This church acknowledges the Holy Scriptures as the norm for the faith and life of the Church. The Holy Scriptures are the divinely inspired record of God's redemptive act in Christ, for which the Old Testament prepared the way and which the New Testament proclaims. In the continuation of this proclamation in the Church, God still speaks through the Holy Scriptures and realizes His redemptive purpose generation after generation.

Section 4. This church accepts the Apostles', the Nicene, and the Athanasian creeds as true declarations of the faith of the Church.

Section 5. This church accepts the Unaltered Augsburg Confession, and Luther's Small Catechism as true witnesses to the Gospel, and acknowledges as one with it in faith and doctrine all churches that likewise accept the teachings of these symbols.

Section 6. This church accepts the other symbolical books of the evangelical Lutheran church, the Apology of the Augsburg Confession, the Smalcald Articles, Luther's Large Catechism, and the Formula of Concord as further valid interpretations of the confession of the church.

Section 7. This church affirms that the Gospel transmitted by the Holy Scriptures, to which the creeds and confessions bear witness, is the true treasure of the Church, the substance of its proclamation, and the basis of its unity and continuity. The Holy Spirit uses the proclamation of the Gospel and the administration of the Sacraments to create and sustain Christian faith and fellowship. As this occurs, the Church fulfills its divine mission and purpose.

Notes: *This confession is found in the constitution of the church (1962). It is noteworthy because of the manner in which it offers varied reflections upon the Bible and various Lutheran doctrinal documents.*

* * *

CONFESSION (LUTHERAN CHURCH-MISSOURI SYNOD)

The Synod, and every member of the Synod, accepts without reservation:

1. The Scriptures of the Old and the New Testament as the written Word of God and the only rule and norm of faith and of practice;

2. All the Symbolical Books of the Evangelical Lutheran Church as a true and unadulterated statement and exposition of the Word of God, to wit: the three Ecumenical Creeds (the Apostles' Creed, the Nicene Creed, the Athanasian Creed), the Unaltered Augsburg Confession, the Apology of the Augsburg Confession, the Smalcald Articles, the Large Catechism of Luther, the Small Catechism of Luther, and the Formula of Concord.

Notes: *One of two documents from the Missouri Synod, this brief statement is from the church's constitution. It stands in stark contrast to the like confessions from the constitutions of the American Lutheran Church and the Lutheran Church in America.*

* * *

BRIEF STATEMENT OF THE DOCTRINAL POSITION OF THE MISSOURI SYNOD [LUTHERAN CHURCH-MISSOURI SYNOD (1932)]

OF THE HOLY SCRIPTURES.

1. We teach that the Holy Scriptures differ from all other books in the world in that they are the Word of God. They are the Word of God because the holy men of God who wrote the Scriptures wrote only that which the Holy Ghost communicated to them by inspiration, 2 Tim. 3, 16; 2 Pet. 1, 21. We teach also that the verbal inspiration of the Scriptures is not a so-called "theological deduction," but that it is taught by direct statements of the Scriptures, 2 Tim. 3, 16; John 10, 35; Rom. 3, 2; 1 Cor. 2, 13. Since the Holy Scriptures are the Word of God, it goes without saying that they contain no errors or contradictions, but that they are in all their parts and words the infallible truth, also in those parts which treat of historical, geographical, and other secular matters, John 10, 35.

2. We furthermore teach regarding the Holy Scriptures that they are given by God to the Christian Church for the foundation of faith, Eph. 2, 20. Hence the Holy Scriptures are the sole source from which all doctrines proclaimed in the Christian Church must be taken and therefore, too, the sole rule and norm by which all teachers and doctrines must be examined and judged.—With the Confessions of our Church we teach also that the "rule of faith" (*analogia fidei*) according to which the Holy Scriptures are to be understood are the clear passages of *Scriptures themselves* which set forth the individual doctrines. (Apologie. *Triglotta*, p. 441, § 60; Mueller, p. 284.) The rule of faith is not the man-made so-called "totality of Scripture" (*"Ganzes der Schrift"*).

3. We reject the doctrine which under the name of science has gained wide popularity in the Church of our day, that Holy Scripture is not in all its parts the Word of God, but in part the Word of God and in part the word of man and hence does, or at least might, contain error. We reject this erroneous doctrine as horrible and blasphemous, since it flatly contradicts Christ and His holy apostles, sets up men as judges over the Word of God, and thus over-

throws the foundation of the Christian Church and its faith.

OF GOD.

4. On the basis of the Holy Scriptures we teach the sublime article of the Holy Trinity; that is, we teach that the one true God, Deut. 6, 4; 1 Cor. 8, 4, is the Father and the Son and the Holy Ghost, three distinct *persons*, but of one and the same divine *essence*, equal in power, equal in eternity, equal in majesty, because each person possesses the one divine essence *entire*, Col. 2, 9; Matt. 28, 19. We hold that all teachers and communions that deny the doctrine of the Holy Trinity are outside the pale of the Christian Church. The Triune God is the God who is *gracious* to man, John 3, 16-18; 1 Cor. 12, 3. Since the Fall no man can believe in the "fatherhood" of God except he believe in the eternal Son of God, who became man and reconciled us to God by His vicarious satisfaction, 1 John 2, 23; John 14, 6. Hence we warn against Unitarianism, which in our country has to a great extent impenetrated the sects and is being spread particularly also through the influence of the lodges.

OF CREATION.

5. We teach that God has created heaven and earth, and that in the manner and in the space of time recorded in the Holy Scriptures, especially Gen. 1 and 2, namely, by His almighty creative word, and in six days. We reject every doctrine which denies or limits the work of creation as taught in Scripture. In our days it is denied or limited by those who assert, ostensibly in deference to science, that the world came into existence through a process of evolution; that is, that it has, in immense periods of time, developed more or less out of itself. Since no man was present when it pleased God to create the world, we must look, for a reliable account of creation, to God's own record, found in God's own book, the Bible. We accept God's own record with full confidence and confess with Luther's Catechism: "I believe that God has made me and all creatures."

OF MAN AND OF SIN.

6. We teach that the first man was not brutelike nor merely capable of intellectual development, but that God created man *in His own image*, Gen. 1, 26. 27; Eph. 4, 24; Col. 3, 10, that is, in true knowledge of God and in true righteousness and holiness and endowed with a truly scientific knowledge of nature, Gen. 2, 19-23.

7. We furthermore teach that sin came into the world by the fall of the first man, as described Gen. 3. By this Fall not only he himself, but also all his natural offspring have lost the original knowledge, righteousness, and holiness, and thus all men are sinners already by birth, dead in sins, inclined to all evil, and subject to the wrath of God, Rom. 5, 12. 18; Eph. 2, 1-3. We teach also that men are unable, through any efforts of their own or by the aid of "culture and science," to reconcile themselves to God and thus to conquer death and damnation.

OF REDEMPTION.

8. We teach that in the fulness of time the eternal Son of God *was made man* by assuming, from the Virgin Mary through the operation of the Holy Ghost, a human nature like unto ours, yet without sin, and receiving it into His divine person. Jesus Christ is therefore "true God, begotten of the Father from eternity, and also true man, born of the Virgin Mary," true God and true man in *one* undivided and indivisible person. The purpose of this miraculous incarnation of the Son of God was that He might become the *Mediator* between God and men, both fulfilling the divine Law and suffering and dying in the place of mankind. In this manner God has reconciled the whole sinful world unto Himself, Gal. 4, 4. 5; 3, 13; 2 Cor. 5, 18. 19.

OF FAITH IN CHRIST.

9. Since God has reconciled the whole world unto Himself through the vicarious life and death of His Son and has commanded that the reconciliation effected by Christ be proclaimed to men in the Gospel, to the end that they may *believe* it, 2 Cor. 5, 18.19; Rom. 1, 5, therefore faith in Christ is the only way for men to obtain personal reconciliation with God, that is, forgiveness of sins, as both the Old and the New Testament Scriptures testify, Acts 10,43; John 3,16—18.36. By this faith in Christ, through which men obtain the forgiveness of sins, is not meant any human effort to fulfil the Law of God after the example of Christ, but faith in the Gospel, that is, in the forgiveness of sins, or justification, which was fully earned for us by Christ and is offered in the Gospel. This faith justifies, not inasmuch as it is a work of man, but inasmuch as it lays hold of the grace offered, the forgiveness of sins, Rom. 4, 16.

OF CONVERSION.

10. We teach that conversion consists in this, that a man, having learned from the Law of God that he is a lost and condemned sinner, *is brought to faith in the Gospel*, which offers him forgiveness of sins and eternal salvation for the sake of Christ's vicarious satisfaction, Acts 11,21; Luke 24,46.47; Acts 26,18.

11. All men, since the Fall, are dead in sins, Eph. 2, 1—3, and inclined only to evil, Gen. 6, 5; 8, 21; Rom. 8, 7. For this reason, and particularly because men regard the Gospel of Christ, crucified for the sins of the world, as foolishness, 1 Cor. 2, 14, faith in the Gospel, or conversion to God, is neither wholly nor in the least part the work of man, but the work of God's grace and almighty power alone, Phil. 1, 29; Eph. 2, 8; 1, 19;—Jer. 31, 18. Hence Scripture calls the faith of man, or his conversion, a raising from the dead, Eph. 1, 20; Col. 2, 12, a being born of God, John 1, 12.13, a new birth by the Gospel, 1 Pet. 1,23—25, a work of God like the creation of light at the creation of the world, 2 Cor. 4, 6.

12. On the basis of these clear statements of the Holy Scriptures we reject every kind of *synergism*, that is, the doctrine that conversion is wrought not by the grace and power of God alone, but in part also by the cooperation of man himself, by man's right conduct, his right attitude, his right self-determination, his lesser guilt or less evil conduct as compared with others, his refraining from wilful resistance, or anything else whereby man's conversion and salvation is taken out of the gracious hands of God and made to depend on what man does or leaves undone. For this refraining from wilful resistance or from any kind of resistance is also solely a work of grace, which "changes unwilling into willing men," Ezek. 36, 26; Phil. 2, 13. We reject also the doctrine that man is able to decide for conversion through "powers imparted by grace," since this doctrine presupposes that *before* conversion man still possesses spiritual powers by which he can make the right use of such "powers imparted by grace."

13. On the other hand, we reject also the *Calvinistic* perversion of the doctrine of conversion, that is, the doctrine that God does not desire to convert and save all hearers of the Word, but only a portion of them. Many hearers of the Word indeed remain unconverted and are not saved, not because God does not earnestly desire their conversion and salvation, but solely because they stubbornly resist the gracious operation of the Holy Ghost, as Scripture teaches, Acts 7, 51; Matt. 23, 37; Acts 13, 46.

14. As to the question why not all men are converted and saved, seeing that God's grace is universal and all men are equally and utterly corrupt, we confess that we cannot answer it. From Scripture we know only this: A man owes his conversion and salvation, not to any lesser guilt or better conduct on his part, but solely to the grace of God. But any man's non-conversion is due to himself alone: it is the result of his obstinate resistance against the converting operation of the Holy Ghost, Hos. 13, 9.

15. Our refusal to go beyond what is revealed in these two Scriptural truths is not "masked Calvinism" ("Cryptocalvinism"), but *precisely* the Scriptural teaching of the Lutheran Church as it is presented in detail in the Formula of Concord (*Triglot*, p. 1081, §§ 57-59. 60 b. 62. 63; M., p. 716 f.): "That one is hardened, blinded, given over to a reprobate mind, while another, who is indeed in the same guilt, is converted again, etc.,—in these and similar questions Paul fixes a certain limit to us how far we should go, namely, that in the one part we should recognize God's *judgment*. For they are well-deserved penalties of sins when God so punishes a land or nation for despising His Word that the punishment extends also to their posterity, as is to be seen in the Jews. And thereby God in some lands and persons exhibits His severity to those that are His in order to indicate what we all would have well deserved and would be worthy and worth, since we act wickedly in opposition to God's Word and often grieve the Holy Ghost sorely; in order that we may live in the fear of God and acknowledge and praise God's *goodness*, to the exclusion of, and contrary to, our merit in and with *us*, to whom He gives His Word and with whom He leaves it and whom He does not harden and reject. . . . And this His righteous, well-deserved judgment He displays in some countries, nations, and persons in order that, when we are placed alongside of them and compared with them (*quam simillimi illis deprehensi, i.e.*, and found to be most similar to them), we may learn the more diligently to recognize and praise God's pure, unmerited grace in the vessels of mercy. . . . When we proceed thus far in this article, we remain on the right way, as it is written, Hos. 13, 9: 'O Israel, thou hast destroyed thyself; but in Me is thy help.' However, as regards these things in this disputation which would soar too high and beyond these limits, we should with Paul place the finger upon our lips and remember and say, Rom. 9, 20: 'O man, who art thou that repliest against God?' " The Formula of Concord describes the mystery which confronts us here not as a mystery in man's heart (a "psychological" mystery), but teaches that, when we try to understand why "one is hardened, blinded, given over to a reprobate mind, while another, who is indeed in the same guilt, is converted again," we enter the domain of the unsearchable judgments of God and ways past finding out, which are not revealed to us in His Word, but which we shall know in eternal life, 1 Cor. 13, 12.

16. Calvinists solve this mystery, which God has not revealed in His Word, by denying the *universality* of grace; synergists, by denying that salvation is by grace *alone*. Both solutions are utterly vicious, since they contradict Scripture and since every poor sinner stands in need of, and must cling to, both the unrestricted *universal grace* and the unrestricted "by grace *alone*," lest he despair and perish.

OF JUSTIFICATION.

17. Holy Scripture sums up all its teachings regarding the love of God to the world of sinners, regarding the salvation wrought by Christ, and regarding faith in Christ as the only way to obtain salvation, in the article of *justification*. Scripture teaches that God has already declared the whole world to be righteous in Christ, Rom. 7, 19; 2 Cor. 5, 18-21; Rom. 4,25; that therefore not for the sake of their good works, but without the works of the Law, by grace, for Christ's sake, He *justifies*, that is, *accounts* as righteous, all those who believe in Christ, that is, believe, accept, and rely on, the fact that for Christ's sake their sins are forgiven. Thus the Holy Ghost testifies through St. Paul: "There is no difference; for all have sinned and come short of the glory of God, being justified freely by His grace, through the redemption that is in Christ Jesus," Rom. 3:23, 24. And again: "Therefore

we conclude that a man is justified by faith, without the deeds of the Law," Rom. 3, 28.

18. Through this doctrine alone Christ is given the *honor* due Him, namely, that through His holy life and innocent suffering and death He is our Savior. And through this doctrine alone can poor sinners have the abiding *comfort* that God is assuredly gracious to them. We reject *as apostasy from the Christian religion* all doctrines whereby man's own works and merit are mingled into the article of justification before God. For the Christian religion is the faith that we have forgiveness of sins and salvation through faith in Christ Jesus, Acts 10, 43.

19. We reject as apostasy from the Christian religion not only the doctrine of the *Unitarians*, who promise the grace of God to men on the basis of their moral efforts; not only the gross work-doctrine of the papists, who expressly teach that good works are necessary to obtain justification; but also the doctrine of the *synergists*, who indeed use the terminology of the Christian Church and say that man is justified "by faith," "by faith alone," but again mix human works into the article of justification by ascribing to man a cooperation with God in the kindling of faith and thus stray into papistic territory.

OF GOOD WORKS.

20. Before God only those works are good which are done for the glory of God and the good of man, according to the rule of the divine Law. Such works, however, no man performs unless he first believes that God has forgiven him his sins and has given him eternal life by grace, for Christ's sake, without any works of his own, John 15, 4. 5. We reject as a great folly the assertion, frequently made in our day, that works must be placed in the fore, and "faith in dogmas"—meaning the Gospel of Christ Crucified for the sins of the world—must be relegated to the rear. Since good works never precede faith, but are always and in every instance the *result* of faith in the Gospel, it is evident that the only means by which we Christians can become rich in good works (and God would have us to be rich in good works, Titus 2, 14) is unceasingly to remember the grace of God which we have received in Christ, Rom. 12, 1; 2 Cor. 8, 9. Hence we reject as unchristian and foolish any attempt to produce good works by the compulsion of the Law or through carnal motives.

OF THE MEANS OF GRACE.

21. Although God is present and operates everywhere throughout all creation and the whole earth is therefore full of the *temporal* bounties and blessings of God, Col. 1, 17; Acts 17, 28; 14, 17, still we hold with Scripture that God offers and communicates to men the *spiritual* blessings purchased by Christ, namely, the forgiveness of sins and the treasures and gifts connected therewith, only through the external means of grace ordained by Him. These means of grace are the Word of the Gospel, in every form in which it is brought to man, and the Sacraments of Holy Baptism and of the Lord's Supper. The Word

of the Gospel promises and applies the grace of God, works faith and thus regenerates man, and gives the Holy Ghost, Acts 20, 24; Rom. 10, 17; 1 Pet. 1, 23; Gal. 3, 2. Baptism, too, is applied for the remission of sins and is therefore a washing of regeneration and renewing of the Holy Ghost, Acts 2, 38; 22, 16; Titus 3, 5. Likewise the object of the Lord's Supper, that is, of the ministration of the body and blood of Christ, is none other than the communication and sealing of the forgiveness of sins, as the words declare: "Given for you," and: "Shed for you for the remission of sins," Luke 22, 19. 20; Matt. 26, 28, and: "This cup is the New Testament in My blood," 1 Cor. 11, 23; Jer. 31, 31-34 ("New Covenant").

22. Since it is only through the external means ordained by Him that God has promised to communicate the grace and salvation purchased by Christ, the Christian Church must not remain at home with the means of grace entrusted to it, but go into the whole world with the preaching of the Gospel and the administration of the Sacraments, Matt. 28, 19.20; Mark 16, 15.16. For the same reason also the churches at home should never forget that there is no other way of winning souls for the Church and keeping them with it than the faithful and diligent use of the divinely ordained means of grace. Whatever activities do not either directly apply the Word of God or subserve such application we condemn as "new methods," unchurchly activities, which do not build, but harm, the Church.

23. We reject as a dangerous error the doctrine, which disrupted the Church of the Reformation, that the grace and the Spirit of God are communicated not through the external means ordained by Him, but by an *immediate* operation of grace. This erroneous doctrine bases the forgiveness of sins, or justification, upon a fictitious "infused grace," that is, upon a quality of man, and thus again establishes the work-doctrine of the papists.

OF THE CHURCH.

24. We believe that there is *one* holy Christian Church on earth, the Head of which is Christ and which is gathered, preserved, and governed by Christ through the Gospel.

The members of the Christian Church are the *Christians*, that is, all those who have despaired of their own righteousness before God and believe that God forgives their sins for Christ's sake. The Christian Church, in the proper sense of the term, is composed of believers only, Acts 5, 14; 26, 18; which means that no person in whom the Holy Ghost has wrought faith in the Gospel, or—which is the same thing—in the doctrine of justification, can be divested of his membership in the Christian Church; and, on the other hand, that no person in whose heart this faith does not dwell can be invested with such membership. All unbelievers, though they be in external communion with the Church and even hold the office of teacher or any other office in the Church, are not members of the Church, but, on the

BRIEF STATEMENT OF THE DOCTRINAL POSITION OF
THE MISSOURI SYNOD [LUTHERAN CHURCH-
MISSOURI SYNOD (1932)] (continued)

contrary, dwelling-places and instruments of Satan, Eph. 2,2. This is also the teaching of our Lutheran Confessions: "It is certain, however, that the wicked are in the power of the devil and members of the kingdom of the devil, as Paul teaches, Eph. 2, 2, when he says that 'the devil now worketh in the children of disobedience,'" etc. (Apology. *Triglot*, p. 231, § 16; M., p. 154.)

25. Since it is by faith in the Gospel alone that men become members of the Christian Church, and since this faith cannot be seen by men, but is known to God alone, 1 Kings 8, 39; Acts 1, 24; 2 Tim. 2, 19, therefore the Christian Church on earth is *invisible*, Luke 17, 20, and will remain invisible till Judgment Day, Col. 3, 3.4. In our day some Lutherans speak of two sides of the Church, taking the means of grace to be its "visible side." It is true, the means of grace are necessarily related to the Church, seeing that the Church is created and preserved through them. But the means of grace are not for that reason a part of the Church; for the Church in the proper sense of the word consists only of *believers*, Eph. 2, 19.20; Acts 5, 14. Lest we abet the notion that the Christian Church in the proper sense of the term is an external institution, we shall continue to call the means of grace the "marks" of the Church. Just as wheat is to be found only where it has been sown, so the Church can be found only where the Word of God is in use.

26. We teach that this Church, which is the invisible communion of all believers, is to be found not only in those external church communions which teach the Word of God purely in every part, but also where, along with error, so much of the Word of God still remains that men may be brought to the knowledge of their sins and to faith in the forgiveness of sins, which Christ has gained for all men, Mark 16, 16; Samaritans: Luke 17, 16; John 4, 25.

27. *Local Churches or Local Congregations.*—Holy Scripture, however, does not speak merely of the *one* Church, which embraces the believers of all places, as in Matt. 16, 18; John 10, 16, but also of churches in the *plural*, that is, of *local churches*, as in 1 Cor. 16, 19; 1, 2; Acts 8, 1: the churches of Asia, the church of God in Corinth, the church in Jerusalem. But this does not mean that there are *two kinds* of churches; for the local churches also, in as far as they are churches, consist solely of believers, as we see clearly from the addresses of the epistles to local churches; for example, "Unto the church which is at Corinth, to *them that are sanctified* in Christ Jesus, called to be *saints*," 1 Cor. 1, 2; Rom. 1, 7, etc. The visible society, containing hypocrites as well as believers, is called a church only in an improper sense, Matt. 13, 47-50. 24-30. 38-43.

28. *On Church-Fellowship.*—Since God ordained that His Word *only*, without the admixture of human doctrine, be taught and believed in the Christian Church, 1 Pet. 4, 11; John 8, 31. 32; 1 Tim. 6, 3. 4, all Christians are required by God to discriminate between orthodox and heterodox church-bodies, Matt. 7, 15, to have church-fellowship only with orthodox church-bodies, and, in case they have strayed into heterodox church-bodies, to leave them, Rom. 16, 17. We repudiate *unionism*, that is, church-fellowship with the adherents of false doctrine, as disobedience to God's command, as causing divisions in the Church, Rom. 16, 17; 2 John 9, 10, and as involving the constant danger of losing the Word of God entirely, 2 Tim. 2, 17-21.

29. The orthodox character of a church is established not by its mere name nor by its outward acceptance of, and subscription to, an orthodox creed, but by the doctrine which is *actually* taught in its pulpits, in its theological seminaries, and in its publications. On the other hand, a church does not forfeit its orthodox character through the casual intrusion of errors, provided these are combated and eventually removed by means of doctrinal discipline, Acts 20, 30; 1 Tim. 1, 3.

30. *The Original and True Possessors of All Christian Rights and Privileges.*—Since the Christians are the Church, it is self-evident that they alone *originally* possess the spiritual gifts and rights which Christ has gained for, and given to, His Church. Thus St. Paul reminds all believers: "All things are yours," 1 Cor. 3, 21.22, and Christ Himself commits to all believers the keys of the kingdom of heaven, Matt. 16, 13-19; 18, 17-20; John 20, 22. 23, and commissions all believers to preach the Gospel and to administer the Sacraments, Matt. 28, 19. 20; 1 Cor. 11, 23-25. Accordingly, we reject all doctrines by which this spiritual power or any part thereof is adjudged as *originally* vested in certain individuals or bodies, such as the Pope, or the bishops, or the order of the ministry, or the secular lords, or councils, or synods, etc. The officers of the Church publicly administer their offices only by virtue of delegated powers, conferred on them by the original possessors of such powers, and such administration remains under the supervision of the latter, Col. 4, 17. Naturally all Christians have also the right and the duty to judge and decide matters of doctrine, not according to their own notions, of course, but according to the Word of God, 1 John 4, 1; 1 Pet. 4, 11.

OF THE PUBLIC MINISTRY.

31. By the public ministry we mean the office by which the Word of God is preached and the Sacraments are administered *by order and in the name* of a Christian congregation. Concerning this office we teach that it is a *divine ordiance*; that is, the Christians of a certain locality must apply the means of grace not only privately and within the circle of their families nor merely in their common intercourse with fellow-Christians, John 5, 39; Eph. 6, 4; Col. 3, 16, but they are also required, by the divine order, to make provision that the Word of God be publicly preached in their midst, and the Sacraments administered

according to the institution of Christ, by persons qualified for such work, whose qualifications and official functions are exactly defined in Scripture, Titus 1,5; Acts 14,23; 20,28; 2 Tim. 2,2.

32. Although the office of the ministry is a divine ordinance, it possesses no other power than the power of the Word of God, 1 Pet. 4,11; that is to say, it is the duty of Christians to yield unconditional obedience to the office of the ministry whenever, and as long as, the minister proclaims to them the Word of God, Heb. 13,17; Luke 10,16. If, however, the minister, in his teachings and injunctions, were to go beyond the Word of God, it would be the duty of Christians not to obey, but to disobey him, so as to remain faithful to Christ, Matt. 23,8. Accordingly, we reject the false doctrine ascribing to the office of the ministry the right to demand obedience and submission in matters which Christ has not commanded.

33. Regarding *ordination* we teach that it is not a divine, but a commendable ecclesiastical ordinance. (Smalcald Articles. *Triglot*, p. 525, § 70; M., p. 342.)

OF CHURCH AND STATE.

34. Although both Church and State are ordinances of God, yet they must not be commingled. Church and State have entirely different aims. By the Church, God would save men, for which reason the Church is called the "mother" of believers, Gal. 4,26. By the State, God would maintain external order among men, "that we may lead a quiet and peaceable life in all godliness and honesty," 1 Tim. 2,2. It follows that the means which Church and State employ to gain their ends are entirely different. The Church may not employ any other means than the preaching of the Word of God, John 18, 11.36; 2 Cor. 10,4. The State, on the other hand, makes laws bearing on civil matters and is empowered to employ for their execution also the sword and other corporal punishments, Rom. 13,4.

Accordingly we condemn the policy of those who would have the power of the State employed "in the interest of the Church" and who thus turn the Church into a secular dominion; as also of those who, aiming to govern the State by the Word of God, seek to turn the State into a Church.

OF THE ELECTION OF GRACE.

35. By election of grace we mean this truth, that all those who by the grace of God alone, for Christ's sake, through the means of grace, are brought to faith, are justified, sanctified, and preserved in faith *here in time*, that all these have already from eternity been endowed by God with faith, justification, sanctification, and preservation in faith, and this *for the same reason*, namely, by grace alone, for Christ's sake, and by way of the means of grace. That this is the doctrine of Holy Scripture is evident from Eph. 1,3-7; 2 Thess. 2,13.14; Acts 13,48; Rom. 8,28-30; 2 Tim 1,9; Matt. 24, 22-24 (cp. Form. of Conc. *Triglot*, p. 1065, §§ 5. 8. 23; M., p. 705).

36. Accordingly we reject as an anti-Scriptural error the doctrine that not alone the grace of God and the merit of Christ are the cause of the election of grace, but that God has, in addition, found or regarded something good *in us* which prompted or caused Him to elect us, this being variously designated as "good works," "right conduct," "proper self-determination," "refraining from wilful resistance," etc. Nor does Holy Scripture know of an election "by foreseen faith," "in view of faith," as though the faith of the elect were to be placed before their election; but according to Scripture the faith which the elect have in time belongs to the spiritual blessings with which God has endowed them by His eternal election. For Scripture teaches, Acts 13,48: "And as many as were ordained unto eternal life believed." Our Lutheran Confession also testifies (*Triglot*, p. 1065, § 8; M., p. 705): "The eternal election of God, however, not only foresees and foreknows the salvation of the elect, but is also, from the gracious will and pleasure of God in Christ Jesus, a cause which procures, works, helps, and promotes our salvation and what pertains thereto; and upon this our salvation is so founded that the gates of hell cannot prevail against it, Matt. 16,18, as is written John 10,28: 'Neither shall any man pluck My sheep out of My hand'; and again, Acts 13,48: 'And as many as were ordained to eternal life believed.' "

37. But as earnestly as we maintain that there is an election of *grace*, or a predestination to salvation, so decidedly do we teach, on the other hand, that there is no election of wrath, or predestination to *damnation*. Scripture plainly reveals the truth that the love of God for the world of lost sinners is universal, that is, that it embraces all men without exception, that Christ has fully reconciled all men unto God, and that God earnestly desires to bring all men to faith, to preserve them therein, and thus to save them, as Scripture testifies, 1 Tim. 2,4: "God will have all men to be saved and to come to the knowledge of the truth." No man is lost because God had predestinated him to eternal damnation.—Eternal election is a cause why the elect are brought to faith in time, Acts 13,48; but election is *not* a cause why men remain unbelievers when they hear the Word of God. The reason assigned by Scripture for this sad fact is that these men judge *themselves* unworthy of everlasting life, putting the Word of God from them and obstinately resisting the Holy Ghost, whose earnest will it is to bring also them to repentance and faith by means of the Word, Acts 13, 46; 7, 51; Matt. 23, 37.

38. To be sure, it is necessary to observe the Scriptural distinction between the election of grace and the universal will of grace. This universal gracious will of God embraces all men; the election of grace, however, does not embrace all, but only a definite number, whom "God hath from the beginning chosen to salvation," 2 Thess. 2, 13, the "remnant," the "seed" which "the Lord left," Rom. 9, 27—29, the "election," Rom. 11, 7; and while the universal

BRIEF STATEMENT OF THE DOCTRINAL POSITION OF
THE MISSOURI SYNOD [LUTHERAN CHURCH-
MISSOURI SYNOD (1932)] (continued)

will of grace is frustrated in the case of most men,
Matt. 22, 14; Luke 7, 30, the election of grace attains
its end with all whom it embraces, Rom. 8, 28-30.
Scripture, however, while distinguishing between the
universal will of grace and the election of grace does
not place the two in opposition to each other. On the
contrary, it teaches that the grace dealing with those
who are lost is altogether earnest and fully efficacious for conversion. Blind reason indeed declares
these two truths to be contradictory; but we impose
silence on our reason. The seeming disharmony will
disappear in the light of heaven, 1 Cor. 13, 12.

39. Furthermore, by election of grace, Scripture does not
mean that *one* part of God's counsel of salvation
according to which He will receive into heaven those
who persevere in faith unto the end, but, on the
contrary, Scripture means this, that God, before the
foundation of the world, from pure grace, because of
the redemption of Christ, has chosen for His own a
definite number of persons out of the corrupt mass
and has determined to bring them, through Word
and Sacrament, to faith and salvation.

40. Christians can and should be assured of their eternal
election. This is evident from the fact that Scripture
addresses them as the chosen ones and comforts
them with their election, Eph. 1, 4; 2 Thess. 2, 13.
This assurance of one's personal election, however,
springs only from faith in the Gospel, from the
assurance that God so loved the world that He gave
His only-begotten Son, that whosoever believeth in
Him should not perish, but have everlasting life. For
God sent not His Son into the world to *condemn* the
world; on the contrary, through the life, suffering,
and death of His Son He fully *reconciled* the whole
world of sinners unto Himself. Faith in this truth
leaves no room for the fear that God might still
harbor thoughts of wrath and damnation concerning
us. Scripture inculcates that in Rom. 8, 32.33: "He
that spared not His own Son, but delivered Him up
for us all, how shall He not with Him also freely give
us all things? Who shall lay anything to the charge of
God's elect? It is God that justifieth." Luther's
pastoral advice is therefore in accord with Scripture:
"Gaze upon the wounds of Christ and the blood shed
for you; there predestination will shine forth." (St.
Louis Ed., II, 181; on Gen. 26, 9.) That the Christian
obtains the personal assurance of his eternal election
in this way is taught also by our Lutheran Confessions (Formula of Concord. *Triglot*, p. 1071, § 26;
M., p. 709): "Of this we should not judge according
to our reason nor according to the Law or from any
external appearance. Neither should we attempt to
investigate the secret, concealed abyss of divine
predestination, but should give heed to the revealed
will of God. For He has made known unto us the
mystery of His will and made it manifest through
Christ that it might be preached, Eph. 1, 9 ff.; 2 Tim.

1, 9 f."—In order to insure the proper method of
viewing eternal election and the Christian's assurance of it, the Lutheran Confessions set forth at
length the principle that election is not to be
considered "in a bare manner (*nude*), as though God
only held a muster, thus: 'This one shall be saved,
that one shall be damned'" (Formula of Concord.
Triglot, p. 1065, § 9; M., p. 706); but "the Scriptures
teach this doctrine in no other way than to direct us
thereby to the *Word*, Eph. 1, 13; 1 Cor. 1, 7; exhort
to repentance, 2 Tim. 3, 16; urge to godliness, Eph. 1,
14; John 15, 3; strengthen faith and assure us of our
salvation, Eph. 1, 13; John 10, 27 f.; 2 Thess. 2, 13 f."
(Formula of Concord. *Triglot*, p. 1067, § 12; M., p.
707).—To sum up, just as God in time draws the
Christians unto Himself through the Gospel, so He
had already in His eternal election endowed them
with "sanctification of the Spirit and belief of the
truth," 2 Thess. 2, 13. Therefore: If, by the grace of
God, you believe in the Gospel of the forgiveness of
your sins for Christ's sake, you are to be certain that
you also belong to the number of God's elect, even as
Scripture, 2 Thess. 2,13, addresses the believing
Thessalonians as the chosen of God and gives thanks
to God for their election.

OF SUNDAY.

41. We teach that in the New Testament God has
abrogated the Sabbath and all the holy-days prescribed for the Church of the Old Covenant, so that
neither "the keeping of the Sabbath nor of any other
day" nor the observance of at least one specific day
of the seven days of the week is ordained or
commanded by God, Col. 2, 16; Rom. 14, 5
(Augsburg Confession. *Triglot*, p. 91, §§ 51-60; M.,
p. 66).

The observance of Sunday and other church festivals
is an ordinance of the Church, made by virtue of
Christian liberty. (Augsburg Confession; *Triglot*, p.
91, §§ 51-53. 60; M., p. 66. Large Catechism; *Triglot*,
p. 603, §§ 83.85.89; M., p. 401.) Hence Christians
should not regard such ordinances as ordained by
God and binding upon the conscience, Col. 2, 16;
Gal. 4, 10. However, for the sake of Christian love
and peace they should willingly observe them, Rom.
14, 13; 1 Cor. 14, 40. (Augsburg Confession. *Triglot*,
p. 91, §§ 53-56; M., p. 67.)

OF THE MILLENNIUM.

42. With the Augsburg Confession (Art. XVII) we reject
every type of Millennialism, or Chiliasm, the opinions that Christ will return visibly to this earth a
thousand years before the end of the world and
establish a dominion of the Church over the world;
or that before the end of the world the Church is to
enjoy a season of special prosperity; or that before
the general resurrection on Judgment Day a number
of departed Christians or martyrs are to be raised
again to reign in glory in this world; or that before
the end of the world a universal conversion of the
Jewish nation (of Israel according to the flesh) will
take place.

Over against this, Scripture clearly teaches, and we teach accordingly, that the kingdom of Christ on earth will remain under the cross until the end of the world, Acts 14, 22; John 16, 33; 18, 36; Luke 9, 23; 14, 27; 17, 20-37; 2 Tim. 4, 18; Heb. 12,28; Luke 18,8; that the second visible coming of the Lord will be His final advent, His coming to judge the quick and the dead, Matt. 24, 29.30; 25, 31; 2 Tim. 4, 1; 2 Thess. 2, 8; Heb. 9, 26-28; that there will be but one resurrection of the dead, John 5, 28; 6, 39.40; that the time of the Last Day is, and will remain, unknown, Matt. 24, 42; 25, 13; Mark 13, 32.37; Acts 1, 7, which would not be the case if the Last Day were to come a thousand years after the beginning of a millennium; and that there will be no general conversion, a conversion *en masse*, of the Jewish nation, Rom. 11, 7; 2 Cor. 3, 14; Rom. 11, 25; 1 Thess. 2, 16.

According to these clear passages of Scripture we reject the whole of Millennialism, since it not only contradicts Scripture, but also engenders a false conception of the kingdom of Christ, turns the hope of Christians upon earthly goals, 1 Cor. 15, 19; Col. 3, 2, and leads them to look upon the Bible as an obscure book.

OF THE ANTICHRIST.

43. As to the Antichrist we teach that the prophecies of the Holy Scriptures concerning the Antichrist, 2 Thess. 2, 3-12; 1 John 2, 18, have been fulfilled in the Pope of Rome and his dominion. All the features of the Antichrist as drawn in these prophecies, including the most abominable and horrible ones, for example, that the Antichrist "as God sitteth in the temple of God," 2 Thess. 2,4; that he anathematizes the very heart of the Gospel of Christ, that is, the doctrine of the forgiveness of sins by grace alone, for Christ's sake alone, through faith alone, without any merit or worthiness in man (Rom. 3, 20-28; Gal. 2, 16); that he recognizes only those as members of the Christian Church who bow to his authority; and that, like a deluge, he had inundated the whole Church with his antichristian doctrines till God revealed him through the Reformation,—these very features are the outstanding characterics of the Papacy. (Of. Smalcald Articles. *Triglot*, p. 515, §§ 39-41; p. 401, § 45; M., pp. 336. 258). Hence we subscribe to the statement of our Confessions that the Pope is "the very Antichrist." (Smalcald Articles. *Triglot*, p. 475, § 10; M., p. 308).

OF OPEN QUESTIONS.

44. Those questions in the domain of Christian doctrine may be termed open questions which Scripture answers either not at all or not clearly. Since neither an individual nor the Church as a whole is permitted to develop or augment the Christian doctrine, but are rather ordered and commanded by God to continue in the doctrine of the apostles, 2 Thess. 2, 15; Acts 2, 42, open questions must remain open questions.— Not to be included in the number of open questions are the following: the doctrine of the Church and the Ministry, of Sunday, of Chiliasm, and of Antichrist, these doctrines being clearly defined in Scripture.

OF THE SYMBOLS OF THE LUTHERAN CHURCH.

45. We accept as our confessions all the symbols contained in the Book of Concord of the year 1580.—The symbols of the Lutheran Church are not a rule of faith beyond, and supplementary to, Scripture, but a confession of the doctrines of Scripture over against those who deny these doctrines.

46. Since the Christian Church cannot make doctrines, but can and should simply profess the doctrine revealed in Holy Scripture, the doctrinal decisions of the symbols are binding upon the conscience not because our Church has made them nor because they are the outcome of doctrinal controversies, but only because they are the doctrinal decisions of Holy Scripture itself.

47. Those desiring to be admitted into the public ministry of the Lutheran Church pledge themselves to teach according to the symbols not "in so far as," but "because," the symbols agree with Scripture. He who is unable to accept as Scriptural the doctrines set forth in the Lutheran symbols and their rejection of the corresponding errors must not be admitted into the ministry of the Lutheran Church.

48. The confessional obligation covers all doctrines, not only those that are treated *ex professo*, but also those that are merely introduced in support of other doctrines.

The obligation does not extend to historical statements, "purely exegetical questions," and other matters not belonging to the doctrinal content of the symbols. All *doctrines* of the symbols are based on clear statements of Scripture.

Notes: *This statement was adopted by the Lutheran Church-Missouri Synod in 1932, at which time the church was considering closer relations with other Lutheran bodies, especially the American Lutheran Church. The statement has become one standard for judging orthodoxy in the synod. Its authority approaches that of the documents mentioned in the constitution, even though in 1962 the synod declared it unconstitutional to bind pastors and college professors to any statement beyond the Bible and The Book of Concord.*

* * *

WE BELIEVE (WISCONSIN EVANGELICAL LUTHERAN SYNOD)

I. GOD AND HIS REVELATION

1. We believe that there is only one true God (John 17:3). He has made Himself known as the Triune God, one God in three persons. This is evident from Jesus' command to His disciples to baptize "in the name of the Father, and of the Son, and of the Holy Ghost" (Matt. 28:19). Whoever does not worship this God worships a false god, a god who does not

WE BELIEVE (WISCONSIN EVANGELICAL LUTHERAN SYNOD) (continued)

exist, for Jesus said: 'He that honoreth not the Son honoreth not the Father which hath sent him" (John 5:23).

2. We believe that God has revealed Himself in nature, for "the heavens declare the glory of God; and the firmament showeth his handiwork" (Ps. 19:1). "For the invisible things of him from the creation of the world are clearly seen, being understood by the things that are made, even his eternal power and Godhead" (Rom. 1:20). So there is no excuse for the atheist. However, we have in nature only a partial revelation of God and one that is wholly insufficient for salvation.

3. We believe that God has given us the full revelation of Himself in His Son, our Lord Jesus Christ. "No man hath seen God at any time; the only-begotten Son, which is in the bosom of the Father, he hath declared him" (John 1:18). Particularly has God revealed Himself in Jesus as the Savior God, who "so loved the world that he gave his only-begotten Son, that whosoever believeth in him should not perish, but have everlasting life" (John 3:16).

4. We believe that God has given the Holy Scriptures to proclaim His grace in Christ to man. In the Old Testament God repeatedly promised His people a divine Deliverer from sin, death, and hell. The New Testament proclaims that this promised Deliverer has come in the person of Jesus of Nazareth. The Scriptures testify of Christ. Jesus Himself says of the Scriptures: "They are they which testify of me" (John 5:39).

5. We believe that God gave us the Scriptures through men whom He chose and used with the language they knew and the style of writing they had. He used Moses and the Prophets to write the Old Testament in Hebrew (some portions in Aramaic) and the Evangelists and Apostles to write the New Testament in Greek.

6. We believe that in a miraculous way that goes beyond all human investigation God the Holy Ghost inspired these men to write His Word. These "holy men of God spoke as they were moved by the Holy Ghost" (II Pet. 1:21). What they said, was spoken "not in the words which man's wisdom teacheth, but which the Holy Ghost teacheth" (I Cor. 2:13). Every thought they expressed, every word they used, was given them by the Holy Spirit by inspiration. St. Paul wrote to Timothy: "All scripture is given by inspiration of God" (II Tim. 3:16). We therefore believe in the verbal inspiration of the Scriptures, not a mechanical dictation, but a word-for-word inspiration.

7. We believe that Scripture is a unified whole, true and without error in everything it says; for our Savior said: "The scripture cannot be broken" (John 10:35). We believe that it, therefore, is the infallible authority and guide for everything we believe and do. We

believe that it is fully sufficient, clearly teaching us all we need to know for salvation, making us "wise unto salvation through faith which is in Christ Jesus" (II Tim. 3:15), equipping us for every good work (II Tim. 3:17). No other revelations are to be expected.

8. We believe and accept Scripture on its own terms, accepting as factual history what it presents as history, recognizing a metaphor where Scripture itself indicates one, and reading as poetry what is evident as such. We believe that Scripture must interpret Scripture, clear passages throwing light on those less easily understood. We believe that no authority, be it man's reason, science, or scholarship, may stand in judgment over Scripture. Sound scholarship will faithfully search out the true meaning of Scripture without presuming to pass judgment on it.

9. We believe that the three ecumenical creeds, the Apostles', the Nicene, and the Athanasian, as well as the Lutheran Confessions as contained in the Book of Concord of 1580, give expression to the true doctrine of Scripture. Since the doctrines they confess are drawn from Scripture alone, we feel ourselves bound to them in our faith and life. Therefore all preaching and teaching in our churches and schools must be in harmony with these Confessions.

10. We reject any thought that makes only part of Scripture God's Word, that allows for the possibility of factual error in Scripture, also in so-called nonreligious matters (for example, historical, geographical).

11. We reject all views that fail to acknowledge the Holy Scriptures as God's revelation and Word. We likewise reject all views that see in them merely a human record of God's revelations as He encounters man in history apart from the Scriptures, and so a record subject to human imperfections.

12. We reject the emphasis upon Jesus as the Word of God (John 1:1) to the exclusion of the Scriptures as God's Word.

13. We reject every effort to reduce the Confessions contained in the Book of Concord to historical documents that have little or no confessional significance for the Church today. We likewise reject any claim that the Church is bound only to those doctrines in Scriptures that have found expression in these Confessions.

This is what Scripture teaches about God and His Revelation. This we believe, teach, and confess.

II. CREATION, MAN, AND SIN

1. We believe that the universe, the world, and man came into existence in the beginning when God created heaven and earth and all creatures (Gen. 1,2). Further testimony of this event is found in other passages of the Old and New Testaments (for example, Exod. 20:11; Heb. 11:3). All this happened in the course of six normal days by the power of God's almighty word when He said, "Let there be."

2. We believe that the Bible presents a true and historical account of Creation.

3. We believe that God created man in His own image (Gen. 1:26), that is, holy and righteous. Man's thoughts, desires, and will were in full harmony with God (Col. 3:10; Eph. 4:24), and he was given the capacity to "subdue" God's creation (Gen. 1:28).

4. We believe that man lost this divine image when he yielded to the temptation of Satan and disobeyed God's command. This brought upon him the judgment of God, "Thou shalt surely die" (Gen. 2:17). Since that time mankind is conceived and born in sin (Ps. 51:5), "flesh born of flesh" (John 3:6), and inclined to all evil (Gen. 8:21). Being dead in sin (Eph. 2:1) man is unable to reconcile himself to God by his own efforts and deeds.

5. We reject the theories of evolution as an explanation of the origin of the universe and man, and all attempts to interpret the Scriptural account of Creation so as to harmonize it with such theories.

6. We reject interpretations that reduce the first chapters of Genesis to a narration of symbolical myths and to poetic accounts that are without factual historical content.

7. We reject all views that see inherent goodness in man, that consider his natural bent only a weakness which is not sinful, and that fail to recognize his total spiritual depravity (Rom. 3:9-18).

This is what Scripture teaches about Creation, Man, and Sin. This we believe, teach, and confess.

III. CHRIST AND REDEMPTION

1. We believe that Jesus Christ is the eternal Son of God, who was with the Father from all eternity (John 1:1,2). In the fullness of time He took a true and complete, yet sinless, human nature to Himself (Gal. 4:4) when He was conceived as a holy child in the Virgin Mary through a miracle of the Holy Spirit. The angel testified: "That which is conceived in her is of the Holy Ghost" (Matt. 1:20). Jesus Christ is that unique person in whom the true God and a true human nature are inseparably united in one, the holy God-man, Immanuel.

2. We believe that He at all times possessed the fullness of the Godhead, all divine power, wisdom, and glory (Col. 2:9). This was evident at times when He performed miracles (John 2:11). But while He lived on earth, He took on the form of a servant, humbling Himself by laying aside the continuous and full display and use of His divine characteristics. During this time we see Him living as a man among men, enduring suffering, and humbling Himself to the shameful death on the cross (Phil. 2:7, 8). We believe that He rose again from the grave with a glorified body, ascended, and is exalted on high to rule with power over the world, with grace in His Church, with glory in eternity (Phil. 2:9-11).

3. We believe that Jesus Christ, the God-man, was sent by the Father to humble Himself for the redemption of mankind and that He was exalted as evidence that

His mission was accomplished. Jesus came to fulfill the Law perfectly (Matt. 5:17), so that by His perfect obedience all men should be accounted righteous (Rom. 5:19). He came to bear "the iniquity of us all" (Isa. 53:6), ransoming us by His sacrifice for sin on the altar of the cross (Matt. 20:28). We believe that He is the God-appointed Substitute for man in all of this: His righteousness is accepted by the Father as our righteousness; His death for sin, as our death for sin (II Cor. 5:21). We believe that His resurrection gives full assurance that God has accepted this atonement in our behalf (Rom. 4:25).

4. We believe that in Christ, God reconciled the "*world*" unto himself" (II Cor. 5:19), that Jesus is "the Lamb of God, which taketh away the sin of the *world*"(John 1:29). The mercy and grace of God are all-embracing; the reconciliation through Christ is universal; the forgiveness of sins has been gained as an accomplished fact for all men. Because of the substitutionary work of Christ, God has justified, that is, declared the verdict of "not guilty" upon all mankind. This forms the firm, objective basis for the sinner's assurance of salvation.

5. We reject any teaching that limits the work of Christ as to either its scope or its completeness, thereby failing to recognize the universality of redemption or the full payment of the ransom.

6. We reject the views which see in the Gospel accounts the early Church's proclamation and interpretation of Jesus Christ rather than a true account of what actually happened in history. We reject the attempts to make the historicity of events in Christ's life, such as His virgin birth, His miracles, or His bodily resurrection, appear unimportant or even doubtful. We reject the attempts to stress a "present encounter with the living Christ" in such a way that Jesus' redemptive work in the fullness of time, as recorded in Scripture, would lose its importance.

This the Scripture teaches about Christ and Redemption. This we believe, teach, and confess.

IV. JUSTIFICATION BY FAITH

1. We believe that God has justified, that is, declared all sinners righteous in His eyes for the sake of Christ. This is the central message of Scripture upon which the very existence of the Church depends. It is a message relevant to men of all times and places, of all races and social strata, for "judgment came upon all men to condemnation" (Rom. 5:18). All need justification before God, and Scripture proclaims that all are justified, for "by the righteousness of one the free gift came upon all men unto justification of life" (Rom. 5:18).

2. We believe that the individual receives this free gift of forgiveness throught Christ, not by works, but only by faith (Eph. 2:8,9). Justifying faith is a firm trust in Christ and His redemptive work. This faith justifies, not because of any inherent virtue, but only because of the salvation prepared by God in Christ, which it embraces (Rom. 3:28; 4:5). On the other

hand, although Jesus died for all, Scripture tells us that "he that believeth not shall be damned" (Mark 16:16). The unbeliever loses the forgiveness won by Christ.

3. We believe that man cannot work this justifying faith, or trust, in his own heart, because "natural man receiveth not the things of the Spirit of God; for they are foolishness unto him" (I Cor. 2:14). In fact, "the carnal mind is enmity against God" (Rom. 8:7). It is the Holy Ghost who moves the heart trustingly to recognize that "Jesus is the Lord" (I Cor. 12:3). This the Holy Spirit works by means of the Gospel (Rom. 10:17). We believe, therefore, that man's conversion is entirely the work of God's grace.

4. We believe that already in eternity God chose those individuals whom He would in time convert through the Gospel of Christ and preserve in the faith to eternal life (Eph. 1:4-6; Rom. 8:29,30). This election to faith and salvation in no way was caused by anything in man, but shows how completely salvation is ours by grace alone (Rom. 11:5,6).

5. We reject every teaching that makes man somehow responsible for his salvation. We reject all efforts to present faith as a condition man must fulfill to complete his justification. We likewise reject any teaching which says that it does not matter what one believes so long as one has faith.

6. We reject any suggestion that the doctrine of justification by faith can no longer be meaningful to "modern man," together with all attempts of man to justify himself or his existence before God.

7. We reject the false and blasphemous conclusion that those who are lost were elected by God to damnation, for God "will have all men to be saved" (I Tim. 2:4).

This is what Scripture teaches about Justification by Faith. This we believe, teach, and confess.

V. GOOD WORKS AND PRAYER

1. We believe that faith in Jesus Christ is a living force within the Christian that must produce works that are pleasing to God. "Faith, if it hath not works, is dead" (Jas. 2:17). A Christian as a branch in Christ the Vine brings forth good fruit (John 15:5).

2. We believe that faith does not set up its own standards to determine what is pleasing to God (Matt. 15:9). True faith, instructed by the Word of God, delights to do only that which conforms to the holy will of God. It recognizes that God's will finds its fulfillment in perfect love, "for love is the fulfilling of the law" (Rom. 13:10).

3. We believe that these works which are the fruits of faith must be distinguished from the works of civic righteousness performed by unbelievers. When unbelievers perform works that outwardly appear as good and upright before men, these works are not good in the sight of God, for "without faith it is impossible to please him" (Heb. 11:6). While we recognize the value of mere civic righteousness for human society, we know that the unbeliever through his works of civic righteousness cannot even begin to do his duty to God.

4. We believe that in this world even the best works of a Christian are still tainted with sin. The flesh, the Old Adam, still afflicts the Christian so that he fails to do the good he would, and does the evil he would not (Rom. 7:19). He must confess that all his righteousnesses are as filthy rags (Isa. 64:6). For the sake of Christ, however, these imperfect efforts of Christians are graciously considered holy and acceptable by our heavenly Father.

5. We believe that also a life of prayer is a fruit of faith. Confidently, through faith in their Savior, Christians address the heavenly Father in petition and praise, presenting their needs and giving thanks. Such prayers are a delight to our God, and He will grant our petitions according to His wisdom.

6. We reject every thought that the good works of Christians contribute toward gaining salvation.

7. We reject every attempt to abolish the unchanging Law of God as an absolute standard by which to measure man's conduct.

8. We reject the "new morality" as a device of Satan to destroy the knowledge of God's holy will and to undermine the consciousness of sin.

9. We reject any view that considers prayer a means of grace or that looks upon it as helpful simply because of its psychological effect upon the one who prays.

10. We reject the view that all prayers are acceptable to God, and we hold the prayers of all who know not Christ to be vain babblings addressed to false gods.

This is what Scripture teaches about Good Works and Prayer. This we believe, teach, and confess.

VI. THE MEANS OF GRACE

1. We believe that God bestows all spiritual blessings upon sinners by special means, ordained by Him. These are the Means of Grace, the Gospel in Word and Sacrament.

2. We believe that through the Gospel of Christ's atoning sacrifice for sinners the Holy Spirit works faith in the heart of man, whose heart by nature is enmity against God. "So then faith cometh by hearing, and hearing by the word of God" (Rom. 10:17). This Spirit-wrought faith, or regeneration, brings about a renewal in man and makes of him an heir of eternal salvation.

3. We believe that also through Baptism the Holy Spirit applies the Gospel to sinful man, regenerating him (Titus 3:5) and cleansing him from all iniquity (Acts 2:38). The Lord points to the blessing of Baptism when He promises: "He that believeth and is baptized shall be saved" (Mark 16:16). We believe that the blessing of Baptism is meant for all people (Matt. 28:19), including infants, who are sinful (John

3:6) and therefore need the regeneration effected through Baptism (John 3:5).

4. We believe that all who partake of the Sacrament of the Lord's Supper receive the true body and blood of Christ "in, with, and under" the bread and wine. This is true because, when the Lord instituted this Sacrament, He said: "This is my body which is given for you. . . . This cup is the new testament in my blood, which is shed for you" (Luke 22:19, 20). As we partake of His body and blood, given and shed for us, we by faith receive the comfort and assurance that our sins are indeed forgiven and that we are truly His own.

5. We believe that the Lord gave His Word and the Sacraments to His disciples for a purpose. He commanded them: "Go ye therefore, and teach all nations, baptizing them in the name of the Father, and of the Son, and of the Holy Ghost" (Matt. 28:19). It is by these Means that He preserves and extends the holy Christian Church throughout the world. We should therefore be diligent and faithful in the use of these divinely ordained Means of Grace in our own midst and in our mission efforts. These are the only means through which immortal souls are brought to faith and to salvation.

6. We reject any views that look for the revelation of the grace of God and salvation apart from the Gospel as found in the Scriptures. We likewise reject the view that the Law is a means of grace.

7. We reject all teachings that see in the Sacrament of the Altar nothing more than signs and symbols for faith, thereby denying that Christ's true body and blood are received in the Lord's Supper.

8. We reject the claim that unbelievers and hypocrites do not receive the true body and blood of Jesus in the Sacrament, as well as the view that to eat the body of Christ in the Sacrament is nothing else than to receive Christ spiritually by faith. We reject the view that the body and blood of Christ are present in the Sacrament through the act of consecration as such, apart from the reception of the elements.

9. We reject the teaching that the real presence of Jesus' body and blood in the Sacrament means merely that the person of Christ is present in His Supper even as He is present in the Gospel.

This is what Scripture teaches about the Means of Grace. This we believe, teach, and confess.

VII. THE CHURCH AND ITS MINISTRY

1. We believe that there is one holy Christian Church, which is the Temple of God (I Cor. 3:16), the Body of Christ (Eph. 1:23; 4:12). The members of this one Church are all those who are "children of God by faith in Christ Jesus" (Gal. 3:26). Whoever believes that Jesus died for his sin and rose again for his justification (Rom. 4:25) belongs to Christ's Church. The Church, then, consists only of believers, or saints, whom God accepts as holy for the sake of Jesus' imputed righteousness (II Cor. 5:21). These saints are scattered throughout the world. Every true believer, regardless of the nation or race or church body to which he belongs, is a member of the holy Christian Church.

2. We believe that the holy Christian Church is a reality, although it is not an external, visible organization. Because "man looketh on the outward appearance, but the Lord looketh on the heart" (I Sam. 16:7), only the Lord knows "them that are his" (II Tim. 2:19). The members of the holy Christian Church are known only to God; we cannot distinguish between true believers and hypocrites. The holy Christian Church is therefore invisible and cannot be identified with any one church body or the sum total of all church bodies.

3. We believe that the presence of the holy Christian Church nevertheless can be recognized. Wherever the Gospel is preached and the Sacraments are administered, the holy Christian Church is present, for through the Means of Grace true faith is produced and preserved (Isa. 55:10,11). Moreover, where these Means are in use, we are confident that the Church is present, for the Lord has entrusted them only to His Church of believers (Matt. 28:19,20). The Means of Grace are therefore called the marks of the Church.

4. We believe that it is the Lord's will that Christians gather together for mutual edification and spiritual growth (Heb. 10:24,25) and for carrying out the whole of the Lord's commission (Mark 16:15). Since these visible gatherings (for example, congregations, synods) confess themselves to the marks of the Church and make use of them, they are called churches. They bear this name, however, only because of the true believers present in them (I Cor. 1:2).

5. We believe that the holy Christian Church is one, united by a common faith, for all true believers have "one Lord, one faith, one baptism, one God and Father of all" (Eph. 4:5,6). Since this is a unity of faith in the heart, it is seen only by God.

6. We believe that God bids us on our part to acknowledge oneness in faith among God's saints on earth only as they by word and deed reveal (confess) the faith of their hearts. Their unity becomes evident when they agree in their confession to the doctrine revealed in Scripture. We believe, furthermore, that the individual through his membership in a church body confesses himself to the doctrine and practice of that body. To assert that unity exists where there is no agreement in confession is to presume to look into man's heart. This only God can do. It is not necessary that all agree on matters of church ritual or organization. About these the New Testament gives no commands.

7. We believe that those who have become evident as united in faith will give recognition to their fellowship in Christ and seek to express it as occasion permits. They may express their fellowship by joint worship, by joint proclamation of the Gospel, by joining in Holy Communion, by joint prayer, by joint

church work. We believe that we cannot practice religious fellowship with those whose confession reveals that error is taught or tolerated, supported or defended. The Lord bids us avoid persistent errorists (Rom. 16:17, 18).

8. We believe that every Christian is a priest and king before God (I Pet. 2:9). All believers have direct and equal access to the throne of grace through Christ, our Mediator (Eph. 2:18). To all believers God has given the Means of Grace to use. All Christians are to show forth the praises of Him who has called us out of darkness into His marvelous light (I Pet. 2:9). In this sense all Christians are ministers of the Gospel.

9. We believe that it is the will of God that the Church in accordance with good order (I Cor. 14:40) call qualified men (I Tim. 3) into the public ministry. They are to preach the Word and adminster the Sacraments publicly, that is, not merely as individuals who possess the universal priesthood, but by order and in the name of fellow Christians. These men are the called servants of Christ, ministers of the Gospel, and not lords over God's heritage, His believers (I Pet. 5:3). Through its call the Church in Christian liberty designates the place, form, and scope of service. We believe that when the Church calls men into this public ministry, it is the Lord Himself acting through the Church (Acts 20:28).

10. We reject any attempt to identify the holy Christian Church with an outward organization, and likewise any claim that the Church must function in the world through specific organizational forms.

11. We reject any views that see in the Church, as the Body of Christ, an extension of Christ's incarnation.

12. We reject as false ecumenicity any views that look for the true unity of the Church in some form of external or organizational union, as we oppose all movements toward such union made at the expense of confessional integrity.

13. We reject the contention that religious fellowship may be practiced without confessional agreement.

This is what Scripture teaches about the Church and its Ministry. This we believe, teach, and confess.

VIII. THE CHURCH AND THE STATE

1. We believe that not only the Church, but also the State, that is, all governmental authority, has been instituted by God. "The powers that be are ordained of God" (Rom. 13:1). Christians will, therefore, for conscience's sake be obedient to the government that rules over them (Rom. 13:5) unless the government commands them to disobey God (Acts 5:29).

2. We believe that God has given to each, the Church and the State, responsibilities that do not conflict with one another. To the Church the Lord has assigned the responsibility of calling sinners to repentance, of proclaiming forgiveness through the cross of Christ, of encouraging believers in their Christian living. The purpose is to lead the elect of God through faith in Christ to eternal salvation. To the State the Lord has assigned the keeping of good order and peace, the arranging of all civil matters among men (Rom. 13:3,4). The purpose is "that we may lead a quiet and peaceable life in all godliness and honesty" (I Tim. 2:2).

3. We believe that the only means God has given to the Church to carry out its assigned purpose is His revealed Word in the Holy Scriptures (Mark 16:15). Only by preaching the Law and the Gospel, sin and grace, the wrath of God against sin and the mercy of God in Christ, will men be converted and made wise to salvation. We believe that the means given to the State to fulfill its assignment are civil law and force, set up and used according to the light of reason (Rom. 13:4). The light of reason also includes the natural knowledge of God, the inscribed law, and conscience.

4. We believe the proper relation is preserved between the Church and the State and the welfare of all is properly served only when each, the Church and the State, remains within its divinely assigned sphere and uses its divinely entrusted means. The Church is not to exercise civil authority nor to interfere with the State as the State carries out its responsibilities. The State is not to become a messenger of the Gospel nor to interfere with the Church in its preaching mission. The Church is not to attempt to use the civil law and force in leading men to Christ. The State is not to seek to govern by means of the Gospel. On the other hand, the Church and the State may participate in one and the same endeavor as long as each remains within its assigned place and uses its entrusted means.

5. We reject any attempt on the part of the State to restrict the free exercise of religion.

6. We reject any views that look to the Church to guide and influence the State directly in the conduct of its affairs.

7. We reject any attempt on the part of the Church to seek the financial assistance of the State in carrying out its saving purpose.

8. We reject any views that hold that a citizen is free to disobey such laws of the State with which he disagrees on the basis of personal judgment.

This is what Scripture teaches about the Church and the State. This we believe, teach, and confess.

IX. JESUS' RETURN AND THE JUDGMENT

1. We believe that Jesus, true God and true man, who rose from death and ascended to the right hand of the Father, will come again. He will return visibly, in like manner as His Disciples saw Him go into heaven (Acts 1:11).

2. We believe that no one can know the exact time of Jesus' return. This knowledge is hidden even from the angels in heaven (Matt. 24:36). Nevertheless, our Lord has given us signs to keep us in constant

expectation of His return. He has told us to take heed to ourselves and to watch lest that Day come upon us unawares (Luke 21:34).

3. We believe that at Jesus' return this present world will come to an end. "Nevertheless, we, according to his promise, look for new heavens and a new earth, wherein dwelleth righteousness" (II Pet. 3:13).

4. We believe that when Jesus returns and His voice is heard throughout the earth, all the dead will rise and together with those still living must appear before His throne of judgment. The unbelievers will be condemned to an eternity in hell. Those who by faith have been cleansed in the blood of Christ will be with Jesus forever in the blessed presence of God in heaven (John 5:28, 29).

5. We reject every form of millenialism, since it has no valid Scriptural basis and leads Christians to set their hopes upon the kingdom of Christ as an earthly kingdom. We likewise reject as unscriptural any hopes that the Jews will all be converted in those final days, or that all men will ultimately enjoy eternal bliss.

6. We reject any denial of a bodily resurrection and of the reality of hell.

7. We reject as contrary to the clear revelation of Scripture all attempts to interpret eschatological passages in the New Testament (those that speak of the end of the world, Jesus' second coming, and the judgment) symbolically, or to see these eschatological events taking place, not in the end of time, but concurrently with history.

This is what Scripture teaches about Jesus' Return and the Judgment. This we believe, teach, and confess.

Notes: *The most conservative of the major Lutheran bodies, the Wisconsin Synod's statement of faith is noteworthy both for its clear affirmation concerning scripture and scriptural authority (as opposed to liberal-modernist and neo-orthodox interpretations) and for its statements on millennialism in reaction to fundamentalism. It also chastizes those Lutherans who think of* The Book of Concord *as merely an historical statement of relative normative value today.*

Chapter 5

Reformed-Presbyterian Family

Reformed

THE BELGIC CONFESSION

Article I. THERE IS ONLY ONE GOD

We all believe with the heart and confess with the mouth that there is one only simple and spiritual Being, which we call God; and that He is eternal, incomprehensible, invisible, immutable, infinite, almighty, perfectly wise, just, good, and the overflowing fountain of all good.

Article II. BY WHAT MEANS GOD IS MADE KNOWN UNTO US

We know Him by two means: First, by the creation, preservation, and government of the universe; which is before our eyes as a most elegant book, wherein all creatures, great and small, are as so many characters leading us to *see clearly the invisible things of God*, even *his everlasting power and divinity*, as the apostle Paul says (Rom. 1:20). All which things are sufficient to convince men and leave them without excuse. Second, He makes Himself more clearly and fully known to us by His holy and divine Word, that is to say, as far as is necessary for us to know in this life, to His glory and our salvation.

Article III. THE WRITTEN WORD OF GOD

We confess that this Word of God was not sent nor delivered by the will of man, but that *men spake from God, being moved by the Holy Spirit*, as the apostle Peter says; and that afterwards God, from a special care which He has for us and our salvation, commanded His servants, the prophets and apostles, to commit His revealed word to writing; and He Himself wrote with His own finger the two tables of the law. Therefore we call such writings holy and divine Scriptures.

Article IV. CANONICAL BOOKS OF THE HOLY SCRIPTURE

We believe that the Holy Scriptures are contained in two books, namely, the Old and the New Testament, which are canonical, against which nothing can be alleged. These are thus named in the Church of God.

The books of the Old Testament are the five books of Moses, to wit: Genesis, Exodus, Leviticus, Numbers, Deuteronomy; the book of Joshua, Judges, Ruth, the two books of Samuel, the two of the Kings, two books of the Chronicles, commonly called Paralipomenon, the first of Ezra, Nehemiah, Esther; Job, the Psalms of David, the three books of Solomon, namely, the Proverbs, Ecclesiastes, and the Song of Songs; the four great prophets, Isaiah, Jeremiah, Ezekiel, and Daniel; and the twelve lesser prophets, namely, Hosea, Joel, Amos, Obadiah, Jonah, Micah, Nahum, Habakkuk, Zephaniah, Haggai, Zechariah, and Malachi.

Those of the New Testament are the four evangelists, to wit: Matthew, Mark, Luke, and John; the Acts of the Apostles; the fourteen epistles of the apostle Paul, namely, one to the Romans, two to the Corinthians, one to the Galatians, one to the Ephesians, one to the Philippians, one to the Colossians, two to the Thessalonians, two to Timothy, one to Titus, one to Philemon, and one to the Hebrews; the seven epistles of the other apostles, namely, one of James, two of Peter, three of John, one of Jude; and the Revelation of the apostle John.

Article V. WHENCE THE HOLY SCRIPTURES DERIVE THEIR DIGNITY AND AUTHORITY

We receive all these books, and these only, as holy and canonical, for the regulation, foundation, and confirmation of our faith; believing without any doubt all things contained in them, not so much because the Church receives and approves them as such, but more especially because the Holy Spirit witnesses in our hearts that they are from God, and also because they carry the evidence thereof in themselves. For the very blind are able to perceive that the things foretold in them are being fulfilled.

Article VI. THE DIFFERENCE BETWEEN THE CANONICAL AND APOCRYPHAL BOOKS

We distinguish those sacred books from the apocryphal, viz.: the third and fourth books of Esdras, the

THE BELGIC CONFESSiON (continued)

books of Tobit, Judith, Wisdom, Jesus Sirach, Baruch, the Appendix to the book of Esther, the Song of the Three Children in the Furnace, the History of Susannah, of Bell and the Dragon, the Prayer of Manasseh, and the two books of the Maccabees. All of which the Church may read and take instruction from, so far as they agree with the canonical books; but they are far from having such power and efficacy that we may from their testimony confirm any point of faith or of the Christian religion; much less may they be used to detract from the authority of the other, that is, the sacred books.

Article VII. THE SUFFICIENCY OF THE HOLY SCRIPTURES TO BE THE ONLY RULE OF FAITH

We believe that those Holy Scriptures fully contain the will of God, and that whatsoever man ought to believe unto salvation is sufficiently taught therein. For since the whole manner of worship which God requires of us is written in them at large, it is unlawful for any one, though an apostle, to teach otherwise than we are now taught in the Holy Scriptures: *nay, though it were an angel from heaven*, as the apostle Paul says. For since it is forbidden to *add unto or take away anything from the Word of God*, it does thereby evidently appear that the doctrine thereof is most perfect and complete in all respects.

Neither may we consider any writings of men, however holy these men may have been, of equal value with those divine Scriptures, nor ought we to consider custom, or the great multitude, or antiquity, or succession of times and persons, or councils, decrees or statutes, as of equal value with the truth of God, since the truth is above all; *for all men are of themselves liars, and more vain than vanity itself.* Therefore we reject with all our hearts whatsoever does not agree with this infallible rule, as the apostles have taught us, saying, *Prove the spirits, whether they are of God.* Likewise: *If any one cometh unto you, and bringeth not this teaching, receive him not into your house.*

Article VIII. GOD IS ONE IN ESSENCE, YET DISTINGUISHED IN THREE PERSONS

According to this truth and this Word of God, we believe in one only God, who is the one single essence, in which are three persons, really, truly, and eternally distinct according to their incommunicable properties; namely, the Father, and the Son, and the Holy Spirit. The Father is the cause, origin, and beginning of all things visible and invisible; the Son is the word, wisdom, and image of the Father; the Holy Spirit is the eternal power and might, proceeding from the Father and the Son. Nevertheless, God is not by this distinction divided into three, since the Holy Scriptures teach us that the Father, and the Son, and the Holy Spirit have each His personality,

distinguished by Their properties; but in such wise that these three persons are but one only God.

Hence, then, it is evident that the Father is not the Son, nor the Son the Father, and likewise the Holy Spirit is neither the Father nor the Son. Nevertheless, these persons thus distinguished are not divided, nor intermixed; for the Father has not assumed the flesh, nor has the Holy Spirit, but the Son only. The Father has never been without His Son, or without His Holy Spirit. For They are all three co-eternal and co-essential. There is neither first nor last; for They are all three one, in truth, in power, in goodness, and in mercy.

Article IX. THE PROOF OF THE FOREGOING ARTICLE OF THE TRINITY OF PERSONS IN ONE GOD

All this we know as well from the testimonies of Holy Writ as from their operations, and chiefly by those we feel in ourselves. The testimonies of the Holy Scriptures that teach us to believe this Holy Trinity are written in many places of the Old Testament, which are not so necessary to enumerate as to choose them out with discretion and judgment.

In Genesis, chap. 1:26, 27, God says: *Let us make man in our image, after our likeness*, etc. *And God created man in his own image, male and female created he them.* And Gen. 3:22, *Behold, the man is become as one of us.* From this saying, Let *us* make man in *our* image, it appears that there are more persons than one in the Godhead; and when He says, *God* created, He signifies the unity. It is true, He does not say how many persons there are, but that which appears to us somewhat obscure in the Old Testament is very plain in the New. For when our Lord was baptized in Jordan, the voice of the Father was heard, saying, *This is my beloved Son*; the Son was seen in the water, and the Holy Spirit appeared in the shape of a dove. This form is also instituted by Christ in the baptism of all believers: *Make disciples of all the nations, baptizing them into the name of the Father and of the Son and of the Holy Spirit.* In the Gospel of Luke the angel Gabriel thus addressed Mary, the mother of our Lord: *The Holy Spirit shall come upon thee, and the power of the Most High shall overshadow thee; wherefore also the holy thing which is begotten shall be called the Son of God.* Likewise: *The grace of the Lord Jesus Christ, and the love of God, and the communion of the Holy Spirit, be with you all.* And (A.V.): *There are three that bear record in heaven, the Father, the Word, and the Holy Ghost: and these three are one.*

In all these places we are fully taught that there are three persons in one only divine essence. And although this doctrine far surpasses all human understanding, nevertheless we now believe it by means of the Word of God, but expect hereafter to enjoy the perfect knowledge and benefit thereof in heaven.

Moreover, we must observe the particular offices and operations of these three persons towards us. The

Father is called our Creator, by His power; the Son is our Savior and Redeemer, by His blood; the Holy Spirit is our Sanctifier, by His dwelling in our hearts.

This doctrine of the Holy Trinity has always been affirmed and maintained by the true Church since the time of the apostles to this very day against the Jews, Mohammedans, and some false Christians and heretics, as Marcion, Manes, Praxeas, Sabellius, Samosatenus, Arius, and such like, who have been justly condemned by the orthodox fathers. Therefore, in this point, we do willingly receive the three creeds, namely, that of the Apostles, of Nicea, and of Athanasius; likewise that which, conformable thereunto, is agreed upon by the ancient fathers.

Article X. JESUS CHRIST IS TRUE AND ETERNAL GOD

We believe that Jesus Christ according to His divine nature is the only begotten Son of God, begotten from eternity, not made, nor created (for then He would be a creature), but co-essential and co-eternal with the Father, *the very image of his substance and the effulgence of his glory,* equal unto Him in all things. He is the Son of God, not only from the time that He assumed our nature but from all eternity, as these testimonies, when compared together, teach us. Moses says that God created the world; and St. John says that all things were made by that Word which he calls God. The apostle says that God made the world by His Son; likewise, that God created all things by Jesus Christ. Therefore it must needs follow that He who is called God, the Word, the Son, and Jesus Christ, did exist at that time when all things were created by Him. Therefore the prophet Micah says: *His goings forth are from of old, from everlasting.* And the apostle: *He hath neither beginning of days nor end of life.* He therefore is that true, eternal, and almighty God whom we invoke, worship, and serve.

Article XI. THE HOLY SPIRIT IS TRUE AND ETERNAL GOD

We believe and confess also that the Holy Spirit from eternity proceeds from the Father and the Son; and therefore neither is made, created, nor begotten, but only proceeds from both; who in order is the third person of the Holy Trinity; of one and the same essence, majesty, and glory with the Father and the Son; and therefore is the true and eternal God, as the Holy Scriptures teach us.

Article XII. THE CREATION OF ALL THINGS, ESPECIALLY THE ANGELS

We believe that the Father by the Word, that is, by His Son, has created of nothing the heaven, the earth, and all creatures, when it seemed good unto Him; giving unto every creature its being, shape, form, and several offices to serve its Creator; that He also still upholds and governs them by His eternal providence and infinite power for the service of mankind, to the end that man may serve his God.

He also created the angels good, to be His messengers and to serve His elect; some of whom are fallen from that excellency in which God created them into everlasting perdition, and the others have by the grace of God remained stedfast and continued in their first state. The devils and evil spirits are so depraved that they are enemies of God and every good thing; to the utmost of their power as murderers watching to ruin the Church and every member thereof, and by their wicked stratagems to destroy all; and are, therefore, by their own wickedness adjudged to eternal damnation, daily expecting their horrible torments.

Therefore we reject and abhor the error of the Sadducees, who deny the existence of spirits and angels; and also that of the Manichees, who assert that the devils have their origin of themselves, and that they are wicked of their own nature, without having been corrupted.

Article XIII. THE PROVIDENCE OF GOD AND HIS GOVERNMENT OF ALL THINGS

We believe that the same good God, after He had created all things, did not forsake them or give them up to fortune or chance, but that He rules and governs them according to His holy will, so that nothing happens in this world without His appointment; nevertheless, God neither is the Author of nor can be charged with the sins which are committed. For His power and goodness are so great and incomprehensible that He orders and executes His work in the most excellent and just manner, even then when devils and wicked men act unjustly. And as to what He does surpassing human understanding, we will not curiously inquire into farther than our capacity will admit of; but with the greatest humility and reverence adore the righteous judgments of God, which are hid from us, contenting ourselves that we are pupils of Christ, to learn only those things which He has revealed to us in His Word, without transgressing these limits.

This doctrine affords us unspeakable consolation, since we are taught thereby that nothing can befall us by chance, but by the direction of our most gracious and heavenly Father; who watches over us with a paternal care, keeping all creatures so under His power that *not a hair of our head (for they are all numbered), nor a sparrow can fall to the ground without the will of our Father,* in whom we do entirely trust; being persuaded that He so restrains the devil and all our enemies that without His will and permission they cannot hurt us.

And therefore we reject that damnable error of the Epicureans, who say that God regards nothing but leaves all things to chance.

Article XIV. THE CREATION AND FALL OF MAN, AND HIS INCAPACITY TO PERFORM WHAT IS TRULY GOOD

We believe that God created man out of the dust of the earth, and made and formed him after His own

THE BELGIC CONFESSION (continued)

image and likeness, good, righteous, and holy, capable in all things to will agreeably to the will of God. But *being in honor, he understood it not*, neither knew his excellency, but wilfully subjected himself to sin and consequently to death and the curse, giving ear to the words of the devil. For the commandment of life, which he had received, he transgressed; and by sin separated himself from God, who was his true life; having corrupted his whole nature; whereby he made himself liable to corporal and spiritual death. And being thus become wicked, perverse, and corrupt in all his ways, he has lost all his excellent gifts which he had received from God, and retained only small remains thereof, which, however, are sufficient to leave man without excuse; for all the light which is in us is changed into darkness, as the Scriptures teach us, saying: *The light shineth in the darkness, and the darkness apprehended it not*; where St. John calls men darkness.

Therefore we reject all that is taught repugnant to this concerning the free will of man, since man is but a slave to sin, and *can receive nothing, except it have been given him from heaven*. For who may presume to boast that he of himself can do any good, since Christ says: *No man can come to me, except the Father that sent me draw him*? Who will glory in his own will, who understands that *the mind of the flesh is enmity against God*? Who can speak of his knowledge, since *the natural man receiveth not the things of the Spirit of God*? In short, who dare suggest any thought, since he knows that *we are not sufficient of ourselves to account anything as of ourselves, but that our sufficiency is of God*? And therefore what the apostle says ought justly to be held sure and firm, that *God worketh in us both to will and to work, for his good pleasure*. For there is no understanding nor will conformable to the divine understanding and will but what Christ has wrought in man; which He teaches us, when He says: *Apart from me ye can do nothing*.

Article XV.   ORIGINAL SIN

We believe that through the disobedience of Adam original sin is extended to all mankind; which is a corruption of the whole nature and a hereditary disease, wherewith even infants in their mother's womb are infected, and which produces in man all sorts of sin, being in him as a root thereof, and therefore is so vile and abominable in the sight of God that it is sufficient to condemn all mankind. Nor is it altogether abolished or wholly eradicated even by baptism; since sin always issues forth from this woeful source, as water from a fountain; notwithstanding it is not imputed to the children of God unto condemnation, but by His grace and mercy is forgiven them. Not that they should rest securely in sin, but that a sense of this corruption should make believers often to sigh, desiring to be delivered from this body of death.

Wherefore we reject the error of the Pelagians, who assert that sin proceeds only from imitation.

Article XVI.   ETERNAL ELECTION

We believe that, all the posterity of Adam being thus fallen into perdition and ruin by the sin of our first parents, God then did manifest Himself such as He is; that is to say, merciful and just: merciful, since He delivers and preserves from this perdition all whom He in His eternal and unchangeable counsel of mere goodness has elected in Christ Jesus our Lord, without any respect to their works; just, in leaving others in the fall and perdition wherein they have involved themselves.

Article XVII.   THE RECOVERY OF FALLEN MAN

We believe that our most gracious God, in His admirable wisdom and goodness, seeing that man had thus thrown himself into physical and spiritual death and made himself wholly miserable, was pleased to seek and comfort him, when he trembling fled from His presence, promising him that He would give His Son (who would be *born of a woman) to bruise the head of the serpent* and to make him blessed.

Article XVIII.   THE INCARNATION OF JESUS CHRIST

We confess, therefore, that God has fulfilled the promise which He made to the fathers by the mouth of His holy prophets, when He sent into the world, at the time appointed by Him, His own only-begotten and eternal Son, who *took upon Him the form of a servant* and *became like unto man*, really assuming the true human nature with all its infirmities, sin excepted; being conceived in the womb of the blessed virgin Mary by the power of the Holy Spirit without the means of man; and did not only assume human nature as to the body, but also a true human soul, that He might be a real man. For since the soul was lost as well as the body, it was necessary that He should take both upon Him, to save both.

Therefore we confess (in opposition to the heresy of the Anabaptists, who deny that Christ assumed human flesh of His mother) that Christ *partook of the flesh and blood of the children*; that He is a *fruit of the loins of David after the flesh; born of the seed of David according to the flesh; a fruit of the womb of Mary; born of a woman; a branch of David; a shoot of the root of Jesse; sprung from the tribe of Judah*; descended from the Jews according to the flesh; of the seed of Abraham, since (A.V.) *he took on him the seed of Abraham*, and *was made like unto his brethren in all things, sin excepted*; so that in truth He is our IMMANUEL, that is to say, *God with us*.

Article XIX.   THE UNION AND DISTINCTION OF THE TWO NATURES IN THE PERSON OF CHRIST

We believe that by this conception the person of the Son is inseparably united and connected with the human nature; so that there are not two Sons of God, nor two persons, but two natures united in one single person; yet each nature retains its own distinct properties. As, then, the divine nature has always remained uncreated, without beginning of days or end of life, filling heaven and earth, so also has the human nature not lost its properties but remained a creature, having beginning of days, being a finite nature, and retaining all the properties of a real body. And though He has by His resurrection given immortality to the same, nevertheless He has not changed the reality of His human nature; forasmuch as our salvation and resurrection also depend on the reality of His body.

But these two natures are so closely united in one person that they were not separated even by His death. Therefore that which He, when dying, commended into the hands of His Father, was a real human spirit, departing from His body. But in the meantime the divine nature always remained united with the human, even when He lay in the grave; and the Godhead did not cease to be in Him, any more than it did when He was an infant, though it did not so clearly manifest itself for a while. Wherefore we confess that He is very God and very man: very God by His power to conquer death; and very man that He might die for us according to the infirmity of His flesh.

Article XX. GOD HAS MANIFESTED HIS JUSTICE AND MERCY IN CHRIST

We believe that God, who is perfectly merciful and just, sent His Son to assume that nature in which the disobedience was committed, to make satisfaction in the same, and to bear the punishment of sin by His most bitter passion and death. God therefore manifested His justice against His Son when He laid our iniquities upon Him, and poured forth His mercy and goodness on us, who were guilty and worthy of damnation, out of mere and perfect love, giving His Son unto death for us, and raising Him for our justification, that through Him we might obtain immortality and life eternal.

Article XXI. THE SATISFACTION OF CHRIST, OUR ONLY HIGH PRIEST, FOR US

We believe that Jesus Christ is ordained with an oath to be an everlasting High Priest, after the order of Melchizedek; and that He has presented Himself in our behalf before the Father, to appease His wrath by His full satisfaction, by offering Himself on the tree of the cross, and pouring out His precious blood to purge away our sins, as the prophets had foretold. For it is written: *He was wounded for our transgressions, he was bruised for our iniquities; the chastisement of our peace was upon him; and with his stripes we are healed. He was led as a lamb to the slaughter, and numbered with the transgressors*; and condemned by Pontius Pilate as a malefactor, though he had first declared Him innocent. Therefore, He *restored that which he took not away*, and *suffered, the righteous for the unrighteous*, as well in His body as in His soul, feeling the terrible punishment which our sins

had merited; insomuch that *his sweat became as it were great drops of blood falling down upon the ground*. He called out: *My God, my God, why hast thou forsaken me*? and has suffered all this for the remission of our sins.

Wherefore we justly say with the apostle Paul that we know nothing *save Jesus Christ, and him crucified; we count all things but loss and refuse for the excellency of the knowledge of Christ Jesus our Lord*, in whose wounds we find all manner of consolation. Neither is it necessary to seek or invent any other means of being reconciled to God than this only sacrifice, once offered, by which *he hath perfected forever them that are sanctified*. This is also the reason why He was called by the angel of God, JESUS, that is to say, SAVIOR, because He would *save his people from their sins*.

Article XXII. OUR JUSTIFICATION THROUGH FAITH IN JESUS CHRIST

We believe that, to attain the true knowledge of this great mystery, the Holy Spirit kindles in our hearts an upright faith, which embraces Jesus Christ with all His merits, appropriates Him, and seeks nothing more besides Him. For it must needs follow, either that all things which are requisite to our salvation are not in Jesus Christ, or if all things are in Him, that then those who possess Jesus Christ through faith have complete salvation in Him. Therefore, for any to assert that Christ is not sufficient, but that something more is required besides Him, would be too gross a blasphemy; for hence it would follow that Christ was but half a Savior.

Therefore we justly say with Paul, that we *are justified by faith* alone, or *by faith apart from works*. However, to speak more clearly, we do not mean that faith itself justifies us, for it is only an instrument with which we embrace Christ our righteousness. But Jesus Christ, imputing to us all His merits, and so many holy works which He has done for us and in our stead, is our righteousness. And faith is an instrument that keeps us in communion with Him in all His benefits, which, when they become ours, are more than sufficient to acquit us of our sins.

Article XXIII. WHEREIN OUR JUSTIFICATION BEFORE GOD CONSISTS

We believe that our salvation consists in the remission of our sins for Jesus Christ's sake, and that therein our righteousness before God is implied; as David and Paul teach us, declaring this to be the blessedness of man that *God imputes righteousness to him apart from works*. And the same apostle says that we are *justified freely by his grace, through the redemption that is in Christ Jesus*.

And therefore we always hold fast this foundation, ascribing all the glory to God, humbling ourselves before Him, and acknowledging ourselves to be such as we really are, without presuming to trust in any thing in ourselves, or in any merit of ours, relying and resting upon the obedience of Christ crucified

THE BELGIC CONFESSION (continued)

alone, which becomes ours when we believe in Him. This is sufficient to cover all our iniquities, and to give us confidence in approaching to God; freeing the conscience of fear, terror, and dread, without following the example of our first father, Adam, who, trembling, attempted to cover himself with fig-leaves. And, verily, if we should appear before God, relying on ourselves or on any other creature, though ever so little, we should, alas! be consumed. And therefore every one must pray with David: *O Jehovah, enter not into judgment with thy servant; for in thy sight no man living is righteous.*

Article XXIV. MAN'S SANCTIFICATION AND GOOD WORKS

We believe that this true faith, being wrought in man by the hearing of the Word of God and the operation of the Holy Spirit, regenerates him and makes him a new man, causing him to live a new life, and freeing him from the bondage of sin. Therefore it is so far from being true that this justifying faith makes men remiss in a pious and holy life, that on the contrary without it they would never do anything out of love to God, but only out of self-love or fear of damnation. Therefore it is impossible that this holy faith can be unfruitful in man; for we do not speak of a vain faith, but of such a faith which is called in Scripture a *faith working through love*, which excites man to the practice of those works which God has commanded in His Word.

These works, as they proceed from the good root of faith, are good and acceptable in the sight of God, forasmuch as they are all sanctified by His grace. Nevertheless they are of no account towards our justification, for it is by faith in Christ that we are justified, even before we do good works; otherwise they could not be good works, any more than the fruit of a tree can be good before the tree itself is good.

Therefore we do good works, but not to merit by them (for what can we merit?); nay, we are indebted to God for the good works we do, and not He to us, since it is He who *worketh in us both to will and to work, for his good pleasure*. Let us therefore attend to what is written: *When ye shall have done all the things that are commanded you, say, We are unprofitable servants; we have done that which it was our duty to do.* In the meantime we do not deny that God rewards good works, but it is through His grace that He crowns His gifts.

Moreover, though we do good works, we do not found our salvation upon them; for we can do no work but what is polluted by our flesh, and also punishable; and although we could perform such works, still the remembrance of one sin is sufficient to make God reject them. Thus, then, we would always be in doubt, tossed to and fro without any certainty, and our poor consciences would be contin-

ually vexed if they relied not on the merits of the suffering and death of our Savior.

Article XXV. THE ABOLISHING OF THE CEREMONIAL LAW

We believe that the ceremonies and symbols of the law ceased at the coming of Christ, and that all the shadows are accomplished; so that the use of them must be abolished among Christians; yet the truth and substance of them remain with us in Jesus Christ, in whom they have their completion. In the meantime we still use the testimonies taken out of the law and the prophets to confirm us in the doctrine of the gospel, and to regulate our life in all honorableness to the glory of God, according to His will.

Article XXVI. CHRIST'S INTERCESSION

We believe that we have no access unto God but alone through the only Mediator and Advocate, Jesus Christ the righteous; who therefore became man, having united in one person the divine and human natures, that we men might have access to the divine Majesty, which access would otherwise be barred against us. But this Mediator, whom the Father has appointed between Him and us, ought in no wise to affright us by His majesty, or cause us to seek another according to our fancy. For there is no creature, either in heaven or on earth, who loves us more than Jesus Christ; who, though *existing in the form of God*, yet *emptied himself, being made in the likeness of men and of a servant* for us, and *in all things was made like unto his brethren*. If, then, we should seek for another mediator who would be favorably inclined towards us, whom could we find who loved us more than He who laid down His life for us, even *while we were His enemies*? And if we seek for one who has power and majesty, who is there that has so much of both as He *who sits at the right hand of God* and *to whom hath been given all authority in heaven and on earth*? And who will sooner be heard than the own well beloved Son of God?

Therefore it was only through distrust that this practice of dishonoring, instead of honoring, the saints was introduced, doing that which they never have done nor required, but have on the contrary stedfastly rejected according to their bounden duty, as appears by their writings. Neither must we plead here our unworthiness; for the meaning is not that we should offer our prayers to God on the ground of our own worthiness, but only on the ground of the excellency and worthiness of the Lord Jesus Christ, whose righteousness is become ours by faith.

Therefore the apostle, to remove this foolish fear, or rather distrust, from us, rightly says that Jesus Christ *in all things was made like unto his brethren, that he might become a merciful and faithful high priest, to make propitiation for the sins of the people. For in that he himself hath suffered being tempted, he is able to succor them that are tempted.* And further to encourage us to go to Him, he says: *Having then a* great high priest, who hath passed through the heavens, Jesus the Son of God, let us hold fast our confession. For we have not a high priest that cannot be touched with the feeling of our infirmities; but one that hath been in all points tempted like as we are, yet without sin. Let us therefore draw near with boldness unto the throne of grace, that we may receive mercy, and may find grace to help us in time of need. The same apostle says: Having boldness to enter into the holy place by the blood of Jesus, let us draw near with a true heart in fulness of faith, etc. Likewise: Christ hath his priesthood unchangeable; wherefore also he is able to save to the uttermost them that draw near unto God through him, seeing he ever liveth to make intercession for them.

What more can be required? since Christ Himself says: I am the way, and the truth, and the life: no one cometh unto the Father, but by me. To what purpose should we, then, seek another advocate, since it has pleased God to give us His own Son as an Advocate? Let us not forsake Him to take another, or rather to seek after another, without ever being able to find him; for God well knew, when He gave Him to us, that we were sinners.

Therefore, according to the command of Christ, we call upon the heavenly Father through Jesus Christ our only Mediator, as we are taught in the Lord's Prayer; being assured that whatever we ask of the Father in His Name will be granted us.

Article XXVII. THE CATHOLIC CHRISTIAN CHURCH

We believe and profess one catholic or universal Church, which is a holy congregation of true Christian believers, all expecting their salvation in Jesus Christ, being washed by His blood, sanctified and sealed by the Holy Spirit.

This Church has been from the beginning of the world, and will be to the end thereof; which is evident from this that Christ is an eternal King, which without subjects He cannot be. And this holy Church is preserved or supported by God against the rage of the whole world; though it sometimes for a while appears very small, and in the eyes of men to be reduced to nothing; as during the perilous reign of Ahab the Lord reserved unto Him seven thousand men who had not bowed their knees to Baal.

Furthermore, this holy Church is not confined, boudn, or limited to a certain place or to certain persons, but is spread and dispersed over the whole world; and yet is joined and united with heart and will, by the power of faith, in one and the same Spirit.

Article XXVIII. EVERY ONE IS BOUND TO JOIN HIMSELF TO THE TRUE CHURCH

We believe, since this holy congregation is an assembly of those who are saved, and outside of it there is no salvation, that no person of whatsoever state or condition he may be, ought to withdraw from it, content to be by himself; but that all men are in duty bound to join and unite themselves with it; maintaining the unity of the Church; submitting themselves to the doctrine and discipline thereof; bowing their necks under the yoke of Jesus Christ; and as mutual members of the same body, serving to the edification of the brethren, according to the talents God has given them.

And that this may be the more effectually observed, it is the duty of all believers, according to the Word of God, to separate themselves from all those who do not belong to the Church, and to join themselves to this congregation, wheresoever God has established it, even though the magistrates and edicts of princes were against it, yea, though they should suffer death or any other corporal punishment. Therefore all those who separate themselves from the same or do not join themselves to it act contrary to the ordinance of God.

Article XXIX. THE MARKS OF THE TRUE CHURCH, AND WHEREIN IT DIFFERS FROM THE FALSE CHURCH

We believe that we ought diligently and circumspectly to discern from the Word of God which is the true Church, since all sects which are in the world assume to themselves the name of the Church. But we speak not here of hypocrites, who are mixed in the Church with the good, yet are not of the Church, though externally in it; but we say that the body and communion of the true Church must be distinguished from all sects that call themselves the Church.

The marks by which the true Church is known are these: If the pure doctrine of the gospel is preached therein; if it maintains the pure administration of the sacraments as instituted by Christ; if church discipline is exercised in punishing of sin; in short, if all things are managed according to the pure Word of God, all things contrary thereto rejected, and Jesus Christ acknowledged as the only Head of the Church. Hereby the true Church may certainly be known, from which no man has a right to separate himself.

With respect to those who are members of the Church, they may be known by the marks of Christians; namely, by faith, and when, having received Jesus Christ the only Savior, they avoid sin, follow after righteousness, love the true God and their neighbor, neither turn aside to the right or left, and crucify the flesh with the works thereof. But this is not to be understood as if there did not remain in them great infirmities; but they fight against them through the Spirit all the days of their life, continually taking their refuge in the blood, death, passion, and obedience of our Lord Jesus Christ, in whom they have remission of sins, through faith in Him.

As for the false Church, it ascribes more power and authority to itself and its ordinances than to the Word of God, and will not submit itself to the yoke of Christ. Neither does it administer the sacraments as appointed by Christ in His Word, but adds to and takes from them, as it thinks proper; it relies more upon men than upon Christ; and persecutes those who live holily according to the Word of God and rebuke it for its errors, covetousness, and idolatry.

These two Churches are easily known and distinguished from each other.

Article XXX. THE GOVERNMENT OF THE CHURCH AND ITS OFFICES

We believe that this true Church must be governed by that spiritual polity which our Lord has taught us in His Word: namely, that there must be ministers or pastors to preach the Word of God and to administer the sacraments; also elders and deacons, who, together with the pastors, form the council of the Church; that by these means the true religion may be preserved, and the true doctrine everywhere propagated, likewise transgressors punished and restrained by spiritual means; also that the poor and distressed may be relieved and comforted, according to their necessities. By these means everything will be carried on in the Church with good order and decency, when faithful men are chosen, according to the rule prescribed by St. Paul in his Epistle to Timothy.

Article XXXI. THE MINISTERS, ELDERS, AND DEACONS

We believe that the ministers of God's Word, the elders, and the deacons ought to be chosen to their respective offices by a lawful election by the Church, with calling upon the name of the Lord, and in that order which the Word of God teaches. Therefore every one must take heed not to intrude himself by improper means, but is bound to wait till it shall please God to call him; that he may have testimony of his calling, and be certain and assured that it is of the Lord.

As for the ministers of God's Word, they have equally the same power and authority wheresoever they are, as they are all ministers of Christ, the only universal Bishop and the only Head of the Church.

Moreover, in order that this holy ordinance of God may not be violated or slighted, we say that every one ought to esteem the ministers of God's Word and the elders of the Church very highly for their work's sake, and be at peace with them without murmuring, strife, or contention, as much as possible.

Article XXXII. THE ORDER AND DISCIPLINE OF THE CHURCH

In the meantime we believe, though it is useful and beneficial that those who are rulers of the Church institute and establish certain ordinances among themselves for maintaining the body of the Church, yet that they ought studiously to take care that they do not depart from those things which Christ, our only Master, has instituted. And therefore we reject all human inventions, and all laws which man would introduce into the worship of God, thereby to bind and compel the conscience in any manner whatever. Therefore we admit only of that which tends to nourish and preserve concord and unity, and to keep all men in obedience to God. For this purpose, excommunication or church discipline is requisite, with all that pertains to it, according to the Word of God.

Article XXXIII. THE SACRAMENTS

We believe that our gracious God, taking account of our weakness and infirmities, has ordained the sacraments for us, thereby to seal unto us His promises, and to be pledges of the good will and grace of God towards us, and also to nourish and strengthen our faith; which He has joined to the Word of the gospel, the better to present to our senses both that which He declares to us by His Word and that which He works inwardly in our hearts, thereby confirming in us the salvation which He imparts to us. For they are visible signs and seals of an inward and invisible thing, by means whereof God works in us by the power of the Holy Spirit. Therefore the signs are not empty or meaningless, so as to deceive us. For Jesus Christ is the true object presented by them, without whom they would be of no moment.

Moreover, we are satisfied with the number of sacraments which Christ our Lord has instituted, which are two only, namely, the sacrament of baptism and the holy supper of our Lord Jesus Christ.

Article XXXIV. HOLY BAPTISM

We believe and confess that Jesus Christ, who is the end of the law, has made an end, by the shedding of His blood, of all other sheddings of blood which men could or would make as a propitiation or satisfaction for sin; and that He, having abolished circumcision, which was done with blood, has instituted the sacrament of baptism instead thereof; by which we are received into the Church of God, and separated from all other people and strange religions, that we may wholly belong to Him whose mark and ensign we bear; and which serves as a testimony to us that He will forever be our gracious God and Father.

Therefore He has commanded all those who are His to be baptized with pure water, *into the name of the Father and of the Son and of the Holy Spirit*, thereby signifying to us, that as water washes away the filth of the body when poured upon it, and is seen on the body of the baptized when sprinkled upon him, so does the blood of Christ by the power of the Holy Spirit internally sprinkle the soul, cleanse it from its sins, and regenerate us from children of wrath unto children of God. Not that this is effected by the external water, but by the sprinkling of the precious blood of the Son of God; who is our Red Sea, through which we must pass to escape the tyranny of Pharaoh, that is, the devil, and to enter into the spiritual land of Canaan.

The ministers, therefore, on their part administer the sacrament and that which is visible, but our Lord gives that which is signified by the sacrament, namely, the gifts and invisible grace; washing, cleansing, and purging our souls of all filth and unrighteousness; renewing our hearts and filling them with all comfort; giving unto us a true assurance of His fatherly goodness; putting on us the new man, and putting off the old man with all his deeds.

We believe, therefore, that every man who is earnestly studious of obtaining life eternal ought to be baptized but once with this only baptism, without ever repeating the same, since we cannot be born twice. Neither does this baptism avail us only at the time when the water is poured upon us and received by us, but also through the whole course of our life.

Therefore we detest the error of the Anabaptists, who are not content with the one only baptism they have once received, and moreover condemn the baptism of the infants of believers, who we believe ought to be baptized and sealed with the sign of the covenant, as the children in Israel formerly were circumcised upon the same promises which are made unto our children. And indeed Christ shed His blood no less for the washing of the children of believers than for adult persons; and therefore they ought to receive the sign and sacrament of that which Christ has done for them; as the Lord commanded in the law that they should be made partakers of the sacrament of Christ's suffering and death shortly after they were born, by offering for them a lamb, which was a sacrament of Jesus Christ. Moreover, what circumcision was to the Jews, baptism is to our children. And for this reason St. Paul calls baptism the *circumcision of Christ*.

Article XXXV. THE HOLY SUPPER OF OUR LORD JESUS CHRIST

We believe and confess that our Savior Jesus Christ did ordain and institute the sacrament of the holy supper to nourish and support those whom He has already regenerated and incorporated into His family, which is His Church.

Now those who are regenerated have in them a twofold life, the one corporal and temporal, which they have from the first birth and is common to all men; the other spiritual and heavenly, which is given them in their second birth, which is effected by the Word of the gospel, in the communion of the body of Christ; and this life is not common, but is peculiar to God's elect. In like manner God has given us, for the support of the bodily and earthly life, earthly and common bread, which is subservient thereto and is common to all men, even as life itself. But for the support of the spiritual and heavenly life which believers have He has sent a living bread, which descended from heaven, namely, Jesus Christ, who nourishes and strengthens the spiritual life of believers when they eat Him, that is to say, when they appropriate and receive Him by faith in the spirit.

In order that He might represent unto us this spiritual and heavenly bread, Christ has instituted an earthly and visible bread as a sacrament of His body, and wine as a sacrament of His blood, to testify by them unto us that, as certainly as we receive and hold this sacrament in our hands and eat and drink the same with our months, by which our life is afterwards nourished, we also do as certainly receive by faith (which is the hand and mouth of our soul) the true body and blood of Christ our only Savior in our souls, for the support of our spiritual life.

Now, as it is certain and beyond all doubt that Jesus Christ has not enjoined to us the use of His sacraments in vain, so He works in us all that He represents to us by these holy signs, though the manner surpasses our understanding and cannot be comprehended by us, as the operations of the Holy Spirit are hidden and incomprehensible. In the meantime we err not when we say that what is eaten and drunk by us is the proper and natural body and the proper blood of Christ. But the manner of our partaking of the same is not by the mouth, but by the spirit through faith. Thus, then, though Christ always sits at the right hand of His Father in the heavens, yet does He not therefore cease to make us partakers of Himself by faith. This feast is a spiritual table, at which Christ communicates Himself with all His benefits to us, and gives us there to enjoy both Himself and the merits of His sufferings and death: nourishing, strengthening, and comforting our poor comfortless souls by the eating of His flesh, quickening and refreshing them by the drinking of His blood.

Further, though the sacraments are connected with the thing signified nevertheless both are not received by all men. The ungodly indeed receives the sacrament to his condemnation, but he does not receive the truth of the sacrament, even as Judas and Simon the sorcerer both indeed received the sacrament but not Christ who was signified by it, of whom believers only are made partakers.

Lastly, we receive this holy sacrament in the assembly of the people of God, with humility and reverence, keeping up among us a holy remembrance of the death of Christ our Savior, with thanksgiving, making there confession of our faith and of the Christian religion. Therefore no one ought to come to this table without having previously rightly examined himself, lest by eating of this bread and drinking of this cup he eat and drink judgment to himself. In a word, we are moved by the use of this holy sacrament to a fervent love towards God and our neighbor.

Therefore we reject all mixtures and damnable inventions which men have added unto and blended with the sacraments, as profanations of them; and affirm that we ought to rest satisfied with the ordinance which Christ and His apostles have taught us, and that we must speak of them in the same manner as they have spoken.

THE BELGIC CONFESSION (continued)

Article XXXVI. THE MAGISTRACY (CIVIL GOVERNMENT)

We believe that our gracious God, because of the depravity of mankind, has appointed kings, princes, and magistrates; willing that the world should be governed by certain laws and policies; to the end that the dissoluteness of men might be restrained, and all things carried on among them with good order and decency. For this purpose He has invested the magistracy with *the sword for the punishment of evil-doers and for the protection of them that do well.*

Their office is not only to have regard unto and watch for the welfare of the civil state, but also to protect the sacred ministry, that the kingdom of Christ may thus be promoted. They must therefore countenance the preaching of the Word of the gospel everywhere, that God may be honored and worshipped by every one, as He commands in His Word.

Moreover, it is the bounden duty of every one, of whatever state, quality, or condition he may be, to subject himself to the magistrates; to pay tribute, to show due honor and respect to them, and to obey them in all things which are not repugnant to the Word of God; to supplicate for them in their prayers that God may rule and guide them in all their ways, and *that we may lead a tranquil and quiet life in all godliness and gravity.*

Wherefore we detest the Anabaptists and other seditious people, and in general all those who reject the higher powers and magistrates and would subvert justice, introduce community of goods, and confound that decency and good order which God has established among men.

Article XXXVII. THE LAST JUDGMENT

Finally, we believe, according to the Word of God, when the time appointed by the Lord (which is unknown to all creatures) is come and the number of the elect complete, that our Lord Jesus Christ will come from heaven, corporally and visibly, as He ascended, with great glory and majesty to declare Himself Judge of the living and the dead, burning this old world with fire and flame to cleanse it.

Then all men will personally appear before this great Judge, both men and women and children, that have been from the beginning of the world to the end thereof, being summoned by *the voice of the archangel, and by the sound of the trump of God.* For all the dead shall be raised out of the earth, and their souls joined and united with their proper bodies in which they formerly lived. As for those who shall then be living, they shall not die as the others, but be changed in the twinkling of an eye, and from corruptible become incorruptible. Then *the books* (that is to say, the consciences) *shall be opened, and the dead judged* according to what they shall have done in this world, whether it be good or evil. Nay, all men *shall give account of every idle word they have spoken,* which the world only counts amusement and jest; and then the secrets and hypocrisy of men shall be disclosed and laid open before all.

And therefore the consideration of this judgment is justly terrible and dreadful to the wicked and ungodly, but most desirable and comfortable to the righteous and elect; because then their full deliverance shall be perfected, and there they shall receive the fruits of their labor and trouble which they have borne. Their innocence shall be known to all, and they shall see the terrible vengeance which God shall execute on the wicked, who most cruelly persecuted, oppressed, and tormented them in this world, and who shall be convicted by the testimony of their own consciences, and shall become immortal, but only to be tormented in *the eternal fire which is prepared for the devil and his angels.*

But on the contrary, the faithful and elect shall be crowned with glory and honor; and the Son of God will confess their names before God His Father and His elect angels; all tears shall be wiped from their eyes; and their cause which is now condemned by many judges and magistrates as heretical and impious will then be known to be the cause of the Son of God. And for a gracious reward, the Lord will cause them to possess such a glory as never entered into the heart of man to conceive.

Therefore we expect that great day with a most ardent desire, to the end that we may fully enjoy the promises of God in Christ Jesus our Lord. AMEN.

Amen, come, Lord Jesus.—Rev. 22:20.

Notes: *During the sixteenth century the Reformed Churches, like the Lutherans, found it necessary and expedient to produce statements clarifying their theological affirmations and their continued allegiance to the historic affirmations (as presented in the creeds) of the early church. Unlike the Lutherans, who collected their authoritative creeds into a single volume* (The Book of Concord), *the various Reformed Churches, representing different nations and languages, prepared their own individual statements of faith. English translations of the most important of the sixteenth-century confessions, originally promulgated between 1523 and 1566, were finally compiled into a single volume by Arthur Cochrane,* Reformed Confessions of the 16th Century *(Philadelphia: Westminster Press, 1966).*

In the United States, two of the sixteenth-century confessions stand out because of their acceptance as official doctrinal statements by Reformed churches with members in the United States. The Belgic Confession of 1561, the main product of Dutch Calvinism, is by far the most accepted in America, as many of the Reformed Churches had their beginnings in Holland.

The Belgic Confession was composed by Guido de Bries (1523-1567) in 1561 as part of an unsuccessful effort to convince the Roman Catholic authorities in the Netherlands that the Reformed Church should be released from persecution at the hands of the Spanish-Catholic authorities. The confession was slightly revised in 1566, and in 1619 it was adopted (along with the Heidelberg Catechism and the

Canons of Dort) as the official doctrinal standard of the Dutch Reformed Church.

The Dutch brought the confession to the United States, where it remains the official standard for the Christian Reformed Church and the Reformed Church in America, as well as for the smaller Netherlands Reformed Congregations, Orthodox Christian Reformed Church, and Protestant Reformed Churches of America.

The text of the confession reproduced here was taken from A Treatise of the Compendium by G. H. Kersten (Grand Rapids, MI: Inheritance Publishing Co., 1956).

* * *

CANONS OF DORT

FIRST HEAD OF DOCTRINE. DIVINE ELECTION AND REPROBATION

Article 1. As all men have sinned in Adam, lie under the curse, and are deserving of eternal death, God would have done no injustice by leaving them all to perish and delivering them over to condemnation on account of sin, according to the words of the apostle: *That every mouth may be stopped, and all the world may be brought under the judgment of God* (Rom. 3:19). And: *For all have sinned, and fall short of the glory of God* (Rom. 3:23). And: *For the wages of sin is death* (Rom. 6:23).

Article 2. But in this the love of God was manifested, that He *sent his only begotten Son into the world, that whosoever believeth on him should not perish, but have eternal life* (1 John 4:9; John 3:16).

Article 3. And that men may be brought to believe, God mercifully sends the messengers of these most joyful tidings to whom He will and at what time He pleases; by whose ministry men are called to repentance and faith in Christ crucified. *How then shall they call on him in whom they have not believed? And how shall they believe in him whom they have not heard? And how shall they hear without a preacher? And how shall they preach except they be sent?* (Rom. 10:14, 15).

Article 4. The wrath of God abides upon those who believe not this gospel. But such as receive it and embrace Jesus the Savior by a true and living faith are by Him delivered from the wrath of God and from destruction, and have the gift of eternal life conferred upon them.

Article 5. The cause or guilt of this unbelief as well as of all other sins is no wise in God, but in man himself; whereas faith in Jesus Christ and salvation through Him is the free gift of God, as it is written: *By grace have ye been saved through faith; and that not of yourselves, it is the gift of God* (Eph. 2:8). Likewise: *To you it hath been granted in the behalf of Christ, not only to believe on him,* etc. (Phil. 1:29).

Article 6. That some receive the gift of faith from God, and others do not receive it, proceeds from God's eternal decree. *For known unto God are all his works from the beginning of the world* (Acts 15:18,

A.V.). *Who worketh all things after the counsel of his will* (Eph. 1:11). According to which decree He graciously softens the hearts of the elect, however obstinate, and inclines them to believe; while He leaves the non-elect in His just judgment to their own wickedness and obduracy. And herein is especially displayed the profound, the merciful, and at the same time the righteous discrimination between men equally involved in ruin; or that decree of election and reprobation, revealed in the Word of God, which, though men of perverse, impure, and unstable minds wrest it to their own destruction, yet to holy and pious souls affords unspeakable consolation.

Article 7. Election is the unchangeable purpose of God, whereby, before the foundation of the world, He has out of mere grace, according to the sovereign good pleasure of His own will, chosen from the whole human race, which had fallen through their own fault from their primitive state of rectitude into sin and destruction, a certain number of persons to redemption in Christ, whom He from eternity appointed the Mediator and Head of the elect and the foundation of salvation. This elect number, though by nature neither better nor more deserving than others, but with them involved in one common misery, God has decreed to give to Christ to be saved by Him, and effectually to call and draw them to His communion by His Word and Spirit; to bestow upon them true faith, justification, and sanctification; and having powerfully preserved them in the fellowship of His Son, finally to glorify them for the demonstration of His mercy, and for the praise of the riches of His glorious grace; as it is written: *Even as he chose us in him before the foundation of the world, that we should be holy and without blemish before him in love: having foreordained us unto adoption as sons through Jesus Christ unto himself, according to the good pleasure of his will, to the praise of the glory of his grace, which he freely bestowed on us in the Beloved* (Eph. 1:4, 5, 6). And elsewhere: *Whom he foreordained, them he also called: and whom he called, them he also justified: and whom he justified, them he also glorified* (Rom. 8:30).

Article 8. There are not various decrees of election, but one and the same decree respecting all those who shall be saved, both under the Old and the New Testament; since the Scripture declares the good pleasure, purpose, and counsel of the divine will to be one, according to which He has chosen us from eternity, both to grace and to glory, to salvation and to the way of salvation, which He has ordained that we should walk therein (Eph. 1:4, 5; 2:10).

Article 9. This election was not founded upon foreseen faith and the obedience of faith, holiness, or any other good quality or disposition in man, as the prerequisite, cause, or condition on which it depended; but men are chosen to faith and to the obedience of faith, holiness, etc. Therefore election is the fountain of every saving good, from which proceed faith, holiness, and the other gifts of salvation, and finally eternal life itself, as its fruits and effects,

CANONS OF DORT (continued)

according to the testimony of the apostle: *He hath chosen us* (not because we were, but) *that we should be holy, and without blemish before him in love* (Eph. 1:4).

Article 10. The good pleasure of God is the sole cause of this gracious election; which does not consist herein that out of all possible qualities and actions of men God has chosen some as a condition of salvation, but that He was pleased out of the common mass of sinners to adopt some certain persons as a peculiar people to Himself, as it is written: *For the children being not yet born, neither having done anything good or bad*, etc., *it was said unto her* (namely, to Rebekah), *The elder shall serve the younger. Even as it is written, Jacob I loved, but Esau I hated* (Rom. 9:11, 12, 13). *And as many as were ordained to eternal life believed* (Acts 13:48).

Article 11. And as God Himself is most wise, unchangeable, omniscient, and omnipotent, so the election made by Him can neither be interrupted nor changed, recalled, or annulled; neither can the elect be cast away, nor their number diminished.

Article 12. The elect in due time, though in various degrees and in different measures, attain the assurance of this their eternal and unchangeable election, not by inquisitively prying into the secret and deep things of God, but by observing in themselves with a spiritual joy and holy pleasure the infallible fruits of election pointed out in the Word of God—such as, a true faith in Christ, filial fear, a godly sorrow for sin, a hungering and thirsting after righteousness, etc.

Article 13. The sense and certainty of this election afford to the children of God additional matter for daily humiliation before Him, for adoring the depth of His mercies, for cleansing themselves, and rendering grateful returns of ardent love to Him who first manifested so great love towards them. The consideration of this doctrine of election is so far from encouraging remissness in the observance of the divine commands or from sinking men in carnal security, that these, in the just judgment of God, are the usual effects of rash presumption or of idle and wanton trifling with the grace of election, in those who refuse to walk in the ways of the elect.

Article 14. As the doctrine of divine election by the most wise counsel of God was declared by the prophets, by Christ Himself, and by the apostles, and is clearly revealed in the Scriptures both of the Old and the New Testament, so it is still to be published in due time and place in the Church of God, for which it was peculiarly designed, provided it be done with reverence, in the spirit of discretion and piety, for the glory of God's most holy Name, and for enlivening and comforting His people, without vainly attempting to investigate the secret ways of the Most High (Acts 20:27; Rom. 11:33, 34; 12:3; Heb. 6:17, 18).

Article 15. What peculiarly tends to illustrate and recommend to us the eternal and unmerited grace of election is the express testimony of sacred Scripture that not all, but some only, are elected, while others are passed by in the eternal decree; whom God, out of His sovereign, most just, irreprehensible, and unchangeable good pleasure, has decreed to leave in the common misery into which they have wilfully plunged themselves, and not to bestow upon them saving faith and the grace of conversion; but, permitting them in His just judgment to follow their own ways, at last, for the declaration of His justice, to condemn and punish them forever, not only on account of their unbelief, but also for all their other sins. And this is the decree of reprobation, which by no means makes God the Author of sin (the very thought of which is blasphemy), but declares Him to be an awful, irreprehensible, and righteous Judge and Avenger thereof.

Article 16. Those in whom a living faith in Christ, an assured confidence of soul, peace of conscience, an earnest endeavor after filial obedience, a glorying in God through Christ, is not as yet strongly felt, and who nevertheless make use of the means which God has appointed for working these graces in us, ought not to be alarmed at the mention of reprobation, nor to rank themselves among the reprobate, but diligently to persevere in the use of means, and with ardent desires devoutly and humbly to wait for a season of richer grace. Much less cause to be terrified by the doctrine of reprobation have they who, though they seriously desire to be turned to God, to please Him only, and to be delivered from the body of death, cannot yet reach that measure of holiness and faith to which they aspire; since a merciful God has promised that He will not quench the smoking flax, nor break the bruised reed. But this doctrine is justly terrible to those who, regardless of God and of the Savior Jesus Christ, have wholly given themselves up to the cares of the world and the pleasures of the flesh, so long as they are not seriously converted to God.

Article 17. Since we are to judge of the will of God from His Word, which testifies that the children of believers are holy, not by nature, but in virtue of the covenant of grace, in which they together with the parents are comprehended, godly parents ought not to doubt the election and salvation of their children whom it pleases God to call out of this life in their infancy (Gen. 17:7; Acts 2:39; 1 Cor. 7:14).

Article 18. To those who murmur at the free grace of election and the just severity of reprobation we answer with the apostle: *Nay but, O man, who art thou that repliest against God?* (Rom. 9:20), and quote the language of our Savior: *Is it not lawful for me to do what I will with mine own?* (Matt. 20:15). And therefore, with holy adoration of these mysteries, we exclaim in the words of the apostle: *O the depth of the riches both of the wisdom and the knowledge of God! how unsearchable are his judgments, and his ways past tracing out! For who hath known the mind of the Lord, or who hath been his counsellor? or who hath first given to him, and it shall be recompensed unto him again? For of him, and through him, and unto him are all things. To him* be the glory for ever. Amen. (Rom. 11:33-36).

REJECTION OF ERRORS

The true doctrine concerning election and reprobation having been explained, the Synod rejects the errors of those:

Paragraph 1. Who teach: That the will of God to save those who would believe and would persevere in faith and in the obedience of faith is the whole and entire decree of election unto salvation, and that nothing else concerning this decree has been revealed in God's Word.

For these deceive the simple and plainly contradict the Scriptures, which declare that God will not only save those who will believe, but that He has also from eternity chosen certain particular persons to whom, above others, He will grant, in time, both faith in Christ and perseverance; as it is written: *I manifested thy name unto the men whom thou gavest me out of the world* (John 17:6). *And as many as were ordained to eternal life believed* (Acts 13:48). And: *Even as he chose us in him before the foundation of the world, that we should be holy and without blemish before him in love* (Eph. 1:4).

Paragraph 2. Who teach: That there are various kinds of election of God unto eternal life: the one general and indefinite, the other particular and definite; and that the latter in turn is either incomplete, revocable, non-decisive, and conditional, or complete, irrevocable, decisive, and absolute. Likewise: That there is one election unto faith and another unto salvation, so that election can be unto justifying faith, without being a decisive election unto salvation.

For this is a fancy of men's minds, invented regardless of the Scriptures, whereby the doctrine of election is corrupted, and this golden chain of our salvation is broken: *And whom he foreordained, them he also called: and whom he called, them he also justified: and whom he justified, them he also glorified* (Rom. 8:30).

Paragraph 3. Who teach: That the good pleasure and purpose of God, of which Scripture makes mention in the doctrine of election, does not consist in this, that God chose certain persons rather than others, but in this, that He chose out of all possible conditions (among which are also the works of the law), or out of the whole order of things, the act of faith which from its very nature is undeserving, as well as its incomplete obedience, as a condition of salvation, and that He would graciously consider this in itself as a complete obedience and count it worthy of the reward of eternal life.

For by this injurious error the pleasure of God and the merits of Christ are made of none effect, and men are drawn away by useless questions from the truth of gracious justification and from the simplicity of Scripture, and this declaration of the apostle is charged as untrue: *Who saved us, and called us with a holy calling, not according to our works, but according to his own purpose and grace, which was given us in Christ Jesus before times eternal* (2 Tim. 1:9).

Paragraph 4. Who teach: That in the election unto faith this condition is beforehand demanded that man should use the light of nature aright, be pious, humble, meek, and fit for eternal life, as if on these things election were in any way dependent.

For this savors of the teaching of Pelagius, and is opposed to the doctrine of the apostle when he writes: *Among whom we also all once lived in the lusts of our flesh, doing the desires of the flesh and of the mind, and were by nature children of wrath, even as the rest; but God, being rich in mercy, for his great love wherewith he loved us, even when we were dead through our trespasses, made us alive together with Christ (by grace have ye been saved), and raised us up with him, and made us to sit with him in the heavenly places, in Christ Jesus; that in the ages to come he might show the exceeding riches of his grace in kindness towards us in Christ Jesus; for by grace have ye been saved through faith; and that not of yourselves, it is the gift of God; not of works, that no man should glory* (Eph. 2:3-9).

Paragraph 5. Who teach: That the incomplete and non-decisive election of particular persons to salvation occurred because of a foreseen faith, conversion, holiness, godliness, which either began or continued for some time; but that the complete and decisive election occurred because of foreseen perseverance unto the end in faith, conversion, holiness, and godliness; and that this is the gracious and evangelical worthiness, for the sake of which he who is chosen is more worthy than he who is not chosen; and that therefore faith, the obedience of faith, holiness, godliness, and perseverance are not fruits of the unchangeable election unto glory, but are conditions which, being required beforehand, were foreseen as being met by those who will be fully elected, and are causes without which the unchangeable election to glory does not occur.

This is repugnant to the entire Scripture, which constantly inculcates this and similar declarations: Election is *not of works, but of him that calleth* (Rom. 9:11). *And as many as were ordained to eternal life believed* (Acts 13:48). *He chose us in him before the foundation of the world, that we should be holy* (Eph. 1:4). *Ye did not choose me, but I chose you* (John 15:16). *But if it is by grace, it is no more of works* (Rom. 11:6). *Herein is love, not that we loved God, but that he loved us, and sent his Son* (1 John 4:10).

Paragraph 6. Who teach: That not every election unto salvation is unchangeable, but that some of the elect, any decree of God notwithstanding, can yet perish and do indeed perish.

CANONS OF DORT (continued)

By this gross error they make God to be changeable, and destroy the comfort which the godly obtain out of the firmness of their election, and contradict the Holy Scripture, which teaches that *the elect can not be led astray* (Matt. 24:24), that Christ *does not lose those whom the Father gave him* (John 6:39), and that *God also glorified those whom he foreordained, called, and justified* (Rom. 8:30).

Paragraph 7. Who teach: That there is in this life no fruit and no consciousness of the unchangeable election to glory, nor any certainty, except that which depends on a changeable and uncertain condition.

For not only is it absurd to speak of an uncertain certainty, but also contrary to the experience of the saints, who by virtue of the consciousness of their election rejoice with the apostle and praise this favor of God (Eph. 1); who according to Christ's admonition rejoice with his disciples that *their names are written in heaven* (Luke 10:20); who also place the consciousness of their election over against the fiery darts of the devil, asking: *Who shall lay anything to the charge of God's elect?* (Rom. 8:33).

Paragraph 8. Who teach: That God, simply by virtue of His righteous will, did not decide either to leave anyone in the fall of Adam and in the common state of sin and condemnation, or to pass anyone by in the communication of grace which is necessary for faith and conversion.

For this is firmly decreed: *He hath mercy on whom he will, and whom he will he hardeneth* (Rom. 9:18). And also this: *Unto you it is given to know the mysteries of the kingdom of heaven, but to them it is not given* (Matt. 13:11). Likewise: *I thank thee, O Father, Lord of heaven and earth, that thou didst hide these things from the wise and understanding, and didst reveal them unto babes; yea, Father, for so it was well-pleasing in thy sight* (Matt. 11:25, 26).

Paragraph 9. Who teach: That the reason why God sends the gospel to one people rather than to another is not merely and solely the good pleasure of God, but rather the fact that one people is better and worthier than another to which the gospel is not communicated.

For this Moses denies, addressing the people of Israel as follows: *Behold unto Jehovah thy God belongeth heaven and the heaven of heavens, the earth, with all that is therein. Only Jehovah had a delight in thy fathers to love them, and he chose their seed after them, even you above all peoples, as at this day* (Deut. 10:14, 15). And Christ said: *Woe unto thee, Chorazin! woe unto thee, Bethsaida! for if the mighty works had been done in Tyre and Sidon which were done in you, they would have repented long ago in sackcloth and ashes* (Matt. 11:21).

SECOND HEAD OF DOCTRINE. THE DEATH OF CHRIST, AND THE REDEMPTION OF MEN THEREBY

Article 1. God is not only supremely merciful, but also supremely just. And His justice requires (as He has revealed Himself in His Word) that our sins committed against His infinite majesty should be punished, not only with temporal but with eternal punishments, both in body and soul; which we cannot escape, unless satisfaction be made to the justice of God.

Article 2. Since, therefore, we are unable to make that satisfaction in our own persons, or to deliver ourselves from the wrath of God, He has been pleased of His infinite mercy to give His only begotten Son for our Surety, who was made sin, and became a curse for us and in our stead, that He might make satisfaction to divine justice on our behalf.

Article 3. The death of the Son of God is the only and most perfect sacrifice and satisfaction for sin, and is of infinite worth and value, abundantly sufficient to expiate the sins of the whole world.

Article 4. This death is of such infinite value and dignity because the person who submitted to it was not only really man and perfectly holy, but also the only begotten Son of God, of the same eternal and infinite essence with the Father and the Holy Spirit, which qualifications were necessary to constitute Him a Savior for us; and, moreover, because it was attended with a sense of the wrath and curse of God due to us for sin.

Article 5. Moreover, the promise of the gospel is that whosoever believes in Christ crucified shall not perish, but have eternal life. This promise, together with the command to repent and believe, ought to be declared and published to all nations, and to all persons promiscuously and without distinction, to whom God out of His good pleasure sends the gospel.

Article 6. And, whereas many who are called by the gospel do not repent nor believe in Christ, but perish in unbelief, this is not owing to any defect or insufficiency in the sacrifice offered by Christ upon the cross, but is wholly to be imputed to themselves.

Article 7. But as many as truly believe, and are delivered and saved from sin and destruction through the death of Christ, are indebted for this benefit solely to the grace of God given them in Christ from everlasting, and not to any merit of their own.

Article 8. For this was the sovereign counsel and most gracious will and purpose of God the Father that the quickening and saving efficacy of the most precious death of His Son should extend to all the elect, for bestowing upon them alone the gift of justifying faith, thereby to bring them infallibly to salvation; that is, it was the will of God that Christ by the blood of the cross, whereby He confirmed the new covenant, should effectually redeem out of every people, tribe, nation, and language, all those, and those only, who were from eternity chosen to salvation and given to Him by the Father; that He should confer upon them faith, which, together with all the other saving gifts of the Holy Spirit, He purchased for them by His death; should purge them from all sin, both original and actual, whether committed before or after believing; and having faithfully preserved them even to the end, should at last bring them, free from every spot and blemish, to the enjoyment of glory in His own presence forever.

Article 9. This purpose, proceeding from everlasting love towards the elect, has from the beginning of the world to this day been powerfully accomplished, and will henceforward still continue to be accomplished, notwithstanding all the ineffectual opposition of the gates of hell; so that the elect in due time may be gathered together into one, and that there never may be wanting a Church composed of believers, the foundation of which is laid in the blood of Christ; which may stedfastly love and faithfully serve Him as its Savior (who, as a bridegroom for his bride, laid down His life for them upon the cross); and which may celebrate His praises here and through all eternity.

REJECTION OF ERRORS

The true doctrine having been explained, the Synod rejects the errors of those:

Paragraph 1. Who teach: That God the Father has ordained His Son to the death of the cross without a certain and definite decree to save any, so that the necessity, profitableness, and worth of what Christ merited by His death might have existed, and might remain in all its parts complete, perfect, and intact, even if the merited redemption had never in fact been applied to any person.

For this doctrine tends to the despising of the wisdom of the Father and of the merits of Jesus Christ, and is contrary to Scripture. For thus says our Savior: *I lay down my life for the sheep, and I know them* (John 10:15, 27). And the prophet Isaiah says concerning the Savior: *When thou shalt make his soul an offering for sin, he shall see his seed, he shall prolong his days, and the pleasure of Jehovah shall prosper in his hand* (Is. 53:10). Finally, this contradicts the article of faith according to which we believe the catholic Christian Church.

Paragraph 2. Who teach: That it was not the purpose of the death of Christ that He should confirm the new covenant of grace through His blood, but only that He should acquire for the Father the mere right to establish with man such a covenant as He might please, whether of grace or of works.

For this is repugnant to Scripture which teaches that *Christ hath become the surety and mediator of a better, that is, the new covenant*, and that *a testament is of force where there hath been death* (Heb. 7:22; 9:15, 17).

Paragraph 3. Who teach: That Christ by His satisfaction merited neither salvation itself for anyone, nor faith, whereby this satisfaction of Christ unto salvation is effectually appropriated; but that He merited for the Father only the authority or the perfect will to deal again with man, and to prescribe new conditions as He might desire, obedience to which, however, depended on the free will of man, so that it therefore might have come to pass that either none or all should fulfil these conditions.

For these adjudge too contemptuously of the death of Christ, in no wise acknowledge the most important fruit or benefit thereby gained, and bring again out of hell the Pelagian error.

Paragraph 4. Who teach: That the new covenant of grace, which God the Father, through the mediation of the death of Christ, made with man, does not herein consist that we by faith, in as much as it accepts the merits of Christ, are justified before God and saved, but in the fact that God, having revoked the demand of perfect obedience of faith, regards faith itself and the obedience of faith, although imperfect, as the perfect obedience of the law, and does esteem it worthy of the reward of eternal life through grace.

For these contradict the Scriptures: *Being justified freely by his grace through the redemption that is in Christ Jesus; whom God set forth* to be a *propitiation, through faith, in his blood* (Rom. 3:24, 25). And these proclaim, as did the wicked Socinus, a new and strange justification of man before God, against the consensus of the whole Church.

Paragraph 5. Who teach: That all men have been accepted unto the state of reconciliation and unto the grace of the covenant, so that no one is worthy of condemnation on account of original sin, and that no one shall be condemned because of it, but that all are free from the guilt of original sin.

For this opinion is repugnant to Scripture which teaches that we are *by nature children of wrath* (Eph. 2:3).

Paragraph 6. Who use the difference between meriting and appropriating, to the end that they may instil into the minds of the imprudent and inexperienced this teaching that God, as far as He is concerned, has been minded to apply to all equally the benefits gained by the death of Christ; but that, while some obtain the pardon of sin and eternal life, and others do not, this difference depends on their own free will, which joins itself to the grace that is offered without exception, and that it is not dependent on the special gift of mercy, which powerfully works in them, that they rather than others should appropriate unto themselves this grace.

For these, while they feign that they present this distinction in a sound sense, seek to instil into the people the destructive poison of the Pelagian errors.

Paragraph 7. Who teach: That Christ neither could die, nor needed to die, and also did not die, for those whom God loved in the highest degree and elected to eternal life, since these do not need the death of Christ.

For they contradict the apostle, who declares: *Christ loved me, and gave himself up for me* (Gal. 2:20). Likewise: *Who shall lay anything to the charge of God's elect? It is God that justifieth; who is he that condemneth? It is Christ Jesus that died* (Rom. 8:33, 34), namely, for them; and the Savior who says: *I lay down my life for the sheep* (John 10:15). And: *This is my commandment, that ye love one another, even as I have loved you. Greater love hath no man than this, that a man lay down his life for his friends* (John 15:12, 13).

THIRD AND FOURTH HEADS OF DOCTRINE. THE CORRUPTION OF MAN, HIS CONVERSION TO GOD, AND THE MANNER THEREOF

Article 1. Man .... ally formed after the image of God. His understanding was adorned with a true and saving knowledge of his Creator, and of spiritual things; his heart and will were upright, all his affections pure, and the whole man was holy. But, revolting from God by the instigation of the devil and by his own free will, he forfeited these excellent gifts; and in the place thereof became involved in blindness of mind, horrible darkness, vanity, and perverseness of judgment; became wicked, rebellious, and obdurate in heart and will, and impure in his affections.

Article 2. Man after the fall begat children in his own likeness. A corrupt stock produced a corrupt offspring. Hence all the posterity of Adam, Christ only excepted, have derived corruption from their original parent, not by limitation, as the Pelagians of old asserted, but by the propagation of a vicious nature, in consequence of the just judgment of God.

Article 3. Therefore all men are conceived in sin, and are by nature children of wrath, incapable of saving good, prone to evil, dead in sin, and in bondage thereto; and without the regenerating grace of the Holy Spirit, they are neither able nor willing to return to God, to reform the depravity of their nature, or to dispose themselves to reformation.

Article 4. There remain, however, in man since the fall, the glimmerings of natural light, whereby he retains some knowledge of God, of natural things, and of the difference between good and evil, and shows some regard for virtue and for good outward behavior. But so far is this light of nature from being sufficient to bring him to a saving knowledge of God and to true conversion that he is incapable of using it aright even in things natural and civil. Nay further, this light, such as it is, man in various ways renders wholly polluted, and hinders in unrighteousness, by doing which he becomes inexcusable before God.

Article 5. In the same light are we to consider the law of the decalogue, delivered by God to His peculiar people, the Jews, by the hands of Moses. For though it reveals the greatness of sin, and more and more convinces man thereof, yet, as it neither points out a remedy nor imparts strength to extricate him from his misery, but, being weak through the flesh, leaves the transgressor under the curse, man cannot by this law obtain saving grace.

Article 6. What, therefore, neither the light of nature nor the law could do, that God performs by the operation of the Holy Spirit through the word or ministry of reconciliation; which is the glad tidings concerning the Messiah, by means whereof it has pleased God to save such as believe, as well under the Old as under the New Testament.

Article 7. This mystery of His will God revealed to but a small number under the Old Testament; under the New Testament (the distinction between various peoples having been removed) He reveals it to many. The cause of this dispensation is not to be ascribed to the superior worth of one nation above another, nor to their better use of the light of nature, but results wholly from the sovereign good pleasure and unmerited love of God. Hence they to whom so great and so gracious a blessing is communicated, above their desert, or rather notwithstanding their demerits, are bound to acknowledge it with humble and grateful hearts, and with the apostle to adore, but in no wise curiously to pry into, the severity and justice of God's judgments displayed in others to whom this grace is not given.

Article 8. As many as are called by the gospel are unfeignedly called. For God has most earnestly and truly declared in His Word what is acceptable to Him, namely, that those who are called should come unto Him. He also seriously promises rest of soul and eternal life to all who come to Him and believe.

Article 9. It is not the fault of the gospel, nor of Christ offered therein, nor of God, who calls men by the gospel and confers upon them various gifts, that those who are called by the ministry of the Word refuse to come and be converted. The fault lies in themselves; some of whom when called, regardless of their danger, reject the Word of life; others, though they receive it, suffer it not to make a lasting impression on their heart; therefore, their joy, arising only from a temporary faith, soon vanishes, and they fall away; while others choke the seed of the Word by perplexing cares and the pleasures of this world, and produce no fruit. This our Savior teaches in the parable of the sower (Matt. 13).

Article 10. But that others who are called by the gospel obey the call and are converted is not to be ascribed to the proper exercise of free will, whereby one distinguishes himself above others equally furnished with grace sufficient for faith and conversion (as the proud heresy of Pelagius maintains); but it must be wholly ascribed to God, who, as He has chosen His own from eternity in Christ, so He calls them effectually in time, confers upon them faith and repentance, rescues them from the power of darkness, and translates them into the kingdom of

His own Son; that they may show forth the praises of Him who has called them out of darkness into His marvelous light, and may glory not in themselves but in the Lord, according to the testimony of the apostles in various places.

Article 11. But when God accomplishes His good pleasure in the elect, or works in them true conversion, He not only causes the gospel to be externally preached to them, and powerfully illuminates their minds by His Holy Spirit, that they may rightly understand and discern the things of the Spirit of God; but by the efficacy of the same regenerating Spirit He pervades the inmost recesses of man; He opens the closed and softens the hardened heart, and circumcises that which was uncircumcised; infuses new qualities into the will, which, though heretofore dead, He quickens; from being evil, disobedient, and refractory, He renders it good, obedient, and pliable; actuates and strengthens it, that like a good tree, it may bring forth the fruits of good actions.

Article 12. And this is that regeneration so highly extolled in Scripture, that renewal, new creation, resurrection from the dead, making alive, which God works in us without our aid. But this is in no wise effected merely by the external preaching of the gospel, by moral suasion, or such a mode of operation that, after God has performed His part, it still remains in the power of man to be regenerated or not, to be converted or to continue unconverted; but it is evidently a supernatural work, most powerful, and at the same time most delightful, astonishing, mysterious, and ineffable; not inferior in efficacy to creation or the resurrection from the dead, as the Scripture inspired by the Author of this work declares; so that all in whose heart God works in this marvelous manner are certainly, infallibly, and effectually regenerated, and do actually believe. Whereupon the will thus renewed is not only actuated and influenced by God, but in consequence of this influence becomes itself active. Wherefore also man himself is rightly said to believe and repent by virtue of that grace received.

Article 13. The manner of this operation cannot be fully comprehended by believers in this life. Nevertheless, they are satisfied to know and experience that by this grace of God they are enabled to believe with the heart and to love their Savior.

Article 14. Faith is therefore to be considered as the gift of God, not on account of its being offered by God to man, to be accepted or rejected at his pleasure, but because it is in reality conferred upon him, breathed and infused into him; nor even because God bestows the power or ability to believe, and then expects that man should by the exercise of his own free will consent to the terms of salvation and actually believe in Christ, but because He who works in man both to will and to work, and indeed all things in all, produces both the will to believe and the act of believing also.

Article 15. God is under no obligation to confer this grace upon any; for how can He be indebted to one who had no previous gifts to bestow as a foundation for such recompense? Nay, how can He be indebted to one who has nothing of his own but sin and falsehood? He, therefore, who becomes the subject of this grace owes eternal gratitude to God, and gives Him thanks forever. Whoever is not made partaker thereof is either altogether regardless of these spiritual gifts and satisfied with his own condition, or is in no apprehension of danger, and vainly boasts the possession of that which he has not. Further, with respect to those who outwardly profess their faith and amend their lives, we are bound, after the example of the apostle, to judge and speak of them in the most favorable manner; for the secret recesses of the heart are unknown to us. And as to others who have not yet been called, it is our duty to pray for them to God, who calls the things that are not as if they were. But we are in no wise to conduct ourselves towards them with haughtiness, as if we had made ourselves to differ.

Article 16. But as man by the fall did not cease to be a creature endowed with understanding and will, nor did sin which pervaded the whole race of mankind deprive him of the human nature, but brought upon him depravity and spiritual death; so also this grace of regeneration does not treat men as senseless stocks and blocks, nor take away their will and its properties, or do violence thereto; but it spiritually quickens, heals, corrects, and at the same time sweetly and powerfully bends it, that where carnal rebellion and resistance formerly prevailed, a ready and sincere spiritual obedience begins to reign; in which the true and spiritual restoration and freedom of our will consist. Wherefore, unless the admirable Author of every good work so deal with us, man can have no hope of being able to rise from his fall by his own free will, by which, in a state of innocence, he plunged himself into ruin.

Article 17. As the almighty operation of God whereby He brings forth and supports this our natural life does not exclude but require the use of means by which God, of His infinite mercy and goodness, has chosen to exert His influence, so also the aforementioned supernatural operation of God by which we are regenerated in no wise excludes or subverts the use of the gospel, which the most wise God has ordained to be the seed of regeneration and food of the soul. Wherefore, as the apostles and the teachers who succeeded them piously instructed the people concerning this grace of God, to His glory and to the abasement of all pride, and in the meantime, however, neglected not to keep them, by the holy admonitions of the gospel, under the influence of the Word, the sacraments, and ecclesiastical discipline; so even now it should be far from those who give or receive instruction in the Church to presume to tempt God by separating what He of His good pleasure has most intimately joined together. For grace is conferred by means of admonitions;

CANONS OF DORT (continued)

and the more readily we perform our duty, the more clearly this favor of God, working in us, usually manifests itself, and the more directly His work is advanced; to whom alone all the glory, both for the means and for their saving fruit and efficacy, is forever due. Amen.

REJECTION OF ERRORS

The true doctrine having been explained, the Synod rejects the errors of those:

Paragraph 1. Who teach: That it cannot properly be said that original sin in itself suffices to condemn the whole human race or to deserve temporal and eternal punishment.

For these contradict the apostle, who declares: *Therefore, as through one man sin entered into the world, and death through sin; and so death passed unto all men, for that all sinned* (Rom. 5:12). And: *The judgment came of one unto condemnation* (Rom. 5:16). And: *The wages of sin is death* (Rom. 6:23).

Paragraph 2. Who teach: That the spiritual gifts or the good qualities and virtues, such as goodness, holiness, righteousness, could not belong to the will of man when he was first created, and that these, therefore, cannot have been separated therefrom in the fall.

For such is contrary to the description of the image of God which the apostle gives in Eph. 4:24, where he declares that it consists in righteousness and holiness, which undoubtedly belong to the will.

Paragraph 3. Who teach: That in spiritual death the spiritual gifts are not separate from the will of man, since the will in itself has never been corrupted, but only hindered through the darkness of the understanding and the irregularity of the affections; and that, these hindrances having been removed, the will can then bring into operation its native powers, that is, that the will of itself is able to will and to choose, or not to will and not to choose, all manner of good which may be presented to it.

This is an innovation and an error, and tends to elevate the powers of the free will, contrary to the declaration of the prophet: *The heart is deceitful above all things, and it is exceedingly corrupt* (Jer. 17:9); and of the apostle: *Among whom* (sons of disobedience) *we also all once lived in the lusts of our flesh, doing the desires of the flesh and of the mind* (Eph. 2:3).

Paragraph 4. Who teach: That the unregenerate man is not really nor utterly dead in sin, nor destitute of all powers unto spiritual good, but that he can yet hunger and thirst after righteousness and life, and offer the sacrifice of a contrite and broken spirit, which is pleasing to God.

For these things are contrary to the express testimony of Scripture: *Ye were dead through your trespasses and sins* (Eph. 2:1, 5). And: *Every imagination of the thoughts of his heart was only evil continually* (Gen.

6:5; 8:21). Moreover, to hunger and thirst after deliverance from misery and after life, and to offer unto God the sacrifice of a broken spirit, is peculiar to the regenerate and those that are called blessed (Ps. 51:17; Matt. 5:6).

Paragraph 5. Who teach: That the corrupt and natural man can so well use the common grace (by which they understand the light of nature), or the gifts still left him after the fall, that he can gradually gain by their good use a greater, that is, the evangelical or saving grace, and salvation itself; and that in this way God on His part shows Himself ready to reveal Christ unto all men, since He applies to all sufficiently and efficiently the means necessary to conversion.

For both the experience of all ages and the Scriptures testify that this is untrue. *He showeth his word unto Jacob, his statutes and his ordances unto Israel. He hath not dealt so with any nation; and as for his ordinances, they have not known them* (Ps. 147:19, 20). *Who in the generations gone by suffered all the nations to walk in their own way* (Acts 14:16). And: *And they* (Paul and his companions) *having been forbidden of the Holy Spirit to speak the word in Asia, when they were come over against Mysia, they assayed to go into Bithynia, and the Spirit of Jesus suffered them not* (Acts 16:6,7).

Paragraph 6. Who teach: That in the true conversion of man no new qualities, powers, or gifts can be infused by God into the will, and that therefore faith, through which we are first converted and because of which we are called believers, is not a quality or gift infused by God but only an act of man, and that it cannot be said to be a gift, except in respect of the power to attain to this faith.

For thereby they contradict the Holy Scriptures, which declare that God infuses new qualities of faith, of obedience, and of the consciousness of His love into our hearts: *I will put my law in their inward parts, and in their heart will I write it* (Jer. 31:33). And: *I will pour water upon him that is thirsty, and streams upon the dry ground; I will pour my Spirit upon thy seed* (Is. 44:3). And: *The love of God hath been shed abroad in our hearts through the Holy Spirit which was given unto us* (Rom. 5:5). This is also repugnant to the constant practice of the Church, which prays by the mouth of the prophet thus: *Turn thou me, and I shall be turned* (Jer. 31:18).

Paragraph 7. Who teach: That the grace whereby we are converted to God is only a gentle advising, or (as others explain it) that this is the noblest manner of working in the conversion of man, and that this manner of working, which consists in advising, is most in harmony with man's nature; and that there is no reason why this advising grace alone should not be sufficient to make the natural man spiritual; indeed, that God does not produce the consent of the will except through this manner of advising; and that the power of the divine working, whereby it surpasses the working of Satan, consists in this that God promises eternal, while Satan promises only temporal goods.

But this is altogether Pelagian and contrary to the whole Scripture, which, besides this, teaches yet another and far more powerful and divine manner of the Holy Spirit's working in the conversion of man, as in Ezekiel: *A new heart also will I give you, and a new spirit will I put within you; and I will take away the stony heart out of your flesh, and I will give you a heart of flesh* (Ezek. 36:26).

Paragraph 8. Who teach: That God in the regeneration of man does not use such powers of His omnipotence as potently and infallibly bend man's will to faith and conversion; but that all the works of grace having been accomplished, which God employs to convert man, man may yet so resist God and the Holy Spirit, when God intends man's regeneration and wills to regenerate him, and indeed that man often does so resist that he prevents entirely his regeneration, and that it therefore remains in man's power to be regenerated or not.

For this is nothing less than the denial of all the efficiency of God's grace in our conversion, and the subjecting of the working of Almighty God to the will of man, which is contrary to the apostles, who teach that *we believe according to the working of the strength of his might* (Eph. 1:19); and that *God fulfils every desire of goodness and every work of faith with power* (2 Thess. 1:11); and that *his divine power hath granted unto us all things that pertain unto life and godliness* (2 Peter 1:3).

Paragraph 9. Who teach: That grace and free will are partial causes which together work the beginning of conversion, and that grace, in order of working, does not precede the working of the will; that is, that God does not efficiently help the will of man unto conversion until the will of man moves and determines to do this.

For the ancient Church has long ago condemned this doctrine of the Pelagians according to the words of the apostle: *So then it is not of him that willeth, nor of him that runneth, but of God that hath mercy* (Rom. 9:16). Likewise: *For who maketh thee to differ? and what hast thou that thou didst not receive?* (I Cor. 4:7). And: *For it is God who worketh in you both to will and to work, for his good pleasure* (Phil. 2:13).

FIFTH HEAD OF DOCTRINE. THE PERSEVERANCE OF THE SAINTS

Article 1. Those whom God, according to His purpose, calls to the communion of His Son, our Lord Jesus Christ, and regenerates by the Holy Spirit, He also delivers from the dominion and slavery of sin, though in this life He does not deliver them altogether from the body of sin and from the infirmities of the flesh.

Article 2. Hence spring forth the daily sins of infirmity, and blemishes cleave even to the best works of the saints. These are to them a perpetual reason to humiliate themselves before God and to flee for refuge to Christ crucified; to mortify the flesh more and more by the spirit of prayer and by holy exercises of piety; and to press forward to the goal of perfection, until at length, delivered from this body of death, they shall reign with the Lamb of God in heaven.

Article 3. By reason of these remains of indwelling sin, and also because the temptations of the world and of Satan, those who are converted could not persevere in that grace if left to their own strength. But God is faithful, who, having conferred grace, mercifully confirms and powerfully preserves them therein, even to the end.

Article 4. Although the weakness of the flesh cannot prevail against the power of God, who confirms and preserves true believers in a state of grace, yet converts are not always so influenced and actuated by the Spirit of God as not in some particular instances sinfully to deviate from the guidance of divine grace, so as to be seduced by and to comply with the lusts of the flesh; they must, therefore, be constant in watching and prayer, that they may not be led into temptation. When these are neglected, they are not only liable to be drawn into great and heinous sins by the flesh, the world, and Satan, but sometimes by the righteous permission of God actually are drawn into these evils. This, the lamentable fall of David, Peter, and other saints described in Holy Scripture, demonstrates.

Article 5. By such enormous sins, however, they very highly offend God, incur a deadly guilt, grieve the Holy Spirit, interrupt the exercise of faith, very grievously wound their consciences, and sometimes for a while lose the sense of God's favor, until, when they change their course by serious repentance, the light of God's fatherly countenance again shines upon them.

Article 6. But God, who is rich in mercy, according to His unchangeable purpose of election, does not wholly withdraw the Holy Spirit from His own people even in their grievous falls; nor suffers them to proceed so far as to lose the grace of adoption and forfeit the state of justification, or to commit the sin unto death or against the Holy Spirit; nor does He permit them to be totally deserted, and to plunge themselves into everlasting destruction.

Article 7. For in the first place, in these falls He preserves in them the incorruptible seed of regeneration from perishing or being totally lost; and again, by His Word and Spirit He certainly and effectually renews them to repentance, to a sincere and godly sorrow for their sins, that they may seek and obtain remission in the blood of the Mediator, may again experience the favor of a reconciled God, through faith adore His mercies, and henceforward more diligently work out their own salvation with fear and trembling.

Article 8. Thus it is not in consequence of their own merits or strength, but of God's free mercy, that they neither totally fall from faith and grace nor

CANONS OF DORT (continued)

continue and perish finally in their backslidings; which, with respect to themselves is not only possible, but would undoubtedly happen; but with respect to God, it is utterly impossible, since His counsel cannot be changed nor His promise fail; neither can the call according to His purpose be revoked, nor the merit, intercession, and preservation of Christ be rendered ineffectual, nor the sealing of the Holy Spirit be frustrated or obliterated.

Article 9. Of this preservation of the elect to salvation and of their preseverance in the faith, true believers themselves may and do obtain assurance according to the measure of their faith, whereby they surely believe that they are and ever will continue true and living members of the Church, and that they have the forgiveness of sins and life eternal.

Article 10. This assurance, however, is not produced by any peculiar revelation contrary to or independent of the Word of God, but springs from faith in God's promises, which He has most abundantly revealed in His Word for our comfort; from the testimony of the Holy Spirit, witnessing with our spirit that we are children and heirs of God (Rom. 8:16); and lastly, from a serious and holy desire to preserve a good conscience and to perform good works. And if the elect of God were deprived of this solid comfort that they shall finally obtain the victory, and of this infallible pledge of eternal glory, they would be of all men the most miserable.

Article 11. The Scripture moreover testifies that believers in this life have to struggle with various carnal doubts, and that under grievous temptations they do not always feel this full assurance of faith and certainty of persevering. But God, who is the Father of all consolation, does not suffer them to be tempted above that they are able, but will with the temptation make also the way of escape, that they may be able to endure it (1 Cor. 10:13), and by the Holy Spirit again inspires them with the comfortable assurance of persevering.

Article 12. This certainty of perseverance, however, is so far from exciting in believers a spirit of pride, or of rendering them carnally secure, that on the contrary it is the real source of humility, filial reverence, true piety, patience in every tribulation, fervent prayers, constancy in suffering and in confessing the truth, and of solid rejoicing in God; so that the consideration of this benefit should serve as an incentive to the serious and constant practice of gratitude and good works, as appears from the testimonies of Scripture and the examples of the saints.

Article 13. Neither does renewed confidence of persevering produce licentiousness or a disregard of piety in those who are recovered from backsliding; but it renders them much more careful and solicitous to continue in the ways of the Lord, which He has ordained, that they who walk therein may keep the assurance of persevering; lest, on account of their abuse of His fatherly kindness, God should turn away His gracious countenance from them (to behold which is to the godly dearer than life, and the withdrawal of which is more bitter than death) and they in consequence thereof should fall into more grievous torments of conscience.

Article 14. And as it has pleased God, by the preaching of the gospel, to begin this work of grace in us, so He preserves, continues, and perfects it by the hearing and reading of His Word, by meditation thereon, and by the exhortations, threatenings, and promises thereof, and by the use of the sacraments.

Article 15. The carnal mind is unable to comprehend this doctrine of the perseverance of the saints and the certainty thereof, which God has most abundantly revealed in His Word, for the glory of His Name and the consolation of pious souls, and which He impresses upon the hearts of the believers. Satan abhors it, the world ridicules it, the ignorant and hypocritical abuse it, and the heretics oppose it. But the bride of Christ has always most tenderly loved and constantly defended it as an inestimable treasure; and God, against whom neither counsel nor strength can prevail, will dispose her so to continue to the end. Now to this one God, Father, Son, and Holy Spirit, be honor and glory forever. Amen.

REJECTION OF ERRORS

The true doctrine having been explained, the Synod rejects the errors of those:

Paragraph 1. Who teach: That the perseverance of the true believers is not a fruit of election, or a gift of God gained by the death of Christ, but a condition of the new covenant, which (as they declare) man before his decisive election and justification must fulfil through his free will.

For the Holy Scripture testifies that this follows out of election, and is given the elect in virtue of the death, the resurrection, and intercession of Christ: *But the election obtained it, and the rest were hardened* (Rom. 11:7). Likewise: *He that spared not his own Son, but delivered him up for us all, how shall he not also with him freely give us all things? Who shall lay anything to the charge of God's elect? It is God that justifieth; who is he that condemneth? It is Christ Jesus that died, yea rather, that was raised from the dead, who is at the right hand of God, who also maketh intercession for us. Who shall separate us from the love of Christ?* (Rom. 8:32-35).

Paragraph 2. Who teach: That God does indeed provide the believer with sufficient powers to persevere, and is ever ready to preserve these in him if he will do his duty; but that, though all things which are necessary to persevere in faith and which God will use to preserve faith are made use of, even then it ever depends on the pleasure of the will whether it will persevere or not.

For this idea contains an outspoken Pelagianism, and while it would make men free, it makes them robbers of God's honor, contrary to the prevailing agreement of the evangelical doctrine, which takes from man all cause of boasting, and ascribes all the praise for this favor to the grace of God alone; and contrary to the apostle, who declares that it is God, *who shall also confirm you unto the end*, that ye be *unreprovable in the day of our Lord Jesus Christ* (1 Cor. 1:8).

Paragraph 3. Who teach: That the true believers and regenerate not only can fall from justifying faith and likewise from grace and salvation wholly and to the end, but indeed often do fall from this and are lost forever.

For this conception makes powerless the grace, justification, regeneration, and continued preservation by Christ, contrary to the expressed words of the apostle Paul: *That, while we were yet sinners, Christ died for us. Much more then, being now justified by his blood, shall we be saved from the wrath* of God *through him* (Rom. 5:8, 9). And contrary to the apostle John: *Whosoever is begotten of God doeth no sin, because his seed abideth in him; and he can not sin, because he is begotten of God* (1 John 3:9). And also contrary to the words of Jesus Christ: *I give unto them eternal life; and they shall never perish, and no one shall snatch them out of my hand. My Father, who hath given* them *to me, is greater than all; and no one is able to snatch* them *out of the Father's hand* (John 10:28, 29).

Paragraph 4. Who teach: That true believers and regenerate can sin the sin unto death or against the Holy Spirit.

Since the same apostle John, after having spoken in the fifth chapter of his first epistle, vs. 16 and 17, of those who sin unto death and having forbidden to pray for them, immediately adds to this in vs. 18: *We know that whosoever is begotten of God sinneth not* (meaning a sin of that character), *but he that was begotten of God keepeth himself, and the evil one toucheth him not* (1 John 5:18).

Paragraph 5. Who teach: That without a special revelation we can have no certainty of future perseverance in this life.

For by this doctrine the sure comfort of the true believers is taken away in this life, and the doubts of the papist are again introduced into the Church, while the Holy Scriptures constantly deduce this assurance, not from a special and extraordinary revelation, but from the marks proper to the children of God and from the very constant promises of God. So especially the apostle Paul: *No creature shall be able to separate us from the love of God, which is in Christ Jesus our Lord* (Rom. 8:39). And John declares: *And he that keepeth his commandments abideth in him, and he in him. And hereby we know that he abideth in us, by the Spirit which he gave us* (1 John 3:24).

Paragraph 6. Who teach: That the doctrine of the certainty of perseverance and of salvation from its own character and nature is a cause of indolence and is injurious to godliness, good morals, prayers, and other holy exercises, but that on the contrary it is praiseworthy to doubt.

For these show that they do not know the power of divine grace and the working of the indwelling Holy Spirit. And they contradict the apostle John, who teaches the opposite with express words in his first epistle: *Beloved, now are we children of God, and it is not yet made manifest what we shall be. We know that, if he shall be manifested, we shall be like him; for we shall see him even as he is. And every one that hath this hope* set *on him purifieth himself, even as he is pure* (1 John 3:2, 3). Furthermore, these are contradicted by the example of the saints, both of the Old and the New Testament, who though they were assured of their perseverance and salvation, were nevertheless constant in prayers and other exercises of godliness.

Paragraph 7. Who teach: That the faith of those who believe for a time does not differ from justifying and saving faith except only in duration.

For Christ Himself, in Matt. 13:20, Luke 8:13, and in other places, evidently notes, besides this duration, a threefold difference between those who believe only for a time and true believers, when He declares that the former receive the seed in stony ground, but the latter in the good ground or heart; that the former are without root, but the latter have a firm root; that the former are without fruit, but that the latter bring forth their fruit in various measure, with constancy and stedfastness.

Paragraph 8. Who teach: That it is not absurd that one having lost his first regeneration is again and even often born anew.

For these deny by this doctrine the incorruptibleness of the seed of God, whereby we are born again; contrary to the testimony of the apostle Peter: *Having been begotten again, not of corruptible seed, but of incorruptible* (Peter 1-23).

Paragraph 9. Who teach: That Christ has in no place prayed that believers should infallibly continue in faith.

For they contradict Christ Himself, who says: *I made supplication for thee* (Simon), *that thy faith fail not* (Luke 22:32), and the evangelist John, who declares that Christ has not prayed for the apostles only, but also for those who through their word would believe: *Holy Father, keep them in thy name*, and: *I pray not that thou shouldest take them from the world, but that thou shouldest keep them from the evil one* (John 17:11, 15, 20).

CONCLUSION

And this is the perspicuous, simple, and ingenuous declaration of the orthodox doctrine respecting the five articles which have been controverted in the Belgic Churches; and the rejection of the errors, with which they have for some time been troubled. This doctrine the Synod judges to be drawn from the Word of God, and to be agreeable to the confession of the Reformed Churches.

CANONS OF DORT (continued)

Whence it clearly appears that some, whom such conduct by no means became, have violated all truth, equity, and charity, in wishing to persuade the public:

'That the doctrine of the Reformed Churches concerning predestination, and the points annexed to it, by its own genius and necessary tendency, leads off the minds of men from all piety and religion; that it is an opiate administered by the flesh and the devil; and the stronghold of Satan, where he lies in wait for all, and from which he wounds multitudes, and mortally strikes through many with the darts both of despair and security; that it makes God the author of sin, unjust, tyrannical, hypocritical; that it is nothing more than an interpolated Stoicism, Manicheism, Libertinism, Turcism; that it renders men carnally secure, since they are persuaded by it that nothing can hinder the salvation of the elect, let them live as they please; and, therefore, that they may safely perpetrate every species of the most atrocious crimes; and that, if the reprobate should even perform truly all the works of the saints, their obedience would not in the least contribute to their salvation; that the same doctrine teaches that God, by a mere arbitrary act of his will, without the least respect or view to any sin, has predestinated the greatest part of the world to eternal damnation, and has created them for this very purpose; that in the same manner in which the election is the fountain and cause of faith and good works, reprobation is the cause of unbelief and impiety; that many children of the faithful are torn, guiltless, from their mothers' breasts, and tyrannically plunged into hell: so that neither baptism nor the prayers of the Church at their baptism can at all profit them;' and many other things of the same kind which the Reformed Churches not only do not acknowledge, but even detest with their whole soul.

Wherefore, this Synod of Dort, in the name of the Lord, conjures as many as piously call upon the name of our Saviour Jesus Christ to judge of the faith of the Reformed Churches, not from the calumnies which on every side are heaped upon it, nor from the private expressions of a few among ancient and modern teachers, often dishonestly quoted, or corrupted and wrested to a meaning quite foreign to their intention; but from the public confessions of the Churches themselves, and from this declaration of the orthodox doctrine, confirmed by the unanimous consent of all and each of the members of the whole Synod. Moreover, the Synod warns calumniators themselves to consider the terrible judgment of God which awaits them, for bearing false witness against the confessions of so many Churches; for distressing the consciences of the weak; and for laboring to render suspected the society of the truly faithful.

Finally, this Synod exhorts all their brethren in the gospel of Christ to conduct themselves piously and religiously in handling this doctrine, both in the universities and churches; to direct it, as well in discourse as in writing, to the glory of the Divine name, to holiness of life, and to the consolation of afflicted souls; to regulate, by the Scripture, according to the analogy of faith, not only their sentiments, but also their language, and to abstain from all those phrases which exceed the limits necessary to be observed in ascertaining the genuine sense of the Holy Scriptures, and may furnish insolent sophists with a just pretext for violently assailing, or even vilifying, the doctrine of the Reformed Churches.

May Jesus Christ, the Son of God, who, seated at the Father's right hand, gives gifts to men, sanctify us in the truth; bring to the truth those who err; shut the mouths of the calumniators of sound doctrine, and endue the faithful ministers of his Word with the spirit of wisdom and discretion, that all their discourses may tend to the glory of God, and the edification of those who hear them. Amen.

Notes: *The Canons of Dort were issued by a synod of the Reformed Church in the Netherlands that met from November 13, 1618, through May 9, 1619. Among the items considered at that synod were the opinions of Jacob Arminius, who had sought to introduce a place for human free-will into the Calvinist theological system. He had proposed these basic ideas: 1) God's foreknowledge as prior to his predestination; 2) partial human depravity; 3) the universality of Christ's atonement; 4) the resistibility of God's grace; and 5) the possibility that a person could fall away from saving grace once received.*

The Synod of Dort (or Dordrecht) responded by declaring faith in 1) God's total and unconditional predestination; 2) complete and utter human depravity; 3) Christ's atonement limited to the saved; 4) the irresistible nature of God's grace; and 5) the guaranteed perseverance of believers. The so-called five points of the synod have frequently been summarized for theological students in a manner appropriate to the Dutch origin of the Canons:

T   Total Depravity
U   Unconditional election (predestination)
L   Limited atonement
I   Irresistible grace
P   Perseverance of the saints

The text of the Canons reproduced here was taken from A Treatise of the Compendium *by G. H. Kersten (Grand Rapids, MI: Inheritance Publishing Co., 1956).*

*   *   *

SECOND HELVETIC CONFESSION (HUNGARIAN REFORMED CHURCH)

CHAPTER 1. OF THE HOLY SCRIPTURE BEING THE TRUE WORD OF GOD

CANONICAL SCRIPTURE. We believe and confess the canonical Scriptures of the holy prophets and apostles of both Testaments to be the true Word of God, and to have sufficient authority of themselves, not of men. For God himself spoke to the fathers, prophets, apostles, and still speaks to us through the Holy Scriptures.

And in this Holy Scripture, the universal Church of Christ has the most complete exposition of all that pertains to a saving faith, and also to the framing of a life acceptable to God; and in this respect it is expressly commanded by God that nothing be either added to or taken from the same.

SCRIPTURE TEACHES FULLY ALL GOD-LINESS. We judge, therefore, that from these Scriptures are to be derived true wisdom and godliness, the reformation and government of churches; as also instruction in all duties of piety; and, to be short, the confirmation of doctrines, and the rejection of all errors, moreover, all exhortations according to that word of the apostle, "All Scripture is inspired by God and profitable for teaching, for reproof," etc. (II Tim. 3:16-17). Again, "I am writing these instructions to you," says the apostle to Timothy, "so that you may know how one ought to behave in the household of God," etc. (I Tim. 3:14-15). *Scripture Is the Word of God*. Again, the selfsame apostle to the Thessalonians: "When," says he, "you received the Word of God which you heard from us, you accepted it, not as the word of men but as what it really is, the Word of God," etc. (I Thess. 2:13). For the Lord himself has said in the Gospel, "It is not you who speak, but the Spirit of my Father speaking through you"; therefore "he who hears you hears me, and he who rejects me rejects him who sent me" (Matt. 10:20; Luke 10:16; John 13:20).

THE PREACHING OF THE WORD OF GOD IS THE WORD OF GOD. Wherefore when this Word of God is now preached in the church by preachers lawfully called, we believe that the very Word of God is proclaimed, and received by the faithful; and that neither any other Word of God is to be invented nor is to be expected from heaven: and that now the Word itself which is preached is to be regarded, not the minister that preaches; for even if he be evil and a sinner, nevertheless the Word of God remains still true and good.

Neither do we think that therefore the outward preaching is to be thought as fruitless because the instruction in true religion depends on the inward illumination of the Spirit, or because it is written "And no longer shall each man teach his neighbor . . . , for they shall all know me" (Jer. 31:34), and "Neither he who plants nor he who waters is anything, but only God who gives the growth" (I Cor. 3:7). For although "no one can come to Christ unless he be drawn by the Father" (John 6:44), and unless the Holy Spirit inwardly illumines him, yet we know that it is surely the will of God that his Word should be preached outwardly also. God could indeed, by his Holy Spirit, or by the ministry of an angel, without the ministry of St. Peter, have taught Cornelius in the Acts; but, nevertheless, he refers him to Peter, of whom the angel speaking says, "He shall tell you what you ought to do."

INWARD ILLUMINATION DOES NOT ELIMINATE EXTERNAL PREACHING. For he that illuminates inwardly by giving men the Holy Spirit, the same one, by way of commandment, said unto his disciples, "Go into all the world, and preach the Gospel to the whole creation" (Mark 16:15). And so in Philippi, Paul preached the Word outwardly to Lydia, a seller of purple goods; but the Lord inwardly opened the woman's heart (Acts 16:14).

And the same Paul, after a beautiful development of his thought, in Rom. 10:17 at length comes to the conclusion. "So faith comes from hearing, and hearing from the Word of God by the preaching of Christ."

At the same time we recognize that God can illuminate whom and when he will, even without the external ministry, for that is in his power: but we speak of the usual way of instructing men, delivered unto us from God, both by commandment and examples.

HERESIES. We therefore detest all the heresies of Artemon, the Manichaeans, the Valentinians, of Cerdon, and the Marcionites, who denied that the Scriptures proceeded from the Holy Spirit; or did not accept some parts of them, or interpolated and corrupted them.

APOCRYPHA. And yet we do not conceal the fact that certain books of the Old Testament were by the ancient authors called *Apocryphal*, and by others *Ecclesiastical*; inasmuch as some would have them read in the churches, but not advanced as an authority from which the faith is to be established. As Augstine also, in his *De Civitate Dei*, book 18, ch. 38, remarks that "in the books of the Kings, the names and books of certain prophets are cited"; but he adds that "they are not in the canon"; and that "those books which we have suffice unto godliness."

CHAPTER II. OF INTERPRETING THE HOLY SCRIPTURES; AND OF FATHERS, COUNCILS, AND TRADITIONS

THE TRUE INTERPRETATION OF SCRIPTURE. The apostle Peter has said that the Holy Scriptures are not of private interpretation (II Peter 1:20), and thus we do not allow all possible interpretations. Nor consequently do we acknowledge as the true or genuine interpretation of the Scriptures what is called the conception of the Roman Church, that is, what the defenders of the Roman Church plainly maintain should be thrust upon all for acceptance. But we hold that interpretation of the Scripture to be orthodox and genuine which is gleaned from the Scriptures themselves (from the nature of the language in which they were written, likewise according to the circumstances in which they were set down, and expounded in the light of like and unlike passages and of many and clearer passages) and which agree with the rule of faith and love, and contributes much to the glory of God and man's salvation.

INTERPRETATIONS OF THE HOLY FATHERS. Wherefore we do not despise the interpretations of the holy Greek and Latin fathers, nor reject their disputations and treatises concerning sacred matters as far as they agree with the Scriptures; but we modestly dissent from them when they are found to set down things differing from, or altogether contrary to, the Scriptures. Neither do we think that we do them any wrong in this matter; seeing that they all, with one consent, will not have their writings equated with the canonical Scriptures, but command us to prove how far they agree or disagree with them, and to accept what is in agreement and to reject what is in disagreement.

COUNCILS. And in the same order also we place the decrees and canons of councils.

Wherefore we do not permit ourselves, in controversies about religion or matters of faith, to urge our case with only the opinions of the fathers or decrees of councils; much less by received customs, or by the large number of those who share the same opinion, or by the prescription of a long time. *Who is the Judge*? Therefore, we do not admit any other judge than God himself, who proclaims by the Holy Scriptures what is true, what is false, what is to be followed, or what to be avoided. So we do assent to the judgments of spiritual men which are drawn from the Word of God. Certainly Jeremiah and other prophets vehemently condemned the assemblies of priests which were set up against the law of God; and diligently admonished us that we should not listen to the fathers, or tread in their path who, walking in their own inventions, swerved from the law of God.

TRADITIONS OF MEN. Likewise we reject human traditions, even if they be adorned with high-sounding titles, as though they were divine and apostolical, delivered to the Church by the living voice of the apostles, and, as it were, through the hands of apostolical men to succeeding bishops which, when compared with the Scriptures, disagree with them; and by their disagreement show that they are not apostolic at all. For as the apostles did not contradict themselves in doctrine, so the apostolic men did not set forth things contrary to the apostles. On the contrary, it would be wicked to assert that the apostles by a living voice delivered anything contrary to their writings. Paul affirms expressly that he taught the same things in all churches (I Cor. 4:17). And, again, "For we write you nothing but what you can read and understand" (II Cor. 1:13). Also, in another place, he testifies that he and his disciples— that is, apostolic men—walked in the same way, and jointly by the same Spirit did all things (II Cor. 12:18). Moreover, the Jews in former times had the traditions of their elders; but these traditions were severely rejected by the Lord, indicating that the keeping of them hinders God's law, and that God is worshipped in vain by such traditions (Matt. 15:1 ff.; Mark 7:1 ff.).

CHAPTER III. OF GOD, HIS UNITY AND TRINITY

GOD IS ONE. We believe and teach that God is one in essence or nature, subsisting in himself, all sufficient in himself, invisible, incorporeal, immense, eternal, Creator of all things both visible and invisible, the greatest good, living, quickening and preserving all things, omnipotent and supremely wise, kind and merciful, just and true. Truly we

detest many gods because it is expressly written: "The Lord your God is one Lord" (Deut. 6:4). "I am the Lord your God. You shall have no other gods before me" (Ex. 20:2-3). "I am the Lord, and there is no other god besides me. Am I not the Lord, and there is no other God beside me? A righteous God and a Savior; there is none besides me" (Isa. 45:5, 21). "The Lord, the Lord, a God merciful and gracious, slow to anger, and abounding in steadfast love and faithfulness" (Ex. 34:6).

GOD IS THREE. Notwithstanding we believe and teach that the same immense, one and indivisible God is in person inseparably and without confusion distinguished as Father, Son and Holy Spirit so, as the Father has begotten the Son from eternity, the Son is begotten by an ineffable generation, and the Holy Spirit truly proceeds from them both, and the same from eternity and is to be worshipped with both. Thus there are not three gods, but three persons, consubstantial, coeternal, and coequal; distinct with respect to hypostases, and with respect to order, the one preceding the other yet without any inequality. For according to the nature or essence they are so joined together that they are one God, and the divine nature is common to the Father, Son and Holy Spirit.

For Scripture has delivered to us a manifest distinction of persons, the angel saying, among other things, to the Blessed Virgin, "The Holy Spirit will come upon you, and the power of the Most High will overshadow you; therefore the child to be born will be called holy, the Son of God" (Luke 1:35). And also in the baptism of Christ a voice is heard from heaven concerning Christ, saying, "This is my beloved Son" (Matt. 3:17). The Holy Spirit also appeared in the form of a dove. (John 1:32.) And when the Lord himself commanded the apostles to baptize, he commanded them to baptize "in the name of the Father, and the Son, and the Holy Spirit" (Matt. 28:19). Elsewhere in the Gospel he said: "The Father will send the Holy Spirit in my name" (John 14:26), and again he said: "When the Counselor comes, whom I shall send to you from the Father, even the Spirit of truth, who proceeds from the Father, he will bear witness to me," etc. (John 15:26). In short, we receive the Apostles' Creed because it delivers to us the true faith.

HERESIES. Therefore we condemn the Jews and Mohammedans, and all those who blaspheme that sacred and adorable Trinity. We also condemn all heresies and heretics who teach that the Son and Holy Spirit are God in name only, and also that there is something created and subservient, or subordinate to another in the Trinity, and that there is something unequal in it, a greater or a less, something corporeal or corporeally conceived, something different with respect to character or will, something mixed or solitary, as if the Son and Holy Spirit were the affections and properties of one God the Father, as the Monarchians, Novatians, Praxeas, Patripassians, Sabellius, Paul of Samosata, Aëtius,

Macedonius, Anthropomorphites, Arius, and such like, have thought.

CHAPTER IV. OF IDOLS OR IMAGES OF GOD, CHRIST AND THE SAINTS

IMAGES OF GOD. Since God as Spirit is in essence invisible and immense, he cannot really be expressed by any art or image. For this reason we have no fear pronouncing with Scripture that images of God are mere lies. Therefore we reject not only the idols of the Gentiles, but also the images of Christians. *Images of Christ.* Although Christ assumed human nature, yet he did not on that account assume it in order to provide a model for carvers and painters. He denied that he had come "to abolish the law and the prophets" (Matt. 5:17). But images are forbidden by the law and the prophets (Deut. 4:15; Isa. 44:9). He denied that his bodily presence would be profitable for the Church, and promised that he would be near us by his Spirit forever (John 16:7). Who, therefore, would believe that a shadow or likeness of his body would contribute any benefit to the pious? (II Cor. 5:5). Since he abides in us by his Spirit, we are therefore the temple of God (I Cor. 3:16). But "what agreement has the temple of God with idols?" (II Cor. 6:16). *Images of Saints.* And since the blessed spirits and saints in heaven, while they lived here on earth, rejected all worship of themselves (Acts 3:12 f.; 14: 11 ff.; Rev. 14:7; 22:9) and condemned images, shall anyone find it likely that the heavenly saints and angels are pleased with their own images before which men kneel, uncover their heads, and bestow other honors?

But in fact in order to instruct men in religion and to remind them of divine things and of their salvation, the Lord commanded the preaching of the Gospel (Mark 16:15)—not to paint and to teach the laity by means of pictures. Moreover, he instituted sacraments, but nowhere did he set up images. *The Scriptures of the Laity.* Furthermore, wherever we turn our eyes, we see the living and true creatures of God which, if they be observed, as is proper, make a much more vivid impression on the beholders than all the images or vain, motionless, feeble and dead pictures made by men, of which the prophet truly said: "They have eyes, but do not see" (Ps. 115:5).

LACTANTIUS. Therefore we approved the judgment of Lactantius, an ancient writer, who says: "Undoubtedly no religion exists where there is an image." *Epiphanius and Jerome.* We also assert that the blessed bishop Epiphanius did right when, finding on the doors of a church a veil on which was painted a picture supposedly of Christ or some saint, he ripped it down and took it away, because to see a picture of a man hanging in the Church of Christ was contrary to the authority of Scripture. Wherefore he charged that from henceforth no such veils, which were contrary to our religion, should be hung in the Church of Christ, and that rather such questionable things, unworthy of the Church of Christ and the faithful people, should be removed.

Moreover, we approve of this opinion of St. Augustine concerning true religion: "Let not the worship of the works of men be a religion for us. For the artists themselves who make such things are better; yet we ought not to worship them" (*De Vera Religione*, cap. 55).

CHAPTER V. OF THE ADORATION, WORSHIP AND INVOCATION OF GOD THROUGH THE ONLY MEDIATOR JESUS CHRIST

GOD ALONE IS TO BE ADORED AND WORSHIPPED. We teach that the true God alone is to be adored and worshipped. This honor we impart to none other, according to the commandment of the Lord, "You shall worship the Lord your God and him only shall you serve" (Matt. 4:10). Indeed, all the prophets severely inveighed against the people of Israel whenever they adored and worshipped strange gods, and not the only true God. But we teach that God is to be adored and worshipped as he himself has taught us to worship, namely, "in spirit and in truth" (John 4:23 f.), not with any superstition, but with sincerity, according to his Word; lest at any time he should say to us: "Who has required these things from your hands?" (Isa. 1:12; Jer. 6:20). For Paul also says: "God is not served by human hands, as though he needed anything," etc. (Acts 17:25).

GOD ALONE IS TO BE INVOKED THROUGH THE MEDIATION OF CHRIST ALONE. In all crises and trials of our life we call upon him alone, and that by the mediation of our only mediator and intercessor, Jesus Christ. For we have been explicitly commanded: "Call upon me in the day of trouble; I will deliver you, and you shall glorify me" (Ps. 1:15). Moreover, we have a most generous promise from the Lord Who said: "If you ask anything of the Father, he will give it to you" (John 16:23), and: "Come to me, all who labor and are heavy laden, and I will give you rest" (Matt. 11:28). And since it is written: "How are men to call upon him in whom they have not believed?" (Rom. 10:14), and since we do believe in God alone, we assuredly call upon him alone, and we do so through Christ. For as the apostle says, "There is one God and there is one mediator between God and men, the man Christ Jesus" (I Tim. 2:5), and, "If any one does sin, we have an advocate with the Father, Jesus Christ the righteous," etc. (I John 2:1).

THE SAINTS ARE NOT TO BE ADORED, WORSHIPPED OR INVOKED. For this reason we do not adore, worship, or pray to the saints in heaven, or to other gods, and we do not acknowledge them as our intercessors or mediators before the Father in heaven. For God and Christ the Mediator are sufficient for us; neither do we give to others the honor that is due to God alone and to his Son, because he has expressly said: "My glory I give to no other" (Isa. 42:8), and because Peter has said: "There is no other name under heaven given among men by which we must be saved," except the name of Christ

(Acts 4:12). In him, those who give their assent by faith do not seek anything outside Christ.

THE DUE HONOR TO BE RENDERED TO THE SAINTS. At the same time we do not despise the saints or think basely of them. For we acknowledge them to be living members of Christ and friends of God who have gloriously overcome the flesh and the world. Hence we love them as brothers, and also honor them; yet not with any kind of worship but by an honorable opinion of them and just praises of them. We also imitate them. For with ardent longings and supplications we earnestly desire to be imitators of their faith and virtues, to share eternal salvation with them, to dwell eternally with them in the presence of God, and to rejoice with them in Christ. And in this respect we approve of the opinion of St. Augustine in *De Vera Religione*: "Let not our religion be the cult of men who have died. For if they have lived holy lives, they are not to be thought of as seeking such honors; on the contrary, they want us to worship him by whose illumination they rejoice that we are fellow-servants of his merits. They are therefore to be honored by way of imitation, but not to be adored in a religious manner," etc.

RELICS OF THE SAINTS. Much less do we believe that the relics of the saints are to be adored and reverenced. Those ancient saints seemed to have sufficiently honored their dead when they decently committed their remains to the earth after the spirit had ascended on high. And they thought that the most noble relics of their ancestors were their virtues, their doctrine, and their faith. Moreover, as they commend these "relics" when praising the dead, so they strive to copy them during their life on earth.

SWEARING BY GOD'S NAME ALONE. These ancient men did not swear except by the name of the only God, Yahweh, as prescribed by the divine law. Therefore, as it is forbidden to swear by the names of strange gods (Ex. 23:13; Deut. 10:20), so we do not perform oaths to the saints that are demanded of us. We therefore reject in all these matters a doctrine that ascribes much too much to the saints in heaven.

CHAPTER VI. OF THE PROVIDENCE OF GOD

ALL THINGS ARE GOVERNED BY THE PROVIDENCE OF GOD. We believe that all things in heaven and on earth, and in all creatures, are preserved and governed by the providence of this wise, eternal and almighty God. For David testifies and says: "The Lord is high above all nations, and his glory above the heavens! Who is like the Lord our God, who is seated on high, who looks far down upon the heavens and the earth?" (Ps. 113:4 ff.). Again: "Thou searchest out . . . all my ways. Even before a word is on my tongue, lo, O Lord, Thou knowest it altogether" (Ps. 139:3 f.). Paul also testifies and declares: "In him we live and move and have our being" (Acts 17:28), and "from him and through him and to him are all things" (Rom.

11:36). Therefore Augustine most truly and according to Scripture declared in his book *De Agone Christi*, cap. 8, "The Lord said, 'Are not two sparrows sold for a penny? And not one of them will fall to the ground without your Father's will'" (Matt. 10:29). By speaking thus, he wanted to show that what men regard as of least value is governed by God's omnipotence. For he who is the truth says that the birds of the air are fed by him and the lilies of the field are clothed by him; he also says that the hairs of our head are numbered. (Matt. 6:26 ff.)

THE EPICUREANS. We therefore condemn the Epicureans who deny the providence of God, and all those who blasphemously say that God is busy with the heavens and neither sees nor cares about us and our affairs. David, the royal prophet, also condemned this when he said: "O Lord, how long shall the wicked exult? They say, 'The Lord does not see; the God of Jacob does not perceive.' Understand, O dullest of the people! Fools, when will you be wise? He who planted the ear, does he not hear? He who formed the eye, does he not see?" (Ps. 94:3, 7-9).

MEANS NOT TO BE DESPISED. Nevertheless, we do not spurn as useless the means by which divine providence works, but we teach that we are to adapt ourselves to them in so far as they are recommended to us in the Word of God. Wherefore we disapprove of the rash statements of those who say that if all things are managed by the providence of God, then our efforts and endeavors are in vain. It will be sufficient if we leave everything to the governance of divine providence, and we will not have to worry about anything or do anything. For although Paul understood that he sailed under the providence of God who had said to him: "You must bear witness also at Rome" (Acts 23:11), and in addition had given him the promise, "There will be no loss of life among you . . . and not a hair is to perish from the head of any of you" (Acts 27:22, 34), yet when the sailors were nevertheless thinking about abandoning ship the same Paul said to the centurion and the soldiers: "Unless these men stay in the ship, you cannot be saved" (Acts 27:31). For God, who has appointed to everything its end, has ordained the beginning and the means by which it reaches its goal. The heathen ascribe things to blind fortune and uncertain chance. But St. James does not want us to say: "Today or tomorrow we will go into such and such a town and trade," but adds: "Instead you ought to say, 'If the Lord wills, we shall live and we shall do this or that'" (James 4:13, 15). And Augustine says: "Everything which to vain men seems to happen in nature by accident, occurs only by his Word, because it happens only at his command" (*Enarrationes in Psalmos* 148). Thus it seemed to happen by mere chance when Saul, while seeking his father's asses, unexpectedly fell in with the prophet Samuel. But previously the Lord had said to the prophet: "Tomorrow I will send to you a man from the land of Benjamin" (I Sam. 9:16).

CHAPTER VII. OF THE CREATION OF ALL THINGS: OF ANGELS, THE DEVIL, AND MAN

GOD CREATED ALL THINGS. This good and almighty God created all things, both visible and invisible, by his co-eternal Word, and preserves them by his co-eternal Spirit, as David testified when he said: "By the word of the Lord the heavens were made, and all their host by the breath of his mouth" (Ps. 33:6). And, as Scripture says, everything that God had made was very good, and was made for the profit and use of man. Now we assert that all those things proceed from one beginning. *Manichaeans and Marcionites*. Therefore, we condemn the Manichaeans and Marcionites who impiously imagined two substances and natures, one good, the other evil; also two beginnings and two gods contrary to each other, a good and an evil one.

OF ANGELS AND THE DEVIL. Among all creatures, angels and men are most excellent. Concerning angels, Holy Scripture declares: "Who makest the winds thy messengers, fire and flame thy ministers" (Ps. 104:4). Also it says: "Are they not all ministering spirits sent forth to serve, for the sake of those who are to obtain salvation?" (Heb. 1:14). Concerning the devil, the Lord Jesus himself testifies: "He was a murderer from the beginning, and has nothing to do with the truth, because there is no truth in him. When he lies, he speaks according to his own nature, for he is a liar and the father of lies" (John 8:44). Consequently we teach that some angels persisted in obedience and were appointed for faithful service to God and men, but others fell of their own free will and were cast into destruction, becoming enemies of all good and of the faithful, etc.

OF MAN. Now concerning man, Scripture says that in the beginning he was made good according to the image and likeness of God; that God placed him in Paradise and made all things subject to him (Gen., ch. 2). This is what David magnificently sets forth in Psalm 8. Moreover, God gave him a wife and blessed them. We also affirm that man consists of two different substances in one person: an immortal soul which, when separated from the body, neither sleeps nor dies, and a mortal body which will nevertheless be raised up from the dead at the last judgment, in order that then the whole man, either in life or in death, abide forever.

THE SECTS. We condemn all who ridicule or by subtle arguments cast doubt upon the immortality of souls, or who say that the soul sleeps or is a part of God. In short, we condemn all opinions of all men, however many, that depart from what has been delivered unto us by the Holy Scriptures in the apostolic Church of Christ concerning creation, angels, and demons, and man.

CHAPTER VIII. OF MAN'S FALL, SIN AND THE CAUSE OF SIN

THE FALL OF MAN. In the beginning, man was made according to the image of God, in righteousness and true holiness, good and upright. But when at the instigation of the serpent and by his own fault he abandoned goodness and righteousness, he became subject to sin, death and various calamities. And what he became by the fall, that is, subject to sin, death and various calamities, so are all those who have descended from him.

SIN. By sin we understand that innate corruption of man which has been derived or propagated in us all from our first parents, by which we, immersed in perverse desires and averse to all good, are inclined to all evil. Full of all wickedness, distrust, contempt and hatred of God, we are unable to do or even to think anything good of ourselves. Moreover, even as we grow older, so by wicked thoughts, words and deeds committed against God's law, we bring forth corrupt fruit worthy of an evil tree (Matt. 12:33 ff.). For this reason by our own deserts, being subject to the wrath of God, we are liable to just punishment, so that all of us would have been cast away by God if Christ, the Deliverer, had not brought us back.

DEATH. By death we understand not only bodily death, which all of us must once suffer on account of sins, but also eternal punishment due to our sins and corruption. For the apostle says: "We were dead through trespasses and sins . . . and were by nature children of wrath, like the rest of mankind. But God, who is rich in mercy . . . even when we were dead through our trespasses, made us alive together with Christ" (Eph. 2:1 ff.). Also: "As sin came into the world through one man and death through sin, and so death spread to all men because all men sinned" (Rom. 5:12).

ORIGINAL SIN. We therefore acknowledge that there is original sin in all men. *Actual Sins*. We acknowledge that all other sins which arise from it are called and truly are sins, no matter by what name they may be called, whether mortal, venial or that which is said to be the sin against the Holy Spirit which is never forgiven (Mark 3:29; I John 5:16). We also confess that sins are not equal; although they arise from the same fountain of corruption and unbelief, some are more serious than others. As the Lord said, it will be more tolerable for Sodom than for the city that rejects the word of the Gospel (Matt. 10:14 f.; 11:20 ff.).

THE SECTS. We therefore condemn all who have taught contrary to this, especially Pelagius and all Pelagians, together with the Jovinians who, with the Stoics, regard all sins as equal. In this whole matter we agree with St. Augustine who derived and defended his view from Holy Scriptures. Moreover, we condemn Florinus and Blastus, against whom Irenaeus wrote, and all who make God the author of sin.

GOD IS NOT THE AUTHOR OF SIN, AND HOW FAR HE IS SAID TO HARDEN. It is expressly written: "Thou art not a God who delights in wickedness. Thou hatest all evildoers. Thou destroyest those who speak lies" (Ps. 5:4 ff.). And again: "When the devil lies, he speaks according to

his own nature, for he is a liar and the father of lies"
(John 8:44). Moreover, there is enough sinfulness
and corruption in us that it is not necessary for God
to infuse into us a new or still greater perversity.
When, therefore, it is said in Scripture that God
hardens, blinds and delivers up to a reprobate mind,
it is to be understood that God does it by a just
judgment as a just Judge and Avenger. Finally, as
often as God in Scripture is said or seems to do
something evil, it is not thereby said that man does
not do evil, but that God permits it and does not
prevent it, according to his just judgment, who could
prevent it if he wished, or because he turns man's evil
into good, as he did in the case of the sin of Joseph's
brethren, or because he governs sins lest they break
out and rage more than is appropriate. St. Augustine
writes in his *Enchiridion*: "What happens contrary to
his will occurs, in a wonderful and ineffable way, not
apart from his will. For it would not happen if he did
not allow it. And yet he does not allow it unwillingly
but willingly. But he who is good would not permit
evil to be done, unless, being omnipotent, he could
bring good out of evil." Thus wrote Augustine.

CURIOUS QUESTIONS. Other questions, such as
whether God willed Adam to fall, or incited him to
fall, or why he did not prevent the fall, and similar
questions, we reckon among curious questions
(unless perchance the wickedness of heretics or of
other churlish men compels us also to explain them
out of the Word of God, as the godly teachers of the
Church have frequently done), knowing that the
Lord forbade man to eat of the forbidden fruit and
punished his transgression. We also know that what
things ᷤre done are not evil with respect to the
providence, will, and power of God, but in respect of
Satan and our will opposing the will of God.

CHAPTER IX. OF FREE WILL, AND THUS OF HUMAN POWERS

In this matter, which has always produced many
conflicts in the Church, we teach that a threefold
condition or state of man is to be considered. *What
Man Was Before the Fall*. There is the state in which
man was in the beginning before the fall, namely,
upright and free, so that he could both continue in
goodness and decline to evil. However, he declined to
evil, and has involved himself and the whole human
race in sin and death, as has been said already. *What
Man Was After the Fall*. Then we are to consider
what man was after the fall. To be sure, his reason
was not taken from him, nor was he deprived of will,
and he was not entirely changed into a stone or a
tree. But they were so altered and weakened that
they no longer can do what they could before the fall.
For the understanding is darkened, and the will
which was free has become an enslaved will. Now it
serves sin, not unwillingly but willingly. And indeed,
it is called a will, not an unwill (ing).

MAN DOES EVIL BY HIS OWN FREE WILL.
Therefore, in regard to evil or sin, man is not forced
by God or by the devil but does evil by his own free
will, and in this respect he has a most free will. But
when we frequently see that the worst crimes and
designs of men are prevented by God from reaching
their purpose, this does not take away man's freedom
in doing evil, but God by his own power prevents
what man freely planned otherwise. Thus Joseph's
brothers freely determined to get rid of him, but they
were unable to do it because something else seemed
good to the counsel of God.

MAN IS NOT CAPABLE OF GOOD PER SE. In
regard to goodness and virtue man's reason does not
judge rightly of itself concerning divine things. For
the evangelical and apostolic Scripture requires
regeneration of whoever among us wishes to be
saved. Hence our first birth from Adam contributes
nothing to our salvation. Paul says: "The unspiritual
man does not receive the gifts of the Spirit of God,"
etc. (I Cor. 2:14). And in another place he denies
that we of ourselves are capable of thinking anything
good (II Cor. 3:5). Now it is known that the mind or
intellect is the guide of the will, and when the guide
is blind, it is obvious how far the will reaches.
Wherefore, man not yet regenerate has no free will
for good, no strength to perform what is good. The
Lord says in the Gospel: "Truly, truly, I say to you,
everyone who commits sin is a slave to sin." (John
8:34.) And the apostle Paul says: "The mind that is
set on the flesh is hostile to God; it does not submit
to God's law, indeed it cannot." (Rom. 8:7.) Yet in
regard to earthly things, fallen man is not entirely
lacking in understanding.

UNDERSTANDING OF THE ARTS. For God in
his mercy has permitted the powers of the intellect to
remain, though differing greatly from what was in
man before the fall. God commands us to cultivate
our natural talents, and meanwhile adds both gifts
and success. And it is obvious that we make no
progress in all the arts without God's blessing. In
any case, Scripture refers all the arts to God; and,
indeed, the heathen trace the origin of the arts to the
gods who invented them.

OF WHAT KIND ARE THE POWERS OF THE
REGENERATE, AND IN WHAT WAY THEIR
WILLS ARE FREE. Finally, we must see whether
the regenerate have free wills, and to what extent. In
regeneration the understanding is illumined by the
Holy Spirit in order that it may understand both the
mysteries and the will of God. And the will itself is
not only changed by the Spirit, but it is also equipped
with faculties so that it wills and is able to do the
good of its own accord. (Rom. 8:1 ff.) Unless we
grant this, we will deny Christian liberty and
introduce a legal bondage. But the prophet has God
saying: "I will put my law within them, and I will
write it upon their hearts" (Jer. 31:33; Ezek. 36:26
f.). The Lord also says in the Gospel: "If the Son
makes you free, you will be free indeed" (John 8:36).
Paul also writes to the Philippians: "It has been

granted to you that for the sake of Christ you should not only believe in him but also suffer for his sake" (Phil. 1:29). Again: "I am sure that he who began a good work in you will bring it to completion at the day of Jesus Christ" (v. 6). Also: "God is at work in you, both to will and to work for his good pleasure" (ch. 2:13).

THE REGENERATE WORK NOT ONLY PASSIVELY BUT ACTIVELY. However, in this connection we teach that there are two things to be observed: First, that the regenerate, in choosing and doing good, work not only passively but actively. For they are moved by God that they may do themselves what they do. For Augustine rightly adduces the saying that "God is said to be our helper. But no one can be helped unless he does something." The Manichaeans robbed man of all activity and made him like a stone or a block of wood.

THE FREE WILL IS WEAK IN THE REGENERATE. Secondly, in the regenerate a weakness remains. For since sin dwells in us, and in the regenerate the flesh struggles against the Spirit till the end of our lives, they do not easily accomplish in all things what they had planned. These things are confirmed by the apostle in Rom., ch. 7, and Gal., ch. 5. Therefore that free will is weak in us on account of the remnants of the old Adam and of innate human corruption remaining in us until the end of our lives. Meanwhile, since the powers of the flesh and the remnants of the old man are not so efficacious that they wholly extinguish the work of the Spirit, for that reason the faithful are said to be free, yet so that they acknowledge their infirmity and do not glory at all in their free will. For believers ought always to keep in mind what St. Augustine so many times inculcated according to the apostle: "What have you that you did not receive? If then you received it, why do you boast as if it were not a gift?" To this he adds that what we have planned does not immediately come to pass. For the issue of things lies in the hand of God. This is the reason Paul prayed to the Lord to prosper his journey (Rom. 1:10). And this also is the reason the free will is weak.

IN EXTERNAL THINGS THERE IS LIBERTY. Moreover, no one denies that in external things both the regenerate and the unregenerate enjoy free will. For man has in common with other living creatures (to which he is not inferior) this nature to will some things and not to will others. Thus he is able to speak or to keep silent, to go out of his house or to remain at home, etc. However, even here God's power is always to be observed, for it was the cause that Balaam could not go as far as he wanted (Num., ch. 24), and Zacharias upon returning from the temple could not speak as he wanted (Luke, ch.1).

HERESIES. In this matter we condemn the Manichaeans who deny that the beginning of evil was for man [created] good, from his free will. We also condemn the Pelagians who assert that an evil man has sufficient free will to do the good that is commanded. Both are refuted by Holy Scripture which says to the former, "God made man upright" and to the latter, "If the Son makes you free, you will be free indeed" (John 8:36).

CHAPTER X. OF THE PREDESTINATION OF GOD AND THE ELECTION OF THE SAINTS

GOD HAS ELECTED US OUT OF GRACE. From eternity God has freely, and of his mere grace, without any respect to men, predestinated or elected the saints whom he wills to save in Christ, according to the saying of the apostle, "God chose us in him before the foundation of the world" (Eph. 1:4). And again: "Who saved us and called us with a holy calling, not in virtue of our works but in virtue of his own purpose and the grace which he gave us in Christ Jesus ages ago, and now has manifested through the appearing of our Saviour Christ Jesus" (II Tim. 1:9 f.).

WE ARE ELECTED OR PREDESTINATED IN CHRIST. Therefore, although not on account of any merit of ours. God has elected us, not directly, but in Christ, and on account of Christ, in order that those who are now ingrafted into Christ by faith might also be elected. But those who were outside Christ were rejected, according to the word of the apostle, "Examine yourselves, to see whether you are holding to your faith. Test yourselves. Do you not realize that Jesus Christ is in you?—unless indeed you fail to meet the test!" (II Cor. 13:5).

WE ARE ELECTED FOR A DEFINITE PURPOSE. Finally, the saints are chosen in Christ by God for a definite purpose, which the apostle himself explains when he says, "He chose us in him for adoption that we should be holy and blameless before him in love. He destined us for adoption to be his sons through Jesus Christ that they should be to the praise of the glory of his grace" (Eph. 1:4 ff.).

WE ARE TO HAVE A GOOD HOPE FOR ALL. And although God knows who are his, and here and there mention is made of the small number of elect, yet we must hope well of all, and not rashly judge any man to be a reprobate. For Paul says to the Philippians, "I thank my God for you all" (now he speaks of the whole Church in Philippi), "because of your fellowship in the Gospel, being persuaded that he who began a good work in you will bring it to completion at the day of Jesus Christ. It is also right that I have this opinion of you all" (Phil. 1:3 ff.).

WHETHER FEW ARE ELECT. And when the Lord was asked whether there were few that should be saved, he does not answer and tell them that few or many should be saved or damned, but rather he exhorts every man to "strive to enter by the narrow door" (Luke 13:24): as if he should say, It is not for you curiously to inquire about these matters, but rather to endeavor that you may enter into heaven by the straight way.

WHAT IN THIS MATTER IS TO BE CONDEMNED. Therefore we do not approve of the impious speeches of some who say, "Few are chosen, and since I do not know whether I am among the number of the few, I will enjoy myself." Others say, "If I am predestinated and elected by God, nothing can hinder me from salvation, which is already certainly appointed for me, no matter what I do. But if I am in the number of the reprobate, no faith or repentance will help me, since the decree of God cannot be changed. Therefore all doctrines and admonitions are useless." Now the saying of the apostle contradicts these men: "The Lord's servant must be ready to teach, instructing those who oppose him, so that if God should grant that they repent to know the truth, they may recover from the snare of the devil, after being held captive by him to do his will" (II Tim. 2:23 ff.).

ADMONITIONS ARE NOT IN VAIN BECAUSE SALVATION PROCEEDS FROM ELECTION. Augustine also shows that both the grace of free election and predestination, and also salutary admonitions and doctrines, are to be preached (*Lib. de Dono Perseverantiae*, cap. 14 ff.).

WHETHER WE ARE ELECTED. We therefore find fault with those who outside of Christ ask whether they are elected. And what has God decreed concerning them before all eternity? For the preaching of the Gospel is to be heard, and it is to be believed; and it is to be held as beyond doubt that if you believe and are in Christ, you are elected. For the Father has revealed unto us in Christ the eternal purpose of his predestination, as I have just now shown from the apostle in II Tim. 1:9-10. This is therefore above all to be taught and considered, what great love of the Father toward us is revealed to us in Christ. We must hear what the Lord himself daily preaches to us in the Gospel, how he calls and says: "Come to me all who labor and are heavy-laden, and I will give you rest" (Matt. 11:28). "God so loved the world, that he gave his only Son, that whoever believes in him should not perish, but have eternal life." (John 3:16.) Also, "It is not the will of my Father that one of these little ones should perish." (Matt. 18:14.)

Let Christ, therefore be the looking glass, in whom we may contemplate our predestination. We shall have a sufficiently clear and sure testimony that we are inscribed in the Book of Life if we have fellowship with Christ, and he is ours and we are his in true faith.

TEMPTATION IN REGARD TO PREDESTINA-TION. In the temptation in regard to predestination, than which there is scarcely any other more dangerous, we are confronted by the fact that God's promises apply to all the faithful, for he says: "Ask, and everyone who seeks, shall receive" (Luke 11:9 f.). This finally we pray, with the whole Church of God. "Our Father who art in heaven" (Matt. 6:9), both because by baptism we are ingrafted into the

body of Christ, and we are often fed in his Church with his flesh and blood unto life eternal. Thereby, being strengthened, we are commanded to work out our salvation with fear and trembling, according to the precept of Paul.

CHAPTER XI. OF JESUS CHRIST, TRUE GOD AND MAN, THE ONLY SAVIOR OF THE WORLD

CHRIST IS TRUE GOD. We further believe and teach that the Son of God, our Lord Jesus Christ, was predestinated or foreordained from eternity by the Father to be the Savior of the world. And we believe that he was born, not only when he assumed flesh of the Virgin Mary, and not only before the foundation of the world was laid, but by the Father before all eternity in an inexpressible manner. For Isaiah said: "Who can tell his generation?" (Ch. 53:8.) And Micah says: "His origin is from of old, from ancient days" (Micah 5:2.) And John said in the Gospel: "In the beginning was the Word, and the Word was with God, and the Word was God," etc. (Ch. 1:1.) Therefore, with respect to his divinity the Son is coequal and consubstantial with the Father; true God (Phil. 2:11), not only in name or by adoption or by any merit, but in substance and nature, as the apostle John has often said: "This is the true God and eternal life" (I John 5:20). Paul also says: "He appointed the Son the heir of all things, through whom also he created the world. He reflects the glory of God and bears the very stamp of his nature, upholding all things by his word of power" (Heb. 1:2 f.). For in the Gospel the Lord himself said: "Father, glorify Thou me in Thy own presence with the glory which I had with Thee before the world was made" (John 17:5). And in another place in the Gospel it is written: "The Jews sought all the more to kill him because he . . . called God his Father, making himself equal with God" (John 5:18).

THE SECTS. We therefore abhor the impious doctrine of Arius and the Arians against the Son of God, and especially the blasphemies of the Spaniard, Michael Servetus, and all his followers, which Satan through them has, as it were, dragged up out of hell and has most audaciously and impiously spread abroad in the world.

CHRIST IS TRUE MAN, HAVING REAL FLESH. We also believe and teach that the eternal Son of the eternal God was made the Son of man, from the seed of Abraham and David, not from the coitus of a man, as the Ebionites said, but was most chastely conceived by the Holy Spirit and born of the ever virgin Mary, as the evangelical history carefully explains to us (Matt., ch. 1). And Paul says: "He took not on him the nature of angels, but of the seed of Abraham." Also the apostle John says that whoever does not believe that Jesus Christ has come in the flesh, is not of God. Therefore, the flesh of Christ was neither imaginary nor brought from heaven, as Valentinus and Marcion wrongly imagined.

A RATIONAL SOUL IN CHRIST. Moreover, our Lord Jesus Christ did not have a soul bereft of sense and reason, as Appollinaris thought, nor flesh without a soul, as Eunomius taught, but a soul with its reason, and flesh with its senses, by which in the time of his passion he sustained real bodily pain, as he himself testified when he said: "My soul is very sorrowful, even to death" (Matt. 26:38). And, "Now is my soul troubled" (John 12:27).

TWO NATURES IN CHRIST. We therefore acknowledge two natures or substances, the divine and the human, in one and the same Jesus Christ our Lord (Heb., ch. 2). And we say that these are bound and united with one another in such a way that they are not absorbed, or confused, or mixed, but are united or joined together in one person—the properties of the natures being unimpaired and permanent.

NOT TWO BUT ONE CHRIST. Thus we worship not two but one Christ the Lord. We repeat: one true God and man. With respect to his divine nature he is consubstantial with the Father, and with respect to the human nature he is consubstantial with us men, and like us in all things, sin excepted (Heb. 4:15).

THE SECTS. And indeed we detest the dogma of the Nestorians who make two of the one Christ and dissolve the unity of the Person. Likewise we thoroughly execrate the madness of Eutyches and of the Monothelites or Monophysites who destroy the property of the human nature.

THE DIVINE NATURE OF CHRIST IS NOT PASSIBLE, AND THE HUMAN NATURE IS NOT EVERYWHERE. Therefore, we do not in any way teach that the divine nature in Christ has suffered or that Christ according to his human nature is still in this world and thus is everywhere. For neither do we think or teach that the body of Christ ceased to be a true body after his glorification, or was deified, and deified in such a way that it laid aside its properties as regards body and soul, and changed entirely into a divine nature and began to be merely one substance.

THE SECTS. Hence we by no means approve of or accept the strained, confused and obscure subtleties of Schwenkfeldt and of similar sophists with their self-contradictory arguments; neither are we Schwenkfeldians.

OUR LORD TRULY SUFFERED. We believe, moreover, that our Lord Jesus Christ truly suffered and died for us in the flesh, as Peter says (I Peter 4:1). We abhor the most impious madness of the Jacobites and all the Turks who execrate the suffering of the Lord. At the same time we do not deny that the Lord of glory was crucified for us, according to Paul's words (I Cor. 2:8).

IMPARTATION OF PROPERTIES. We piously and reverently accept and use the impartation of properties which is derived from Scripture and which has been used by all antiquity in explaining and reconciling apparently contradictory passages.

CHRIST IS TRULY RISEN FROM THE DEAD. We believe and teach that the same Jesus Christ our Lord, in his true flesh in which he was crucified and died, rose again from the dead, and that not another flesh was raised other than the one buried, or that a spirit was taken up instead of the flesh, but that he retained his true body. Therefore, while his disciples thought they saw the spirit of the Lord, he showed them his hands and feet which were marked by the prints of the nails and wounds, and added: "See my hands and my feet, that it is I myself; handle me, and see, for a spirit has not flesh and bones as you see that I have" (Luke 24:39).

CHRIST IS TRULY ASCENDED INTO HEAVEN. We believe that our Lord Jesus Christ, in his same flesh, ascended above all visible heavens into the highest heaven, that is, the dwelling-place of God and the blessed ones, at the right hand of God the Father. Although it signifies an equal participation in glory and majesty, it is also taken to be a certain place about which the Lord, speaking in the Gospel, says: "I go to prepare a place for you" (John 14:2). The apostle Peter also says: "Heaven must receive Christ until the time of restoring all things" (Acts 3:21). And from heaven the same Christ will return in judgment, when wickedness will then be at its greatest in the world and when the Antichrist, having corrupted true religion, will fill up all things with superstition and impiety and will cruelly lay waste the Church with bloodshed and flames (Dan., ch. 11). But Christ will come again to claim his own, and by his coming to destroy the Antichrist, and to judge the living and the dead (Acts 17:31). For the dead will rise again (I Thess. 4:14 ff.), and those who on that day (which is unknown to all creatures [Mark 13:32]) will be alive will be changed "in the twinkling of an eye," and all the faithful will be caught up to meet Christ in the air, so that then they may enter with him into the blessed dwelling-places to live forever (I Cor. 15:51 f.). But the unbelievers and ungodly will descend with the devils into hell to burn forever and never to be redeemed from torments (Matt. 25:46).

THE SECTS. We therefore condemn all who deny a real resurrection of the flesh (II Tim. 2:18), or who with John of Jerusalem, against whom Jerome wrote, do not have a correct view of the glorification of bodies. We also condemn those who thought that the devil and all the ungodly would at some time be saved, and that there would be an end to punishments. For the Lord has plainly declared: "Their fire is not quenched, and their worm does not die" (Mark 9:44). We further condemn Jewish dreams that there will be a golden age on earth before the Day of Judgment, and that the pious, having subdued all their godless enemies, will possess all the kingdoms of the earth. For evangelical truth in Matt., chs. 24 and 25, and Luke, ch. 18, and apostolic teaching in II Thess., ch. 2, and II Tim., chs. 3 and 4, present something quite different.

THE FRUIT OF CHRIST'S DEATH AND RES-SURRECTION. Further by his passion and death and everything which he did and endured for our sake by his coming in the flesh, our Lord reconciled all the faithful to the heavenly Father, made expiation for sins, disarmed death, overcame damnation and hell, and by his resurrection from the dead brought again and restored life and immortality. For he is our righteousness, life and resurrection, in a word, the fulness and perfection of all the faithful, salvation and all sufficiency. For the apostle says: "In him all the fulness of God was pleased to dwell," and, "You have come to fulness of life in him." (Col., chs. 1 and 2.)

JESUS CHRIST IS THE ONLY SAVIOR OF THE WORLD, AND THE TRUE AWAITED MESSI-AH. For we teach and believe that this Jesus Christ our Lord is the unique and eternal Savior of the human race, and thus of the whole world, in whom by faith are saved all who before the law, under the law, and under the Gospel were saved, and however many will be saved at the end of the world. For the Lord himself says in the Gospel: "He who does not enter the sheepfold by the door but climbs in by another way, that man is a thief and a robber. . . . I am the door of the sheep" (John 10:1 and 7). And also in another place in the same Gospel he says: "Abraham saw my day and was glad" (ch. 8:56). The apostle Peter also says: "There is salvation in no one else, for there is no other name under heaven given among men by which we must be saved." We therefore believe that we will be saved through the grace of our Lord Jesus Christ, as our fathers were. (Acts 4:12; 10:43; 15:11.) For Paul also says: "All our fathers ate the same spiritual food, and all drank the same spiritual drink. For they drank from the spiritual Rock which followed them, and the Rock was Christ" (I Cor. 10:3 f.). And thus we read that John says: "Christ was the Lamb which was slain from the foundation of the world" (Rev. 13:8), and John the Baptist testified that Christ is that "Lamb of God, who takes away the sin of the world" (John 1:29). Wherefore, we quite openly profess and preach that Jesus Christ is the sole Redeemer and Savior of the world, the King and High Priest, the true and awaited Messiah, that holy and blessed one whom all the types of the law and predictions of the prophets prefigured and promised; and that God appointed him beforehand and sent him to us, so that we are not now to look for any other. Now there only remains for all of us to give all glory to Christ, believe in him, rest in him alone, despising and rejecting all other aids in life. For however many seek salvation in any other than in Christ alone, have fallen from the grace of God and have rendered Christ null and void for themselves (Gal. 5:4).

THE CREEDS OF FOUR COUNCILS RE-CEIVED. And, to say many things with a few words, with a sincere heart we believe, and freely confess with open mouth, whatever things are defined from the Holy Scriptures concerning the mystery of the incarnation of our Lord Jesus Christ, and are summed up in the Creeds and decrees of the first four most excellent synods convened at Nicea, Constantinople, Ephesus and Chalcedon—together with the Creed of blessed Athanasius, and all similar symbols; and we condemn everything contrary to these.

THE SECTS. And in this way we retain the Christian, orthodox and catholic faith whole and unimpaired; knowing that nothing is contained in the aforesaid symbols which is not agreeable to the Word of God, and does not altogether make for a sincere exposition of the faith.

CHAPTER XII. OF THE LAW OF GOD

THE WILL OF GOD IS EXPLAINED FOR US IN THE LAW OF GOD. We teach that the will of God is explained for us in the law of God, what he wills or does not will us to do, what is good and just, or what is evil and unjust. Therefore, we confess that the law is good and holy.

THE LAW OF NATURE. And this law was at one time written in the hearts of men by the finger of God (Rom. 2:15), and is called the law of nature (*the law of Moses is in two Tables*), and at another it was inscribed by his finger on the two Tables of Moses, and eloquently expounded in the books of Moses (Ex. 20:1 ff.; Deut. 5:6 ff.). For the sake of clarity we distinguish the moral law which is contained in the Decalogue or two Tables and expounded in the books of Moses, the ceremonial law which determines the ceremonies and worship of God, and the judicial law which is concerned with political and domestic matters.

THE LAW IS COMPLETE AND PERFECT. We believe that the whole will of God and all necessary precepts for every sphere of life are taught in this law. For otherwise the Lord would not have forbidden us to add or to take away anything from this law: neither would he have commanded us to walk in a straight path before this law, and not to turn aside from it by turning to the right or to the left (Deut. 4:2; 12:32).

WHY THE LAW WAS GIVEN. We teach that this law was not given to men that they might be justified by keeping it, but that rather from what it teaches we may know (our) weakness, sin and condemnation, and, despairing of our strength, might be converted to Christ in faith. For the apostle openly declares: "The law brings wrath," and, "Through the law comes knowledge of sin" (Rom. 4:15; 3:20), and, "If a law had been given which could justify or make alive, then righteousness would indeed be by the law. But the Scripture (that is, the law) has concluded all under sin, that the promise which was of the faith of Jesus might be given to those who believe. . . . Therefore, the law was our schoolmaster unto Christ, that we might be justified by faith" (Gal. 3:21 ff.).

THE FLESH DOES NOT FULFIL THE LAW.
For no flesh could or can satisfy the law of God and fulfil it, because of the weakness in our flesh which adheres and remains in us until our last breath. For the apostle says again: "God has done what the law, weakened by the flesh, could not do: sending his own Son in the likeness of sinful flesh and for sin" (Rom. 8:3). Therefore, Christ is the perfecting of the law and our fulfilment of it (Rom. 10:4), who, in order to take away the curse of the law, was made a curse for us (Gal. 3:13). Thus he imparts to us through faith his fulfilment of the law, and his righteousness and obedience are imputed to us.

HOW FAR THE LAW IS ABROGATED.
The law of God is therefore abrogated to the extent that it no longer condemns us, nor works wrath in us. For we are under grace and not under the law. Moreover, Christ has fulfilled all the figures of the law. Hence, with the coming of the body, the shadows ceased, so that in Christ we now have the truth and all fulness. But yet we do not on that account contemptuously reject the law. For we remember the words of the Lord when he said: "I have not come to abolish the law and the prophets but to fulfil them" (Matt. 5:17). We know that in the law is delivered to us the patterns of virtues and vices. We know that the written law when explained by the Gospel is useful to the Church, and that therefore its reading is not to be banished from the Church. For although Moses' face was covered with a veil, yet the apostle says that the veil has been taken away and abolished by Christ. *The Sects.* We condemn everything that heretics old and new have taught against the law.

CHAPTER XIII. OF THE GOSPEL, OF JESUS CHRIST, OF THE PROMISES, AND OF THE SPIRIT AND LETTER

THE ANCIENTS HAD EVANGELICAL PROM-ISES.
The Gospel is, indeed, opposed to the law. For the law works wrath and announces a curse, whereas the Gospel preaches grace and blessing. John says: "For the law was given through Moses; grace and truth came through Jesus Christ." (John 1:17.) Yet notwithstanding it is most certain that those who were before the law and under the law, were not altogether destitute of the Gospel. For they had extraordinary evangelical promises such as these are: "The seed of the woman shall bruise the serpent's head" (Gen. 3:15). "In thy seed shall all the nations of the earth be blessed" (Gen. 22:18). "The scepter shall not depart from Judah . . . until he comes" (Gen. 49:10). "The Lord will raise up a prophet from among his own brethren" (Deut. 18:15; Acts 3:22), etc.

THE PROMISES TWOFOLD.
And we acknowledge that two kinds of promises were revealed to the fathers, as also to us. For some were of present or earthly things, such as the promises of the Land of Canaan and of victories, and as the promise today still of daily bread. Others were then and are still now of heavenly and eternal things, namely, divine grace, remission of sins, and eternal life through faith in Jesus Christ.

THE FATHERS ALSO HAD NOT ONLY CAR-NAL BUT SPIRITUAL PROMISES.
Moreover, the ancients had not only external and earthly but also spiritual and heavenly promises in Christ. Peter says: "The prophets who prophesied of the grace that was to be yours searched and inquired about this salvation." (I Peter 1:10.) Wherefore the apostle Paul also said: "The Gospel of God was promised beforehand through his prophets in the holy scriptures" (Rom. 1:2). Thereby it is clear that the ancients were not entirely destitute of the whole Gospel.

WHAT IS THE GOSPEL PROPERLY SPEAK-ING?
And although our fathers had the Gospel in this way in the writings of the prophets by which they attained salvation in Christ through faith, yet the Gospel is properly called glad and joyous news, in which, first by John the Baptist, then by Christ the Lord himself, and afterwards by the apostles and their successors, is preached to us in the world that God has now performed what he promised from the beginning of the world, and has sent, may more, has given us his only Son and in him reconciliation with the Father, the remission of sins, all fulness and everlasting life. Therefore, the history delineated by the four Evangelists and explaining how these things were done or fulfilled by Christ, what things Christ taught and did, and that those who believe in him have all fulness, is rightly called the Gospel. The preaching and writings of the apostles, in which the apostles explain for us how the Son was given to us by the Father, and in him everything that has to do with life and salvation, is also rightly called evangelical doctrine, so that not even today, if sincerely preached, does it lose its illustrious title.

OF THE SPIRIT AND THE LETTER.
That same preaching of the Gospel is also called by the apostle "the spirit" and "the ministry of the spirit" because by faith it becomes effectual and living in the ears, nay more, in the hearts of believers through the illumination of the Holy Spirit (II Cor. 3:6). For the letter, which is opposed to the Spirit, signifies everything external, but especially the doctrine of the law which, without the Spirit and faith, works wrath and provokes sin in the minds of those who do not have a living faith. For this reason the apostle calls it "the ministry of death." In this connection the saying of the apostle is pertinent: "The letter kills, but the Spirit gives life." And false apostles preached a corrupted Gospel, having combined it with the law, as if Christ could not save without the law.

THE SECTS.
Such were the Ebionites said to be, who were descended from Ebion the heretic, and the Nazarites who were formerly called Mineans. All these we condemn, while preaching the pure Gospel and teaching that believers are justified by the Spirit

alone, and not by the law. A more detailed exposition of this matter will follow presently under the heading of justification.

THE TEACHING OF THE GOSPEL IS NOT NEW, BUT MOST ANCIENT DOCTRINE. And although the teaching of the Gospel, compared with the teaching of the Pharisees concerning the law, seemed to be a new doctrine when first preached by Christ (which Jeremiah also prophesied concerning the New Testament), yet actually it not only was and still is an old doctrine (even if today it is called new by the Papists when compared with the teaching now received among them), but is the most ancient of all in the world. For God predestinated from eternity to save the world through Christ, and he has disclosed to the world through the Gospel this his predestination and eternal counsel (II Tim. 2:9 f.). Hence it is evident that the religion and teaching of the Gospel among all who ever were, are and will be, is the most ancient of all. Wherefore we assert that all who say that the religion and teaching of the Gospel is a faith which has recently arisen, being scarcely thirty years old, err disgracefully and speak shamefully of the eternal counsel of God. To them applies the saying of Isaiah the prophet: "Woe to those who call evil good and good evil, who put darkness for light and light for darkness, who put bitter for sweet and sweet for bitter!" (Isa. 5:20).

CHAPTER XIV. OF REPENTANCE AND THE CONVERSION OF MAN

The doctrine of repentance is joined with the Gospel. For so has the Lord said in the Gospel: "Repentance and forgiveness of sins should be preached in my name to all nations" (Luke 24:47). *What Is Repentance?* By repentance we understand (1) the recovery of a right mind in sinful man awakened by the Word of the Gospel and the Holy Spirit, and received by true faith, by which the sinner immediately acknowledges his innate corruption and all his sins accused by the Word of God; and (2) grieves for them from his heart, and not only bewails and frankly confesses them before God with a feeling of shame, but also (3) with indignation abominates them; and (4) now zealously considers the amendment of his ways and constantly strives for innocence and virtue in which conscientiously to exercise himself all the rest of his life.

TRUE REPENTANCE IS CONVERSION TO GOD. And this is true repentance, namely, a sincere turning to God and all good, and earnest turning away from the devil and all evil. *1. Repentance is a gift of God.* Now we expressly say that this repentance is a sheer gift of God and not a work of our strength. For the apostle commands a faithful minister diligently to instruct those who oppose the truth, if "God may perhaps grant that they will repent and come to know the truth" (II Tim. 2:25) *2. Laments sins committed.* Now that sinful woman

who washed the feet of the Lord with her tears, and Peter who wept bitterly and bewailed his denial of the Lord (Luke 7:38; 22:62) show clearly how the mind of a penitent man ought to be seriously lamenting the sins he has committed. *3. Confesses sins to God.* Moreover, the prodigal son and the publican in the Gospel, when compared with the Pharisee, present us with the most suitable pattern of how our sins are to be confessed to God. The former said: " 'Father, I have sinned against heaven and before you: I am no longer worthy to be called your son: treat me as one of your hired servants.' " (Luke 15:8 ff.) And the latter, not daring to raise his eyes to heaven, beat his breast, saying, "God be merciful to me a sinner" (ch. 18:13). And we do not doubt that they were accepted by God into grace. For the apostle John says: "If we confess our sins, he is faithful and just, and will forgive our sins and cleanse us from all unrighteousness. If we say we have not sinned, we make him a liar, and his word is not in us" (I John 1:9 f.).

SACERDOTAL CONFESSION AND ABSOLUTION. But we believe that this sincere confession which is made to God alone, either privately between God and the sinner, or publicly in the Church where the general confession of sins is said, is sufficient, and that in order to obtain forgiveness of sins it is not necessary for anyone to confess his sins to a priest, murmuring them in his ears, that in turn he might receive absolution from the priest with his laying on of hands, because there is neither a commandment nor an example of this in Holy Scriptures. David testifies and says: "I acknowledged my sin to thee, and did not hide my iniquity: I said, 'I will confess my transgressions to the Lord'; then thou didst forgive the guilt of my sin" (Ps. 32:5). And the Lord who taught us to pray and at the same time to confess our sins said: "Pray then like this: Our Father, who art in heaven. . . . forgive us our debts, as we also forgive our debtors" (Matt. 6:12). Therefore it is necessary that we confess our sins to God our Father, and be reconciled with our neighbor if we have offended him. Concerning this kind of confession, the Apostle James says: "Confess your sins to one another" (James 5:16). If, however, anyone is overwhelmed by the burden of his sins and by perplexing temptations, and will seek counsel, instruction and comfort privately, either from a minister of the Church, or from any other brother who is instructed in God's law, we do not disapprove; just as we also fully approve of that general and public confession of sins which is usually said in Church and in meetings for worship, as we noted above, inasmuch as it is agreeable to Scripture.

OF THE KEYS OF THE KINGDOM OF HEAVEN. Concerning the keys of the Kingdom of Heaven which the Lord gave to the apostles, many babble many astonishing things, and out of them forge swords, spears, scepters and crowns, and complete power over the greatest kingdoms, indeed, over souls and bodies. Judging simply according to the Word of the Lord, we say that all properly called ministers possess and exercise the keys or the use of them when they proclaim the Gospel; that is, when they teach, exhort, comfort, rebuke, and keep in discipline the people committed to their trust.

OPENING AND SHUTTING (THE KINGDOM). For in this way they open the Kingdom of Heaven to the obedient and shut it to the disobedient. The Lord promised these keys to the apostles in Matt., ch. 16, and gave them in John, ch. 20, Mark, ch. 16, and Luke, ch. 24, when he sent out his disciples and commanded them to preach the Gospel in all the world, and to remit sins.

THE MINISTRY OF RECONCILIATION. In the letter to the Corinthians the apostle says that the Lord gave the ministry of reconciliation to his ministers (II Cor. 5:18 ff.). And what this is he then explains, saying that it is the preaching or teaching of reconciliation. And explaining his words still more clearly he adds that Christ's ministers discharge the office of an ambassador in Christ's name, as if God himself through ministers exhorted the people to be reconciled to God, doubtless by faithful obedience. Therefore, they exercise the keys when they persuade [men] to believe and repent. Thus they reconcile men to God.

MINISTERS REMIT SINS. Thus they remit sins. Thus they open the Kingdom of Heaven, and bring believers into it: very different from those of whom the Lord said in the Gospel. "Woe to you lawyers! for you have taken away the key of knowledge; you did not enter yourselves, and you hindered those who were entering."

HOW MINISTERS ABSOLVE. Ministers, therefore, rightly and effectually absolve when they preach the Gospel of Christ and thereby the remission of sins, which is promised to each one who believes, just as each one is baptized, and when they testify that it pertains to each one peculiarly. Neither do we think that this absolution becomes more effectual by being murmured in the ear of someone or by being murmured singly over someone's head. We are nevertheless of the opinion that the remission of sins in the blood of Christ is to be diligently proclaimed, and that each one is to be admonished that the forgiveness of sins pertains to him.

DILIGENCE IN THE RENEWAL OF LIFE. But the examples in the Gospel teach us how vigilant and diligent the penitent ought to be in striving for newness of life and in mortifying the old man and quickening the new. For the Lord said to the man he healed of palsy: "See, you are well! Sin no more, that nothing worse befall you" (John 5:14). Likewise to the adulteress whom he set free he said: "Go, and sin no more" (ch. 8:11). To be sure, by these words he did not mean that any man, as long as he lived in the flesh, could not sin; he simply recommends diligence and a careful devotion, so that we should strive by all means, and beseech God in prayers lest we fall back into sins from which, as it were, we have been

resurrected, and lest we be overcome by the flesh, the world and the devil. Zacchaeus the publican, whom the Lord had received back into favor, exclaims in the Gospel: "Behold, Lord, the half of my goods I give to the poor; and if I have defrauded any one of anything, I restore it fourfold" (Luke 19:8). Therefore, in the same way we preach that restitution and compassion, and even almsgiving, are necessary for those who truly repent, and we exhort all men everywhere in the words of the apostle: "Let not sin therefore reign in your mortal bodies, to make you obey their passions. Do not yield your members to sin as instruments of wickedness, but yield yourselves to God as men who have been brought from death to life, and your members to God as instruments of righteousness" (Rom. 6:12 f.).

ERRORS. Wherefore we condemn all impious utterances of some who wrongly use the preaching of the Gospel and say that it is easy to return to God. Christ has atoned for all sins. Forgiveness of sins is easy. Therefore, what harm is there in sinning? Nor need we be greatly concerned about repentance, etc. Notwithstanding we always teach that an access to God is open to all sinners, and that he forgives all sinners of all sins except the one sin against the Holy Spirit (Mark 3:29).

THE SECTS. Wherefore we condemn both old and new Novatians and Catharists.

PAPAL INDULGENCES. We especially condemn the lucrative doctrine of the Pope concerning penance, and against his simony and his simoniacal indulgences we avail ourselves of Peter's judgment concerning Simon: "Your silver perish with you, because you thought you could obtain the gift of God with money! You have neither part nor lot in this matter, for your heart is not right before God" (Acts 8:20 f.).

SATISFACTIONS. We also disapprove of those who think that by their own satisfactions they make amends for sins committed. For we teach that Christ alone by his death or passion is the satisfaction, propitiation or expiation of all sins (Isa., ch. 53; I Cor. 1:30). Yet as we have already said, we do not cease to urge the mortification of the flesh. We add, however, that this mortification is not to be proudly obtruded upon God as a satisfaction for sins, but is to be performed humbly, in keeping with the nature of the children of God, as a new obedience out of gratitude for the deliverance and full satisfaction obtained by the death and satisfaction of the Son of God.

CHAPTER XV. OF THE TRUE JUSTIFICATION OF THE FAITHFUL

WHAT IS JUSTIFICATION? According to the apostle in his treatment of justification, to justify means to remit sins, to absolve from guilt and punishment, to receive into favor, and to pronounce a man just. For in his epistle to the Romans the apostle says: "It is God who justifies; who is to condemn?" (Rom. 8:33). To justify and to condemn are opposed. And in The Acts of the Apostles the apostle states: "Through Christ forgiveness of sins is proclaimed to you, and by him everyone that believes is freed from everything from which you could not be freed by the law of Moses" (Acts 13:38 f.). For in the Law and also in the Prophets we read: "If there is a dispute between men, and they come into court . . . the judges decide between them, acquitting the innocent and condemning the guilty" (Deut. 25:1). And in Isa., ch. 5: "Woe to those . . . who acquit the guilty for a bribe."

WE ARE JUSTIFIED ON ACCOUNT OF CHRIST. Now it is most certain that all of us are by nature sinners and godless, and before God's judgment-seat are convicted of godlessness and are guilty of death, but that, solely by the grace of Christ and not from any merit of ours or consideration for us, we are justified, that is, absolved from sin and death by God the Judge. For what is clearer than what Paul said: "Since all have sinned and fall short of the glory of God, they are justified by his grace as a gift, through the redemption which is in Christ Jesus" (Rom. 3:23 f.).

IMPUTED RIGHTEOUSNESS. For Christ took upon himself and bore the sins of the world, and satisfied divine justice. Therefore, solely on account of Christ's sufferings and resurrection God is propitious with respect to our sins and does not impute them to us, but imputes Christ's righteousness to us as our own (II Cor. 5:19 ff.; Rom. 4:25), so that now we are not only cleansed and purged from sins or are holy, but also, granted the righteousness of Christ, and so absolved from sin, death and condemnation, are at last righteous and heirs of eternal life. Properly speaking, therefore, God alone justifies us, and justifies only on account of Christ, not imputing sins to us but imputing his righteousness to us.

WE ARE JUSTIFIED BY FAITH ALONE. But because we receive this justification, not through any works, but through faith in the mercy of God and in Christ, we therefore teach and believe with the apostle that sinful man is justified by faith alone in Christ, not by the law or any works. For the apostle says: "We hold that a man is justified by faith apart from works of law" (Rom. 3:28). Also: "If Abraham was justified by works, he has something to boast about, but not before God. For what does the scripture say? Abraham believed God, and it was reckoned to him as righteousness. . . . And to one who does not work but believes in him who justifies the ungodly, his faith is reckoned as righteousness" (Rom. 4:2 ff.; Gen. 15:6). And again: "By grace you have been saved through faith: and this is not your own doing, it is the gift of God—not because of works, lest any man should boast," etc. (Eph. 2:8 f.). Therefore, because faith receives Christ our righteousness and attributes everything to the grace of God in Christ, on that account justification is

attributed to faith, chiefly because of Christ and not therefore because it is our work. For it is the gift of God.

WE RECEIVE CHRIST BY FAITH. Moreover, the Lord abundantly shows that we receive Christ by faith in John, ch. 6, where he puts eating for believing, and believing for eating. For as we receive food by eating, so we participate in Christ by believing. *Justification Is Not Attributed Partly to Christ or to Faith, Partly to Us.* Therefore, we do not share in the benefit of justification partly because of the grace of God or Christ, and partly because of ourselves, our love, works or merit, but we attribute it wholly to the grace of God in Christ through faith. For our love and our works could not please God if performed by unrighteous men. Therefore, it is necessary for us to be righteous before we may love and do good works. We are made truly righteous, as we have said, by faith in Christ purely by the grace of God, who does not impute to us our sins, but the righteousness of Christ, or rather, he imputes faith in Christ to us for righteousness. Moreover, the apostle very clearly derives love from faith when he says: "The aim of our command is love that issues from a pure heart, a good conscience, and a sincere faith" (I Tim. 1:5).

JAMES COMPARED WITH PAUL. Wherefore, in this matter we are not speaking of a fictitious, empty, lazy and dead faith, but of a living, quickening faith. It is and is called a living faith because it apprehends Christ who is life and makes alive, and shows that it is alive by living works. And so James does not contradict anything in this doctrine of ours. For he speaks of an empty, dead faith of which some boasted but who did not have Christ living in them by faith (James 2:14 ff.). James said that works justify, yet without contradicting the apostle (otherwise he would have to be rejected) but showing that Abraham proved his living and justifying faith by works. This all the pious do, but they trust in Christ alone and not in their own works. For again the apostle said: "It is no longer I who live, but Christ who lives in me; and the life I now live in the flesh I live by faith in the Son of God, who loved me and gave himself for me. I do not reject the grace of God; for if justification were through the law, then Christ died to no purpose," etc. (Gal. 2:20 f.).

CHAPTER XVI. OF FAITH AND GOOD WORKS, AND OF THEIR REWARD, AND OF MAN'S MERIT

WHAT IS FAITH? Christian faith is not an opinion or human conviction, but a most firm trust and a clear and steadfast assent of the mind, and then a most certain apprehension of the truth of God presented in the Scriptures and in the Apostles' Creed, and thus also of God himself, the greatest good, and especially of God's promise and of Christ who is the fulfilment of all promises.

FAITH IS THE GIFT OF GOD. But this faith is a pure gift of God which God alone of his grace gives to his elect according to his measure when, to whom and to the degree he wills. And he does this by the Holy Spirit by means of the preaching of the Gospel and steadfast prayer. *The Increase of Faith*. This faith also has its increase, and unless it were given by God, the apostles would not have said: "Lord, increase our faith" (Luke 17:5). And all these things which up to this point we have said concerning faith, the apostles have taught before us. For Paul said: "For faith is the υποστασιζ or sure subsistence, of things hoped for, and the ελεγχοζ, that is, the clear and certain apprehension" (Heb. 11:1). And again he says that all the promises of God are Yes through Christ and through Christ are Amen (II Cor. 1:20). And to the Philippians he said that it has been given to them to believe in Christ (Phil. 1:29). Again, God assigned to each the measure of faith (Rom. 12:3). Again: "Not all have faith" and, "Not all obey the Gospel" (II Thess. 3:2; Rom. 10:16). But Luke also bears witness, saying: "As many as were ordained to life believed" (Acts 13:48). Wherefore Paul also calls faith "the faith of God's elect" (Titus 1:1), and again: "Faith comes from hearing, and hearing comes by the Word of God" (Rom. 10:17). Elsewhere he often commands men to pray for faith.

FAITH EFFICACIOUS AND ACTIVE. The same apostle calls faith efficacious and active through love (Gal. 5:6). It also quiets the conscience and opens a free access to God, so that we may draw near to him with confidence and may obtain from him what is useful and necessary. The same [faith] keeps us in the service we owe to God and our neighbor, strengthens our patience in adversity, fashions and makes a true confession, and in a word, brings forth good fruit of all kinds, and good works.

CONCERNING GOOD WORKS. For we teach that truly good works grow out of a living faith by the Holy Spirit and are done by the faithful according to the will or rule of God's Word. Now the apostle Peter says: "Make every effort to supplement your faith with virtue, and virtue with knowledge, and knowledge with self-control," etc. (II Peter 1:5 ff.) But we have said above that the law of God, which is his will, prescribes for us the pattern of good works. And the apostle says: "This is the will of God, your sanctification, that you abstain from immorality . . . that no man transgress, and wrong his brother in business." (I Thess. 4:3 ff.)

WORKS OF HUMAN CHOICE. And indeed works and worship which we choose arbitrarily are not pleasing to God. These Paul calls εθλεοθρησκειαζ (Col. 2:23—'self-devised worship"). Of such the Lord says in the Gospel: "In vain do they worship me, teaching as doctrines the precepts of men" (Matt. 15:9). Therefore, we disapprove of such works, and approve and urge those that are of God's will and commission.

THE END OF GOOD WORKS. These same works ought not to be done in order that we may earn eternal life by them, for, as the apostle says, eternal life is the gift of God. Nor are they to be done for ostentation which the Lord rejects in Matt., ch. 6, nor for gain which he also rejects in Matt., ch. 23, but for the glory of God, to adorn our calling, to show gratitude to God, and for the profit of the neighbor. For our Lord says again in the Gospel: "Let your light so shine before men, that they may see your good works and give glory to your Father who is in heaven" (Matt. 5:16). And the apostle Paul says: "Lead a life worthy of the calling to which you have been called." (Eph. 4:1.) Also: "And whatever you do, in word or deed, do everything in the name of the Lord Jesus, giving thanks to God and to the Father through him (Col. 3:17), and. "Let each of you look not to his own interests, but to the interests of others" (Phil. 2:4), and, "Let our people learn to apply themselves to good deeds, so as to help cases of urgent need, and not to be unfruitful" (Titus 3:14).

GOOD WORKS NOT REJECTED. Therefore, although we teach with the apostle that a man is justified by grace through faith in Christ and not through any good works, yet we do not think that good works are of little value and condemn them. We know that man was not created or regenerated through faith in order to be idle, but rather that without ceasing he should do those things which are good and useful. For in the Gospel the Lord says that a good tree brings forth good fruit (Matt. 12:33), and that he who abides in me bears much fruit (John 15:5). The apostle says: "For we are his workmanship, created in Christ Jesus for good works, which God prepared beforehand, that we should walk in them" (Eph. 2:10), and again: "Who gave himself for us to redeem us from all iniquity and to purify for himself a people of his own who are zealous for good deeds" (Titus 2:14). We therefore condemn all who despise good works and who babble that they are useless and that we do not need to pay attention to them.

WE ARE NOT SAVED BY GOOD WORKS. Nevertheless, as was said above, we do not think that we are saved by good works, and that they are so necessary for salvation that no one was ever saved without them. For we are saved by grace and the favor of Christ alone. Works necessarily proceed from faith. And salvation is improperly attributed to them, but is most properly ascribed to grace. The apostle's sentence is well known: "If it is by grace, then it no longer of works; otherwise grace would no longer be grace. But if it is of works, then it is no longer grace, because otherwise work is no longer work" (Rom. 11:6).

GOOD WORKS PLEASE GOD. Now the works which we do by faith are pleasing to God and are approved by him. Because of faith in Christ, those who do good works which, moreover, are done from God's grace through the Holy Spirit, are pleasing to God. For St. Peter said: "In every nation any one who fears God and does what is right is acceptable to him." (Acts 10:35.) And Paul said: "We have not ceased to pray for you . . . that you may walk worthily of the Lord, fully pleasing to him, bearing fruit in every good work." (Col. 1:9 f.)

WE TEACH TRUE, NOT FALSE AND PHILOSOPHICAL VIRTUES. And so we diligently teach true, not false and philosophical virtues, truly good works, and the genuine service of a Christian. And as much as we can we diligently and zealously press them upon all men, while censuring the sloth and hypocrisy of all those who praise and profess the Gospel with their lips and dishonor it by their disgraceful lives. In this matter we place before them God's terrible threats and then his rich promises and generous rewards—exhorting, consoling and rebuking.

GOD GIVES A REWARD FOR GOOD WORKS. For we teach that God gives a rich reward to those who do good works, according to that saying of the prophet: "Keep your voice from weeping, . . . from your work shall be rewarded" (Jer. 31:16; Isa., ch. 4). The Lord also said in the Gospel: "Rejoice and be glad, for your reward is great in heaven" (Matt. 5:12), and, "Whoever gives to one of these my little ones a cup of cold water, truly, I say to you, he shall not lose his reward" (ch. 10:42). However, we do not ascribe this reward, which the Lord gives, to the merit of the man who receives it, but to the goodness, generosity and truthfulness of God who promises and gives it, and who, although he owes nothing to anyone, nevertheless promises that he will give a reward to his faithful worshippers; meanwhile he also gives them that they may honor him. Moreover, in the works even of the saints there is much that is unworthy of God and very much that is imperfect. But because God receives into favor and embraces those who do works for Christ's sake, he grants to them the promised reward. For in other respects our righteousnesses are compared to a filthy wrap (Isa. 64:6). And the Lord says in the Gospel: "When you have done all that is commanded you, say, 'We are unworthy servants; we have only done what was our duty.'" (Luke 17:10.)

THERE ARE NO MERITS OF MEN. Therefore, although we teach that God rewards our good deeds, yet at the same time we teach, with Augustine, that God does not crown in us our merits but his gifts. Accordingly we say that whatever reward we receive is also grace, and is more grace than reward, because the good we do, we do more through God than through ourselves, and because Paul says: "What have you that you did not receive? If then you received it, why do you boast as if you had not received it?" (I Cor. 4:7). And this is what the blessed martyr Cyprian concluded from this verse: We are not to glory in anything in us, since nothing is our own. We therefore condemn those who defend the merits of men in such a way that they invalidate the grace of God.

CHAPTER XVII. OF THE CATHOLIC AND HOLY CHURCH OF GOD, AND OF THE ONE ONLY HEAD OF THE CHURCH

THE CHURCH HAS ALWAYS EXISTED AND IT WILL ALWAYS EXIST. But because God from the beginning would have men to be saved, and to come to the knowledge of the truth (I Tim. 2:4), it is altogether necessary that there always should have been, and should be now, and to the end of the world, a Church.

WHAT IS THE CHURCH? The Church is an assembly of the faithful called or gathered out of the world: a communion, I say, of all saints, namely, of those who truly know and rightly worship and serve the true God in Christ the Savior, by the Word and Holy Spirit, and who by faith are partakers of all benefits which are freely offered through Christ. *Citizens of One Commonwealth.* They are all citizens of the one city, living under the same Lord, under the same laws, and in the same fellowship of all good things. For the apostle calls them "fellow citizens with the saints and members of the household of God" (Eph. 2:19), calling the faithful on earth saints (I Cor. 4:1), who are sanctified by the blood of the Son of God. The article of the Creed, "I believe in the holy catholic Church, the communion of saints," is to be understood wholly as concerning these saints.

ONLY ONE CHURCH FOR ALL TIMES. And since there is always but one God, and there is one mediator between God and men, Jesus the Messiah, and one Shepherd of the whole flock, one Head of this body, and, to conclude, one Spirit, one salvation, one faith, one Testament or covenant, it necessarily follows that there is only one Church. *The Catholic Church.* We, therefore, call this Church catholic because it is universal, scattered through all parts of the world, and extended unto all times, and is not limited to any times or places. Therefore, we condemn the Donatists who confined the Church to I know not what corners of Africa. Nor do we approve of the Roman clergy who have recently passed off only the Roman Church as catholic.

PARTS OR FORMS OF THE CHURCH. The Church is divided into different parts or forms; not because it is divided or rent asunder in itself, but rather because it is distinguished by the diversity of the numbers that are in it. *Militant and Triumphant.* For the one is called the Church Militant, the other the Church Triumphant. The former still wages war on earth, and fights against the flesh, the world, and the prince of this world, the devil; against sin and death. But the latter, having been now discharged, triumphs in heaven immediately after having overcome all those things and rejoices before the Lord. Notwithstanding both have fellowship and union one with another.

THE PARTICULAR CHURCH. Moreover, the Church Militant upon the earth has always had many particular churches. Yet all these are to be referred to the unity of the catholic Church. This

[Militant] Church was set up differently before the Law among the patriarchs; otherwise under Moses by the Law; and differently by Christ through the Gospel.

THE TWO PEOPLES. Generally two peoples are usually counted, namely, the Israelites and Gentiles, or those who have been gathered from among Jews and Gentiles into the Church. There are also two Testaments, the Old and the New. *The Same Church for the Old and the New People.* Yet from all these people there was and is one fellowship, one salvation in the one Messiah; in whom, as members of one body under one Head, all united together in the same faith, partaking also of the same spiritual food and drink. Yet here we acknowledge a diversity of times, and a diversity in the signs of the promised and delivered Christ; and that now the ceremonies being abolished, the light shines unto us more clearly, and blessings are given to us more abundantly, and a fuller liberty.

THE CHURCH THE TEMPLE OF THE LIVING GOD. This holy Church of God is called the temple of the living God, built of living and spiritual stones and founded upon a firm rock, upon a foundation which no other can lay, and therefore it is called "the pillar and bulwark of the truth" (I Tim. 3:15). *The Church Does Not Err.* It does not err as long as it rests upon the rock Christ, and upon the foundation of the prophets and apostles. And it is no wonder if it errs, as often as it deserts him who alone is the truth. *The Church as Bride and Virgin.* The Church is also called a virgin and the Bride of Christ, and even the only Beloved. For the apostle says: "I betrothed you to Christ to present you as a pure bride to Christ." (II Cor. 11:2.) *The Church as a Flock of Sheep.* The Church is called a flock of sheep under the one shepherd, Christ, according to Ezek., ch. 34, and John, ch. 10. *The Church as the Body.* It is also called the body of Christ because the faithful are living members of Christ under Christ the Head.

CHRIST THE SOLE HEAD OF THE CHURCH. It is the head which has the preeminence in the body, and from it the whole body receives life; by its spirit the body is governed in all things; from it, also, the body receives increase, that it may grow up. Also, there is one head of the body, and it is suited to the body. Therefore the Church cannot have any other head besides Christ. For as the Church is a spiritual body, so it must also have a spiritual head in harmony with itself. Neither can it be governed by any other spirit than by the Spirit of Christ. Wherefore Paul says: "He is the head of the body, the church; he is the beginning, the firstborn from the dead, that in everything he might be preeminent" (Col. 1:18). And in another place: "Christ is the head of the church, his body, and is himself its Savior" (Eph. 5:23). And again: he is "the head over all things for the church, which is his body, the fulness of him who fills all in all" (Eph. 1:22 f.). Also: "We are to grow up in every way into him who is the head, into Christ, from whom the whole body, joined and knit together, makes bodily growth" (Eph. 4:15 f.). And therefore we do not approve of the doctrine of the Roman clergy, who make their Pope at Rome the universal shepherd and supreme head of the Church Militant here on earth, and so the very vicar of Jesus Christ, who has (as they say) all fulness of power and sovereign authority in the Church. *Christ the Only Pastor of the Church.* For we teach that Christ the Lord is, and remains the only universal pastor, and highest Pontiff before God the Father; and that in the Church he himself performs all the duties of a bishop or pastor, even to the world's end; [*Vicar*] and therefore does not need a substitute for one who is absent. For Christ is present with his Church, and is its life-giving Head. *No Primacy in the Church.* He has strictly forbidden his apostles and their successors to have any primacy and dominion in the Church. Who does not see, therefore, that whoever contradicts and opposes this plain truth is rather to be counted among the number of those of whom Christ's apostles prophesied: Peter in II Peter, ch. 2, and Paul in Acts 20:2; II Cor. 11:2; II Thess., ch. 2, and also in other places?

NO DISORDER IN THE CHURCH. However, by doing away with a Roman head we do not bring any confusion or disorder into the Church, since we teach that the government of the Church which the apostles handed down is sufficient to keep the Church in proper order. In the beginning when the Church was without any such Roman head as is now said to keep it in order, the Church was not disordered or in confusion. The Roman head does indeed preserve his tyranny and the corruption that has been brought into the Church, and meanwhile he hinders, resists, and with all the strength he can muster cuts off the proper reformation of the Church.

DISSENSIONS AND STRIFE IN THE CHURCH. We are reproached because there have been manifold dissensions and strife in our churches since they separated themselves from the Church of Rome, and therefore cannot be true churches. As though there were never in the Church of Rome any sects, nor contentions and quarrels concerning religion, and indeed, carried on not so much in the schools as from pulpits in the midst of the people. We know, to be sure, that the apostle said: "God is not a God of confusion but of peace" (I Cor. 14:33), and, "While there is jealousy and strife among you, are you not of the flesh? " Yet we cannot deny that God was in the apostolic Church and that it was a true Church, even though there were wranglings and dissensions in it. The apostle Paul reprehended Peter, an apostle (Gal. 2:11 ff.), and Barnabas dissented from Paul. Great contention arose in the Church of Antioch between them that preached the one Christ, as Luke records in The Acts of the Apostles, ch. 15. And there have at all times been great contentions in the Church, and the most excellent teachers of the Church have differed among themselves about important matters without meanwhile the Church ceasing to be the

Church because of these contentions. For thus it pleases God to use the dissensions that arise in the Church to the glory of his name, to illustrate the truth, and in order that those who are in the right might be manifest (I Cor. 11:19).

OF THE NOTES OR SIGNS OF THE TRUE CHURCH. Moreover, as we acknowledge no other head of the Church than Christ, so we do not acknowledge every church to be the true Church which vaunts herself to be such; but we teach that the true Church is that in which the signs or marks of the true Church are to be found, especially the lawful and sincere preaching of the Word of God as it was delivered to us in the books of the prophets and the apostles, which all lead us unto Christ, who said in the Gospel: "My sheep hear my voice, and I know them, and they follow me; and I give unto them eternal life. A stranger they do not follow, but they flee from him, for they do not know the voice of strangers" (John 10:5, 27, 28).

And those who are such in the Church have one faith and one spirit; and therefore they worship but one God, and him alone they worship in spirit and in truth, loving him alone with all their hearts and with all their strength, praying unto him alone through Jesus Christ, the only Mediator and Intercessor; and they do not seek righteousness and life outside Christ and faith in him. Because they acknowledge Christ the only head and foundation of the Church, and, resting on him, daily renew themselves by repentance, and patiently bear the cross laid upon them. Moreover, joined together with all the members of Christ by an unfeigned love, they show that they are Christ's disciples by persevering in the bond of peace and holy unity. At the same time they participate in the sacraments instituted by Christ, and delivered unto us by his apostles, using them in no other way than as they received them from the Lord. That saying of the apostle Paul is well known to all: "I received from the Lord what I also delivered to you" (I Cor. 11:23 ff.). Accordingly, we condemn all such churches as strangers from the true Church of Christ, which are not such as we have heard they ought to be, no matter how much they brag of a succession of bishops, of unity, and of antiquity. Moreover, we have a charge from the apostles of Christ "to shun the worship of idols" (I Cor. 10:14: I John 5:21), and "to come out of Babylon," and to have no fellowship with her, unless we want to be partakers with her of all God's plagues (Rev. 18:4; II Cor. 6:17).

OUTSIDE THE CHURCH OF GOD THERE IS NO SALVATION. But we esteem fellowship with the true Church of Christ so highly that we deny that those can live before God who do not stand in fellowship with the true Church of God, but separate themselves from it. For as there was no salvation outside Noah's ark when the world perished in the flood; so we believe that there is no certain salvation outside Christ, who offers himself to be enjoyed by the elect in the Church; and hence we teach that those who wish to live ought not to be separated from the true Church of Christ.

THE CHURCH IS NOT BOUND TO ITS SIGNS. Nevertheless, by the signs [of the true Church] mentioned above, we do not so narrowly restrict the Church as to teach that all those are outside the Church who either do not participate in the sacraments, at least not willingly and through contempt, but rather, being forced by necessity, unwillingly abstain from them or are deprived of them; or in whom faith sometimes fails, though it is not entirely extinguished and does not wholly cease; or in whom imperfections and errors due to weakness are found. For we know that God had some friends in the world outside the commonwealth of Israel. We know what befell the people of God in the captivity of Babylon, where they were deprived of their sacrifices for seventy years. We know what happened to St. Peter, who denied his Master, and what is wont to happen daily to God's elect and faithful people who go astray and are weak. We know, moreover, what kind of churches the churches in Galatia and Corinth were in the apostles' time, in which the apostle found fault with many serious offenses; yet he calls them holy churches of Christ (I Cor. 1:2: Gal. 1:2).

THE CHURCH APPEARS AT TIMES TO BE EXTINCT. Yes, and it sometimes happens that God in his just judgment allows the truth of his Word, and the catholic faith, and the proper worship of God to be so obscured and overthrown that the Church seems almost extinct, and no more to exist, as we see to have happened in the days of Elijah (I Kings 19:10, 14), and at other times. Meanwhile God has in this world and in this darkness his true worshippers, and those not a few, but even seven thousand and more (I Kings 19:18; Rev. 7:3 ff.). For the apostle exclaims: "God's firm foundation stands, bearing this seal, 'The Lord knows those who are his,'" etc. (II Tim. 2:19.) Whence the Church of God may be termed invisible; not because the men from whom the Church is gathered are invisible, but because, being hidden from our eyes and known only to God, it often secretly escapes human judgment.

NOT ALL WHO ARE IN THE CHURCH ARE OF THE CHURCH. Again, not all that are reckoned in the number of the Church are saints, and living and true members of the Church. For there are many hypocrites, who outwardly hear the Word of God, and publicly receive the sacraments, and seem to pray to God through Christ alone, to confess Christ to be their only righteousness, and to worship God, and to exercise the duties of charity, and for a time to endure with patience in misfortune. And yet they are inwardly destitute of true illumination of the Spirit, of faith and sincerity of heart, and of perseverance to the end. But eventually the character of these men, for the most part, will be disclosed. For the apostle John says: "They went out from us, but they were not of us: for if they had been of us, they would indeed have continued with us." (I John 2:19.) And although while they simulate piety they are not of the Church, yet they are considered to be in the Church, just as traitors in a state are numbered among its citizens before they are discovered; and as the tares or darnel and chaff are found among the wheat, and as swellings and tumors are found in a sound body, when they are rather diseases and deformities than true members of the body. And therefore the Church of God is rightly compared to a net which catches fish of all kinds, and to a field, in which both wheat and tares are found (Matt. 13:24 ff., 47 ff.).

WE MUST NOT JUDGE RASHLY OR PREMATURELY. Hence we must be very careful not to judge before the time, nor undertake to exclude, reject or cut off those whom the Lord does not want to have excluded or rejected, and those whom we cannot eliminate without loss to the Church. On the other hand, we must be vigilant lest while the pious snore the wicked gain ground and do harm to the Church.

THE UNITY OF THE CHURCH IS NOT IN EXTERNAL RITES. Furthermore, we diligently teach that care is to be taken wherein the truth and unity of the Church chiefly lies, lest we rashly provoke and foster schisms in the Church. Unity consists not in outward rites and ceremonies, but rather in the truth and unity of the catholic faith. This catholic faith is not given to us by human laws, but by Holy Scriptures, of which the Apostles' Creed is a compendium. And, therefore, we read in the ancient writers that there was a manifold diversity of rites, but that they were free, and no one ever thought that the unity of the Church was thereby dissolved. So we teach that the true harmony of the Church consists in doctrines and in the true and harmonious preaching of the Gospel of Christ, and in rites that have been expressly delivered by the Lord. And here we especially urge that saying of the apostle: "Let those of us who are perfect have this mind; and if in any thing you are otherwise minded, God will reveal that also to you. Nevertheless let us walk by the same rule according to what we have attained, and let us be of the same mind" (Phil. 3:15 f.).

CHAPTER XVIII. OF THE MINISTERS OF THE CHURCH, THEIR INSTITUTION AND DUTIES

GOD USES MINISTERS IN THE BUILDING OF THE CHURCH. God has always used ministers for the gathering or establishing of a Church for himself, and for the governing and preservation of the same; and still he does, and always will, use them so long as the Church remains on earth. Therefore, the first beginning, institution, and office of ministers is a most ancient arrangement of God himself, and not a new one of men. *Institution and Origin of Ministers.* It is true that God can, by his power, without any means join to himself a Church from among men;

but he preferred to deal with men by the ministry of men. Therefore ministers are to be regarded, not as ministers by themselves alone, but as the ministers of God, inasmuch as God effects the salvation of men through them.

THE MINISTRY IS NOT TO BE DESPISED. Hence we warn men to beware lest we attribute what has to do with our conversion and instruction to the secret power of the Holy Spirit in such a way that we make void the ecclesiastical ministry. For it is fitting that we always have in mind the words of the apostle: "How are they to believe in him of whom they have not heard? And how are they to hear without a preacher? So faith comes from hearing, and hearing comes by the word of God" (Rom. 10:14, 17). And also what the Lord said in the Gospel: "Truly, truly, I say to you, he who receives any one whom I send receives me; and he who receives me receives him who sent me" (John 13:20). Likewise a man of Macedonia, who appeared to Paul in a vision while he was in Asia, secretly admonished him, saying: "Come over to Macedonia and help us" (Acts 16:9). And in another place the same apostle said: "We are fellow workmen for God; you are God's tillage, God's building" (I Cor. 3:9).

Yet, on the other hand, we must beware that we do not attribute too much to ministers and the ministry; remembering here also the words of the Lord in the Gospel: "No one can come to me unless my Father draws him" (John 6:44), and the words of the apostle: "What then is Paul? What is Apollos? Servants through whom you believed, as the Lord assigned to each. I planted, Apollos watered, but only God gives the growth" (I Cor. 3:5 ff.). *God Moves the Hearts of Men.* Therefore, let us believe that God teaches us by his word, outwardly through his ministers, and inwardly moves the hearts of his elect to faith by the Holy Spirit; and that therefore we ought to render all glory unto God for this whole favor. But this matter has been dealt with in the first chapter of this Exposition.

WHO THE MINISTERS ARE AND OF WHAT SORT GOD HAS GIVEN TO THE WORLD. And even from the beginning of the world God has used the most excellent men in the whole world (even if many of them were simple in worldly wisdom or philosophy, but were outstanding in true theology), namely, the patriarchs, with whom he frequently spoke by angels. For the patriarchs were the prophets or teachers of their age whom God for this reason wanted to live for several centuries, in order that they might be, as it were, fathers and lights of the world. They were followed by Moses and the prophets renowned throughout all the world.

CHRIST THE TEACHER. After these the heavenly Father even sent his only-begotten Son, the most perfect teacher of the world: in whom is hidden the wisdom of God, and which has come to us through the most holy, simple, and most perfect doctrine of all. For he chose disciples for himself whom he made apostles. These went out into the whole world, and everywhere gathered together churches by the preaching of the Gospel, and then throughout all the churches in the world they appointed pastors or teachers according to Christ's command; through their successors he has taught and governed the Church unto this day. Therefore, as God gave unto his ancient people the patriarchs, together with Moses and the prophets, so also to his people of the New Testament he sent his only-begotten Son, and, with him, the apostles and teachers of the Church.

MINISTERS OF THE NEW TESTAMENT. Furthermore, the ministers of the new people are called by various names. For they are called apostles, prophets, evangelists, bishops, elders, pastors, and teachers (I Cor. 12:28; Eph. 4:11). *The Apostles.* The apostles did not stay in any particular place, but throughout the world gathered together different churches. When they were once established, there ceased to be apostles, and pastors took their place, each in his church. *Prophets.* In former times the prophets were seers, knowing the future; but they also interpreted the Scriptures. Such men are also found still today. *Evangelists.* The writers of the history of the Gospel were called Evangelists; but they also were heralds of the Gospel of Christ; as Paul also commended Timothy: "Do the work of an evangelist" (II Tim. 4:5). *Bishops.* Bishops are the overseers and watchmen of the Church, who administer the food and needs of the life of the Church. *Presbyters.* The presbyters are the elders and, as it were, senators and fathers of the Church, governing it with wholesome counsel. *Pastors.* The pastors both keep the Lord's sheepfold, and also provide for its needs. *Teachers.* The teachers instruct and teach the true faith and godliness. Therefore, the ministers of the churches may now be called bishops, elders, pastors, and teachers.

PAPAL ORDERS. Then in subsequent times many more names of ministers in the Church were introduced into the Church of God. For some were appointed patriarchs, others archbishops, others suffragans; also, metropolitans, archdeacons, deacons, subdeacons, acolyts, exorcists, cantors, porters, and I know not what others, as cardinals, provosts, and priors; greater and lesser fathers, greater and lesser orders. But we are not troubled about all these, about how they once were and are now. For us the apostolic doctrine concerning ministers is sufficient.

CONCERNING MONKS. Since we assuredly know that monks, and the orders or sects of monks, are instituted neither by Christ nor by the apostles, we teach that they are of no use to the Church of God, nay rather, are pernicious. For, although in former times they were tolerable (when they were hermits, earning their living with their own hands, and were not a burden to anyone, but like the laity were everywhere obedient to the pastors of the churches),

yet now the whole world sees and knows what they are like. They formulate I know not what vows; but they lead a life quite contrary to their vows, so that the best of them deserves to be numbered among those of whom the apostle said: "We hear that some of you are living an irregular life, mere busybodies, not doing any work" etc. (II Thess. 3:11). Therefore, we neither have such in our churches, nor do we teach that they should be in the churches of Christ.

MINISTERS ARE TO BE CALLED AND ELECTED. Furthermore, no man ought to usurp the honor of the ecclesiastical ministry; that is, to seize it for himself by bribery or any deceits, or by his own free choice. But let the ministers of the Church be called and chosen by lawful and ecclesiastical election; that is to say, let them be carefully chosen by the Church or by those delegated from the Church for that purpose in a proper order without any uproar, dissension and rivalry. Not any one may be elected, but capable men distinguished by sufficient consecrated learning, pious eloquence, simple wisdom, lastly, by moderation and an honorable reputation, according to that apostolic rule which is compiled by the apostle in I Tim., ch. 3, and Titus, ch. 1.

ORDINATION. And those who are elected are to be ordained by the elders with public prayer and laying on of hands. Here we condemn all those who go off of their own accord, being neither chosen, sent, nor ordained (Jer., ch. 23). We condemn unfit ministers and those not furnished with the necessary gifts of a pastor.

In the meantime we acknowledge that the harmless simplicity of some pastors in the primitive Church sometimes profited the Church more than the many-sided, refined and fastidious, but a little too esoteric learning of others. For this reason we do not reject even today the honest, yet by no means ignorant, simplicity of some.

PRIESTHOOD OF ALL BELIEVERS. To be sure, Christ's apostles call all who believe in Christ "priests," but not on account of an office, but because, all the faithful having been made kings and priests, we are able to offer up spiritual sacrifices to God through Christ (Ex. 19:6; I Peter 2:9; Rev. 1:6). Therefore, the priesthood and the ministry are very different from one another. For the priesthood, as we have just said, is common to all Christians; not so is the ministry. Nor have we abolished the ministry of the Church because we have repudiated the papal priesthood from the Church of Christ.

PRIESTS AND PRIESTHOOD. Surely in the new covenant of Christ there is no longer any such priesthood as was under the ancient people: which had an external anointing, holy garments, and very many ceremonies which were types of Christ, who abolished them all by his coming and fulfilling them. But he himself remains the only priest forever, and lest we derogate anything from him, we do not impart the name of priest to any minister. For the

Lord himself did not appoint any priests in the Church of the New Testament who, having received authority from the suffragan, may daily offer up the sacrifice, that is, the very flesh and blood of the Lord, for the living and the dead, but ministers who may teach and administer the sacraments.

THE NATURE OF THE MINISTERS OF THE NEW TESTAMENT.

Paul explains simply and briefly what we are to think of the ministers of the New Testament or of the Christian Church, and what we are to attribute to them. "This is how one should regard us, as servants of Christ and stewards of the mysteries of God" (I Cor. 4:1). Therefore, the apostle wants us to think of ministers as ministers. Now the apostle calls them νπηρεταζ, rowers, who have their eyes fixed on the coxswain, and so men who do not live for themselves or according to their own will, but for others—namely, their masters, upon whose command they altogether depend. For in all his duties every minister of the Church is commanded to carry out only what he has received in commandment from his Lord, and not to indulge his own free choice. And in this case it is expressly declared who is the Lord, namely, Christ; to whom the ministers are subject in all the affairs of the ministry.

MINISTERS AS STEWARDS OF THE MYSTERIES OF GOD.

Moreover, to the end that he might expound the ministry more fully, the apostle adds that ministers of the Church are administrators and stewards of the mysteries of God. Now in many passages, especially in Eph., ch. 3. Paul called the mysteries of God the Gospel of Christ. And the sacraments of Christ are also called mysteries by the ancient writers. Therefore for this purpose are the ministers of the Church called—namely, to preach the Gospel of Christ to the faithful, and to administer the sacraments. We read, also, in another place in the Gospel, of "the faithful and wise steward," whom his master will set over his household, to give them their portion of food at the proper time" (Luke 12:42). Again, elsewhere in the Gospel a man takes a journey in a foreign country and, leaving his house, gives his substance and authority over it to his servants, and to each his work.

THE POWER OF MINISTERS OF THE CHURCH.

Now, therefore, it is fitting that we also say something about the power and duty of the ministers of the Church. Concerning this power some have argued industriously, and to it have subjected everything on earth, even the greatest things, and they have done so contrary to the commandment of the Lord who has prohibited dominion for his disciples and has highly commended humility (Luke 22:24 ff.: Matt. 18:3 f.; 20:25 ff.). There is, indeed, another power that is pure and absolute, which is called the power of right. According to this power all things in the whole world are subject to Christ, who is Lord of all, as he himself has testified when he said: "All authority in heaven and on earth has been given to me" (Matt. 28:18), and again, "I am the first and the last, and behold I am alive for evermore, and I have the keys of Hades and Death" (Rev. 1:18): also, "He has the key of David, which opens and no one shall shut, who shuts and no one opens" (Rev. 3:7).

THE LORD RESERVES TRUE POWER FOR HIMSELF.

This power the Lord reserves to himself, and does not transfer it to any other, so that he might stand idly by as a spectator while his ministers work. For Isaiah says, "I will place on his shoulder the key of the house of David" (Isa. 22:22), and again, "The government will be upon his shoulders" (Isa. 9:6). For he does not lay the government on other men's shoulders, but still keeps and uses his own power, governing all things.

THE POWER OF THE OFFICE AND OF THE MINISTER.

Then there is another power of an office or of ministry limited by him who has full and absolute power. And this is more like a service than a dominion. *The Keys.* For a lord gives up his power to the steward in his house, and for that cause gives him the keys, that he may admit into or exclude from the house those whom his lord will have admitted or excluded. In virtue of this power the minister, because of his office, does that which the Lord has commanded him to do; and the Lord confirms what he does, and wills that what his servant has done will be so regarded and acknowledged, as if he himself had done it. Undoubtedly, it is to this that these evangelical sentences refer: "I will give you the keys of the kingdom of heaven, and whatever you bind on earth shall be bound in heaven, and whatever you loose on earth shall be loosed in heaven" (Matt. 16:19). Again, "If you forgive the sins of any, they are forgiven; if you retain the sins of any, they are retained" (John 20:23). But if the minister does not carry out everything as the Lord has commanded him, but transgresses the bounds of faith, then the Lord certainly makes void what he has done. Wherefore the ecclesiastical power of the ministers of the Church is that function whereby they indeed govern the Church of God, but yet so do all things in the Church as the Lord has prescribed in his Word. When those things are done, the faithful esteem them as done by the Lord himself. But mention has already been made of the keys above.

THE POWER OF MINISTERS IS ONE AND THE SAME, AND EQUAL.

Now the one and an equal power or function is given to all ministers in the Church. Certainly, in the beginning, the bishops or presbyters governed the Church in common; no man lifted up himself above another, none usurped greater power or authority over his fellow-bishops. For remembering the words of the Lord: "Let the leader among you become as one who serves" (Luke 22:26), they kept themselves in humility, and by mutual services they helped one another in the governing and preserving of the Church.

ORDER TO BE PRESERVED.

Nevertheless, for the sake of preserving order some one of the ministers called the assembly together, proposed matters to be laid before it, gathered the opinions of the others, in short, to the best of man's ability took precaution lest any confusion should arise. Thus did St. Peter, as we read in The Acts of the Apostles, who nevertheless was not on that account preferred to the others, nor endowed with greater authority than the rest. Rightly then does Cyprian the Martyr say, in his *De Simplicitate Clericorum*: "The other apostles were assuredly what Peter was, endowed with a like fellowship of honor and power; but [his] primacy proceeds from unity in order that the Church may be shown to be one."

WHEN AND HOW ONE WAS PLACED BEFORE THE OTHERS. St. Jerome also in his commentary upon The Epistle of Paul to Titus, says something not unlike this: "Before attachment to persons in religion was begun at the instigation of the devil, the churches were governed by the common consultation of the elders; but after every one thought that those whom he had baptized were his own, and not Christ's, it was decreed that one of the elders should be chosen, and set over the rest, upon whom should fall the care of the whole Church, and all schismatic seeds should be removed." Yet St. Jerome does not recommend this decree as divine; for he immediately adds: "As the elders knew from the custom of the Church that they were subject to him who was set over them, so the bishops knew that they were above the elders, more from custom than from the truth of an arrangement by the Lord, and that they ought to rule the Church in common with them." Thus far St. Jerome. Hence no one can rightly forbid a return to the ancient constitution of the Church of God, and to have recourse to it before human custom.

THE DUTIES OF MINISTERS. The duties of ministers are various; yet for the most part they are restricted to two, in which all the rest are comprehended: to the teaching of the Gospel of Christ, and to the proper administration of the sacraments. For it is the duty of the ministers to gather together an assembly for worship in which to expound God's Word and to apply the whole doctrine to the care and use of the Church, so that what is taught may benefit the hearers and edify the faithful. It falls to ministers, I say, to teach the ignorant, and to exhort; and to urge the idlers and lingerers to make progress in the way of the Lord. Moreover, they are to comfort and to strengthen the fainthearted, and to arm them against the manifold temptations of Satan; to rebuke offenders; to recall the erring into the way; to raise the fallen; to convince the gainsayers to drive the wolf away from the sheepfold of the Lord; to rebuke wickedness and wicked men wisely and severly; not to wink at nor to pass over great wickedness. And, besides, they are to administer the sacraments, and to commend the right use of them,

and to prepare all men by wholesome doctrine to receive them; to preserve the faithful in a holy unity; and to check schisms; to catechize the unlearned, to commend the needs of the poor to the Church, to visit, instruct, and keep in the way of life the sick and those afflicted with various temptations. In addition, they are to attend to public prayers or supplications in times of need, together with common fasting, that is, a holy abstinence; and as diligently as possible to see to everything that pertains to the tranquility, peace and welfare of the churches.

But in order that the minister may perform all these things better and more easily, it is especially required of him that he fear God, be constant in prayer, attend to spiritual reading, and in all things and at all times be watchful, and by a purity of life to let his light to shine before all men.

DISCIPLINE. And since discipline is an absolute necessity in the Church and excommunication was once used in the time of the early fathers, and there were ecclesiastical judgments among the people of God, wherein this discipline was exercised by wise and godly men, it also falls to ministers to regulate this discipline for edification, according to the circumstances of the time, public state, and necessity. At all times and in all places the rule is to be observed that everything is to be done for edification, decently and honorably, without oppression and strife. For the apostle testifies that authority in the Church was given to him by the Lord for building up and not for destroying (II Cor. 10:8). And the Lord himself forbade the weeds to be plucked up in the Lord's field, because there would be danger lest the wheat also be plucked up with it (Matt. 13:29 f).

EVEN EVIL MINISTERS ARE TO BE HEARD. Moreover, we strongly detest the error of the Donatists who esteem the doctrine and administration of the sacraments to be either effectual or not effectual, according to the good or evil life of the ministers. For we know that the voice of Christ is to be heard, though it be out of the mouths of evil ministers; because the Lord himself said: "Practice and observe whatever they tell you, but not what they do" (Matt. 23:3). We know that the sacraments are sanctified by the institution and the word of Christ, and that they are effectual to the godly, although they be administered by unworthy ministers. Concerning this matter, Augustine, the blessed servant of God, many times argued from the Scriptures against the Donatists.

SYNODS. Nevertheless, there ought to be proper discipline among ministers. In synods the doctrine and life of ministers is to be carefully examined. Offenders who can be cured are to be rebuked by the elders and restored to the right way, and if they are incurable, they are to be deposed, and like wolves driven away from the flock of the Lord by the true shepherds. For, if they be false teachers, they are not to be tolerated at all. Neither do we disapprove of ecumenical councils, if they are convened according to the example of the apostles, for the welfare of the Church and not for its destruction.

THE WORKER IS WORTHY OF HIS REWARD. All faithful ministers, as good workmen, are also worthy of their reward, and do not sin when they receive a stipend, and all things that be necessary for themselves and their family. For the apostle shows in I Cor., ch. 9, and in I Tim., ch. 5, and elsewhere that these things may rightly be given by the Church and received by ministers. The Anabaptists, who condemn and defame ministers who live from their ministry are also refuted by the apostolic teaching.

CHAPTER XIX. OF THE SACRAMENTS OF THE CHURCH OF CHRIST

THE SACRAMENTS [ARE] ADDED TO THE WORD AND WHAT THEY ARE. From the beginning, God added to the preaching of his Word in his Church sacraments or sacramental signs. For thus does all Holy Scripture clearly testify. Sacraments are mystical symbols, or holy rites, or sacred actions, instituted by God himself, consisting of his Word, of signs and of things signified, whereby in the Church he keeps in mind and from time to time recalls the great benefits he has shown to men; whereby also he seals his promises, and outwardly represents, and, as it were, offers unto our sight those things which inwardly he performs for us, and so strengthens and increases our faith through the working of God's Spirit in our hearts. Lastly, he thereby distinguishes us from all other people and religions, and consecrates and binds us wholly to himself, and signifies what he requires of us.

SOME ARE SACRAMENTS OF THE OLD, OTHERS OF THE NEW, TESTAMENT. Some sacraments are of the old, others of the new, people. The sacraments of the ancient people were circumcision, and the Paschal Lamb, which was offered up; for that reason it is referred to the sacrifices which were practiced from the beginning of the world.

THE NUMBER OF SACRAMENTS OF THE NEW PEOPLE. The sacraments of the new people are Baptism and the Lord's Supper. There are some who count seven sacraments of the new people. Of these we acknowledge that repentance, the ordination of ministers (not indeed the papal but apostolic ordination), and matrimony are profitable ordinances of God, but not sacraments. Confirmation and extreme unction are human inventions which the Church can dispense with without any loss, and indeed, we do not have them in our churches. For they contain some things of which we can by no means approve. Above all we detest all the trafficking in which the Papists engage in dispensing the sacraments.

THE AUTHOR OF THE SACRAMENTS. The author of all sacraments is not any man, but God alone. Men cannot institute sacraments. For they pertain to the worship of God, and it is not for man to appoint and prescribe a worship of God, but to accept and preserve the one he has received from God. Besides, the symbols have God's promises annexed to them, which require faith. Now faith rests only upon the Word of God; and the Word of God is like papers or letters, and the sacraments are like seals which only God appends to the letters.

CHRIST STILL WORKS IN SACRAMENTS. And as God is the author of the sacraments, so he continually works in the Church in which they are rightly carried out; so that the faithful, when they receive them from the ministers, know that God works in his own ordinance, and therefore they receive them as from the hand of God; and the minister's faults (even if they be very great) cannot affect them, since they acknowledge the integrity of the sacraments to depend upon the institution of the Lord.

THE AUTHOR AND THE MINISTERS OF THE SACRAMENTS TO BE DISTINGUISHED. Hence in the administration of the sacraments they also clearly distinguish between the Lord himself and the ministers of the Lord, confessing that the substance of the sacraments is given them by the Lord, and the outward signs by the ministers of the Lord.

THE SUBSTANCE OR CHIEF THING IN THE SACRAMENTS. But the principal thing which God promises in all sacraments and to which all the godly in all ages direct their attention (some call it the substance and matter of the sacraments) is Christ the Savior—that only sacrifice, and that Lamb of God slain from the foundation of the world; that rock, also, from which all our fathers drank, by whom all the elect are circumcised without hands through the Holy Spirit, and are washed from all their sins, and are nourished with the very body and blood of Christ unto eternal life.

THE SIMILARITY AND DIFFERENCE IN THE SACRAMENTS OF OLD AND NEW PEOPLES. Now, in respect of that which is the principal thing and the matter itself in the sacraments, the sacraments of both peoples are equal. For Christ, the only Mediator and Savior of the faithful, is the chief thing and very substance of the sacraments in both; for the one God is the author of them both. They were given to both peoples as signs and seals of the grace and promises of God, which should call to mind and renew the memory of God's great benefits, and should distinguish the faithful from all the religions in the world; lastly, which should be received spiritually by faith, and should bind the receivers to the Church, and admonish them of their duty. In these and similar respects, I say, the sacraments of both peoples are not dissimilar, although in the outward signs they are different. And, indeed, with respect to the signs we make a great difference. For ours are more firm and lasting, inasmuch as they will never be changed to the end of the world. Moreover, ours testify that both the substance and the promise have been fulfilled or perfected in Christ; the former signified what was to be fulfilled. Ours are also more simple and less laborious, less sumptuous and involved with ceremonies. Moreover, they belong to a more numerous people, one that is dispersed throughout the whole earth. And since they are more excellent, and by the Holy Spirit kindle greater faith, a greater abundance of the Spirit also ensues.

OUR SACRAMENTS SUCCEED THE OLD WHICH ARE ABROGATED. But now since Christ the true Messiah is exhibited unto us, and the abundance of grace is poured forth upon the people of the New Testament, the sacraments of the old people are surely abrogated and have ceased; and in their stead the symbols of the New Testament are placed—Baptism in the place of circumcision, the Lord's Supper in place of the Paschal Lamb and sacrifices.

IN WHAT THE SACRAMENTS CONSIST. And as formerly the sacraments consisted of the word, the sign, and the thing signified; so even now they are composed, as it were, of the same parts. For the Word of God makes them sacraments, which before they were not. *The Consecration of the Sacraments.* For they are consecrated by the Word, and shown to be sanctified by him who instituted them. To sanctify or consecrate anything to God is to dedicate it to holy uses; that is, to take it from the common and ordinary use, and to appoint it to a holy use. For the signs in the sacraments are drawn from common use, things external and visible. For in baptism the sign is the element of water, and that visible washing which is done by the minister; but the thing signified is regeneration and the cleansing from sins. Likewise, in the Lord's Supper, the outward sign is bread and wine, taken from things commonly used for meat and drink; but the thing signified is the body of Christ which was given, and his blood which was shed for us, or the communion of the body and blood of the Lord. Wherefore, the water, bread, and wine, according to their nature and apart from the divine institution and sacred use, are only that which they are called and we experience. But when the Word of God is added to them, together with invocation of the divine name, and the renewing of their first institution and sanctification, then these signs are consecrated, and shown to be sanctified by Christ. For Christ's first institution and consecration of the sacraments remains always effectual in the Church of God, so that those who do not celebrate the sacraments in any other way than the Lord himself instituted from the beginning still today enjoy that first and all-surpassing consecration. And hence in the celebration of the sacraments the very words of Christ are repeated.

SIGNS TAKE NAME OF THINGS SIGNIFIED. And as we learn out of the Word of God that these signs were instituted for another purpose than the usual use, therefore we teach that they now, in their holy use, take upon them the names of things signified, and are no longer called mere water, bread

or wine, but also regeneration or the washing of water, and the body and blood of the Lord or symbols and sacraments of the Lord's body and blood. Not that the symbols are changed into the things signified, or cease to be what they are in their own nature. For otherwise they would not be sacraments. If they were only the thing signified, they would not be signs.

THE SACRAMENTAL UNION. Therefore the signs acquire the names of things because they are mystical signs of sacred things, and because the signs and the things signified are sacramentally joined together; joined together, I say, or united by a mystical signification, and by the purpose or will of him who instituted the sacraments. For the water, bread, and wine are not common, but holy signs. And he that instituted water in baptism did not institute it with the will and intention that the faithful should only be sprinkled by the water of baptism; and he who commanded the bread to be eaten and the wine to be drunk in the supper did not want the faithful to receive only bread and wine without any mystery as they eat bread in their homes; but that they should spiritually partake of the things signified, and by faith be truly cleansed from their sins, and partake of Christ.

THE SECTS. And, therefore, we do not at all approve of those who attribute the sanctification of the sacraments to I know not what properties and formula or to the power of words pronounced by one who is consecrated and who has the intention of consecrating, and to other accidental things which neither Christ or the apostles delivered to us by word or example. Neither do we approve of the doctrine of those who speak of the sacraments just as common signs, not sanctified and effectual. Nor do we approve of those who despise the visible aspect of the sacraments because of the invisible, and so believe the signs to be superfluous because they think they already enjoy the things themselves, as the Messalians are said to have held.

THE THING SIGNIFIED IS NEITHER INCLUDED IN OR BOUND TO THE SACRAMENTS. We do not approve of the doctrine of those who teach that grace and the things signified are so bound to and included in the signs that whoever participate outwardly in the signs, no matter what sort of persons they be, also inwardly participate in the grace and things signified.

However, as we do not estimate the value of the sacraments by the worthiness or unworthiness of the ministers, so we do not estimate it by the condition of those who receive them. For we know that the value of the sacraments depends upon faith and upon the truthfulness and pure goodness of God. For as the Word of God remains the true Word of God, in which, when it is preached, not only bare words are repeated, but at the same time the things signified or announced in words are offered by God, even if the ungodly and unbelievers hear and understand the words yet do not enjoy the things signified, because they do not receive them by true faith; so the sacraments, which by the Word consist of signs and the things signified, remain true and inviolate sacraments, signifying not only sacred things, but, by God offering, the things signified, even if unbelievers do not receive the things offered. This is not the fault of God who gives and offers them, but the fault of men who receive them without faith and illegitimately; but whose unbelief does not invalidate the faithfulness of God (Rom. 3:3 f.).

THE PURPOSE FOR WHICH SACRAMENTS WERE INSTITUTED. Since the purpose for which sacraments were instituted was also explained in passing when right at the beginning of our exposition it was shown what sacraments are, there is no need to be tedious by repeating what once has been said. Logically, therefore, we now speak severally of the sacraments of the new people.

CHAPTER XX. OF HOLY BAPTISM

THE INSTITUTION OF BAPTISM. Baptism was instituted and consecrated by God. First John baptized, who dipped Christ in the water in Jordan. From him it came to the apostles, who also baptized with water. The Lord expressly commanded them to preach the Gospel and to baptize "in the name of the Father and of the Son and of the Holy Spirit" (Matt. 28:19). And in The Acts, Peter said to the Jews who inquired what they ought to do: "Be baptized every one of you in the name of Jesus Christ for the forgiveness of your sins; and you shall receive the gift of the Holy Spirit" (Acts 2:37 f.). Hence by some baptism is called a sign of initiation for God's people, since by it the elect of God are consecrated to God.

ONE BAPTISM. There is but one baptism in the Church of God; and it is sufficient to be once baptized or consecrated unto God. For baptism once received continues for all of life, and is a perpetual sealing of our adoption.

WHAT IT MEANS TO BE BAPTIZED. Now to be baptized in the name of Christ is to be enrolled, entered, and received into the covenant and family, and so into the inheritance of the sons of God: yes, and in this life to be called after the name of God; that is to say, to be called a son of God; to be cleansed also from the filthiness of sins, and to be granted the manifold grace of God, in order to lead a new and innocent life. Baptism, therefore, calls to mind and renews the great favor God has shown to the race of mortal men. For we are all born in the pollution of sin and are the children of wrath. But God, who is rich in mercy, freely cleanses us from our sins by the blood of his Son, and in him adopts us to be his sons, and by a holy covenant joins us to himself, and enriches us with various gifts, that we might live a new life. All these things are assured by baptism. For inwardly we are regenerated, purified, and renewed by God through the Holy Spirit; and outwardly we receive the assurance of the greatest gifts in the water, by which also those great benefits are represented, and, as it were, set before our eyes to be beheld.

WE ARE BAPTIZED WITH WATER. And therefore we are baptized, that is, washed or sprinkled with visible water. For the water washes dirt away, and cools and refreshes hot and tired bodies. And the grace of God performs these things for souls, and does so invisibly or spirtually.

THE OBLIGATION OF BAPTISM. Moreover, God also separates us from all strange religions and peoples by the symbol of baptism, and consecrates us to himself as his property. We, therefore, confess our faith when we are baptized, and obligate ourselves to God for obedience, mortification of the flesh, and newness of life. Hence, we are enlisted in the holy military service of Christ that all our life long we should fight against the world, Satan, and our own flesh. Moreover, we are baptized into one body of the Church, that with all members of the Church we might beautifully concur in the one religion and in mutual services.

THE FORM OF BAPTISM. We believe that the most perfect form of baptism is that by which Christ was baptized, and by which the apostles baptized. Those things, therefore, which by man's device were added afterwards and used in the Church we do not consider necessary to the perfection of baptism. Of this kind is exorcism, the use of burning lights, oil, salt, spittle, and such other things as that baptism is to be celebrated twice every year with a multitude of ceremonies. For we believe that one baptism of the Church has been sanctified in God's first institution, and that it is consecrated by the Word and is also effectual today in virtue of God's first blessing.

THE MINISTER OF BAPTISM. We teach that baptism should not be administered in the Church by women or midwives. For Paul deprived women of ecclesiastical duties, and baptism has to do with these.

ANABAPTISTS. We condemn the Anabaptists, who deny that newborn infants of the faithful are to be baptized. For according to evangelical teaching, of such is the Kingdom of God, and they are in the covenant of God. Why, then, should the sign of God's covenant not be given to them? Why should those who belong to God and are in his Church not be initiated by holy baptism? We condemn also the Anabaptists in the rest of their peculiar doctrines which they hold contrary to the Word of God. We therefore are not Anabaptists and have nothing in common with them.

CHAPTER XXI. OF THE HOLY SUPPER OF THE LORD

THE SUPPER OF THE LORD. The Supper of the Lord, (which is called the Lord's Table, and the Eucharist, that is, a Thanksgiving) is, therefore, usually called a supper, because it was instituted by Christ at his last supper, and still represents it, and because in it the faithful are spiritually fed and given drink.

THE AUTHOR AND CONSECRATOR OF THE SUPPER. For the author of the Supper of the Lord is not an angel or any man, but the Son of God himself, our Lord Jesus Christ, who first consecrated it to his Church. And the same consecration or blessing still remains among all those who celebrate no other but that very Supper which the Lord instituted, and at which they repeat the words of the Lord's Supper, and in all things look to the one Christ by a true faith, from whose hands they receive, as it were, what they receive through the ministry of the ministers of the Church.

A MEMORIAL OF GOD'S BENEFITS. By this sacred rite the Lord wishes to keep in fresh remembrance that greatest benefit which he showed to mortal men, namely, that by having given his body and shed his blood he has pardoned all our sins, and redeemed us from eternal death and the power of the devil, and now feeds us with his flesh, and gives us his blood to drink, which, being received spiritually by true faith, nourish us to eternal life. And this so great a benefit is renewed as often as the Lord's Supper is celebrated. For the Lord said: "Do this in remembrance of me." This holy Supper also seals to us that the very body of Christ was truly given for us, and his blood shed for the remission of our sins, lest our faith should in any way waver.

THE SIGN AND THING SIGNIFIED. And this is visibly represented by this sacrament outwardly through the ministers, and, as it were, presented to our eyes to be seen, which is invisibly wrought by the Holy Spirit inwardly in the soul. Bread is outwardly offered by the minister, and the words of the Lord are heard: "Take, eat; this is my body"; and, "Take and divide among you. Drink of it, all of you; this is my blood." Therefore the faithful receive what is given by the ministers of the Lord, and they eat the bread of the Lord and drink of the Lord's cup. At the same time by the work of Christ through the Holy Spirit they also inwardly receive the flesh and blood of the Lord, and are thereby nourished unto life eternal. For the flesh and blood of Christ is the true food and drink unto life eternal; and Christ himself, since he was given for us and is our Savior, is the principal thing in the Supper, and we do not permit anything else to be substituted in his place.

But in order to understand better and more clearly how the flesh and blood of Christ are the food and drink of the faithful, and are received by the faithful unto eternal life, we would add these few things. There is more than one kind of eating. There is corporeal eating whereby food is taken into the mouth, is chewed with the teeth, and swallowed into the stomach. In times past the Capernaites thought that the flesh of the Lord should be eaten in this way, but they are refuted by him in John, ch. 6. For as the flesh of Christ cannot be eaten corporeally without infamy and savagery, so it is not food for the stomach. All men are forced to admit this. We therefore disapprove of that canon in the Pope's decrees, *Ego Berengarius (De Consecrat.*, Dist. 2). For neither did godly antiquity believe, nor do we believe, that the body of Christ is to be eaten corporeally and essentially with a bodily mouth.

SPIRITUAL EATING OF THE LORD. There is also a spiritual eating of Christ's body; not such that we think that thereby the food itself is to be changed into spirit, but whereby the body and blood of the Lord, while remaining in their own essence and property, are spiritually communicated to us, certainly not in a corporeal but in a spiritual way, by the Holy Spirit, who applies and bestows upon us these things which have been prepared for us by the sacrifice of the Lord's body and blood for us, namely, the remission of sins, deliverance, and eternal life; so that Christ lives in us and we live in him, and he causes us to receive him by true faith to this end that he may become for us such spiritual food and drink, that is, our life.

CHRIST AS OUR FOOD SUSTAINS US IN LIFE. For even as bodily food and drink not only refresh and strengthen our bodies, but also keeps them alive, so the flesh of Christ delivered for us, and his blood shed for us, not only refresh and strengthen our souls, but also preserve them alive, not in so far as they are corporeally eaten and drunken, but in so far as they are communicated unto us spiritually by the Spirit of God, as the Lord said: "The bread which I shall give for the life of the world is my flesh" (John 6:51), and "the flesh" (namely what is eaten bodily) "is of no avail; it is the spirit that gives life" (v. 63). And: "The words that I have spoken to you are spirit and life."

CHRIST RECEIVED BY FAITH. And as we must by eating receive food into our bodies in order that it may work in us, and prove its efficacy in us—since it profits us nothing when it remains outside us—so it is necessary that we receive Christ by faith, that he may become ours, and he may live in us and we in him. For he says: "I am the bread of life; he who comes to me shall not hunger, and he who believes in me shall never thirst" (John 6:35); and also, "He who eats me will live because of me . . . he abides in me, I in him" (vs. 57, 56).

SPIRITUAL FOOD. From all this it is clear that by spiritual food we do not mean some imaginary food I know not what, but the very body of the Lord given to us, which nevertheless is received by the faithful not corporeally, but spiritually by faith. In this matter we follow the teaching of the Savior himself, Christ the Lord, according to John, ch.6.

EATING NECESSARY FOR SALVATION. And this eating of the flesh and drinking of the blood of the Lord is so necessary for salvation that without it no man can be saved. But this spiritual eating and drinking also occurs apart from the Supper of the

Lord, and as often and wherever a man believes in Christ. To which that sentence of St. Augustine's perhaps applies: "Why do you provide for your teeth and your stomach? Believe, and you have eaten."

SACRAMENTAL EATING OF THE LORD. Besides the higher spiritual eating there is also a sacramental eating of the body of the Lord by which not only spiritually and internally the believer truly participates in the true body and blood of the Lord, but also, by coming to the Table of the Lord, outwardly receives the visible sacrament of the body and blood of the Lord. To be sure, when the believer believed, he first received the life-giving food, and still enjoys it. But therefore, when he now receives the sacrament, he does not receive nothing. For he progresses in continuing to communicate in the body and blood of the Lord, and so his faith is kindled and grows more and more, and is refreshed by spiritual food. For while we live, faith is continually increased. And he who outwardly receives the sacrament by true faith, not only receives the sign, but also, as we said, enjoys the thing itself. Moreover, he obeys the Lord's institution and commandment, and with a joyful mind gives thanks for his redemption and that of all mankind, and makes a faithful memorial to the Lord's death, and gives a witness before the Church, of whose body he is a member. Assurance is also given to those who receive the sacrament that the body of the Lord was given and his blood shed, not only for men in general, but particularly for every faithful communicant, to whom it is food and drink unto eternal life.

UNBELIEVERS TAKE THE SACRAMENT TO THEIR JUDGMENT. But he who comes to this sacred Table of the Lord without faith, communicates only in the sacrament and does not receive the substance of the sacrament whence comes life and salvation; and such men unworthily eat of the Lord's Table. Whoever eats the bread or drinks the cup of the Lord in an unworthy manner will be guilty of the body and blood of the Lord, and eats and drinks judgment upon himself (I Cor. II:26-29). For when they do not approach with true faith, they dishonor the death of Christ, and therefore eat and drink condemnation to themselves.

THE PRESENCE OF CHRIST IN THE SUPPER. We do not, therefore, so join the body of the Lord and his blood with the bread and wine as to say that the bread itself is the body of Christ except in a sacramental way; or that the body of Christ is hidden corporeally under the bread, so that it ought to be worshipped under the form of bread; or yet that whoever receives the sign, receives also the thing itself. The body of Christ is in heaven at the right hand of the Father; and therefore our hearts are to be lifted up on high, and not to be fixed on the bread, neither is the Lord to be worshipped in the bread. Yet the Lord is not absent from his Church when she celebrates the Supper. The sun, which is absent from us in the heavens, is notwithstanding effectually present among us. How much more is the Sun of Righteousness, Christ, although in his body he is absent from us in heaven, present with us, not corporeally, but spiritually, by his vivifying operation, and as he himself explained at his Last Supper that he would be present with us (John, chs. 14; 15; and 16). Whence it follows that we do not have the Supper without Christ, and yet at the same time have an unbloody and mystical Supper, as it was universally called by antiquity.

OTHER PURPOSES OF THE LORD'S SUPPER. Moreover, we are admonished in the celebration of the Supper of the Lord to be mindful of whose body we have become members, and that, therefore, we may be of one mind with all the brethren, live a holy life, and not pollute ourselves with wickedness and strange religions; but, persevering in the true faith to the end of our life, strive to excel in holiness of life.

PREPARATION FOR THE SUPPER. It is therefore fitting that when we would come to the Supper, we first examine ourselves according to the commandment of the apostle, especially as to the kind of faith we have, whether we believe that Christ has come to save sinners and to call them to repentance, and whether each man believes that he is in the number of those who have been delivered by Christ and saved; and whether he is determined to change his wicked life, to lead a holy life, and with the Lord's help to persevere in the true religion and in harmony with the brethren, and to give due thanks to God for his deliverance.

THE OBSERVANCE OF THE SUPPER WITH BOTH BREAD AND WINE. We think that rite, manner, or form of the Supper to be the most simple and excellent which comes nearest to the first institution of the Lord and to the apostles' doctrine. It consists in proclaiming the Word of God, in godly prayers, in the action of the Lord himself, and its repetition, in the eating of the Lord's body and drinking of his blood; in a fitting remembrance of the Lord's death, and a faithful thanksgiving; and in a holy fellowship in the union of the body of the Church.

We therefore disapprove of those who have taken from the faithful one species of the sacrament, namely, the Lord's cup. For these seriously offend against the institution of the Lord who says: "Drink ye all of this"; which he did not so expressly say of the bread.

We are now discussing what kind of mass once existed among the fathers, whether it is to be tolerated or not. But this we say freely that the mass which is now used throughout the Roman Church has been abolished in our churches for many and very good reasons which, for brevity's sake, we do not now enumerate in detail. We certainly could not approve of making a wholesome action into a vain spectacle and a means of gaining merit, and of celebrating it for a price. Nor could we approve of saying that in it the priest is said to effect the very body of the Lord, and really to offer it for the remission of the sins of the living and the dead, and in addition, for the honor, veneration and remembrance of the saints in heaven, etc.

CHAPTER XXII. OF RELIGIOUS AND ECCLESIASTICAL MEETINGS

WHAT OUGHT TO BE DONE IN MEETINGS FOR WORSHIP. Although it is permitted all men to read the Holy Scriptures privately at home, and by instruction to edify one another in the true religion, yet in order that the Word of God may be properly preached to the people, and prayers and supplication publicly made, also that the sacraments may be rightly administered, and that collections may be made for the poor and to pay the cost of all the Church's expenses, and in order to maintain social intercourse, it is most necessary that religious or Church gatherings be held. For it is certain that in the apostolic and primitive Church, there were such assemblies frequented by all the godly.

MEETINGS FOR WORSHIP NOT TO BE NEGLECTED. As many as spurn such meetings and stay away from them, despise true religion, and are to be urged by the pastors and godly magistrates to abstain from stubbornly absenting themselves from sacred assemblies.

MEETINGS ARE PUBLIC. But Church meetings are not to be secret and hidden, but public and well attended, unless persecution by the enemies of Christ and the Church does not permit them to be public. For we know how under the tyranny of the Roman emperors the meetings of the primitive Church were held in secret places.

DECENT MEETING PLACES. Moreover, the places where the faithful meet are to be decent, and in all respects fit for God's Church. Therefore, spacious buildings or temples are to be chosen, but they are to be purged of everything that is not fitting for a church. And everything is to be arranged for decorum, necessity, and godly decency, lest anything be lacking that is required for worship and the necessary works of the Church.

MODESTY AND HUMILITY TO BE OBSERVED IN MEETINGS. And as we believe that God does not dwell in temples made with hands, so we know that on account of God's Word and sacred use places dedicated to God and his worship are not profane, but holy, and that those who are present in them are to conduct themselves reverently and modestly, seeing that they are in a sacred place, in the presence of God and his holy angels.

THE TRUE ORNAMENTATION OF SANCTUARIES. Therefore, all luxurious attire, all pride, and everything unbecoming to Christian humility, discipline and modesty, are to be banished from the sanctuaries and places of prayer of Christians. For the true ornamentation of churches does not consist in ivory, gold, and precious stones, but in the frugality, piety, and virtues of those who are in the Church. Let all things be done decently and in order in the church, and finally, let all things be done for edification.

WORSHIP IN THE COMMON LANGUAGE. Therefore, let all strange tongues keep silence in gatherings for worship, and let all things be set forth in a common language which is understood by the people gathered in that place.

CHAPTER XXIII. OF THE PRAYERS OF THE CHURCH, OF SINGING, AND OF CANONICAL HOURS

COMMON LANGUAGE. It is true that a man is permitted to pray privately in any language that he understands, but public prayers in meetings for worship are to be made in the common language known to all. *Prayer*. Let all the prayers of the faithful be poured forth to God alone, through the mediation of Christ only, out of faith and love. The priesthood of Christ the Lord and true religion forbid the invocation of saints in heaven or to use them as intercessors. Prayer is to be made for magistracy, for kings, and all that are placed in authority, for ministers of the Church, and for all needs of churches. In calamities, especially of the Church, unceasing prayer is to be made both privately and publicly.

FREE PRAYER. Moreover, prayer is to be made voluntarily, without constraint or for any reward. Nor is it proper for prayer to be superstitiously restricted to one place, as if it were not permitted to pray anywhere except in a sanctuary. Neither is it necessary for public prayers to be the same in all churches with respect to form and time. Each Church is to exercise its own freedom. Socrates, in his history, says, "In all regions of the world you will not find two churches which wholly agree in prayer." (*Hist. ecclesiast.* V.22, 57.) The authors of this difference, I think, were those who were in charge of the Churches at particular times. Yet if they agree, it is to be highly commended and imitated by others.

THE METHOD TO BE EMPLOYED IN PUBLIC PRAYERS. As in everything, so also in public prayers there is to be a standard lest they be excessively long and irksome. The greater part of meetings for worship is therefore to be given to evangelical teaching, and care is to be taken lest the congregation is wearied by too lengthy prayers and when they are to hear the preaching of the Gospel they either leave the meeting or, having been exhausted, want to do away with it altogether. To such people the sermon seems to be overlong, which otherwise is brief enough. And therefore it is appropriate for preachers to keep to a standard.

SINGING. Likewise moderation is to be exercised where singing is used in a meeting for worship. That song which they call the Gregorian Chant has many foolish things in it; hence it is rightly rejected by many of our churches. If there are churches which have a true and proper sermon but no singing, they ought not to be condemned. For all churches do not have the advantage of singing. And it is well known from testimonies of antiquity that the custom of singing is very old in the Eastern Churches whereas it was late when it was at length accepted in the West.

CANONICAL HOURS. Antiquity knew nothing of canonical hours, that is, prayers arranged for certain hours of the day, and sung or recited by the Papists, as can be proved from their breviaries and by many arguments. But they also have not a few absurdities, of which I say nothing else; accordingly they are rightly omitted by churches which substitute in their place things that are beneficial for the whole Church of God.

CHAPTER XXIV. OF HOLY DAYS, FASTS AND THE CHOICE OF FOODS

THE TIME NECESSARY FOR WORSHIP. Although religion is not bound to time, yet it cannot be cultivated and exercised without a proper distribution and arrangement of time. Every Church, therefore, chooses for itself a certain time for public prayers, and for the preaching of the Gospel, and for the celebration of the sacraments; and no one is permitted to overthrow this appointment of the Church at his own pleasure. For unless some due time and leisure is given for the outward exercise of religion, without doubt men would be drawn away from it by their own affairs.

THE LORD'S DAY. Hence we see that in the ancient churches there were not only certain set hours in the week appointed for meetings, but that also the Lord's Day itself, ever since the apostles' time, was set aside for them and for a holy rest, a practice now rightly preserved by our Churches for the sake of worship and love.

SUPERSTITION. In this connection we do not yield to the Jewish observance and to superstitions. For we do not believe that one day is any holier than another, or think that rest in itself is acceptable to God. Moreover, we celebrate the Lord's Day and not the Sabbath as a free observance.

THE FESTIVALS OF CHRIST AND THE SAINTS. Moreover, if in Christian liberty the churches religiously celebrate the member of the Lord's nativity, circumcision, passion, resurrection, and of his ascension into heaven, and the sending of the Holy Spirit upon his disciples, we approve of it highly. But we do not approve of feasts instituted for men and for saints. Holy days have to do with the first Table of the Law and belong to God alone. Finally, holy days which have been instituted for the saints and which we have abolished, have much that is absurd and useless, and are not to be tolerated. In the meantime, we confess that the remembrance of saints, at a suitable time and place, is to be profitably commended to the people in sermons, and the holy examples of the saints set forth to be imitated by all.

FASTING. Now, the more seriously the Church of Christ condemns surfeiting, drunkenness, and all kinds of lust and intemperance, so much the more strongly does it commend to us Christian fasting. For fasting is nothing else than the abstinence and moderation of the godly, and a discipline, care and chastisement of our flesh undertaken as a necessity for the time being, whereby we are humbled before God, and we deprive the flesh of its fuel so that it may the more willingly and easily obey the Spirit. Therefore, those who pay no attention to such things do not fast, but imagine that they fast if they stuff their stomachs once a day, and at a certain or prescribed time abstain from certain foods, thinking that by having done this work they please God and do something good. Fasting is an aid to the prayers of the saints and for all virtues. But as is seen in the books of the prophets, the fast of the Jews who fasted from food but not from wickedness did not please God.

PUBLIC AND PRIVATE FASTING. Now there is a public and a private fasting. In olden times they celebrated public fasts in calamitous times and in the affliction of the Church. They abstained altogether from food till the evening, and spent all that time in holy prayers, the worship of God, and repentance. These differed little from mourning, and there is frequent mention of them in the Prophets and especially by Joel in ch. 2. Such a fast should be kept at this day, when the Church is in distress. Private fasts are undertaken by each one of us, as he feels himself withdrawn from the Spirit. For in this manner he withdraws the flesh from its fuel.

CHARACTERISTICS OF FASTING. All fasts ought to proceed from a free and willing spirit, and from genuine humility, and not feigned to gain the applause or favor of men, much less that a man should wish to merit righteousness by them. But let every one fast to this end, that he may deprive the flesh of its fuel in order that he may the more zealously serve God.

LENT. The fast of Lent is attested by antiquity but not at all in the writings of the apostles. Therefore it ought not, and cannot, be imposed on the faithful. It is certain that formerly there were various forms and customs of fasting. Hence, Irenaeus, a most ancient writer, says: "Some think that a fast should be observed one day only, others two days, but others more, and some forty days. This diversity in keeping this fast did not first begin in our times, but long before us by those, as I suppose, who did not simply keep to what had been delivered to them from the beginning, but afterwards fell into another custom either through negligence or ignorance" (*Fragm.* 3, ed. Stieren, I. 824 f.). Moreover, Socrates, the historian, says: "Because no ancient text is found concerning this matter, I think the apostles left this to every man's own judgment, that every one might do what is good without fear or constraint" (*Hist. ecclesiast.* V.22, 40).

CHOICE OF FOOD. Now concerning the choice of foods, we think that in fasting all things should be denied to the flesh whereby the flesh is made more insolent, and by which it is greatly pleased, and by which it is inflamed with desire whether by fish or meat or spices or delicacies and excellent wines. Moreover, we know that all the creatures of God were made for the use and service of men. All things which God made are good, and without distinction are to be used in the fear of God and with proper moderation (Gen. 2:15 f.). For the apostle says: "To the pure all things are pure" (Titus 1:15), and also: "Eat whatever is sold in the meat market without raising any question on the ground of conscience" (I Cor. 10:25). The same apostle calls the doctrine of those who teach to abstain from meats "the doctrine of demons"; for "God created foods to be received with thanksgiving by those who believe and know this truth that everything created by God is good, and nothing is to be rejected if it is received with thanksgiving" (I Tim. 4:1 ff.). The same apostle, in the epistle to the Colossians, reproves those who want to acquire a reputation for holiness by excessive abstinence (Col. 2:18 ff.).

SECTS. Therefore we entirely disapprove of the Tatians and the Encratites, and all the disciples of Eustathius, against whom the Gangrian Synod was called.

CHAPTER XXV. OF CATECHIZING AND OF COMFORTING AND VISITING THE SICK

YOUTH TO BE INSTRUCTED IN GODLINESS. The Lord enjoined his ancient people to exercise the greatest care that young people, even from infancy, be properly instructed. Moreover, he expressly commanded in his law that they should teach them, and that the mysteries of the sacraments should be explained. Now since it is well known from the writings of the Evangelists and apostles that God has no less concern for the youth of his new people, when he openly testifies and says: "Let the children come to me; for to such belongs the kingdom of heaven" (Mark 10:14), the pastors of the churches act most wisely when they early and carefully catechize the youth, laying the first grounds of faith, and faithfully teaching the rudiments of our religion by expounding the Ten Commandments, the Apostles' Creed, the Lord's Prayer, and the doctrine of the sacraments, with other such principles and chief heads of our religion. Here let the Church show her faith and diligence in bringing the children to be catechized, desirous and glad to have her children well instructed.

THE VISITATION OF THE SICK. Since men are never exposed to more grievous temptations than when they are harassed by infirmities, are sick and are weakened by diseases of both soul and body, surely it is never more fitting for pastors of churches to watch more carefully for the welfare of their flocks than in such diseases and infirmities. Therefore let them visit the sick soon, and let them be called in good time by the sick, if the circumstance itself would have required it. Let them comfort and confirm them in the true faith, and then arm them against the dangerous suggestions of Satan. They should also hold prayer for the sick in the home and, if need be, prayers should also be made for the sick in the public meeting; and they should see that they happily depart this life. We said above that we do not approve of the Popish visitation of the sick with extreme unction because it is absurd and is not approved by canonical Scriptures.

CHAPTER XXVI. OF THE BURIAL OF THE FAITHFUL, AND OF THE CARE TO BE SHOWN FOR THE DEAD; OF PURGATORY, AND THE APPEARING OF SPIRITS

THE BURIAL OF BODIES. As the bodies of the faithful are the temples of the Holy Spirit which we truly believe will rise again at the Last Day, Scriptures command that they be honorably and without superstition committed to the earth, and also that honorable mention be made of those saints who have fallen asleep in the Lord, and that all duties of familial piety be shown to those left behind, their widows and orphans. We do not teach that any other care be taken for the dead. Therefore, we greatly disapprove of the Cynics, who neglected the bodies of the dead or most carelessly and disdainfully cast them into the earth, never saying a good word about the deceased, or caring a bit about those whom they left behind them.

THE CARE FOR THE DEAD. On the other hand, we do not approve of those who are overly and absurdly attentive to the deceased; who, like the heathen, bewail their dead (although we do not blame that moderate mourning which the apostle permits in I Thess. 4:13, judging it to be inhuman not to grieve at all); and who sacrifice for the dead, and mumble certain prayers for pay, in order by such ceremonies to deliver their loved ones from the torments in which they are immersed by death, and then think they are able to liberate them by such incantations.

THE STATE OF THE SOUL DEPARTED FROM THE BODY. For we believe that the faithful, after bodily death, go directly to Christ, and, therefore, do not need the eulogies and prayers of the living for the dead and their services. Likewise we believe that unbelievers are immediately cast into hell from which no exit is opened for the wicked by any services of the living.

PURGATORY. But what some teach concerning the fire of purgatory is opposed to the Christian faith, namely, "I believe in the forgiveness of sins, and the life everlasting," and to the perfect purgation through Christ, and to these words of Christ our Lord: "Truly, truly, I say to you, he who hears my word and believes him who sent me, has eternal life; he shall not come into judgment, but has passed from death to life" (John 5:24). Again: "He who has bathed does not need to wash, except for his feet, but he is clean all over, and you are clean" (John 13:10).

THE APPARITION OF SPIRITS. Now what is related of the spirits or souls of the dead sometimes appearing to those who are alive, and begging certain duties of them whereby they may be set free, we count those apparitions among the laughingstocks, crafts, and deceptions of the devil, who, as he can transform himself into an angel of light, so he strives either to overthrow the true faith or to call it into doubt. In the Old Testament the Lord forbade the seeking of the truth from the dead, and any sort of commerce with spirits. (Deut. 18:11.) Indeed, as evangelical truth declares, the glutton, being in torment, is denied a return to his brethren, as the divine oracle declares in the words: "They have Moses and the prophets; let them hear them. If they hear not Moses and the prophets, neither will they be convinced if some one should rise from the dead" (Luke 16:29 ff.).

CHAPTER XXVII. OF RITES, CEREMONIES AND THINGS INDIFFERENT

CEREMONIES AND RITES. Unto the ancient people were given at one time certain ceremonies, as a kind of instruction for those who were kept under the law, as under a schoolmaster or tutor. But when Christ, the Deliverer, came and the law was abolished, we who believe are no more under the law (Rom. 6:14), and the ceremonies have disappeared; hence the apostles did not want to retain or to restore them in Christ's Church to such a degree that they openly testified that they did not wish to impose any burden upon the Church. Therefore, we would seem to be bringing in and restoring Judaism if we were to increase ceremonies and rites in Christ's Church according to the custom in the ancient Church. Hence, we by no means approve of the opinion of those who think that the Church of Christ must be held in check by many different rites, as if by some kind of training. For if the apostles did not want to impose upon Christian people ceremonies or rites which were appointed by God, who, I pray, in his right mind would obtrude upon them the inventions devised by man? The more the mass of rites is increased in the Church, the more is detracted not only from Christian liberty, but also from Christ, and from faith in him, as long as the people seek those things in ceremonies which they should seek in the only Son of God, Jesus Christ, through faith. Wherefore a few moderate and simple rites, that are not contrary to the Word of God, are sufficient for the godly.

DIVERSITY OF RITES. If different rites are found in churches, no one should think that for this reason the churches disagree. Socrates says: "It would be impossible to put together in writing all the rites of churches throughout cities and countries. No religion observes the same rites, even though it embraces the same doctrine concerning them. For those who

are of the same faith disagree among themselves about rites." *(Hist. ecclesiast.* V.22, 30, 62.) This much says Socrates. And we, today, having in our churches different rites in the celebration of the Lord's Supper and in some other things, nevertheless do not disagree in doctrine and faith; nor is the unity and fellowship of our churches thereby rent asunder. For the churches have always used their liberty in such rites, as being things indifferent. We also do the same thing today.

THINGS INDIFFERENT. But at the same time we admonish men to be on guard lest they reckon among things indifferent what are in fact not indifferent, as some are wont to regard the mass and the use of images in places of worship as things indifferent. "Indifferent," wrote Jerome to Augustine, "is that which is neither good nor bad, so that, whether you do it or not, you are neither just nor unjust." Therefore, when things indifferent are wrested to the confession of faith, they cease to be free; as Paul shows that it is lawful for a man to eat flesh if someone does not remind him that it was offered to idols; for then it is unlawful, because he who eats it seems to approve idolatry by eating it (I Cor. 8:9 ff.; 10:25 ff.).

CHAPTER XXVIII. OF THE POSSESSIONS OF THE CHURCH

THE POSSESSIONS OF THE CHURCH AND THEIR PROPER USE. The Church of Christ possesses riches through the munificence of princes and the liberality of the faithful who have given their means to the Church. For the Church has need of such resources and from ancient time has had resources for the maintenance of things necessary for the Church. Now the true use of the Church's wealth was, and is now, to maintain teaching in schools and in religious meetings, along with all the worship, rites, and buildings of the Church; finally, to maintain teachers, scholars, and ministers, with other necessary things, and especially for the succor and relief of the poor. *Management.* Moreover, God-fearing and wise men, noted for the management of domestic affairs, should be chosen to administer properly the Church's possessions.

THE MISUSE OF THE CHURCH'S POSSESSIONS. But if through misfortune or through the audacity, ignorance or avarice of some persons the Church's wealth is abused, it is to be restored to a sacred use by godly and wise men. For neither is an abuse, which is the greatest sacrilege, to be winked at. Therefore, we teach that schools and institutions which have been corrupted in doctrine, worship and morals must be reformed, and that the relief of the poor must be arranged dutifully, wisely, and in good faith.

CHAPTER XXIX. OF CELIBACY, MARRIAGE AND THE MANAGEMENT OF DOMESTIC AFFAIRS

SINGLE PEOPLE. Those who have the gift of celibacy from heaven, so that from the heart or with their whole soul are pure and continent and are not aflame with passion, let them serve the Lord in that calling, as long as they feel endued with that divine gift; and let them not lift up themselves above others, but let them serve the Lord continuously in simplicity and humility (I Cor. 7:7 ff.). For such are more apt to attend to divine things than those who are distracted with the private affairs of a family. But if, again, the gift be taken away, and they feel a continual burning, let them call to mind the words of the apostle: "It is better to marry than to be aflame" (I Cor. 7:9).

MARRIAGE. For marriage (which is the medicine of incontinency, and continency itself) was instituted by the Lord God himself, who blessed it most bountifully, and willed man and woman to cleave one to the other inseparably, and to live together in complete love and concord (Matt. 19:4 ff.). Whereupon we know that the apostle said: "Let marriage be held in honor among all, and let the marriage bed be undefiled." (Heb. 13:4.) And again: "If a girl marries, she does not sin" (I Cor. 7:28). *The sects.* We therefore condemn polygamy, and those who condemn second marriages.

HOW MARRIAGES ARE TO BE CONTRACTED. We teach that marriages are to be lawfully contracted in the fear of the Lord, and not against the laws which forbid certain degrees of consanguinity, lest the marriages should be incestuous. Let marriages be made with consent of the parents, or of those who take the place of parents, and above all for that purpose for which the Lord instituted marriages. Moreover, let them be kept holy with the utmost faithfulness, piety, love and purity of those joined together. Therefore let them guard against quarrels, dissensions, lust and adultery.

MATRIMONIAL FORUM. Let lawful courts be established in the Church, and holy judges who may care for marriages, and may repress all unchastity and shamefulness, and before whom matrimonial disputes may be settled.

THE REARING OF CHILDREN. Children are to be brought up by the parents in the fear of the Lord; and parents are to provide for their children, remembering the saying of the apostle: "If anyone does not provide for his relatives, he has disowned the faith and is worse than an unbeliever" (I Tim. 5:8). But especially they should teach their children honest trades or professions by which they may support themselves. They should keep them from idleness and in all these things instill in them true faith in God, lest through a lack of confidence or too much security or filthy greed they become dissolute and achieve no success.

And it is most certain that those works which are done by parents in true faith by way of domestic duties and the management of their households are in God's sight holy and truly good works. They are

no less pleasing to God than prayers, fasting and almsgiving. For thus the apostle has taught in his epistles, especially in those to Timothy and Titus. And with the same apostle we account the doctrine of those who forbid marriage or openly castigate or indirectly discredit it, as if it were not holy and pure, among the doctrine of demons.

We also detest an impure single life, the secret and open lusts and fornications of hypocrites pretending to be continent when they are the most incontinent of all. All these God will judge. We do not disapprove of riches or rich men, if they be godly and use their riches well. But we reject the sect of the Apostolicals, etc.

CHAPTER XXX. OF THE MAGISTRACY

THE MAGISTRACY IS FROM GOD. Magistracy of every kind is instituted by God himself for the peace and tranquillity of the human race, and thus it should have the chief place in the world. If the magistrate is opposed to the Church, he can hinder and disturb it very much; but if he is a friend and even a member of the Church, he is a most useful and excellent member of it, who is able to benefit it greatly, and to assist it best of all.

THE DUTY OF THE MAGISTRATE. The chief duty of the magistrate is to secure and preserve peace and public tranquillity. Doubtless he will never do this more successfully than when he is truly God-fearing and religious; that is to say, when, according to the example of the most holy kings and princes of the people of the Lord, he promotes the preaching of the truth and sincere faith, roots out lies and all superstition, together with all impiety and idolatry, and defends the Church of God. We certainly teach that the care of religion belongs especially to the holy magistrate.

Let him, therefore, hold the Word of God in his hands, and take care lest anything contrary, to it is taught. Likewise let him govern the people entrusted to him by God with good laws made according to the Word of God, and let him keep them in discipline, duty and obedience. Let him exercise judgment by judging uprightly. Let him not respect any man's person or accept bribes. Let him protect widows, orphans and the afflicted. Let him punish and even banish criminals, impostors and barbarians. For he does not bear the sword in vain. (Rom. 13:4.)

Therefore, let him draw this sword of God against all malefactors, seditious persons, thieves, murderers, oppressors, blasphemers, perjured persons, and all those whom God has commanded him to punish and even to execute. Let him suppress stubborn heretics (who are truly heretics), who do not cease to blaspheme the majesty of God and to trouble, and even to destroy the Church of God.

WAR. And if it is necessary to preserve the safety of the people by war, let him wage war in the name of God; provided he has first sought peace by all means possible, and cannot save his people in any other way except by war. And when the magistrate does these things in faith, he serves God by those very works which are truly good, and receives a blessing from the Lord.

We condemn the Anabaptists, who, when they deny that a Christian may hold the office of a magistrate, deny also that a man may be justly put to death by the magistrate, or that the magistrate may wage war, or that oaths are to be rendered to a magistrate, and such like things.

THE DUTY OF SUBJECTS. For as God wants to effect the safety of his people by the magistrate, whom he has given to the world to be, as it were, a father, so all subjects are commanded to acknowledge this favor of God in the magistrate. Therefore let them honor and reverence the magistrate as the minister of God; let them love him, favor him, and pray for him as their father; and let them obey all his just and fair commands. Finally, let them pay all customs and taxes, and all other such dues faithfully and willingly. And if the public safety of the country and justice require it, and the magistrate of necessity wages war, let them even lay down their life and pour out their blood for the public safety and that of the magistrate. And let them do this in the name of God willingly, bravely and cheerfully. For he who opposes the magistrate provokes the severe wrath of God against himself.

SECTS AND SEDITIONS. We, therefore, condemn all who are contemptuous of the magistrate—rebels, enemies of the state, seditious villains, finally, all who openly or craftily refuse to perform whatever duties they owe.

We beseech God, our most merciful Father in heaven, that he will bless the rulers of the people, and us, and his whole people, through Jesus Christ, our only Lord and Savior; to whom be praise and glory and thanksgiving, for all ages. Amen.

Notes: *Of the several Reformed churches in the United States, only the Hungarian Reformed Church, following the lead of the Reformed Church in Hungary, adopted what is possibly the most popular statement of the Reformed faith in Europe, the Second Helvetic Confession, as one of its official doctrinal statements. The confession was originally promulgated in 1566 and was written by Heinrich Bullinger, a reformer in Zurich, Switzerland. First published in Latin and German, it was soon translated in most European languages, including Hungarian, and was officially adopted by the Reformed Church in Hungary in 1642. It should also be noted that the Second Helvetic Confession was placed in* The Book of Confessions *mandated in 1967 by the United Presbyterian Church in the U.S.A. and has continued to appear in subsequent editions.*

Presbyterian

WESTMINSTER CONFESSION

CHAPTER I. OF THE HOLY SCRIPTURE.

I. Although the light of nature, and the works of creation and providence, do so far manifest the goodness, wisdom, and power of God, as to leave men inexcusable; yet are they not sufficient to give that knowledge of God, and of his will, which is necessary unto salvation; therefore it pleased the Lord, at sundry times, and in divers manners, to reveal himself, and to declare that his will unto his Church; and afterwards, for the better preserving and propagating of the truth, and for the more sure establishment and comfort of the Church against the corruption of the flesh, and the malice of Satan and of the world, to commit the same wholly unto writing; which maketh the holy Scripture to be most necessary; those former ways of God's revealing his will unto his people being now ceased.

II. Under the name of the holy Scripture, or the Word of God written, are now contained all the Books of the Old and New Testament, which are these:

OF THE OLD TESTAMENT

Genesis	Ecclesiastes
Exodus	The Song of Songs
Leviticus	Isaiah
Numbers	Jeremiah
Deuteronomy	Lamentations
Joshua	Ezekiel
Judges	Daniel
Ruth	Hosea
I. Samuel	Joel
II. Samuel	Amos
I. Kings	Obadiah
II. Kings	Jonah
I. Chronicles	Micah
II. Chronicles	Nahum
Ezra	Habakkuk
Nehemiah	Zephaniah
Esther	Haggai
Job	Zechariah
Psalms	Malachi
Proverbs	

WESTMINSTER CONFESSION (continued)

OF THE NEW TESTAMENT

The Gospels according to

Matthew	Thessalonians II
Mark	To Timothy I
Luke	To Timothy II
John	To Titus
The Acts of the	To Philemon
Apostles	The Epistle to the Hebrews
Paul's Epistles to	The Epistle of James
the Romans	The First and Second
Corinthians I	Epistles of Peter
Corinthians II	The First, Second, and
Galatians	Third Epistles of John
Ephesians	The Epistle of Jude
Philippians	The Revelation
Colossians	
Thessalonians I	

All which are given by inspiration of God, to be the rule of faith and life.

III. The books commonly called Apocrypha, not being of divine inspiration, are no part of the Canon of the Scripture; and therefore are of no authority in the Church of God, nor to be any otherwise approved, or made use of, than other human writings.

IV. The authority of the holy Scripture, for which it ought to be believed and obeyed, dependeth not upon the testimony of any man or church, but wholly upon God (who is truth itself), the Author thereof; and therefore it is to be received, because it is the Word of God.

V. We may be moved and induced by the testimony of the Church to an high and reverent esteem of the holy Scripture; and the heavenliness of the matter, the efficacy of the doctrine, the majesty of the style, the consent of all the parts, the scope of the whole (which is to give all glory to God), the full discovery it makes of the only way of man's salvation, the many other incomparable excellencies, and the entire perfection thereof, are arguments whereby it doth abundantly evidence itself to be the Word of God; yet, notwithstanding, our full persuasion and assurance of the infallible truth, and divine authority thereof, is from the inward work of the Holy Spirit, bearing witness by and with the Word in our hearts.

VI. The whole counsel of God, concerning all things necessary for his own glory, man's salvation, faith, and life, is either expressly set down in Scripture, or by good and necessary consequence may be deduced from Scripture: unto which nothing at any time is to be added, whether by new revelations of the Spirit, or traditions of men. Nevertheless we acknowledge the inward illumination of the Spirit of God to be necessary for the saving understanding of such things as are revealed in the Word; and that there are some circumstances concerning the worship of God, and government of the Church, common to human actions and societies, which are to be ordered by the light of nature and Christian prudence, according to the general rules of the Word, which are always to be observed.

VII. All things in Scripture are not alike plain in themselves, nor alike clear unto all; yet those things which are necessary to be known, believed, and observed, for salvation, are so clearly propounded and opened in some place of Scripture or other, that not only the learned, but the unlearned, in a due use of the ordinary means, may attain unto a sufficient understanding of them.

VIII. The Old Testament in Hebrew (which was the native language of the people of God of old), and the New Testament in Greek (which at the time of the writing of it was most generally known to the nations), being immediately inspired by God, and by his singular care and providence kept pure in all ages, are therefore authentical; so as in all controversies of religion the Church is finally to appeal unto them. But because these original tongues are not known to all the people of God who have right unto, and interest in the Scriptures, and are commanded, in the fear of God, to read and search them, therefore they are to be translated into the vulgar language of every nation unto which they come, that the Word of God dwelling plentifully in all, they may worship him in an acceptable manner, and, through patience and comfort of the Scriptures, may have hope.

IX. The infallible rule of interpretation of Scripture is the Scripture itself; and therefore, when there is a question about the true and full sense of any Scripture (which is not manifold, but one), it must be searched and known by other places that speak more clearly.

X. The Supreme Judge, by which all controversies of religion are to be determined, and all decrees of councils, opinions of ancient writers, doctrines of men, and private spirits, are to be examined, and in whose sentence we are to rest, can be no other but the Holy Spirit speaking in the Scripture.

CHAPTER II. OF GOD, AND OF THE HOLY TRINITY.

I. There is but one only living and true God, who is infinite in being and perfection, a most pure spirit, invisible, without body, parts, or passions, immutable, immense, eternal, incomprehensible, almighty, most wise, most holy, most free, most absolute, working all things according to the counsel of his own immutable and most righteous will, for his own glory; most loving, gracious, merciful, long-suffering, abundant in goodness and truth, forgiving iniquity, transgression, and sin; the rewarder of them that diligently seek him; and withal most just and terrible in his judgments; hating all sin, and who will by no means clear the guilty.

II. God hath all life, glory, goodness, blessedness, in and of himself; and is alone in and unto himself all-sufficient, not standing in need of any creatures which he hath made, nor deriving any glory from them, but only manifesting his own glory in, by, unto, and upon them: he is the alone foundation of all being, of whom, through whom, and to whom are all things; and hath most sovereign dominion over them, to do by them, for them, or upon them whatsoever himself pleaseth. In his sight all things are open and manifest; his knowledge is infinite, infallible, and independent upon the creature; so as nothing is to him contingent or uncertain. He is most holy in all his counsels, in all his works, and in all his commands. To him is due from angels and men, and every other creature, whatsoever worship, service, or obedience, he is pleased to require of them.

III. In the unity of the Godhead there be three persons, of one substance, power, and eternity: God the Father, God the Son, and God the Holy Ghost. The Father is of none, neither begotten nor proceeding; the Son is eternally begotten of the Father; the Holy Ghost eternally proceeding from the Father and the Son.

CHAPTER III. OF GOD'S ETERNAL DECREE.

I. God from all eternity did, by the most wise and holy counsel of his own will, freely and unchangeably ordain whatsoever comes to pass; yet so as thereby neither is God the author of sin, nor is violence offered to the will of the creatures, nor is the liberty or contingency of second causes taken away, but rather established.

II. Although God knows whatsoever may or can come to pass upon all supposed conditions, yet hath he not decreed any thing because he foresaw it as future, or as that which would come to pass upon such conditions.

III. By the decree of God, for the manifestation of his glory, some men and angels are predestinated unto everlasting life, and others foreordained to everlasting death.

IV. These angels and men, thus predestinated and foreordained, are particularly and unchangeably designed; and their number is so certain and definite that it can not be either increased or diminished.

V. Those of mankind that are predestinated unto life, God, before the foundation of the world was laid, according to his eternal and immutable purpose, and the secret counsel and good pleasure of his will, hath chosen in Christ, unto everlasting glory, out of his mere free grace and love, without any foresight of faith or good works, or perseverance in either of them, or any other thing in the creature, as conditions, or causes moving him thereunto; and all to the praise of his glorious grace.

VI. As God hath appointed the elect unto glory, so hath he, by the eternal and most free purpose of his will, foreordained all the means thereunto. Wherefore they who are elected, being fallen in Adam, are redeemed by Christ, are effectually called unto faith in Christ by his Spirit working in due season; are justified, adopted, sanctified, and kept by his power through faith unto salvation. Neither are any other redeemed by Christ, effectually called, justified, adopted, sanctified, and saved, but the elect only.

VII. The rest of mankind God was pleased, according to the unsearchable counsel of his own will, whereby he extendeth or withholdeth mercy as he pleaseth, for the glory of his sovereign power over his creatures, to pass by, and to ordain them to dishonor and wrath for their sin, to the praise of his glorious justice.

VIII. The doctrine of this high mystery of predestination is to be handled with special prudence and care, that men attending the will of God revealed in his Word, and yielding obedience thereunto, may, from the certainty of their effectual vocation, be assured of their eternal election. So shall this doctrine afford matter of praise, reverence, and admiration of God; and of humility, diligence, and abundant consolation to all that sincerely obey the gospel.

CHAPTER IV. OF CREATION.

I. It pleased God the Father, Son, and Holy Ghost, for the manifestation of the glory of his eternal power, wisdom, and goodness, in the beginning, to create or make of nothing the world, and all things therein, whether visible or invisible, in the space of six days, and all very good.

II. After God had made all other creatures, he created man, male and female, with reasonable and immortal souls, endued with knowledge, righteousness, and true holiness, after his own image, having the law of God written in their hearts, and power to fulfill it; and yet under a possibility of transgressing, being left to the liberty of their own will, which was subject unto change. Beside this law written in their hearts, they received a command not to eat of the tree of the knowledge of good and evil; which while they kept they were happy in their communion with God, and had dominion over the creatures.

CHAPTER V. OF PROVIDENCE.

I. God, the great Creator of all things, doth uphold, direct, dispose, and govern all creatures, actions, and things, from the greatest even to the least, by his most wise and holy providence, according to his infallible foreknowledge and the free and immutable counsel of his own will, to the praise of the glory of his wisdom, power, justice, goodness, and mercy.

II. Although in relation to the foreknowledge and decree of God, the first cause, all things come to pass immutably and infallibly, yet by the same providence he ordereth them to fall out, according to the nature of second causes, either necessarily, freely, or contingently.

III. God, in his ordinary providence, maketh use of means, yet is free to work without, above, and against them, at his pleasure.

IV. The almighty power, unsearchable wisdom, and infinite goodness of God so far manifest themselves in his providence that it extendeth itself even to the first fall, and all other sins of angels and men, and that not by a bare permission, but such as hath joined with it a most wise and powerful bounding, and otherwise ordering and governing of them, in a manifold dispensation, to his own holy ends; yet so as the sinfulness thereof proceedeth only from the creature, and not from God; who, being most holy and righteous, neither is nor can be the author or approver of sin.

V. The most wise, righteous, and gracious God doth oftentimes leave for a season his own children to manifold temptations and the corruption of their own hearts, to chastise them for their former sins, or to discover unto them the hidden strength of corruption and deceitfulness of their hearts, that they may be humbled; and to raise them to a more close and constant dependence for their support unto himself, and to make them more watchful against all future occasions of sin, and for sundry other just and holy ends.

VI. As for those wicked and ungodly men whom God, as a righteous judge, for former sins, doth blind and harden, from them he not only withholdeth his grace, whereby they might have been enlightened in their understandings and wrought upon in their hearts, but sometimes also withdraweth the gifts which they had, and exposeth them to such objects as their corruption makes occasion of sin; and withal, gives them over to their own lusts, the temptations of the world, and the power of Satan; whereby it comes to pass that they harden themselves, even under those means which God useth for the softening of others.

VII. As the providence of God doth, in general, reach to all creatures, so, after a most special manner, it taketh care of his Church, and disposeth all things to the good thereof.

CHAPTER VI. OF THE FALL OF MAN, OF SIN, AND OF THE PUNISHMENT THEREOF.

I. Our first parents, being seduced by the subtilty and temptation of Satan, sinned in eating the forbidden fruit. This their sin God was pleased, according to his wise and holy counsel, to permit, having purposed to order it to his own glory.

II. By this sin they fell from their original righteousness and communion with God, and so became dead in sin, and wholly defiled in all the faculties and parts of soul and body.

III. They being the root of all mankind, the guilt of this sin was imputed, and the same death in sin and corrupted nature conveyed to all their posterity descending from them by ordinary generation.

IV. From this original corruption, whereby we are utterly indisposed, disabled, and made opposite to all good, and wholly inclined to all evil, do proceed all actual transgressions.

V. This corruption of nature, during this life, doth remain in those that are regenerated; and although it be through Christ pardoned and mortified, yet both itself and all the motions thereof are truly and properly sin.

VI. Every sin, both original and actual, being a transgression of the righteous law of God, and contrary thereunto, doth, in its own nature, bring guilt upon the sinner, whereby he is bound over to the wrath of God and curse of the law, and so made subject to death, with all miseries spiritual, temporal, and eternal.

CHAPTER VII. OF GOD'S COVENANT WITH MAN.

I. The distance between God and the creature is so great that although reasonable creatures do owe obedience unto him as their Creator, yet they could never have any fruition of him as their blessedness and reward but by some voluntary condescension on God's part, which he hath been pleased to express by way of covenant.

II. The first covenant made with man was a covenant of works, wherein life was promised to Adam, and in him to his posterity, upon condition of perfect and personal obedience.

III. Man by his fall having made himself incapable of life by that covenant, the Lord was pleased to make a second, commonly called the covenant of grace: wherein he freely offered unto sinners life and salvation by Jesus Christ, requiring of them faith in him that they may be saved, and promising to give unto all those that are ordained unto life his Holy Spirit, to make them willing and able to believe.

IV. This covenant of grace is frequently set forth in the Scripture by the name of a testament, in reference to the death of Jesus Christ the testator, and to the everlasting inheritance, with all things belonging to it, therein bequeathed.

V. This covenant was differently administered in the time of the law and in the time of the gospel: under the law it was administered by promises, prophecies, sacrifices, circumcision, the paschal lamb, and other types and ordinances delivered to the people of the Jews, all foresignifying Christ to come, which were for that time sufficient and efficacious, through the operation of the Spirit, to instruct and build up the elect in faith in the promised Messiah, by whom they had full remission of sins and eternal salvation; and is called the Old Testament.

VI. Under the gospel, when Christ the substance was exhibited, the ordinances in which this covenant is dispensed are the preaching of the word and the administration of the sacraments of Baptism and the Lord's Supper; which, though fewer in number, and administered with more simplicity and less outward glory, yet in them it is held forth in more fullness, evidence, and spiritual efficacy, to all nations, both Jews and Gentiles; and is called the New Testament. There are not, therefore, two covenants of grace differing in substance, but one and the same under various dispensations.

CHAPTER VIII. OF CHRIST THE MEDIATOR.

I. It pleased God, in his eternal purpose, to choose and ordain the Lord Jesus, his only-begotten Son, to be the Mediator between God and man, the Prophet, Priest, and King; the Head and Saviour of his Church, the Heir of all things, and Judge of the world; unto whom he did, from all eternity, give a people to be his seed, and to be by him in time redeemed, called, justified, sanctified, and glorified.

II. The Son of God, the second person in the Trinity, being very and eternal God, of one substance, and equal with the Father, did, when the fullness of time was come, take upon him man's nature, with all the essential properties and common infirmities thereof, yet without sin: being conceived by the power of the Holy Ghost in the womb of the Virgin Mary, of her substance. So that two whole, perfect, and distinct natures, the Godhead and the manhood, were inseparably joined together in one person, without conversion, composition, or confusion. Which person is very God and very man, yet one Christ, the only mediator between God and man.

III. The Lord Jesus, in his human nature thus united to the divine, was sanctified and anointed with the Holy Spirit above measure; having in him all the treasures of wisdom and knowledge, in whom it pleased the Father that all fullness should dwell; to the end that, being holy, harmless, undefiled, and full of grace and truth, he might be thoroughly furnished to execute the office of a mediator and surety. Which office he took not unto himself, but was thereunto called by his Father, who put all power and judgment into his hand, and gave him commandment to execute the same.

IV. This office the Lord Jesus did most willingly undertake, which, that he might discharge, he was made under the law, and did perfectly fulfill it; endured most grievous torments immediately in his soul, and most painful sufferings in his body; was crucified, and died; was buried, and remained under the power of death, yet saw no corruption. On the third day he arose from the dead, with the same body in which he suffered; with which also he ascended into heaven, and there sitteth at the right hand of his Father, making intercession; and shall return to judge men and angels at the end of the world.

V. The Lord Jesus, by his perfect obedience and sacrifice of himself, which he through the eternal Spirit once offered up unto God, hath fully satisfied the justice of his Father, and purchased not only reconciliation, but an everlasting inheritance in the kingdom of heaven, for all those whom the Father hath given unto him.

VI. Although the work of redemption was not actually wrought by Christ till after his incarnation, yet the virtue, efficacy, and benefits thereof were communicated unto the elect, in all ages successively, from the beginning of the world, in and by those promises, types, and sacrifices, wherein he was revealed, and signified to be the seed of the woman which should bruise the serpent's head, and the lamb slain from the beginning of the world, being yesterday and to-day the same and forever.

VII. Christ, in the work of mediation, acteth according to both natures; by each nature doing that which is proper to itself; yet, by reason of the unity of the person, that which is proper to one nature is sometimes, in Scripture, attributed to the person denominated by the other nature.

VIII. To all those for whom Christ hath purchased redemption he doth certainly and effectually apply and communicate the same; making intercession for them, and revealing unto them, in and by the Word, the mysteries of salvation; effectually persuading them by his Spirit to believe and obey; and governing their hearts by his Word and Spirit; overcoming all their enemies by his almighty power and wisdom, in such manner and ways as are most consonant to his wonderful and unsearchable dispensation.

CHAPTER IX. OF FREE-WILL.

I. God hath endued the will of man with that natural liberty, that is neither forced nor by any absolute necessity of nature determined to good or evil.

II. Man, in his state of innocency, had freedom and power to will and to do that which is good and well-pleasing to God, but yet mutably, so that he might fall from it.

III. Man, by his fall into a state of sin, hath wholly lost all ability of will to any spiritual good accompanying salvation; so as a natural man, being altogether averse from that good, and dead in sin, is not able, by his own strength, to convert himself, or to prepare himself thereunto.

IV. When God converts a sinner, and translates him into the state of grace, he freeth him from his natural bondage under sin, and by his grace alone enables him freely to will and to do that which is spiritually good; yet so as that, by reason of his remaining corruption, he doth not perfectly, nor only, will that which is good, but doth also will that which is evil.

V. The will of man is made perfectly and immutably free to good alone, in the state of glory only.

CHAPTER X. OF EFFECTUAL CALLING.

I. All those whom God hath predestinated unto life, and those only, he is pleased, in his appointed and accepted time, effectually to call, by his Word and Spirit, out of that state of sin and death, in which they are by nature, to grace and salvation by Jesus Christ; enlightening their minds, spiritually and savingly, to understand the things of God; taking away their heart of stone, and giving unto them an heart of flesh; renewing their wills, and by his almighty power determining them to that which is good, and effectually drawing them to Jesus Christ; yet so as they come most freely, being made willing by his grace.

II. This effectual call is of God's free and special grace alone, not from any thing at all foreseen in man; who is altogether passive therein, until, being quickened and renewed by the Holy Spirit, he is thereby enabled to answer this call, and to embrace the grace offered and conveyed in it.

III. Elect infants, dying in infancy, are regenerated and saved by Christ through the Spirit, who worketh when, and where, and how he pleaseth. So also are all other elect persons, who are incapable of being outwardly called by the ministry of the Word.

IV. Others, not elected, although they may be called by the ministry of the Word, and may have some common operations of the Spirit, yet they never truly come unto Christ, and therefore can not be saved: much less can men, not professing the Christian religion, be saved in any other way whatsoever, be they never so diligent to frame their lives according to the light of nature and the law of that religion they do profess; and to assert and maintain that they may is very pernicious, and to be detested.

CHAPTER XI. OF JUSTIFICATION.

I. Those whom God effectually calleth he also freely justifieth; not by infusing righteousness into them, but by pardoning their sins, and by accounting and accepting their persons as righteous: not for any thing wrought in them, or done by them, but for Christ's sake alone; nor by imputing faith itself, the act of believing, or any other evangelical obedience to them, as their righteousness; but by imputing the obedience and satisfaction of Christ unto them, they receiving and resting on him and his righteousness by faith; which faith they have not of themselves, it is the gift of God.

II. Faith, thus receiving and resting on Christ and his righteousness, is the alone instrument of justification; yet is it not alone in the person justified, but

is ever accompanied with all other saving graces, and is no dead faith, but worketh by love.

III. Christ, by his obedience and death, did fully discharge the debt of all those that are thus justified, and did make a proper, real, and full satisfaction to his Father's justice in their behalf. Yet inasmuch as he was given by the Father for them, and his obedience and satisfaction accepted in their stead, and both freely, not for anything in them, their justification is only of free grace; that both the exact justice and rich grace of God might be glorified in the justification of sinners.

IV. God did, from all eternity, decree to justify all the elect, and Christ did, in the fullness of time, die for their sins, and rise again for their justification: nevertheless, they are not justified until the Holy Spirit doth, in due time, actually apply Christ unto them.

V. God doth continue to forgive the sins of those that are justified; and although they can never fall from the state of justification, yet they may by their sins fall under God's fatherly displeasure, and not have the light of his countenance restored unto them, until they humble themselves, confess their sins, beg pardon, and renew their faith and repentance.

VI. The justification of believers under the Old Testament was, in all these respects, one and the same with the justification of believers under the New Testament.

CHAPTER XII. OF ADOPTION.

All those that are justified God vouchsafeth, in and for his only Son Jesus Christ, to make partakers of the grace of adoption; by which they are taken into the number, and enjoy the liberties and privileges of the children of God; have his name put upon them; receive the Spirit of adoption; have access to the throne of grace with boldness; are enabled to cry, Abba, Father; are pitied, protected, provided for, and chastened by him as by a father; yet never cast off, but sealed to the day of redemption, and inherit the promises, as heirs of everlasting salvation.

CHAPTER XIII. OF SANCTIFICATION.

I. They who are effectually called and regenerated, having a new heart and a new spirit created in them, are further sanctified, really and personally, through the virtue of Christ's death and resurrection, by his Word and Spirit dwelling in them; the dominion of the whole body of sin is destroyed, and the several lusts thereof are more and more weakened and mortified, and they more and more quickened and strengthened, in all saving graces, to the practice of true holiness, without which no man shall see the Lord.

II. This sanctification is throughout in the whole man, yet imperfect in this life; there abideth still some remnants of corruption in every part, whence ariseth a continual and irreconcilable war, the flesh lusting against the spirit, and the spirit against the flesh.

III. In which war, although the remaining corruption for a time may much prevail, yet, through the continual supply of strength from the sanctifying Spirit of Christ, the regenerate part doth overcome; and so the saints grow in grace, perfecting holiness in the fear of God.

CHAPTER XIV. OF SAVING FAITH.

I. The grace of faith, whereby the elect are enabled to believe to the saving of their souls, is the work of the Spirit of Christ in their hearts, and is ordinarily wrought by the ministry of the Word; by which also, and by the administration of the sacraments and prayer, it is increased and strengthened.

II. By this faith a Christian believeth to be true whatsoever is revealed in the Word, for the authority of God himself speaking therein; and acteth differently upon that which each particular passage thereof containeth; yielding obedience to the commands, trembling at the threatenings, and embracing the promises of God for this life and that which is to come. But the principal acts of saving faith are accepting, receiving, and resting upon Christ alone for justification, sanctification, and eternal life, by virtue of the covenant of grace.

III. This faith is different in degrees, weak or strong; may be often and many ways assailed and weakened, but gets the victory; growing up in many to the attainment of a full assurance through Christ, who is both the author and finisher of our faith.

CHAPTER XV. OF REPENTANCE UNTO LIFE.

I. Repentance unto life is an evangelical grace, the doctrine whereof is to be preached by every minister of the gospel, as well as that of faith in Christ.

II. By it a sinner, out of the sight and sense, not only of the danger, but also of the filthiness and odiousness of his sins, as contrary to the holy nature and righteous law of God, and upon the apprehension of his mercy in Christ to such as are penitent, so grieves for and hates his sins as to turn from them all unto God, purposing and endeavoring to walk with him in all the ways of his commandments.

III. Although repentance be not to be rested in as any satisfaction for sin, or any cause of the pardon thereof, which is the act of God's free grace in Christ; yet is it of such necessity to all sinners that none may expect pardon without it.

IV. As there is no sin so small but it deserves damnation, so there is no sin so great that it can bring damnation upon those who truly repent.

V. Men ought not to content themselves with a general repentance, but it is every man's duty to endeavor to repent of his particular sins particularly.

VI. As every man is bound to make private confession of his sins to God, praying for the pardon thereof, upon which, and the forsaking of them, he shall find mercy; so he that scandalizeth his brother, or the Church of Christ, ought to be willing, by a private or public confession and sorrow for his sin, to declare his repentance to those that are offended, who are thereupon to be reconciled to him, and in love to receive him.

CHAPTER XVI. OF GOOD WORKS.

I. Good works are only such as God hath commanded in his holy Word, and not such as, without the warrant thereof, are devised by men out of blind zeal, or upon any pretense of good intention.

II. These good works, done in obedience to God's commandments, are the fruits and evidences of a true and lively faith; and by them believers manifest their thankfulness, strengthen their assurance, edify their brethren, adorn the profession of the gospel, stop the mouths of the adversaries, and glorify God, whose workmanship they are, created in Christ Jesus thereunto, that, having their fruit unto holiness, they may have the end, eternal life.

III. Their ability to do good works is not at all of themselves, but wholly from the Spirit of Christ. And that they may be enabled thereunto, besides the graces they have already received, there is required an actual influence of the same Holy Spirit to work in them to will and to do of his good pleasure; yet are they not hereupon to grow negligent, as if they were not bound to perform any duty unless upon a special motion of the Spirit; but they ought to be diligent in stirring up the grace of God that is in them.

IV. They who in their obedience attain to the greatest height which is possible in this life, are so far from being able to supererogate and to do more than God requires, as that they fall short of much which in duty they are bound to do.

V. We can not, by our best works, merit pardon of sin, or eternal life at the hand of God, by reason of the great disproportion that is between them and the glory to come, and the infinite distance that is between us and God, whom by them we can neither profit nor satisfy for the debt of our former sins; but when we have done all we can, we have done but our duty, and are unprofitable servants; and because, as they are good, they proceed from his Spirit; and as they are wrought by us, they are defiled and mixed with so much weakness and imperfection that they can not endure the severity of God's judgment.

VI. Yet notwithstanding, the persons of believers being accepted through Christ, their good works also are accepted in him, not as though they were in this life wholly unblamable and unreprovable in God's sight; but that he, looking upon them in his Son, is pleased to accept and reward that which is sincere, although accompanied with many weaknesses and imperfections.

VII. Works done by unregenerate men, although for the matter of them they may be things which God commands, and of good use both to themselves and others; yet because they proceed not from a heart purified by faith, nor are done in a right manner, according to the Word, nor to a right end, the glory of God; they are therefore sinful, and can not please God, or make a man meet to receive grace from God. And yet their neglect of them is more sinful and displeasing unto God.

CHAPTER XVII. OF THE PERSEVERANCE OF THE SAINTS.

I. They whom God hath accepted in his Beloved, effectually called and sanctified by his Spirit, can neither totally nor finally fall away from the state of grace; but shall certainly persevere therein to the end, and be eternally saved.

II. This perseverance of the saints depends, not upon their own free-will, but upon the immutability of the decree of election, flowing from the free and unchangeable love of God the Father; upon the efficacy of the merit and intercession of Jesus Christ; the abiding of the Spirit and of the seed of God within them; and the nature of the covenant of grace: from all which ariseth also the certainty and infallibility thereof.

III. Nevertheless they may, through the temptations of Satan and of the world, the prevalency of corruption remaining in them, and the neglect of the means of their preservation, fall into grievous sins; and for a time continue therein: whereby they incur God's displeasure, and grieve his Holy Spirit; come to be deprived of some measure of their graces and comforts; have their hearts hardened, and their consciences wounded; hurt and scandalize others, and bring temporal judgments upon themselves.

CHAPTER XVIII. OF THE ASSURANCE OF GRACE AND SALVATION.

I. Although hypocrites and other unregenerate men may vainly deceive themselves with false hopes and carnal presumptions of being in the favor of God and estate of salvation, which hope of theirs shall perish: yet such as truly believe in the Lord Jesus, and love him in sincerity, endeavoring to walk in all good conscience before him, may in this life be certainly assured that they are in a state of grace, and may rejoice in the hope of the glory of God, which hope shall never make them ashamed.

II. This certainty is not a bare conjectural and probable persuasion, grounded upon a fallible hope; but an infallible assurance of faith, founded upon the divine truth of the promises of salvation, the inward evidence of those graces unto which these promises are made, the testimony of the Spirit of adoption witnessing with our spirits that we are the children of God: which Spirit is the earnest of our inheritance, whereby we are sealed to the day of redemption.

III. This infallible assurance doth not so belong to the essence of faith, but that a true believer may wait long, and conflict with many difficulties before he be partaker of it: yet, being enabled by the Spirit to know the things which are freely given him of God, he may, without extraordinary revelation, in the right use of ordinary means, attain thereunto. And therefore it is the duty of every one to give all diligence to make his calling and election sure; that thereby his heart may be enlarged in peace and joy in the Holy Ghost, in love and thankfulness to God, and in strength and cheerfulness in the duties of obedience, the proper fruits of this assurance: so far is it from inclining men to looseness.

IV. True believers may have the assurance of their salvation divers ways shaken, diminished, and intermitted; as, by negligence in preserving of it; by falling into some special sin, which woundeth the conscience, and grieveth the Spirit; by some sudden or vehement temptation; by God's withdrawing the light of his countenance, and suffering even such as fear him to walk in darkness and to have no light: yet are they never utterly destitute of that seed of God, and life of faith, that love of Christ and the brethren, that sincerity of heart and conscience of duty, out of which, by the operation of the Spirit, this assurance may in due time be revived, and by the which, in the mean time, they are supported from utter despair.

CHAPTER XIX. OF THE LAW OF GOD.

I. God gave to Adam a law, as a covenant of works, by which he bound him and all his posterity to personal, entire, exact, and perpetual obedience; promised life upon the fulfilling, and threatened death upon the breach of it; and endued him with power and ability to keep it.

II. This law, after his fall, continued to be a perfect rule of righteousness; and, as such, was delivered by God upon mount Sinai in ten commandments, and written in two tables; the first four commandments containing our duty towards God, and the other six our duty to man.

III. Beside this law, commonly called moral, God was pleased to give to the people of Israel, as a Church under age, ceremonial laws, containing several typical ordinances, partly of worship, prefiguring Christ, his graces, actions, sufferings, and benefits; and partly holding forth divers instructions of moral duties. All which ceremonial laws are now abrogated under the New Testament.

IV. To them also, as a body politic, he gave sundry judicial laws, which expired together with the state of that people, not obliging any other, now, further than the general equity thereof may require.

V. The moral law doth forever bind all, as well justified persons as others, to the obedience thereof; and that not only in regard of the matter contained in it, but also in respect of the authority of God the Creator who gave it. Neither doth Christ in the gospel any way dissolve, but much strengthen, this obligation.

VI. Although true believers be not under the law as a covenant of works, to be thereby justified or condemned; yet is it of great use to them, as well as to others; in that, as a rule of life, informing them of the will of God and their duty, it directs and binds them to walk accordingly; discovering also the sinful pollutions of their nature, hearts, and lives; so as, examining themselves thereby, they may come to further conviction of, humiliation for, and hatred against sin; together with a clearer sight of the need they have of Christ, and the perfection of his obedience. It is likewise of use to the regenerate, to restrain their corruptions, in that it forbids sin; and the threatenings of it serve to show what even their sins deserve, and what afflictions in this life they may expect for them, although freed from the curse thereof threatened in the law. The promises of it, in like manner, show them God's approbation of obedience, and what blessings they may expect upon the performance thereof; although not as due to them by the law as a covenant of words: so as a man's doing good, and refraining from evil, because the law encourageth to the one, and deterreth from the other, is no evidence of his being under the law, and not under grace.

VII. Neither are the forementioned uses of the law contrary to the grace of the gospel, but do sweetly comply with it: the Spirit of Christ subduing and enabling the will of man to do that freely and cheerfully which the will of God, revealed in the law, requireth to be done.

CHAPTER XX. OF CHRISTIAN LIBERTY, AND LIBERTY OF CONSCIENCE.

I. The liberty which Christ hath purchased for believers under the gospel consists in their freedom from the guilt of sin, the condemning wrath of God, the curse of the moral law; and in their being delivered from this present evil world, bondage to Satan, and dominion of sin, from the evil of afflictions, the sting of death, the victory of the grave, and everlasting damnation; as also in their free access to God, and their yielding obedience unto him, not out of slavish fear, but a child-like love and willing mind. All which were common also to believers under the law; but under the New Testament the liberty of Christians is further enlarged in their freedom from the yoke of the ceremonial law, to which the Jewish Church was subjected; and in greater boldness of access to the throne of grace, and in fuller communications of the free Spirit of God, than believers under the law did ordinarily partake of.

II. God alone is Lord of the conscience, and hath left it free from the doctrines and commandments of men which are in any thing contrary to his Word, or beside it in matters of faith or worship. So that to believe such doctrines, or to obey such commands out of conscience, is to betray true liberty of conscience; and the requiring of an implicit faith, and an absolute and blind obediene, is to destroy liberty of conscience, and reason also.

III. They who, upon pretense of Christian liberty, do practice any sin, or cherish any lust, do thereby destroy the end of Christian liberty; which is, that, being delivered out of the hands of our enemies, we might serve the Lord without fear, in holiness and righteousness before him, all the days of our life.

IV. And because the power which God hath ordained, and the liberty which Christ hath purchased, are not intended by God to destroy, but mutually to uphold and preserve one another; they who, upon pretense of Christian liberty, shall oppose any lawful power, or the lawful exercise of it, whether it be civil or ecclesiastical, resist the ordinance of God. And for their publishing of such opinions, or maintaining of such practices, as are contrary to the light of nature, or to the known principles of Christianity, whether concerning faith, worship, or conversation; or to the power of godliness; or such erroneous opinions or practices, as, either in their own nature, or in the manner of publishing or maintaining them, are destructive to the external peace and order which Christ hath established in the Church; they may lawfully be called to account, and proceeded against by the censures of the Church, and by the power of the Civil Magistrate.

CHAPTER XXI. OF RELIGION WORSHIP AND THE SABBATH-DAY.

I. The light of nature showeth that there is a God, who hath lordship and sovereignty over all; is good, and doeth good unto all; and is therefore to be feared, loved, praised, called upon, trusted in, and served with all the heart, and with all the soul, and with all the might. But the acceptable way of worshiping the true God is instituted by himself, and so limited to his own revealed will, that he may not be worshiped according to the imaginations and devices of men, or the suggestions of Satan, under any visible representations or any other way not prescribed in the Holy Scripture.

II. Religious worship is to be given to God, the Father, Son, and Holy Ghost; and to him alone: not to angels, saints, or any other creature: and since the fall, not without a Mediator; nor in the mediation of any other but of Christ alone.

III. Prayer with thanksgiving, being one special part of religious worship, is by God required of all men; and that it may be accepted, it is to be made in the name of the Son, by the help of his Spirit, according to his will, not with understanding, reverence, humility, fervency, faith, love, and perseverance; and, if vocal, in a known tongue.

IV. Prayer is to be made for things lawful, and for all sorts of men living, or that shall live hereafter; but not for the dead, nor for those of whom it may be known that they have sinned the sin unto death.

V. The reading of the Scriptures with godly fear; the sound preaching; and conscionable hearing of the Word, in obedience unto God with understanding, faith, and reverence; singing of psalms with grace in the heart; as, also, the due administration and worthy receiving of the sacraments instituted by Christ; are all parts of the ordinary religious worship of God: besides religious oaths, vows, solemn fastings, and thanksgivings upon several occasions; which are, in their several times and seasons, to be used in an holy and religious manner.

VI. Neither prayer, nor any other part of religious worship, is now under the gospel, either tied unto or made more acceptable by any place in which it is performed, or towards which it is directed: but God is to be worshiped every where in spirit and truth; as in private families daily, and in secret each one by himself, so more solemnly in the public assemblies, which are not carelessly or willfully to be neglected or foresaken, when God, by his Word or providence, calleth thereunto.

VII. As it is of the law of nature, that, in general, a due proportion of time be set apart for the worship of God; so, in his Word, by a positive, moral, and perpetual commandment, binding all men in all ages, he hath particularly appointed one day in seven for a Sabbath, to be kept holy unto him: which, from the beginning of the world to the resurrection of Christ, was the last day of the week; and, from the resurrection of Christ, was changed into the first day of the week, which in Scripture is called the Lord's day, and is to be continued to the end of the world, as the Christian Sabbath.

VIII. This Sabbath is then kept holy unto the Lord, when men, after a due preparing of their hearts, and ordering of their common affairs beforehand, do not only observe an holy rest all the day from their own works, words, and thoughts, about their worldly employments and recreations; but also are taken up the whole time in the public and private exercises of his worship, and in the duties of necessity and mercy.

CHAPTER XXII. OF LAWFUL OATHS AND VOWS.

I. A lawful oath is a part of religious worship, wherein, upon just occasion, the person swearing solemnly calleth God to witness what he asserteth or promiseth; and to judge him according to the truth or falsehood of what he sweareth.

II. The name of God only is that by which men ought to swear, and therein it is to be used with all holy fear and reverence; therefore to swear vainly or rashly by that glorious and dreadful name, or to swear at all by any other thing, is sinful, and to be abhorred. Yet as, in matters of weight and moment, an oath is warranted by the Word of God, under the New Testament, as well as under the Old, so a lawful oath, being imposed by lawful authority, in such matters ought to be taken.

III. Whosoever taketh an oath ought duly to consider the weightiness of so solemn an act, and therein to avouch nothing but what he is fully persuaded is the truth. Neither may any man bind himself by oath to any thing but what is good and just, and what he believeth so to be, and what he is able and resolved to perform. Yet it is a sin to refuse an oath touching any thing that is good and just, being imposed by lawful authority.

IV. An oath is to be taken in the plain and common sense of the words, without equivocation or mental reservation. It can not oblige to sin; but in any thing not sinful, being taken, it binds to performance, although to a man's own hurt: nor is it to be violated, although made to heretics or infidels.

V. A vow is of the like nature with a promissory oath, and ought to be made with the like religious care, and to be performed with the like faithfulness.

VI. It is not to be made to any creature, but to God alone: and that it may be accepted, it is to be made voluntarily, out of faith and conscience of duty, in way of thankfulness for mercy received, or for the obtaining of what we want; whereby we more strictly bind ourselves to necessary duties, or to other things, so far and so long as they may fitly conduce thereunto.

VII. No man may vow to do any thing forbidden in the Word of God, or what would hinder any duty therein commanded, or which is not in his own power, and for the performance whereof he hath no promise or ability from God. In which respect, popish monastical vows of perpetual single life, professed poverty, and regular obedience, are so far from being degrees of higher perfection, that they are superstitious and sinful snares, in which no Christian may entangle himself.

CHAPTER XXIII. OF THE CIVIL MAGISTRATE.

I. God, the Supreme Lord and King of all the world, hath ordained civil magistrates to be under him, over the people, for his own glory and the public good, and to this end hath armed them with the power of the sword, for the defense and encouragement of them that are good, and for the punishment of evil-doers.

II. It is lawful for Christians to accept and execute the office of a magistrate when called thereunto; in the managing whereof, as they ought especially to maintain piety, justice, and peace, according to the wholesome laws of each commonwealth, so, for that end, they may lawfully, now under the New Testament, wage war upon just and necessary occasion.

III. The civil magistrate may not assume to himself the administration of the Word and Sacraments, or the power of the keys of the kingdom of heaven: yet he hath authority, and it is his duty to take order, that unity and peace be preserved in the Church, that the truth of God be kept pure and entire, that all blasphemies and heresies be suppressed, all corruptions and abuses in worship and discipline prevented or reformed, and all the ordinances of God duly settled, administered, and observed. For the better effecting whereof he hath power to call synods, to be present at them, and to provide that whatsoever is transacted in them be according to the mind of God.

IV. It is the duty of people to pray for magistrates, to honor their persons, to pay them tribute and other dues, to obey their lawful commands, and to be subject to their authority, for conscience's sake. Infidelity or difference in religion doth not make void the magistrate's just and legal authority, nor free the people from their due obedience to him: from which ecclesiastical persons are not exempted; much less hath the Pope any power or jurisdiction over them in their dominions, or over any of their people; and least of all to deprive them of their dominions or lives, if he shall judge them to be heretics, or upon any other pretense whatsoever.

CHAPTER XXIV. OF MARRIAGE AND DIVORCE.

I. Marriage is to be between one man and one woman: neither is it lawful for any man to have more than one wife, nor for any woman to have more than one husband at the same time.

II. Marriage was ordained for the mutual help of husband and wife; for the increase of mankind with a legitimate issue, and of the church with an holy seed; and for preventing of uncleanness.

III. It is lawful for all sorts of people to marry who are able with judgment to give their consent. Yet it is the duty of Christians to marry only in the Lord. And, therefore, such as profess the true reformed religion should not marry with infidels, Papists, or other idolaters: neither should such as are godly be unequally yoked, by marrying with such as are notoriously wicked in their life, or maintain damnable heresies.

IV. Marriage ought not to be within the degrees of consanguinity or affinity forbidden in the Word; nor can such incestuous marriages ever be made lawful by any law of man, or consent of parties, so as those persons may live together, as man and wife. The man may not marry any of his wife's kindred nearer in blood than he may of his own, nor the woman of her husband's kindred nearer in blood than of her own.

V. Adultery or fornication, committed after a contract, being detected before marriage, giveth just occasion to the innocent party to dissolve that contract. In the case of adultery after marriage, it is lawful for the innocent party to sue out a divorce, and after the divorce to marry another, as if the offending party were dead.

VI. Although the corruption of man be such as is apt to study arguments, unduly to put asunder those whom God hath joined together in marriage; yet nothing but adultery, or such willful desertion as can no way be remedied by the Church or civil magistrate, is cause sufficient of dissolving the bond of marriage; wherein a public and orderly course of proceeding is to be observed; and the persons concerned in it, not left to their own wills and discretion in their own case.

CHAPTER XXV. OF THE CHURCH.

I. The catholic or universal Church, which is invisible, consists of the whole number of the elect, that have been, are, or shall be gathered into one, under Christ the head thereof; and is the spouse, the body, the fullness of him that filleth all in all.

II. The visible Church, which is also catholic or universal under the gospel (not confined to one nation as before under the law) consists of all those, throughout the world, that profess the true religion, and of their children; and is the kingdom of the Lord Jesus Christ, the house and family of God, out of which there is no ordinary possibility of salvation.

III. Unto this catholic visible Church Christ hath given the ministry, oracles, and ordinances of God, for the gathering and perfecting of the saints, in this life, to the end of the world: and doth by his own presence and Spirit, according to his promise, make them effectual thereunto.

IV. This catholic Church hath been sometimes more, sometimes less visible. And particular churches, which are members thereof, are more or less pure, according as the doctrine of the gospel is taught and embraced, ordinances administered, and public worship performed more or less purely in them.

V. The purest churches under heaven are subject both to mixture and error; and some have so degenerated as to become no churches of Christ, but synagogues of Satan. Nevertheless, there shall be always a Church on earth to worship God according to his will.

VI. There is no other head of the Church but the Lord Jesus Christ: nor can the Pope of Rome, in any sense be head thereof; but is that Antichrist, that man of sin and son of perdition, that exalteth himself in the Church against Christ, and all that is called God.

CHAPTER XXVI. OF THE COMMUNION OF SAINTS.

I. All saints that are united to Jesus Christ their head, by his Spirit and by faith, have fellowship with him in his graces, sufferings, death, resurrection, and glory: and being united to one another in love, they have communion in each other's gifts and graces, and are obliged to the performance of such duties, public and private, as do conduce to their mutual good, both in the inward and outward man.

II. Saints, by profession, are bound to maintain an holy fellowship and communion in the worship of God, and in performing such other spiritual services as tend to their mutual edification; as also in relieving each other in outward things, according to their several abilities and necessities. Which communion, as God offereth opportunity, is to be extended unto all those who, in every place, call upon the name of the Lord Jesus.

III. This communion which the saints have with Christ, doth not make them in anywise partakers of the substance of his Godhead, or to be equal with Christ in any respect: either of which to affirm is impious and blasphemous. Nor doth their communion one with another, as saints, take away or infringe the title or propriety which each man hath in his goods and possessions.

CHAPTER XXVII. OF THE SACRAMENTS.

I. Sacraments are holy signs and seals of the covenant of grace, immediately instituted by God, to represent Christ and his benefits, and to confirm our interest in him: as also to put a visible difference between those that belong unto the Church and the rest of the world; and solemnly to engage them to the service of God in Christ, according to his Word.

II. There is in every sacrament a spiritual relation or sacramental union, between the sign and the thing signified; whence it comes to pass that the names and the effects of the one are attributed to the other.

III. The grace which is exhibited in or by the sacraments, rightly used, is not conferred by any power in them; neither doth the efficacy of a sacrament depend upon the piety or intention of him that doth administer it, but upon the work of the Spirit, and the word of institution, which contains, together with a precept authorizing the

use thereof, a promise of benefit to worthy receivers.

IV. There be only two sacraments ordained by Christ our Lord in the gospel, that is to say, Baptism and the Supper of the Lord: neither of which may be dispensed by any but by a minister of the Word lawfully ordained.

V. The sacraments of the Old Testament, in regard of the spiritual things thereby signified and exhibited, were, for substance, the same with those of the New.

CHAPTER XXVIII. OF BAPTISM.

I. Baptism is a sacrament of the New Testament, ordained by Jesus Christ, not only for the solemn admission of the party baptized into the visible Church, but also to be unto him a sign and seal of the covenant of grace, of his ingrafting into Christ, of regeneration, of remission of sins, and of his giving up unto God, through Jesus Christ, to walk in newness of life: which sacrament is, by Christ's own appointment, to be continued in his Church until the end of the world.

II. The outward element to be used in this sacrament is water, wherewith the party is to be baptized in the name of the Father, and of the Son, and of the Holy Ghost, by a minister of the gospel lawfully called thereunto.

III. Dipping of the person into the water is not necessary; but baptism is rightly administered by pouring or sprinkling water upon the person.

IV. Not only those that do actually profess faith in and obedience unto Christ, but also the infants of one or both believing parents are to be baptized.

V. Although it be a great sin to condemn or neglect this ordinance, yet grace and salvation are not so inseparably annexed unto it, as that no person can be regenerated or saved without it, or that all that are baptized are undoubtedly regenerated.

VI. The efficacy of baptism is not tied to that moment of time wherein it is administered; yet, notwithstanding, by the right use of this ordinance the grace promised is not only offered, but really exhibited and conferred by the Holy Ghost, to such (whether of age or infants) as that grace belongeth unto, according to the counsel of God's own will, in his appointed time.

VII. The sacrament of baptism is but once to be administered to any person.

CHAPTER XXIX. OF THE LORD'S SUPPER.

I. Our Lord Jesus, in the night wherein he was betrayed, instituted the sacrament of his body and blood, called the Lord's Supper, to be observed in his Church, unto the end of the world; for the perpetual remembrance of the sacrifice of himself in his death, the sealing all benefits thereof unto true believers, their spiritual nourishment and growth in him, their further engagement in, and to all duties which they owe unto him; and to be a bond and pledge of their communion with him, and with each other, as members of his mystical body.

II. In this sacrament Christ is not offered up to his Father, nor any real sacrifice made at all for remission of sins of the quick or dead, but only a commemoration of that one offering up of himself, by himself, upon the cross, once for all, and a spiritual oblation of all possible praise unto God for the same; so that the Popish sacrifice of the mass, as they call it, is most abominably injurious to Christ's one only sacrifice, the alone propitiation for all the sins of the elect.

III. The Lord Jesus hath, in this ordinance, appointed his ministers to declare his word of institution to the people, to pray, and bless the elements of bread and wine, and thereby to set them apart from a common to an holy use; and to take and break the bread, to take the cup, and (they communicating also themselves) to give both to the communicants; but to none who are not then present in the congregation.

IV. Private masses, or receiving this sacrament by a priest, or any other, alone; as likewise the denial of the cup to the people; worshiping the elements, the lifting them up, or carrying them about for adoration, and the reserving them for any pretended religious use, are all contrary to the nature of this sacrament, and to the institution of Christ.

V. The outward elements in this sacrament, duly set apart to the uses ordained by Christ, have such relation to him crucified, as that truly, yet sacramentally only, they are sometimes called by the name of the things they represent, to wit, the body and blood of Christ; albeit, in substance and nature, they still remain truly, and only, bread and wine, as they were before.

VI. That doctrine which maintains a change of the substance of bread and wine, into the substance of Christ's body and blood (commonly called transubstantiation) by consecration of a priest, or by any other way, is repugnant, not to Scripture alone, but even to common-sense and reason; overthroweth the nature of the sacrament; and hath been, and is the cause of manifold superstitions, yea, of gross idolatries.

VII. Worthy receivers, outwardly partaking of the visible elements in this sacrament, do then also inwardly by faith, really and indeed, yet not carnally and corporally, but spiritually, receive and feed upon Christ crucified, and all benefits of his death: the body and blood of Christ being then not corporally or carnally in, with, or under the bread and wine; yet as really, but spiritually, present to the faith of believers in that ordinance, as the elements themselves are, to their outward senses.

VIII. Although ignorant and wicked men receive the outward elements in this sacrament, yet they receive not the thing signified thereby; but by their unworthy coming thereunto are guilty of the body and blood of the Lord, to their own damnation. Wherefore all ignorant and ungodly persons, as they are unfit to enjoy communion with him, so are they unworthy of the Lord's table, and can not, without great sin against Christ, while they remain such, partake of these holy mysteries, or be admitted thereunto.

CHAPTER XXX. OF CHURCH CENSURES.

I. The Lord Jesus, as king and head of his Church, hath therein appointed a government in the hand of Church officers, distinct from the civil magistrate.

II. To these officers the keys of the kingdom of heaven are committed, by virtue whereof they have power respectively to retain and remit sins, to shut that kingdom against the impenitent, both by the Word and censures, and to open it unto penitent sinners, by the ministry of the gospel, and by absolution from censures, as occasion shall require.

III. Church censures are necessary for the reclaiming and gaining of offending brethren; for deterring of others from the like offenses; for purging out of that leaven which might infect the whole lump; for vindicating the honor of Christ, and the holy profession of the gospel; and for preventing the wrath of God, which might justly fall upon the Church, if they should suffer his covenant, and the seals thereof, to be profaned by notorious and obstinate offenders.

IV. For the better attaining of these ends, the officers of the Church are to proceed by admonition, suspension from the Sacrament of the Lord's Supper for a season, and by excommunication from the Church, according to the nature of the crime and demerit of the person.

CHAPTER XXXI. OF SYNODS AND COUNCILS.

I. For the better government and further edification of the Church, there ought to be such assemblies as are commonly called synods or councils.

II. As magistrates may lawfully call a synod of ministers and other fit persons to consult and advise with about matters of religion; so, if magistrates be open enemies to the Church, the ministers of Christ, of themselves, by virtue of their office, or they, with other fit persons, upon delegation from their churches, may meet together in such assemblies.

III. It belongeth to synods and councils, ministerially, to determine controversies of faith, and cases of conscience; to set down rules and directions for the better ordering of the public worship of God, and government of his Church; to receive complaints in cases of maladministration, and authoritatively to determine the same: which decrees and determinations, if consonant to the Word of God, are to be received with reverence and submission, not only for their agreement with the Word, but also for the power whereby they are made, as being an ordinance of God, appointed thereunto in his Word.

IV. All synods or councils since the apostles' times, whether general or particular, may err, and many have erred; therefore they are not to be made the rule of faith or practice, but to be used as a help in both.

V. Synods and councils are to handle or conclude nothing but that which is ecclesiastical: and are not to intermeddle with civil affairs which concern the commonwealth, unless by way of humble petition in cases extraordinary; or by way of advice for satisfaction of conscience, if they be thereunto required by the civil magistrate.

CHAPTER XXXII. OF THE STATE OF MEN AFTER DEATH, AND OF THE RESURRECTION OF THE DEAD.

I. The bodies of men, after death, return to dust, and see corruption; but their souls (which neither die nor sleep), having an immortal subsistence, immediately return to God who gave them. The souls of the righteous, being then made perfect in holiness, are received into the highest heavens, where they behold the face of God in light and glory, waiting for the full redemption of their bodies: and the souls of the wicked are cast into hell, where they remain in torments and utter darkness, reserved to the judgment of the great day. Besides these two places for souls separated from their bodies, the Scripture acknowledgeth none.

II. At the last day, such as are found alive shall not die, but be changed; and all the dead shall be raised up with the self-same bodies, and none other, although with different qualities, which shall be united again to their souls forever.

III. The bodies of the unjust shall, by the power of Christ, be raised to dishonor; the bodies of the just, by his Spirit, unto honor, and be made conformable to his own glorious body.

CHAPTER XXXIII. OF THE LAST JUDGMENT.

I. God hath appointed a day wherein he will judge the world in righteousness by Jesus Christ, to whom all power and judgment is given of the Father. In which day, not only the apostate angels shall be judged, but likewise all persons, that have lived upon earth, shall appear before the tribunal of Christ, to give an account of their thoughts, words, and deeds; and to receive according to what they have done in the body, whether good or evil.

II. The end of God's appointing this day, is for the manifestation of the glory of his mercy in the eternal salvation of the elect; and of his justice in the damnation of the reprobate, who are wicked and disobedient. For then shall the righteous go into everlasting life, and receive that fullness of joy and refreshing which shall come from the presence of the Lord: but the wicked, who know not God, and obey not the gospel of Jesus Christ, shall be cast into eternal torments, and be punished with everlasting destruction from the presence of the Lord, and from the glory of his power.

III. As Christ would have us to be certainly persuaded that there shall be a day of judgment, both to deter all men from sin, and for the greater consolation of the godly in their adversity: so will he have that day unknown to men, that they may shake off all carnal security, and be always watchful, because they know not at what hour the Lord will come; and may be ever prepared to say, Come, Lord Jesus, come quickly. Amen.

> Charles Herle, Prolocutor.
> Cornelius Burges, Assessor.
> Herbert Palmer, Assessor.
> Henry Robroughe, Scriba.
> Adoniram Byfield, Scriba.

Notes: *The confession was written in the middle of the seventeenth century by the British and Scottish church leaders gathered at Westminster (1644-49) in the midst of the civil strife that would see the king of England beheaded and the establishment of a Protestant commonwealth. Those gathered produced three major documents: a longer and shorter catechism, and the Westminster Confession. The Westminster Confession soon became the definitive theological standard of the English-speaking Reformed movement, i.e., Presbyterianism.*

Transported to the United States, the confession soon encountered problems on the issues of church and state relations. After the American Revolution, revisions of the several articles on civil magistrates and on synods and councils were required. The Westminster Confession has remained the standard of most Presbyterian church bodies in the United States to the present, though a variety of statements on its use and authority have been issued at various times, usually upon the merger of two churches. In 1967 the United Presbyterian Church in the U.S.A. adopted a new contemporary statement of faith, the Confession of 1967, and at the same time ordered the production of The Book of Confessions. *This action removed the Westminster Confession from the place of honor it had held as the only confession within the church's constitution and set it in the midst of eight other creeds. Many interpreted the church's action as reducing the Westminster Confession's authority to that of a mere historical precedence. The Book of Confessions has been retained by the new Presbyterian Church (U.S.A.).*

The Westminster Confession has been adopted by the Bible Presbyterian Church, the Orthodox Presbyterian Church, the Presbyterian Church in America, and the Reformed Presbyterian Church of North America. Substantive revisions of the Westminster Confession were made prior to its adoption by the Associate Reformed Presbyterian Church and the Cumberland Presbyterian Church. Subsequently, the Cumberland Presbyterian Church completely rewrote its confession.

* * *

THE CONFESSION OF FAITH (CUMBERLAND PRESBYTERIAN CHURCH)

HOLY SCRIPTURES

1. The Holy Scriptures comprise all the books of the Old and the New Testament which are received as canonical, and which are given by inspiration of God to be the rule of faith and practice, and are these:

OLD TESTAMENT

Genesis	Ecclesiastes
Exodus	Song of Solomon
Leviticus	Isaiah
Numbers	Jeremiah
Deuteronomy	Lamentations
Joshua	Ezekiel
Judges	Daniel
Ruth	Hosea
I. Samuel	Joel
II. Samuel	Amos
I. Kings	Obadiah
II. Kings	Jonah
I. Chronicles	Micah
II. Chronicles	Nahum
Ezra	Habakkuk
Nehemiah	Zephaniah
Esther	Haggai
Job	Zechariah
Psalms	Malachi
Proverbs	

NEW TESTAMENT

Matthew	I. Timothy
Mark	II. Timothy
Luke	Titus
John	Philemon
The Acts	Hebrews
Romans	James
I. Corinthians	I. Peter
II. Corinthians	II. Peter
Galatians	I. John
Ephesians	II. John
Philippians	III. John
Colossians	Jude
I. Thessalonians	Revelation
II. Thessalonians	

2. The authority of the Holy Scriptures depends not upon the testimony of any man or Church, but upon God alone.

3. The whole counsel of God, concerning all things necessary for his own glory—in creation, providence, and man's salvation—is either expressly stated in the Scriptures, or by necessary consequence may be deduced therefrom; unto which nothing at any time is to be added by man, or from the traditions of men; nevertheless, we acknowledge the inward illumination of the Spirit of God to be necessary for the saving understanding of such things as are revealed in the word.

4. The best rule of interpretation of the Scriptures is the comparison of scripture with scripture.

THE HOLY TRINITY

5. There is but one living and true God, a self-existent Spirit, infinite, eternal, and unchangeable in his being, wisdom, power, holiness, justice, goodness, and truth.

6. God has all life, glory, goodness, and blessedness in himself; not standing in need of any creatures which he has made, nor deriving any essential glory from them; and has most sovereign dominion over them to do whatsoever he may please.

7. In the unity of the Godhead there are three persons of one substance, power, and eternity; God the Father, Son, and Holy Spirit.

DECREES OF GOD

8. God, for the manifestation of his glory and goodness, by the most wise and holy counsel of his own will, freely and unchangeably ordained or determined what he himself would do, what he would require his intelligent creatures to do, and what should be the awards, respectively, of the obedient and the disobedient.

9. Though all Divine decrees may not be revealed to men, yet it is certain that God has decreed nothing contrary to his revealed will or written word.

CREATION

10. It pleased God, for the manifestation of the glory of his eternal power, wisdom, and goodness, to create the world and all things therein, whether visible or invisible: and all very good.

11. After God had made all other creatures, he created man in his own image; male and female created he them, enduing them with intelligence, sensibility, and will; they having the law of God written in their hearts, and power to fulfill it, being upright and free from all bias to evil.

PROVIDENCE

12. God the Creator upholds and governs all creatures and things by his most wise and holy providence.

13. God, in his providence, ordinarily works through the instrumentality of laws or means, yet is free to work with and above them, at his pleasure.

14. God never leaves nor forsakes his people; yet when they fall into sin he chastises them in various ways, and makes even their own sin the occasion of discovering unto them their weakness and their need of greater watchfulness and dependence upon him for supporting grace.

15. God's providence over the wicked is not designed to lead them to destruction, but to a knowledge of his goodness, and of his sovereign power over them, and thus to become a means of their repentance and reformation, or to be a warning to others; and if the wicked make it an occasion of hardening their hearts, it is because of their perversity, and not from necessity.

THE CONFESSION OF FAITH (CUMBERLAND
PRESBYTERIAN CHURCH) (continued)

16. While the providence of God, in general, embraces all creatures, it does, in a special manner, extend to his Church.

FALL OF MAN

17. Our first parents, being seduced by the subtlety and temptation of Satan, sinned in eating the forbidden fruit; whereupon, God was pleased, for his own glory and the good of mankind, to reveal the Covenant of Grace in Christ, by which a gracious probation was established for all men.

18. By this sin they fell from their original uprightness, lost their communion with God, and so became dead in sin and defiled in all the faculties of their moral being. They being the root of all mankind, sin entered into the world through their act, and death by sin, and so death passed upon all men.

19. From this original corruption also proceeds actual transgression.

20. The remains of this corrupt nature are felt by those who are regenerated, nor will they altogether cease to operate and disturb during the present life.

21. Sin, being a transgression of the law of God, brings guilt upon the transgressor, and subjects him to the wrath of God and to endless torment, unless pardoned through the mediation of Christ.

GOD'S COVENANT WITH MAN

22. The first covenant made with man was a Covenant of Works, wherein life was promised to Adam upon condition of perfect and personal obedience.

23. Man, by his fall, having made himself incapable of life by that covenant, the Lord was pleased to make the second, commonly called the Covenant of Grace, wherein he freely offers unto sinners life and salvation by Jesus Christ, requiring of them faith in him, that they may be saved. This covenant is frequently set forth in the Scriptures by the name of a testament, in reference to the death of Jesus Christ, the testator, and to the everlasting inheritance, with all things belonging to it, therein bequeathed.

24. Under the Old Testament dispensation the Covenant of Grace was administered by promises, prophecies, sacrifices, circumcision, the paschal lamb, and other types and ordinances delivered to the Jews—all foresignifying Christ to come—which were sufficient, through the operation of the Holy Spirit, to instruct them savingly in the knowledge of God, and build them up in the faith of the Messiah.

25. Under the New Testament dispensation, wherein Christ, the substance, is set forth, the ordinances in which the Covenant of Grace is dispensed are the preaching of the Word and the administration of the sacraments of Baptism and the Lord's Supper, which are administered with more simplicity, yet in them it is held forth in more fullness and spiritual efficacy to all nations, Jews and Gentiles.

26. As children were included with their parents in the Covenant of Grace under the Old Testament dispensation, so are they included in it under the New, and should, as under the Old, receive the appropriate sign and seal thereof.

CHRIST THE MEDIATOR

27. Jesus Christ, the only-begotten Son of God, was verily appointed before the foundation of the world to be the Mediator between God and man, the Prophet, Priest, and King, the heir of all things, the propitiation for the sins of all mankind, the Head of his Church, the Judge of the world, and the Savior of all true believers.

28. The Son of God, the second person in the Trinity, did, when the fullness of time was come, take upon himself man's nature, yet without sin, being very God and very man, yet one Christ, the only Mediator between God and man.

29. Jesus Christ, in his human nature, thus united to the Divine, was sanctified and anointed with the Holy Spirit above measure, having in him all the treasures of wisdom and knowledge, in whom it pleased the Father that all fulness should dwell, to the end that, being holy, harmless, undefiled, and full of grace and truth, he might be thoroughly furnished to execute the office of a Mediator and Surety.

30. That he might discharge the office of Mediator Jesus Christ was made under the law, which he perfectly fulfilled, was crucified, died, and was buried, and remained under the power of death for a time, yet saw no corruption. On the third day he arose from the dead, and afterward ascended to heaven, where he sits on the right hand of God, making intercession for transgressors.

31. Jesus Christ, by his perfect obedience and sacrifice of himself, which he, through the Eternal Spirit once offered unto God, became the propitiation for the sins of the whole world, so God can be just in justifying all who believe in Jesus.

32. Although the work of redemption was not actually wrought by Christ until after his incarnation, yet the benefits thereof were communicated unto the believer, in all ages, successively, from the beginning of the world, by the Holy Spirit, and through such instrumentalities as God was pleased to employ.

33. Jesus Christ tasted death for every man, and now makes intercession for transgressors, by virtue of which the Holy Spirit is given to convince of sin and enable man to believe and obey, governing the hearts of believers by his word and Spirit, overcoming all their enemies, by his almighty power and wisdom, in such manner and ways as are most consonant to his wonderful and unsearchable dispensation.

FREE WILL

34. God, in creating man in his own likeness, endued him with intelligence, sensibility, and will, which form the basis of moral character, and render man capable of moral government.

35. The freedom of the will is a fact of human consciousness, and is the sole ground of human accountability. Man, in his state of innocence, was both free and able to keep the Divine law, also to violate it. Without any constraint, from either physical or moral causes, he did violate it.

36. Man, by disobedience, lost his innocence, forfeited the favor of God, became corrupt in heart and inclined to evil. In this state of spiritual death and condemnation, man is still free and responsible; yet, without the illuminating influences of the Holy Spirit, he is unable either to keep the law or lay hold upon the hope set before him in the gospel.

37. When the sinner is born of God, he loves him supremely, and steadfastly purposes to do his will; yet, because of remaining corruption, and of his imperfect knowledge of moral and spiritual things, he often wills what in itself is sinful. This imperfect knowledge and corruption remain, in greater or less force, during the present life; hence the conflict between the flesh and the spirit.

DIVINE INFLUENCE

38. God the Father, having set forth his Son Jesus Christ as a propitiation for the sins of the world, does most graciously vouchsafe a manifestation of the Holy Spirit with the same intent to every man.

39. The Holy Spirit, operating through the written word, and through such other means as God in his wisdom may choose, or directly, without means, so moves upon the hearts of men as to enlighten, reprove, and convince them of sin, of their lost estate, and of their need of salvation; and, by so doing, inclines them to come to Christ.

40. This call of the Holy Spirit is purely of God's free grace alone, and not because of human merit, and is antecedent to all desire, purpose, and intention on the part of the sinner to come to Christ; so that while it is possible for all to be saved with it, none can be saved without it.

41. This call is not irresistible, but is effectual in those only who, in penitence and faith, freely surrender themselves wholly to Christ, the only name whereby men can be saved.

REPENTANCE UNTO LIFE

42. Repentance unto life is a change of mind and feeling toward God, induced by the agency of the Holy Spirit, wherein the sinner resolutely purposes to forsake all sin, to turn unto God, and to walk in all his commandments.

43. There is no merit in repentance, or in any other human exercise; yet God is pleased to require all men to repent.

44. As all men are required to make full and frank confession of sin to God, so he that gives grounds of offense to the Church, or trespasses against his brother, should confess his errors, make amendment and due restitution, so far as is in his power.

SAVING FAITH

45. Saving faith, including assent to the truth of God's holy word, is the act of receiving and resting upon Christ alone for salvation, and is accompanied by contrition for sin and a full purpose of heart to turn from it and to live unto God.

46. While there is no merit in faith, yet it is the condition of salvation. It is not of the nature of good works, from which it must be distinguished.

47. This faith may be tried in many ways, but the believer has the promise of ultimate victory through Christ.

JUSTIFICATION

48. All those who truly repent of their sins, and in faith commit themselves to Christ, God freely justifies; not by infusing righteousness into them, but by pardoning their sins and by counting and accepting their persons as righteous; not for any thing wrought in them or done by them, but for Christ's sake alone; not by imputing faith itself, or any other evangelical obedience, to them as their righteousness, but by imputing the obedience and satisfaction of Christ unto them, they receiving and resting on him and his righteousness by faith.

49. Justification is purely of God's free grace, and is a full pardon for all sins, and exemption from all their penal consequences; but it imparts no moral qualities or merits to the believer, being strictly a legal transaction. Though of free grace alone, it is conditioned upon faith, and is assured to none but penitent and true believers, who, being justified, have peace with God through our Lord Jesus Christ.

50. God continues to forgive the sins of those who are justified, and although he will never permit them to fall from the state of justification, yet they may, by their sins, fall under God's fatherly displeasure, and not have the light of his countenance restored unto them until they humble themselves, confess their sins, and renew their consecration to God.

REGENERATION

51. Those who believe in the Lord Jesus Christ are regenerated, or born from above, renewed in spirit, and made new creatures in Christ.

52. The necessity for this moral purification arises out of the enmity of the human heart against God, its insubordination to his law, and its consequent incapacity to love and glorify God.

53. Regeneration is of God's free grace alone, and is the work of the Holy Spirit, who, by taking of the things which are Christ's and showing them unto the sinner, enables him to lay hold on Christ. This renewal of the heart by the Holy Spirit is not of the nature of a physical but of a moral work—a purification of the heart by faith.

54. All infants dying in infancy, and all persons who have never had the faculty of reason, are regenerated and saved.

ADOPTION

55. All those who are regenerated, and are thus changed into the image of his Son, God the Father is pleased to make partakers of the grace of adoption, by which they are taken into the number, and enjoy the liberties and privileges, of the children of God; have his name put upon them; receive the Spirit of adoption; have access to the throne of grace with boldness; are enabled to cry, Abba, Father; are pitied, protected, provided for, and chastened by him, as by a father, yet never cast off, but sealed to the day of redemption, and inherit the promises as heirs of everlasting salvation.

SANCTIFICATION

56. Sanctification is a doctrine of the Holy Scriptures, and it is the duty and privilege of believers to avail themselves of its inestimable benefits, as taught in the word of God. A state of sinless perfection in this life is not authorized by the Scriptures, and is a dogma of dangerous tendency.

GROWTH IN GRACE

57. Growth in grace is secured by personal consecration to the service of God, regular attention to the means of grace, the reading of the Holy Scriptures, prayer, the ministrations of the sanctuary, and all known Christian duties. By such means the believer's faith is much increased, his tendency to sin weakened, the lusts of the flesh mortified, and he more and more strengthened in all saving graces, and in the practice of holiness, without which no man shall see the Lord.

GOOD WORKS

58. Good works are such only as God has commanded in his word, and not such as may be devised by men out of blind zeal, or any pretense of good intention.

59. Those who, in their obedience and love, attain the greatest height in this life, still fall short of that perfection which the Divine law requires; yet their good works are accepted of God, who, looking upon them in his Son, is pleased to accept and reward that which is sincere, although accompanied with many weaknesses and imperfections.

PRESERVATION OF BELIEVERS

60. Those whom God has justified, he will also glorify; consequently, the truly regenerated soul will not totally fall away from a state of grace, but will be preserved to everlasting life.

61. The preservation of believers depends on the unchangeable love and power of God, the merits, advocacy, and intercession of Jesus Christ, the abiding of the Holy Spirit and seed of God within them, and the nature of the Covenant of Grace. Nevertheless, true believers, through the temptations of Satan, the world, and the flesh, and the neglect of the means of grace, may fall into sin, incur God's displeasure, and grieve the Holy Spirit, and thus be deprived of some measure of their graces and comforts, and have their consciences wounded; but the Christian will never rest satisfied therein.

CHRISTIAN ASSURANCE

62. Those who truly believe in the Lord Jesus Christ, and love him in sincerity, endeavoring to walk in all good conscience before him, may, in this life, be certainly assured that they are in a state of grace, and may rejoice in the hope of the glory of God, which hope shall never make them ashamed.

63. This assurance is founded upon the Divine promises, the consciousness of peace with God, the testimony of the Holy Spirit witnessing with their spirits that they are the children of God, and is the earnest of their inheritance.

64. This comfortable assurance of salvation is not an invariable accompaniment of faith in Christ; hence the believer may have many sore conflicts before he is made a partaker of it; yet he may, by the right use of the means of grace—through the agency of the Holy Spirit—attain thereunto; therefore, it is the duty of every one to give diligence to make his calling and election sure.

65. As this assurance may be very much strengthened by full consecration to God and fidelity in his service, so it may be weakened by worldly-mindedness and negligence in Christian duty, which result in darkness and in doubt; yet true believers have the promise of God that he will never leave nor forsake them.

THE LAW OF GOD

66. The moral law is the rule of duty growing immediately out of the relations of rational creatures to their Creator and to each other. These relations being the product of the Divine purpose, the law has its ultimate source in the will of the Creator.

67. This law is of universal and perpetual obligation, and is written primarily upon the hearts of all accountable beings. It was sufficiently known to Adam to enable him to know and do the will of God, and thus, by the righteousness of works, secure eternal life.

68. After Adam's fall, and that of his posterity through him, a written form of the law became necessary. This was given in the Decalogue, or Ten Commandments, a summary of which is given in these words: Thou shalt love the Lord thy God with all thy heart, and with all thy soul, and with all thy strength, and with all thy mind, and thy neighbor as thyself.

69. This law is not set aside, but rather established, by the gospel, which is the Divine expedient by which sinners are saved, and the end of the law fully met. It accordingly remains in full force as the rule of conduct. It must not, therefore, be confounded with the ceremonial law, which was abolished under the New Testament dispensation.

70. The penalties of this law are the natural and subjective sequences of transgression, and, unless set aside by the provisions of the gospel, must of

necessity be eternal; and such are they declared to be by the Holy Scriptures. These moral retributions must be distinguished from judicial punishments, which are arbitrary, objective, and temporary, and are always inflicted as occasion may require, for administrative purposes.

CHRISTIAN LIBERTY

71. The liberty that Christ has secured to believers under the gospel consists in freedom from the guilt and penal consequences of sin, in their free access to God, and in their yielding obedience to him, not from a slavish fear, but from a cheerful and confiding love.

72. God, who alone is Lord of the conscience, has left it free, in matters of faith and worship, from such opinions and commandments of men as may be contrary to his word.

73. Those who, upon pretense of Christian liberty, practice any sin, or cherish any lust, do thereby destroy the end of Christian liberty, which is, that being delivered from the dominion of sin, we may serve the Lord without fear in righteousness all our days.

74. Those who, upon a similar pretense, shall oppose the proper exercise of any lawful authority, whether civil or ecclesiastical, and thereby resist the ordinance of God, may lawfully be called to account, and be subjected to the censures of the Church.

RELIGIOUS WORSHIP

75. Religious worship is to be rendered to God the Father, Son, and Holy Spirit, and to him alone; not to angels, saints, or any other creature; and, since the fall, this worship is acceptable only through the mediation of the Lord Jesus Christ.

76. Prayer with thanksgiving, being one special part of religious worship, is required of all men; and, by the help of the Holy Spirit, is made efficacious through Christ, when offered according to his will. Prayer is to be made for things lawful, and for the living, but not for the dead.

77. The reading of the Holy Scriptures, attendance upon the ministrations of the word, the use of psalms and sacred songs, the proper observance of the Christian sacraments, visiting the sick, contributing to the relief of the poor, and the support and spread of the gospel, are all proper acts of religious worship. Religious vows, solemn fastings and thanksgivings, are also acts of religious worship, and are of much benefit when properly performed.

78. God is to be worshiped in spirit and in truth, in secret, in private families daily, and in the public assembly.

CHRISTIAN STEWARDSHIP

79. Christian stewardship consists in the recognition that all of life is a trust from God and is to be used for his glory and the advancement of his kingdom. It extends to all gifts which God has bestowed upon man including time, talents, and substance.

80. The motive of Christian stewardship is love toward both God and man and the desire for the propagation of the gospel.

81. Tithing as a principle of stewardship is both a duty and a privilege of every believer. While not expressly commanded in the New Testament, it was endorsed by Christ himself and may be legitimately deduced from the epistles.

82. Tithing is, when rightly practiced, an act of Christian devotion and a means of grace for the believer and is blessed of God in the propagation of the gospel.

83. While tithing is a duty and privilege of every believer, it should be regarded as the minimum basis of Christian giving and not necessarily as the full measure of one's devotion to Christ.

84. Every man must give an account to God of his stewardship.

SABBATH-DAY

85. God has been pleased to appoint one day in seven to be kept holy unto him, which, from the beginning of the world to the resurrection of Christ was the last day of the week; and, after the resurrection of Christ, was changed unto the first day of the week, which in the Scriptures is called the Lord's-day.

86. The Sabbath is kept holy unto the Lord by resting from employments and recreations of a secular character, by the public and private worship of God, and by works of necessity and mercy.

LAWFUL OATHS AND VOWS

87. The name of God only is that by which men ought to swear, and therein it is to be used with all reverence; therefore, to swear vainly or rashly by that glorious and dreadful name, or to swear at all by any other thing, is sinful. Yet, an oath is warranted by the word of God, under the New Testament as well as under the Old, when imposed by lawful authority.

88. Whosoever takes an oath ought duly to consider the weightiness of so solemn an act, and therein to avouch nothing but what he is fully persuaded is the truth. Neither may a man bind himself by oath to any thing but what is good and just, or what he believes so to be, and what he is able and resolved to perform.

89. An oath is to be taken in the plain and common sense of the words, without equivocation or mental reservation. It cannot oblige to sin; but in any thing not sinful, being taken, it binds to performance, although to a man's own hurt.

90. A vow is of a like nature with an oath, and ought to be made with the like religious care, and to be performed with the like faithfulness. No man may vow to do any thing forbidden in the word of God, or what would hinder any duty therein commanded, or which is not in his own power, and for the performance whereof he has no promise or ability from God.

CIVIL GOVERNMENT

91. God, the Supreme Lord and King of all the world, has ordained civil officers to be under him over the people, for his own glory and the public good; and, to this end, has armed them with power for the defense of the innocent and the punishment of evil-doers.

92. It is lawful for Christians to accept civil offices when called thereunto, in the management whereof they ought especially to maintain piety, justice, and peace, according to the wholesome laws of each Commonwealth.

93. Civil officers may not assume to themselves the administration of the word and the sacraments, or in the least interfere in matters of faith; yet it is their duty to protect the Church of our common Lord, without giving preference to any denomination of Christians. And, as Jesus Christ has appointed a government and discipline in his Church, no law of any Commonwealth should interfere therewith, but should provide that all religious and ecclesiastical assemblies shall be held without molestation or disturbance.

94. It is the duty of the people to pray for magistrates, to obey their lawful commands, and to be subject to their authority for conscience's sake.

MARRIAGE AND DIVORCE

95. Marriage is to be between one man and one woman; neither is it lawful for any man to have more than one wife, nor for any woman to have more than one husband, at the same time.

96. Marriage was ordained for the mutual help of husband and wife, and for the benefit of the human race.

97. Marriages ought not to be within the degrees of consanguinity or affinity forbidden in the word of God, nor can such marriages be justified by the human law.

98. The marriage relation should not be dissolved for any cause not justified by the teachings of the word of God, and any immorality in relation to its dissolution is cognizable by the Church-courts.

THE CHURCH

99. The universal Church, which is invisible, consists of all those who have become children of God by faith, and joint-heirs with Christ, who is the head thereof.

100. The visible Church consists of those who hold to the fundamental doctrines of Christianity in respect to matters of faith and morals, and have entered into formal covenant with God and some organized body of Christians for the maintenance of religious worship. The children of such are included in the covenant relations of their parents, and are properly under the special care of the Church.

101. Unto this visible Church Christ has given the ministry, the word, and the ordinances for its edification, and, by his own presence in spirit, makes them effectual thereunto. The Lord Jesus Christ is the only head of his Church on earth.

CHRISTIAN COMMUNION

102. All those united to Christ by faith have fellowship with him, and, being united to one another in love, have communion one with another, and are required to bear one another's burdens, and so fulfill the law of Christ.

103. While it is required of all Christians to live in fellowship, it is the especial duty of those belonging to the same denomination; and also to co-operate in sustaining public worship, and whatever measures are adjudged best for the spiritual interests of the Church and the glory of God.

THE SACRAMENTS

104. As under the Old Testament dispensation two sacraments were ordained, Circumcision and the Passover; so, under the New, there are but two—that is to say, Baptism and the Lord's Supper.

BAPTISM

105. Water-baptism is a sacrament of the New Testament, ordained by Jesus Christ as a sign or symbol of the baptism of the Holy Spirit, and as the seal of the Covenant of Grace.

106. The outward element to be used in this sacrament is water, wherewith the party is to be baptized in the name of the Father, and of the Son, and of the Holy Spirit, by an ordained minister of the gospel.

107. Baptism is rightly administered by pouring or sprinkling water upon the person, yet the validity of this sacrament does not depend upon any particular mode of administration.

108. The proper subjects of water-baptism are believing adults; also infants, one or both of whose parents or guardians are believers.

109. There is no saving efficacy in water-baptism, yet it is a duty of all believers to confess Christ in this solemn ordinance, and it is also the duty of all believing parents to consecrate their children to God in baptism.

THE LORD'S SUPPER

110. The sacrament, commonly called the Lord's Supper, was instituted by the Lord Jesus Christ at the close of his last passover supper, as a perpetual remembrance of his passion and death on the cross, by which sacrifice of himself he was made the propitiation for the sins of the whole world.

111. In this sacrament no sacrifice of any kind is offered for sin, but the one perfect offering of Christ as a sufficient sacrifice is set forth and commemorated by appropriate symbols. These symbols are bread and wine, which, though figuratively called the body and blood of Christ, nevertheless remain, after consecration, literal bread and wine, and give no countenance

to the doctrines of consubstantiation and transubstantiation.

112. As in this sacrament the communicants have visibly set before them symbols of the Saviour's passion, they should not approach the holy communion without due self-examination, reverence, humility, and gratitude.

113. All who love the Lord Jesus in sincerity and in truth should, on all suitable occasions, express their devotion to him by the use of the symbols of his death. But none who have not faith to discern the Lord's body should partake of his holy communion.

CHURCH AUTHORITY

114. The Lord Jesus, as king and head of his Church, has therein appointed a government intrusted to Church-officers distinct from the civil government.

115. By Divine appointment the officers of the visible church have the power to admit members into its communion, to admonish, suspend, or expel the disorderly and to restore those who, in the judgment of charity, have repented of their sins.

CHURCH COURTS

116. Church-government implies the existence of Church-courts, invested with legislative, judicial, and executive authority; and the Scriptures recognize such institutions, some of subordinate and some of superior authority, each having its own particular sphere of duties and privileges in reference to matters ministerial and ecclesiastical, yet all subordinate to the same general design.

117. It is the prerogative of these courts, ministerially, to determine controversies of faith and questions of morals, to set down rules and directions for the better ordering of the public worship of God and government of his Church, to receive complaints in cases of maladministration, and authoritatively to determine the same, which determinations are to be received with reverence and submission.

DEATH AND THE RESURRECTION

118. The bodies of men, after death, return to dust; but their spirits, being immortal, return to God who gave them. The spirits of the righteous are received into heaven, where they behold the face of God in light and glory, waiting for the full redemption of their bodies; and the spirits of the wicked are cast into hell, where they are reserved to the judgment of the great day. The Scriptures speak of no other place for departed spirits.

119. At the resurrection, those who are alive shall not die, but shall be changed; and all the dead shall be raised up, spiritual and immortal, and spirits and bodies be reunited forever. There shall be a resurrection both of the just and the unjust: of the unjust to dishonor, and of the just unto honor; the bodies of the latter shall be fashioned like unto Christ's glorious body.

THE JUDGMENT

120. God has appointed a day wherein he will judge the world in righteousness by Jesus Christ—to whom all power and judgment are given by the Father—in which not only the apostate angels shall be judged, but likewise all persons who have lived upon earth shall appear before the tribunal of Christ, and shall receive according to what they have done, whether good or evil.

121. After the judgment, the wicked shall go away into eternal punishment, but the righteous into eternal life.

Notes: *The Cumberland Presbyterian Church emerged on the American frontier at the period usually termed the Second Great Awakening. From the Methodist example, it developed an Arminian theological perspective and followed the practice of formally using untrained ministers, which placed its leaders in conflict with the older Presbyterian authorities on the East Coast. Seeing the need to organize separately, the leaders wished to create a church that was Presbyterian but at the same time did not hold to the strong Calvinist doctrines of limited atonement and predestination.*

In 1814 the new church adopted a confession of faith that was little more than the Westminster Confession modified to eliminate the prime features of what was termed "hyper-Calvinism," i.e., the doctrines of universal foreordination, unconditional election, and rebrobation and limited atonement. [The text of these early revisions can be found in Philip Schaff's The Creeds of Christendom. (New York: Harper & Brothers, 1877).] However, so integral were these doctrines to the Westminster position that expunging them completely could only be accomplished with a complete rewriting. That rewriting was not done until the 1880s, and the new confession was accepted in 1883. The continuing Cumberland Presbyterian Church has retained the rewritten confession, reproduced here without the Biblical footnotes. This confession is also used by the Second Cumberland Presbyterian Church in the U.S.

The Arminian emphasis on universal atonement, the free grace of God, and free will had been passed to the Cumberland Presbyterian Church by the Methodists. However, one Methodist emphasis, that on human perfectability, was not accepted by the Presbyterians and is specifically denied by them.

* * *

THE CONFESSION OF 1967 [PRESBYTERIAN CHURCH (U.S.A.)]

PREFACE

The Church confesses its faith when it bears a present witness to God's grace in Jesus Christ.

In every age the church has expressed its witness in words and deeds as the need of the time required. The earliest examples of confession are found within the Scriptures. Confessional statements have taken such varied forms as hymns, liturgical formulas, doctrinal definitions, catechisms, theological systems in summary, and declarations of purpose against threatening evil.

Confessions and declarations are subordinate standards in the church, subject to the authority of Jesus Christ, the Word of God, as the Scriptures bear witness to him. No one type of confession is exclusively valid, no one statement is irreformable. Obedience to Jesus Christ alone identifies the one universal church and supplies the continuity of its tradition. This obedience is the ground of the church's duty and freedom to reform itself in life and doctrine as new occasions, in God's Providence, may demand.

The United Presbyterian Church in the United States of America acknowledges itself aided in understanding the gospel by the testimony of the church from earlier ages and from many lands. More especially it is guided by the Nicene and Apostles' Creeds from the time of the early church; the Scots Confession, the Heidelberg Catechism, and the Second Helvetic Confession from the era of the Reformation; the Westminster Confession and Shorter Catechism from the seventeenth century, and the Shorter Catechism from the seventeenth century, and the Theological Declaration of Barmen from the twentieth century.

The purpose of the Confession of 1967 is to call the church to the unity in confession and mission which is required of disciples today. This Confession is not a "system of doctrine," nor does it include all the traditional topics of theology. For example, the Trinity and the Person of Christ are not redefined but are recognized and reaffirmed as forming the basis and determining the structure of the Christian faith.

God's reconciling work in Jesus Christ and the mission of reconciliation to which he has called his church are the heart of the gospel in any age. Our generation stands in peculiar need of reconciliation in Christ. Accordingly this Confession of 1967 is built upon that theme.

THE CONFESSION

In Jesus Christ God was reconciling the world to himself. Jesus Christ is God with man. He is the eternal Son of the Father, who became man and lived among us to fulfill the work of reconciliation. He is present in the church by the power of the Holy Spirit to continue and complete his mission. This work of God, the Father, Son and Holy Spirit, is the foundation of all confessional statements about God, man and the World. Therefore the church calls men to be reconciled to God and to one another.

Part I. GOD'S WORK OF RECONCILIATION

Section A. THE GRACE OF OUR LORD JESUS CHRIST

1. JESUS CHRIST. In Jesus of Nazareth true humanity was realized once for all. Jesus, a Palestinian Jew, lived among his own people and shared their needs, temptations, joys, and sorrows. He expressed the love of God in word and deed and became a brother to all kinds of sinful men. But his complete obedience led him into conflict with his people. His life and teaching judged their goodness, religious aspirations, and national hopes. Many rejected him and demanded his death. In giving himself freely for them He took upon himself the judgment under which all men stand convicted. God raised him from the

dead, vindicating him as Messiah and Lord. The victim of sin became victor, and won the victory over sin and death for all men.

God's reconciling act in Jesus Christ is a mystery which the Scriptures describe in various ways. It is called the sacrifice of a lamb, a shepherd's life given for his sheep, atonement by a priest; again it is ransom of a slave, payment of debt, vicarious satisfaction of a legal penalty, and victory over the powers of evil. These are expressions of a truth which remains beyond the reach of all theory in the depths of God's love for man. They reveal the gravity, cost, and sure achievement of God's reconciling work.

The risen Christ is the savior for all men. Those joined to him by faith are set right with God and commissioned to serve as his reconciling community. Christ is head of this community, the church, which began with the apostles and continues through all generations.

The same Jesus Christ is the judge of all men. His judgment discloses the ultimate seriousness of life and gives promise of God's final victory over the power of sin and death. To receive life from the risen Lord is to have life eternal; to refuse life from him is to choose the death which is separation from God. All who put their trust in Christ face divine judgment without fear, for the judge is their redeemer.

2. THE SIN OF MAN. The reconciling act of God in Jesus Christ exposes the evil in men as sin in the sight of God. In sin men claim mastery of their own lives, turn against God and their fellowmen, and become exploiters and despoilers of the world. They lose their humanity in futile striving and are left in rebellion, despair, and isolation.

Wise and virtuous men through the ages have sought the highest good in devotion to freedom, justice, peace, truth and beauty. Yet all human virtue, when seen in the light of God's love in Jesus Christ, is found to be infected by self-interest and hostility. All men, good and bad alike, are in the wrong before God and helpless without his forgiveness. Thus all men fall under God's judgment. No one is more subject to that judgment than the man who assumes that he is guiltless before God or morally superior to others.

God's love never changes. Against all who oppose him, God expresses his love in wrath. In the same love God took on himself judgment and shameful death in Jesus Christ, to bring men to repentance and new life.

Section B. THE LOVE OF GOD

God's sovereign love is a mystery beyond the reach of man's mind. Human thought ascribes to God superlatives of power, widsom, and goodness. But God reveals his love in Jesus Christ by showing power in the form of a servant, wisdom in the folly of the cross, and goodness in receiving sinful men. The power of God's love in Christ to transform the world discloses that the Redeemer is the Lord and Creator who made all things to serve the purpose of his love.

God has created the world of space and time to be the sphere of his dealings with men. In its beauty and vastness, sublimity and awfulness, order and disorder, the world reflects to the eye of faith the majesty and mystery of its Creator.

God has created man in a personal relation with himself that man may respond to the love of the Creator. He has created male and female and given them a life which proceeds from birth to death in a succession of generations and in a wide complex of social relations. He has endowed man with capacities to make the world serve his needs and to enjoy its good things. Life is a gift to be received with gratitude and a task to be pursued with courage. Man is free to seek his life within the purpose of God: to develop and protect the resources of nature for the common welfare, to work for justice and peace in society, and in other ways to use his creative powers for the fulfillment of human life.

God expressed his love for all mankind through Israel, whom he chose to be his covenant people to serve him in love and faithfulness. When Israel was unfaithful, he disciplined the nation with his judgments and maintained his cause through prophets, priests, teachers, and true believers. These witnesses called all Israelites to a destiny in which they would serve God faithfully and become a light to the nations. The same witnesses proclaimed the coming of a new age, and a true servant of God in whom God's purpose for Israel and for mankind would be realized.

Out of Israel God in due time raised up Jesus. His faith and obedience were the response of the perfect child of God. He was the fulfillment of God's promise to Israel, the beginning of the new creation, and the pioneer of the new humanity. He gave history its meaning and direction and called the church to be his servant for the reconciliation of the world.

Section C. THE COMMUNION OF THE HOLY SPIRIT

God the Holy Spirit fulfills the work of reconciliation in man. The Holy Spirit creates and renews the church as the community in which men are reconciled to God and to one another. He enables them to receive forgiveness as they forgive one another and to enjoy the peace of God as they make peace among themselves. In spite of their sin, he gives them power to become representatives of Jesus Christ and his gospel of reconciliation to all men.

1. THE NEW LIFE. The reconciling work of Jesus was the supreme crisis in the life of mankind. His cross and resurrection become personal crisis and present hope for men when the gospel is proclaimed and believed. In this experi-

ence the Spirit brings God's forgiveness to men, moves them to respond in faith, repentance, and obedience, and initiates the new life in Christ.

The new life takes shape in a community in which men know that God loves and accepts them in spite of what they are. They therefore accept themselves and love others, knowing that no man has any ground on which to stand except God's grace.

The new life does not release a man from conflict with unbelief, pride, lust, fear. He still has to struggle with disheartening difficulties and problems. Nevertheless, as he matures in love and faithfulness in his life with Christ, he lives in freedom and good cheer, bearing witness on good days and evil days, confident that the new life is pleasing to God and helpful to others.

The new life finds its direction in the life of Jesus, his deeds and words, his struggles against temptation, his compassion, his anger, and his willingness to suffer death. The teaching of apostles and prophets guides men in living this life, and the Christian community nurtures and equips them for their ministries.

The members of the church are emissaries of peace and seek the good of man in cooperation with powers and authorities in politics, culture, and economics. But they have to fight against pretensions and injustices when these same powers endanger human welfare. Their strength is in their confidence that God's purpose rather than man's schemes will finally prevail.

Life in Christ is life eternal. The resurrection of Jesus is God's sign that he will consummate his work of creation and reconciliation beyond death and bring to fulfillment the new life begun in Christ.

2. THE BIBLE. The one sufficient revelation of God is Jesus Christ, the Word of God incarnate, to whom the Holy Spirit bears unique and authoritative witness through the Holy Scriptures, which are received and obeyed as the word of God written. The Scriptures are not a witness among others, but the witness without parallel. The church has received the books of the Old and New Testaments as prophetic and apostolic testimony in which it hears the word of God and by which its faith and obedience are nourished and regulated.

The New Testament is the recorded testimony of apostles to the coming of the Messiah, Jesus of Nazareth, and the sending of the Holy Spirit to the church. The Old Testament bears witness to God's faithfulness in his covenant with Israel and points the way to the fulfillment of his purpose in Christ. The Old Testament is indispensable to understand the New, and is not itself fully understood without the New.

The Bible is to be interpreted in the light of its witness to God's work of reconciliation in Christ. The Scriptures, given under the guidance of the Holy Spirit, are nevertheless the words of men, conditioned by the language, thought forms, and literary fashions of the places and times at which they were written. They reflect views of life, history, and the cosmos which were then current. The church, therefore, has an obligation to approach the Scriptures with literary and historical understanding. As God has spoken his word in diverse cultural situations, the church is confident that he will continue to speak through the Scriptures in a changing world and in every form of human culture.

God's word is spoken to his church today where the Scriptures are faithfully preached and attentively read in dependence on the illumination of the Holy Spirit and with readiness to receive their truth and direction.

Part II. THE MINISTRY OF RECONCILIATION

Section A. THE MISSION OF THE CHURCH

1. DIRECTION. To be reconciled to God is to be sent into the world as his reconciling community. This community, the church universal, is entrusted with God's message of reconciliation and shares his labor of healing the enmities which separate men from God and from each other. Christ has called the church to this mission and given it the gift of the Holy Spirit. The church maintains continuity with the apostles and with Israel by faithful obedience to his call.

    The life, death, resurrection, and promised coming of Jesus Christ has set the pattern for the church's mission. His life as man involves the church in the common life of men. His service to men commits the church to work for every form of human well-being. His suffering makes the church sensitive to all the sufferings of mankind so that it sees the face of Christ in the faces of men in every kind of need. His crucifixion discloses to the church God's judgment on man's inhumanity to man and the awful consequences of its own complicity in injustice. In the power of the risen Christ and the hope of his coming the church sees the promise of God's renewal of man's life in society and of God's victory over all wrong.

    The church follows this pattern in the form of its life and in the method of its action. So to live and serve is to confess Christ as Lord.

2. FORMS AND ORDER. The institutions of the people of God change and vary as their mission requires in different times and places. The unity of the church is compatible with a wide variety of forms, but it is hidden and distorted when variant forms are allowed to harden into sectarian divisions, exclusive denominations, and rival factions.

Wherever the church exists, its members are both gathered in corporate life and dispersed in society for the sake of mission in the world.

The church gathers to praise God, to hear his word for mankind, to baptize and to join the Lord's Supper, to pray for and present the world to him in worship, to enjoy fellowship, to receive instruction, strength, and comfort, to order and organize its own corporate life, to be tested, renewed, and reformed, and to speak and act in the world's affairs as may be appropriate to the needs of the time.

The church disperses to serve God wherever its members are, at work or play, in private or in the life of society. Their prayer and Bible study are part of the church's worship and theological reflection. Their witness is the church's evangelism. Their daily action in the world is the church in mission to the world. The quality of their relation with other persons is the measure of the church's fidelity.

Each member is the church in the world, endowed by the Spirit with some gift of ministry and is responsible for the integrity of his witness in his own particular situation. He is entitled to the guidance and support of the Christian community and is subject to its advice and correction. He in turn, in his own competence, helps to guide the church.

In recognition of special gifts of the Spirit and for the ordering of its life as a community, the church calls, trains, and authorizes certain members for leadership and oversight. The persons qualified for these duties in accordance with the polity of the church are set apart by ordination or other appropriate acts and thus made responsible for their special ministries.

The church thus orders its life as an institution with a constitution, government, officers, finances and administrative rules. These are instruments of mission, not ends in themselves. Different orders have served the gospel, and none can claim exclusive validity. A presbyterian polity recognizes the responsibility of all members for ministry and maintains the organic relation of all congregations in the church. It seeks to protect the church from exploitation by ecclesiastical or secular power and ambition. Every church order must be open to such reformation as may be required to make it a more effective instrument of the mission of reconciliation.

3. REVELATION AND RELIGION. The church in its mission encounters the religions of men and in that encounter becomes conscious of its own human character as a religion. God's revelation to Israel, expressed within Semitic culture, gave rise to the religion of the Hebrew people. God's revelation in Jesus Christ called forth the response of Jews and Greeks and came to expression within Judaism and Hellenism as

the Christian religion. The Christian religion as distinct from God's revelation of himself, has been shaped throughout its history by the cultural forms of its environment.

The Christian finds parallels between other religions and his own and must approach all religions with openness and respect. Repeatedly God has used the insight of non-Christians to challenge the church to renewal. But the reconciling word of the gospel is God's judgment upon all forms of religion, including the Christian. The gift of God in Christ is for all men. The church, therefore, is commissioned to carry the gospel to all men whatever their religion may be and even when they profess none.

4. RECONCILIATION IN SOCIETY. In each time and place there are particular problems and crises through which God calls the church to act. The church, guided by the Spirit, humbled by its own complicity, and instructed by all attainable knowledge, seeks to discern the will of God and learn how to obey in these concrete situations. The following are particularly urgent at the present time.

a. God has created the peoples of the earth to be one universal family. In his reconciling love he overcomes the barriers between brothers and breaks down every form of discrimination based on racial or ethnic difference, real or imaginary. The church is called to bring all men to receive and uphold one another as persons in all relationships of life: in employment, housing, education, leisure, marriage, family, church, and the exercise of political rights. Therefore the church labors for the abolition of all racial discrimination and ministers to those injured by it. Congregations, individuals, or groups of Christians who exclude, dominate, or patronize their fellowmen, however subtly, resist the Spirit of God and bring contempt on the faith which they profess.

b. God's reconciliation in Jesus Christ is the ground of the peace, justice, and freedom among nations which all powers of government are called to serve and defend. The church, in its own life, is called to practice the forgiveness of enemies and to commend to the nations as practical politics the search for cooperation and peace. This requires the pursuit of fresh and responsible relations across every line of conflict, even at risk to national security, to reduce areas of strife and to broaden international understanding. Reconciliation among nations becomes peculiarly urgent as countries develop nuclear, chemical and biological weapons, diverting their manpower and resources from constructive uses and risking the annihilation of mankind. Although nations may serve God's purposes in history, the church which identifies the sovereignty of any one nation or

any one way of life with the cause of God denies the Lordship of Christ and betrays its calling.

c. The reconciliation of man through Jesus Christ makes it plain that enslaving poverty in a world of abundance is an intolerable violation of God's good creation. Because Jesus identified himself with the needy and exploited, the cause of the world's poor is the cause of his disciples. The church cannot condone poverty, whether it is the product of unjust social structures, exploitation of the defenseless, lack of national resources, absence of technological understanding, or rapid expansion of populations. The church calls every man to use his abilities, his possessions, and the fruits of technology as gifts entrusted to him by God for the maintenance of his family and the advancement of the common welfare. It encourages those forces in human society that raise men's hopes for better conditions and provide them with opportunity for a decent living. A church that is indifferent to poverty, or evades responsibility in economic affairs, or is open to one social class only, or expects gratitude for its beneficence makes a mockery of reconciliation and offers no acceptable worship to God.

d. The relationship between man and woman exemplifies in a basic way God's ordering of the interpersonal life for which he created mankind. Anarchy in sexual relationships is a symptom of man's alienation from God, his neighbor, and himself. Man's perennial confusion about the meaning of sex has been aggravated in our day by the availability of new means for birth control and the treatment of infection, by the pressures of urbanization, by the exploitation of sexual symbols in mass communication, and by world overpopulation. The church, as the household of God, is called to lead men out of this alienation into the responsible freedom of the new life in Christ. Reconciled to God, each person has joy in and respect for his own humanity and that of other persons; a man and woman are enabled to marry, to commit themselves to a mutually shared life, and to respond to each other in sensitive and lifelong concern; parents receive the grace to care for children in love and to nurture their individuality. The church comes under the judgment of God and invites rejection by man when it fails to lead men and women into the full meaning of life together, or withholds the compassion of Christ from those caught in the moral confusion of our time.

Section B. THE EQUIPMENT OF THE CHURCH

Jesus Christ has given the church preaching and teaching, praise and prayer, and Baptism and the Lord's Supper as means of fulfilling its service of God among men. These gifts remain, but the church

THE CONFESSION OF 1967 [PRESBYTERIAN CHURCH
(U.S.A.)] (continued)

is obliged to change the forms of its service in ways appropriate to different generations and cultures.

1. PREACHING AND TEACHING. God instructs his church and equips it for mission through preaching and teaching. By these, when they are carried on in fidelity to the Scriptures and dependence upon the Holy Spirit, the people hear the word of God and accept and follow Christ. The message is addressed to men in particular situations. Therefore effective preaching, teaching, and personal witness require disciplined study of both the Bible and the contemporary world. All acts of public worship should be conducive to men's hearing of the gospel in a particular time and place and responding with fitting obedience.

2. PRAISE AND PRAYER. The church responds to the message of reconciliation in praise and prayer. In that response it commits itself afresh to its mission, experiences a deepening of faith and obedience, and bears open testimony to the gospel. Adoration of God is acknowledgment of the Creator by the creation. Confession of sin is admission of all men's guilt before God and of their need for his forgiveness. Thanksgiving is rejoicing in God's goodness to all men and in giving for the needs of others. Petitions and intercessions are addressed to God for the continuation of his goodness, the healing of men's ills, and their deliverance from every form of oppression. The arts, especially music and architecture, contribute to the praise and prayer of a Christian congregation when they help men to look beyond themselves to God and to the world which is the object of his love.

3. BAPTISM. By humble submission to John's baptism Christ joined himself to men in their need and entered upon his ministry of reconciliation in the power of the Spirit. Christian baptism marks the receiving of the same Spirit by by all his people. Baptism with water represents not only cleansing from sin but a dying with Christ and a joyful rising with him to new life. It commits all Christians to die each day to sin and to live for righteousness. In baptism the church celebrates the renewal of the covenant with which God has bound his people to himself. By baptism individuals are publicly received into the church to share in its life and ministry, and the church becomes responsible for their training and support in Christian discipleship. When those baptized are infants the congregation, as well as the parents, has a special obligation to nurture them in the Christian life, leading them to make, by a public profession, a personal response to the love of God shown forth in their baptism.

4. THE LORD'S SUPPER. The Lord's Supper is a celebration of the reconciliation of men with God and with one another in which they joyfully eat and drink together at the table of their Savior. Jesus Christ gave his church this remembrance of his dying for sinful men so that by participation in it they have communion with him and with all who shall be gathered to him. Partaking in him as they eat the bread and drink the wine in accordance with Christ's appointment, they receive from the risen and living Lord the benefits of his death and resurrection. They rejoice in the foretaste of the kingdom which he will bring to consummation at his promised coming and go out from the Lord's Table with courage and hope for the service to which he has called them.

PART III. THE FULFILLMENT OF
RECONCILIATION

God's redeeming work in Jesus Christ embraces the whole of man's life: social and cultural, economic and political, scientific and technological, individual and corporate. It includes man's natural environment as exploited and despoiled by sin. It is the will of God that his purpose for human life shall be fulfilled under the rule of Christ and all evil be banished from his creation.

Biblical visions and images of the rule of Christ such as a heavenly city, a Father's house, a new Heaven and earth, a marriage feast, and an unending day culminate in the image of the kingdom. The kingdom represents the triumph of God over all that resists his will and disrupts his creation. Already God's reign is present as a ferment in the world, stirring hope in men and preparing the world to receive its ultimate judgment and redemption.

With an urgency born of this hope the church applies itself to present tasks and strives for a better world. It does not justify limited progress with the kingdom of God on earth nor does it despair in the face of disappointment and defeat. In steadfast hope the church looks beyond all partial achievement to the final triumph of God.

"Now to him who by the power at work within us is able to do far more abundantly than all we ask or think, to him be glory in the church and in Christ Jesus to all generations, forever and ever. Amen."

Notes: *In 1967 the United Presbyterian Church in the U.S.A. adopted a new statement of faith. Hailed by the majority as a contemporary statement of the Christian tradition, it was denounced by others as a departure from the standards of the Westminster Confession. While affirming many of the traditional statements of the Westminster Confession, it provided a latitude on a number of theological questions. Contemporaneously with the passing of the confession, the church authorized the publication of* The Book of Confessions, *which included this new confession, the Westminster Confession, six other confessions, and the Heidelberg Catechism. In the act of recognizing the ancient creeds, other Reformed documents, and the twentieth-century Barmen declaration, the church dislodged the Westminster Confession from its unique role as the principal definer of Presbyterian faith to become but one of many acceptable statements. The Book of Confessions continues to be used by the Presbyterian Church (U.S.A.).*

THE SCOTS CONFESSION (1560)

CHAPTER I. GOD

We confess and acknowledge one God alone, to whom alone we must cleave, whom alone we must serve, whom only we must worship, and in whom alone we put our trust. Who is eternal, infinite, immeasurable, incomprehensible, omnipotent, invisible; one in substance and yet distinct in three persons, the Father, the Son, and the Holy Ghost. By whom we confess and believe all things in heaven and earth, visible and invisible, to have been created, to be retained in their being, and to be ruled and guided by his inscrutable providence for such end as his eternal wisdom, goodness, and justice have appointed, and to the manifestation of his own glory.

CHAPTER II. THE CREATION OF MAN

We confess and acknowledge that our God has created man, i.e., our first father, Adam, after his own image and likeness, to whom he gave wisdom, lordship, justice, free will, and self-consciousness, so that in the whole nature of man no imperfection could be found. From this dignity and perfection man and woman both fell; the woman being deceived by the serpent and man obeying the voice of the woman, both conspiring against the sovereign majesty of God, who in clear words had previously threatened death if they presumed to eat of the forbidden tree.

CHAPTER III. ORIGINAL SIN

By this transgression, generally known as original sin, the image of God was utterly defaced in man, and he and his children because by nature hostile to God, slaves to Satan, and the servants to sin. And thus everlasting death has had, and shall have, power and dominion over all who have not been, are not, or shall not be reborn from above. This rebirth is wrought by the power of the Holy Ghost creating in the hearts of God's chosen ones an assured faith in the promise of God revealed to us in his Word; by this faith we grasp Christ Jesus with the graces and blessings promised in him.

CHAPTER IV. THE REVELATION OF THE PROMISE

We constantly believe that God, after the fearful and horrible departure of man from his obedience, did seek Adam again, call upon him, rebuke and convict him of his sin, and in the end made unto him a most joyful promise, that "the seed of the woman should bruise the head of the serpent," that is, that he should destroy the works of the devil. This promise was repeated and made clearer from time to time, it was embraced with joy, and most constantly received by all the faithful from Adam to Noah, from Noah to Abraham, from Abraham to David, and so onwards to the incarnation of Christ Jesus: all (we mean the believing fathers under the law) did see the joyful day of Christ Jesus, and did rejoice.

CHAPTER V. THE CONTINUANCE, INCREASE, AND PRESERVATION OF THE KIRK

We most surely believe that God preserved, instructed, multiplied, honored, adorned, and called from death to life his Kirk in all ages since Adam until the coming of Christ Jesus in the flesh. For he called Abraham from his father's country, instructed him, and multiplied his seed; he marvelously preserved him, and more marvelously delivered his seed from the bondage and tyranny of Pharaoh; to them he gave his laws, constitutions, and ceremonies; to them he gave the land of Canaan; after he had given them judges, and afterwards, Saul, he gave David to be king, to whom he gave promise that of the fruit of his loins should one sit forever upon his royal throne. To this same people from time to time he sent prophets, to recall them to the right way of their God, from which sometimes they strayed by idolatry. And although, because of their stubborn contempt for righteousness he was compelled to give them into the hands of their enemies, as had previously been threatened by the mouth of Moses, so that the holy city was destroyed, the temple burned with fire, and the whole land desolate for seventy years, yet in mercy he restored them again to Jerusalem, where the city and temple were rebuilt, and they endured against all temptations and assaults of Satan till the Messiah came according to the promise.

CHAPTER VI. THE INCARNATION OF CHRIST JESUS

When the fullness of time came God sent his Son, his eternal wisdom, the substance of his own glory, into this world, who took the nature of humanity from the substance of a woman, a virgin, by means of the Holy Ghost. And so was born the "just seed of David," the "Angel of the great counsel of God," the very Messiah promised, whom we confess and acknowledge to be Emmanuel, true God and true man, two perfect natures united and joined in one person. So by our Confession we condemn the damnable and pestilent heresies of Arius, Marcion, Eutyches, Nestorius, and such others as did either deny the eternity of his Godhead, or the truth of his humanity, or confounded them, or else divided them.

CHAPTER VII. WHY THE MEDIATOR HAD TO BE TRUE GOD AND TRUE MAN

We acknowledge and confess that this wonderful union between the Godhead and the humanity in Christ Jesus did arise from the eternal and immutable decree of God from which all our salvation springs and depends.

CHAPTER VIII. ELECTION

That same eternal God and Father, who by grace alone chose us in his Son Christ Jesus before the foundation of the world was laid, appointed him to be our head, our brother, our pastor, and the great bishop of our souls. But since the opposition between the justice of God and our sins was such that no flesh by itself could or might have attained unto God, it behooved the Son of God to descend unto us and take himself a body of our body, flesh of our flesh, and bone of our bone, and so become the Mediator between God and man, giving power to as many as believe in him to be the sons of God; as he himself says, "I ascend to my Father and to your Father, to my God and to your God." By this most holy brotherhood whatever we have lost in Adam is restored to us again. Therefore we are not afraid to call God our Father, not so much because he has created us, which we have in common with the reprobate, as because he has given unto us his only Son to be our brother, and given us grace to acknowledge and embrace him as our only Mediator. Further, it behooved the Messiah and Redeemer to be true God and true man, because he was able to undergo the punishment of our transgressions and to present himself in the presence of his Father's judgment, as in our stead, to suffer for our transgression and disobedience, and by death to overcome him that was the author of death. But because the Godhead alone could not suffer death, and neither could manhood overcome death, he joined both together in one person, that the weakness of one should suffer and be subject to death—which we had deserved—and the infinite and invincible power of the other, that is, of the Godhead, should triumph, and purchase for us life, liberty, and perpetual victory. So we confess, and most undoubtedly believe.

CHAPTER IX. CHRIST'S DEATH, PASSION, AND BURIAL

That our Lord Jesus offered himself a voluntary sacrifice unto his Father for us, that he suffered contradiction of sinners, that he was wounded and plagued for our transgressions, that he, the clean innocent Lamb of God, was condemned in the presence of an earthly judge, that we should be absolved before the judgment seat of our God; that he suffered not only the cruel death of the cross, which was accursed by the sentence of God; but also that he suffered for a season the wrath of his Father which sinners had deserved. But yet we avow that he remained the only, well beloved, and blessed Son of his Father even in the midst of his anguish and torment which he suffered in body and soul to make full atonement for the sins of his people. From this we confess and avow that there remains no other sacrifice for sin; if any affirm so, we do not hesitate to say that they are blasphemers against Christ's death and the everlasting atonement thereby purchased for us.

CHAPTER X. THE RESURRECTION

We undoubtedly believe, since it was impossible that the sorrows of death should retain in bondage the Author of life, that our Lord Jesus crucified, dead, and buried, who descended into hell, did rise again for our justification, and the destruction of him who was the author of death, and brought life again to us who were subject to death and its bondage. We know that his resurrection was confirmed by the testimony of his enemies, and by the resurrection of the dead, whose sepulchres did open, and they did rise and appear to many within the city of Jerusalem. It was also confirmed by the testimony of his angels, and by the senses and judgment of his apostles and of others, who had conversation, and did eat and drink with him after his resurrection.

CHAPTER XI. THE ASCENSION

We do not doubt but that the selfsame body which was born of the virgin, was crucified, dead, and buried, and which did rise again, did ascend into the heavens, for the accomplishment of all things, where in our name and for our comfort he has received all power in heaven and earth, where he sits at the right hand of the Father, having received his kingdom, the only advocate and mediator for

us. Which glory, honor, and prerogative, he alone amongst the brethren shall possess till all his enemies are made his footstool, as we undoubtedly believe they shall be in the Last Judgment. We believe that the same Lord Jesus shall visibly return for this Last Judgment as he was seen to ascend. And then, we firmly believe, the time of refreshing and restitution of all things shall come, so that those who from the beginning have suffered violence, injury, and wrong, for righteousness' sake, shall inherit that blessed immortality promised them from the beginning. But, on the other hand, the stubborn, disobedient, cruel persecutors, filthy persons, idolators, and all sorts of unbelieving, shall be cast into the dungeon of utter darkness, where their worm shall not die, nor their fire be quenched. The rememberance of that day, and of the Judgment to be executed in it, is not only a bridle by which our carnal lusts are restrained but also such inestimable comfort that neither the threatening of worldly princes, nor the fear of present danger or of temporal death, may move us to renounce and forsake that blessed society which we, the members, have with our Head and only Mediator, Christ Jesus: whom we confess and avow to be the promised Messiah, the only Head of his Kirk, our just Lawgiver, our only High Priest, Advocate, and Mediator. To which honors and offices, if man or angel presume to intrude themselves, we utterly detest and abhor them, as blasphemous to our sovereign and supreme Governor, Christ Jesus.

CHAPTER XII. FAITH IN THE HOLY GHOST

Our faith and its assurance do not proceed from flesh and blood, that is to say, from natural powers within us, but are the inspiration of the Holy Ghost; whom we confess to be God, equal with the Father and with his Son, who sanctifies us, and brings us into all truth by his own working, without whom we should remain forever enemies to God and ignorant of his Son, Christ Jesus. For by nature we are so dead, blind, and perverse, that neither can we feel when we are pricked, see the light when it shines, nor assent to the will of God when it is revealed, unless the Spirit of the Lord Jesus quicken that which is dead, remove the darkness from our minds, and bow our stubborn hearts to the obedience of his blessed will. And so, as we confess that God the Father created us when we were not, as his Son our Lord Jesus redeemed us when we were enemies to him, so also do we confess that the Holy Ghost does sanctify and regenerate us, without respect to any merit proceeding from us, be it before or be it after our regeneration. To put this even more plainly: as we willingly disclaim any honor and glory for our own creation and redemption, so do we willingly also for our regeneration and sanctification; for by ourselves we are not capable of thinking one good thought, but he who has begun the work in us alone continues us in it, to the praise and glory of his undeserved grace.

CHAPTER XIII. THE CAUSE OF GOOD WORKS

The cause of good works, we confess, is not our free will, but the Spirit of the Lord Jesus, who dwells in our hearts by true faith, brings forth such works as God has prepared for us to walk in. For we most boldly affirm that it is blasphemy to say that Christ abides in the hearts of those in whom is no spirit of sanctification. Therefore we do not hesitate to affirm that murderers, oppressors, cruel persecuters, adulterers, filthy persons, idolators, drunkards, thieves, and all workers of iniquity, have neither true faith nor anything of the Spirit of the Lord Jesus, so long as they obstinately continue in wickedness. For as soon as the Spirit of the Lord Jesus, whom God's chosen children receive by true faith, takes possession of the heart of any man, so soon does he regenerate and renew him, so that he begins to hate what before he loved, and to love what he hated before. Thence comes that continual battle which is between the flesh and the Spirit in God's children, while the flesh and the natural man, being corrupt, lust for things pleasant and delightful to themselves, are envious in adversity and proud in prosperity, and every moment prone and ready to offend the majesty of God. But the Spirit of God, who bears witness to our spirit that we are the sons of God, makes us resist filthy pleasures and groan in God's presence for deliverance from this bondage of corruption, and finally to triumph over sin so that it does not reign in our mortal bodies. Other men do not share this conflict since they do not have God's Spirit, but they readily follow and obey sin and feel no regrets, since they act as the devil and their corrupt nature urge. But the sons of God fight against sin; sob and mourn when they find themselves tempted to do evil; and, if they fall, rise again with earnest and unfeigned repentance. They do these things, not by their own power, but by the power of the Lord Jesus, apart from whom they can do nothing.

CHAPTER XIV. THE WORKS WHICH ARE COUNTED GOOD BEFORE GOD

We confess and acknowledge that God has given to man his holy law, in which not only all such works as displease and offend his godly majesty are forbidden, but also those which please him and which he has promised to reward are commanded. These works are of two kinds. The one is done to the honor of God, the other to the profit of our neighbor, and both have the revealed will of God as their assurance. To have one God, to worship and honor him, to call upon him in all our troubles, to reverence his holy Name, to hear his Word and to believe it, and to share in his holy sacraments, belong to the first kind. To honor father, mother, princes, rulers, and superior powers; to love them, to support them, to obey their orders if they are not contrary to the commands of God, to save the lives of the innocent, to repress tyranny, to defend the oppressed, to keep our bodies clean and holy, to live in soberness and temperance, to deal justly with all men in word and deed, and, finally, to repress any desire to harm our neighbor, are the good works of the second kind, and these are most pleasing and acceptable to God as he has commanded them himself. Acts to the contrary are sins, which always displease him and provoke him to anger, such as, not to call upon him alone when we have need, not to hear his Word with reverence, but to condemn and despise it, to have or worship idols, to maintain and defend idolatry, lightly to esteem the reverend name of God, to profane, abuse, or condemn the sacraments of Christ Jesus, to disobey or resist any whom God has placed in authority, so long as they do not exceed the bounds of their office, to murder, or to consent thereto, to bear hatred, or to let innocent blood be shed if we can prevent it. In conclusion, we confess and affirm that the breach of any other commandment of the first or second kind is sin, by which God's anger and displeasure are kindled against the proud, unthankful world. So that we affirm good works to be those alone which are done in faith and at the command of God who, in his law, has set forth the things that please him. We affirm that evil works are not only those expressly done against God's command, but also, in religious matters and the worship of God, those things which have no other warrant than the invention and opinion of man. From the beginning God has rejected such, as we learn from the words of the prophet Isaiah and of our master. Christ Jesus, "In vain do they worship Me, teaching the doctrines and commandments of men."

CHAPTER XV. THE PERFECTION OF THE LAW AND THE IMPERFECTION OF MAN

We confess and acknowledge that the law of God is most just, equal, holy, and perfect, commanding those things which, when perfectly done, can give life and bring man to eternal felicity; but our nature is so corrupt, weak, and imperfect, that we are never able perfectly to fulfill the works of the law. Even after we are reborn, if we say that we have no sin, we deceive ourselves and the truth of God is not in us. It is therefore essential for us to lay hold on Christ Jesus, in his righteousness and his atonement, since he is the end and consummation of the Law and since it is by him that we are set at liberty so that the curse of God may not fall upon us, even though we do not fulfill the Law in all points. For as God the Father beholds us in the body of his Son Christ Jesus, he accepts our imperfect obedience as if it were perfect, and covers our works, which are defiled with many stains, with the righteousness of his Son. We do not mean that we are so set at liberty that we owe no obedience to the Law—for we have already acknowledged its place—but we affirm that no man on earth, with the sole exception of Christ Jesus, has given, gives, or shall give in action that obedience to the Law which the Law requires. When we have done all things we must fall down and unfeignedly confess that we are unprofitable servants. Therefore, whoever boasts of the merits of his own works or puts his trust in works of supererogation, boasts of what does not exist, and puts his trust in damnable idolatry.

CHAPTER XVI. THE KIRK

As we believe in one God, Father, Son, and Holy Ghost, so we firmly believe that from the beginning there has been, now is, and to the end of the world shall be, one Kirk, that is to say, one company and multitude of men chosen by God, who rightly worship and embrace him by true faith in Christ Jesus, who is the only Head of the Kirk, even as it is the body and spouse of Christ Jesus. This Kirk is catholic, that is, universal, because it contains the chosen of all ages, of all realms, nations and tongues, be they of the Jews or be they of the Gentiles, who have communion and society with God the Father, and with his Son, Christ Jesus, through the sanctification of his Holy Spirit. It is therefore called the communion, not of profane persons, but of saints, who, as citizens of the heavenly Jerusalem, have the fruit of inestimable benefits, one God, one Lord

THE SCOTS CONFESSION (1560) (continued)

Jesus, one faith, and one baptism. Out of this Kirk there is neither life nor eternal felicity. Therefore we utterly abhor the blasphemy of those who hold that men who live according to equity and justice shall be saved, no matter what religion they profess. For since there is neither life nor salvation without Christ Jesus: so shall none have part therein but those whom the Father has given unto his Son Christ Jesus, and those who in time come to him, avow his doctrine, and believe in him. (We include the children with the believing parents.) This Kirk is invisible, known only to God, who alone knows whom he has chosen, and includes both the chosen who are departed, the Kirk triumphant, those who yet live and fight against sin and Satan, and those who shall live hereafter.

CHAPTER XVII. THE IMMORTALITY OF SOULS

The chosen departed are in peace, and rest from their labors; not that they sleep and are lost in oblivion as some fanatics hold, for they are delivered from all fear and torment, and all the temptations to which we and all God's chosen are subject in this life, and because of which we are called the Kirk Militant. On the other hand, the reprobate and unfaithful departed have anguish, torment, and pain which cannot be expressed. Neither the one nor the other is in such sleep that they feel no joy or torment, as is testified by Christ's parable in St. Luke XVI, his words to the thief, and the words of the souls crying under the altar. "O Lord, thou that art righteous and just, how long shalt thou not revenge our blood upon those that dwell in the earth?"

CHAPTER XVIII. THE NOTES BY WHICH THE TRUE KIRK SHALL BE DETERMINED FROM THE FALSE, AND WHO SHALL BE JUDGE OF DOCTRINE

Since Satan has labored from the beginning to adorn his pestilent synagogue with the title of the Kirk of God, and has incited cruel murderers to persecute, trouble, and molest the true Kirk and its members, as Cain did to Abel, Ishmael to Isaac, Esau to Jacob, and the whole priesthood of the Jews to Christ Jesus himself and his apostles after him. So it is essential that the true Kirk be distinguished from the filthy synagogues by clear and perfect notes lest we, being deceived, receive and embrace, to our own condemnation, the one for the other. The notes, signs, and assured tokens whereby the spotless bride of Christ is known from the horrible harlot, the false Kirk, we state, are neither antiquity, usurped title lineal succession, appointed place, nor the numbers of men approving an error. For Cain was before Abel and Seth in age and title; Jerusalem had precedence above all other parts of the earth, for in it were priests lineally descended from Aaron, and greater numbers followed the scribes, pharisees, and priests, than unfeignedly believed and followed Christ Jesus and his doctrine . . . and yet no man of judgment, we suppose, will hold that any of the forenamed were the Kirk of God. The notes of the true Kirk, therefore, we believe, confess, and avow to be first, the true preaching of the Word of God, in which God has revealed himself to us, as the writings of the prophets and apostles declare; secondly, the right administration of the sacraments of Christ Jesus, with which must be associated the Word and promise of God to seal and confirm them in our hearts; and lastly, ecclesiastical discipline uprightly ministered, as God's Word prescribes, whereby vice is repressed and virtue nourished. Then wherever these notes are seen and continue for any time, be the number complete or not, there, beyond any doubt, is the true Kirk of Christ, who, according to his promise, is in its midst. This is not that universal Kirk of which we have spoken before, but particular Kirks, such as were in Corinth, Galatia, Ephesus, and other places where the ministry was planted by Paul and which he himself called Kirks of God. Such Kirks, we the inhabitants of the realm of Scotland confessing Christ Jesus, do claim to have in our cities, towns, and reformed districts because of the doctrine taught in our Kirks, contained in the written Word of God, that is, the Old and New Testaments, in those books which were originally reckoned canonical. We affirm that in these all things necessary to be believed for the salvation of man are sufficiently expressed. The interpretation of Scripture, we confess, does not belong to any private or public person, nor yet to any Kirk for pre-eminence or precedence, personal or local, which it has above others, but pertains to the Spirit of God by whom the Scriptures were written. When controversy arises about the right understanding of any passage or sentence of Scripture, or for the reformation of any abuse within the Kirk of God, we ought not so much to ask what men have said or done before us, as what the Holy Ghost uniformly speaks within the body of the Scriptures and what Christ Jesus himself did and commanded. For it is agreed by all that the Spirit of God, who is the Spirit of unity, cannot contradict himself. So if the interpretation or opinion of any theologian, Kirk, or council, is contrary to the plain Word of God written in any other passage of the Scripture, it is most certain that this is not the true understanding and meaning of the Holy Ghost, although councils, realms, and nations have approved and received it. We dare not receive or admit any interpretation which is contrary to any principal point of our faith, or to any other plain text of Scripture, or to the rule of love.

CHAPTER XIX. THE AUTHORITY OF THE SCRIPTURES

As we believe and confess the Scriptures of God sufficient to instruct and make perfect the man of God, so do we affirm and avow their authority to be from God, and not to depend on men or angels. We affirm, therefore, that those who say the Scriptures have no other authority save that which they have received from the Kirk are blasphemous against God and injurious to the true Kirk, which always hears and obeys the voice of her own Spouse and Paster, but takes not upon her to be mistress over the same.

CHAPTER XX. GENERAL COUNCILS, THEIR POWER, AUTHORITY, AND THE CAUSE OF THEIR SUMMONING

As we do not rashly condemn what good men, assembled together in general councils lawfully gathered, have set before us; so we do not receive uncritically whatever has been declared to men under the name of the general councils, for it is plain that, being human, some of them have manifestly erred, and that in matters of great weight and importance. So far then as the council confirms its decrees by the plain Word of God, so far do we reverence and embrace them. But if men, under the name of a council, pretend to forge for us new articles of faith, or to make decisions contrary to the Word of God, then we must utterly deny them as the doctrine of devils, drawing our souls from the voice of the one God to follow the doctrines and teachings of men. The reason why the general councils met was not to make any permanent law which God had not made before, nor yet to form new articles for our belief, nor to give the Word of God authority; much less to make that to be his Word, or even the true interpretation of it, which was not expressed previously by his holy will in his Word; but the reason for councils, at least of those that deserve that name, was partly to refute heresies, and to give public confession of their faith to the generations following, which they did by the authority of God's written Word, and not by any opinion or prerogative that they could not err by reason of their numbers. This, we judge, was the primary reason for general councils. The second was that good policy and order should be constituted and observed in the Kirk where, as in the house of God, it becomes all things to be done decently and in order. Not that we think any policy or order of ceremonies can be appointed for all ages, times, and places; for as ceremonies which men have devised are but temporal, so they may, and ought to be, changed, when they foster superstition rather than edify the Kirk.

CHAPTER XXI. THE SACRAMENTS

As the fathers under the Law, besides the reality of the sacrifices, had two chief sacraments, that is, circumcision and the passover, and those who rejected these were not reckoned among God's people; so do we acknowledge and confess that now in the time of the gospel we have two chief sacraments, which alone were instituted by the Lord Jesus and commanded to be used by all who will be counted members of his body, that is, Baptism and the Supper or Table of the Lord Jesus, also called the Communion of His Body and Blood. These sacraments, both of the Old Testament and of the New, were instituted by God not only to make a visible distinction between his people and those who were without the Covenant, but also to exercise the faith of his children and, by participation of these sacraments, to seal in their hearts the assurance of his promise, and of that most blessed conjunction, union, and society, which the chosen have with their Head, Christ Jesus. And so we utterly condemn the vanity of those who affirm the sacraments to be nothing else than naked and bare signs. No, we assuredly believe that by Baptism we are engrafted into Christ Jesus, to be made partakers of his righteousness, by which our sins are covered and remitted, and also that in the Supper rightly used, Christ Jesus is so joined with us that he becomes the very nourishment and food of our souls. Not that we imagine any transubstantiation of bread into Christ's body, and of wine into his natural blood, as the Romanists have perniciously taught and wrongly believed: but this union and conjunction which we have with the body and blood of Christ Jesus in the right use of the sacraments is wrought by means of the Holy Ghost, who by true faith carries us above all things that are visible, carnal, and earthly, and makes us feed upon the body and blood of Christ Jesus, once broken and shed for us but now in heaven, and appearing for us in the presence of his Father. Notwithstanding the distance between his glorified body in heaven and mortal men on earth, yet we must assuredly believe that the bread which we break is the communion of Christ's body and the cup which we bless the communion of his blood. Thus we confess and believe without doubt that the faithful, in the right use of the Lord's Table, do so eat the body and drink the blood of the Lord Jesus that he remains in them and they in him; they are so made flesh of his flesh and bone of his bone that as the eternal Godhood has given to the flesh of Christ Jesus, which by nature was corruptible and mortal, life and immortality, so the eating and drinking of the flesh and blood of Christ Jesus does the like for us. We grant that this is neither given to us merely at the time nor by the power and virtue of the sacrament alone, but we affirm that the faithful, in the right use of the Lord's Table, have such union with Christ Jesus as the natural man cannot apprehend. Further we affirm that although the faithful, hindered by negligence and human weakness, do not profit as much as they ought in the actual moment of the Supper, yet afterwards it shall bring forth fruit, being living seed sown in good ground; for the Holy Spirit, who can never be separated from the right institution of the Lord Jesus, will not deprive the faithful of the fruit of that mystical action. Yet all this, we say again, comes of that true faith which apprehends Christ Jesus, who alone makes the sacrament effective in us. Therefore, if anyone slanders us by saying that we affirm or believe the sacraments to be symbols and nothing more, they are libelous and speak against the plain facts. On the other hand we readily admit that we make a distinction between Christ Jesus in his eternal substance and the elements of the sacramental signs. So we neither worship the elements, in place of that which they signify, nor yet do we despise them or undervalue them, but we use them with great reverence, examining ourselves diligently before we participate, since we are assured by the mouth of the apostle that "whosoever shall eat this bread, and drink this cup of the Lord, unworthily, shall be guilty of the body and blood of the Lord."

CHAPTER XXII. THE RIGHT ADMINISTRATION OF THE SACRAMENTS

Two things are necessary for the right administration of the sacraments. The first is that they should be ministered by lawful ministers, and we declare that these are men appointed to preach the Word, unto whom God has given the power to preach the gospel, and who are lawfully called by some Kirk. The second is that they should be ministered in the elements and manner which God has appointed. Otherwise they cease to be the sacraments of Christ Jesus. This is why we abandon the teaching of the Roman Church and withdraw from its sacraments; firstly, because their ministers are not true ministers of Christ Jesus (indeed they even allow women, whom the Holy Ghost will not permit to preach in the congregation to baptize) and, secondly, because they have so adulterated both the sacraments with their own additions that no part of Christ's original act remains in its original simplicity. The addition of oil, salt, spittle, and such like in baptism, are merely human additions. To adore or venerate the sacrament, to carry it through streets and towns in procession, or to reserve it in a special case, is not the proper use of Christ's sacrament but an abuse of it. Christ Jesus said. "Take ye, eat ye," and "Do this in remembrance of Me." By these words and commands he sanctified bread and wine to be the sacrament of his holy body and blood, so that the one should be eaten and that all should drink of the other, and not that they should be reserved for worship or honored as God, as the Romanists do. Further, in withdrawing one part of the sacrament—the blessed cup—from the people, they have committed sacrilege. Moreover, if the sacraments are to be rightly used it is essential that the end and purpose of their institution should be understood, not only by the minister but by the recipients. For if the recipient does not understand what is being done, the sacrament is not being rightly used, as is seen in the case of the Old Testament sacrifices. Similarly, if the teacher teaches false doctrine which is hateful to God, even though the sacraments are his own ordinance, they are not rightly used, since wicked men have used them for another end than what God commanded. We affirm that this has been done to the sacraments in the Roman Church, for there the whole action of the Lord Jesus is adulterated in form, purpose, and meaning. What Christ Jesus did, and commanded to be done, is evident from the Gospels and from St. Paul; what the priest does at the altar we do not need to tell. The end and purpose of Christ's institution, for which it should be used, is set forth in the words. "Do this in remembrance of Me," and "For as often as ye eat this bread and drink this cup ye do show"—that is, extol, preach, magnify, and praise—"the Lord's death, till He come." But let the words of the mass, and their own doctors and teachings witness, what is the purpose and meaning of the mass; it is that, as mediators between Christ and his Kirk, they should offer to God the Father, a sacrifice in propitiation for the sins of the living and of the dead. This doctrine is blasphemous to Christ Jesus and would deprive his unique sacrifice, once offered on the cross for the cleansing of all who are to be sanctified, of its sufficiency; so we detest and renounce it.

CHAPTER XXIII. TO WHOM SACRAMENTS APPERTAIN

We hold that baptism applies as much to the children of the faithful as to those who are of age and discretion, and so we condemn the error of the Anabaptist, who deny that children should be baptized before they have faith and understanding. But we hold that the Supper of the Lord is only for those who are of the household of faith and can try and examine themselves both in their faith and their duty to their neighbors. Those who eat and drink at that holy table without faith, or without peace and goodwill to their brethren, eat unworthily. This is the reason why ministers in our Kirk make public and individual examination of those who are to be admitted to the table of the Lord Jesus.

CHAPTER XXIV. THE CIVIL MAGISTRATE

We confess and acknowledge that empires, kingdoms, dominions, and cites are appointed and ordained by God; the powers and authorities in them, emperors in empires, kings in their realms, dukes and princes in their dominions, and magistrates in cities, are ordained by God's holy ordinance for the manifestation of his own glory and for the good and well being of all men. We hold that any men who conspire to rebel or to overturn the civil powers, as duly established, are not merely enemies to humanity but rebels against God's will. Further, we confess and acknowledge that such persons as are set in authority are to be loved, honored, feared, and held in the highest respect, because they are the lieutenants of God, and in their councils God himself doth sit and judge. They are the judges and princes to whom God has given the sword for the praise and defense of good men and the punishment of all open evil doers. Moreover, we state that the preservation and purification of religion is particularly the duty to kings, princes, rulers, and magistrates. They are not only appointed for civil government but also to maintain true religion and to suppress all idolatry and superstition. This may be seen in David, Jehosaphat. Hezekiah, Josiah, and others highly commended for their zeal in that cause.

Therefore we confess and avow that those who resist the supreme powers, so long as they are acting in their own spheres, are resisting God's ordinance and cannot be held guiltless. We further state that so long as princes and rulers vigilantly fulfill their office, anyone who denies them aid, counsel, or service, denies it to God, who by his lieutenant craves it of them.

CHAPTER XXV. THE GIFTS FREELY GIVEN TO THE KIRK

Although the Word of God truly preached, the sacraments rightly ministered, and discipline executed according to the Word of God, are certain and infallible signs of the true Kirk, we do not mean that every individual person in that company is a chosen member of Christ Jesus. We acknowledge and confess that many weeds and tares are sown among the corn and grow in great abundance in its midst, and that the reprobate may be found in the fellowship of the chosen and may take an outward part with them in the benefits of the Word and sacraments. But since they only confess God for a time with their mouths and not with their hearts, they lapse, and do not continue to the end. Therefore they do not share the fruits of Christ's death, resurrection, and ascension. But such as unfeignedly believe with the heart and boldly confess the Lord Jesus with their mouths shall certainly receive his gifts. Firstly, in this life, they shall receive remission of sins and that by faith in Christ's blood alone; for though sin shall remain and continually abide in our mortal bodies, yet it shall not be counted against us, but be pardoned, and covered with Christ's righteousness. Secondly, in the general judgment, there shall be given to every man and woman resurrection of the flesh. The seas shall give up her dead, and the earth those who are buried within her. Yea, the Eternal, our God, shall stretch out his hand on the dust, and the dead shall arise incorruptible, and in the very substance of the selfsame flesh which every man now bears, to receive according to their works, glory or punishment. Such as now delight in vanity, cruelty, filthiness, superstition, or idolatry, shall be condemned to the fire unquenchable, in which those who now serve the devil in all abominations shall be tormented forever, both in body and in spirit. But such as continue in well doing to the end, boldly confessing the Lord Jesus, shall receive glory, honor, and immortality, we constantly believe, to reign forever in life everlasting with Christ Jesus, to whose glorified body all his chosen shall be made like, when he shall appear again in judgment and shall render up the Kingdom to God his Father, who then shall be and ever shall remain, all in all things, God blessed forever. To whom, with the Son and the Holy Ghost, be all honor and glory, now and ever. Amen.

Arise, O Lord, and let thine enemies be confounded; let them flee from thy presence that hate thy godly Name. Give thy servants strength to speak thy Word with boldness, and let all nations cleave to the true knowledge of thee. Amen.

Notes: *Following the acceptance of the new Confession of 1967, the United Presbyterian Church in the U.S.A., now a constituent part of the Presbyterian Church (U.S.A.), adopted a variety of confessional statements to stand beside the Westminster Confession. These additional statements serve as expressions of the church's full participation in the broad Western Christian tradition as well as the Reformed Church tradition, which the church inherited through sixteenth-century reformers John Calvin (in Geneva) and John Knox (in Scotland). The Scots Confession, originally published in 1560, is a reflection of that Scottish heritage. In several places it deals with issues of grave concern in the sixteenth century, such as the authority of general councils of the Roman Church, one of which had recently met at Trent.*

*   *   *

THE THEOLOGICAL DECLARATION OF BARMEN

I. AN APPEAL TO THE EVANGELICAL CONGREGATIONS AND CHRISTIANS IN GERMANY

The Confessional Synod of the German Evangelical Church met in Barmen, May 29-31, 1934. Here representatives from all the German Confessional Churches met with one accord in a confession of the one Lord of the one, holy, apostolic Church. In fidelity to their Confession of Faith, members of Lutheran. Reformed, and United Churches sought a common message for the need and temptation of the Church in our day. With gratitude to God they are convinced that they have been given a common word to utter. It was not their intention to found a new Church or to form a union. For nothing was farther from their minds than the abolition of the confessional status of our Churches. Their intention was, rather, to withstand in faith and unanimity the destruction of the Confession of Faith, and thus of the Evangelical Church in Germany. In opposition to attempts to establish the unity of the German Evangelical Church by means of false doctrine, by

the use of force and insincere practices, the Confessional Synod insists that the unity of the Evangelical Churches in Germany can come only from the Word of God in faith through the Holy Spirit. Thus alone is the Church renewed.

Therefore the Confessional Synod calls upon the congregations to range themselves behind it in prayer, and steadfastly to gather around those pastors and teachers who are loyal to the Confessions.

Be not deceived by loose talk, as if we meant to oppose the unity of the German nation! Do not listen to the seducers who pervert our intentions, as if we wanted to break up the unity of the German Evangelical Church or to forsake the Confessions of the Fathers!

Try the spirits whether they are of God! Prove also the words of the Confessional Synod of the German Evangelical Church to see whether they agree with Holy Scripture and with the Confessions of the Fathers. If you find that we are speaking contrary to Scripture, then do not listen to us! But if you find that we are taking our stand upon Scripture, then let no fear or temptation keep you from treading with us the path of faith and obedience to the Word of God, in order that God's people be of one mind upon earth and that we in faith experience what he himself has said: "I will never leave you, nor forsake you." Therefore, "Fear not, little flock, for it is your Father's good pleasure to give you the kingdom."

II. THEOLOGICAL DECLARATION CONCERNING THE PRESENT SITUATION OF THE GERMAN EVANGELICAL CHURCH

According to the opening words of its constitution of July 11, 1933, the German Evangelical Church is a federation of Confessional Churches that grew out of the Reformation and that enjoy equal rights. The theological basis for the unification of these Churches is laid down in Article 1 and Article 2(1) of the constitution of the German Evangelical Church that was recognized by the Reich Government on July 14, 1933:

> Article 1. The inviolable foundation of the German Evangelical Church is the gospel of Jesus Christ as it is attested for us in Holy Scripture and brought to light again in the Confessions of the Reformation. The full powers that the Church needs for its mission are hereby determined and limited.

> Article 2 (1). The German Evangelical Church is divided into member Churches (*Landeskirchen*).

We, the representatives of Lutheran, Reformed, and United Churches, of free synods, Church assemblies, and parish organizations united in the Confessional Synod of the German Evangelical Church, declare that we stand together on the ground of the German Evangelical Church as a federation of German Confessional Churches. We are bound together by the confession of the one Lord of the one, holy, catholic, and apostolic Church.

We publicly declare before all evangelical Churches in Germany that what they hold in common in this Confession is grievously imperiled, and with it the unity of the German Evangelical Church. It is threatened by the teaching methods and actions of the ruling Church party

THE THEOLOGICAL DECLARATION OF BARMEN (continued)

of the "German Christians" and of the Church administration carried on by them. These have become more and more apparent during the first year of the existence of the German Evangelical Church. This threat consists in the fact that the theological basis, in which the German Evangelical Church is united, has been continually and systematically thwarted and rendered ineffective by alien principles, on the part of the leaders and spokesmen of the "German Christians" as well as on the part of the Church administration. When these principles are held to be valid, then, according to all the Confessions in force among us, the Church ceases to be the Church and the German Evangelical Church, as a federation of Confessional Churches, becomes intrinsically impossible.

As members of Lutheran, Reformed, and United Churches we may and must speak with one voice in this matter today. Precisely because we want to be and to remain faithful to our various Confessions, we may not keep silent, since we believe that we have been given a common message to utter in a time of common need and temptation. We commend to God what this may mean for the interrelations of the Confessional Churches.

In view of the errors of the "German Christians" of the present Reich Church government which are devastating the Church and are also thereby breaking up the unity of the German Evangelical Church, we confess the following evangelical truths:

1. "I am the way, and the truth, and the life; no one comes to the Father, but by me." (John 14:6). "Truly, truly, I say to you, he who does not enter the sheepfold by the door but climbs in by another way, that man is a thief and a robber . . . I am the door; if anyone enters by me, he will be saved." (John 10:1, 9.)

   Jesus Christ, as he is attested for us in Holy Scripture, is the one Word of God which we have to hear and which we have to trust and obey in life and in death.

   We reject the false doctrine, as though the Church could and would have to acknowledge as a source of its proclamation, apart from and besides this one Word of God, still other events and powers, figures and truths, as God's revelation.

2. "Christ Jesus, whom God made our wisdom, our righteousness and sanctification and redemption." (1 Cor. 1:30.)

   As Jesus Christ is God's assurance of the forgiveness of all our sins, so in the same way and with the same seriousness he is also God's mighty claim upon our whole life. Through him befalls us a joyful deliverance from the godless fetters of this world for a free, grateful service to his creatures.

   We reject the false doctrine, as though there were areas of our life in which we would not belong to Jesus Christ, but to other lords—areas in which we would not need justification and sanctification through him.

3. "Rather, speaking the truth in love, we are to grow up in every way into him who is the head, into Christ, from whom the whole body [is] joined and knit together." (Eph. 4:15, 16.)

   The Christian Church is the congregation of the brethren in which Jesus Christ acts presently as the Lord in Word and sacrament through the Holy Spirit. As the Church of pardoned sinners, it has to testify in the midst of a sinful world, with its faith as with its obedience, with its message as with its order, that it is solely his property, and that it lives and wants to live solely from his comfort and from his direction in the expectation of his appearance.

   We reject the false doctrine, as though the Church were permitted to abandon the form of its message and order to its own pleasure or to changes in prevailing ideological and political convictions.

4. "You know that the rules of the Gentiles lord it over them, and their great men exercise authority over them. It shall not be so among you; but whoever would be great among you must be your servant." (Matt. 20:25, 26.)

   The various offices in the Church do not establish a dominion of some over the others; on the contrary, they are for the exercise of the ministry entrusted to and enjoined upon the whole congregation.

   We reject the false doctrine, as though the Church, apart from this ministry, could and were permitted to give to itself, or allow to be given to it, special leaders vested with ruling powers.

5. "Fear God. Honor the emperor." (1 Peter 2:17.) Scripture tells us that, in the as yet unredeemed world in which the Church also exists, the State has by divine appointment the task of providing for justice and peace. [It fulfills this task] by means of the threat and exercise of force, according to the measure of human judgment and human ability. The Church acknowledges the benefit of this divine appointment in gratitude and reverence before him. It calls to mind the Kingdom of God, God's commandment and righteousness, and thereby the responsibility both of rulers and of the ruled. It trusts and obeys the power of the Word by which God upholds all things.

   We reject the false doctrine, as though the State, over and beyond its special commission, should and could become the single and totalitarian order of human life, thus fulfilling the Church's vocation as well.

   We reject the false doctrine, as though the Church, over and beyond its special commission, should and could appropriate the characteristics, the tasks, and the dignity of the State, thus itself becoming an organ of the State.

6. "Lo, I am with you always, to the close of the age." (Matt. 28:20.) "The word of God is not fettered." (II Tim. 2:9.)

   The Church's commission, upon which its freedom is founded, consists in delivering the message of the free grace of God to all people in Christ's stead, and therefore in the ministry of his own Word and work through sermon and sacrament.

We reject the false doctrine, as though the Church in human arrogance could place the Word and work of the Lord in the service of any arbitrarily chosen desires, purposes, and plans.

The Confessional Synod of the German Evangelical Church declares that it sees in the acknowledgment of these truths and in the rejection of these errors the indispensable theological basis of the German Evangelical Church as a federation of Confessional Churches. It invites all who are able to accept its declaration to be mindful of these theological principles in their decisions in Church politics. It entreats all whom it concerns to return to the unity of faith, love, and hope.

Notes: *One of several statements added to* The Book of Confessions *of the United Presbyterian Church in the U.S.A. [now a constituent part of the Presbyterian Church (U.S.A.)], the Barmen declaration was a statement in defiance of Adolf Hitler. It was issued in 1934 by the Confessing Church, a segment of the German Evangelical Church which opposed the attempted co-optation of the church by the new Nazi regime. The Confessing Church, which consisted of elements of the Lutheran, Reformed, and United Churches, opposed the so-called German Christians, that segment of the church supporting Hitler.*

*   *   *

Congregationalism

KANSAS CITY STATEMENT OF 1913 (CONGREGATIONAL CHURCHES)

FAITH. "We believe in God the Father, Infinite in wisdom, goodness and love; and in Jesus Christ, His Son, our Lord and Saviour, who for us and our salvation lived and died and rose again and liveth evermore; and in the Holy Spirit, who taketh of the things of Christ and revealeth them to us, renewing, comforting, and inspiring the souls of men. We are united in striving to know the will of God as taught in the Holy Scriptures, and in our purpose to walk in the ways of the Lord, made known or to be made known to us. We hold it to be the mission of the Church of Christ to proclaim the gospel to all mankind, exalting the worship of the one true God, and laboring for the progress of knowledge, the promotion of justice, the reign of peace, and the realization of human brotherhood. Depending, as did our fathers, upon the continued guidance of the Holy Spirit to lead us into all truth, we work and pray for the transformation of the world into the kingdom of God; and we look with faith for the triumph of righteousness and the life everlasting.

POLITY. "We believe in the freedom and responsibility of the individual soul, and the right of private judgment. We hold to the autonomy of the local church and its independence of all ecclesiastical control. We cherish the fellowship of the churches, united in district, state, and national bodies, for counsel and cooperation in matters of common concern.

THE WIDER FELLOWSHIP. "While affirming the liberty of our churches, and the validity of our ministry, we hold to the unity and catholicity of the Church of Christ, and will unite with all its branches in hearty cooperation; and will earnestly seek, so far as in us lies, that the prayer of the Lord for His disciples may be answered, that 'they all may be one'."

Notes: *The Congregational Church tradition underwent a variety of organizational changes during the twentieth century, which added to the confessional heritage passed on by eighteenth-century New England congregationalism and the Reformed Church of Germany. The mergers that ultimately produced the United Church of Christ (UCC) in the middle of the twentieth century clearly reaffirmed the UCC's place in the larger Reformed-Presbyterian family. The mergers also bequeathed to the UCC a present-mindedness symbolized in a new creedal statement that both summarized the previous creeds and assigned them to their historical era. The texts of these Congregational confessions and statements of faith promulgated prior to the twentieth century have been compiled by Williston Walker in* The Creeds and Platforms of Congregationalism *(Philadelphia: Pilgrim Press, 1969).*

The only creedal statement written before the various mergers and schisms of the twentieth century and retaining some visible life in the Congregational churches is the statement passed by the National Council of the Congregational Church in 1913 at Kansas City. It grew out of the increased liberalism (modernism) in theological matters beginning to dominate the Congregational Churches.

The annual meeting of the National Council of Congregational Churches in 1913 adopted a statement of faith reflective of the growing liberal Protestant theological perspective. The statement is noteworthy for what it does not affirm; for example, there is no clear affirmation of either the Trinity or the authority of the Scriptures. The authors left considerable room for theological divergence on most issues. The statement has survived within the liturgy of the United Church of Christ, printed in the hymnal as an alternative along with the Apostles' and Nicene Creeds. It is also widely used by churches of the National Association of Congregational Christian Churches, consisting largely of congregations that refused to enter the United Church of Christ. These churches had an organizational, rather than a theological, complaint with the UCC.

*   *   *

BELIEFS OF THE CONSERVATIVE CONGREGATIONAL CHRISTIAN CONFERENCE

We believe in . . .

THE BIBLE

We believe the Bible, consisting of the Old and New Testaments, to be the only inspired, inerrant, infallible, authoritative Word of God written.

BELIEFS OF THE CONSERVATIVE CONGREGATIONAL
CHRISTIAN CONFERENCE (continued)

THE TRINITY

We believe that there is one God, eternally existent in three persons: Father, Son, and Holy Spirit.

JESUS CHRIST

We believe in the deity of Christ, in His virgin birth, in His sinless life, in His miracles, in His vicarious and atoning death through His shed blood, in His bodily resurrection, in His ascension to the right hand of the Father, and in His personal return in power and glory.

SALVATION

We believe that for salvation of lost and sinful man regeneration by the Holy Spirit is absolutely essential.

THE HOLY SPIRIT

We believe in the present ministry of the Holy Spirit by Whose indwelling power and fullness the Christian is enabled to live a godly life in this present evil world.

THE RESURRECTION

We believe in the resurrection of both the saved and the lost; they that are saved unto the resurrection of life, and they that are lost unto the resurrection of damnation.

SPIRITUAL UNITY

We believe in the spiritual unity of all believers in Christ.

Notes: *Reacting to the theological liberalism in the main body of congregationalism, the congregations of the Conservative Congregational Christian Church reorganized around a more evangelical theological perspective. Their beliefs specifically affirm many of the beliefs deleted from the Kansas City Statement of 1913, as well as those from the Statement of Faith of the United Church of Christ.*

*   *   *

STATEMENT OF FAITH OF THE MIDWEST CONGREGATIONAL CHRISTIAN CHURCH

1. We believe the Bible to be the inspired, the only infallible, authoritative word of God.

2. We believe that there is one God, eternally existent in three persons, Father, Son and Holy Ghost.

3. We believe in the deity of our Lord Jesus Christ, in His virgin birth, in His sinless life, in His miracles in His vicarious and atoning death through His shed blood, in His bodily resurrection, in His ascension to the right hand of the Father, and in His personal return in power and glory.

4. We believe that for the salvation of lost and sinful man regeneration by the Holy Spirit is absolutely essential.

5. We believe in the present ministry of the Holy Spirit by whose indwelling the Christian is enabled to live a Godly life.

6. We believe in the resurrection of both the saved and the lost; they that are saved unto the resurrection of life and they that are lost unto the resurrection of damnation.

7. We believe in the spiritual unity of believers in our Lord Jesus Christ.

Notes: *Like the Conservative Congregational Christian Conference, the Midwest Congregational Christian Church adopted a very conservative theological position, as reflected in its statement of faith.*

*   *   *

THE BASIS OF UNION (UNITED CHURCH OF CANADA)

DOCTRINE

We, the representatives of the Presbyterian, the Methodist, and the Congregational branches of the Church of Christ in Canada, do hereby set forth the substance of the Christian faith, as commonly held among us. In doing so, we build upon the foundation laid by the apostles and prophets, Jesus Christ Himself being the chief cornerstone. We affirm our belief in the Scriptures of the Old and New Testaments as the primary source and ultimate standard of Christian faith and life. We acknowledge the teaching of the great creeds of the ancient Church. We further maintain our allegiance to the evangelical doctrines of the Reformation, as set forth in common in the doctrinal standards adopted by the Presbyterian Church in Canada, by the Congregational Union of Ontario and Quebec, and by the Methodist Church. We present the accompanying statement as a brief summary of our common faith and commend it to the studious attention of the members and adherents of the negotiating Churches, as in substance agreeable to the teaching of the Holy Scriptures.

ARTICLE I. OF GOD. We believe in the one only living and true God, a Spirit, infinite, eternal and unchangeable, in His being and perfections; the Lord Almighty, who is love, most just in all His ways, most glorious in holiness, unsearchable in wisdom, plenteous in mercy, full of compassion, and abundant in goodness and truth. We worship Him in the unity of the Godhead and the mystery of the Holy Trinity, the Father, the Son and the Holy Spirit, three persons of the same substance, equal in power and glory.

ARTICLE II. OF REVELATION. We believe that God has revealed Himself in nature, in history, and in the heart of man; that He has been graciously pleased to make clearer revelation of Himself to men of God who spoke as they were moved by the Holy Spirit; and that in the fullness of time He has perfectly revealed Himself in Jesus Christ, the Word made flesh, who is the brightness of the Father's glory and the express image of His person. We receive the Holy Scriptures of the Old and New Testaments, given by inspiration of God, as containing the only infallible rule of faith and life, a faithful record of God's gracious revelations, and as the sure witness to Christ.

ARTICLE III. OF THE DIVINE PURPOSE. We believe that the eternal, wise, holy and loving purpose of God so embraces all events that, while the freedom of man is not taken away, nor is God the author of sin, yet in His providence He makes all things work together in the fulfilment of His sovereign design and the manifestation of His glory.

ARTICLE IV. OF CREATION AND PROVIDENCE. We believe that God is the creator, upholder and governor of all things; that He is above all His works and in them all; and that He made man in His own image, meet for fellowship with Him, free and able to choose between good and evil, and responsible to his Maker and Lord.

ARTICLE V. OF THE SIN OF MAN. We believe that our first parents, being tempted, chose evil, and so fell away from God and came under the power of sin, the penalty of which is eternal death; and that, by reason of this disobedience, all men are born with a sinful nature, that we have broken God's law and that no man can be saved but by His grace.

ARTICLE VI. OF THE GRACE OF GOD. We believe that God, out of His great love for the world, has given His only begotten Son to be the Saviour of sinners, and in the Gospel freely offers His all-sufficient salvation to all men. We believe also that God, in His own good pleasure, gave to His Son a people, an innumerable multitude, chosen in Christ unto holiness, service and salvation.

ARTICLE VII. OF THE LORD JESUS CHRIST. We believe in and confess the Lord Jesus Christ, the only Mediator between God and man, who, being the Eternal Son of God, for us men and for our salvation became truly man, being conceived of the Holy Spirit and born of the Virgin Mary, yet without sin. Unto us He has revealed the Father, by His word and Spirit, making known the perfect will of God. For our redemption He fulfilled all righteousness, offered Himself a perfect sacrifice on the Cross, satisfied Divine justice and made propitiation for the sins of the whole world. He rose from the dead and ascended into Heaven, where He ever intercedes for us. In the hearts of believers He abides for ever as the indwelling Christ; above us and over us all He rules; wherefore, unto Him we render love, obedience and adoration as our Prophet, Priest and King.

ARTICLE VIII. OF THE HOLY SPIRIT. We believe in the Holy Spirit, the Lord and Giver of life, who proceeds from the Father and the Son, who moves upon the hearts of men to restrain them from evil and to incite them unto good, and whom the Father is ever willing to give unto all who ask Him. We believe that He has spoken by holy men of God in making known His truth to men for their salvation; that, through our exalted Saviour, He was sent forth in power to convict the world of sin, to enlighten men's minds in the knowledge of Christ, and to persuade and enable them to obey the call of the Gospel; and that He abides with the Church, dwelling in every believer as the spirit of truth, of power, of holiness, of comfort and of love.

ARTICLE IX. OF REGENERATION. We believe in the necessity of regeneration, whereby we are made new creatures in Christ Jesus by the Spirit of God, who imparts spiritual life by the gracious and mysterious operation of His power, using as the ordinary means the truths of His word and the ordinances of divine appointment in ways agreeable to the nature of man.

ARTICLE X. OF FAITH AND REPENTANCE. We believe that faith in Christ is a saving grace whereby we receive Him, trust in Him and rest upon Him alone for salvation as He is offered to us in the Gospel, and that this saving faith is always accompanied by repentance, wherein we confess and forsake our sins with full purpose of and endeavor after a new obedience to God.

ARTICLE XI. OF JUSTIFICATION AND SONSHIP. We believe that God, on the sole ground of the perfect obedience and sacrifice of Christ, pardons those who by faith receive Him as their Saviour and Lord, accepts them as righteous and bestows upon them the adoption of sons, with a right to all privileges therein implied, including a conscious assurance of their sonship.

ARTICLE XII. OF SANCTIFICATION. We believe that those who are regenerated and justified grow in the likeness of Christ through fellowship with Him, the indwelling of the Holy Spirit, and obedience to the truth; that a holy life is the fruit and evidence of saving faith; and that the believer's hope of continuance in such a life is in the preserving grace of God. And we believe that in this growth in grace Christians may attain that maturity and full assurance of faith whereby the love of God is made perfect in us.

ARTICLE XIII. OF PRAYER. We believe that we are encouraged to draw near to God, our Heavenly Father, in the name of His Son, Jesus Christ, and on our own behalf and of others to pour out our hearts humbly yet freely before Him, as becomes His beloved children, giving Him the honour and praise due His holy name, asking Him to glorify Himself on earth as in Heaven, confessing unto Him our sins and seeking of Him every gift needful for this life and for our everlasting salvation. We believe also that, inasmuch as all true prayer is prompted by His Spirit, He will in response thereto grant us every blessing according to His unsearchable wisdom and the riches of His grace in Jesus Christ.

ARTICLE XIV. OF THE LAW OF GOD. We believe that the moral law of God, summarized in the Ten Commandments, testified to by the prophets and unfolded in the life and teachings of Jesus Christ, stands for ever in truth and equity, and is not made void by faith, but on the contrary is established thereby. We believe that God requires of every man to do justly, to love mercy, and to walk humbly with God; and that only through this harmony with the will of God shall be fulfilled that brotherhood of man wherein the Kingdom of God is to be made manifest.

ARTICLE XV. OF THE CHURCH. We acknowledge one holy Catholic Church, the innumerable company of saints of every age and nation, who being united by the Holy Spirit to Christ their Head are one body in Him and have communion with their Lord and with one another. Further, we receive it as the will of Christ that His Church on earth should exist as a visible and sacred brotherhood, consisting of those who profess faith in Jesus Christ and obedience to Him, together with their children, and other baptized children, and organized for the confession of His name, for the public worship of God, for the administration of the sacraments, for the upbuilding of the saints, and

for the universal propagation of the Gospel; and we
acknowledge as a part, more or less pure, of this universal
brotherhood, every particular Church throughout the
world which professes this faith in Jesus Christ and
obedience to Him as divine Lord and Saviour.

ARTICLE XVI. OF THE SACRAMENTS. We acknowledge two sacraments, Baptism and the Lord's Supper,
which were instituted by Christ, to be of perpetual
obligation as signs and seals of the covenant ratified in His
precious blood, as means of grace, by which, working in
us, He doth not only quicken, but also strengthen and
comfort our faith in Him, and as ordinances through the
observance of which His Church is to confess her Lord
and be visibly distinguished from the rest of the world.

(1) Baptism with water into the name of the Father and
of the Son and of the Holy Spirit is the sacrament by
which are signified and sealed our union to Christ
and participation in the blessings of the new covenant. The proper subjects of baptism are believers
and infants presented by their parents or guardians
in the Christian faith. In the latter case the parents or
guardians should train up their children in the
nurture and admonition of the Lord and should
expect that their children will, by the operation of
the Holy Spirit, receive the benefits which the
sacrament is designed and fitted to convey. The
Church is under the most solemn obligation to
provide for their Christian instruction.

(2) The Lord's Supper is the sacrament of communion
with Christ and with His people, in which bread and
wine are given and received in thankful remembrance of Him and His sacrifice on the Cross; and
they who in faith receive the same do, after a
spiritual manner, partake of the body and blood of
the Lord Jesus Christ to their comfort, nourishment
and growth in grace. All may be admitted to the
Lord's Supper who make a credible profession of
their faith in the Lord Jesus Christ and of obedience
to His law.

ARTICLE XVII. OF THE MINISTRY. We believe that
Jesus Christ, as the Supreme Head of the Church, has
appointed therein a ministry of the word and sacraments,
and calls men and women to this ministry; that the
Church, under the guidance of the Holy Spirit, recognizes
and chooses those whom He calls, and should thereupon
duly ordain them to the work of the ministry.

**ARTICLE XVIII. OF CHURCH ORDER AND FEL-
LOWSHIP.** We believe that the Supreme and only Head of
the Church is the Lord Jesus Christ; that its worship,
teaching, discipline and government should be administered according to His will by persons chosen for their
fitness and duly set apart to their office; and that although
the visible Church may contain unworthy members and is
liable to err, yet believers ought not lightly to separate
themselves from its communion, but are to live in
fellowship with their brethen, which fellowship is to be
extended, as God gives opportunity, to all who in every
place call upon the name of the Lord Jesus.

**ARTICLE XIX. OF THE RESURRECTION, THE
LAST JUDGMENT AND THE FUTURE LIFE.** We
believe that there shall be a resurrection of the dead, both
of the just and of the unjust, through the power of the Son
of God, who shall come to judge the living and the dead;
that the finally impenitent shall go away into eternal
punishment and the righteous into life eternal.

**ARTICLE XX. OF CHRISTIAN SERVICE AND THE
FINAL TRIUMPH.** We believe that it is our duty as
disciples and servants of Christ, to further the extension of
His Kingdom, to do good unto all men, to maintain the
public and private worship of God, to hallow the Lord's
Day, to preserve the inviolability of marriage and the
sanctity of the family, to uphold the just authority of the
State, and so to live in all honesty, purity and charity, that
our lives shall testify of Christ. We joyfully receive the
word of Christ, bidding His people go into all the world
and make disciples of all nations, declaring unto them that
God was in Christ reconciling the world unto Himself, and
that He will have all men to be saved, and come to the
knowledge of the truth. We confidently believe that by His
power and grace all His enemies shall finally be overcome,
and the kingdoms of this world be made the Kingdom of
our God and of His Christ.

Notes: *Prepared in the first decade of the twentieth century,
The Basis of Union formed part of the early agreement of
the churches that eventually merged in 1925 to create the
United Church of Canada. This statement shows minimal
influence from either the Twenty-five Articles of Religion of
the Methodists or the Westminster Confession of the
Presbyterians. Rather, it draws upon the Brief Statement of
the Reformed Faith, issued in 1905 by the Presbyterian
Church in the U.S.A., and the Articles of Faith of the
Presbyterian Church in England, issued in 1890.*

*   *   *

STATEMENT OF FAITH OF THE UNITED CHURCH OF CHRIST

We believe in God, the Eternal Spirit, Father of our Lord
Jesus Christ and our Father, and to his deeds we testify:

He calls the worlds into being, creates man in his own
image and sets before him the ways of life and death.

He seeks in holy love to save all people from aimlessness
and sin.

He judges men and nations by his righteous will declared
through prophets and apostles.

In Jesus Christ, the man of Nazareth, our crucified and
risen Lord, he has come to us and shared our common lot,
conquering sin and death and reconciling the world to
himself.

He bestows upon us his Holy Spirit, creating and renewing
the Church of Jesus Christ, binding in covenant faithful
people of all ages, tongues, and races.

He calls us into his Church to accept the cost and joy of
discipleship, to be his servants in the service of men, to
proclaim the gospel to all the world and resist the powers
of evil, to share in Christ's baptism and eat at his table, to
join him in his passion and victory.

He promises to all who trust him forgiveness of sins and fullness of grace, courage in the struggle for justice and peace, his presence in trial and rejoicing, and eternal life in his kingdom which has no end.

Blessing and honor, glory and power be unto him. Amen

Notes: *Carrying on the liberal Protestant theological tradition that had produced the Kansas City Statement of 1913 and had dominated congregationalism in the twentieth century, the United Church of Christ adopted a new creed in 1960 as part of its basis of union. By doing this the church affirmed the creed's role as a "testimony" to faith rather than a "creed" and pointed out that the statement was never to be used as a test for prospective members or ministers seeking ordination.*

Chapter 6

Pietist-Methodist Family

Scandinavian Pietism

CONFESSION OF THE EVANGELICAL COVENANT CHURCH

The Covenant Church believes in the Holy Scriptures, the Old and the New Testament, as the Word of God and the only perfect rule for faith, doctrine, and conduct.

PREFACE TO THE CHURCH'S CONSTITUTION

The Covenant Church adheres to the affirmations of the Protestant Reformation regarding the Holy Scriptures, the Old and the New Testament, as the Word of God and the only perfect rule for faith, doctrine, and conduct. It has traditionally valued the historic confessions of the Christian church, particularly the Apostles' Creed, while at the same time it has emphasized the sovereignty of the Word over all creedal interpretations. It has especially cherished the pietistic restatement of the doctrine of justification by faith as basic to its dual task of evangelism and Christian nurture, the New Testament emphasis upon personal faith in Jesus Christ as Savior and Lord, the reality of a fellowship of believers which recognizes but transcends theological differences, and the belief in baptism and the Lord's Supper as divinely ordained sacraments of the church. While the denomination has traditionally practiced the baptism of infants, in conformity with its principle of freedom it has given room to divergent views. The principle of personal freedom, so highly esteemed by the Covenant, is to be distinguished from the individualism that disregards the centrality of the Word of God and the mutual responsibilities and disciplines of the spiritual community.

Notes: *The churches of the Pietist-Methodist Family did not have many essential doctrinal disagreements with the Lutheran and Reformed churches out of which they came. Their main emphases were personal religion and the practice of the Christian faith. In creating their doctrinal statements, the Pietist-Methodist churches assumed the existence of the lengthy Reformation confessions, which formed a broad basis of agreement. Their statements moved to affirm, in principle, the perspective of the Reformation,*

without commiting the churches to every particular of the lengthier statements. The emphasis upon precise theological formulas, exemplified in The Book of Concord *and the* Westminster Confession, *was seen as not productive of piety. The statements also contained controversial opinions about certain issues without threatening the essentials of faith.*

The statement of pietistic churches, therefore, tended to be much shorter than those produced in the sixteenth and seventeenth centuries by the Lutheran and Reformed churches. Possibly the briefest is that of the Evangelical Covenant Church, which has less than thirty words. The preface to the church's constitution gives some content to the brief confession.

* * *

CREED (EVANGELICAL FREE CHURCH OF AMERICA)

The Evangelical Free Church of America believes:

1. The Scriptures, both Old and New Testaments, to be the inspired Word of God, without error in the original writings, the complete revelation of His will for the salvation of men, and the Divine and final authority for all Christian faith and life.

2. In one God, Creator of all things, infinitely perfect and eternally existing in three persons, Father, Son and Holy Spirit.

3. That Jesus Christ is true God and true man, having been conceived of the Holy Ghost and born of the Virgin Mary. He died on the cross a sacrifice for our sins according to the Scriptures. Further, He arose bodily from the dead, ascended into heaven, where at the right hand of the Majesty on High, He now is our High Priest and Advocate.

4. That the ministry of the Holy Spirit is to glorify the Lord Jesus Christ, and during this age to convict men, regenerate the believing sinner, indwell, guide, instruct, and empower the believer for godly living and service.

5. That man was created in the image of God but fell into sin and is therefore lost and only through

CREED (EVANGELICAL FREE CHURCH OF AMERICA) (continued)

regeneration by the Holy Spirit can salvation and spiritual life be obtained.

6. That the shed blood of Jesus Christ and His resurrection provide the only ground for justification and salvation for all who believe, and only such as receive Jesus Christ are born of the Holy Spirit, and thus become children of God.

7. That water baptism and the Lord's Supper are ordinances to be observed by the Church during the present age. They are however, not to be regarded as means of salvation.

8. That the true Church is composed of all such persons who through saving faith in Jesus Christ have been regenerated by the Holy Spirit and are united together in the body of Christ of which He is the head.

9. That only those who are thus members of the true Church shall be eligible for membership in the local church.

10. That Jesus Christ is the Lord and Head of the Church, and that every local church has the right under Christ to decide and govern its own affairs.

11. In the personal and premillennial and imminent coming of our Lord Jesus Christ and that this "Blessed Hope" has a vital bearing on the personal life and service of the believer.

12. In the bodily resurrection of the dead; of the believer to everlasting blessedness and joy with the Lord, of the unbeliever to judgment and everlasting conscious punishment.

Notes: *The statement of beliefs adopted by the Evangelical Free Church grew out of the statements of two bodies that merged to form the church in 1950: the Swedish Evangelical Free Church and the Norwegian-Danish Free Church Association. The statement of the merged church, in its position on scriptural authority, christology, and premillennialism, showed the strong influence of the fundamentalist movement in the early twentieth century.*

* * *

THE MORAVIAN COVENANT FOR CHRISTIAN LIVING (THE MORAVIAN CHURCH)

PREFACE

This Moravian Covenant for Christian Living is an attempt to state in clear arrangement and contemporary form a document which has long served the Moravian Church. The Church today has need of a clear statement of its faith and life through which each member may become aware of the nature of his/her Christian commitment. Such a document can become an invaluable aid in the instruction of both new and present members and a meaningful guide in the expression of the Christian life. That such a revision of the Agreement should have been made is entirely in harmony with the spirit of the early Moravian Church which believed that all forms should be updated and made relevant to the present life of the Church.

The Moravian Covenant in its original form was adopted by the Moravian Church at Herrnhut, Saxony, as the Brotherly Agreement on May 12 of the year that marked the Church's spiritual renewal, 1727. The Covenant was not intended to be a "discipline" forced on the congregation from above, but rather an "agreement" into which the members entered voluntarily. This spirit pervades the new Covenant which in itself is only a recommended form, to be voluntarily accepted by each of the local congregations before it becomes effective for their congregational life.

Most of the Covenant deals with the Christian life, and since it is in terms of everyday life that the Christian witness is often most effectively borne, the document is subtitled, "Principles by Which We Live and Bear Our Witness." The theme of "witness" is carried out in all the sections. The introductory section, "Ground of Our Witness," deals briefly with the faith and doctrine of the Moravian Church, something that is not explicitly dealt with in older forms of the Covenant. Section I, "The Witness of the Christian Life," describes the "how" of the life in Christ and thus forms a basis for all that follows. The following sections then consider various areas of Christian responsibility. Section II deals largely with Christian responsibility in the local congregation and in relation to Christians of other churches; III, responsibility in the home; IV, one's duties as a citizen; and V, as a Christian in the world.

Variations in the form of the Moravian Covenant recommended by Synod may be adopted only with the approval of the Provincial Elders' Conference.

THE GROUND OF OUR WITNESS

We are called into a Christian fellowship by the Lord Jesus Christ, according to the eternal purpose of God the Father (Eph. 3:11) by the Holy Spirit (Acts 2:18-21), and as members of Christ's Body, the Church, to serve all people by proclaiming the gospel and witnessing to our faith by word and deed.

The Holy Scriptures are and shall remain the only source and rule of our doctrine, faith, and practice.

With the universal Christian Church, we share our faith in the Triune God, who revealed himself in the Lord Jesus Christ as the only Saviour of all people. We particularly declare his living presence and Lordship over the Church, joy in the benefits of his life, sufferings, death and resurrection and emphasize a close bond of fellowship with each other in his name. We believe that Christ is present with us in Word and Sacrament. We decline to determine as binding what the Scriptures have left undetermined, or to argue about mysteries impenetrable to human reason. In this regard, we hold to the principles: "In essentials, unity; in non-essentials, liberty; and in all things, charity."

We thankfully recognize the value of the historic creeds of the Christian Church in calling upon believers in every age to give an obedient and fearless testimony, recognizing Jesus Christ as Lord. A Moravian confession of faith is to be found in the Easter Morning Liturgy.

I. THE WITNESS OF THE CHRISTIAN LIFE

1. We believe that as in baptism we have been united with Christ in his death and resurrection, so we have died to sin and should walk in newness of life. (Romans 6:1-11)

2. When seeking guidance we find that the simplest expression of Christian living is contained in the earliest of Christian confessions, "Jesus Christ is Lord." This implies that obedience is due him as an absolute Ruler and Lord of our lives. Not only his teachings (e.g. Matt. 5-7), but even more, the example of his life (Phil. 2:5; Eph. 4:20) provide an understanding of the obedience that he desires. Although the early Church, guided by the Spirit of Jesus, did not develop a code covering all issues, it offered guidance in various areas of Christian living. (e.g. Col. 3:1-4:6; I Peter 2:11-3:12; Eph. 4:1-6:20)

3. Living the Christian life depends not only on our own effort but upon God our Father, who in Jesus Christ accepts us as heirs of God (Gal. 4:4-7) and strengthens and sustains us. (Phil. 4:13)

4. We realize that our Christian faith must continually be nourished if it is to remain living and vital. Therefore, we desire to grow in our Christian lives through family devotions, personal prayer and study, and the opportunities for spiritual development offered by the church.

II. THE WITNESS OF A LIVING CHURCH

A. THE MORAVIAN UNITY

1. RECOGNITION OF AUTHORITY

   As members of the Moravian Church we will abide by the decisions made by the official boards of our congregation, and agree to be governed, both as individuals and as a congregation, by the enactments of the Unity Synod of the Moravian Church and of the Synods of the Province to which our congregation belongs.

2. STEWARDSHIP

   a. We deem it a sacred responsibility and genuine opportunity to be faithful stewards of all God has entrusted to us: our time, our talents, and our financial resources. We view all of life as a sacred trust to be used wisely.

   b. We will support, according to our ability, the financial needs of the local congregation, the District, the Province, and the Unity. We will consider the support of the benevolent causes of the Moravian Church, both at home and abroad as a privilege, an opportunity, and a responsibility.

   c. We will also recognize the support of worthy causes outside of the Church as part of our stewardship.

3. PERSONAL RELATIONSHIPS

   a. Since disciples of Jesus are to be known by the love they have to one another (John 13:35), we will cherish Christian love as of prime importance.

   b. We will be eager to maintain the unity of the Church, realizing that God has called us from many and varied backgrounds, we recognize the possibility of disagreements or differences. Often these differences enrich the Church, but sometimes they divide. We consider it to be our responsibility to demonstrate within the congregational life the unity and togetherness created by God who made us one. How well we accomplish this will be a witness to our community as to the validity of our faith.

   c. We will endeavor to settle our differences with others in a Christian manner (Gal. 6:1), amicably, and with mediation, and if at all possible avoid resort to a court of law. (Matt. 18:15-17)

4. WORSHIP AND SUNDAY OBSERVANCE

   a. Remembering that worship is one of our proper responses to Almighty God, an experience designed for our benefit, and a part of our Christian witness, we and our children will faithfully attend the worship services of the Church.

   b. We, therefore, will be careful to avoid unnecessary labor on Sunday and plan that the recreations in which we engage on that day do not interfere with our own attendance or that of others at divine worship.

5. HOLY COMMUNION

   In the celebration of this Sacrament we receive the renewed assurance of the forgiveness of our sins, and of our fellowship with Christ; unite with one another as members of his body; and rejoice in the hope of his return in glory. Therefore, we will commune faithfully and thus renew our pledge of allegiance to him.

B. THE UNITY WE SEEK

1. We will have fellowship, in all sincerity, with children of God in other Christian churches, and will carefully avoid all disputes respecting opinions and ceremonies peculiar to one or another church. In this fellowship we will cooperate with other churches in the support of public charities or Christian enterprises, which have a just claim upon us as followers of the Lord Jesus Christ.

2. We realize that it is the Lord's will that the Church of Jesus Christ should give evidence of and seek unity in him with zeal and love. We see how such unity has been promised us and laid upon us as a charge. We recognize that through the grace of Christ the different denominations have received many gifts and that the Church of Christ may be enriched by these many and varied contributions. It is our desire that we may learn from one another and rejoice together in the riches of the love of Christ and the manifold wisdom of God. We welcome every step that brings us nearer the goal of unity in him.

III. THE WITNESS OF THE CHRISTIAN HOME

A. MARRIAGE

1. We regard it as a sacred obligation to hold to the ideal of Christian marriage given by our Lord in his teaching. We consider it essential, therefore, that all persons contemplating marriage should receive premarital counseling and that our young people should be instructed, beginning in adolescence, in the meaning and obligation of true Christian marriage; this instruction to be given through the Church and the home.

2. We regard Christian marriage as an indissoluble union, which requires the lifelong loyalty of the man and the woman towards each other. Because any breaking of the marriage bond involves sin against God and causes human suffering, it is the duty of husband and wife to meet all frictions, offenses, and disagreements with a forgiving spirit that persistently works for reconciliation. Furthermore, if at any time the stability of their marriage is threatened, they are to seek the counsel of their pastor or of other spiritual leaders in the church as soon as possible and before any other action is taken.

B. FAMILY LIFE

1. As parents, remembering that our children are the property of the Lord Jesus Christ, (Acts 20:28; I Peter 1:19) we will bring them up in the nurture and admonition of the Lord (Eph. 6:4) and take all possible care to preserve them from every evil influence. For this reason we will seek to approve ourselves as followers of the Lord Jesus Christ, setting an example for our children. We will give faithful attention to the spiritual development of our children, both in the home and in the church. We will endeavor to conduct regular family devotions.

IV. THE WITNESS OF A CHRISTIAN CITIZEN

A. RECOGNITION OF CIVIL AUTHORITY

We will be subject to the civil authorities as the powers ordained of God, in accordance with the admonitions of Scripture (Rom. 13:1; I Peter 2:13-14) and will in nowise evade the taxes and other obligations which are lawfully required of us (Rom. 13:7).

B. RESPONSIBILITIES

Considering it a special privilege to live in a democratic society, we will faithfully fulfill the responsibilities of our citizenship, among which are intelligent and well-informed voting, a willingness to assume public office, guiding the decisions of government by the expression of our opinions, and supporting good government by our personal efforts.

C. A HIGHER LOYALTY

Though giving our loyalty to the state of which we are citizens, we do recognize a higher loyalty to God and conscience. (Acts 5:29)

D. PEACEMAKERS

For the sake of the peace which we have with God, we earnestly desire to live peaceably with all people and to seek the peace of the places where we dwell.

V. OUR WITNESS IN THE WORLD

A. LOVE TOWARD ALL

We will not hate, despise, slander or otherwise injure anyone. We will ever strive to manifest love towards all people, to treat them in a kind and friendly manner, and in our dealings with them to approve ourselves upright, honest, and conscientious, as becomes children of God. Together with the universal Christian Church, we have a concern for this world, opening our heart and hand to our neighbors with the message of the love of God, and being ever ready to minister of our substance to their necessities. (Matt. 25:40)

B. OUR MANNER OF LIFE

We will at all times be ready cheerfully to witness to our faith (I Peter 3:15, 16) and if need be, to suffer reproach for Christ's sake (Luke 6:22, 23). Being aware that our witness is made both by what we do and what we avoid doing, we will endeavor to let our manner of life "be worthy of the gospel of Christ," (Phil. 1:27) "not being conformed to this world." (Rom. 12:2) But in our yearning for the redemption of the whole creation, we will seek to meet the needs of the world in self-giving love, and as true yokefellows of Jesus Christ, willingly share in the fellowship of his sufferings, walking in his strength, by whom all things "are given us that pertain to life and godliness." (II Peter 1:3)

C. TEMPERANCE IN ALL THINGS

Remembering the admonition of Scripture to be temperate in all things (I Cor. 9:25), we shall endeavor to look upon our bodies as temples of God's spirit (I Cor. 6:19). We must also remember to respect the welfare of others who may be affected by our actions (Rom. 14:20, 21). We are aware of the problems that can be caused by the intemperate use of such things as alcoholic beverages, food, tobacco, drugs, and other things. We consider it the responsibility of every Christian to decide most carefully how they can be used in good conscience. We regard intemperance in any area of living as being inconsistent with the Christian life.

D. UNITY

1. Christian: We recognize no distinction between those who are one in the Lord. We believe that God in Jesus Christ calls his people out of "every race, kindred and tongue," pardons them beneath the Cross, and brings them into a living fellowship with himself. We regard it as a commandment of our Lord to bear public witness to this and to

demonstrate by word and deed that we are one in Christ.

2. Universal: Because we hold that all people are God's creatures (Gen. 1:27) and that he has made of one blood all nations (Acts 17:26) we oppose any discrimination based on color, race, creed or land of origin and declare that we should treat everyone with love and respect.

E. OTHER AREAS

We realize that all areas of Christian life and conduct cannot be covered in this statement of principles by which we live and bear our witness, and we call attention, therefore, to the Christian's responsibility to follow Christ as Lord of all areas of life.

VI. DISCIPLINE

We make it a duty of the Board of Elders, which is charged with the spiritual welfare of the congregation, to see that this "Moravian Covenant" be adhered to and faithfully observed; and we will cooperate with the Board of Elders in its efforts to maintain the discipline of the congregation. As a redemptive community we will be much more concerned in aiding than censuring those who falter, being conscious of our own need for correction and forgiveness.

Notes: *The Moravian Covenant is a revised form of "The Brotherly Agreement," a document originally adopted in 1727. True to its pietist heritage, the Covenant centers on the Christian life and action more than belief. The preface gives some explanation of its history and emphases. The text is the one adopted in 1982 by the Northern Province Synod of the Moravian Church.*

*   *   *

United Methodism

THE TWENTY-FIVE ARTICLES OF RELIGION (UNITED METHODIST CHURCH)

Article I. OF FAITH IN THE HOLY TRINITY

There is but one living and true God, everlasting, without body or parts, of infinite power, wisdom, and goodness; the maker and preserver of all things, both visible and invisible. And in unity of this Godhead there are three persons, of one substance, power, and eternity—the Father, the Son, and the Holy Ghost.

Article II. OF THE WORD, OR SON OF GOD, WHO WAS MADE VERY MAN

The Son, who is the Word of the Father, the very and eternal God, of one substance with the Father, took man's nature in the womb of the blessed Virgin; so that two whole and perfect natures, that is to say, the Godhead and Manhood, were joined together in one person, never to be divided; whereof is one Christ, very God and very Man, who truly suffered, was crucified, dead, and buried, to reconcile his Father to us, and to be a sacrifice, not only for original guilt, but also for the actual sins of men.

Article III. OF THE RESURRECTION OF CHRIST

Christ did truly rise again from the dead, and took again his body, with all things appertaining to the perfection of man's nature, wherewith he ascended into heaven, and there sitteth until he return to judge all men at the last day.

Article IV. OF THE HOLY GHOST

The Holy Ghost, proceeding from the Father and the Son, is of one substance, majesty, and glory with the Father and the Son, very and eternal God.

Article V. OF THE SUFFICIENCY OF THE HOLY SCRIPTURES FOR SALVATION

The Holy Scripture containeth all things necessary to salvation; so that whatsoever is not read therein, nor may be proved thereby, is not to be required of any man that it should be believed as an article of faith, or be thought requisite or necessary to salvation. In the name of the Holy Scripture we do understand those canonical books of the Old and New Testament of whose authority was never any doubt in the Church. The names of the canonical books are:

Genesis, Exodus, Leviticus, Numbers, Deuteronomy, Joshua, Judges, Ruth, The First Book of Samuel, The Second Book of Samuel, The First Book of Kings, The Second Book of Kings, The First Book of Chronicles, The Second Book of Chronicles, The Book of Ezra, The Book of Nehemiah, The Book of Esther, The Book of Job, The Psalms, The Proverbs, Ecclesiastes or the Preacher, Cantica or Songs of Solomon, Four Prophets the Greater, Twelve Prophets the Less.

All the books of the New Testament, as they are commonly received, we do receive and account canonical.

Article VI. OF THE OLD TESTAMENT

The Old Testament is not contrary to the New; for both in the Old and New Testament everlasting life is offered to mankind by Christ, who is the only Mediator between God and man, being both God and Man. Wherefore they are not to be heard who feign that the old fathers did look only for transitory promises. Although the law given from God by Moses as touching ceremonies and rites doth not bind Christians, nor ought the civil precepts thereof of necessity be received in any commonwealth; yet notwithstanding, no Christian whatsoever is free from the obedience of the commandments which are called moral.

Article VII. OF ORIGINAL OR BIRTH SIN

Original sin standeth not in the following of Adam (as the Pelagians do vainly talk), but it is the corruption of the nature of every man, that naturally is engendered of the offspring of Adam, whereby man is very far gone from original righteousness, and of his own nature inclined to evil, and that continually.

Article VIII. OF FREE WILL

The condition of man after the fall of Adam is such that he cannot turn and prepare himself, by his own natural strength and works, to faith, and calling upon God; wherefore we have no power to do good work, pleasant and acceptable to God, without the grace of God by Christ preventing us, that we may have a good will, and working with us, when we have that good will.

Article IX. OF THE JUSTIFICATION OF MAN

We are accounted righteous before God only for the merit of our Lord and Saviour Jesus Christ, by faith, and not for our own works or deservings. Wherefore, that we are justified by faith, only, is a most wholesome doctrine, and very full of comfort.

Article X. OF GOOD WORKS

Although good works, which are the fruits of faith, and follow after justification, cannot put away our sins, and endure the severity of God's judgment; yet are they pleasing and acceptable to God in Christ, and spring out of a true and lively faith, insomuch that by them a lively faith may be as evidently known as a tree is discerned by its fruit.

Article XI. OF WORKS OF SUPEREROGATION

Voluntary works—besides, over and above God's commandments—which they call works of supererogation, cannot be taught without arrogancy and impiety. For by them men do declare that they do not only render unto God as much as they are bound to do, but that they do more for his sake than the bounden duty is required; whereas Christ saith plainly: When you have done all that is commanded you, say, We are unprofitable servants.

Article XII. OF SIN AFTER JUSTIFICATION

Not every sin willingly committed after justification is the sin against the Holy Ghost, and unpardonable. Wherefore, the grant of repentance is not to be denied to such as fall into sin after justification. After we have received the Holy Ghost, we may depart from grace given, and fall into sin, and, by the grace of God, rise again and amend our lives. And therefore they are to be condemned who say they can no more sin as long as they live here; or deny the place of forgiveness to such as truly repent.

Article XIII. OF THE CHURCH

The visible Church of Christ is a congregation of faithful men in which the pure Word of God is preached, and the Sacraments duly administered according to Christ's ordinance, in all those things that of necessity are requisite to the same.

Article XIV. OF PURGATORY

The Romish doctrine concerning purgatory, pardon, worshiping, and adoration, as well of images as of relics, and also invocation of saints, is a fond thing, vainly invented, and grounded upon no warrant of Scripture, but repugnant to the Word of God.

Article XV. OF SPEAKING IN THE CONGREGATION IN SUCH A TONGUE AS THE PEOPLE UNDERSTAND

It is a thing plainly repugnant to the Word of God, and the custom of the primitive Church, to have public prayer in the church, or to minister the Sacraments, in a tongue not understood by the people.

Article XVI. OF THE SACRAMENTS

Sacraments ordained of Christ are not only badges or tokens of Christian men's profession, but rather they are certain signs of grace, and God's good will toward us, by which he doth work invisibly in us, and doth not only quicken, but also strengthen and confirm, our faith in him.

There are two Sacraments ordained of Christ our Lord in the Gospel; that is to say, Baptism and the Supper of the Lord.

Those five commonly called sacraments, that is to say, confirmation, penance, orders, matrimony, and extreme unction, are not to be counted for Sacraments of the Gospel; being such as have partly grown out of the *corrupt* following of the apostles, and partly are states of life allowed in the Scriptures, but yet have not the like nature of Baptism and the Lord's Supper, because they have not any visible sign or ceremony ordained of God.

The Sacraments were not ordained of Christ to be gazed upon, or to be carried about; but that we should duly use them. And in such only as worthily receive the same, they have a wholesome effect or operation; but they that receive them unworthily, purchase to themselves condemnation, as St. Paul saith.

Article XVII. OF BAPTISM

Baptism is not only a sign of profession and mark of difference whereby Christians are distinguished from others that are not baptized; but it is also a sign of regeneration or the new birth. The baptism of young children is to be retained in the church.

Article XVIII. OF THE LORD'S SUPPER

The Supper of the Lord is not only a sign of the love that Christians ought to have among themselves one to another, but rather is a sacrament of our redemption by Christ's death; insomuch that, to such as rightly, worthily, and with faith receive the same, the bread which we break is a partaking of the body of Christ; and likewise the cup of blessing is a partaking of the blood of Christ.

Transubstantiation, or the change of the substance of bread and wine in the Supper of our Lord, cannot be proved by Holy Writ, but is repugnant to the plain words of Scripture, overthroweth the nature of a sacrament, and hath given occasion to many superstitions.

The body of Christ is given, taken, and eaten in the Supper, only after a heavenly and spiritual manner. And the mean whereby the body of Christ is received and eaten in the Supper is faith.

The Sacrament of the Lord's Supper was not by Christ's ordinance reserved, carried about, lifted up, or worshiped.

Article XIX. OF BOTH KINDS

The cup of the Lord is not to be denied to the lay people; for both the parts of the Lord's Supper, by Christ's ordinance and commandment, ought to be administered to all Christians alike.

Article XX. OF THE ONE OBLATION OF CHRIST, FINISHED UPON THE CROSS

The offering of Christ, once made, is that perfect redemption, propitiation, and satisfaction for all the sins of the whole world, both original and actual; and there is none other satisfaction for sin but that alone. Wherefore the sacrifice of masses, in the which it is commonly said that the priest doth offer Christ for the quick and the dead, to have remission of pain or guilt, is a blasphemous fable and dangerous deceit.

Article XXI. OF THE MARRIAGE OF MINISTERS

The ministers of Christ are not commanded by God's law either to vow the estate of single life, or to abstain from marriage; therefore it is lawful for them, as for all other Christians, to marry at their own discretion, as they shall judge the same to serve best to godliness.

Article XXII. OF THE RITES AND CEREMONIES OF CHURCHES

It is not necessary that rites and ceremonies should in all places be the same, or exactly alike; for they have been always different, and may be changed according to the diversity of countries, times, and men's manners, so that nothing be ordained against God's Word. Whosoever, through his private judgment, willingly and purposely doth openly break the rites and ceremonies of the church to which he belongs, which are not repugnant to the Word of God, and are ordained and approved by common authority, ought to be rebuked openly, that others may fear to do the like, as one that offendeth against the common order of the church, and woundeth the consciences of weak brethren.

Every particular church may ordain, change, or abolish rites and ceremonies, so that all things may be done to edification.

Article XXIII. OF THE RULERS OF THE UNITED STATES OF AMERICA

The President, the Congress, the general assemblies, the governors, and the councils of state, *as the delegates of the people*, are the rulers of the United States of America, according to the division of power made to them by the Constitution of the United States and by the constitutions of their respective states. And the said states are a sovereign and independent nation, and ought not to be subject to any foreign jurisdiction.

Article XXIV. OF CHRISTIAN MEN'S GOODS

The riches and goods of Christians are not common as touching the right, title, and possession of the same, as some do falsely boast. Notwithstanding, every man ought, of such things as he possesseth, liberally to give alms to the poor, according to his ability.

Article XXV. OF A CHRISTIAN MAN'S OATH

As we confess that vain and rash swearing is forbidden Christian men by our Lord Jesus Christ and James his apostle, so we judge that the Christian religion doth not prohibit, but that a man may swear when the magistrate requireth, in a cause of faith and charity, so it be done according to the prophet's teaching, in justice, judgment, and truth.

Notes: *Following the American Revolution, John Wesley prepared doctrinal materials to guide the newly independent Methodists residing in the former British colonies in the New World. Among the items were twenty-five articles of religion. Wesley took them directly from the Thirty-nine Articles of the Church of England (still in use today by most Anglican churches in the United States), deleting what he considered less essential statements, including the more*

controversial articles on eschatology. The Twenty-five Articles were adopted by the Methodist Episcopal Church in 1784 and remain part of the constitution of the United Methodist Church.

The United Methodist Church, in the persona of the General Conference, its highest legislative body, is bound by what are termed the six restrictive rules. The first of these states: "The General Conference shall not revoke, alter, or change our Articles of Religion or establish any new standards or rule of doctrine contrary to our present existing and established standards of doctrine." Deletion of one of these restrictive rules takes almost unanimous consent of the church. These restrictive rules have been retained by most of the churches that have broken away from what is now known as the United Methodist Church. The rules have also helped perpetuate the Twenty-five Articles in the face of periodic attempts to rewrite doctrinal statements.

The Twenty-five Articles of Religion have been among the most influential documents in American religious history. Beyond their service to the multi-million member United Methodist Church and its antecedents, they have served as a base from which many of the holiness and pentecostal churches have begun their doctrinal formulations (though most have now moved considerably beyond the articles).

The articles also are held, in some cases with minor changes or additions, by the Congregational Methodist Church, the Evangelical Methodist Church, the Evangelical Methodist Church of America, the First Congregational Methodist Church of the U.S.A., the Southern Methodist Church, the African Methodist Episcopal Church, the African Methodist Episcopal Zion Church, the African Union First Colored Methodist Protestant Church, the Christian Methodist Episcopal Church, and the Reformed Zion Union Apostolic Church.

*   *   *

CHANGES, ADDITIONS, AND FOOTNOTES TO THE *TWENTY-FIVE ARTICLES OF RELIGION* (UNITED METHODIST CHURCH)

OF SANCTIFICATION

Sanctification is that renewal of our fallen nature by the Holy Ghost, received through faith in Jesus Christ, whose blood of atonement cleanseth from all sin; whereby we are not only delivered from the guilt of sin, but are washed from its pollution, saved from its power, and are enabled, through grace, to love God with all our hearts and to walk in his holy commandments blameless.

OF THE DUTY OF CHRISTIANS TO THE CIVIL AUTHORITY

It is the duty of all Christians, and especially of all Christian ministers, to observe and obey the laws and commands of the governing or supreme authority of the country of which they are citizens or subjects or in which they reside, and to use all laudable means to encourage and enjoin obedience to the powers that be.

Notes: *The Methodist Protestant Church (1828-1939), one of the church bodies participating in the series of mergers that led to the formation of United Methodism, added a* *statement on sanctification to the Articles of Religion. That statement is carried in* The Book of Discipline *of the United Methodist Church with a note: "The following Article from the Methodist Protestant Church* Discipline *is placed here by the Uniting Conference (1939). It was not one of the Articles of Religion voted upon by the three churches [which united at that time]."*

A second article was also added in 1939. It grew out of the problems arising from the stated allegiance of the Methodist Church to the government of the United States. A note is appended: "The following provision was adopted by the Uniting Conference. This statement seeks to interpret to our churches in foreign lands Article XXIII of the Articles of Religion. It is a legislative enactment but is not part of the Constitution."

* * *

CONFESSION OF FAITH (UNITED METHODIST CHURCH)

Article I. GOD

1. We believe in the one true, holy and living God, Eternal Spirit, who is Creator, Sovereign and Preserver of all things visible and invisible. He is infinite in power, wisdom, justice, goodness and love, and rules with gracious regard for the well-being and salvation of men, to the glory of his name. We believe the one God reveals himself as the Trinity: Father, Son and Holy Spirit, distinct but inseparable, eternally one in essence and power.

Article II. JESUS CHRIST

2. We believe in Jesus Christ, truly God and truly man, in whom the divine and human natures are perfectly and inseparably united. He is the eternal Word made flesh, the only begotten Son of the Father, born of the Virgin Mary by the power of the Holy Spirit. As ministering Servant he lived, suffered and died on the cross. He was buried, rose from the dead and ascended into heaven to be with the Father, from whence he shall return. He is eternal Savior and Mediator, who intercedes for us, and by him all men will be judged.

Article III. THE HOLY SPIRIT

3. We believe in the Holy Spirit who proceeds from and is one in being with the Father and the Son. He convinces the world of sin, of righteousness and of judgment. He leads men through faithful response to the Gospel into the fellowship of the church. He comforts, sustains and empowers the faithful and guides them into all truth.

Article IV. THE HOLY BIBLE

4. We believe the Holy Bible, Old and New Testaments, reveals the Word of God as far as it is necessary for our salvation. It is to be received through the Holy Spirit as the true rule and guide for faith and practice. Whatever is not revealed in or established by the Holy Scriptures is not to be made an article of faith nor is it to be taught as essential to salvation.

Article V. THE CHURCH

5. We believe the Christian church is the community of all true believers under the Lordship of Christ. We believe it is one, holy, apostolic and catholic. It is the redemptive fellowship in which the Word of God is preached by men divinely called, and the sacraments are duly administered according to Christ's own appointment. Under the discipline of the Holy Spirit the church exists for the maintenance of worship, the edification of believers and the redemption of the world.

Article VI. THE SACRAMENTS

6. We believe the sacraments, ordained by Christ, are symbols and pledges of the Christian's profession and of God's love toward us. They are means of grace by which God works invisibly in us, quickening, strengthening and confirming our faith in him. Two sacraments are ordained by Christ our Lord, namely, Baptism and the Lord's Supper.

We believe Baptism signifies entrance into the household of faith, and is a symbol of repentance and inner cleansing from sin, a representation of the new birth in Christ Jesus and a mark of Christian discipleship.

We believe children are under the atonement of Christ and as heirs of the kingdom of God are acceptable subjects for Christian baptism. Children of believing parents through baptism become the special responsibility of the church. They should be nurtured and led to personal acceptance of Christ, and by profession of faith confirm their baptism.

We believe the Lord's Supper is a representation of our redemption, a memorial of the sufferings and death of Christ, and a token of love and union which Christians have with Christ and with one another. Those who rightly, worthily and in faith eat the broken bread and drink the blessed cup partake of the body and blood of Christ in a spiritual manner until he comes.

Article VII. SIN AND FREE WILL

7. We believe man is fallen from righteousness and, apart from the grace of our Lord Jesus Christ, is destitute of holiness and inclined to evil. Except a man be born again, he cannot see the kingdom of God. In his own strength, without divine grace, man cannot do good works pleasing and acceptable to God. We believe, however, man influenced and empowered by the Holy Spirit is responsible in freedom to exercise his will for good.

Article VIII. RECONCILIATION THROUGH CHRIST

8. We believe God was in Christ reconciling the world to himself. The offering Christ freely made on the cross is the perfect and sufficient sacrifice for the sins

of the whole world, redeeming man from all sin, so that no other satisfaction is required.

Article IX. JUSTIFICATION AND REGENERATION

9. We believe we are never accounted righteous before God through our works or merit, but that penitent sinners are justified or accounted righteous before God only by faith in our Lord Jesus Christ.

   We believe regeneration is the renewal of man in righteousness through Jesus Christ, by the power of the Holy Spirit, whereby we are made partakers of the divine nature and experience newness of life. By this new birth the believer becomes reconciled to God and is enabled to serve him with the will and the affections.

   We believe, although we have experienced regeneration, it is possible to depart from grace and fall into sin; and we may even then, by the grace of God, be renewed in righteousness.

Article X. GOOD WORKS

10. We believe good works are the necessary fruits of faith and follow regeneration but they do not have the virtue to remove our sins or to avert divine judgment. We believe good works, pleasing and acceptable to God in Christ, spring from a true and living faith, for through and by them faith is made evident.

Article XI. SANCTIFICATION AND CHRISTIAN PERFECTION

11. We believe sanctification is the work of God's grace through the Word and the Spirit, by which those who have been born again are cleansed from sin in their thoughts, words and acts, and are enabled to live in accordance with God's will, and to strive for holiness without which no one will see the Lord.

   Entire sanctification is a state of perfect love, righteousness and true holiness which every regenerate believer may obtain by being delivered from the power of sin, by loving God with all the heart, soul, mind and strength, and by loving one's neighbor as one's self. Through faith in Jesus Christ this gracious gift may be received in this life both gradually and instantaneously, and should be sought earnestly by every child of God.

   We believe this experience does not deliver us from the infirmities, ignorance and mistakes common to man, nor from the possibilities of further sin. The Christian must continue on guard against spiritual pride and seek to gain victory over every temptation to sin. He must respond wholly to the will of God so that sin will lose its power over him; and the world, the flesh and the devil are put under his feet. Thus he rules over these enemies with watchfulness through the power of the Holy Spirit.

Article XII. THE JUDGMENT AND THE FUTURE STATE

12. We believe all men stand under the righteous judgment of Jesus Christ, both now and in the last day. We believe in the resurrection of the dead; the righteous to life eternal and the wicked to endless condemnation.

Article XIII. PUBLIC WORSHIP

13. We believe divine worship is the duty and privilege of man who, in the presence of God, bows in adoration, humility and dedication. We believe divine worship is essential to the life of the church, and that the assembling of the people of God for such worship is necessary to Christian fellowship and spiritual growth.

   We believe the order of public worship need not be the same in all places but may be modified by the church according to circumstances and the needs of men. It should be in a language and form understood by the people, consistent with the Holy Scriptures to the edification of all, and in accordance with the order and DISCIPLINE of the Church.

Article XIV. THE LORD'S DAY

14. We believe the Lord's Day is divinely ordained for private and public worship, for rest from unnecessary work, and should be devoted to spiritual improvement, Christian fellowship and service. It is commemorative of our Lord's resurrection and is an emblem of our eternal rest. It is essential to the permanence and growth of the Christian church, and important to the welfare of the civil community.

Article XV. THE CHRISTIAN AND PROPERTY

15. We believe God is the owner of all things and that the individual holding of property is lawful and is a sacred trust under God. Private property is to be used for the manifestation of Christian love and liberality, and to support the Church's mission in the world. All forms of property, whether private, corporate or public, are to be held in solemn trust and used responsibly for human good under the sovereignty of God.

Article XVI. CIVIL GOVERNMENT

16. We believe civil government derives its just powers from the sovereign God. As Christians we recognize the governments under whose protection we reside and believe such governments should be based on, and be responsible for, the recognition of human rights under God. We believe war and bloodshed are contrary to the gospel and spirit of Christ. We believe it is the duty of Christian citizens to give moral strength and purpose to their respective governments through sober, righteous and godly living.

Notes: *In 1968, the United Methodist Church accepted the Confession of Faith of the Evangelical United Brethren (formed in 1946), originally adopted in 1962, as one of its standards of doctrine. At the same time it added a new restrictive rule to the constitution: "The General Conference shall not revoke, alter, or change our Confession of Faith."*

A MODERN AFFIRMATION (UNITED METHODIST CHURCH)

MINISTER: Where the Spirit of the Lord is, there is the one true Church, apostolic and universal, whose holy faith let us now declare:

MINISTER AND PEOPLE: We believe in God the Father, infinite in wisdom, power and love, whose mercy is over all his works, and whose will is ever directed to his children's good.

We believe in Jesus Christ, Son of God and Son of man, the gift of the Father's unfailing grace, the ground of our hope, and the promise of our deliverance from sin and death.

We believe in the Holy Spirit as the divine presence in our lives, whereby we are kept in perpetual remembrance of the truth of Christ, and find strength and help in time of need.

We believe that this faith should manifest itself in the service of love as set forth in the example of our blessed Lord, to the end that the kingdom of God may come upon the earth. Amen.

Notes: *The United Methodist Church includes a variety of creedal affirmations in its* Hymnal *and* The Book of Worship, *used in the liturgies of its member churches. Among these affirmations are the Apostles' and Nicene Creeds, as well as the Creed of the Church of South Korea. These affirmations do not represent doctrinal standards, like the Twenty-five Articles, and they have never been presented to or voted upon by the General Conference with such intent. They merely appear as additional liturgical resources. However, their inclusion does represent the diversity of opinion that has appeared within the church during this century.*

Added by the Methodist Episcopal Church in the early twentieth century, the creed called "A Modern Affirmation" is similiar to the Congregational Church statement adopted in 1913 in that it does not require ministers and members who repeat it to affirm certain traditional Christian beliefs, especially those debated by theologians in the twentieth century such as the Trinity or the substitutionary atonement of Christ. The affirmation has emerged as a substitute for the Apostles' Creed and is commonly repeated in many United Methodist Church worship services.

* * *

Non-Episcopal Methodism

ADDITIONS TO THE *TWENTY-FIVE ARTICLES OF RELIGION* (ASBURY BIBLE CHURCHES)

OF SEGREGATION

We do not believe that integration, for which so many are clamoring, is the answer to current social problems. In fact, it is our opinion that integration would produce more problems than it would solve. In the light of the present moral and spiritual crisis, and also in the light of Scriptural teaching, we believe in the segregation of the races and practice the principle of segregation in our churches. The practice of this principle, however, does not mean that our churches are not vigorously missionary and evangelistic in their ministries, nor that we would not endeavor to win to Christ and nurture in Christ ANYONE so long as, where differing races are involved, we do so on an INDIVIDUAL, rather than a SOCIAL, basis.

"[God] hath made of one blood all nations of men for to dwell on all the face of the earth, and hath determined the times before appointed, AND THE BOUNDS OF THEIR HABITATION . . . " (Acts 17:26).

OF SEPARATION

We believe that, in these days of apostasy, the Church should be separated from compromising situations in the world.

Such being the case, no independent Methodist church can consistently hold membership in, or otherwise be connected with, the National Council of Churches (NCC), the World Council of Churches (WCC), or even the National Association of Evangelicals (NAE). In regard to the NCC and the WCC, the apostasy of churches and denominations in those organizations would prohibit an independent Methodist church from being a part thereof. So would the ecumenical world church movement in which the NCC and the WCC are actively engaged. (Such a world church, so-called, would not be a church at all, in the true sense of the word, for every vestige of the fundamentals of the Faith has to be forfeited for the sake of the 'unity' to be effected by this monstrous ecclesiastical-political machine.) In regard to the NAE, this organization is now off-limits to independent Methodist churches, inasmuch as ecumenism and also neo-evangelicalism (modernism disguised as fundamentalism) are characteristics of the NAE as it is presently constituted. The NAE, therefore, is now a compromise organization, and independent Methodist churches are not to compromise. Furthermore, it is now possible for a church or denomination to hold membership in the NAE and also the NCC and the WCC.

We heartily urge that independent Methodist churches seek membership in the American Council of Christian Churches (ACCC). This Council was formed in 1941 to combat the NCC [then the Federal Council of Churches], along with other kindred organizations and enterprises. The ACCC has maintained—and continues to maintain— an aggressive attempt to expose evil wherever it is found, to preserve the integrity of the Scriptures, and to staunchly oppose those who try to destroy such integrity.

Cooperative church and ministerial activities with churches and denominations in the NCC, WCC and NAE are unthinkable for independent Methodist churches, on any level of local church activity or in any kind or degree of participation.

Notes: *The Asbury Bible Churches, the congregations served by the John Wesley Fellowship (a ministerial fellowship), and many otherwise independent Methodist congregations (particularly those in the southeastern United States), have taken their doctrinal statement from* Guidelines for Independent Methodist Church, *compiled by Thomas L. Baird (Colonial Heights, VA: The Author, 1971). This volume, in turn, was taken largely from* The Doctrines and Discipline of the Southern Methodist Church. *The doctrinal section of the* Guidelines *includes the Twenty-five Articles of Religion common to Methodism as well as the additional doctrinal statements made by the Southern Methodist Church (SMC), with two exceptions. The SMC statement on racial segregation have been rewritten and expanded, and a statement on biblical "separation" from apostacy was added.*

* * *

OUR BELIEFS (ASSOCIATION OF INDEPENDENT METHODISTS)

We believe the Bible is the infallible Word of God, inerrant in the originals.

We believe that there is one God, eternally existent in three persons, Father, Son and Holy Spirit.

We believe in the deity of Jesus Christ, His virgin birth, His blood-atoning death, His bodily resurrection, His ascension and His premillennial return.

We believe that Jesus Christ is the only Savior and the only Way to salvation and everlasting life.

We believe that salvation is by grace through faith in the blood atonement of Christ with repentance of sins.

We believe in the Biblical account of creation and all other supernatural acts of God recorded in the Scriptures.

We believe that man was created a free moral agent and remains so all the days of his life, with the God given freedom to choose or reject God throughout one's life.

We believe and practice two ordinances: Baptism (choice of mode) and the Lord's Supper.

We believe in the resurrection of both the saved and the lost; the saved to eternal life and the lost to eternal damnation.

We hold to the traditional twenty-five articles of belief.

We believe in free America. We love and respect our nation, its' leaders, its' laws, its' flag and its' Constitution.

We believe that the believer may be cleansed from all sin through the sanctifying power of the blood of Christ and the work of the Holy Spirit.

Notes: *The Association of Independent Methodists represents a very conservative group who rejected the merger of the Methodist Episcopal Church, South, with what it considered a very liberal (in both doctrine and social policy) Methodist Episcopal Church. The Association's statement of beliefs follows that of nineteenth-century Methodism in general, though its statement on Biblical authority reflects some Protestant fundamentalist influence.*

* * *

DOCTRINAL STATEMENT (BIBLE PROTESTANT CHURCH)

1. We believe the Bible in the original tongues to be the verbally inspired Word of God, and the only infallible rule of faith and Practice, (2 Timothy 3:14-16).

2. We believe that God is Triune; that there are three eternal, co-equal, Divine persons in the Godhead, and these three are one God, (Matthew 28:19).

3. We believe in the Deity of the Lord Jesus Christ; that He was conceived of the Holy Spirit and born of the Virgin Mary, (John 1 and Matthew 1).

4. We believe that the only way to be saved is by faith in the blood sacrifice, death and resurrection of Jesus Christ, the Son of God, and that to those who thus become His sheep He says, "I give unto them eternal life; and they shall never perish, neither shall any man pluck them out of my hand," (John 10:28, Ephesians 2:8,9).

5. We believe that our Lord Jesus Christ ascended into Heaven, and is now seated at the right hand of the Father; that He ever liveth to make intercession for all that come to God by Him, (Acts 1:9-11, Hebrews 4:14, Ephesians 1:20,21).

6. We believe that the Church which is the Body of Christ began with the descent of the Holy Spirit on the Day of Pentecost and that each one who receives the Lord Jesus Christ as his personal Saviour is a member of the Body of Christ, and is indwelled by the Holy Spirit, (I Corinthians 12:12-28, 6:19,20).

7. We believe that the Gospel commission is for the Church; that the Lord's Supper and water Baptism are Divine Institutions and that Christ desires us to practice them in this age, (Matthew 28:18-20, I Corinthians 11:23-29).

8. We believe that Christ may at any moment return in the air to rapture the Saints, and that a tribulation period of approximately seven years shall follow, after which He will come to the earth with His Saints, and rule for a thousand years. After this the wicked will be judged and cast into the lake of fire, (I Thessalonians 4:13-18, I Corinthians 15:51-57, Daniel 9:27, Matthew 24:15-21, 24:27, 25:46, Revelation 19:11, 20:10-15).

9. We believe that Satan is a person, the author of the fall, and that he shall be eternally punished, (Job 1:7, Genesis 3:1-19, Revelation 20:10).

10. We believe in the bodily resurrection of the dead, both of the just and the unjust; and in the eternal conscious punishment of the lost and the eternal joy of the saved, (Revelation 20:11-15, 22:12-14, I Corinthians 15:1-58).

Notes: *The Bible Protestant Church consists of congregations that rejected the merger of the Methodist Protestant Church in 1939. Subsequently, its doctrinal position moved toward Protestant fundamentalism.*

ARTICLES OF FAITH AND PRACTICE (CHURCH OF DANIEL'S BAND)

1. THE HOLY TRINITY

There is but one living and true God, everlasting in infinite power, wisdom and goodness; the maker and preserver of all things, visible and invisible. And in unity of this godhead there are three persons of one substance, power and eternity-the Father, the Son (the Word) and the Holy Ghost. I Cor. viii, 4-6; John xvii, 3, 1; Tim. i, John iv, 24.

2. THE WORD, OR SON OF GOD

The Son, who is the Word of Father, the very and eternal God of one substance with the Father, took man's nature in the womb of the blessed virgin, so that two whole and perface natures, that is to say, the godhead and manhood were joined together one person never to be divided whereof is one Christ God and very man who truly suffered, was crucified, dead and buried to reconcile us to his Father and to be a sacrifice not only for original guilt but also for the actual sins of men. John i, 14-18; chap. iii, 16; Luke i, 27-31, 35; Gal. iv, 4-5; Heb. vii, 27; Rom. v, 10.

3. RESURRECTION OF CHRIST

Christ did truly rise from the dead, taking his body with all things appertained to the perfection of man's nature, wherewith he ascended into heaven, and there sitteth until he return to judge all men at the last day. Acts x, 39-42.

4. THE HOLY GHOST

The Holy Ghost, proceeding from the Father and the Son, is one of substance, majesty and glory, with the Father and the Son, very and eternal God. Acts ii, 2-4.

5. THE SUFFICIENCY OF THE HOLY SCRIPTURES FOR SALVATION

The Holy Scriptures contain all things necessary to salvation, for it is written, "search the scriptures, for in them ye think ye have eternal life, and they are they which testify of me." John v, 39. By the Holy Scriptures we do mean and understand those canonical Books of the Old and New Testament of whose authority there is no doubt in the church. 2 Tim. iii, 15-17.

6. OF THE OLD TESTAMENT

The Old Testament is not contrary to the new; for both in the Old and New Testaments everlasting life is offered to mankind through Christ, who is the only mediator between God and man. Wherefore, they are not to be heard, who feign that the old fathers did look for only transitory promises. 1 Tim. ii, 5; Heb. xi, 39-40.

7. OF ORIGINAL AND ACQUIRED DEPRAVITY

Original depravity is the corruption of the moral nature inherited by every human being, because of Adam's disobedience to the law of God, whereby every man is wholly gone from original righteousness, and without grace, inclined to evil and that continually. Acquired depravity is all the thoughts of our defiled minds resulting from the original depravity of our moral nature. Tit. i, 15; Matt. xv, 19; Rom. iii, 10-18.

8. OF FREE WILL

Man having become so completely ruined, has neither the will nor the power to turn to God, and if left to himself would remain in his wretched and miserable condition forever. But blessed thought, the grace of God that bringeth salvation, hath appeared to all men; hence, God graciously employs the means of enlightening and awakening the mind of the sinner to a sense of his poverty and wretchedness through preaching (1 Cor. 1, 21) it pleased God by the foolishness of preaching to save them that believe. John vi, 44.

9. OF REPENTANCE

This consists of Godly sorrow for sin, and forsaking it by turning to God. 2 Cor. vii, 9, 10.

10. OF CONVERSION

This consists in the forgiveness of actual transgressions of the law, and the regeneration "which is the new birth" of the soul by the Holy Ghost, in which all the corruption of the past sinful life is removed, and the new life implanted. John i, 13.

11. OF ENTIRE SANCTIFICATION

This entire cleansing is the work of the Holy Ghost by which the hereditary body of sin, or inherited depravity, is removed from the flesh. Romans, viii, 21; 2 Cor. iv, 10-11; 1 John iv, 2-3; 2 John i, 7.

12. OF GOOD WORK

Good works are not a condition of salvation, but are the natural fruits of regeneration. Matt. v, 16.

13. OF SIN AFTER CONVERSION

Not every error fallen into after conversion is unpardonable; wherefore repentance is granted to such as fall into error; they may fall therein, and by the grace of God, rise again to obedience. 1 John Chp. 2, verse 1.

14. OF THE RESURRECTION OF THE DEAD

There will be a resurrection of the dead, both of the just and the unjust, at which time the souls and bodies of men will be united to receive together a just retribution for the deeds done in the body in this life. 1 Thess. iv, 14, 15, 17; Rev. xx, 6.

15. FUTURE REWARD AND PUNISHMENT

God has appointed a day in which He will judge the world in righteousness by Jesus Christ according to the Gospel. The righteous shall have in Heaven an inheritance incorruptible, undefiled and that fadeth not away. The wicked shall go away into everlasting punishment, where the worm dieth not, and their fire is not quenched. Matt. xxv, 45-46; Rev. xxi, 6-8.

16. THE CHURCH OF JESUS CHRIST

The Church of Jesus Christ consists of all people that are born again. John iii, 3.

17. SACRAMENTS

Sacraments ordained of Christ are badges and tokens of Christian man's professions, and to them who rightly discern the Lord's body; they are a means used of him to strengthen and confirm our love.. Matt. xxvi, 26, 27, 28; Matt. xxviii, 19; 1 Cor. xi, 26, 26. There are two sacraments ordained of Christ our Lord in the Gospel, that is to say, Baptism, and the Supper of the Lord.

18. OF BAPTISM

Baptism is not only a sign of profession, and mark of difference, whereby Christians are distinguished from others who are not baptised, but is also a sign of regeneration or new birth. Liberty of conscience will be allowed as to the mode of baptism, except in the baptism of young children, the mode shall be left with the preacher. Matt. iii, 11; Acts x, 47-48.

19. OF THE LORD'S SUPPER

The Supper of the Lord is a sign of love that his children have for one another, and when rightly discerned as an emblem of the broken body of Christ, does communicate grace and love to the heart. 1 Cor. x. 16.

20. OF THE RITES AND CEREMONIES OF CHURCHES

It is not necessary that rites and ceremonies should in all places be the same or exactly alike; for they have always been different and may be changed according to the diversities of countries, times and men's manners, so that nothing be ordained against God's word. Each particular church may ordain, change or abolish rites and ceremonies so that all things be done to edification. Roman xiv, 4, 17; Acts xv, 10; Gal. v, 1, 13; 1 Peter ii, 16.

21. OF CHRISTIAN MEN'S GOODS

The goods of Christians are not common as touching the rights, title and possession of the same, as some do falsely boast. But what they have belongs to God, and as his stewards they should use that entrusted to their care with an eye single to his glory. Romans xv, 26; 1 Timothy vi, 17-18; James i, 10; Acts iv, 32.

22. OF DIVINE HEALING

The scriptures plainly declare, "The prayer of faith shall save the sick" All of God's children should be exorted to lay hold upon this promise. James v, 14; Acts iii, 1-9.

23. OF ORDINATION

A minister must set in the class three Consecutive years before Ordination Amendment, if it be necessary we can ordain any minister born in our own organization at any time.

24. OF THE SUPPORT OF THE GOSPEL

The support of the Gospel consists in the offering of ourselves a living sacrific to God, with all that God has instrusted us with as stewards, to be used with an eye single to his glory. Phil. iv, 10-13; Rom. xii, 1-2; 2 Cor. xi, 9; 2 Cor. ix, 5-9.

25. OF MARRIAGE

Holy Matrimony is a sacred institution of divine origin, and no believer should enter into this sacred agreement without positive leadings from God in harmony with His Word which commands his children to marry "only in the Lord". 2 Cor. vi, 14; Duet. xxii, 10.

26. OF DIVORCE

See Matthew, nineteenth chapter, third to twelfth verses inclusive.

27. OF INTEMPERANCE

Intemperance is excess in any kind of action or indulgence; any exertion of body or mind, or any indulgence of appetites or passions which is injurious to the person or contrary to the law of God. 1 Cor. ix, 25.

28. OF CONFORMITY TO THE WORLD

We are as Christians earnestly and lovingly exhorted to be not conformed to this world, but to be transformed by the renewing of our minds, that we may prove what is that good and acceptable and perfect will of God. See Romans xii, 2.

29. OF THE CALL TO THE MINISTRY

There is abundant evidence in the scriptures that God calls whom he will to preach the Gospel, both men and women. And such as he calls and qualifies only can be effective in bringing souls into the Kingdom of God. Consequently the sisters called should have all the privileges given the brethren. Rom. x, 15.

30. LAYING ON OF HANDS

We recognize scriptural authority for the laying on of hands for the gift of the Holy Ghost, for the healing of the sick and in setting apart for the work of the ministry of those called of God. James v, 14; Acts vi, 5-6; Acts xix, 6.

31. OF SALARIED MINISTERS

We believe it to be the duty of the societies to support their ministers, as the laborer is worthy of his hire.

32. OF QUORUM

That when any Annual Conference is called six members present will constitute a quorum.

33. MINISTER SUPPORT

That the classes desiring a minister to serve them should be responsible for the minister getting to the next Annual Conference.

34. PRESIDENT TRANSPORTATION

That the church circuits raise ten dollars or more and send the same to the President to bear his expenses to and from the quarterly conference.

> Amendment to the above resolution: That the amount raised by the church circuit for the President's expenses in case of his absence can be given to the one substituting in his place. Also, if the church circuit cannot raise the ten dollars, but the President is willing to travel for less, the matter can be settled between them.

35. GENERAL FUND

That each and every class of the Church of Daniel's Band take up one offering each and every month for fund and this money be sent to the conference secretary to be used for the building of new classes. Secretary to notify each class who are a month in arrears.

> Amendment to the above resolution: That the head evangelist of the Annual Conference appointed to spend the money sent the order to the President, Secretary, and Treasurer of the Annual Conference.

36. CHARGING AN ELDER

That there shall be no charges brought against an Elder only in writing and before calling for reports it should be the duty of the investigating committee to thoroughly investigate both sides of the question separately and also together before any action is taken.

37. OF BANK FAILURE

That any money held by the Church Conference Treasurer belonging to the Church of Daniel's Band shall not be held responsible for money lost in bank failures only to the amount the bank may refund.

Notes: *The statement of the small Church of Daniel's Band, formed in 1893, reflects a desire to make the church's position clear on many matters neglected by the Methodist Articles of Religion, as well as some decisions on financial matters of immediate concern at the time.*

* * *

ADDITIONS TO THE *TWENTY-FIVE ARTICLES OF RELIGION* (CONGREGATIONAL METHODIST CHURCH)

As far as respects civil affairs, we believe it the duty of Christians, and especially all Christian ministers, to be subject to the supreme authority of the country where they may reside, and to use all laudable means to enjoin obedience to the powers that be, and therefore it is expected that all our preachers and people, who may be under the British, or any other government, will behave themselves as peaceable and orderly subjects.

Article XXVI. REGENERATION.

"Whereas justification is the judicial act on God's part in that He declares the sinner no longer exposed to the penalty of a broken law because of a new faith relationship to Jesus Christ, regeneration is the instantaneous imparta-tion of spiritual life to the human soul by the Holy Ghost. This experience of grace, sometimes called the (new birth) prepares the human soul for the functions of the new life."

Article XXVII. SANCTIFICATION.

"Entire sanctification is that second definite work of grace, subsequent to regeneration, whereby the heart of a justified person is cleansed from the original or Adamic nature, and is filled with the Holy Ghost."

Article XXVIII. FINANCIAL PLAN FOR THE CHURCH.

The Lord has given the church a financial plan which we believe to be storehouse tithing and free will offerings. (All tithes should go through the church treasury.)

Article XXIX. ETERNAL RETRIBUTION.

The wicked shall have their part in the lake which burneth with fire and brimstone and that everlastingly.

Article XXX. RESURRECTION OF THE DEAD.

There are two resurrections. The first shall be at the pre-millennial second coming of Jesus Christ in which the saved dead shall be resurrected and living saints raptured. The second shall be after the millennium when the unsaved dead will be resurrected at the Great White Throne Judgment.

Notes: *The Congregational Methodist Church, as have most Methodist bodies expanding into foreign lands, experienced difficulties with Article XXIII of the Twenty-five Articles of Religion, which countenanced allegiance to the government of the United States. The church dealt with that problem by placing an addendum to Article XXIII.*

In 1957 the church added five more articles of religion covering, among other matters, sanctification, finances, and eschatology. These additional articles were not accepted by the First Congregational Methodist Church of America, which had left the Congregational Methodist Church in 1941.

* * *

ADDITIONS TO THE *TWENTY-FIVE ARTICLES OF RELIGION* (EVANGELICAL METHODIST CHURCH)

XXIII. OF THE DUTY OF CHRISTIANS TO THE CIVIL AUTHORITY.

It is the duty of all Christians, and especially of all Christian ministers, to observe and obey the laws and commands of the governing or supreme authority of the country of which they are citizens or subjects, or in which they reside, and to use all laudable means to encourage and enjoin obedience to the powers that be.

XXVI. PERFECT LOVE.

46. Perfect love is that renewal of our fallen nature by the Holy Spirit, received through faith in Jesus Christ, whose blood of atonement cleanseth from all sin; whereby we are not only delivered from the guilt of sin, but are washed from its pollution, saved from its power, and are enabled, through grace, to love God with all our hearts and to walk in His holy commandments blameless.

Notes: *The Evangelical Methodist Church adopted the Twenty-five Articles of Religion common to all Methodists, and subsequently prepared a substitute for Article XXIII, "Of the Rulers of the United States of America," for use by member churches in foreign lands. In addition, the church added an article and explanatory footnote on the distinctly Wesleyan doctrine of "Perfect Love."*

* * *

ADDITIONS TO THE *TWENTY-FIVE ARTICLES OF RELIGION* (EVANGELICAL METHODIST CHURCH OF AMERICA)

Article XXIII. OF THE DUTY OF CHRISTIANS TO THE CIVIL AUTHORITY.

It is the duty of all Christians, and especially of all Christian ministers, to observe and obey the laws and commands of the governing or supreme authority of the country of which they are citizens or subjects, or in which they reside, so long as they are not contrary to the Word of God. (Acts 5:29)

Notes: *Like many Methodist bodies who adopted the Twenty-five Articles of Religion, a new article for members in foreign lands has been adopted as a substitute for Article XXIII, "Of the Rulers of the United States of America."*

* * *

ARTICLES OF RELIGION (FUNDAMENTAL METHODIST CHURCH)

1. OF FAITH IN THE HOLY TRINITY

There is but one living and true God, everlasting, of infinite power, wisdom and goodness, the maker and preserver of all things, visible and invisible. And in unity of this Godhead, there are three persons of one substance, power and eternity—the Father, the Son, and the Holy Ghost.

2. OF THE WORD, OR THE SON OF GOD, WHO WAS MADE VERY MAN

The Son, who is the Word of the Father, the very and eternal God, of one substance with the Father, took man's nature in the womb of the blessed virgin; so that two whole and perfect natures, that is to say, the Godhead and manhood, were joined together in one person, never to be divided, whereof is one Christ, very God and very man who truly suffered, was crucified, died, and was buried, to reconcile us to God, and to be a sacrifice, not only for original guilt, but also for the actual sins of men.

3. OF THE RESURRECTION OF CHRIST

Christ did truly rise again from the dead, and took again his body, with all things appertaining to the perfection of man's nature, wherewith he ascended into heaven, and there sitteth until he returns to judge all men at the last day.

4. OF THE HOLY GHOST

The Holy Ghost, proceeding from the Father and the Son is of one substance, majesty and glory with the Father and the Son, very and eternal God.

5. THE SUFFICIENCY OF THE HOLY SCRIPTURES FOR SALVATION

The Holy Scriptures contain all things necessary to salvation; so whatsoever is not read therein, nor may be proved thereby, is not to be required of any man that it should be believed as an article of faith, or be thought requisite or necessary to salvation. In the name of the Holy Scriptures, we do understand those canonical books of the Old and New Testament, of whose authority was never any doubt in the church.

The names of the canonical books are: Genesis, Exodus, Leviticus, Numbers, Deuteronomy, Joshua, Judges, Ruth, the First Book of Samuel, the Second Book of Samuel, the First Book of Kings, the Second Book of Kings, the First Book of Chronicles, the Second Book of Chronicles, the Book of Ezra, the Book of Nehemiah, the Book of Esther, the Book of Job, the Psalms, the Proverbs, Ecclesiastes (or the Preacher), Cantica (or Song of Solomon), Four Prophets the Greater, Twelve Prophets the Less; all the books of the New Testament, as they are commonly received, we do receive and account canonical.

6. OF THE OLD TESTAMENT

The Old Testament is not contrary to the New; for in both the Old and New Testament everlasting life is offered to mankind by Christ, who is the only Mediator between God and man, being both God and man. Wherefore they are not to be heard who feign that the old fathers did look for only transitory promises. Although the law given from God by Moses as touching ceremonies and rites doth not bind Christians, nor ought the civil precepts thereof of necessity be received in any commonwealth, yet notwithstanding, no Christian whatsoever is free from obedience of the commandments which are called moral.

7. OF ORIGINAL SIN

Original sin is the corruption of the nature of every man that naturally is engendered of the offspring of Adam, whereby man is very far gone from the original righteousness, and of his own nature inclined to evil, and that continually.

8. OF FREE WILL

The condition of man after the fall of Adam is such that he cannot turn and prepare himself, by his own natural strength and works, to faith and calling upon God; wherefore, we have no power to do good works, pleasant and acceptable to God, without the grace of God by Christ enabling us, that we may have a good will, and working with us, when we have that good will.

9. OF JUSTIFICATION

We are accounted righteous before God, only for the merit of our Lord and Saviour Jesus Christ, by faith, and not for our own works or deservings. Wherefore, that we are justified by faith only is a most wholesome doctrine, and very full of comfort.

10. OF SANCTIFICATION

Sanctification is the setting apart of the regenerated person by the Holy Ghost (or spirit) received through faith in Jesus Christ, whose blood of atonement cleanseth from all sin; whereby we are not only delivered from the guilt of sin, but are washed from its pollution, saved from its power. It is also the continuing of God's grace by which the Christian may constantly grow in grace and in the knowledge of our Lord and Savior Jesus Christ.

11. OF GOOD WORKS

Although good works, which are the fruits of faith, and follow after justification, cannot put away our sins, and endure the severity of God's judgments; yet they are pleasing and acceptable to God in Christ, and spring out of a true and lively faith, insomuch that by them a lively faith may be as evidently known as a tree is discerned by its fruit.

12. OF WORKS OF SUPEREROGATION

Voluntary works—besides, over and above God's commandments—which are called works of supererogation, cannot be taught without arrogancy and impiety. For by them men do declare that they do not only render unto God as much as they are bound to do, but that they do more for his sake than of bounden duty is required;

whereas, Christ saith plainly, "When ye have done all that is commanded of you, say, 'We are unprofitable servants'."

13. OF SIN AFTER JUSTIFICATION

Not every sin willingly committed after justification is the sin against the Holy Ghost, and unpardonable. Wherefore, the grant of repentance is not to be denied to such as fall into sin after justification. After we have received the Holy Ghost, we may depart from grace given, and fall into sin, and by the grace of God rise again and amend our lives. And therefore they are to be condemned who say they can no more sin as long as they live here; or deny the place of forgiveness to such as truly repent.

14. OF THE CHURCH

The visible Church of Christ is a congregation of faithful men in which the pure Word of God is preached, and the ordinances duly administered according to Christ's command in all those things that of necessity are requisite to the same.

15. OF PURGATORY

The Romish doctrine concerning purgatory, pardon, worshiping and adoration, as well of images, as of relics, and also invocation of saints, is a fond thing vainly invented and grounded upon no warrant of Scripture, but repugnant to the word of God.

16. OF SPEAKING

It is a thing plainly repugnant to the Word of God, and the custom of the primitive church, to have the prayer in the church, or to minister the ordinances, in a tongue not understood by the people.

17. OF THE ORDINANCES

Ordinances of Christ are not only badges or tokens of Christian men's professions: but rather they are certain signs of grace and God's good-will towards us, by which he doth work invisibly in us, and doth not only quicken, but also strengthen and confirm our faith in him.

There are two ordinances of Christ our Lord in the Gospel; that is to say, Baptism and the Supper of the Lord.

18. OF BAPTISM

Baptism by Immersion is not only a sign of profession and mark of difference, whereby Christians are distinguished from others that are not baptized, but it is also a sign of regeneration or the new birth. It is not to be considered the door into the Fundamental Methodist Church. The dedication of young children may be retained in the church, but they are not to be baptized.

19. OF THE LORD'S SUPPER

The Supper of the Lord is not only a sign of the love that Christians ought to have among themselves one to another, but rather is an ordinance of our redemption by Christ's death; insomuch, that to such as rightly, worthily, and with faith receive the same, the bread which we break is a partaking of the body of Christ; and likewise the cup of blessing is the partaking of the blood of Christ.

Transubstantiation, or the change of the substance of bread and wine in the Supper of our Lord, cannot be proved by Holy Writ, but is repugnant to the Plain words of Scripture, overthroweth the nature of the ordinance, and hath given occasion to many superstitions.

The body of Christ is given, taken, and eaten in the Supper, only after a heavenly and spiritual manner. And the means whereby the body of Christ is received and eaten in the Supper is faith.

The Lord's Supper was not by Christ's ordinance reserved, carried about, lifted up, or worshiped.

20. OF BOTH KINDS

The cup of the Lord is not to be denied to the lay people; for both parts of the Lord's Supper by Christ's ordinance and commandment ought to be administered to all Christians alike.

21. OF THE ONE OBLIGATION OF CHRIST FINISHED ON THE CROSS

The offering of Christ, once made, is that perfect redemption, propitiation and satisfaction for all the sins of the whole world, both original and actual; and there is none other satisfaction for sin but that alone. Wherefore the sacrifice of masses, in the which it is commonly said that the priest doth offer Christ for the quick and the dead, to have remission of pain or guilt, is a blasphemous fable and dangerous deceit.

22. OF THE RESURRECTION OF THE DEAD

There shall be two resurrections of the dead, one of the just and the other of the unjust, at which time the souls and bodies will be reunited to receive a just retribution for the deeds done in this life. These resurrections shall be a thousand years apart, according to the Scriptures. (I Thess. 4:16, 17. Rev. 20:5)

23. OF THE JUDGMENTS

There will be a judgment of the saints following the first resurrection at the judgment seat of Christ; then there will be the judgment of the wicked at the great White Throne judgment to adjudge them to everlasting punishment suited to the demerit of their sins. (II Cor. 5:10, Rev. 20:1, 15)

24. OF THE MARRIAGE OF MINISTERS

The ministers of Christ are not commanded by God's law either to vow the state of single life, or to abstain from marriage; therefore, it is lawful for them, as for all Christians, to marry at their own discretion, as they shall judge the same to serve best to godliness.

25. OF THE RITES AND CEREMONIES OF CHURCHES

It is not necessary that rites and ceremonies should in all places be the same, or exactly alike; for they have been always different, and may be changed according to the diversity of countries, times and men's manners, so that nothing be ordained against God's Word. Whosoever, through his private judgment, willingly and purposely doth openly break the rites and ceremonies of the Church to which he belongs, which are not repugnant to the Word of God, and are ordained and approved by common authority, ought to be rebuked openly (that others may fear to do the like), as one that offendeth against the common order of the Church, and woundeth the consciences of weak brethren.

26. OF THE RULERS OF THE UNITED STATES OF AMERICA

The President, the Congress, the General Assemblies, the Governors and the Councils of State, as the delegates of the people, are the rulers of the United States of America, according to the division of power made to them by the Constitution of the United States, and by the Constitution of their respective states. And the said states are a sovereign and independent nation, and ought not to be subject to any foreign jurisdiction.

27. OF CHRISTIAN MEN'S GOODS

The riches and goods of Christians are not common, as touching the right, title and possession of the same, as some do falsely boast. Notwithstanding, every man ought, of such things as he possesseth, liberally to give alms to the poor, according to his ability.

28. OF A CHRISTIAN MAN'S OATH

As we confess that vain and rash swearing is forbidden Christian men by our Lord Jesus Christ, and James his Apostle, so we judge that the Christian religion doth not prohibit, but that a man may swear, or affirm, when the magistrate requireth, in a cause of faith and charity, so it be done according to the prophet's teaching, in justice, judgment and truth.

(Note affixed by the General Conference at Ash Grove, Missouri August 1964)

These articles of religion set forth the doctrinal teachings of the Fundamental Methodist Church, and those who enter the ministry thereof thereby avow their acceptance of the teachings thus formulated; and good faith towards the Church forbids any teaching on their part which is at variance with them.

Notes: *While based upon the Twenty-five Articles of Religion of the United Methodist Church, the Articles of Religion of the Fundamental Methodist Church make enough additions and changes to warrant its inclusion in its entirety. Noteworthy are an article against the practice of speaking in tongues (Pentecostalism) and several on eschatology.*

* * *

ADDITIONS TO THE *TWENTY-FIVE ARTICLES OF RELIGION* (SOUTHERN METHODIST CHURCH)

OF PREVENIENT (PRECEDING) GRACE

40. We believe that God must take the initiative if man is to be saved. We believe that since the race fell in Adam and lost all claims to consideration before God, along with the ability in its own strength to return to God, we have in the blessings of life, health, friends, fruitful seasons, prosperity, the delay of punishment, the presence and influence of the Bible, the Holy Spirit, and the church, manifestations of the prevenient grace of God. Prevenient grace is not sufficient for salvation, yet it reveals the goodness of God to all sinful creatures. We believe that the prevenient grace of God constitutes the medium through which the Holy Spirit can operate upon the sinner, and that which makes the soul susceptible to the saving grace of Christ. In other words, we hold that God, in His grace, makes it possible for *all* men to be saved.

Titus 2:11, "For the grace of God that bringeth salvation hath appeared to all men." Gen. 3:8, 9; Isa. 59:15, 16; Rom. 2:4; Prov. 1:23; Isa. 31:6; Eze. 14:6; 18:32; Joel 2:13, 14; Matt. 18:3; Acts 3:19; I Kings 8:47; Matt. 3:2; Mark 1:15; Luke 13:3, 5; Acts 2:38; 17:30; II Chr. 20:20; Isa. 43:10; John 1:9; 6:29; 14:1; Acts 16:31; Phil. 1:29; I John 3:23.

OF REPENTANCE

41. We believe that salvation comes to the individual soul as the free, undeserved gift of God through faith in Christ as a personal Saviour. We do not believe that the sinner is in a proper attitude for the reception of salvation until there is first a change of mind, will, and emotions concerning sin, and this results in a godly sorrow for sin in the heart of the individual.

These changes concerning one's sins constitute the grace of repentance, which grace is wrought in the sinner by the Holy Spirit, and which leads the sinner to forsake his sins and to seek the justifying mercy of God in Christ.

Acts 17:30, "God . . . commandeth all men every where to repent." Rom. 3:20; cf. 1:32; Psm. 51:3,7; Job 42:56; Psm. 51:1,2; II Cor. 7:9, 10; Matt 3:8, 11; Rom. 2:4; II Peter 3:9; Acts 2:38; Rev. 2:5; Acts 11:18; 5:31; II Tim. 2:25; Matt. 11:20, 21; Luke 16:30, 31; Rev. 3:19; John 3:5; Acts 20:21.

OF FAITH

42. We believe that after the Spirit of God has implanted within the human soul the grace of repentance, there remains a condition, on the part of the sinner, namely, belief in the Lord Jesus Christ as personal Saviour.

This belief is infinitely more than a mere mental assent to any doctrine concerning either the person of Christ or of any of His miraculous or atoning works.

Rom. 10:10, "For with the heart man believeth unto righteousness; and with the mouth confession is made unto salvation." Acts 16:31; Eph. 2:8, 9; Rom. 5:1; cf. 9:30, 32; Gal. 3:5, 14; I Peter 1:5; Rom. 11:20; II Cor. 1:24; I John 5:4; Isa. 7:9; II Cor. 5:7; Heb. 11:6; John 16:9; Rom. 14:23; John 7:38; Acts 27:24, 25; Heb. 11:1; Eccl. 1:13; Dan. 2:30; I Kings 3:9; Ex. 35:29; Prov. 4:23; Rom. 10:14; Psm. 9:10; John 2:23. 24; Rom. 10:17; 1:19, 20; 10:14; Psm. 106:12, 13; Matt. 13:20, 21; Mark 12:32-34; John 5:35; Prov. 23:26; Matt. 11:28, 29; Luke 14:26, 33; John 1:12; 4:14; 6:53, 54; Rev. 3:20; II Peter 1:1; John 5:47; Acts 4:4; Heb. 12:2; Judges 6:14; Matt. 25:29; II Thess. 3:2.

OF REGENERATION

43. When the penitent, believing soul is justified through the atoning merits of the blood of Christ, simultaneously there takes place within that soul the washing of regeneration, which work is the act of the Holy Ghost, and which results in the new creation of the whole spiritual being.

This definite change in the sinner is referred to in the Word of God as "the new birth" or "being born again." Although the believer is truly born of God and is definitely His child at the time of regeneration, he is but a babe in Christ, and God desires that His babes reach maturity. If there is to be maturity, the seed of holiness that has been sown in the heart in regeneration must be permitted to germinate and spring up, and with a prayerful cultivation and studying of God's Word, under the bountiful showers of God's grace, produce a full harvest of the fruit of the Spirit.

II Cor. 5:17, "Therefore if any man be in Christ, he is a new creature; old things are passed away; behold, all things are become new." John 3:3; James 1:18; John 3:14-16; I Peter 1:3; I Cor. 4:15; Titus 3:5; I John 3:9; 5:4, 18; 5:1; Psm. 119:97; Matt. 5:44; 7:11; Rom. 8:16, 17.

OF THE WITNESS OF THE SPIRIT

44. We believe that a penitent sinner is saved the moment he believes upon Christ as his personal Saviour, however; he cannot have full assurance that he has passed from death unto life until the Holy Spirit, Himself, gives him this assurance. Our souls must hear a more authoritative voice and have a more compelling evidence than that which came from our own feeble human senses.

Rom. 8:16, "The Spirit itself beareth witness with our spirit, that we are the children of God." John 3:5, 6; Titus 3:5; I John 1:3; I Cor. 1:9; Gal. 4:6; John 16:12, 13; I Cor. 2:12.

OF CHRISTIAN PERFECTION OR SANCTIFICATION OR CONSECRATION OR DEDICATION OR PERFECT LOVE OR TOTAL YIELDEDNESS

45. Christian perfection is that work of the Holy Spirit which is subsequent to regeneration, and is wrought when the believer presents himself a living sacrifice, holy and acceptable unto God, and is thus enabled through grace to love God with all his heart. Methodists have always been very clear and positive in their teachings that this is not angelic, adamic, faultless perfection, but rather that Christian perfection where the soul is filled with the love of God and all its faculties are spiritualized through the fullness of God's presence within. While in this state, God is loved with every faculty of one's being, and one's neighbors are loved as one's self.

I John 1:9, "If we confess our sins, He is faithful and just to forgive us our sins, and to cleanse us from all unrighteousness." Gen. 17:1; Duet. 36; Psm. 138; Ezek. 36:25-29; Matt. 5:48; Luke 1:74, 75; John 17:2-23; Rom. 8:3, 4; 11:26; I Cor. 6:11; 14:20; Eph. 4:13, 24; 5:25-27; Phil. 2:5, 7; Col. 4:12; I Thess. 3:10; 5:23; II Thess. 2:13; II Tim. 3:17; Titus 2:12; Heb. 9:13, 14; 10:14, 18:22; James 1:27; 4:8; I Peter 1:10; II Peter 1:4; I John 1:7; 3:8, 9; 4:17, 18; Jude 24.

OF THE UNIVERSALITY OF THE ATONEMENT

46. We believe that God is a mighty God, and that He is unlimited in greatness, grandeur, and power; that He is loving and benevolent and is seeking wholeheartedly and continuously for the highest well-being and the eternal happiness of all His moral creatures. We believe that in keeping with His benevolent nature, God has given His only begotten Son, not for a few favored ones, but for the whole world, that "whosoever believeth in Him should not perish, but have everlasting life," John 3:16.

We believe that in order to enable His moral creatures to avail themselves of this salvation in His Son, God has given to everyone a power of choice—the ability to choose or reject salvation and spiritual life in Christ. This power being given to Adam, it will be possessed by each one of his sons and daughters throughout all time.

We believe that even though God foreknows all things, His foreknowledge in no way affects the destiny of any soul. Even though the Holy Spirit works upon the will, mind, and emotions of man, He does not work to the point of absolute compulsion. Man's will, mind, and emotions, being aroused and fully awakened by the Holy Spirit, must cooperate with Him. There must be a full and mutual agreement between the two before the human party can become the beneficiary of salvation. God works, while the believing heart of man responds. "For it is God which worketh in you both to will and to do of His good pleasure," Phil. 2:13.

Thus, we do not believe in unconditional predestination, but we do believe that when the conditions of salvation are fully met by the sinner, that sinner is then elected to be saved.

I Tim. 4:10; John 1:29; I Tim. 2:6; Titus 2:11; II Peter 2:1; 3:9; Heb. 2:9; I John 2:2; II Cor. 5:18-20.

OF PERSEVERANCE

47. We believe that every true child of God, being a free moral agent, may, and will be saved eternally, if he meets the divine conditions of repentance and faith until the last. Habitual and final failure to meet these basic conditions will bring eternal loss. We believe also that although a Christian is now in a state of salvation, and would be saved eternally if called before God in his present state, he must be kept under the saving power of the Holy Ghost until the last, if he would be saved eternally hereafter. All who in their obedience to the Holy Spirit faithfully meet

these conditions until death will inherit everlasting life.

Heb. 6:4-6, "For it is impossible for those who were once enlightened . . . if they shall fall away, to renew them again unto repentance . . . " I Chron. 28:9; Ezek. 18:24, 33; 12:13, 18; Matt. 5:13; Luke 9:62; John 15:1-6; Rom. 11:20-22; I Cor. 9:27; 10:12; I Tim. 1:19, 20; 5:12, 15; II Tim. 1:14, 15; Heb. 4:1, 11; 10:26-29, 38, 39; 12:14, 15; II Peter 1:8-10; 2:18-22; Rev. 2:4, 5; 3:10, 11.

OF THE CHURCH

48. The visible church of Christ is a congregation of faithful men, in which the pure Word of God is preached, and the sacraments duly administered according to Christ's ordinance, in all those things that of necessity are requisite to the same.

By the invisible church is understood all those who are known of Christ as belonging to Him, whether they have joined the visible church or not.

I Cor. 12:27, "Now ye are the body of Christ, and members in particular." II Tim. 2:19; Eph. 4:12, 13; 5:26, 27; Heb. 12:22-24; I John 3:2, 3; Rev. 19:7, 8; I Tim. 3:15; Col. 2:16-19.

OF INSPIRATION

49. We believe in the original manuscripts of the Bible as the inerrant Word of God, verbally inspired; by this we mean that inexplicable power which the divine Spirit put forth of old on the authors of Holy Scripture, in order to guide them even in the employment of the words they used, and to preserve them alike from all error and from all omission. We recognize the King James Version of the Bible as a trustworthy translation and we recommend that it be read from the pulpit.

I Peter 1:23, "Being born again . . . by the word of God, which liveth and abideth for ever." Deut. 27:26; II Kings 17:13; Psm. 19:7; 33:4; 119:89; Isa. 8:20; Gal. 3:10; II Peter 3:15, 16; II Tim. 3:16; II Peter 1:20, 21; John 10:34, 35; Luke 24:44; Matt. 5:17; 10:34; 12:34; 15:25; I Cor. 14:21; James 4:5; I John 3:24; Jude 19; Acts 2:4; I Cor. 2:13; 14:37; Gal. 1:12; I Thess. 2:13; 4:2, 8; Rev. 21:5; 22:6, 18, 19.

OF EVANGELIZATION OF THE WORLD

50. We believe in the evangelization of the world, placing emphasis upon the task of reaching the individual with the gospel and its implications, and that no humanitarian and philanthropic schemes may be substituted for the preaching of the Cross.

Mark 16:15, ". . . go ye into all the world, and preach the gospel to every creature." Matt. 28:19; Luke 24:46-48; Acts 1:8; 15:14; Rom. 11:25; Matt. 9:38; Phil. 4:15-18; Rom. 10:15; Matt. 5:13-16; I Cor. 3:9, 10; Eph. 4:11-16; Rev. 22:17.

OF CREATION

51. We believe in the Genesis account of creation, which teaches that all things found their origin in God, Who created by His own fiat instantaneously every living thing after its kind.

Gen. 1:1, 2, "In the beginning God created the heaven and the earth. And the earth was without form, and void . . . " Neh. 9:6; Col. 1:16, 17; Job 38:7; Ezek. 28:12-15; Isa. 14:9-14, 26; 5:18; Psm. 102:18; 139:13-16; Isa. 43:1, 7; 54:16; Ezek. 21:30; John 1:3; Acts 17:24; Rom. 11:36; Eph. 3:9; Rev. 4:11; Psm. 10:30; 148:5.

OF THE SECOND COMING OF CHRIST

52. We believe, according to Scripture, in the sure return of the Lord Jesus Christ; that his second coming will be a literal, bodily, personal, imminent, and premillennial return; that His coming for His bride, the church, constitutes the "blessed hope" set before us, for which we should be constantly looking.

Acts 1:11, ". . . this same Jesus, which is taken up from you into heaven, shall so come in like manner as ye have seen him go into heaven." John 14:1-3; Job 19:25-27; Dan. 12:1-4; Psm. 17:15; Isa. 11:1-12; Zech. 14:1-11; Matt. 24:1-51; 26:64; Mark 13:26-37; Luke 17:26-37; 21:24-36; Acts 1:9-11; I Cor. 1:7, 8; I Thess. 4:13-18; Titus 2:11-14; Heb. 9:27, 28; James 5:7, 8; II Peter 3:1-14; I John 3:2, 3; Jude 14; Rev. 1:7; 19:11-16; 22:6, 7, 12, 20.

OF SATAN, ANGELS, AND DEMONS

53. We believe in the reality of the person of good angels, bad angels, demons, and of Satan, "that old serpent, called the Devil, and Satan, which deceiveth the whole world." Rev. 12:9.

OF TITHING

54. We subscribe heartily to the scriptural command to give the tithe of all our increases to the Lord and the ongoing of His work on earth. Of course, we acknowledge that this law does not bind one saved by grace, but we hasten to say that this would be a poor excuse to do less for One whom we profess to love and One who gave His all for our salvation. We wish to state further that we believe that we are not giving until we have first tithed. We should also remember that God challenges us to try Him and see that He will pour upon those who do more than they can receive. So we conclude that a professed Christian who does not tithe is falling far short of the goal set for us, and thus misses the fullness of the abundant life in Christ.

OF SEGREGATION

55. The Southern Methodist Church is a segregated church. We do not believe that integration, for which so many are clamoring, is the answer to current social problems. In fact, it is our opinion that integration would produce more problems than it would solve.

OF SEPARATION

56. We believe that in these days of apostasy the church should be separated from compromising situations in the world. II Cor. 6:11-18; I Cor. 3:1-3; Rom. 16:17; II Thess. 3:6-9, 14, 15; Eph. 5:11; Titus 3:10, 11; Acts 15:19-29; II John 9-11.

ADDITIONS TO THE *TWENTY-FIVE ARTICLES OF RELIGION* (SOUTHERN METHODIST CHURCH) (continued)

Notes: *Besides the addition of a statement on civic duty for foreign members of the church, the Southern Methodist Church has added a variety of doctrinal statements to the Twenty-five Articles of Religion. These are set apart from the articles in a separate section of* The Doctrine and Discipline of the Southern Methodist Church *under the heading, "Other Southern Methodist Beliefs." Included is a belief in racial segregation.*

*   *   *

CONFESSIONAL STATEMENT (WESLEY BIBLICAL SEMINARY)

"We hold the following:

"1. The supreme authority of the Word of God which stands written in the sixty-six books of the Holy Bible, all therein being divinely inspired by Almighty God and therefore without error or defect in the autographs. Believing the Bible to be the Word of God written, the only infallible rule of faith and practice, Wesley Biblical Seminary asserts the authority of Scripture alone over the life of the Church and its individual members. We therefore believe that a reverent and loyal approach to the study of the Bible recognizes and affirms its full inspiration and its absolute trustworthiness as the divinely revealed and authoritative Word of God.

"2. The one true God as Creator, Sustainer and Sovereign Ruler of the Universe, eternally existent in the Holy Trinity of Father, Son, and Holy Spirit, each with personality and deity.

"3. The Son of God, our Lord Jesus Christ, as manifested in the flesh through a miraculous conception by the Holy Spirit and virgin birth, who lived a sinless life and then died on Calvary, making a full and satisfactory atonement for the sins of all men, rose bodily the third day, ascended into Heaven and is enthroned at God's right hand as our abiding Intercessor.

"4. The Holy Spirit as the Lord and Giver of life, taking the things of Jesus Christ and applying them to man and to his salvation and service. Assurance of personal salvation and the fruit of the Spirit are clearly distinguished from the gifts of the Spirit which are for the edification of the Church and which carry no guarantee of personal holiness or destiny.

"5. The special original creation of man in God's image and likeness and the willful disobedience through which man became deeply fallen and tragically lost apart from God's redeeming grace.

"6. The privilege and necessity of each person's being made a new creature in Christ by the life-giving Holy Spirit, adopted into God's family, and delivered from the penalty and practice of sinning. In this context sinning is regarded as known, willful violation of the will of God.

"7. The second definite work of grace subsequent to regeneration, accomplished by the baptism with the Holy Spirit, thereby purifying the heart from original sin and empowering for continuous growth in grace, victorious living and fruitful service. The result of this epochal experience—termed perfect love and/or entire sanctification—is maintained by faith as expressed in continuous obedience to God's revealed will, thus giving perfect cleansing moment by moment (Acts 15:8-9; I Thessalonians 5:23; I John 1:7-9; 4:13-21). Life in the Spirit is dynamically expressed in maturing and enabling grace to progress from glory to glory in personal holiness and Christian mission (II Corinthians 3:18).

"8. The possibility of forfeiting divine grace and being lost since persons are Christians solely by their willing response to the gracious call and enablings of the Holy Spirit. However, backsliders may be restored to their forfeited state of grace if they truly repent and return to the Lord in obedient faith.

"9. The Church as the living body of Christ, constituting all who are united by faith to Him as members of His body and who are under the commandment to love one another with pure and fervent hearts. While in its spiritual essence the Church is an organism created by the Holy Spirit, it is also a divine-human institution functioning visibly on earth. As an institution its divinely assigned mission is the universal proclamation of the Gospel. Application of the Gospel in the political, social, and economic needs of mankind is inherently proper, but secondary and subservient to its primarily spiritual commission.

"10. At the end of this Age, the return of Jesus Christ to gather His Church, to judge the world and to rule over all in righteousness.

"11. The everlasting blessedness of all who die in Christ and the everlasting pain and loss of all others.

"12. The obligation of all who are truly Christ's to live righteously, joyously, and sacrificially, to endeavor to bring salvation to all persons everywhere, and to express compassionate love in ministering to every kind of human need.

"13. No change shall be allowed or made in this Doctrinal Statement of Wesley Biblical Seminary."

Notes: *The Wesley Biblical Seminary is closely associated with the Methodist Protestant Church. Wesley's position is representative of a conservative holiness position held by Methodists in various conservative denominations across the South and to a lesser extent, the United States. Each member of the faculty must ascribe to the statement.*

Black Methodism

ADDITIONS TO THE *TWENTY-FIVE ARTICLES OF RELIGION* (AFRICAN METHODIST EPISCOPAL CHURCH)

FOOTNOTE TO ARTICLE XXIII

Obedience to Civil Government, however, is one of the principal duties of all men, and was honored by our Lord and His Apostles. Though differing in form and policy, all righteous governments rightfully command the obedience, loyalty, support, and defense of all Christian men and women as that they control and protect.

SPECIAL DECLARATION ON APOSTOLIC SUCCESSION

WHEREAS, We have heard with deep regret the dogma of Apostolic Succession and the distinct and separate priesthood of the ministry preached in our pulpit, and

WHEREAS, There are those among us members of this body who are said to be seeking reordination at the hands of the Episcopal Bishops, and Bishops of the Protestant Episcopal Church, and

WHEREAS, We have strong reasons for believing that what is thus reported has some foundation in fact, therefore be it

Resolved, By this, Eighteenth General Conference now assembled, that we set forth the following declarations and that any person or persons who are not in harmony with the same or cannot subscribe thereto are hereby declared out of harmony with the standards of Methodism and are liable to impeachment for propagating error and sowing dissension to wit:

We hold and believe that there is no separate priesthood under the Christian symbol set over the Church. That the sacerdotal theory of the Christian ministry is a dishonor to our Lord Jesus and is especially condemned by the tenor of the Epistle to the Hebrews.

Second—That while there is a separate ministry in the New Testament representing the universal priesthood or membership of the Church, yet as has been affirmed above, each and every member is a king and priest under God.

Third—That we recognize the two orders and the one office in our church to be the regularly ordained ministry, and that we are satisfied with the ordinations of the same, holding it to be valid and true in every respect.

Fourth—That the doctrine of Apostolic Succession, according to our belief as Methodists, is erroneous. That there is an uninterrupted succession of ministers which the divine eye can trace up to the Apostolic times, there can be no doubt. But it is utterly impossible to prove that in any part of the world there is a ministry that can trace its orders up through episcopal hands to the Apostles.

Fifth—"That the Apostles had and could have no successors from the fact that their authority, indicated in two ways, was first to teach Christianity by words and writing, for which they had the gift of inspiration in a special sense; and secondly, to found the church, for which they had the power of the keys of binding and loosing, that is, of

uttering unchangeable decrees of ecclesiastical government; that a succession of such men would not have been in harmony with the known will of Christ."

Sixth—That there is an identity between the Bishops and Elders or Presbyters as is evident from Acts 20:17-28; Titus 1:5-7; First Peter 5:1, 2; Phil. 1:1; First Timothy 3:1-8. But as every body must have a head, the Bishops among us are Primus Inter Pares—"Chief among the Elders."

Seventh—That a reordination of any Bishop, Elder, or Deacon by any other ecclesiastical authority cannot and will not be tolerated in the African Methodist Episcopal Church.

Eighth—Any person or persons who shall violate these Declarations by preaching the Dogma of Apostolic Succession shall be guilty of a breach of Discipline and shall be tried and, if found guilty, be suspended or expelled at the discretion of the committee before whom such person or persons shall be tried.

RITUALISM

WHEREAS, We believe that the doctrines, practices, usages, and genius of American Methodism as believed, observed, and conformed to by the founders of African Methodism and their successors to the present day, should in their entirety without modification, restriction, or enlargement, be believed, practiced, and conformed to by us and by those entrusted with the continued preservation and development of African Methodism in its historic and progressive relations, and

WHEREAS, We further believe that in all things essential as touching the doctrines, government, services, order and work of the African Methodist Episcopal Church there should be oneness of purpose, concurrent opinion, continuity of methods and harmony of feeling and relation between the several factors that compose the whole,

Resolved: First—we hold as the result of our best knowledge based upon the facts of history and the teachings of experience, (the same resulting primarily from the origin and development of American Methodism and secondarily from Methodism), that it is highly expedient we set forth the concurrent beliefs, practices, and usages of African Methodism; and in view of this, we do not hesitate to affirm that the Dogma of Apostolic Succession is foreign and repugnant to the concurrent beliefs and teachings of the African Methodist Episcopal Church, and that no Bishop or preacher shall be allowed to publicly proclaim opinions and views favorable thereto.

Second—As touching the usages and practices of the African Methodist Episcopal Church, we are free to aver that while it is desirable to secure uniformity in the order of the public services and to enlist, so far as possible, the thought and spirit of the people in the same, and while we grant that the orderly repetition of the Decalogue, the Apostles' Creed, and the Responsive Reading of the Scriptures may conduce to the attainment therefore, we strenuously deny that the presence and use of heavy and prosy ritualistic service in our public congregations will in any sense increase their spiritual interest and we deprecate any and all efforts that favor the introduction of extreme ritualism in connection with our public services.

ADDITIONS TO THE *TWENTY-FIVE ARTICLES OF RELIGION*
(AFRICAN METHODIST EPISCOPAL CHURCH) (continued)

Third—That all laws or parts of laws in conflict with the spirit and language of these resolutions be and the same are hereby repealed. General Conference, 1884.

Notes: *As a group, the black Methodist denominations have retained in their constitution the restrictive rule preventing any changes in the Twenty-five Articles of Religion. However, that has not prevented the churches from adopting explanatory footnotes and additional doctrinal statements, even though these may not share the status of the Articles of Religion.*

The African Methodist Church has adopted a footnote to Article XXIII of the Articles of Religion for the benefit of foreign members. In addition, it has adopted statements on apostolic succession and ritualism. These follow the Articles of Religion in the Church's Discipline, but are set apart in a separate section.

* * *

ADDITIONS TO THE *TWENTY-FIVE ARTICLES OF RELIGION* (AFRICAN METHODIST EPISCOPAL ZION CHURCH)

XXIII. OF THE RULERS OF THE UNITED STATES OF AMERICA

23. The President, the Congress, the General Assemblies, the Governors and the Councils of State as the Delegates of the People, are the Rulers of the United States of America, according to the division of power made to them by the Constitution of the United States, and by the Constitutions of their respective States. And the said States are a sovereign and independent Nation, and ought not to be subject to any foreign jurisdiction. As far as it respects civil affairs, we believe it the duty of Christians, and especially all Christian Ministers, to be subject to the supreme authority of the country where they may reside and to use all laudable means to enjoin obedience to the powers that be; and, therefore, it is expected that all our Preachers and People who may be under any foreign Government will behave themselves as peaceable and orderly subjects.

Notes: *Though bound by a restrictive rule preventing the alteration of the Articles of Religion, the AMEZ Church added material to Article XXIII.*

* * *

ADDITIONS TO THE *TWENTY-FIVE ARTICLES OF RELIGION* (CHRISTIAN METHODIST EPISCOPAL CHURCH)

As far as it respects civil affairs we believe it the duty of Christians and especially all Christian ministers, to be subject to the supreme authority of the country where they reside, and to use all laudable means to enjoin obedience to the powers that be and therefore it is expected that all our preachers and people, who may be under any foreign government, will behave themselves as peaceable and orderly subjects.

Notes: *Like the United Methodist Church and African Methodist Episcopal Church, the Christian Methodist Episcopal Church has added a footnote to Article XXIII for the benefit of foreign members.*

* * *

German Methodism

CONFESSION OF FAITH OF THE CHURCH OF THE UNITED BRETHREN

In the name of God we declare and confess before all men, that we believe in the only true God, the Father, the Son, and the Holy Ghost; that these three are one—the Father in the Son, the Son in the Father, and the Holy Ghost equal in essence or being with both; that this triune God created the heavens and the earth and all that in them is, visible as well as invisible, and furthermore sustains, governs, protects and supports the same.

We believe in Jesus Christ; that He is very God and man; that He became incarnate by the power of the Holy Ghost in the Virgin Mary and was born of her; that He is the Savior and Mediator of the whole human race, if they with full faith in Him accept the grace proffered in Jesus; that this Jesus suffered and died on the cross for us, was buried, arose again on the third day, ascended into heaven, and sitteth on the right hand of God to intercede for us; and that He shall come again at the last day to judge the quick and the dead.

We believe in the Holy Ghost; that He is equal in being with the Father and the Son, and that He comforts the faithful, and guides them into all truth.

We believe in a holy Christian church, the communion of saints, the resurrection of the body, and life everlasting.

We believe that the Holy Bible, Old and New Testaments, is the Word of God; that it contains the only true way of our salvation; that every true Christian is bound to acknowledge and receive it with the influence of the Spirit of God as the only rule and guide; and that without faith in Jesus Christ, true repentance, forgiveness of sins and following after Christ, no one can be a true Christian.

We also believe that what is contained in the Holy Scriptures, to-wit; the fall in Adam and redemption through Jesus Christ, shall be preached throughout the world.

We believe that the ordinances, viz: baptism and the remembrance of the sufferings and death of our Lord Jesus Christ, are to be in use and practiced by all Christian societies; and that it is incumbent on all the children of God particularly to practice them; but the manner in which, ought always to be left to the judgment and understanding of every individual. Also the example of washing feet is left to the judgment of every one to practice or not; but it is not becoming of any of our preachers or members to traduce any of their brethren whose judgment and understanding in these respects is different from their own, either in public or in private. Whosoever shall make himself guilty in this respect, shall be considered a traducer of his brethren, and shall be answerable for the same.

Notes: *Methodism spread through the German-American community in the early nineteenth century via two groups, the United Brethren in Christ and the Evangelical Association. Both eventually authored their own doctrinal statements. The association experienced a major schism in 1894. However, the two factions reunited in 1922 to emerge as the Evangelical Church. In 1946 the United Brethren and Evangelical Church merged to become the Evangelical United Brethren. In 1962 that church replaced the prior doctrinal statements of both churches with a new Confession of Faith, which is now a part of the doctrinal standards of the United Methodist Church.*

The United Brethren had originally adopted its Confession of Faith in 1841. In 1885 several changes made in the constitution, including some in the confession, were among the causes of a schism by conservatives who retained the unaltered constitution. The conservative group continues to exist as the Church of the United Brethren.

* * *

ARTICLES OF RELIGION (EVANGELICAL CONGREGATIONAL CHURCH)

The following Articles contain our confession of Christian Faith:

101. OF GOD

There is but one true and living God, an eternal Being, a Spirit without body, indivisible, of infinite power, wisdom, and goodness, the Creator and Preserver of all things, visible and invisible. In this Godhead there is a Trinity, of one substance and power, and co-eternal, namely, the Father, the Son, and the Holy Ghost.

102. OF JESUS CHRIST

The Lord Jesus Christ, who is the only begotten Son of God, was born of the Virgin Mary, grew into perfect manhood and became acquainted with all the infirmities, temptations, and sorrows of men. In Him dwelt all the fullness of the Godhead, so that, uniting Deity and humanity in one Christ, He is sole Mediator between God and man. He gave His life a ransom for all, and by His death on the cross made a full, perfect and sufficient sacrifice, oblation, and satisfaction for the sins of the whole world. He rose from the dead and ascended into heaven, wherein He abideth, our great High-Priest and King, and must reign until all things are put in subjection under him.

103. OF THE HOLY SPIRIT

The Holy Spirit, proceeding from the Father and the Son, and of the same eternal nature, power, and glory, is everywhere present with men to convict of sin, work newness of life in them that believe, and lead them into all truth.

104. OF THE HOLY SCRIPTURES

By the Holy Scriptures we understand those canonical books of the Old and New Testaments, which the church has at all times received as such. These books in order are as follows:

The Old Testament

Genesis, Exodus, Leviticus, Numbers, Deuteronomy, Joshua, Judges, Ruth, I Samuel, II Samuel, I Kings, II Kings, I Chronicles, II Chronicles, Ezra, Nehemiah, Esther, Job, the Psalms, the Proverbs of Solomon, Ecclesiastes, Song of Solomon, Isaiah, Jeremiah, Lamentations, Ezekiel, Daniel, Hosea, Joel, Amos, Obadiah, Jonah, Micah, Nahum, Habakkuk, Zephaniah, Haggai, Zechariah, Malachi.

The New Testament

Matthew, Mark, Luke, John, The Acts, Epistle to the Romans, I Corinthians, II Corinthians, Galatians, Ephesians, Philippians, Colossians, I Thessalonians, II Thessalonians, I Timothy, II Timothy, Titus, Philemon, Hebrews, Epistle of James, I Peter, II Peter, I John, II John, III John, Jude, Revelation.

These Scriptures, given by Divine inspiration, contain the will of God concerning us in all things necessary to our salvation; so that whatever is not contained therein nor can be proved thereby is not to be enjoined on any as an article of faith.

105. OF HUMAN DEPRAVITY

All men have sinned, and they inherit a depravity of nature which is continually propagated in the entire race of Adam. This corruption of nature so far removes them from the original righteousness of man that of themselves they have no ability to recover from their fallen condition, but are continually inclined to that which is evil.

106. OF SALVATION THROUGH CHRIST

The love of God has made salvation possible to all through the mediation of Jesus Christ, whereby every man is graciously provided with freedom of will to accept or reject the offer of eternal life.

107. OF REPENTANCE

Repentance is sorrow for sin, wrought in the heart by the power of the Holy Spirit. The awakened sinner is thereby made to recognize the holiness of God, the righteousness of His law and the guilt and shame of his own perverse nature. Thus deeply humbled he turns unto God and forsakes his sins.

108. OF JUSTIFICATION

Justification is that act of God by which, when we yield ourselves in full confidence to our Saviour, Jesus Christ, we are freely acquitted from the guilt of sin and accounted righteous in His sight. We are accordingly justified, not by works which we perform, but by faith in Him who died for us.

109. OF REGENERATION

Regeneration is that work of the Holy Spirit wrought in us whereby we are made partakers of the divine nature and experience newness of life in Christ Jesus. By this new birth the believer becomes a child of God, receives the spirit of adoption and is made an heir of the kingdom of heaven.

110. OF THE WITNESS OF THE SPIRIT

The witness of the Spirit is an inward impression on the soul, whereby the Spirit of God, the heavenly Comforter, immediately convinces the regenerate believer that he has passed from death unto life, that his sins are all forgiven, and that he is a child of God.

111. OF SANCTIFICATION

Entire sanctification, or Christian perfection, is a state of righteousness and true holiness, which every regenerate believer may attain. It consists in being cleansed from all sin, loving God with all the heart, soul, mind, and strength, and loving our neighbor as ourselves. This gracious state of perfect love is attainable in this life by faith, both gradually and instantaneously, and should be earnestly sought by every child of God; but it does not deliver us from the infirmities, ignorance and mistakes which are common to man.

112. OF GOOD WORKS

The Holy Spirit dwelling in man begets within him love, joy, peace, long suffering, gentleness, temperance, and all other ennobling virtues, and these show themselves in numerous outward acts, which become so many evidences of a living faith. Although such good works cannot put away sin, they are ever well-pleasing and acceptable in the sight of God.

113. OF APOSTASY

The gracious help of God is pledged to all those who continue steadfast in faith; but, on account of man's free will, which no power may coerce, apostasy from God is possible so long as we continue in the flesh. Wherefore, constant watchfulness, prayer, and holy living are necessary on the part of man, lest he fall away from the grace of God, grieve and quench the Holy Spirit, and lose his soul at last.

114. OF IMMORTALITY

The soul of man is immortal, and, on its separation from the body at death, continues in a conscious state of existence in the world of spirits. It there either enters into bliss or undergoes torment, according to its character as formed and fixed in the present life.

115. OF THE RESURRECTION

Christ did truly rise from the dead, and took again his own body, and ascended into heaven. Likewise, all the dead shall be raised up by the power of God through Christ, both the just and the unjust; but those who have done good shall come forth unto an eternal life of glory, and those who have wrought wickedness shall be adjudged to everlasting punishment.

116. OF THE FINAL JUDGMENT

God has appointed a day in which He will judge all men by Jesus Christ, to whom is committed the judgment of this world. We must all, accordingly, appear before the judgment-seat of Christ and have our eternal destiny determined according to our works.

117. OF HEAVEN

Our Lord and Saviour Jesus Christ has provided for those who are redeemed by His grace a heavenly and eternal rest, into which He purposes ultimately to gather them and dwell with them in unspeakable glory. There shall be no more sorrow, pain or death, and the glorified saints shall see God and walk in His light forever.

118. OF HELL

The incorrigible sinner, having rejected Christ and all the offers and opportunities of grace, is without God, and without hope in the world, and makes himself a child of Satan. When he dies his soul awakes to the torment of hell, from which there is no promise or hope of deliverance, but the sentence of everlasting punishment prepared for the devil and his angels.

119. OF THE CHURCH

The Holy General Church consists of the great body of believers who confess the Lord Jesus Christ and have life in Him. The individual church is a congregation or society of Christian believers, in which the pure worship of God is maintained, His holy word is preached, and His commandments and ordinances are sacredly observed.

120. OF THE MINISTRY

The ministry of the Gospel is a sacred office and calling, ordained by Christ for the proclamation of His truth in all the world and for the orderly administration of the sacraments, the worship, and the discipline of the Church. No man may assume this office without the conviction of a divine call thereto, and the recognition and ratification of that call by the Church.

121. OF BAPTISM

The sacrament of baptism is the formal application of water to an infant, or to an adult believer, in the name of the Father, and of the Son, and of the Holy Spirit, as a visible sign and seal that the person so consecrated stands in a holy covenant relation to God and His people.

122. OF THE LORD'S SUPPER

The Lord's Supper is not merely a token of love and union that Christians ought to have among themselves, but is a sacrament instituted in memory of the sufferings and death of Christ, whereby those who rightly and worthily receive the same partake of the body and blood of Christ by faith, not in a bodily but in a spiritual manner, in eating the broken bread and in drinking the blessed cup. We thereby also continually show forth our Christian faith and hope.

123. OF CHURCH POLITY

The Lord Jesus Christ ordained no particular form of government for His church, so that whatever polity, rules, regulations, rites, and ceremonies are adopted and approved by common authority, and are not repugnant to the word of God, may be acknowledged as sufficient to constitute a true church of the living God. Such polity, rules, rites, and ceremonies may be lawfully changed from time to time, as the needs of men and the diversity of nations, countries, and manners may require.

124. OF CIVIL GOVERNMENT

Civil government is an ordinance of God, grounded in the necessities of human nature and essential to the maintenance of public order, the security of personal rights, and the punishment of evil-doers. It is the duty of all men to be subject to the supreme authority of the country in which they reside and to respect and honor the civil magistrates.

125. OF THE EVANGELIZATION OF THE WORLD

The Gospel is designed for all nations, its field of operation is the whole world, and the Church and people of God are under solemn obligation to make known its saving truth and power among the heathen. To this great work we are impelled and encouraged by the command of the Lord and the promises and prophecies of the Holy Scriptures.

130. CHAPTER II - CHRISTIAN PERFECTION

131. TAUGHT IN THE WORD OF GOD

We believe that the doctrine of Christian Perfection is clearly taught in the Word of God. For this reason it is accepted as one of the cherished doctrines of the Evangelical Congregational Church. God said to Abram, as recorded in Genesis 17:1: "I am God Almighty; walk before me and be blameless." Our Lord and Saviour expressly said to His disciples, as recorded in Matthew 5:48: "Be perfect, therefore, as your heavenly Father is perfect." Furthermore, to effect this great end was plainly one of the leading purposes of God in instituting the Church and calling laborers into His vineyard. Hear Paul to the Ephesians, "It was he who gave some to be apostles, some to be prophets, some to be evangelists, and some to be pastors and teachers, to prepare God's people for works of service, so that the body of Christ may be built up, until we all reach unity in the faith and in the knowledge of the Son of God and become mature attaining to the whole measure of the fullness of Christ." Ephesians 4:11-13. Paul further taught with much emphasis that the best way to attain to this high standard was to preach the sinless Christ as our pattern of perfection. See Colossians 1:28: "We proclaim him, admonishing and teaching everyone with all wisdom so that we may present everyone perfect in Christ."

131.1. SUMMARY OF JOHN WESLEY'S TEACHING

As to the character of this work of grace, when attainable, and its effect upon its possessor, that most excellent summary given by John Wesley in the year 1764, fully meets our views. This statement was made after the thought and experience of Mr. Wesley had attained their full ripeness, for he was then within a few years of the close of his life. He had given much thought to this doctrine, and finally, after a careful review of the whole subject, wrote the sum of what he had observed in a number of brief propositions, to which we as a body of Christians most heartily subscribe. These propositions are as follows as found in A PLAIN ACCOUNT OF CHRISTIAN PERFECTION, Rev. John Wesley, 1764:

1. "There is such a thing as perfection; for it is again and again mentioned in the Scriptures.

2. It is not so early as justification; for justified persons are to 'go on unto perfection'. (Hebrews 6:1).

3. It is not so late as death; for St. Paul speaks of living men that were perfect. (Phillippians 3:15).

4. It is not absolute. Absolute perfection belongs not to man, nor to angels, but to God alone.

5. It does not make a man infallible; no one is infallible while he remains in the body.

6. Is it sinless? It is not worth while to contend for a term. It is 'salvation from sin.'

7. It is 'perfect love'. (1 John 4:18) This is the essence of it; its properties or inseparable fruits are, rejoicing evermore, praying without ceasing, and in every thing giving thanks, (1 Thessalonians 5:16, etc.)

8. It is improvable. It is so far from . . . being incapable of increase, that one perfected in love may grow in grace far swifter than he did before.

9. It is losable, capable of being lost; of which we have numerous instances . . .

10. It is constantly both preceded and followed by a gradual work.

11. But is it in itself instantaneous or not? In examining this, let us go on step by step. An instantaneous change has been wrought in some believers; no one can deny this. Since that change, they enjoy perfect love; they feel this and this alone; they 'rejoice evermore, pray without ceasing, and in everything give thanks' . . . But in some this change was not instantaneous. They did not perceive the instant when it was wrought. It is often difficult to perceive the instant when a man dies; yet there is an instant when life ceases. And if even sin ceases, there must be a last moment of its existence, and a first moment of our deliverance from it.

'But if they have this love now they will lose it.' They may; but they need not. And whether they do or no, they have it now; they now experience what we teach. They now are all love; they now rejoice, pray and praise without ceasing.

'However, sin is only suspended in them; it is not destroyed.' Call it which you please; they are all love today; and they take no thought for the morrow.

'But this doctrine has been much abused.' So has that of justification by faith. But that is no reason for giving up either this or any other Scriptural doctrine . . .

'But those who think they are saved from sin say they have no need of the merits of Christ.' They say just the contrary. Their language is 'Every moment, Lord, I need the merit of thy death.' They never before had so deep, so unspeakable a conviction of the need of Christ in all His offices as they have now."

Notes: *In 1922 the majority of the United Evangelical Church, which had broken away from the Evangelical Association in 1894, reunited with the Association to form the Evangelical Church. The new church's Articles of Religion were derived from those of the Evangelical*

ARTICLES OF RELIGION (EVANGELICAL
  CONGREGATIONAL CHURCH) (continued)

Association but rewritten to include additional emphasis on the subjective side of the Christian faith. This new emphasis is detailed in the articles on regeneration, repentance, the witness of the Spirit, sanctification, and the work of the Holy Spirit. Appended to the articles is a lengthy explanation of the doctrine of Christian perfection.

*   *   *

CONFESSION OF FAITH (UNITED CHRISTIAN CHURCH)

1. We believe the Church of God is a community of Saints united together for the worship of God according to Scripture Matt. 18:17; Rom. 16:1; Acts 14:23; 1 Cor. 1:2. We believe no church to be scripturally organized without a competent number of elders, Tit. 1:5 and deacons, Acts 6:1-5; 20:17, 28. We believe the Bible, the Old and New Testament, to be the Word of God, a revelation from God to man and the only authoritative rule of faith and practice. Luke 16:29; 2 Tim. 3:16; 2 Pet. 1:19.

2. She believes in one supreme God consisting of Father, Son, and Holy Spirit and that these three are one. Matt. 28:19; 1 John 5:7.

3. She believes in the Fall and Depravity of man. Rom. 3:10, 23; 5:10; 8:7.

4. She believes in the redemption of man through the atonement of Jesus Christ. Rom. 3:25; 5:6; 2 Cor. 5:19.

5. She believes in the gifts and office work of the Holy Spirit to enlighten, regenerate, and sanctify the believers, body, soul, and spirit. John 17:17.

6. She believes that man is justified by faith in Christ and not by the works of the law. Rom. 3:28; 4:4.

7. She believes in the new birth without which no man can see the kingdom of God. John 3:5.

8. She believes in three ordinances in the church of God; baptism, the Lord's supper, and feet-washing. Acts 2:38; 1 Cor. 11:23; John 13:1-14.

9. She believes that faith is essential to baptism, and that it should be done in the water if possible. 1 Pet. 3:21; Acts 8:37, 38.

10. She believes that the Lord's supper should be administered to believers only, 1 Cor. 11:23; and if it could be done, always in the evening.

11. She believes that the church, if she can, ought to relieve and take care of her own poor. Acts 6:1; 11:29.

12. She believes that all wars are sinful and unholy and in which the saints of God ought never participate. Matt. 5:39; 26:52; 2 Cor. 10:4.

13. She believes that the saints of God should not sue and go to law with each other. Matt. 5:40; 1 Cor. 6:1.

14. She believes that all governments are ordained of God and that Christians ought to be subject to the same in all things, except what is manifestly unscriptural; and that appeals to the law—for rights, liberty, and life are not inconsistent with the Christian religion. Rom. 13:1; Acts 25:11-31.

15. She believes in the resurrection of the dead, both of the just and the unjust. John 5:28, 29; Acts 24:15.

16. She believes in the immortality of the soul, in a universal and eternal judgment and in future and everlasting rewards and punishments. Matt. 25:3-46; Mark 8:36; Luke 16:19-31.

Notes: *Breaking away from the United Brethren in 1877, the United Christian Church adopted its own distinct confession. It espoused the unique (for Methodism) beliefs in pacifism, foot washing, and the exclusivity of the Lord's Supper (closed communion for believers only), which was to be held only in the evening.*

*   *   *

British Methodism

REVISION OF THE *TWENTY-FIVE ARTICLES OF RELIGION* (METHODIST CHURCH, CANADA; METHODIST CHURCH OF CANADA)

XXIII. OF THE CIVIL GOVERNMENT

21. We believe it is the duty of all Christians to be subject to the powers that be; for we are commanded by the Word of God to respect and obey the Civil Government: we should therefore not only fear God, but honour the King.

Notes: *Canadian Methodists adopted the Twenty-five Articles of Religion common to Methodism in North America, but as with all Methodist churches outside of the United States, had to revise the twenty-third article, which in the statement adopted by the Methodist Episcopal Church (now the United Methodist church) professed loyalty to the government of the United States of America.*

Chapter 7

Holiness Family

STATEMENT OF FAITH (NATIONAL HOLINESS ASSOCIATION)

We believe:

1. That both Old and New Testaments constitute the divinely-inspired word of God, inerrant in the originals, and the final authority for life and truth;

2. That there is one God, eternally existent in the Holy Trinity of Father, Son, and Holy Spirit, each with personality and deity;

3. That the Son, our Lord Jesus Christ, manifested in the flesh through the virgin birth, died on Calvary for the redemption of the human family, all of whom may be saved from sin through faith in Him;

4. That men, although created by God in His own image and likeness, fell into sin through disobedience and "so death passed upon all men, for that all have sinned" (Romans 5:12);

5. In the salvation of the human soul, including the new birth; and in a subsequent work of God in the soul, a crisis, wrought by faith, whereby the heart is cleansed from all sin and filled with the Holy Spirit; this gracious experience is retained by faith as expressed in a constant obedience to God's revealed will, thus giving us perfect cleansing moment by moment (1 John 1:7-9). We stand for the Wesleyan position;

6. That the church is the body of Christ, that all who are united by faith to Christ are members of the same, and that, having thus become members one of another, it is our solemn and covenant duty to fellowship with one another in peace, and to love one another with pure and fervent hearts;

7. That our Lord Jesus Christ in His literal resurrection from the dead is the living guarantee of the resurrection of all human beings, the believing saved to conscious eternal joy, and the unbelieving lost to conscious eternal punishment;

8. That our Lord Jesus Christ, in fulfillment of His own promise, both angelically and apostolically attested, will personally return in power and great glory.

Notes: *Emerging out of the holiness revival that spread through Methodism after the Civil War, the holiness churches developed a special emphasis upon the doctrine of sanctification. Succinctly stated, they teach that after a person is justified (born again), God's Holy Spirit continues to work in the believer. The believer is said to grow in grace. Held out as a possibility toward which Christians strive, sanctification is experienced as a second definite act of grace in the Christian's life through the action of the Holy Spirit. This second blessing, as it is frequently termed, makes the person perfect in love.*

In the late nineteenth century, Methodist leaders attacked several basic assumptions underlying the holiness system. Most importantly, they emphasized the process of conversion, as opposed to the instantaneous conversion often precipitated around a personal crisis. While believing in the possibility of the Christian's process of growth through grace, they shied away from any affirmation of the possibility of perfection in this life. Finally, they talked of numerous "blessings" given as part of the Christian life, as opposed to a special "second blessing."

The trend of Methodist theology to deny holiness emphases, and the growing opposition of bishops and presiding elders to holiness advocates, led to the establishment of distinctly holiness churches in the late nineteenth century. Joining the holiness movement were some of the previously existing independent Methodist denominations (i.e., the Free Methodist Church and the Wesleyan Methodist Church) which had strong holiness leanings and had been drawn into the revival.

Among the earliest structures of the holiness revival was the National Camp Meeting Association for the Promotion of Holiness, popularly called the National Holiness Association, founded in 1867. In the early years it promoted camp meetings across the United States. By the beginning of the twentieth century it had become the common meeting ground between holiness denominations and individuals who held a holiness doctrine but remained in "non-holiness" churches.

STATEMENT OF FAITH (CHRISTIAN HOLINESS ASSOCIATION)

The Christian Holiness Association is a body of churches, organizations, and individuals who accept the inspiration and infallibility of sacred Scripture and evangelical doctrine that pertains to divine revelation, the incarnation, the resurrection, the second coming of Christ, the Holy Spirit, and the Church as affirmed in the historic Christian creeds. The particular concern of this fellowship is the biblical doctrine of sanctification identified historically in what is known as the Wesleyan position.

The Association believes that personal salvation includes both the new birth and entire sanctification wrought by God in the heart by faith. Entire sanctification is a crisis experience subsequent to conversion which results in a heart cleansed from all sin and filled with the Holy Spirit. This grace is witnessed to by the Holy Spirit. It is maintained by that faith which expresses itself in constant obedience to God's revealed will and results in a moment by moment cleansing.

Notes: *In 1970 the National Holiness Association, following the entry of several groups from outside the United States, changed its name to the Christian Holiness Association. At that time, it also adopted a new brief statement of faith.*

*   *   *

Nineteenth-Century Holiness

ARTICLES OF RELIGION (AMERICAN RESCUE WORKERS)

1. We believe in one Supreme God, who is "from everlasting to everlasting," who is infinitely perfect, benevolent and wise, who is omnipotent, omnipresent, and omnicient, and who is the Creator and Ruler of heaven and earth.

2. We believe in a Triune God—the Father, the Son and the Holy Ghost. We believe these three Persons are one, and while separate in office, are undivided in essence, co-equal in power and glory, and that all men everywhere ought to worship and serve this Triune God.

3. We believe the contents of the Bible to have been given by inspiration of God, and the Scriptures form the divine rule of all true, godly faith and Christian practice.

4. We believe that Jesus Christ, when upon earth, was truly man and yet was as truly God, the Divine and human being blended in the one being, hence His ability to feel and suffer as a man and yet supremely love and triumph as the Godhead.

5. We believe that our first parents were created without sin, but by listening to the tempter and obeying his voice fell from grace and lost their purity and peace; and that in consequences of their disobedience and fall all men have become sinful by propensity and are consequently exposed to the wrath of God.

6. We believe that Jesus Christ, the only begotten Son of God, by the sacrifice of His life, made an atonement for all men, and that whosoever will call upon Him and accept His overtures of grace may be saved.

7. We believe that in order to be saved it is necessary (a) to repent toward God, (b) to believe with the heart in Jesus Christ, and (c) to become regenerated through the operation of the Holy Spirit.

8. We believe that the Holy Ghost gives to each person thus saved the inward witness of acceptance by God.

9. We believe that the Scriptures teach and urge all Christians to be cleansed in heart from inbred sin, so that they may walk uprightly and "serve Him without fear in holiness, and righteousness before Him all the days of our lives."

10. We believe the soul shall never die; and that we shall be raised again; that the world shall be judged by God, and that the punishment of the wicked will be eternal and the joy and reward of the righteous will be everlasting before the throne of God.

The American Rescue Workers, Inc., believe in two sacraments —Baptism and the Lord's Supper.

Baptism may be administered by sprinkling, pouring or immersion according: as the Candidate may elect.

Notes: *Most of the large holiness bodies have their roots in groups which emerged in the nineteenth century. One of these groups, The American Rescue Workers, was founded by former members of the Salvation Army. While retaining the Army's military bearing, it has rejected the Army's peculiar stance in regard to the sacraments.*

*   *   *

SUMMARY OF DOCTRINE (BIBLE HOLINESS MOVEMENT)

We believe there is One God—the Father, Son and Holy Spirit;

That the Bible is the inspired and authoritative Word of God;

That man is born spiritually and morally depraved;

That the atonement provided by the sufferings and death of our Lord Jesus Christ is universal;

That all men may be saved who repent and believe the Gospel;

That it is the privilege of every believer to be sanctified wholly;

That it is the privilege of the entirely sanctified to be anointed with the Holy Spirit and made effective witnesses;

That all true Christians should lead godly lives in conformity with the Holy Scriptures;

And that Jesus Christ will come again in the end of the world to raise the dead and judge all mankind.

Notes: *The Bible Holiness Movement has roots in the Salvation Army. Its brief statement affirms the central affirmations of the holiness tradition while avoiding any mention of the Army's controversial position on the sacraments.*

*   *   *

DOCTRINAL STATEMENT (CHRISTIAN AND MISSIONARY ALLIANCE)

Qualifications for membership shall consist of:

1. Satisfactory evidence of regeneration;
2. Belief in God the Father, Son and Holy Spirit; in the verbal inspiration of the Holy Scriptures as originally given; in the vicarious atonement of the Lord Jesus Christ; in the eternal salvation of all who believe in Him and the eternal punishment of all who reject Him;
3. Acceptance of the doctrines of the Lord Jesus Christ as Saviour, Sanctifier, Healer and Coming King.

The following doctrinal statement shall be adopted in all of our home and foreign Bible schools:

1. The Scriptures of the Old and New Testaments are the inspired Word of God. They contain a complete revelation of His will for the salvation of men, and constitute the Divine and only rule of Christian faith and practice.—2 Timothy 3:16-17; 2 Peter 1:21.
2. There is one God, Who is infinitely perfect, existing eternally in three persons: Father, Son and Holy Spirit.
3. Jesus Christ is true God and true man. He was conceived by the Holy Ghost and born of the Virgin Mary. He died upon the cross, the just for the unjust, as a substitutionary sacrifice, and all who believe in Him are justified on the ground of His shed blood. He arose from the dead according to the Scriptures. He is now at the right hand of the Majesty on high as our great High Priest, and He will return again to establish His Kingdom of righteousness and justice.
4. The Holy Spirit is a Divine Person, the Executive of the Godhead, the Comforter sent by the Lord Jesus Christ to indwell, to guide, and to teach the believer, and to convince the world of sin, of righteousness, and of judgment.
5. Man was originally created in the likeness and image of God; he fell through disobedience, incurring thereby both physical and spiritual death. All men are born with a sinful nature, are separated from the life of God, and can be saved only through the atoning work of the Lord Jesus Christ. The portion of the impenitent and unbelieving is existence forever in conscious torment; and that of the believer, in everlasting joy and bliss.
6. Salvation has been provided through Jesus Christ for all men; and those who receive Him are born again of the Holy Spirit, obtain the gift of eternal life, and become the children of God.
7. There shall be a bodily resurrection of the just and of the unjust; for the former, a resurrection unto life; for the latter, a resurrection unto judgment.
8. The Church consists of all those who have believed on the Lord Jesus Christ, are washed in His blood, and have been born again of the Holy Spirit. It has been commissioned of the Lord to witness in His name, to comfort and build up its members in the holy faith, and especially to fulfill the terms of the Great Commission to go forth into all the world as a witness, preaching the Gospel to all nations.
9. It is the will of God that each believer should be filled with the Holy Spirit and thus be sanctified wholly, being separated from sin and the world and fully consecrated to the will of God, thereby receiving power for holy living and effective service. This is recognized as an experience wrought in the life subsequent to conversion.
10. Provision is made in the redemption of the Lord Jesus Christ for the healing of the mortal body in accordance with His Word. The anointing with oil, as set forth in the fifth chapter of James, is to be practiced by the Church in this present age.
11. The premillennial coming of the Lord Jesus Christ is a practical truth which should be preached, showing its relation to the personal life and the service of the believer.

Notes: *The Christian and Missionary Alliance was founded by Albert Benjamin Simpson, a former Presbyterian minister who had been healed at a holiness camp meeting. He is rightfully credited as being one of the major spokespersons for the revival of the healing ministry in twentieth-century Christianity. In conjunction with his mature ministry, he developed a theology centering on the work of Christ as Saviour, Sanctifier, Healer, and Coming King. This theology was known as the four-fold gospel and became the distinguishing feature of the alliance's holiness doctrine. The constitution of the alliance spells out the minimal doctrinal essentials in its statement on membership. However, the more complete presentation of the alliance's position is found in the doctrinal statement mandated for adoption for all Bible schools associated with the alliance.*

*   *   *

ARTICLES OF FAITH (CHRIST'S SANCTIFIED HOLY CHURCH)

That there is but one uncreated, unoriginated, infinite and eternal Being, the Creator, Preserver and Governor of all things. That there is in this infinite essence a plurality of what is commonly called persons, not separately subsisting but essentially belonging to the Godhead, which persons are commonly termed the Father, Son and Holy Ghost, and are generally named the Trinity. That the sacred Scriptures or Holy Books which form the Old and New Testaments, contain a full revelation of the will of God in relation to man, and alone sufficient for everything relative to the faith and practice of the Christian, and were given by the inspiration of God. That man was created in

ARTICLES OF FAITH (CHRIST'S SANCTIFIED HOLY
  CHURCH) (continued)

righteousness and true holiness, without any moral imperfection or any kind of propensity to sin, but free to stand or fall, but he fell from this state, became morally corrupt in his nature, and transmitted his moral defilment to all his posterity. That to counteract the evil principle and bring man into a saveable state, God, from his infinite love, formed the purpose of redeeming man from his lost estate by Jesus Christ and in the interim sent His holy spirit to enlighten, strive with and convince men of sin, righteousness and judgment. That in due time Jesus, the Christ, the Son of God, the Savior of the world, became incarnated and sojourned among men, teaching the purest truth and working the most stupendous, beneficent miracles. That this divine person, foretold by the prophets and described by the evangelists and apostles, is really and properly God, having by the inspired writers assigned to Him every attribute essential to the Deity, being one with Him who is called God, Jehovah, etc. That He is also a perfect man in consequence of his incarnation, and in that man or manhood dwelt all the fullness of the Godhead bodily; so His nature is twofold—divine and human, or God manifested in the flesh. That His human nature is derived from the blessed Virgin Mary through the creative energy of the Holy Ghost, but His divine nature, because God is infinite and eternal, uncreated, underived, and unbegotten, which, were it otherwise, He could not be God in any proper sense of the word. That, as He took upon Himself the nature of man, He died for the whole human race without respect of person equally for all and every person. That, on the third day after His crucifixion and burial He arose from the dead, and after showing Himself many days to His disciples and others, He ascended to heaven, where as God manifest in the flesh, He continues and shall continue to be mediator for the human race till the consummation of all things. That there is no salvation but through Him, and that throughout the Scriptures His passion and death are obtained by the shedding of His blood. That no human being since the fall either has or can have merit or worthiness of or by himself, and therefore has nothing to claim from God, but in the way of His mercy through Christ, therefore pardon and holiness and every other blessing promised in the Gospel have been purchased by His sacrificial death, and are given to man, not on account of anything he has done, or suffered, or can do, but for His sake or through His merit alone. That these blessings are received by faith, because not of works, nor of sufferings, that the power to believe or grace of faith is the free gift of God, without which none can believe, but that the act of faith or actual believing is the act of the soul under the influence of that power, but this power to believe, like all other gifts of God, may be slighted, not used or misused, in consequence of which is that declaration, He that believeth and is baptized shall be saved, but he that believeth not shall be damned (Mark xvi, 16). That justification or the pardon of all actual sin is an instantaneous act of God's infinite mercy in behalf of a penitent soul, trusting only in the merits of Jesus Christ. That this act is absolute in respect of all past actual sins, all being forgiven where any are forgiven. That the souls of all

believers or justified persons must be purified and cleansed from all inbred sin. That moral corruption of the natural human heart, by the precious blood of Jesus Christ, here in this life without which none are prepared for heaven, and that we must live under the continual influence of the grace of Christ, without sinning against God, all evil tempers and sinful propensities being destroyed and the heart being filled with pure love of God; and man being sanctified by the Holy Ghost and received instantaneously as justification. That unless a person live and walk in the spirit of perfect obedience to God's Holy Law, he will fall from the grace of God and forfeit all his Christian privileges and rights, which state of backsliding he may pursue, and if so, perish everlastingly. That the whole period of human life is a state of probation, in every part of which a sinner may repent and turn to God, and in every part of it a believer may, if he wills, give way to sin and fall from the grace attained, and that this possibility of attainments in grace or falling from them are essential to a state of trial or probation. That all the promises and threatenings of the Word of God are conditional as they regard man in reference to his being here and hereafter, and on this ground alone the Sacred Writings can be consistently interpreted or rightly judged. That man is a free agent, never being impelled by any necessitating influence, either to do evil or good, but has it continually in his power to choose the life or death that is set before him, on which ground he is an accountable being and answerable for his own actions, and on this ground also he is alone capable of being rewarded or punished. That his free will is a necessary constituent of his rational soul, without which man must be a mere machine, either the sport of blind chance or a mere patient of an irresistible necessity, and consequently not accountable for any acts to which he was irresistibly impelled. That every human being has this freedom of will with a sufficiency of light and power to direct its operations, and that this powerful light is not inherent in any man's nature, but is graciously bestowed by Him who is a true light, that lighteth every man that cometh into the world. That Jesus Christ has made by His once offering Himself upon the cross as a sufficient sacrifice, oblation and satisfaction for the sins of the whole world, and that His gracious Spirit strives with and enlightens all men, thus putting them in a saveable state; therefore every human soul may be saved. If they are not it is their own fault.

Q.—What is conversion?
Ans.—It is pardon of all past willful sins.

Q.—What are the fruits of conversion?
Ans.—It gives a hungering and thirsting for holiness; the power to become the sons of God.

Q.—Does sin still remain in the heart at conversion?
Ans.—It does, yea, the seed of all sin until they are entirely sanctified.

Q.—Is any soul born of God at conversion?
Ans.—No! Whosoever is born of God doth not commit sin, neither willful nor through error. Unless they are converted from the error of their way, they will go to hell.

Q.—Why are not the people converted from the error of their way, which is inbred sin?

Ans.—Because they have been taught by professing ministers that they are saved at conversion.

Q.—Why is it that the whole world is not saved?

Ans.—The word of God teaches, If they had stood in My counsel, and had caused My people to hear My words, then they should have turned them from the evil of their way.

Q.—Who is the Father of them that say they are saved, and say they sin every day?

Ans.—He that commiteth sin is of the devil.

Q.—Was any soul ever saved at any moment until it was entirely sanctified?

Ans.—No. Without holiness no man shall see the Lord. And again, He that abideth not in Me is cast forth as a branch, and is withered, and men gather them and they are cast into the fire and are burned.

Q.—What is the one Lord, one Faith, one Baptism?

Ans.—It is to be baptized in Jesus Christ by being sanctified and made holy.

Q.—Can any soul be saved without keeping the commandments?

Ans.—No. They that offend in the least are guilty of the whole. So everyone that is forgiven and not sanctified is lost.

Q.—Can anyone be saved without loving God?

Ans.—No. The Scriptures teach that if ye love Me ye will keep My word, which is the commandments, and every one that keepeth the commandments is sanctified and made holy.

Q.—Do persons still have the carnal mind in them after they are converted?

Ans.—Yes, and they are still the enemy of God, for His Word says the carnal mind is enmity to God. It is not subject to God, neither indeed can be. Then to be carnal-minded is death, but to be spiritual-minded is life and peace.

Q.—Can anyone be Christ's disciple without forsaking all that he hath?

Ans.—No.

Q.—When do persons forsake all?

Ans.—Not until they are sanctified.

Q.—Can a person be holy without being sanctified?

Ans.—No. The Word of God teaches us to abstain from all appearance of evil, and the very God of peace sanctify you wholly. So no one is holy unless he is sanctified.

Q.—Are people taught of God who have to study all the week to get up a sermon for Sunday?

Ans.—No, for God has said, Settle it in your hearts not to premeditate before what ye shall say, for I will give you a mouth and wisdom which all your adversaries may not be able to gainsay nor resist. And again—Open your mouth wide and I will fill it.

Q.—What kind of a discipline will be used at the millennial year?

Ans.—This very one, for the millennial year has already come with all Sanctified Holy people.

Q.—Does anyone know God at conversion?

Ans.—No. He that sinneth hath neither seen Him, neither known Him.

Q.—What is sanctification?

Ans.—It is to love the Lord thy God with all thy heart, with all thy soul, and with all thy mind, and with all thy strength, and thy neighbor as thyself.

Notes: *Two groups share the name "Christ's Sanctified Holy Church." The older one, founded in 1887, has its headquarters in South Carolina and is predominantly composed of whites. The other, organized in 1904, is headquartered in Louisiana and predominantly composed of blacks. The statement reproduced here is taken from the South Carolina group. It is not known whether or not the Louisiana group uses the same statement.*

* * *

ARTICLES OF FAITH [CHURCH OF GOD (HOLINESS)]

ARTICLE I

There is one God over all, the same yesterday, today, and forever; the Creator of all things, and in whom all things consist. (Deut. 6:4; Heb. 11:3).

ARTICLE II

There is one Savior, Jesus Christ, the only begotten Son of God, who is the Supreme Head of the Church, which He redeemed unto God by His own blood. (Matt. 3:16, 17).

ARTICLE III

There is one Holy Spirit, the third person of the Holy Trinity, who is now the representative of the Godhead on earth, who came from the Father and the Son, to convict the world of sin, of righteousness, and of judgment. (John 14:16, 17, 26; 15:26).

God the Father, God the Son, and God the Holy Spirit are three persons, united and inseparable, of one substance and eternal. (Matt. 28:19; II Cor. 13:14).

ARTICLE IV

We emphatically affirm the divine inspiration of the Holy Scriptures, both Old and New Testaments, infallibly true as originally inspired, constituting our only divinely authorized rule of faith and practice. (II Tim. 3:16; II Pet. 1:21).

ARTICLES OF FAITH [CHURCH OF GOD
(HOLINESS)] (continued)

ARTICLE V

Man, in his natural state, is sinful, apart from saving grace, and consequently is in need of salvation. (Gen. 6:5; Psa. 14:2, 3; Matt. 15:19; Rom. 3:9-23).

ARTICLE VI

The Scriptures declare the necessity of repentance, implying a previous conviction for sins, followed by a hearty sorrow for them and immediate abandonment thereof, together with suitable confession to God and men, and prompt and honest restitution of all that is due to others, according to his ability; and all such gracious states and experiences, constituting scriptural repentance, etc., must be inwrought by the efficient grace of the Holy Ghost. (Isaiah 55:6, 7; Matt. 9:13; Luke 13:3, 5; Acts 17:30, 31; II Cor. 7:10; Ezek. 33:15).

ARTICLE VII

Justification is a legal act on the part of God, including the forgiveness of sins and the impartation of personal righteousness, through faith in the Lord Jesus Christ. (Jer. 36:3; Psalm 130:4; Acts 13:38, 39; Rom. 5:1; I John 3:7; Rev. 19:8; Rom. 8:16).

ARTICLE VIII

Regeneration is the quickening to spiritual life by the Holy Ghost, of the sinner who is dead in trespasses and sins, which gracious act of the Divine Spirit accompanies justification. (Isa. 55:3; John 3:3, 5; Eph. 2:1; Col. 2:13; Titus 3:15).

ARTICLE IX

The Scriptures affirm the necessity of entire sanctification, or deliverance from inbred sin, implying the complete purification of the nature from depravity, or inherited sin, and the complete renewal of the nature in holiness, whereby the child of God is enabled to love God perfectly, and to serve Him in righteousness and true holiness. This gracious act of purification, or entire sanctification, is accomplished instantaneously for the believer by the Holy Spirit, and is distinct from, and takes place subsequent to, the believer's regeneration, being preceded by a definite conviction of remaining inbred sin, an entire and unreserved consecration of the whole being to God, and a definite faith in the Lord Jesus Christ for the entire sanctification of the nature. (Lev. 11:44, 45; Luke 1:73-75; John 17:17; I Thess. 4:3; 5:23, 24; Heb. 10:14, 15).

This work of entire sanctification attended by the infilling of the Holy Spirit, is witnessed to directly by the Holy Spirit, and not by any special manifestations or gifts, such as speaking in unknown tongues.

ARTICLE X

The New Testament Scriptures teach that there is one true Church, which is composed only of those who have savingly believed in the Lord Jesus Christ, and who willingly submit themselves to His divine order concerning the ministries of the Church through the instrumentalities of God-chosen elders and deacons, ordained in the Church by laying on of the hands of the presbytery. The attributes of the Church are unity, spirituality, visibility, and catholicity. (Matt. 16:18; Eph. 4:4; Col. 1:18; I Tim. 3:1-7; Titus 1:5).

ARTICLE XI

The second advent of our Savior, Jesus Christ, is premillennial and visible. The children of God are admonished to look for the personal coming of Christ with confident hope, and with the assurance that at His appearing they will become the happy partakers of His glory in the Kingdom prepared for them from the foundation of the world. (Dan. 7:13, 14; Matt. 24:30, 31; Acts 1:11; I Thess. 4:15-17; 22:20).

ARTICLE XII

The Scriptures affirm the resurrection of the body, the judgment of all mankind, the everlasting punishment of the wicked, and the eternal happiness of the righteous, (John 5:28, 29; I Cor. 15:52-55; Rom. 14:10; II Cor. 5:10; Rev. 20:12, 13; John 14:1-3; Psa. 9:17; Matt. 25:46; Rev. 21:8).

ARTICLE XIII

We urge our people to embrace the Bible doctrine of Divine healing and to offer the prayer of faith for the healing of the sick, according to James 5:14-16; Acts 4:10, 14; Luke 9:2; 10:9.

ARTICLE XIV

Recognizing the fact that water baptism is an outward sign of an inward work of grace wrought in the heart by the Holy Ghost, we recommend that this ordinance be observed by all born-again children of God.

ARTICLE XV

Believing that the sacrament of the Lord's Supper represents our redemption through Christ, we recommend that this ordinance be reverently observed.

Notes: *The Church of God (Holiness) was among the first of the holiness churches to emerge after the Civil War and a leading exponent of what became known as the "come out" [of denominations] movement. The church has adopted a premillennial eschatology indicative of the influence of Protestant fundamentalism.*

* * *

ARTICLES OF FAITH (CHURCH OF THE NAZARENE)

I. THE TRIUNE GOD

We believe in one eternally existent, infinite God, Sovereign of the universe; that He only is God, creative and administrative, holy in nature, attributes, and purpose; that He, as God, is Triune in essential being, revealed as Father, Son, and Holy Spirit.

II. JESUS CHRIST

We believe in Jesus Christ, the Second Person of the Triune Godhead; that He was eternally one with the Father; that He became incarnate by the Holy Spirit and was born of the Virgin Mary, so that two whole and perfect natures, that is to say the Godhead and manhood, are thus united in one person very God and very man, the God-man.

We believe that Jesus Christ died for our sins, and that He truly arose from the dead and took again His body, together with all things appertaining to the perfection of man's nature, wherewith He ascended into heaven and is there engaged in intercession for us.

III. THE HOLY SPIRIT

We believe in the Holy Spirit, the Third Person of the Triune Godhead, that He is ever present and efficiently active in and with the Church of Christ, convincing the world of sin, regenerating those who repent and believe, sanctifying believers, and guiding into all truth as it is in Jesus.

IV. THE HOLY SCRIPTURES

We believe in the plenary inspiration of the Holy Scriptures, by which we understand the sixty-six books of the Old and New Testaments given by divine inspiration, inerrantly revealing the will of God concerning us in all things necessary to our salvation, so that whatever is not contained therein is not to be enjoined as an article of faith.

V. ORIGINAL SIN, OR DEPRAVITY

We believe that original sin, or depravity, is that corruption of the nature of all the offspring of Adam by reason of which every one is very far gone from original righteousness or the pure state of our first parents at the time of their creation, is averse to God, is without spiritual life, and inclined to evil, and that continually. We further believe that original sin continues to exist with the new life of the regenerate, until eradicated by the baptism with the Holy Spirit.

VI. ATONEMENT

We believe that Jesus Christ, by His sufferings, by the shedding of His own blood, and by His meritorious death on the Cross, made a full atonement for all human sin, and that this atonement is the only ground of salvation, and that it is sufficient for every individual of Adam's race. The atonement is graciously efficacious for the salvation of the irresponsible and for the children in innocency, but is efficacious for the salvation of those who reach the age of responsibility only when they repent and believe.

VII. FREE AGENCY

We believe that man's creation in Godlikeness included ability to choose between right and wrong, and that thus he was made morally responsible; that through the fall of Adam he became depraved so that he cannot now turn and prepare himself by his own natural strength and works to faith and calling upon God. But we also believe that the grace of God through Jesus Christ is freely bestowed upon all men, enabling all who will to turn from sin to righteousness, believe on Jesus Christ for pardon and cleansing from sin, and follow good works pleasing and acceptable in His sight.

We believe that man, though in the possession of the experience of regeneration and entire sanctification, may fall from grace and apostatize and, unless he repent of his sin, be hopelessly and eternally lost.

VIII. REPENTANCE

We believe that repentance, which is a sincere and thorough change of the mind in regard to sin, involving a sense of personal guilt and a voluntary turning away from sin, is the demand of all who have by act or purpose become sinners against God. The Spirit of God gives to all who will repent the gracious help of penitence of heart and hope of mercy, that they may believe unto pardon and spiritual life.

IX. JUSTIFICATION, REGENERATION, AND ADOPTION

We believe that justification is the gracious and judicial act of God by which He grants full pardon of all guilt and complete release from the penalty of sins committed, and acceptance as righteous, to all who believe on Jesus Christ and receive Him as Lord and Saviour.

We believe that regeneration, or the new birth, is that gracious work of God whereby the moral nature of the repentant believer is spiritually quickened and given a distinctively spiritual life, capable of faith, love, and obedience.

We believe that adoption is that gracious act of God by which the justified and regenerated believer is constituted a son of God.

We believe that justification, regeneration, and adoption are simultaneous in the experience of seekers after God and are obtained upon the condition of faith, preceded by repentance; and that to this work and state of grace the Holy Spirit bears witness.

X. ENTIRE SANCTIFICATION

We believe that entire sanctification is that act of God, subsequent to regeneration, by which believers are made free from original sin, or depravity, and brought into a state of entire devotement to God, and the holy obedience of love made perfect.

It is wrought by the baptism with the Holy Spirit, and comprehends in one experience the cleansing of the heart from sin and the abiding indwelling presence of the Holy Spirit, empowering the believer for life and service.

Entire sanctification is provided by the blood of Jesus, is wrought instantaneously by faith, preceded by entire consecration; and to this work and state of grace the Holy Spirit bears witness.

This experience is also known by various terms representing its different phases, such as "Christian perfection," "perfect love," "heart purity," "the baptism with the Holy Spirit," "the fullness of the blessing," and "Christian holiness."

XI. SECOND COMING OF CHRIST

We believe that the Lord Jesus Christ will come again; that we who are alive at His coming shall not precede them that are asleep in Christ Jesus; but that, if we are abiding in Him, we shall be caught up with the risen saints to meet the Lord in the air, so that we shall ever be with the Lord.

XII. RESURRECTION, JUDGMENT, AND DESTINY

We believe in the resurrection of the dead, that the bodies both of the just and of the unjust shall be raised to life and united with their spirits—"they that have done good, unto the resurrection of life; and they that have done evil, unto the resurrection of damnation."

We believe in future judgment in which every man shall appear before God to be judged according to his deeds in this life.

We believe that glorious and everlasting life is assured to all who savingly believe in, and obediently follow, Jesus Christ our Lord; and that the finally impenitent shall suffer eternally in hell.

XIII. BAPTISM

We believe that Christian baptism is a sacrament signifying acceptance of the benefits of the atonement of Jesus Christ, to be administered to believers as declarative of their faith in Jesus Christ as their Saviour, and full purpose of obedience in holiness and righteousness.

Baptism being the symbol of the New Testament, young children may be baptized, upon request of parents or guardians who shall give assurance for them of necessary Christian training.

Baptism may be administered by sprinkling, pouring, or immersion, according to the choice of the applicant.

XIV. THE LORD'S SUPPER

We believe that the Memorial and Communion Supper instituted by our Lord and Saviour Jesus Christ is essentially a New Testament sacrament, declarative of His sacrificial death, through the merits of which believers have life and salvation and promise of all spiritual blessings in Christ. It is distinctively for those who are prepared for reverent appreciation of its significance and by it they show forth the Lord's death till He come again. It being the Communion feast, only those who have faith in Christ and love for the saints should be called to participate therein.

XV. DIVINE HEALING

We believe in the Bible doctrine of divine healing and urge our people to seek to offer the prayer of faith for the healing of the sick. Providential means and agencies when deemed necessary should not be refused.

Notes: *Beginning as a single mission in Los Angeles pastored by a man who had already finished a lengthy and distinguished career as a Methodist minister [Phineas F. Bresee], the Church of the Nazarene has become one of the largest of the holiness denominations. The statements on "Entire Sanctification" and "Healing" reflect, in part, the church's attempt to distinguish itself from Pentecostalism.*

*   *   *

STATEMENT OF DOCTRINE [CHURCHES OF GOD (INDEPENDENT HOLINESS PEOPLE)]

1. The scriptural truth concerning the naturally sinful condition of all men, apart from saving grace, and their consequent need of salvation.—Gen. 6:5; Psa. 14:2, 3; Matt. 15:19; Rom 3:9-18.

2. The atonement, in that Jesus Christ has made full and complete satisfaction for all. He "tasted death for every man", so that all may be saved who will, upon scriptural conditions, accept Him as their Saviour.—John 3:16; Rom. 5:18; 1 Tim. 2:6; 2 Pet. 3:9.

3. The necessity of repentance, implying a previous conviction for sins, followed by hearty sorrow for and immediate abandonment thereof, together with suitable confession to God and men, and a prompt and honest restitution of all that is due unto others, according to ability; all which gracious states and experiences, as containing true scriptural repentance, must be inwrought by the efficient grace of the Holy Ghost.—Isa. 55:6, 7; Ezek. 33:15; Matt. 9: 13; Luke 13:3-5; Acts 17:30, 31; 2 Cor. 7: 10,11.

4. Justification, implying forgiveness, through faith in the Lord Jesus Christ.—Jer. 36:3; Psa. 130:4; Acts 13:38, 39; Rom. 5:1, 8:16; 1 John 4:7; Rev. 19:8.

5. Regeneration, being the quickening into spiritual life, by the Holy Ghost, of the sinner who is dead in trespasses and sins, which gracious work of the Divine Spirit accompanies justification.—Isa. 55:3; John 3:3-5; Eph. 2:1; Col. 2:13; Titus 3:15.

6. Entire sanctification, being deliverance from inborn sin, implying the complete purification of the nature from depravity, or inherited sin, and the complete renewal of the nature in holiness, whereby the child of God is enabled perfectly to love God, and to serve Him in righteousness and true holiness. This gracious work of purification, or entire sanctification, is accomplished instantaneouly, for the believer, by the Holy Spirit, and is distinct from, and takes place subsequent to, the believer's justification, being preceded by a definite conviction of remaining inward sin, an entire and unreserved consecration of the whole being to God, and a definite faith in the Lord Jesus Christ for the entire sanctification of the nature, and is witnessed to by the Holy Ghost.—Lev. 11:44, 45; Luke 1:73-75; Heb. 10:14, 15.

The work of entire sanctification thus inwrought by the Holy Ghost, through the believer's faith in the Lord Jesus Christ, includes all possibilities of gracious experience in the present life, and neither do the Scriptures teach that said holy estate is to be followed in this world by other super-added and distinctive experiences, as of special divine enlightenment independent of, and superior to, the written Word of God; present immortality or deathlessness; the experience of a present physical resurrection; the consequent glorification of the body and spirit, or other kindred hallucinations which have no warrant from Scripture, but are superinduced by neglect of, or disobedience to, the plainly written truths of God's Word, and imply a willing or wilful following of satanic delusion. Nor does the experience of entire sanctification involve an impossibility of falling away.

7. The institution of the holy Sabbath, or Lord's Day; its sanctity and perpetuity, implying obligation of due and proper observance on the part of all men, according to God's holy commandment. The Convention would express utter disapproval of public

teaching or private conduct, whether under the name of holiness or otherwise, that has a tendency to secularize the holy Sabbath, to weaken or destroy the sense of its sanctity and its perpetual obligation as ordained of God, or to impair either the sacred or civil sanction of the holy day whose proper observance has ever been attended with the evident blessing of God and with national and individual prosperity.—Ex. 20:8-11; Mark 2:27, 28; Luke 6:5; Acts 20:7; 1 Cor. 16:1, 2.

8. The ordinances of the church are but two—baptism of water and the Lord's Supper, which are heartily received and conscientiously observed, as instituted by the head of the church, our Lord and Saviour Jesus Christ.—Matt. 28:19. 20; 1 Cor. 11: 23, 24.

9. The second literal personal advent of our Saviour, Jesus Christ, who will come actually and visibly in like manner as He ascended, for whose personal coming the children of God are admonished to look with confident hope, and with the blessed assurance that when He shall come to be glorified in His saints, and admired by all them that believe, they will become the happy partakers of His glory in the Kingdom prepared for them from the foundation of the world.—Dan. 7:13, 14; Matt. 24:30, 31; Acts 1:11; 1 Thess. 4:15-17; Rev. 1:7, 22:20.

10. The resurrection of the body, according to the Scriptures, which declare that all who die shall live again; that the saints who are alive at the coming of the Lord shall be changed in a moment, in the twinkling of an eye, and shall be glorified, and that all who are dead shall hear the voice of the Son of God, and shall rise again.—Isa. 26:19; Dan. 12:2; John 5:28, 29; 1 Cor. 15:52-55; Job 14:14, 15.

11. The future and final judgment, in which all who have lived shall be summoned into the presence of the Lord, there to be judged for the deeds done in the body.—Rom. 14:10; 2 Cor. 5:10; Rev. 20:12, 13; 22:11; Acts 17:30, 31; Heb. 9:27.

12. The final glorification of the saints, at the coming of our Lord Jesus Christ, which is yet future, and can only be realized when Christ shall come, in the glory of the Father, to end the dispensation and to receive His saints to Himself, that where He is, there they may be also, according to His own blessed promise.—Matt. 13:43; John 14:13; 17:24; Rev. 21:1-4.

13. The final rejection, condemnation and eternal punishment of all impenitent and unsaved persons.—Psa. 9:17; Prov. 14:32; Matt. 25:26; 2 Thess. 1:7-9; Rev. 20:14, 15.

Notes: *Closely related to the Church of God (Holiness), the Independent Holiness People differ primarily on matters of organization. However, unlike the Church of God (Holiness), their statement makes no reference to premillennialism or the nature of Biblical authority.*

PRINCIPLES OF FAITH (EMMANUEL ASSOCIATION)

GOD THE FATHER

There is but one living and true God (Isa. 45:21, 22; Deut. 6:4), everlasting (Psalm 90:2), of infinite power, wisdom, and goodness—the Maker and Preserver of all things visible and invisible. And in the unity of this Godhead there are three Persons (I John 5:7; II Cor. 13:14) equal in power and eternity—the Father, the Son, and the Holy Ghost (John 1:1; 15:26).

GOD THE SON

The Son of God is the Word, the eternal and true God, one with the Father (John 1:1-3), who took man's nature upon Him by being conceived of the Holy Ghost and born of the Virgin Mary; so that both natures—divine and human—were perfectly and inseparably joined in Him (John 1:14; Phil. 2:6-8). Therefore He is Christ the Anointed, very God and very Man, who suffered, was crucified, died, and was buried, and rose again (He "is risen again, who is even at the right hand of God, who also maketh intercession for us" [Rom. 8:34]), and thus presented Himself a sacrifice for both our original sin (Rom. 6:6; Heb. 10:10) and actual sins (Gal. 1:4; Eph. 1:7; I Peter 3:18), in order to reconcile us to the Eternal Father (II Cor. 5:19).

GOD THE HOLY GHOST

The Holy Ghost proceeds from the Father and the Son (John 15:26), and is one with Them, ever present and efficiently active in and with the Church of Christ. As the Executive of the God-head He convinces the world of sin (John 16:8), regenerates those who repent (John 3:5), sanctifies believers (Acts 15:8, 9), and guides all into the truth as the truth is in Jesus (John 16:13).

THE HOLY SCRIPTURES

We understand the sixty-six canonical books of the Old and New Testaments to be the Word of God, given by divine inspiration (II Tim. 3:16; II Peter 1:20), revealing the will of God concerning us in all things necessary to our salvation (John 5:39; II John 10); so that whatever is not contained therein is not to be enjoined as an article of faith (Isa. 8:20).

ORIGINAL SIN

Original sin, or total depravity, is that corruption of the nature of all the offspring of Adam by reason of which everyone is destitute of original righteousness (I Cor. 15:22; Rom. 5:12, 18; 3:12), and is inclined to evil and that continually (Gen. 6:5; 8:2). In the Scriptures it is designated as "the carnal mind" (Rom. 8:7), "our old man" (Rom. 6:6), "the flesh" (Rom. 8:5, 8), "sin that dwelleth in me" (Rom. 7:17), and similar expressions. It continues to exist after regeneration, though subdued, until eradicated and destroyed (I John 3:8) by the mighty baptism of the Holy Ghost and Fire.

The condition of man since the fall of Adam is such that he can not turn and prepare himself by his own natural strength and works to faith and calling upon God; wherefore, we have no power to do good works pleasant and acceptable unto God, without the grace of God, which is freely given by Christ to all men without respect of persons (Titus 2:11, 12), assisting us. "For it is God which worketh in you both to will and to do of his good pleasure."

FAITH

Living faith is the gift of God (Eph. 2:8) imparted to the obedient heart through the Word of God (Rom. 10:17) and the ministry of the Holy Ghost (Eph. 2:18). This faith becomes effective as it is exercised by man with the aid of the Spirit, which aid is always assured when the heart has met the divine condition (Heb. 5:9). Living faith is to be distinguished from intellectual confidence which may be in the possession of any unawakened soul (Rom. 10:1-4).

JUSTIFICATION AND REGENERATION

Though these two phases of the New Birth occur simultaneously, they are, in fact, two separate and distinct acts. Justification is that gracious and judicial act of God whereby a soul is granted complete absolvence from all guilt and a full release from the penalty of sin (Rom. 3:23-25). This act of divine grace is wrought by faith in the merits of our Lord and Saviour Jesus Christ (Rom. 5:1). Regeneration is the impartation of divine life which is manifested in that radical change in the moral character of man from the love and life of sin to the love of God and the life of righteousness (II Cor. 5:17; I Peter 1:23).

CONSECRATION

Consecration necessary for entire sanctification is the total abandonment of the redeemed soul to the whole will of God (Rom. 12:1; 6:11, 13, 22). As such it takes place after the work of regeneration and must be completed before the soul is sanctified. While the act of consecration depends wholly upon the individual, the scope of consecration must be dictated by the Holy Spirit (Acts 5:32). In saying that consecration is the act of the creature, it must be understood that every step in grace is undertaken through the assistance of the Holy Spirit (I Peter 1:22). This consecration becomes so deep that it includes perfect submission to the crucifixion of the body of sin (Rom. 6:6; Gal. 2:20; 5:24).

ENTIRE SANCTIFICATION OR THE BAPTISM WITH THE HOLY GHOST

Entire sanctification is that second definite, instantaneous work of grace subsequent to regeneration (John 17:9; Eph. 1:12, 13) wrought in the heart of the justified person through faith by the baptism of the Holy Ghost fire, whereby the heart of the believer is cleansed from all original sin, and purified by the filling of the Holy Ghost (Acts 15:8, 9; Rom. 15:16).

THE WITNESS OF THE SPIRIT

The witness of the Spirit is that inward impression wrought on the soul whereby the Spirit of God immediately and directly assures our spirit that Bible conditions are met for salvation and that the work of grace is complete in the soul (Rom. 8:15, 16). Therefore none should think that they are either saved or sanctified until the Spirit of God has added His testimony (I John 5:10). And if we take care to

walk with God and not grieve the Holy Spirit, we shall have an abiding testimony (Eph. 4:30).

SIN AFTER JUSTIFICATION

Not every sin wilfully committed after justification is blasphemy against the Holy Ghost, and is unpardonable. Therefore the grant of repentance is not to be denied to such as fall into sin after justification (James 5:19, 20).

SIN AFTER ENTIRE SANCTIFICATION

After we have received the Holy Ghost, any careless attitude toward the covenant that we entered when we were sanctified shall cause us to depart from grace given, and to fall into sin. Only through deep repentance, which God may permit, shall we then turn to God and receive forgiveness of our sins.

WATER BAPTISM

As revealed in the Gospel, water baptism bore a twofold testimony. First, that the candidate had been a partaker of divine grace, which qualified him to enter into fellowship with the children of God. Second, that his testimony was accepted by the one who baptized him (Matt. 3:7; Acts 8:35-38; 10:47, 48).

It is not to be held as being essential in bringing either justifying or sanctifying grace to one's heart, for the apostle administered it to Cornelius, who had previously received the baptism of the Holy Ghost.

The individual conscience should be satisfied as to the mode.

THE LORD'S SUPPER

The Lord's Supper was instituted by our Saviour with bread and the fruit of the vine on the night of His betrayal (Luke 22:19, 20). In observing it, we commemorate the fact that His body was broken and His blood was shed upon the cross, to redeem us from the curse of sin and death (I Cor. 11:23-29).

The elements used are representative, and the means whereby the body of Christ is received and eaten in the supper is faith. God has directed that each one examine himself before partaking, and so let him eat of that bread and drink of that cup (Matt. 26:26-29; I Cor. 10:16; 11:20-29).

HEALING

We believe and embrace the scriptural doctrine of healing for the body, and maintain that it is the privilege of every child of God to be healed in answer to the prayer of faith, according to James 5:14, 15. Yet we are not to sever fellowship from, or pass judgment on, those who use other providential means for the restoration of health (James 5:16; Acts 4:14; Matt. 10:8; Luke 9:2; II Cor. 12:9; John 9:1-34).

THE CHRISTIAN SABBATH

We believe the Christian Sabbath to be of divine origin. The Jewish Sabbath was obligatory upon those living under the law of Moses until the time of its consummation. We recognize the first day of the week as being the Christian Sabbath under the present dispensation (Rev. 1:10; I Cor. 16:2), the observance of which we hold obligatory and sacredly binding upon the followers of the

Lord Jesus, in commemoration of the glorious victory achieved through His resurrection from the dead on that eventful day. It was also duly and persistently observed by the Apostolic Church (Acts 20:7; I Cor. 16:2), and was the day upon which the Holy Ghost was poured out on the disciples.

THE SECOND COMING OF THE LORD

We believe that the coming of our Lord is to be personal and premillennial, also that it is imminent (Acts 1:9-11; I Thess. 4:14-17; Matt. 25:13; Rev. 22:12). We must distinguish between the Rapture—His coming in the air to receive His saints, which may occur at any moment—and the Revelation—His coming down to earth with His saints (II Thess. 1:7-10; Matt. 24:27; 26:29; Rev. 20:4), which latter will not occur until after the gathering of Israel, the manifestation of Antichrist, and other prophesied events (II Thess. 2:8-10; Rev. 19:20).

Notes: The principles of the association are based upon, but differ from many points contained in, the statement of belief of its parent, the Pilgrim Holiness Church. The differences are not so much in doctrine as in standards of conduct (the association being more strict). The principles deleted some articles (such as the one on "Eternal Security") and added others (such as the one on the "Christian Sabbath"). The Pilgrim Holiness Church merged with the Wesleyan Methodist Church in 1968 to form the Wesleyan Church. At that time, the Pilgrim Holiness Church's statement of belief was replaced by that of the Wesleyan Church.

* * *

ARTICLES OF RELIGION [FREE METHODIST CHURCH (PRIOR TO 1974)]

I. OF FAITH IN THE HOLY TRINITY

21. There is but one living and true God, everlasting, without body or parts, of infinite power, wisdom, and goodness the maker and preserver of all things, visible and invisible. And in unity of this Godhead there are three persons of one substance, power, and eternity—the Father, the Son, and the Holy Ghost.

II. OF THE WORD, OR SON OF GOD, WHO WAS MADE VERY MAN

22. The Son, who is the Word of the Father, the very and eternal God, of one substance with the Father, took man's nature in the womb of the blessed virgin so that the two whole and perfect natures, that is to say, the Godhead and manhood, were joined together in one person, never to be divided, whereof is one Christ, very God and very man, who truly suffered, was crucified, dead, and buried, to be the one mediator between God and man, by the sacrifice of Himself both for original sin and for the actual transgressions of men.

III. OF THE RESURRECTION OF CHRIST

23. Christ did truly rise again from the dead, and took again His body, with all things appertaining to the perfection of man's nature, wherewith He ascended into heaven, and there sitteth until He returns to judge all men at the last day.

IV. OF THE HOLY GHOST

24. The Holy Ghost, proceeding from the Father and the Son, is of one substance, majesty, and glory with the Father and the Son, very and eternal God.

V. THE SUFFICIENCY OF THE HOLY SCRIPTURES FOR SALVATION

25. The Holy Scriptures contain all things necessary to salvation; so that whatsoever is not read therein, nor may be proved thereby, is not to be required of any man, that it should be believed as an article of faith, or be thought requisite or necessary to salvation. By the term Holy Scriptures we understand those canonical books of the Old and New Testaments of whose authority there was never any doubt in the Church.

The names of the canonical books are: Genesis, Exodus, Leviticus, Numbers, Deuteronomy, Joshua, Judges, Ruth, I and II Samuel, I and II Kings, I and II Chronicles, Ezra, Nehemiah, Esther, Job, Psalms, Proverbs, Ecclesiastes, Song of Solomon, Isaiah, Jeremiah, Lamentations, Ezekiel, Daniel, Hosea, Joel, Amos, Obadiah, Jonah, Micah, Nahum, Habakkuk, Zephaniah, Haggai, Zechariah, Malachi.

All the books of the New Testament, as they are commonly received, we do receive and account canonical: Matthew, Mark, Luke, John, Acts, Romans, I and II Corinthians, Galatians, Ephesians, Philippians, Colossians, I and II Thessalonians, I and II Timothy, Titus, Philemon, Hebrews, James, I and II Peter, I, II, and III John, Jude, Revelation.

VI. OF THE OLD TESTAMENT

26. The Old Testament is not contrary to the New; for in both the Old and New Testaments everlasting life is offered to mankind by Christ, who is the only mediator between God and man. Wherefore they are not to be heard who feign that the old fathers did look only for transitory promises. Although the law given from God by Moses, as touching ceremonies and rites, doth not bind Christians, nor ought the civil precepts thereof, of necessity to be received in any commonwealth; yet, notwithstanding, no Christian whatsoever is free from obedience to the commandments which are called moral.

VII. OF ORIGINAL OR BIRTH SIN

27. Original sin standeth not in the following of Adam, as the Pelagians do vainly talk, but it is the corruption of the nature of every man that naturally is engendered of the offspring of Adam, whereby man is very far gone from original righteousness, and of his own nature inclined to evil and that continually.

VIII. OF FREE WILL

28. The condition of man after the fall of Adam is such that he cannot turn and prepare himself by his own natural strength and works to faith and calling upon God, wherefore we have no power to do good works, pleasing and acceptable to God, without the grace of God by Christ enabling us, that we may have a good

will, and working with us, when we have that good will.

IX. OF THE JUSTIFICATION AND REGENERATION OF MAN

29. We are accounted righteous before God only for the merit of our Lord and Saviour Jesus Christ by faith, and not for our own works or deservings; wherefore, that we are justified by faith only, is a most wholesome doctrine, and very full of comfort. Concurrently with justification we are regenerated by the Holy Spirit, who imparts spiritual life and renews us after the image of Him who created us.

X. OF GOOD WORKS

30. Although good works, which are the fruits of faith and follow after justification, cannot put away our sins and endure the severity of God's judgments, yet they are pleasing and acceptable to God in Christ, and spring out of a true and lively faith, insomuch that by them a lively faith may be as evidently known as a tree is discerned by its fruit.

XI. OF WORKS OF SUPEREROGATION

31. Voluntary works—besides, over and above God's commandments—which are called works of supererogation, cannot be taught without arrogancy and impiety. For by them men do declare that they do not only render unto God as much as they are bound to do, but that they do more for His sake than of bounden duty is required; whereas Christ saith plainly, "When ye have done all that is commanded you, say, We are unprofitable servants."

XII. OF SIN AFTER JUSTIFICATION

32. Not every sin willingly committed after justification is the sin against the Holy Ghost, and unpardonable. Wherefore the grant of repentance is not to be denied to such as fall into sin after justification. After we have received the Holy Ghost, we may depart from grace given, and fall into sin, and by the grace of God rise again and amend our lives. Therefore, they are to be condemned who say they can no more sin as long as they live here, or who deny the place of foregiveness to such as truly repent.

XIII. OF ENTIRE SANCTIFICATION

33. Entire sanctification is that work of the Holy Spirit, subsequent to regeneration, by which the fully consecrated believer, upon exercise of faith in the atoning blood of Christ, is cleansed in that moment from all inward sin and empowered for service. The resulting relationship is attested by the witness of the Holy Spirit and is maintained by obedience and faith. Entire sanctification enables the believer to love God with all his heart, soul, strength, and mind, and his neighbor as himself, and prepares him for greater growth in grace.

XIV. FUTURE REWARD AND PUNISHMENT

34. God has appointed a day in which He will judge the world in righteousness by Jesus Christ, according to the gospel. The righteous shall have in heaven an inheritance incorruptible, undefiled, and that fadeth not away. The wicked shall go away into everlasting punishment, where their worm dieth not, and the fire is not quenched.

XV. OF SPEAKING IN THE CONGREGATION IN SUCH A TONGUE AS THE PEOPLE UNDERSTAND

35. It is a thing plainly repugnant to the Word of God and the custom of the primitive Church to have public prayer in the church or to minister the sacrament in a tongue not understood by the people.

XVI. OF THE CHURCH

36. The visible Church of Christ is a congregation of faithful men, in which the pure Word of God is preached, and the sacraments are duly administered, according to Christ's ordinance, in all those things that of necessity are requisite to the same.

XVII. OF THE SACRAMENTS

37. Sacraments ordained of Christ are not only badges or tokens of Christian men's profession, but they are also certain signs of grace, and of God's good will toward us, by the which He doth work invisibly in us, and doth not only quicken but also strengthen and confirm our faith in Him.

XVIII. OF BAPTISM

38. Baptism is not only a sign of profession and mark of difference, whereby Christians are distinguished from others who are not baptized, but it is also a sign of regeneration or the new birth. The baptism of young children is to be retained in the church.

XIX. OF THE LORD'S SUPPER

39. The Supper of the Lord is not merely a sign of the love that Christians ought to have among themselves one to another, but rather is a sacrament of our redemption by Christ's death, insomuch that, to such as rightly, worthily, and with faith receive the same, the bread which we break is a partaking of the body of Christ; and likewise the cup of blessing is a partaking of the blood of Christ.

Transubstantiation, or the change of the substance of bread and wine in the Supper of our Lord, cannot be proved by Holy Writ, but is repugnant to the plain word of the Scripture, overthroweth the nature of a sacrament, and hath given occasion to many superstitions.

The body of Christ is given, taken, and eaten in the Supper only after a heavenly and spiritual manner; and the means whereby the body of Christ is received and eaten in the Supper, is faith. The sacrament of the Lord's Supper was not by Christ's ordinance reserved, carried about, lifted up, or worshipped.

XX. OF THE ONE OBLATION OF CHRIST, FINISHED UPON THE CROSS

40. The offering of Christ, once made, is a perfect redemption, propitiation, and satisfaction for all the sins of the whole world, both original and actual; and there is none other satisfaction for sin but that alone.

Wherefore the sacrifice of the masses, in the which it is said that the priest doth offer Christ for the quick and the dead, to have remission of pain or guilt, is a blasphemous and dangerous deceit.

XXI. OF THE RITES AND CEREMONIES OF CHURCHES

41. It is not necessary that rites and ceremonies should in all places be the same, or exactly alike; for they have been always different, and may be changed according to the diversity of countries, times, and men's manners, so that nothing be ordained against God's Word. Whosoever through his private judgment, willingly and purposely doth openly break the rites and ceremonies of the church to which he belongs, which are not repugnant to the Word of God, and are ordained and approved by common authority, ought to be rebuked openly, that others may fear to do the like, as one that offendeth against the common order of the church, and woundeth the conscience of the weak brethren. We recognize the right of every denomination to ordain, change, or abolish rites and ceremonies so that all things may be done to edification.

XXII. OF CHRISTIAN MEN'S GOODS

42. The riches and goods of Christians are not common, as touching the right, title, and possession of the same, as some do falsely boast. Notwithstanding, every man ought, of such things as he possesseth, liberally to give alms to the poor according to his ability.

XXIII. OF A CHRISTIAN MAN'S OATH

43. As we confess that vain and rash swearing is forbidden Christian men by our Lord Jesus Christ, and James the apostle; so we hold that the Christian religion doth not prohibit, but that a man may take oath when the magistrate requireth in a case of faith and charity, so it be done according to the prophet's teaching, in justice, judgment, and truth.

Notes: *In 1974 the Free Methodist Church adopted a newly-written set of Articles of Religion. Prior to that time, it had adopted a modified version of the Twenty-five Articles of Religion common to Methodism. The Free Methodist revisions included additions to several articles (Of Justification and Regeneration of Man), deletions from some (Of the Sacraments), the addition of two articles (Of Entire Sanctification, Future Reward and Punishment), and the deletion of four articles (Of Purgatory, Of Both Kinds, Of the Marriage of Ministers, and Of the Rulers of the United States). A footnote to the article "Of a Christian Man's Oath" upholds the rights of members who have a conscientious objection to oath-taking.*

These articles became the basis for the articles of religion of the Evangelical Wesleyan Church whose original members left the Free Methodist Church in the early 1960s.

ARTICLES OF RELIGION [FREE METHODIST CHURCH (1974)]

GOD

I. THE HOLY TRINITY

101. We believe in the one living and true God, the maker and preserver of all things. And in the unity of this Godhead there are three persons: the Father, the Son, and the Holy Spirit. These three are one in eternity, deity, and purpose; everlasting, of infinite power, wisdom, and goodness.

II. THE FATHER

102. We believe the Father is the cause of all that exists whether of matter or spirit. He with the Son and the Holy Spirit made man to bear his image. By intention he relates to man as Father, thereby forever declaring his goodwill toward man. He is, according to the New Testament, the one who both seeks and receives penitent sinners.

III. THE SON

HIS INCARNATION

103. We believe God was himself in Jesus Christ to reconcile man to God. Conceived by the Holy Spirit, born of the Virgin Mary, he joined together the deity of God and the humanity of man. Jesus of Nazareth was God in human flesh, truly God and truly man. He came to save us. For us the Son of God suffered, was crucified, dead and buried. He poured out his life as a blameless sacrifice for our sin and transgressions. We gratefully acknowledge that he is our Savior, the one perfect mediator between God and man.

HIS RESURRECTION AND EXALTATION

104. We believe Jesus Christ is risen victorious from the dead. His resurrected body became more glorious, not hindered by ordinary human limitations. Thus he ascended into heaven. There he sits as our exalted Lord at the right hand of God the Father, where he intercedes for us until all his enemies shall be brought into complete subjection. He will return to judge all men. Every knee will bow and every tongue confess Jesus Christ is Lord, to the glory of God the Father.

IV. THE HOLY SPIRIT

HIS PERSON

105. We believe the Holy Spirit is the third person of the Trinity. Proceeding from the Father and the Son, he is one with them, the eternal Godhead; equal in deity, majesty, and power. He is God effective in creation, in life, and in the church. The incarnation and ministry of Jesus Christ were accomplished by the Holy Spirit. He continues to reveal, interpret, and glorify the Son.

HIS WORK IN SALVATION

106. We believe the Holy Spirit is the administrator of the salvation planned by the Father and provided by the Son's death, resurrection, and ascension. He is the effective agent in our conviction, regeneration, sanc-

tification, and glorification. He is our Lord's ever-present self, indwelling, assuring, and enabling the believer.

HIS RELATION TO THE CHURCH

107. We believe the Holy Spirit is poured out upon the church by the Father and the Son. He is the church's life and witnessing power. He bestows the love of God and makes real the lordship of Jesus Christ in the believer so that both his gifts of words and service may achieve the common good and build and increase the church. In relation to the world he is the Spirit of truth, and his instrument is the Word of God.

THE SCRIPTURES
V. SUFFICIENCY

108. We believe the Holy Scriptures are God's record, uniquely inspired by the Holy Spirit. They have been given without error faithfully recorded by holy men of God as moved by the Holy Spirit, and subsequently transmitted without corruption of any essential doctrine. They are the authoritative record of the revelation of God's acts in creation, in history, in our salvation, and especially in his Son, Jesus Christ.

We believe this written Word fully reveals the will of God concerning man in all things necessary to salvation and Christian living; so that whatever is not found therein, nor can be proved thereby, is not to be required of one as an article of faith or as necessary to salvation.

VI. AUTHORITY OF THE OLD TESTAMENT

109. We believe the Old Testament is not contrary to the New. Both Testaments bear witness to God's salvation in Christ; both speak of God's will for his people. The ancient laws for ceremonies and rites, and the civil precepts for the nation Israel are not necessarily binding on Christians today. But, on the example of Jesus we are obligated to obey the moral commandments of the Old Testament.

The books of the Old Testament are: Genesis, Exodus, Leviticus, Numbers, Deuteronomy, Joshua, Judges, Ruth, I Samuel, II Samuel, I Kings, II Kings, I Chronicles, II Chronicles, Ezra, Nehemiah, Esther, Job, Psalms, Proverbs, Ecclesiastes, The Song of Solomon, Isaiah, Jeremiah, Lamentations, Ezekiel, Daniel, Hosea, Joel, Amos, Obadiah, Jonah, Micah, Nahum, Habakkuk, Zephaniah, Haggai, Zechariah, Malachi.

VII. NEW TESTAMENT

110. We believe the New Testament fulfills and interprets the Old Testament. It is the record of the revelation of God in Jesus Christ and the Holy Spirit. It is God's final word regarding man, his sin, and his salvation, the world, and destiny.

The books of the New Testament are: Matthew, Mark, Luke, John, Acts, Romans, I Corinthians, II Corinthians, Galatians, Ephesians, Philipians, Colos-

sians, I Thessalonians, II Thessalonians, I Timothy, II Timothy, Titus, Philemon, Hebrews, James, I Peter, II Peter, I John, II John, III John, Jude, Revelation.

MAN
VIII. A FREE MORAL PERSON

111. We believe God created man in his own image, innocent, morally free and responsible to choose between good and evil, right and wrong. By the sin of Adam, man as the offspring of Adam is corrupted in his very nature so that from birth he is inclined to sin. He is unable by his own strength and work to restore himself in right relationship with God and to merit eternal salvation. God, the Omnipotent, provides all the resources of the Trinity to make it possible for man to respond to his grace through faith in Jesus Christ as Savior and Lord. By God's grace and help man is enabled to do good works with a free will.

IX. LAW OF LIFE AND LOVE

112. We believe God's law for all human life, personal and social, is expressed in two divine commands: Love the Lord God with all your heart, and love your neighbor as yourself. These commands reveal what is best for man in his relationship with God, persons, and society. They set forth the principles of human duty in both individual and social action. They recognize God as the only Sovereign. All men as created by him and in his image have the same inherent rights regardless of sex, race, or color. Men should therefore give God absolute obedience in their individual, social, and political acts. They should strive to secure to everyone respect for his person, his rights, and his greatest happiness in the possession and exercise of the right within the moral law.

X. GOOD WORKS

113. We believe good works are the fruit of faith in Jesus Christ, but works cannot save us from our sins nor from God's judgment. As expressions of Christian faith and love, our good works performed with reverence and humility are both acceptable and pleasing to God. However, good works do not earn God's grace.

SALVATION
XI. CHRIST'S SACRIFICE

114. We believe Christ offered once and for all the one perfect sacrifice for the sins of the whole world. No other satisfaction for sin is necessary; none other can atone.

XII. THE NEW LIFE IN CHRIST

115. We believe a new life and a right relationship with God are made possible through the redemptive acts of God in Jesus Christ. God, by his Spirit, acts to impart new life and put us into a relationship with himself as we repent and our faith responds to his grace. Justification, regeneration, and adoption speak significantly to entrance into and continuance in the new life.

JUSTIFICATION

116. Justification is a legal term that emphasizes that by our new relationship in Jesus Christ we are in fact accounted righteous, being freed from both the guilt and the penalty of our sins.

REGENERATION

117. Regeneration is a biological term which illustrates that by our new relationship in Christ we do in fact have a new life and a new spiritual nature capable of faith, love, and obedience to Christ Jesus as Lord. The believer is born again. He is a new creation. The old life is past; a new life is begun.

ADOPTION

118. Adoption is a filial term full of warmth, love, and acceptance. It denotes that by our new relationship in Christ we have become his wanted children freed from the mastery of both sin and Satan. The believer has the witness of the Spirit that he is a child of God.

XIII. ENTIRE SANCTIFICATION

119. We believe entire sanctification to be that work of the Holy Spirit, subsequent to regeneration, by which the fully consecrated believer, upon exercise of faith in the atoning blood of Christ, is cleansed in that moment from all inward sin and empowered for service. The resulting relationship is attested by the witness of the Holy Spirit and is maintained by faith and obedience. Entire sanctification enables the believer to love God with all his heart, soul, strength, and mind, and his neighbor as himself, and it prepares him for greater growth in grace.

XIV. RESTORATION

120. We believe the Christian may be sustained in a growing relationship with Jesus as Savior and Lord. However, he may grieve the Holy Spirit in the relationships of life without returning to the dominion of sin. When he does, he must humbly accept the correction of the Holy Spirit, trust in the advocacy of Jesus, and mend his relationships.

The Christian can sin willfully and sever his relationship with Christ. Even so by repentance before God, forgiveness is granted and the relationship with Christ restored, for not every sin is the sin against the Holy Spirit and unpardonable. God's grace is sufficient for those who truly repent and, by his enabling, amend their lives. However, forgiveness does not give the believer liberty to sin and escape the consequences of sinning.

God has given responsibility and power to the church to restore a penitent believer through loving reproof, counsel, and acceptance.

THE CHURCH

XV. THE CHURCH

121. We believe the church is created by God; it is the people of God. Christ Jesus is its Lord and Head; the Holy Spirit is its life and power. It is both divine and human, heavenly and earthly, ideal and imperfect. It is an organism, not an unchanging institution. It exists to fulfill the purposes of God in Christ. It redemptively ministers to persons. Christ loved the church and gave himself for it that it should be holy and without blemish. The church is a fellowship of the redeemed and the redeeming, preaching the Word of God and administering the sacraments according to Christ's instruction. The Free Methodist Church purposes to be representative of what the church of Jesus Christ should be on earth. It therefore requires specific commitment regarding the faith and life of its members. In its requirements it seeks to honor Christ and obey the written Word of God.

XVI. THE LANGUAGE OF WORSHIP

122. We believe that according to the Word of God and the custom of the early church, public worship and prayer and the administration of the sacraments should be in a language understood by the people. The Reformation applied this principle to provide for the use of the common language of the people. It is likewise clear that the Apostle Paul places the strongest emphasis upon rational and intelligible utterance in worship. We cannot endorse practices which plainly violate these scriptural principles.

XVII. THE HOLY SACRAMENTS

123. We believe water baptism and the Lord's Supper are the sacraments of the church commanded by Christ. They are means of grace through faith, tokens of our profession of Christian faith, and signs of God's gracious ministry toward us. By them, he works within us to quicken, strengthen, and confirm our faith.

BAPTISM

124. We believe water baptism is a sacrament of the church, commanded by our Lord, signifying acceptance of the benefits of the atonement of Jesus Christ to be administered to believers, as declaration of their faith in Jesus Christ as Savior.

Baptism is a symbol of the new covenant of grace as circumcision was the symbol of the old covenant; and, since infants are recognized as being included in the atonement, we hold that they may be baptized upon the request of parents or guardians who shall give assurance for them of necessary Christian training. They shall be required to affirm the vow for themselves before being accepted into church membership.

THE LORD'S SUPPER

125. We believe the Lord's Supper is a sacrament of our redemption by Christ's death. To those who rightly, worthily, and with faith receive it, the bread which we break is a partaking of the body of Christ; and likewise the cup of blessing is a partaking of the blood of Christ. The supper is also a sign of the love and unity that Christians have among themselves.

Christ, according to his promise, is really present in the sacrament. But his body is given, taken, and eaten only after a heavenly and spiritual manner. No change is effected in the element; the bread and wine are not literally the body and blood of Christ. Nor is the body and blood of Christ literally present with the elements. The elements are never to be considered objects of worship. The body of Christ is received and eaten in faith.

LAST THINGS

XVIII. THE KINGDOM OF GOD

126. We believe that the kingdom of God is a prominent Bible theme providing the Christian with both his task and hope. Jesus announced its presence. The kingdom is realized now as God's reign is established in the hearts and lives of believers.

The church, by its prayers, example, and proclamation of the gospel, is the appointed and appropriate instrument of God in building his kingdom.

But the kingdom is also future and is related to the return of Christ when judgment will fall upon the present order. The enemies of Christ will be subdued; the reign of God will be established; a total cosmic renewal which is both material and moral shall occur; and the hope of the redeemed will be fully realized.

XIX. THE RETURN OF CHRIST

127. We believe the return of Christ is certain and may occur at any moment. It is not given us to know the hour. At his return he will fulfill all prophecies concerning his final triumph over all evil. The believer's response is joyous expectation, watchfulness, readiness, and diligence.

XX. RESURRECTION

128. We believe in the bodily resurrection from the dead of both the just and the unjust, they that have done good unto the resurrection of life; they that have done evil unto the resurrection of damnation. The resurrected body will be a spiritual body, but the person will be whole and identifiable. The resurrection of Christ is the guarantee of resurrection unto life to those who are in him.

XXI. JUDGMENT

129. We believe God has appointed a day in which he will judge the world in righteousness in accordance with the gospel and men's deeds in this life.

XXII. FINAL DESTINY

130. We believe the eternal destiny of man is determined by God's grace and man's response, not by arbitrary decrees of God. For those who trust him and obediently follow Jesus as Savior and Lord, there is a heaven of eternal glory and the blessedness of Christ's presence. But for the finally impenitent there is a hell of eternal suffering and of separation from God.

131. The doctrines of the Free Methodist Church are based upon the Holy Scriptures and are derived from their total biblical context. The references below are appropriate passages related to the given articles.

They are listed in their biblical sequence and are not intended to be exhaustive.

GOD

I. HOLY TRINITY

Genesis 1:1-2; Exodus 3:13-15; Deuteronomy 6:4; Matthew 28:19; John 1:1-3; 5:19-23; 8:58; 14:9-11; 15:26; 16:13-15; II Corinthians 13:14.

II. FATHER

Genesis 1:26-27; Psalm 103:13-14; Isaiah 40:28-29; 64:8; Matthew 6:8; 18:14; Luke 15:11-32; John 4:23; I John 1:3.

III. SON - HIS INCARNATION

Matthew 1:21; 20:28; 26:27-28; Luke 1:35; 19:10; John 1:1, 10, 14; II Corinthians 5:18-19; Philippians 2:5-8; Hebrews 2:17; 9:14-15.

SON - HIS RESURRECTION AND EXALTATION

Matthew 25:31-32; Luke 24:1-7; 24:39; John 20:19; Acts 1:9-11; 2:24; Romans 8:33-34; II Corinthians 5:10; Philippians 2:9-11; Hebrews 1:1-4.

IV. HOLY SPIRIT - HIS PERSON

Matthew 28:19; John 4:24; 14:16-17, 26; 15:26; 16:13-15

HOLY SPIRIT - HIS WORK IN SALVATION

John 16:7-8; Acts 15:8-9; Romans 8:9, 14-16; I Corinthians 3:16; II Corinthians 3:17-18; Galatians 4:6.

HOLY SPIRIT - HIS RELATION TO THE CHURCH

Acts 5:3-4; Romans 8:14; I Corinthians 12:4-7; II Peter 1:21.

THE SCRIPTURES

V. SUFFICIENCY

Deuteronomy 4:2; 28:9; Psalm 19:7-11; John 14:26; 17:17; Romans 15:4; II Timothy 3:14-17; Hebrews 4:12; James 1:21.

VI. AUTHORITY OF THE OLD TESTAMENT

Matthew 5:17-18; Luke 10:25-28; John 5:39, 46-47; Acts 10:43; Galatians 5:3-4; I Peter 1:10-12.

VII. NEW TESTAMENT

Matthew 24:35; Mark 8:38; John 14:24; Hebrews 2:1-4; II Peter 1:16-21; I John 2:2-6; Revelation 21:5; 22:19.

MAN

VIII. MAN: A FREE MORAL PERSON

Genesis 1:27; Psalm 51:5; 130:3; Romans 5:17-19; Ephesians 2:8-10.

IX. LAW OF LIFE AND LOVE

Matthew 22:35-40; John 15:17; Galatians 3:28; I John 4:19-21.

X. GOOD WORKS

Matthew 5:16; 7:16-20; Romans 3:27-28; Ephesians 2:10; II Timothy 1:8-9; Titus 3:5.

SALVATION

XI. CHRIST'S SACRIFICE

Luke 24:46-48; John 3:16; Acts 4:12; Romans 5:8-11; Galatians 2:16; 3:2-3; Ephesians 1:7-8; 2:13; Hebrews 9:11-14, 25-26; 10:8-14.

XII. THE NEW LIFE IN CHRIST

John 1:12-13; 3:3-8; Acts 13:38-39; Romans 8:15-17; Ephesians 2:8-9; Colossians 3:9-10.

JUSTIFICATION

Psalm 32:1-2; Acts 10:43; Romans 3:21-26, 28; 4:2-5; 5:8-9; I Corinthians 6:11; Philippians 3:9.

REGENERATION

Ezekiel 36:26-27; John 5:24; Romans 6:4; II Corinthians 5:17; Ephesians 4:22-24; Colossians 3:9-10; Titus 3:4-5; I Peter 1:23.

ADOPTION

Romans 8:15-17; Galatians 4:4-7; Ephesians 1:5-6; I John 3:1-3.

XIII. ENTIRE SANCTIFICATION

Leviticus 20:7-8; John 14:16-17; 17:19; Acts 1:8; 2:4; 15:8-9; Romans 5:3-5; 8:12-17; 12:1-2; I Corinthians 6:11; 12:4-11; Galatians 5:22-25; Ephesians 4:22-24; I Thessalonians 4:7; 5:23-24; II Thessalonians 2:13; Hebrews 10:14.

XIV. RESTORATION

Matthew 12:31-32; 18:21-22; Romans 6:1-2; Galatians 6:1; I John 1:9; 2:1-2; 5:16-17; Revelation 2:5; 3:19-20.

THE CHURCH

XV. THE CHURCH

Matthew 16:15-18; 18:17; Acts 2:41-47; 9:31; 12:5; 14:23-26; 15:22; 20:28; I Corinthians 1:2; 11:23; 12:28; 16:1; Ephesians 1:22-23; 2:19-22; 3:9-10; 5:22-23; Colossians 1:18; I Timothy 3:14-15.

XVI. THE LANGUAGE OF WORSHIP

Nehemiah 8:5, 6, 8; Matthew 6:7; I Corinthians 14:6-9; I Corinthians 14:23-25.

XVII. THE HOLY SACRAMENTS

Matthew 26:26-29; 28:19; Acts 22:16; Romans 4:11; I Corinthians 10:16-17; 11:23-26; Galatians 3:27.

BAPTISM

Acts 2:38, 41; 8:12-17; 9:18; 16:33; 18:8; 19:5; John 3:5; I Corinthians 12:13; Galatians 3:27-29; Colossians 2:11-12; Titus 3:5.

THE LORD'S SUPPER

Mark 14:22-24; John 6:53-58; Acts 2:46; I Corinthians 5:7-8; 10:16; 11:20, 23-29.

LAST THINGS

XVIII. THE KINGDOM OF GOD.

Matthew 6:10, 19-20; 24:14; Acts 1:8; Romans 8:19-23; I Corinthians 15:20-25; Philippians 2:9-10; I Thessalonians 4:15-17; II Thessalonians 1:5-12; II Peter 3:3-10; Revelation 14:6; 21:3-8; 22:1-5, 17.

XIX. THE RETURN OF CHRIST

Matthew 24:1-51; 26:64; Mark 13:26-27; Luke 17:26-37; John 14:1-3; Acts 1:9-11; I Thessalonians 4:13-18; Titus 2:11-14; Hebrews 9:27-28; Revelation 1:7; 19:11-16; 22:6-7, 12, 20.

XX. RESURRECTION

John 5:28-29; I Corinthians 15:20, 51-57; II Corinthians 4:13-14.

XXI. JUDGMENT

Matthew 25:31-46; Luke 11:31-32; Acts 10:42; 17:31; Romans 2:15-16; 14:10-11; II Corinthians 5:6-10; Hebrews 9:27-28; 10:26-31; II Peter 3:7.

XXII. DESTINY

Mark 9:42-48; John 14:3; Hebrews 2:1-3; Revelation 20:11-15; 21:22-27.

Notes: *The new articles, rewritten in a more confessional style, were adopted by the Free Methodist Church in 1974. They reflect the twentieth-century debate over the nature of biblical authority and expand the statements on eschatological issues. They also added a lengthy set of scriptural references as a grounding for the new articles.*

* * *

WE BELIEVE (HOLINESS CHRISTIAN CHURCH)

1. In one God, the Creator of all things and man; eternally existing in three Persons, in a threefold relationship, that of the Father, Son and Holy Spirit.

2. That Jesus Christ was begotten by the Holy Spirit, born of the Virgin Mary, and became God in the flesh.

3. That man was created in the image of God, that he sinned and thereby incurred not only physical death, but also the spiritual death which is separation from God. That Adam's sin is imputed to the whole race of mankind, and that all human beings are born with a sinful nature and in the case of those who reach the state of moral responsibility, become sinners before God in thought, word and deed.

4. That Jesus Christ died for our sins (the sins of all men) according to the Scriptures as a substitutionary sacrifice, and that all who believe in Him are freely justified and stand before God accepted in the character and merit of Jesus Christ, with a transformation of life and conduct.

5. That God has provided through the Lord Jesus Christ for a complete cleansing from the sin nature and that this work is subsequent to the new birth, wherein the believer is filled with the Holy Spirit.

6. In the bodily resurrection of Jesus Christ, in His ascension into heaven, and in His present life He is the Head of the Church, the Lord of the individual believer, the High Priest over the house of God, and the Advocate of the family of God.

7. In the personal imminent and premillennial second coming of Christ; first, to receive His own unto Himself, and later to set up His earthly kingdom and

to reign over redeemed Israel and all nations of the world; that is, to bring peace and blessing to the whole world.

8. In the bodily resurrection of the just and the unjust, the everlasting blessedness of the saved, and the everlasting punishment of the unsaved.

9. In the Scriptures of the Old and New Testaments as verbally inspired of God and inerrant in the original writings, and that they are the Word of God and the final authority for faith and conduct.

* * *

ARTICLES OF FAITH (METROPOLITAN CHURCH ASSOCIATION)

I. THE APOSTLES' CREED

I believe in God the Father Almighty, Maker of Heaven and earth; and in Jesus Christ His only Son our Lord, who was conceived by the Holy Ghost; born of the virgin Mary; suffered under Pontius Pilate; was crucified, dead and buried; the third day He rose from the dead; He ascended into Heaven, and sitteth at the right hand of God the Father Almighty; from thence He shall come to judge the quick and the dead.

I believe in the Holy Ghost, the holy catholic church, the communion of saints, the forgiveness of sins, the resurrection of the body and the life everlasting. Amen.

II. THE HOLY TRINITY

There is but one living and true God, existing from eternity, of infinite power, wisdom and goodness, the Maker and Preserver of all things visible and invisible. The Godhead consists of three persons, of one substance and power and eternity—the Father, the Son and the Holy Ghost.

III. JESUS CHRIST THE SON

The Son, who is the Word of the Father, the very and eternal God of one substance with the Father, took man's nature in the womb of the blessed virgin, so that the two whole and perfect natures, that is to say, the Godhead and manhood, were joined together in one Person, never to be divided, whereof is one Christ, very God and very man.

IV. RESURRECTION OF CHRIST

Christ did truly rise from the dead and took again His body, with all things pertaining to the completeness of man's nature, wherewith He ascended into Heaven, and there sitteth on the right hand of God until He shall return to judge all men at the last day.

V. THE HOLY GHOST

The Holy Ghost, proceeding from the Father and the Son, is of one substance, majesty and glory with the Father and the Son, very and eternal God.

VI. THE HOLY SCRIPTURES

The Holy Scriptures contain all things necessary to salvation; so that whatsoever is not read therein, nor may be proved thereby, is not to be required of any man, that it should be believed as an article of faith or be thought requisite or necessary to salvation. By the term "the Holy Scriptures" we understand those canonical books of the Old and New Testament given in the King James version, of whose authority there never was any doubt in the church.

VII. MANKIND

Man, in the person of Adam, was made in the image of God, created a holy being. By transgressing God's law, his nature became depraved, and this condition has been transmitted to all mankind; so that man is very far gone from original righteousness and of his own nature inclined to evil, and that continually.

VIII. OF FREE WILL

The condition of man after the fall is such that, unassisted by divine grace, he cannot find his way back to God and holiness. The office of the Holy Ghost is to draw mankind to God and to work God's grace in the soul. All men can, if they will, yield to the Holy Spirit and turn from sin to God and holiness.

IX. OF THE ATONEMENT

The atonement is the satisfaction made to God for the sins of all mankind, original and actual, by the mediation of Christ, and especially by His passion and death; so that pardon might be granted to all, while the divine perfections are kept in harmony, the authority of the Sovereign is upheld, and the strongest motives are brought to bear upon sinners to lead them to repentance and to faith in Christ, the necessary conditions of pardon, and to a life of obedience, by the gracious aid of the Holy Spirit.

X. JUSTIFICATION

We are justified by faith only, through the merit of our Lord and Savior Jesus Christ, and are accounted righteous before God, not by our own works and deservings but by virtue of the shed blood of Christ.

XI. OF GOOD WORKS

Although good works, which are the fruits of faith and follow after justification, cannot put away our sins or endure the severity of God's judgments, yet they are pleasing and acceptable to God in Christ, and spring out of a true and lively faith; insomuch that by them a lively faith is evidently known, as a tree is discerned by its fruits.

XII. SIN AFTER JUSTIFICATION

Not every sin willingly committed after justification is the sin against the Holy Ghost and unpardonable. While it is possible for a person never to fall into sin after being justified, yet is is possible to fall, and by the grace of God to be restored again. After we have received the Holy Ghost in the grace of entire sanctification, we may depart from grace given and fall into sin, and by the grace of God be restored to justification and holiness. This is not intended in any way to countenance the teaching commonly known as the doctrine of the final perseverance of the saints, and again, as the doctrine of eternal security, which teaches that once having received grace it is impossible so to fall away from God as to be finally lost.

XIII. ENTIRE SANCTIFICATION

Justified persons, while they do not outwardly commit sin, are nevertheless conscious of sin still remaining in the heart. They feel a natural tendency to evil, a proneness to depart from God and to cleave to the things of earth. Those who are sanctified wholly are saved from all inward sin, from evil thoughts and evil tempers. No wrong temper, none contrary to pure love, remains in the soul. All their thoughts, words and actions are governed by pure love.

Entire sanctification takes place subsequently to justification, and is the work of God wrought instantaneously in the soul through faith in the shed blood of Christ.

XIV. FUTURE REWARDS AND PUNISHMENTS

God hath appointed a day in which He will judge the world in righteousness by Jesus Christ, according to the Gospel. The righteous shall have in Heaven an inheritance incorruptible and that fadeth not away. The wicked shall go away into everlasting punishment, where the worm dieth not and the fire is not quenched.

XV. THE CHURCH

The church is the body of Christ. It is not a material structure but is composed of those who are born of the Spirit and washed in the blood of Christ. The visible church of Christ is a congregation of godly men in which the pure Word of God is preached and the sacraments are duly administered, according to Christ's ordinance.

XVI. OF BAPTISM

Baptism is a sign of profession and mark of difference whereby Christians are distinguished from others. It is not essential to salvation, but it serves as the outward sign of an inward work of regeneration wrought by the Holy Ghost, and is to be administered to all that require it. We hereby repudiate the doctrine known as baptismal regeneration, teaching that saving grace is communicated only in the act of baptism.

XVII. OF THE LORD'S SUPPER

The supper of the Lord is a sacrament of our redemption by Christ's death, and its observance shows forth His death till He come. It is a sign, too, of the love that Christians ought to have among themselves, one to another. It is a certain means of grace, by the which He doth work invisibly in us, and doth not only quicken but also strengthens and confirms our faith in Him.

XVIII. OF CHRIST'S SECOND COMING

Of this glorious event, commonly spoken of as the second coming of Christ, Jesus often spoke, and His apostles. It will be premillennial, and the world will be found in a state of sin and rebellion. It will be sudden and visible. It will close the day of grace, thus shutting off all hope of any second probation for those in sin. We repudiate any view of Christ's second coming that militates against the Scripture commands for present holiness of heart and life.

Notes: *After the initial restatement of the Apostles' Creed, these articles are condensed from the Twenty-five Articles of Religion common to Methodism. Two articles on eschatology have been added, including the statement on "Future Rewards and Punishments," borrowed from the Free Methodist Church. The statement on scripture has been altered to affirm the exclusive use of the King James Version of the Bible.*

* * *

THE STATEMENTS OF FAITH OF THE MISSIONARY CHURCH

GOD. There is but one eternal, all powerful, all knowing, and everywhere present triune God—Father, Son and Holy Spirit—who is the Creator and Sustainer of all things. (Deuteronomy 6:4, 5; I Timothy 2:5)

JESUS CHRIST. He is God Incarnate, yet human, lived a sinless life, died to make atonement for the sins of all mankind, was bodily resurrected and is now Mediator at the right hand of the Father, is assuredly coming in power and glory for His believing followers, and is the only Savior of men. (John 1:1,14; Titus 2:11-14)

HOLY SPIRIT. He convicts the world of sin, righteousness and judgment; regenerates all who repent of their sins and believe on the Lord Jesus Christ; and sanctifies, empowers, teaches, guides, and comforts the believers. (John 16:7,8,12-15)

BIBLE. To us, the Bible is the divinely inspired Word of God and thus authoritative in all matters of Christian faith and practice. (II Timothy 3:16; II Peter 1:20,21)

SALVATION. Salvation is genuine repentance of sin and faith in the atoning work of Christ. It brings forgiveness to the penitent, makes him a partaker of the divine nature and gives peace with God. We call this new birth. (Titus 3:5; I Peter 1:3-5)

CHURCH. We believe in the invisible and universal Church as an organism, composed of all believers in the Lord Jesus Christ who have been vitally united by faith to Christ, its living Head and sovereign Lord. (Matthew 16:18; Hebrews 12:22-24)

ORDINANCES. We also believe that the Christian ordinances are two, baptism and the Lord's Supper, and that they are outward rites appointed by Christ to be administered in each church, not as a means of salvation, but as a visible sign and seal of its reality. (Acts 2:36; I Corinthians 11:23-34)

SERVICE. Service includes witnessing to one's faith in Christ and meeting social physical needs in the name of Christ. (I Peter 3:8; Matthew 25:40)

Notes: *The Missionary Church is a holiness church with roots in the Mennonite Church. It sees itself as sound and pure in Biblical interpretation, avoiding extremes while maintaining a balance of teaching that encourages holy living and service.*

* * *

CREED (MISSIONARY METHODIST CHURCH)

1. That the Holy Scriptures are of Divine origin, and are given to us by Inspiration for our instruction, edification and final sanctification.

CREED (MISSIONARY METHODIST CHURCH) (continued)

2. That Christ is the Head of the Church, and the Holy Scriptures the only guide to our faith.

3. That all who believe in the Scriptures and follow Christ are entitled to membership in the Missionary Methodist Church.

4. That God having made man to choose between good and evil, it is his right and duty, acting upon his judgment, based upon the Word of God to choose that society or church, which accords with his judgment and the Holy Scriptures.

5. That no member of these societies shall be tried for any cause or deprived of the benefits of the church, except for those things forbidden in the Holy Scriptures.

6. That ministers, deacons, elders and stewards in the church are of Divine origin, and all elders in the church are equal in rank.

7. That the church has only the right to enforce such rules and regulations as are plainly taught in the Holy Scriptures.

8. That all inherent power to make laws and regulations for the government of the church, is vested in the ministers and members; this power, however, may be delegated to representatives, for the purpose of better organization.

9. That it is the duty of both members and ministers, of these societies, to stand for the right and oppose the wrong at all times.

10. That it is the solemn duty of all ministers to be faithful to their trust, and the duty of the members to regard the ministers as those sent of God, to minister in Holy things.

11. That all ministers and members are to be temperate in all things, and do none of those things that would cause a weaker brother to fall, or bring reproach upon the cause for which we stand, and bring His name into disrepute among men.

12. That we believe in a missionary movement upon the world, for that all mankind are brethren, and our duty to our brother must needs be that we go or send the Gospel to every nation.

Notes: *The Missionary Methodist Church has two doctrinal documents. Its articles of faith derive from the Articles of Religion of the Wesleyan Methodist Church, from whence the Missionary Methodist Church came. The creed deals with issues not covered in the articles.*

*   *   *

ARTICLES OF FAITH (MISSIONARY METHODIST CHURCH)

1. FAITH IN THE HOLY TRINITY.

We believe that there is but one GOD, infinitely and eternally the Maker and Preserver of all mankind. And of this Godhead, there are three persons, of one power and eternity—God, the Father; God, the Son (or Word); and

God, the Holy Ghost. Genesis, 1:1; John, 1:1; John 3:16; Acts, 5:3-4.

2. THE SON OF GOD.

We believe that Jesus Christ is the only begotten Son of God, and was conceived by the Holy Ghost, born of the Virgin Mary, suffered and was crucified at the hands of the Jews and Gentiles—was dead and buried—to be a sacrifice for original and actual sins of all mankind, and to reconcile us to God. Luke, 1 and 2; Mark, 15; and 2 Corinthians, 5:17-19.

3. THE RESURRECTION OF CHRIST.

Now if Christ be preached that He rose from the dead how say some among you that there is no resurrection of the dead? But if there be no resurrection of the dead, then is Christ not risen: And if Christ be not risen, then is our preaching vain, and your faith is also vain . . . But now is Christ risen from the dead and become the first fruits of them that slept. 1 Corinthians, 15:12-14; 20. He then ascended into heaven and there sitteth on the right hand of God, until he shall so come in like manner as he went into heaven, to judge all men on the final day. Psalms, 16; 8:10; Matthew, 28:5-7; Psalms, 24:7-10; Ephesians, 4:8-10.

4. THE HOLY GHOST. (OR SPIRIT).

The Holy Ghost (or Spirit) is the third Person in the Divine Trinity, the Spirit of God proceeding from the Father. Genesis, 1:2; Job, 33:4; John 4:24-26; 16, 17, 26.

5. SUFFICIENCY OF HOLY SCRIPTURES.

All things necessary to salvation, are contained in the Holy Scriptures. Nothing is required of man as an article of faith if it is not found in the Holy Scriptures, or may not be proved thereby. We understand the names of the Old and New Testament Books to be those whose authority is no doubt in the Church, as being and containing the Holy Scriptures.

The Books of the Old Testament are: Genesis, Exodus, Leviticus, Numbers, Deuteronomy, Joshua, Judges, Ruth, 1 Samuel, 2 Samuel, 1 Kings, 2 Kings, 1 Chronicles, 2 Chronicles, Ezra, Nehemiah, Esther, Job, Psalms, Proverbs, Ecclesiastes, The Song of Solomon, Isaiah, Jeremiah, Lamentations, Ezekiel, Daniel, Hosea, Joel, Amos, Obadiah, Jonah, Micah, Nahum, Habakkuk, Zephaniah, Haggai, Zechariah, Malachi.

The books of the New Testament are: Matthew, Mark, Luke, John, The Acts, Romans, I Corinthians, 2 Corinthians, Galatians, Ephesians, Philippians, Colossians, I Thessalonians, 2 Thessalonians, I Timothy, 2 Timothy, Titus, Philemon, Hebrews, James, I Peter, 2 Peter, I John, 2 John, 3 John, Jude, Revelation. Psalms, 19:7-8; also 119; Luke, 24:27; 2 Timothy, 3-16; Revelation 22:14 and 19; Hebrews, 4:12.

6. THE OLD TESTAMENT.

Some would do away with the Old Testament, but without the Old Testament, we could not interpret some things in the New Testament. The New Testament in the Old Testament is concealed, the Old Testament in the New Testament is revealed. As touching some of the civil, ceremonial, and sacrificial rites, given in the law, they are not binding upon Christians now, notwithstanding, no

Christian may ignore or disregard the moral and ethical commandments.

7. RELATIVE DUTIES.

Under the Old Covenant, God commanded, saying, Thou shalt not avenge, nor bear any grudge against the children of thy people, but thou shalt love thy neighbor as thyself: I am the Lord. Leviticus 19:18. Under the New Covenant, His Son Jesus said "Love your enemies, bless them that curse you, do good to them that hate you, and pray for them which despitefully use you and persecute you." Matthew, 5:44. We are to do no wrong toward the stranger, the fatherless, nor the widow; but we are to show love, peace and friendship toward all our neighbors. Psalms 15; Luke, 10:25-37.

8. THE CORRUPT NATURE.

The Scriptures plainly teach that the natural man is corrupt, that he was born in that state, and is continually inclined to sin, and needs the grace of God to elevate and lift him to a higher plane. Genesis, 8:21; Psalms, 51:5; Jeremiah, 17:9; Romans, 3:10-12; Ephesians, 2:1-3.

9. THE WILL AND CHOICE.

God has mercifully endowed all his created intelligence with the power of will and choice, or free moral agency, called the "King of man"—that which chooses and shapes destiny. Deut. 30:19; Joshua, 24:15; John, 5:40; Revelation, 22:17. However this will is always subservient to the will of God; for we do not have power to do acceptable works before God, except by the grace of God; working in us through His Son, and our Saviour, Jesus Christ. Prov. 16:1; Jeremiah, 10:23; Matthew, 16:17; John 6:44.

10. MAN JUSTIFIED.

All have sinned and come short of the glory of God, says the Scriptures. Therefore we can stand before God, in a state of justification, only by faith, in the meritorious and vicarious blood of His Son, Jesus Christ. Romans, 3:23; 5:1; Ephesians, 2:8-9; Hebrews, 11.

11. GOOD WORKS.

Although good works are not altogether religion, they have a part in revealing our prosperity and fruitfulness in the Gospel, for we are created in Christ Jesus unto good works, and if professing Godliness, God is able to make all grace abound toward you; that ye always having all sufficiency in all things may abound to every good work. 2 Corinthians, 9:8; Colossians, 1:10; 2 Timothy, 2:21; Titus, 3:8.

12. SIN AFTER JUSTIFICATION.

For thus saith the Lord: "when the righteous turneth away from his righteousness, and committeth iniquity; in his trespass that he hath trespassed, and in his sin that he hath sinned, in them shall he die." Ezekial, 18:24. Now this is to be understood of as eternal death, appears when a righteous man turneth away from his righteousness, and committeth iniquity and dieth in them. (Here is temporal or physical death.) For his iniquity that he hath done he shall die. (Here is eternal death.) Now justification is an act of God's free grace, wherein he pardoned all our sins, and accepted us as righteous in his sight, only for the righteousness of Christ imputed to us and received by faith alone. Justification is to make righteous. Scripturally, however, this belongs to the field of regeneration, rather than to that of justification. According to the Bible usage, justification is the act of counting, declaring or pronouncing one righteous, or free from guilt and exposure to punishment. Romans, 4:25; 5:16-18.

13. REGENERATION OR THE NEW BIRTH.

Regeneration is an act of the Holy Spirit, by which we obtain the new birth or salvation through faith in Jesus Christ. The word means "begetting again," and the result is that "old things are passed away; behold, all things are become new."—John, 3:1-13; Titus, 3:5.

14. HOLINESS AND ENTIRE SANCTIFICATION.

We believe and teach entire sanctification to be synonymous with the Baptism with the Holy Ghost, Heart Purity, Christian Perfection and Holiness. 1 Thessalonians, 5:23; Joel, 2:28-29; Acts, 2; Psalms, 24:4; Matthew, 5:8; Genesis, 17:1; Matthew, 5:48; Leviticus, 20:7; Hebrews, 12:14. It is that work of grace wrought in the heart of man, by the Holy Ghost, subsequent to regeneration, when the believer presents himself a living sacrifice, holy, and acceptable to God; thus enabling him to love the Lord with all the heart, soul, mind and strength, and to walk in all his holy commandments, blameless. Titus, 2:11-12; John, 17:1-23; Romans, 12:1-2; Ephesians, 5:25-27.

15. SACRAMENTS OF THE CHURCH.

Baptism, the Supper of the Lord, and the Washing of the Brethren's feet, are recognized by our Church, as sacraments ordained of our Lord, as a token of Christian profession. Not merely an outward form, but to vivify and ratify our faith in Him. For Scriptural proof, see: Matthew, 26:26-28; Matthew 28:19; Mark, 14:22; 24; John, 13; 1 Corinthians, 10:16; 11:23-26; 1 Timothy 5:10.

16. BAPTISM.

Baptism, is the sacrament, ordinance or rite, commanded by Christ, in which water is used to initiate the recipient into the Christian faith. Christ himself, did not baptize, but His disciples. John baptized with water, Christ with the Holy Ghost and with fire. Jesus was baptized by John. The word "baptism" means, dipping, bathing, therefore we grant the candidiate the choice of immersion, or sprinkling. Matt. 18:19; John, 4:2; Matt. 3:1-12; Luke, 3:16.

17. THE SUPPER OF THE LORD.

The Supper of the Lord is practiced by Christians to show their love to each other and their love and faith to God for the redemption provided through Jesus Christ's atoning death. It is a medium of grace communicated to the heart of all who rightly and worthily receive it. And He took bread and gave thanks and brake it, and gave unto them saying, "This is my body which is given for you; this do in remembrance of me." Likewise also the cup after supper saying, "This cup is the new Testament in my blood, which is shed for you." Luke, 22:19-20. See also 1 Corinthians, 11:23-29.

18. THE OFFERING OF CHRIST ON THE CROSS.

Jesus Christ made the perfect and supreme sacrifice on the cross for the salvation of all people of all time. He finished

ARTICLES OF FAITH (MISSIONARY METHODIST
   CHURCH) (continued)

the plan of salvation. Therefore being justified by faith, we
have peace through our Lord Jesus Christ. Romans 5:1.
For when we were yet without strength, in due time Christ
died for the ungodly. Romans, 5:6. For as by one man's
disobedience many were made sinners, so by the obedience
of one shall many be made righteous. Romans, 5:19. For
the wages of sin is death, but the gift of God is eternal life
through Jesus Christ our Lord. Romans, 6:23. For with
the heart man believeth unto righteousness; and with the
mouth confession is made unto salvation. Romans, 10:10.
This is the stone which was set at naught of you builders,
which is become the head of the corner. Neither is there
salvation in any other; for there is none other name under
heaven given among men, whereby we must be saved.
Acts, 4:11-12.

19. CHURCH RITES AND CEREMONIES.

Our rites and ceremonies may be different from others in
some respects. But we know as the customs of men change
it may require the changing of rites and ceremonies in the
churches, for so it has been down through the ages of time,
so long as it does not contravene the Word of God. Acts,
15:10, 28, 29; Romans, 14:1-6; Galatians, 5:13.

20. RESURRECTION OF THE DEAD.

There will be a resurrection of the dead; the just unto the
resurrection of life, and the unjust unto the resurrection of
damnation. At this time the soul and body of every man
will be reunited, and shall appear before the Judgment seat
of Christ; that every one may receive the things done in the
body, according to that he hath done, whether it be good
or bad. Dan. 12:2; 2 Cor. 5:10; Rev. 20:4-6; vs. 12 and 13.

21. THE GENERAL OR FINAL JUDGMENT.

At the end of time there is to be a final or general
judgment, at which time the dead shall be judged and
rewarded according to their works in this life. Jesus Christ
is to be the Judge, and the righteous will receive a crown of
life for their righteous works, and be received into heaven
to be forever, with Christ. The wicked shall be judged for
their evil deeds and rewarded with eternal punishment in
hell. 2 Cor. 5:10; Heb. 9:27; Rev. 20:11-12.

Notes: *These articles derive from those of the Wesleyan
Methodist Church, though the wording has been altered in
almost every item. The church practices foot washing as a
third ordinance.*

*　　*　　*

DOCTRINES OF THE SALVATION ARMY

We believe that the Scriptures of the Old and New
Testaments were given by inspiration of God and that they
only constitute the divine rule of Christian faith and
practice.

We believe there is only one God who is infinitely perfect
the Creator Preserver and Governor of all things and who
is the only proper object of religious worship.

We believe that there are three persons in the Godhead the
Father the Son and the Holy Ghost undivided in essence
and co-equal in power and glory.

We believe that in the person of Jesus Christ the divine and
human natures are united so that He is truly and properly
God and truly and properly man.

We believe that our first parents were created in a state of
innocency but by their disobedience they lost their purity
and happiness and that in consequence of their fall all men
have become sinners totally depraved and as such are
justly exposed to the wrath of God.

We believe that the Lord Jesus Christ has by His suffering
and death made an atonement for the whole world so that
whosoever will may be saved.

We believe that repentance toward God faith in our Lord
Jesus Christ and regeneration by the Holy Spirit are
necessary to salvation.

We believe that we are justified by grace through faith in
our Lord Jesus Christ and that he that believeth hath the
witness in himself.

We believe that continuance in a state of salvation depends
upon continued obedient faith in Christ.

We believe that it is the privilege of all believers to be
'wholly sanctified' and that their 'whole spirit and soul and
body' may 'be preserved blameless unto the coming of our
Lord Jesus Christ' (1 Thess. 5:23).

We believe in the immortality of the soul in the resurrection of the body in the general judgment at the end of the
world in the eternal happiness of the righteous and in the
endless punishment of the wicked.

Notes: *Known publicly for modelling its organization on the
military, within holiness circles the Salvation Army is
known for not observing any sacraments. The Army does
not mention sacraments in its statement of beliefs.*

*　　*　　*

DOCTRINES OF THE VOLUNTEERS OF AMERICA

1.　We believe in one supreme God, who is "from
   everlasting to everlasting," who is infinitely perfect,
   benevolent and wise, who is omnipotent and omnipresent, and who is creator and ruler of heaven and
   earth.

2.　We believe in a Triune God,—The Father, Son and
   the Holy Ghost. We believe these three Persons are
   one, and while separate in office, are undivided in
   essence, co-equal in power and glory, and that all
   men everywhere ought to worship and serve this
   Triune God.

3.　We believe the contents of the Bible to have been
   given by inspiration of God, and the Scriptures form
   the Divine rule of all true, Godly faith and Christian
   practice.

4.　We believe that Jesus Christ, when upon earth, was
   truly man and yet was as truly God—The Divine
   and human being blended in the one Being, hence

His ability to feel and suffer as a man and yet supremely love and triumph as the Godhead.

5. We believe that our first parents were created without sin, but by listening to the tempter and obeying his voice fell from grace and lost their purity and peace; and that in consequence of their disobedience and fall all men have become sinful by propensity and are consequently exposed to the wrath of God.

6. We believe that Jesus Christ, the only begotten Son of God, by the sacrifice of His life, made an atonement for all men, and that whosoever will call upon Him and accept His overtures of grace shall be saved.

7. We believe that in order to be saved it is necessary (a) to repent toward God; (b) to believe with the heart in Jesus Christ; and (c) to become regenerated through the operation of the Holy Spirit.

8. We believe that the Spirit beareth witness with our spirit, that we are the children of God, thus giving the inward witness of acceptance by God.

9. We believe that the Scriptures teach and urge all Christians to be cleansed in heart from inbred sin, so that they may walk uprightly and serve Him without fear in holiness and righteousness all the days of their lives.

10. We believe the soul shall never die; that we shall be raised again; that the world shall be judged by God; and that the punishment of the wicked shall be eternal, and the joy and reward of the righteous will be everlasting before the throne of God.

Notes: *Organized by former members of the Salvation Army, the Volunteers of America rejected the Army's position on the sacraments and adopted the observation of both baptism and the Lord's Supper. Like the Army, the sacramental issue is not dealt with in the Volunteers' doctrinal statement.*

*　　*　　*

ARTICLES OF RELIGION (WESLEYAN CHURCH)

I. FAITH IN THE HOLY TRINITY

8. There is but one living and true God, everlasting, of infinite power, wisdom and goodness; the Maker and Preserver of all things, visible and invisible. And in unity of this Godhead there are three persons of one substance, power and eternity—the Father, the Son (the Word), and the Holy Ghost.

Gen. 1:1; 17:1; Ex. 3:13-15; 33:20; Deut. 6:4; Psalms 90:2; 104:24; Isa. 9:6; Jer. 10:10; John 1:1, 2; 4:24; 5:18; 10:30; 16:13; 17:3; Acts 5:3, 4; Rom. 16:27; I Cor. 8:4, 6; 2 Cor. 13:14; Eph. 2:18; Phil. 2:6; Col. 1:16; I Tim. 1:17; I John 5:7, 20, Rev. 19:13.

II. THE SON OF GOD

9. The only begotten Son of God was conceived by the Holy Ghost, born of the Virgin Mary, suffered under Pontius Pilate, was crucified, dead and buried—to be a sacrifice, not only for original guilt, but also for the actual sins of men, and to reconcile us to God.

Mark 15; Luke 1:27, 31, 35; John 1:14, 18; 3:16, 17; Acts 4:12; Rom. 5:10, 18; I Cor. 15:3; 2 Cor. 5:18, 19; Gal. 1:4; 2:20; 4:4, 5; Eph. 5:2; I Tim. 1:15; Heb. 2:17; 7:27; 9:28; 10:12; I Peter 2:24; I John 2:2; 4:14.

III. THE RESURRECTION OF CHRIST

10. Christ did truly rise again from the dead, taking His body with all things appertaining to the perfection of man's nature, wherewith He ascended into heaven, and there sitteth until He returns to judge all men at the last day.

Psalms 16:8-10; Matt. 27:62-66; 28:5-9, 16, 17; Mark 16:6, 7, 12; Luke 24:4-8, 23; John 20:26-29; 21; Acts 1:2; 2:24-31; 10:40; Rom. 8:34; 14:9, 10; 1 Cor. 15:6, 14; Heb. 13:20.

IV. THE HOLY GHOST

11. The Holy Ghost proceeding from the Father and the Son is of one substance, majesty and glory with the Father and the Son, very and eternal God.

Job 33:4; Matt. 28:19; John 4:24-26; Acts 5:3; 4; Rom. 8:9; 2 Cor. 3:17; Gal. 4:6.

V. THE SUFFICIENCY AND FULL AUTHORITY OF THE HOLY SCRIPTURES FOR SALVATION

12. The Holy Scriptures contain all things necessary to salvation; so that whatsoever is not read therein, nor may be proved thereby, is not to be required of any man, that it should be believed as an article of faith, or be thought requisite or necessary to salvation. In the name of the Holy Scriptures, we do understand the books of the Old and New Testaments. These Scriptures we do hold to be the inspired and infallibly written Word of God, fully inerrant in their original manuscript and superior to all human authority.

The canonical books of the Old Testament are:

Genesis, Exodus, Leviticus, Numbers, Deuteronomy, Joshua, Judges, Ruth, 1 Samuel, 2 Samuel, 1 Kings, 2 Kings, 1 Chronicles, 2 Chronicles, Ezra, Nehemiah, esther, Job, Psalms, Proverbs, Ecclesiastes, The Song of Solomon, Isaiah, Jeremiah, Lamentations, Ezekiel, Daniel, Hosea, Joel, Amos, Obadiah, Jonah, Micah, Nahum, Habakkuk, Zephaniah, Haggai, Zechariah and Malachi.

The canonical books of the New Testament are:

Matthew, Mark, Luke, John, The Acts, The Epistle to the Romans, 1 Corinthians, 2 Corinthians, Galatians, Ephesians, Philippians, Colossians, 1 Thessalonians, 2 Thessalonians, I Timothy, 2 Timothy, Titus, Philemon, Hebrews, James, 1 Peter, 2 Peter, 1 John, 2 John, 3 John, Jude and Revelation.

Psalms 19:7; Luke 24:27; John 17:17; Acts 17:2, 11; Rom. 1:2; 15:4; 16:26; Gal. 1:8; I Thess. 2:13; 2 Tim. 3:15-17; Heb. 4:12; James 1:21; 1 Peter 1:23; 2 Peter 1:19-21; Rev. 22:14, 19.

VI. THE OLD TESTAMENT

13. The Old Testament is not contrary to the New; for both in the Old and New Testaments everlasting life is offered to mankind through Christ, Who is the only Mediator between God and man. Wherefore they are not to be heard, who feign that the old fathers did look only for transitory promises. Although the law given from God by Moses, as touching ceremonies and rites, doth not bind Christians, nor ought the civil precepts thereof of necessity be received in any commonwealth, yet not withstanding no Christian whatsoever is free from the obedience of the commandments which are called moral.

    Matt. 5:17-19; 22:37-40; Luke 24:27, 44; John 1:45; 5:46; Rom. 15:8; 2 Cor. 1:20; Eph. 2:15, 16; 1 Tim. 2:5; Heb. 10:1; 11:39; I John 2:3-7.

VII. RELATIVE DUTIES

14. Those two great commandments which require us to love the Lord our God with all the heart, and our neighbors as ourselves, contain the sum of the divine law as it is revealed in the Scriptures: they are the measure and perfect rule of human duty, as well for the ordering and directing of families and nations, and all other social bodies, as for individual acts, by which we are required to acknowledge God as our only Supreme Ruler, and all men as created by Him, equal in all natural rights. Wherefore all men are bound so to order all their individual and social and political acts as to render to God entire and absolute obedience, and to secure to all men the enjoyment of every natural right, as well as to promote the greatest happiness of each in the possession and exercise of such rights.

    Lev. 19:18, 34; Deut. 1:15, 17; 2 Sam. 23:3; Job 29:16; 31:13, 14; Jer. 21:12; 22:3; Matt. 5:44-47; 7:12; Luke 6:27-29, 35; John 13:34, 35; Acts 10:34, 35; 17:26; Rom. 12:9; 13:1, 7, 8, 10; Gal. 5:14; 6:10; Titus 3:1; James 2:8; 1 Peter 2:17; 1 John 2:5; 4:12, 13; 2 John 6.

VIII. ORIGINAL OR BIRTH SIN

15. Original sin standeth not in the following of Adam (as the Pelagians do vainly talk), but it is the corruption of the nature of every man, that naturally is engendered of the offspring of Adam, whereby man is wholly gone from original righteousness, and of his own nature inclined to evil, and that continually.

    Gen. 8:21; Psalms 51:5; Jer. 17:9; Mark 7:21-23; Rom. 3:10-12; 5:12, 18, 19; Eph. 2:1-3.

IX. FREE WILL

16. The condition of man after the fall of Adam is such that he cannot turn and prepare himself, by his own natural strength and work, in faith and calling upon God; wherefore we have no power to do good works, pleasant and acceptable to God, without the grace of God by Christ working in us, that we may have a good will, and working with us when we have that good will.

    Prov. 16:1; 20:24; Jer. 10:23; Matt. 16:17; John 6:44, 65; 15:5; Rom. 5:6, 7, 8; Eph. 2:5-9; Phil. 2:13; 4:13.

X. JUSTIFICATION OF MAN

17. We are accounted righteous before God only for the merit of our Lord and Saviour Jesus Christ, by faith, and not our own works or deservings. Wherefore, that we are justified by faith only is a most wholesome doctrine, and very full of comfort.

    Acts 13:38, 39; 15:11; 16:31; Rom. 3:28; 4:2-5; 5:1, 2, 9; Eph. 2:6, 9; Phil. 3:9; Heb. 11.

XI. GOOD WORKS

18. Although good works, which are the fruit of faith and follow after justification, cannot put away our sins and endure the severity of God's judgment, yet they are pleasing and acceptable to God in Christ, and spring out of a true and lively faith, insomuch that by them a lively faith may be as evidently known as a tree is discerned by its fruit.

    Matt. 5:16; 7:16-20; John 15:8; Rom. 3:20; 4:2, 4, 6; Gal. 2:16; Phil. 1:11; Titus 3:5; James 2:18, 22; 1 Peter 2:9, 12.

XII. SIN AFTER JUSTIFICATION

19. Not every sin willingly committed after justification is the sin against the Holy Ghost, and unpardonable. Wherefore repentance is not denied to such as fall into sin after justification; after we have received the Holy Ghost we may depart from grace given and fall into sin, and by the grace of God rise again to amend our lives. And therefore, they are to be condemned who say they can no more sin as long as they live here, or deny the place of forgiveness to such as truly repent.

    Psa. 32:5; 95:7, 11; Eccl. 7:20; Jer. 3:13-15; Matt. 24:12; John 5:14; Gal. 5:4, 7; Eph. 5:14; Heb. 3:7-13, 15; James 3:2, 8; I John 1:8, 9; 2:12; Rev. 2:5.

XIII. REGENERATION

20. Regeneration is that work of the Holy Spirit by which the pardoned sinner becomes a child of God; this work is received through faith in Jesus Christ, whereby the regenerate are delivered from the power of sin which reigns over all the unregenerate, so that they love God and through grace serve Him with the will and affections of the heart-receiving the Spirit of adoption whereby we cry, Abba Father.

    John 1:12, 13; 3:3, 5; Rom. 8:15, 17; Gal. 3:26; 4:5, 7; Eph. 1:5; 2:5, 19; 4:24; Col. 3:10; Titus 3:5; James 1:18; I Peter 1:3, 4; 2 Peter 1:4; I John 3:1.

XIV. ENTIRE SANCTIFICATION

21. Entire sanctification is that work of the Holy Spirit by which the child of God is cleansed from all inbred sin through faith in Jesus Christ. It is subsequent to regeneration, and is wrought when the believer presents himself a living sacrifice, holy and acceptable unto God, and is thus enabled through grace to

love God with all the heart and to walk in His holy commandments blameless.

Gen. 17:1; Deut. 30:6; Psa. 130:8; Ezek. 36:25-29; Matt. 5:48; Luke 1:74, 75; John 17:2-23; Rom. 8:3, 4; 11:26; 1 Cor. 6:11; 14:20; Eph. 4:13, 24; 5:25-27; Phil. 2:5, 7; Col. 4:12; I Thess. 3:10; 5:23; 2 Thess. 2:13; 2 Tim. 3:17; Titus 2:12; Heb. 9:13, 14; 10:14, 18-22; James 1:27; 4:8; I Peter 1: 10; 2 Peter 1:4; 1 John, 1:7, 9; 3:8, 9; 4:17, 18; Jude 24.

XV. THE SACRAMENTS

22. Sacraments ordained of Christ are not only tokens of Christian profession, but they are certain signs of grace and God's good will toward us, by which He doth work invisibly in us, and doth not only quicken but also strengthen and confirm our faith in Him.

There are two sacraments ordained of Christ our Lord in the Gospel: that is to say, Baptism, and the Supper of the Lord.

Matt. 26:26-28; 28:19; Mark 14:22-24; Rom. 2:28, 29; 4:11; 1 Cor. 10:16; 11:23-26; Gal. 3:27.

XVI. BAPTISM

23. Baptism is not only a sign of profession and mark of difference whereby Christians are distinguished from others who are not baptized, but it is also a sign of regeneration or new birth. The baptism of young children is to be retained in the Church.

Num. 8:7; Isa. 52:15; Ezek. 36:25; Matt. 3:13-17; Mark 1:10; 16:16; John 3:22, 26; 4:1, 2; Acts 2:38, 41; 8:12, 13-17; 9:18; 16:33; 18:8; 19:5; 22:16; I Cor. 12:13; Gal. 3:27-29; Col. 2:11, 12; Titus 3:5.

XVII. THE LORD'S SUPPER

24. The Supper of the Lord is not only a sign of love that Christians ought to have among themselves one to another, but rather it is a Sacrament of our redemption by Christ's death; insomuch that to such as rightly, worthily and with faith receive the same, it is made a medium through which God doth communicate grace to the heart.

Luke 22:19, 20; John 6:53, 56; 1 Cor. 5:7, 8; 10:3, 4, 16; 11:28.

XVIII. THE ONE OBLATION OF CHRIST FINISHED UPON THE CROSS

25. The offering of Christ, once made, is that perfect redemption and propitiation for all the sins of the whole world, both original and actual; and there is none other satisfaction for sin but that alone. Wherefore, to expect salvation on the ground of our own works, or by suffering the pains our sins deserve, either in the present or future state, is derogatory to Christ's offering for us, and a dangerous deceit.

Acts 4:12; Rom. 5:8; 8:34; Gal. 2:16; 3:2, 3, 11; 1 Tim. 2:5, 6; Heb. 7:23-27; 9:11-15, 24-28; 10:14.

XIX. THE RITES AND CEREMONIES OF CHURCHES

26. It is not necessary that rites and ceremonies should in all places be the same or exactly alike, for they have always been different and may be changed according to the diversities of countries, times, and men's manners, so that nothing be ordained against God's Word.

Every particular church may ordain, change or abolish rites and ceremonies, so that all things may be done to edification.

Acts 15:10, 28, 29; Rom. 14:2-6, 15, 17, 21; 1 Cor. 1:10; 12:25; 14:26; 2 Cor. 13:11; Gal. 5:1, 13; Col. 2:16, 17; 2 Thess. 3:6, 14; I Tim. 1:4, 6; I Peter 2:16.

XX. THE SECOND COMING OF CHRIST

27. The doctrine of the second coming of Christ is a very precious truth, and this good hope is a powerful inspiration to holy living and godly effort for the evangelization of the world. We believe the Scriptures teach the coming of Christ to be a bodily return to the earth and that He will cause the fulfillment of all prophecies made concerning His final and complete triumph over all evil. Faith in the imminence of Christ's return is a rational and inspiring hope to the people of God.

Job 19:25-27; Daniel 12:1-4; Psalm 17:15; Isaiah 11:1-12; Zech. 14:1-11; Matt. 24:1-51; Matt. 26:64; Mark 13:26-37; Luke 17:26-37; Luke 21:24-36; John 14:1-3; Acts 1:9-11; 1 Cor. 1:7, 8; 1 Thess. 4:13-18; Titus 2:11-14; Hebrews 9:27, 28; James 5:7, 8; 2 Pet. 3:1-14; 1 John 3:2, 3; Jude 14; Revelation 1:7; Revelation 19:11-16; Revelation 22:6, 7, 12, 20.

XXI. THE RESURRECTION OF THE DEAD

28. We hold the scriptural statements concerning the resurrection of the dead to be true and worthy of universal acceptance. We believe the bodily resurrection of Jesus Christ was a fact of history and a miracle of supreme importance. We understand the manner of the resurrection of mankind to be the resurrection of the righteous dead, at Christ's second coming, and the resurrection of the wicked at a later time, as stated in Revelation 20:4-6. Resurrection will be the reuniting of soul and body preparatory to final reward or punishment.

Job 19:25-27; Psalms 17:15; Daniel 12:2; Matthew 22:30-32; Matthew 28:1-20; Luke 14:14; John 5:28, 29; Acts 23:6-8; Romans 8:11; 1 Corinthians 6:14; 1 Corinthians 15; 2 Corinthians 4:14; 2 Corinthians 5:1-11; 1 Thessalonians 4:14-17; Revelation 20:4-6.

XXII. THE JUDGMENT OF MANKIND

29. The Scriptures reveal God as the Judge of all mankind and the acts of His judgment to be based on His omniscience and eternal justice. His administration of judgment will culminate in the final meeting of mankind before His throne of great majesty and power, where records will be examined and final rewards and punishments will be administered.

Ecclesiastes 12:14; Romans 14:10, 11; 2 Corinthians 5:10; Acts 17:31; Romans 2:16; Matthew 10:15; Luke 11:31, 32; Acts 10:42; 2 Timothy 4:1; Hebrews 9:27; Matthew 25:31-46; Revelation 20:11, 12, 13; 2 Peter 3:7.

ARTICLES OF RELIGION (WESLEYAN CHURCH) (continued)

It is not to be understood that a dissenting understanding on the subject of the millennium shall be held to break or hinder either church fellowship or membership.

APPENDIX A

THE REAFFIRMATION OF THE DOCTRINES OF OUR FAITH

30. Be It Resolved, That the General Conference of the Wesleyan Methodist Connection (or Church) of America, now in its twenty-first quadrennial session, do hereby declare and reaffirm our faith and adherence to those Doctrines that have been held as fundamental.

1st. We reaffirm our faith in the Bible, as the inerrant and inspired Word of God, containing a sufficient revelation of God's will to man in order to secure his eternal salvation and perfect in its system of religion and moral teachings and precepts.

2nd. We reaffirm our faith in the Deity of Jesus Christ, Who was supernaturally conceived by the Holy Ghost, and born of the virgin Mary, free from moral taint of nature, and perfect in His life and conduct.

3rd. We reaffirm our faith in the expiatory death, and vicarious atonement of Christ, which adjusted matters in the government of God so that mercy and grace could be extended to the sinner.

4th. We reaffirm our faith in the resurrection of Jesus Christ from the dead; that He arose with the same body that was placed in the tomb, supernaturally transformed from its physical properties to that of spiritual.

5th. We reaffirm our faith in His ascension to the right hand of the Father, and that He now occupies the throne of His mediation.

6th. We reaffirm our faith in the doctrine and promise of His second coming "in like manner" as He went away.

7th. We reaffirm our faith in the creation of man by the immediate creative act of God, according to the Bible narrative, and not by the process of evolutionary transition from a lower order of animalism to his present physical and intellectual condition.

8th. We reaffirm our faith in the doctrine of the fall of man from that holy state in which he was created, to his present sinful and depraved state, "and of his own nature is inclined to evil and that continually."

9th. We reaffirm our faith in the doctrine of regeneration, or the "new birth," by which the sinner becomes a child of God through faith in Jesus Christ, by which the sinner is delivered from the power of sin, and is enabled through grace to love and serve God.

10th. We reaffirm our faith in the doctrine of entire sanctification, by which work of grace the heart is cleansed by the Holy Spirit from all inbred sin through faith in Jesus Christ when the believer presents himself a living sacrifice, holy and acceptable unto God, and is enabled through grace to love God with all his heart and to walk in His holy commandments blameless. By the act of cleansing it is to be interpreted and taught by the ministry and teachers that it is not a "suppression" or a "counteraction" of "inbred sin" so as to "make it inoperative"; but "to destroy" or "to eradicate" from the heart so that the believer not only has a right to heaven, but is so conformed to God's nature that he will enjoy God and heaven forever. These terms are what we hold that cleansing from all sin implies.

[Adopted by the General Conference held at Fairmount, Indiana, in 1923.]

Notes: *These articles replace the statements of both the Pilgrim Holiness Church and the Wesleyan Methodist Church, which merged in 1968 to form the Wesleyan Church. Of particular interest is the detailed statement on sanctification.*

* * *

ARTICLES OF RELIGION [WESLEYAN METHODIST CHURCH (1968)]

I. OF FAITH IN THE HOLY TRINITY.

There is but one living and true God, everlasting, of infinite power, wisdom, and goodness; the maker and preserver of all things, visible and invisible. And in unity of this Godhead there are three persons of one substance, power, and eternity;—the Father, the Son, [the Word] and the Holy Ghost.

II. OF THE SON OF GOD.

The only begotten Son of God was conceived by the Holy Ghost, born of the Virgin Mary, suffered under Pontius Pilate, was crucified, dead, and buried, to be a sacrifice, not only for original guilt, but also for the actual sins of men, and to reconcile us to God.

III. OF THE RESURRECTION OF CHRIST.

Christ did truly rise again from the dead, taking his body, with all things appertaining to the perfection of man's nature, wherewith he ascended into heaven, and there sitteth until he return to judge all men at the last day.

IV. OF THE HOLY GHOST.

The Holy Ghost proceeding from the Father and the Son, is of one substance, majesty, and glory, with the Father and the Son, very and eternal God.

V. THE SUFFICIENCY OF THE HOLY SCRIPTURES FOR SALVATION.

The Holy Scriptures contain all things necessary to salvation: so that whatsoever is not read therein, nor may be proved thereby, is not to be required of any man, that it should be believed as an article of faith, or be thought requisite or necessary to salvation. In the name of the Holy Scriptures, we do understand these canonical books of the

Old and New Testament, of whose authority there is no doubt in the Church.

The canonical books of the Old Testament are—

Genesis	Proverbs
Exodus	Ecclesiastes
Leviticus	The Song of Solomon
Numbers	Isaiah
Deuteronomy	Jeremiah
Joshua	Lamentations
Judges	Ezekiel
Ruth	Daniel
I. Samuel	Hosea
II. Samuel	Joel
1. Kings	Amos
II. Kings	Obadiah
I. Chronicles	Jonah
II. Chronicles	Micah
Ezra	Nahum
Nehemiah	Habakkuk
Esther	Zephaniah
Job	Haggai
Psalms	Zachariah
	Malachi

The canonical books of the New Testament are—

Matthew	II. Thessalonians
Mark	I. Timothy
Luke	II. Timothy
John	Titus
The Acts	Philemon
The Epistles to the	Hebrews
Romans	James
I. Corinthians	I. Peter
II. Corinthians	II. Peter
Galatians	I. John
Ephesians	II. John
Philippians	III. John
Colossians	Jude
I. Thessalonians	Revelation

VI. OF THE OLD TESTAMENT.

The Old Testament is not contrary to the New; for both in the Old and New Testament, everlasting life is offered to mankind through Christ, who is the only Mediator between God and man. Wherefore they are not to be heard, who feign that the old fathers did look only for transitory promises. Although the law given from God by Moses, as touching ceremonies and rites, doth not bind Christians, nor ought the civil precepts thereof of necessity be received in any commonwealth; yet, notwithstanding, no Christian, whatsoever is free from the obedience of the commandments which are called moral.

VII. OF RELATIVE DUTIES.

Those two great commandments which require us to love the Lord our God with all our hearts, and our neighbor as ourselves, contain the sum of the divine law as it is revealed in the Scriptures, and are the measure and perfect rule of human duty, as well for the ordering and directing of families and nations, and all other social bodies, as for individual acts; by which we are required to acknowledge God as our only supreme ruler, and all men as created by him, equal in all natural rights. Wherefore all men are bound so to order all their individual and social acts, as to render to God entire and absolute obedience, and to secure to all men the enjoyment of every natural right, as well as to promote the greatest happiness of each in the possession and exercise of such rights.

VIII. OF ORIGINAL OR BIRTH SIN.

Original sin standeth not in the following of Adam, (as the Pelagians do vainly talk,) but it is the corruption of the nature of every man, that naturally is engendered of the offspring of Adam, whereby man is wholly gone from original righteousness, and of his own nature inclined to evil, and that continually.

IX. OF FREE WILL.

The condition of man after the fall of Adam is such, that he cannot turn and prepare himself, by his own natural strength and works, to faith, and calling upon God; wherefore we have no power to do good works, pleasant and acceptable to God, without the grace of God by Christ working in us, that we may have a good will, and working with us, when we have that good will.

X. OF THE JUSTIFICATION OF MAN.

We are accounted righteous before God, only for the merit of our Lord and Saviour Jesus Christ by faith, and not for our own works or deservings:—Wherefore, that we are justified by faith, only, is a most wholesome doctrine, and very full of comfort.

XI. OF GOOD WORKS.

Although good works, which are the fruit of faith, and follow after justification, cannot put away our sins, and endure the severity of God's judgments; yet are they pleasing and acceptable to God in Christ, and spring out of a true and lively faith, insomuch that by them a lively faith may be as evidently known as a tree is discerned by its fruit.

XII. OF SIN AFTER JUSTIFICATION.

Not every sin willingly committed after justification is the sin against the Holy Ghost, and unpardonable. Wherefore, repentance is not denied to such as fall into sin after justification; after we have received the Holy Ghost, we may depart from grace given, and fall into sin, and, by the grace of God, rise again to amend our lives. And therefore they are to be condemned, who say they can no more sin as long as they live here; or deny the place of forgiveness to such as truly repent.

XIII. OF SANCTIFICATION.

Sanctification is that renewal of our fallen natures by the Holy Ghost, received through faith in Jesus Christ, whose blood of atonement cleanseth from all sin; whereby we are not only delivered from the guilt of sin, but are washed from its pollution, saved from its power, and are enabled, through grace, to love God with all our hearts, and to walk in his holy commandments blameless.

XIV. OF THE SACRAMENTS.

Sacraments ordained of Christ, are not only badges or tokens of Christian men's profession, but they are certain signs of grace, and God's good will toward us, by which he doth work invisibly in us, and doth not only quicken, but also strengthen and confirm our faith in him.

ARTICLES OF RELIGION [WESLEYAN METHODIST CHURCH (1968)] (continued)

There are two sacraments ordained of Christ our Lord, in the Gospel; that is to say, Baptism and the Supper of the Lord.

XV. OF BAPTISM.

Baptism is not only a sign of profession, and mark of difference, whereby Christians are distinguished from others that are not baptized, but it is also a sign of regeneration or the new birth. The baptism of young children is to be retained in the Church.

XVI. OF THE LORD'S SUPPER.

The supper of the Lord is not only a sign of the love that Christians ought to have among themselves one to another, but rather it is a sacrament of our redemption by Christ's death: insomuch that, to such as rightly, worthily, and with faith receive the same, it is made a medium through which God doth communicate grace to the heart.

XVII. OF THE ONE OBLATION OF CHRIST FINISHED UPON THE CROSS.

The offering of Christ, once made, is that perfect redemption and propitiation for all the sins of the whole world, both original and actual: and there is none other satisfaction for sin but that alone. Wherefore to expect salvation on the ground of our own works, or by suffering the pains our sins deserve, either in the present or future state, is derogatory to Christ's offering for us, and a dangerous deceit.

XVIII. OF THE RITES AND CEREMONIES OF CHURCHES.

It is not necessary that rites and ceremonies should in all places be the same, or exactly alike: for they have always been different, and may be changed according to the diversity of countries, times, and men's manners, so that nothing be ordained against God's word.

Every particular Church may ordain, change, or abolish rites and ceremonies, so that all things may be done to edification.

XIX. OF THE RESURRECTION OF THE DEAD.

There will be a general resurrection of the dead, both of the just and the unjust, at which time the souls and bodies of men will be re-united to receive together a just retribution for the deeds done in the body in this life.

XX. OF THE GENERAL JUDGMENT.

There will be a general judgment at the end of the world, when God will judge all men by Jesus Christ, and receive the righteous into his heavenly kingdom, where they shall be forever secure and happy; and adjudge the wicked to everlasting punishment suited to the demerit of their sins.

Notes: *At the time of its formation in the 1840s, the Wesleyan Methodist Church adopted a set of articles taken from the Twenty-five Articles of Religion of what was then the Methodist Episcopal Church. Although the Wesleyan Methodist Church adopted a restrictive rule concerning the revision of the Articles of Religion, the procedures were more lax than those of the Methodist Episcopal Church. Over the years the original twenty articles of the Wesleyan Methodist*

Church (including articles on sanctification and relative duties, added at the original general conference) were increased by the addition of an article on the second coming of Christ. These additions, plus numerous wording changes, produced the version of the articles taken into the church's 1968 merger with the Pilgrim Holiness Church that resulted in the formation of the Wesleyan Church. At the time of merger, both the Articles of Religion of the Wesleyan Methodist Church and the Statement of Faith of the Pilgrim Holiness Church were replaced by the Articles of Religion of the Wesleyan Church.

The Articles of Religion of the Wesleyan Methodist Church were adopted by the Allegheny Wesleyan Methodist Connection, formed in 1968 by members of the Wesleyan Methodist Church who did not wish to participate in the merger with the Pilgrim Holiness Church. The connection considers itself a continuing Wesleyan Methodist Church.

* * *

Twentieth-Century Holiness

ARTICLES OF FAITH (EVANGELICAL CHURCH OF NORTH AMERICA)

ARTICLE I. OF THE HOLY TRINITY

1. There is but one true and living God, an eternal Being, a Spirit without body, indivisible, of infinite power, wisdom, and goodness; the Creator and Preserver of all things visible and invisible. And in this Godhead there is a Trinity, of one substance and power, and co-eternal; namely, the Father, the Son, and the Holy Spirit.

ARTICLE II. OF THE SON OF GOD

2. Jesus Christ is truly God and truly man, in Whom the divine and human natures are perfectly and inseparably united. He is the eternal Word made flesh, the only begotten Son of the Father, born of the Virgin Mary by the power of the Holy Spirit. As ministering Servant, He lived, suffered and died on the cross. He was buried, rose from the dead and ascended into heaven to be with the Father, from whence He shall return. He is eternal Savior and Mediator, who intercedes for us, and by Him all men will be judged.

ARTICLE III. OF THE RESURRECTION OF CHRIST

3. Christ did truly rise from the dead, and took again His body, with all things appertaining to the perfection of Man's nature; and with the same body He ascended into heaven, and is seated there until He returns, at the last day, to judge all men.

ARTICLE IV. OF THE HOLY SPIRIT

4. The Holy Spirit proceeds from the Father and the Son, as the true and eternal God, of one substance, majesty, and glory with the Father and the Son; He convinces the world of sin, of righteousness, and of

judgment and comforts the faithful and guides them into all truth.

ARTICLE V. OF THE HOLY SCRIPTURES

5. The Holy Scriptures are the divinely inspired Word of God, written; they contain the will of God so far as it is necessary for us to know for our salvation, so that whatsoever is not contained therein, nor can be proved thereby, is not to be enjoined on any as an article of faith, or as a doctrine essential to salvation. By the Holy Scriptures we understand those canonical books of the Old and New Testament, which the church has at all times received as follows:

THE NAMES OF THE CANONICAL BOOKS

The Old Testament

Genesis	The First Book of Kings
Exodus	The Second Book of Kings
Leviticus	The First Book of
Numbers	Chronicles
Deuteronomy	The Second Book of
Joshua	Chronicles
Judges	The Book of Ezra
Ruth	Amos
The First Book of	The Book of Nehemiah
Samuel	The Book of Esther
The Second Book	The Book of Job
of Samuel	The Psalms
Ecclesiastes	The Proverbs of Solomon
The Song of	Obadiah
Solomon	Jonah
Isaiah	Micah
Jeremiah	Nahum
Lamentations	Habakkuk
Ezekiel	Zephaniah
Daniel	Haggai
Hosea	Zechariah
Joel	Malachi

The New Testament

Matthew	1 Timothy
Mark	2 Timothy
Luke	Titus
John	Philemon
The Acts	Hebrews
Romans	James
1 Corinthians	1 Peter
2 Corinthians	2 Peter
Galatians	1 John
Ephesians	2 John
Philippians	3 John
Colossians	Jude
1 Thessalonians	Revelation
2 Thessalonians	

ARTICLE VI. OF THE OLD TESTAMENT

6. The Old Testament is not contrary to the New. In both the Old as well as the New Testament, everlasting life is offered to mankind by Christ, who being both God and man, is the only Mediator between God and man.

We are, therefore, not to listen to those who teach that the fathers of the ancient covenant grounded their expectations only on the temporal promises. Though the law given from God by Moses, as touching ceremonies and rites, does not bind Christians, nor ought the civil precepts thereof necessarily be received in any commonwealth; yet no Christian is exempt from obeying the ten commandments, which are also called the moral law.

ARTICLE VII. OF DEPRAVITY

7. Man is fallen from original righteousness, and, apart from the grace of our Lord Jesus Christ, is not only entirely destitute of holiness, but is inclined to evil, and that continually; and except a man be born again, he cannot see the Kingdom of God.

ARTICLE VIII. OF PREVENIENT GRACE AND FREE WILL

8. The condition of man since the fall of Adam is so wretched that he cannot turn to God by the mere powers of his nature; and hence we cannot, by our own natural strength, do any good works pleasing and acceptable in the sight of God, without the grace of God by Christ assisting us and influencing us, that we may have a good will, and working with us, when we have that good will.

ARTICLE IX. OF JUSTIFICATION BY FAITH

9. We are never accounted righteous before God on account of our works or merits, but only for the merit of our Lord and Savior, Jesus Christ, and by faith in His name. Wherefore, it is a most wholesome doctrine, and full of comfort, that we are justified by faith only.

ARTICLE X. OF REGENERATION AND ADOPTION

10. Regeneration is the renewal of the heart of man after the image of God, through the Word, by the act of the Holy Spirit, by which the believer receives the Spirit of adoption, and is enabled to serve God with the will and the affections. The witness of the Spirit is an inward impression on the soul, whereby the Spirit of God, the heavenly Comforter, immediately convinces the regenerate believer that he has passed from death unto life, that his sins are all forgiven, and that he is a child of God.

ARTICLE XI. OF GOOD WORKS

11. Although good works are the fruits of faith and follow justification, they have not the virtue to put away our sins, or to avert the judgment, or endure the severity of God's justice; yet they are pleasing and acceptable to God in Christ, spring from a true and living faith, for through and by them a living faith may be as evidently known, as a tree is discerned by its fruits.

ARTICLE XII. OF SIN AFTER JUSTIFICATION

12. Not every sin willingly committed after justification is therefore the sin against the Holy Spirit, which is unpardonable. They cannot all be precluded from repentance who fall into sin after justification, nor can reacceptance straightway be denied them. After we have received the Holy Spirit, it may happen that we depart from grace, and fall into sin; and we may even then, by the grace of God, rise again and amend

our lives. Therefore, the doctrine of those is to be rejected, who say that they can no more fall into sin so long as they live here, or who deny forgiveness to such as truly repent.

ARTICLE XIII. OF ENTIRE SANCTIFICATION

13. Entire sanctification is that work of the Holy Spirit by which the child of God is cleansed from all inbred sin through faith in Jesus Christ. It is subsequent to regeneration and is wrought instantaneously by faith when the believer consecrates himself a living sacrifice, holy and acceptable unto God. The evidence of this gracious work is love out of a pure heart thus enabling us to love God with all of the heart, soul, mind and strength, and our neighbor as ourselves, and to walk in God's holy commandments blameless.

There is a clear distinction that must be made between consecration and entire sanctification. Consecration is that more or less gradual process of devoting oneself to God, by the help of the Holy Spirit, that comes to a completion at a point in time. Total consecration of necessity precedes and prepares the way for that act of faith which brings God's instantaneous sanctifying work to the soul.

We believe this gracious work does not deliver us from the infirmities, ignorance and mistakes common to man, nor from the possibilities of further sin. The Christian must continue to guard against the temptation to spiritual pride and seek to gain victory over this and every temptation to sin.

ARTICLE XIV. OF THE CHURCH

14. The visible Church of Christ is the community of true believers, among whom the Word of God is preached in its purity, and the means of grace are duly administered, according to Christ's own appointment.

ARTICLE XV. OF THE CHRISTIAN SABBATH

15. We believe that the Christian Sabbath is divinely appointed; that it is commemorative of our Lord's resurrection from the grave and is an emblem of our eternal rest; that it is essential to the welfare of the civil community, and to the permanence and growth of the Christian Church, and that it should be reverently observed as a day of holy rest and of social and public worship.

ARTICLE XVI. OF THE LANGUAGE TO BE USED IN PUBLIC WORSHIP

16. The use of any language in any public service which is not understood by the people is plainly repugnant to the Word of God and the customs of the early Church.

ARTICLE XVII. OF THE SACRAMENTS

17. Baptism and the Lord's Supper are the only sacraments ordained by Christ. They were ordained by Christ that we should duly use, but not abuse them. And in such persons only as properly receive the same, they produce a wholesome effect; while such as

receive them improperly they bring upon themselves condemnation, as Paul writes in reference to the Lord's Supper. (I Corinthians 11:29).

(a) Holy Baptism. Baptism is a token of the Christian profession, whereby Christians are distinguished from others, and whereby they obligate themselves to observe every Christian duty; it is also a sign of internal cleansing, or the new birth.

(b) The Lord's Supper. The Supper of the Lord is a token of love and union that Christians ought to have among themselves; it is also a mystery or a representation of our redemption by the sufferings and death of Christ; insomuch that such as rightly, properly and faithfully receive the same, partake of the body and blood of Christ by faith, not in a bodily, but in a spiritual manner, in eating the broken bread, and in drinking the cup. The changing of the bread and wine into the body and blood of Christ, cannot be supported by Holy Writ, but is contrary to the plain words of Scriptures.

ARTICLE XVIII. OF THE ONE SACRIFICE OF CHRIST

18. The offering which was once made by Christ on the Cross is the perfect redemption, propitiation, and satisfaction for the sins of the whole world, both original and actual; so that there is no other satisfaction required but that alone.

ARTICLE XIX. OF THE RITES AND CEREMONIES OF THE CHURCH

19. It is by no means necessary that ceremonies and rites should in all places be the same; for they have always been different, and may be changed according to the diversity of countries, times, and national customs, provided that nothing be introduced contrary to God's ordinances. Whosoever, through his private judgment, willingly and purposely breaks the ordinances, ceremonies and rites of the church to which he belongs (if they are not contrary to the Word of God, and are ordained by proper authority), ought to be rebuked openly, as one that offends against the order of the Church and wounds the consciences of the weaker brethren, in order that others may be deterred from similar audacity.

ARTICLE XX. OF CIVIL GOVERNMENT

20. We recognize the sovereign governments under whose protection our members reside. The sovereignty of these governments should be respected. Generally speaking, war and bloodshed are not in keeping with the Gospel and Spirit of Christ, nevertheless, at times, in order to preserve orderly governments in the world, war is the unpleasant alternative. As Christian citizens it is our duty to give moral strength and purpose to our respective nations through sober, righteous and godly living.

ARTICLE XXI. OF CHRISTIANS' PROPERTY

21. The property of Christians is not to be considered as common, in regard to the right, title, and possession of the same, as some do erroneously pretend, but as

lawful possessions. Notwithstanding, everyone ought, of the things he possesses to give to the poor and needy and manifest Christian love and liberality toward them.

ARTICLE XXII. OF THE SECOND COMING OF CHRIST

22. The Scriptures teach the coming of Christ to be a bodily return to the earth and that He will cause the fulfillment of all prophecies made concerning His final and complete triumph over all evil. Faith in the imminence of Christ's return is a rational and inspiring hope to the people of God.

ARTICLE XXIII. OF THE LAST JUDGMENT

23. Jesus Christ will come in the last day to judge all mankind by a righteous judgment; God will give unto the believers eternal life and happiness, and rest, peace, and joy without end. But God will bid the impenitent and ungodly depart to the devil and his angels, to endure everlasting damnation, punishment, and pain, torment and misery. We are, therefore, not to agree to the doctrine of those who maintain that devils and ungodly men will not have to suffer eternal punishment.

Notes: *In 1968 when the Methodist Church and the Evangelical United Brethren merged to become the United Methodist Church, some former members of the Brethren declined to join the merger. They established the Evangelical Church of North America. For their statement of belief they returned to the articles of religion of the Evangelical Church, one of the bodies that had merged in 1946 to found the Evangelical United Brethren. To those articles, they added statements concerning the sabbath and the second coming of Christ and made some minor changes in wording. The article on sanctification was condensed from a lengthy statement that the Evangelical Church had appended to its articles.*

*   *   *

BIBLICAL DOCTRINES (GOSPEL MISSION CORPS)

INTRODUCTION

We believe in the fundamental doctrines of evangelical, orthodox Christianity. We shall not lay great stress on the study of dogma and theorizing, but will preach and teach sound, wholesome doctrine, upholding our "common salvation," earnestly contending "for the faith once delivered unto the saints" (Jude 3), and guarding against liberalism, modernism, and other heresies. We will emphasize the necessity of the New Birth (John 3:3) and a transformed life through Christ (II Corinthians 5:17).

However, doctrine is important, and neither the Church of Christ nor its ministry can be effective without it. No doubt there will be, and already are, numerous ones in the area who, as men did in the time of Christ, "question among themselves, saying: 'What thing is this? What new doctrine is this?'" (Mark 1:27; see also Acts 17:19). Let us assure them as far as we possibly can, by the grace of God in our lives and in our testimony, both as individual

members of the Body of Christ (I Corinthians 12:27), and as a fellowship in the Gospel (Phillippians 1:5-6 & 27), that we accept the teachings of the Bible as our way of life. We are a part of the Holy Christian Church, and therefore we are "ambassadors" in bonds to the Truth (John 14:6); our message is: "Be ye reconciled to God" (II Corinthians 5:20).

Yet within the unity of the Spirit there must be the principles of the Faith, and thus we are reminded of St. Paul's admonition to the young pastor-evangelist, Timothy: "Take heed unto thyself (discipline), and unto the doctrine; continue in them: for in doing this thou shalt both save thyself, and them that hear thee" (I Timothy 4:16).

Following we shall state briefly the fundamental Biblical Doctrines of The Gospel Mission Corps:

1. We believe that the Scriptures of the Old and New Testaments have been given to man by the divine inspiration of God, and that they are the only sufficient revelation and rule of faith and practice.

2. We believe in the unity and trinity of the one, only, and true Lord God Jehovah, eternally existent in three Divine Personalities: the Father Almighty, Creator of the universe and all therein; Jesus Christ, His only begotten Son, our Saviour and Messiah; and the Holy Spirit, our Comforter and Sanctifier.

3. We believe the Son of God, Jesus Christ, took upon Himself by the instrumentality of the Holy Spirit, man's true human nature, but remained sinless, and that without losing His divinity He was born of the Virgin Mary, and came among men "not to condemn the world, but that the world through Him might be saved."

4. We believe in repentance toward God and faith toward our Lord Jesus Christ, and in regeneration by the Holy Spirit, thus bringing to personal experience the new birth, or justification "by grace through faith" for the salvation and eternal welfare of the soul.

5. We believe that "Jesus Christ died for our sins and rose again for our justification," and that personal faith in His shed blood brings complete cleansing and deliverance from the guilt and power of all confessed and forsaken sin.

6. We believe in the "deeper life"—a victorious Christian experience through sanctification, or the baptism of the Holy Spirit, for all who are fully consecrated to the Lord, and in growing in grace experienced by complete surrender and obedience to God and continued faith and fellowship with Christ; this is both the duty and privilege of every believer to be filled with the Holy Ghost, be kept by the power of God, and to do His will.

7. We believe in the immortality of the soul and the resurrection of the body.

8. We believe in the present intercessory ministry of Christ, His spiritual presence within and among His followers, and in His pre-millenial, visible, literal, and glorious return to earth, otherwise known as the

BIBLICAL DOCTRINES (GOSPEL MISSION
CORPS) (continued)

Secong Coming of Christ, which event may be at any moment and will climax this age or dispensation of grace.

9. We believe in the future judgment of mankind and the world, and in the eternal conscious destiny of each individual; Heaven is the prepared Home for the righteous (those who are saved from sin), and Hell is the place of punishment for the unsaved (those who remain in sin by either rejecting or neglecting Christ).

10. We believe that the message of the Gospel is being spread throughout the world in preparation for the end of the age, that God is gathering out a people for His name and preparing His Church to be the Bride of Christ, and also that the national and spiritual restoration of the Jews is a fulfillment of prophecy and a principal sign of the last times in which we are now living.

11. We believe in the spiritual unity of all born-again, Bible-believing Christians, and that the true Church is the body of believers, a militant and united fellowship of all men, women, and children—whether they be Jews or Gentiles—who have been brought "from darkness to light, from the power of Satan unto God, that they may receive forgiveness of sins, and inheritance among them who are sanctified by faith" in Christ; it is the brotherhood of saints, disciples of Jesus by belief in and obedience to His Word, regardless of race, nationality, or denominational affiliation.

12. We believe in water baptism as the believer's testimony and as the act of obedience to Christ's command, although not necessary for regeneration; the candidate is given preference as to the mode of pouring, immersion, or sprinkling, but the required form is "in the name of the Father, and of the Son, and of the Holy Ghost."

13. We believe in the sacrament, or ordinance of the Lord's Supper, as the holy communion of the body and blood of Jesus Christ, Who commanded: "This do in remembrance of Me;" as a memorial of His death and passion until He comes again in glory, the bread (unleavened) and the cup (unfermented wine) are to be partaken of only by believers, and then after careful self-examination and prayer.

14. We believe marriage is a divinely ordained institution, the bonds of which are sacred and not to be broken in this life; the wedded life of believers is to be within the fellowship of Christ.

15. We believe that infants and children of Christians should be dedicated to the Lord by their parents or guardians, and be trained and nourished in the ways of God; "Forbid them not," said Jesus, to come unto Him early in life.

16. We believe Christ is the Great Physician, and He provides deliverance and divine healing according to His will for the physical and the mental afflictions of mankind; His Word tells us to lay hands on the sick, anoint them with oil in the name of the Lord, and pray in faith for their well-being. Some cases are cured instantaneously, some gradually, and others are like Paul's "thorn in the flesh". . . . "My grace is sufficient."

17. We believe that concerning family relationships, upright business dealings, proper employment, civic affairs, and other worthy responsibilities, it is the duty of Christians to be subject to the appropriate authorities, first as faithful and obedient followers of Jesus Christ, and then as good citizens of our Country. We stress loyalty to our nation, respectful obedience to sound legislation, responsible participation and co-operation in legitimate community, social and educational activities, and in Christ-honoring personal, family, and group living, work, and service. However, we feel that being required to swear by oath to a statement of truth, and also the taking up of arms or weapons for the intent purpose of destroying human life, are both contrary to what Christ allows of His disciples.

18. We believe in the efficacy of prayer, the necessity of private and public worship, the enjoyment of praise to God, the privilege of Christian fellowship, the importance of Bible study, teaching, preaching, witnessing, and service as all a part of God's plan for His people. We gladly acknowledge that in the midst of these changing times in which we live, we can trust "Jesus Christ the same yesterday, and today, and for ever," and while human ideas and ideologies come and go, we can learn that "these three" "now abide—faith, hope, and divine love. . . . but the greatest of these is divine love."

CONCLUSION

"The preaching of these and kindred truths has been instrumental in the salvation of souls down the ages. It is not theory, not new philosophies of religion that are needed, but the old truths faithfully preached and reinforced by holy living. True religion consists in one's personal relationship with Christ. He is our Priest, making expiation for our sins and purging away defilement. He is our Prophet, instructing us in the way of life. He is our King, ruling over us."

(From the pen of Bishop Alma White, in the book—*The New Testament Church,* ch. III p. 46.)

REPENT ye, and BELIEVE the Gospel. (Mark 1:15)

Notes: *The doctrines of the Gospel Mission Corps are based upon those of the Pillar of Fire, the founder having been a member of that organization at one time.*

* * *

DOCTRINAL STATEMENT (GRACE AND HOPE MISSION)

WE BELIEVE:

1. "All scripture is given by inspiration of God, and is profitable for doctrine, for reproof, for correction, for instruction in righteousness." 2 Tim. 3:16.

2. There is one living and true God, the Creator and Preserver of all things, who is infinite in being and perfection, almighty, all-wise, all-holy, working all things according to the counsel of His most holy will, and for His own eternal glory and praise.

3. In the unity of the Godhead there are three persons: God the Father, God the Son and God the Holy Spirit, equal in power and divine perfection.

4. Our first parents being seduced by the subtilty and temptation of Satan fell from their sinless state, and as a consequence the sentence of death was placed upon the entire human race. Ps. 14:3.

5. Man's salvation is all through God's grace and mercy. He was willing to sacrifice His only begotten Son, the spotless Lamb of God as a sin-offering, that He might make full atonement for all sin. On the cross He shed His blood and tasted death for every man and all who believe in Him are fully justified. Isa. 53:5, 6.

6. Conversion or regeneration implies a new birth, a new man in Christ Jesus, it is nothing short of a miracle of grace. The Holy Spirit convicts and leads sinners to repentance and faith in the Lord Jesus Christ; by simply believing on the Lord Jesus Christ they are saved.

7. Sanctification is the work of the Holy Spirit, the third Person of the Trinity, whereby the believer is separated from ungodliness, unto a life of holiness. The divine injunction is—"Walk in the Spirit and ye shall not fulfill the desires of the flesh." Gal. 5:16.

8. The Word of God faithfully warns us against backsliding, as we find recorded in Heb. 10:26-29, Rom. 11:22 and Eze. 18:26-29. The Bible assures the backslider of forgiveness and cleansing from sin according to 1 John 2:1 and 1 John 1:9.

9. The return of the Lord Jesus Christ is the comforting hope of the church. "Unto them that look for him shall he appear the second time, without sin unto salvation." Heb. 9:28.

10. As to the resurrection of the just and the unjust: "The hour is coming, in which all that are in the graves shall hear his voice, and shall come forth; they that have done good, unto the resurrection of life; and they that have done evil unto the resurrection of damnation." John 5:28, 29.

* * *

STATEMENT OF DOCTRINE (KENTUCKY MOUNTAIN HOLINESS ASSOCIATION)

Kentucky Mountain Bible Institute is definitely committed to the Wesleyan interpretation of Christian doctrine including the following positions:

* the divine, plenary inspiration of the Holy Scriptures, inerrant in the original.

* the deity of Jesus Christ, His virgin birth, vicarious atonement, bodily resurrection, and personal pre-millenial return.

* the deity of the Holy Spirit.

* the fall of man.

* the universal inheritance of the carnal nature.

* justification by faith.

* sanctification as an instantaneous work of grace wrought in the believer through faith subsequent to regeneration and witnessed to by the Holy Spirit. The heart is cleansed from all sin and filled with the pure love of God. This excludes all speaking in unknown tongues either in private or in public.

* the resurrection and glorification of the saints and the eternal punishment of the wicked.

Notes: *This statement is derived from that of the Association's school.*

* * *

THE STATEMENT OF BELIEFS OF THE MEGIDDO MISSION

Megiddo means

"a place of troops" (Gesenius' Hebrew Lexicon); "a place of God" (Young's Analytical Concordance). Megiddo was and is a town in Palestine, strategically located, and the scene of frequent warfare. In the spiritual parallel, it is a place where soldiers engaged in spiritual warfare gather to renew their strength and courage (II Cor. 10:4-5).

WE BELIEVE

—in God the Creator of all things, all men, and all life.

WE BELIEVE

—in the Bible as containing the genuine revelation of God and His purposes for men, and as being our only source of divine knowledge today.

WE BELIEVE

—in Christ the Son of God and our Perfect Example, who was born of a Virgin, ministered among men, was crucified, resurrected, and taken to heaven, and who shall shortly return to be king of the whole earth.

WE BELIEVE

—in life as the gift of God, and in our sacred responsibility to use it for God and His coming Kingdom.

WE BELIEVE

—in all mankind as providing the nucleus from which a superior, God-honoring people shall be chosen to receive the blessings of immortal life.

WE BELIEVE

—in ourselves as capable of fulfilling the demands and disciplines given us in the law of God, thus perfecting that high quality of character which God has promised to reward with life everlasting in His heavenly Kingdom on earth.

WE BELIEVE

—in the promise of God, that a new age is coming—is near—when the earth will be filled with His glory, His people, and His will be done here as it is now done in heaven.

* * *

STATEMENT OF FAITH (ORIENTAL MISSIONARY SOCIETY HOLINESS CONFERENCE OF NORTH AMERICA)

We believe that:

1. THE GODHEAD

The Godhead eternally exists in three persons—the Father, the Son, and the Holy Spirit. These three are one God; of precisely identical nature, attributes and perfection.

A. GOD THE FATHER

God the Father Almighty, creator, preserver, and ruler of the universe, in His essential nature, is Spirit, and to His essential attribute is absolutely holy, and to His essential character, is love.

B. GOD THE SON, JESUS CHRIST

Jesus Christ, the eternal Son, was conceived by the Holy Spirit and born of the Virgin Mary, thereby having a truly divine nature in one person, and is the only mediator between God and man.

To accomplish salvation, He lived a sinless life, completely fulfilling righteousness and offered Himself a substitutionary sacrifice for the sin of the world, satisfying divine justice.

He was crucified under Pontius Pilate, died, and was buried. On the third day, He arose bodily from the dead. He ascended into heaven where in His glorified state, He intercedes for believers. He shall come again personally and visibly to judge the world in righteousness and to establish His kingdom.

C. GOD THE HOLY SPIRIT

The Holy Spirit is the third person of the Godhead. His ministry is to reveal Christ through the Word of God; to fulfill salvation in the regeneration and sanctification of the believers; to direct and empower the church in fulfillment of the Great Commission; and to convict the world of sin, of righteousness and of judgment.

II. THE BIBLE

The Bible, both the Old and New Testaments, the Word of God, is a divinely inspired revelation. It is the supreme and final authority in matters pertaining to faith and practice.

III. MAN

Man was created in the image of God, and he disobeyed God, thereby incurring spiritual death which is separation from God. Man is saved from the condition of spiritual death only by the grace of God through faith in Christ and His redemptive act, and by the ministry of the Holy Spirit. His spiritual growth and maturity is initiated by God's Spirit and by a conscious act of dedication on the part of the believer, and is effected by the indwelling of the Holy Spirit.

IV. THE CHURCH

The Church consists of all who have been regenerated through faith in Christ and have been united into one body under Christ, the Head thereof. It is called to worship God; to preach the Gospel; to administer baptism and holy communion by its duly appointed ministers; to care for and nurture the believers.

Notes: *Over the years of its existence, the Oriental Missionary Society Holiness Conference of North America has moved away from its unique holiness beginning to an emphasis on the common affirmations of evangelical Christianity. Its statement deals with only the most essential issues.*

* * *

APOSTOLIC DOCTRINES (PILLAR OF FIRE CHURCH)

We believe in the fundamental doctrines of the orthodox denominations. We do not lay great stress on the study of systematic theology, but preach wholesome, practical doctrine, guarding against liberalism and latter-day heresies. We are contending for the faith once delivered to the saints (Jude 3). We emphasize the necessity of a vital Christian experience and a transformed life. But doctrine is important, and neither the Church nor the ministry will be effective without it.

1. We believe that the Scriptures are given by inspiration of God, and that they are "the only sufficient rule of faith and practise." The tendency is to eliminate the supernatural from the Bible. It is our business to preach the Word and not to criticize it.

2. We believe in "repentance toward God and faith toward our Lord Jesus Christ." Repentance is giving up a wrong way and taking up a right way; that is, ceasing from sin. Repentance, like the pain of a physical malady, leads the patient to the great Physician. John the Baptist, the forerunner of Christ, said, "Repent ye," and this implied renunciation of all sin.

3. We believe in justification by faith. How is a man justified before God? is the old question ever recurring. Faith is the one condition, for by the deeds of the law shall no man be justified. Faith must be preceded by an absolute surrender to the will of God. Then, when one stands on believing ground, one beholds Christ as the bleeding sacrifice to take away sin, and divine life is imparted. Holy living then becomes an evidence of the change.

    Justification by faith is the doctrine that sent the thunders of the Reformation around the world. A justified person lives without knowingly committing sin. He may ignorantly transgress the law, but in this case sin is not imputed. "Whosoever is born of God doth not commit sin." "Whosoever abideth in him sinneth not" (1 John 3:6, 9).

4. We believe in Christian perfection, or entire sanctification, which is the cleansing of the believer's heart from inbred sin, or spiritual defilement, so that the whole spirit, soul and body may be preserved blameless unto the coming of our Lord Jesus Christ. This is the second work of grace, called by Mr. Wesley the second blessing. Sanctification is preceded by perfect consecration, and is an act of faith, and therefore instantaneous (Acts 26:18; 1 Thess. 5:23). We do not preach absolute perfection in the sense that one is free from mistakes and infirmities, but Christian perfection, which is purity of heart and life. This is the fundamental doctrine of the New Testament. It is that "holiness, without which no man shall see the Lord" (Heb. 12:14). It is the doctrine of the old-time Methodists, and for the propagation of it, John Wesley said God had raised them up. This experience is identical with the baptism of the Holy Ghost.

5. We believe in the immortality of the soul and the resurrection of the body. Soul-sleep, annihilation, no-hellism, and the denial of a literal resurrection are latter-day heresies and are soul-destroying. The Scriptures teach that there are to be at least two resurrections. There is to be a resurrection unto life, and a resurrection unto damnation (John 5:29). At Christ's coming the sanctified dead and the living saints are to be caught up to meet Him in the air (1 Cor. 15:22-23; 1 Thess 4:16-17). Paul speaks of "the resurrection out of the dead ones," or, as another has translated it, "the out-resurrection." It must be this "better resurrection" that he wished to obtain (Phil. 3:11; Heb. 11:35; Rev. 20:5-6).

6. We believe in the Judgments as taught in the Scriptures. The time is coming when all the wrongs of earth must be righted; the uneven scales of Justice will find their balance, and man will be dealt with according to the deeds done in the body. Christ paid the debt on Calvary for all who will accept (John 19:17-18). Those who repent and continue to the end do not come into judgment, except it be to receive their reward (John 5:24, R.V.). The soul undergoes a deep heart searching in seeking the experience of holiness. Jacob had his judgment day, in a sense, at the brookside when he wrestled all night in prayer (Gen. 32:24). There is next the judgment of the Church, or Bride of Christ, which takes place when she is caught up in the clouds to meet the Lord. This may be called a judgment of works. Paul says, "For we shall all stand before the judgment seat of Christ" (Rom. 14:10). When Christ shall come again, faithful Christians will be rewarded according to their works (Luke 14:14; Rev. 22:12). The next is the judgment of nations, which takes place when Christ returns with His Bride. This will be at Jerusalem. The last judgment is that of the great white throne (Rev. 20:12-15). The saints will be associated with Christ in this judgment and hence will not be a part of it. It will be for the wicked dead who will be raised after the Millennium and be brought before the Judge to receive their final sentence, prior to their banishment

to the lake of fire (Acts 17:31). That will be a momentous hour, when the secrets of all ages will be unfolded before men, angels, and devils.

7. We believe in water baptism; not that it is essential to salvation, but that it is an outward sign of regeneration, or of divine life that is imparted to the soul in the new birth. We believe that either pouring or sprinkling is scriptural, and will immerse those who prefer that mode.

8. We believe in the sacrament of the Lord's Supper, and administer the same to those who have knowledge of sins forgiven or are earnestly seeking to be delivered from their sins. It is a means of grace, inasmuch as Jesus said, "This do in remembrance of me."

9. We believe that marriage is a divine institution and should not be entered into indiscreetly. Those who wish to give their lives up to the service of the Master should not enter into such relationship unless in so doing they can better glorify His name.

10. We believe in divine healing for the body, a doctrine very much abused, and yet clearly taught in the Scriptures. While there are many false teachers and many false movements, such as Christian Science, Mormonism, Spiritualism, Russellism, Seventh Day-ism, and the so-called Pentecostal Tongues, or Latter Rain—Four-square Gospel—working miracles through demoniacal power, there are those who are divinely healed in answer to prayer (James 5:14-16). As a Church we have great reason to rejoice for the physical deliverances we have witnessed through the power of the great Physician.

11. We believe in the premillennial coming of the Lord and the Restoration of the Jews. More than three hundred times, Christ's second coming is mentioned in the New Testament. It is the polar star of the Church and the hope of every believer. By His return we mean His visible appearing on earth at the close of the Gentile Age to reign a thousand years. This is the kingdom symbolized by Daniel's stone cut out of the mountain, and which is to fall upon the feet of the image and grind it to powder. The figure implies a sudden catastrophe, which harmonizes with the tribulation spoken of in the gospels. We are now nearing the time of the end, when the Jews will be restored and the overthrow of the Gentile dominion is to take place.

12. We believe the wicked will go into eternal punishment and the righteous into life everlasting (Matt. 25:46). Heaven is a prepared place for a prepared people. "Blessed are the pure in heart: for they shall see God." The natural heart would fain believe there is no future punishment, but between the holy and the unholy in the other world there is an impassable gulf (Luke 16:26). And it is written also, "He which is filthy, let him be filthy still. . . . Without are dogs, and sorcerers, and whoremongers, and murderers, and idolaters, and whosoever loveth and maketh a lie" (Rev. 22:11, 15). There is to be a place of punishment for the incorrigible somewhere in the

universe. God calls it the place of outer darkness where there is weeping and wailing and gnashing of teeth.

The preaching of these and kindred truths has been instrumental in the salvation of souls down the ages. It is not theory, not new philosophies of religion that are needed, but the old truths faithfully preached and reinforced by holy living. True religion consists in one's personal relationship with Christ. He is our Priest, making expiation for our sins and purging away defilement. He is our Prophet, instructing us in the way of life. He is our King, ruling over us.

The New Testament Church is built on Christ. It is a regenerated Church, a Spirit-baptized Church, a joyful, witnessing Church, going forth with girded loins and burning lamp, carrying the salvation of a lost world upon its heart, and looking forward to the blessed hope and glorious appearing of our Lord and Savior Jesus Christ (Titus 2:13). It is as fair as the moon, clear as the sun, and terrible as an army with banners (Cant. 6:10).

Notes: *This statement of belief is taken from* The New Testament Church *by Bishop Alma White, founder of the Pillar of Fire Church. The Pillar of Fire had originally adopted a set of articles of religion based upon the Twenty-five Articles of Religion of the Methodist Episcopal Church. The present statement reflects that religious heritage as well as the debates that led to the founding of an independent church. There is also an affirmation of premillennialism.*

*　　*　　*

ARTICLES OF FAITH (SANCTIFIED CHURCH OF CHRIST)

I. THE HOLY TRINITY

1. God the Father: We believe there is but one true God everlasting and eternal, of infinite power, wisdom and goodness; the Maker and Preserver of all things visible and invisible. In unity of and in this Godhead there are three persons, of one substance and power,—the Father, the Son and the Holy Ghost.

2. God the Son: We believe that in due time, Jesus the Christ, the Son of God, the Saviour of the world became incarnated and sojourned among men, teaching the purest of truth and working the most amazing and beneficient miracles. That this divine person, foretold by the prophets and described by the Evangelists and Apostles is really and properly God, having assigned to Him by the inspired writers every attribute essential to the Deity, being one with Him who is called God, Jehovah, etc.

That He is also a perfect man in consequence of His incarnation and in that man, or manhood, dwelt all the fulness of the Godhead bodily; so His nature is two-fold—divine and human, or God manifest in the flesh.

We believe that His human nature is derived from the Blessed Virgin Mary through the creative energy of the Holy Ghost, so that two whole or perfect natures, that is to say, the Godhead and manhood are united in one person, never to be divided, whereof is one Christ very God and very man who truly suffered, was crucified and buried to reconcile His Father to us and to be a vicarious sacrifice, not only for sins of commission but also for the original or inherent sin.

We further believe that on the third day after His crucifixion and burial, Jesus Christ arose from the dead and took again His body with all things appertaining to the perfection of man's nature, wherewith He ascended into Heaven and there sitteth at the right hand of God, as the mediator until the consummation of all things (Luke 1:27; 35; John 3:16; Acts 4:12).

3. God the Holy Ghost: We believe in the Holy Ghost, the Third Person of the Triune Godhead, proceeding from the Father and the Son as the true and eternal God, of one substance, majesty and glory with the Father and the Son. He is ever present and efficiently active in and with the church or Christ, convincing the world of sin, of righteousness and of judgment and guiding into all truth as it is in Jesus (John 16:8; 3:5-9; Acts 15:8-9).

II. THE SACRED SCRIPTURES

4. We believe that the sacred scriptures or Holy Books which constitute the old and new testament are the inerrant and inspired word of God (II Tim. 3:16) and that they contain a full revelation of the will of God in relation to man concerning us in all things necessary to our salvation, so that whatever is not contained therein nor may be proved thereby, is not to be enjoined as an article of faith (II Peter 1:20-21).

III. FREE MORAL AGENCY

5. We believe in the beginning man was created in righteousness and true holiness without any moral imperfection or any kind of propensity to sin but with the divine right of choice, free to stand or fall and thus was made morally responsible, that man fell from this state, became corrupt in His nature and transmitted his defilement to all his posterity.

6. We further believe that man, though in the possession of the experience of forgiveness and sanctification, may fall from grace; and unless he repent of his sins and be cleansed from the nature of sin, be hopelessly and eternally lost.

IV. ORIGINAL OR INHERENT SIN

7. We believe that original sin or depravity is that corruption of every man's nature that is naturally engendered of the off-spring of Adam. Man is inclined to evil and that continually. (Gen. 6:5; Rom. 5:12-18) The scripture hath concluded all under sin (I John 1:8, Rom. 5:12) that the promise by faith of Jesus Christ might be given to all that believe (Rev. 22:17; John 3:16). God does not forgive original sin in us and it continues to exist, though suppressed,

after we have been forgiven of sins of commission and will remain within the nature of man until eradicated or destroyed by the Baptism with the Holy Ghost (I John 1:9; 3:8; Acts 15:8-9).

V. THE ATONEMENT

8. We believe that Jesus Christ, by the sacrificial shedding of His blood through an expiatory death on the cross made a full atonement for all sin (Rom. 5:8-11), and that this atonement is the only ground for salvation, it being sufficient for every individual of Adam's race. The atonement is graciously efficacious for the salvation of the irresponsible from birth, or for the righteous who have become irresponsible (Rom. 4:15) and to children in innocency (Mark 10:14) but is efficacious for the salvation of those who reach the age of responsibility only when they repent and believe (Luke 24:47; Acts 17:30).

VI. FAITH

9. We believe that there is no salvation except through faith in Jesus Christ and that this faith is a gift from God and without it, it is impossible to please God (Eph. 2:8; Heb. 11:6). No human since the fall of Adam has or ever can, through his own righteousness or works merit salvation (Eph. 2:9; Titus 3:5), but is saved by a living faith that becomes effective when it is exercised by man with the aid of the Spirit, which aid is assured, when the heart has met the divine condition (Heb. 5:9).

VII. REPENTANCE

10. We believe that genuine repentance toward God consists in a knowledge of, a sorrow for, and a voluntary confession and forsaking of sin. This is brought about by the knowledge of the goodness and severity of God, through the medium of the truth and the convincing power of the Holy Spirit. It is demanded of all who have by act or purpose become sinners against God. The Spirit of God gives to all who will repent the gracious help of penitence of heart and hope of mercy, that they may believe unto pardon and spiritual life (Matt. 3:2; Rom. 3:23; II Cor. 7:10; John 16:7-11; Luke 13:5; Acts 11:18).

VIII. JUSTIFICATION

11. We believe that justification is that gracious and judicial act of God in which He grants full pardon from the penalty of sins committed in behalf of a penitent soul, trusting only in the merits of the shed blood of Jesus Christ (Rom. 5:1). That this act is absolute in respect of all past sins of commission, all being forgiven where any are forgiven.

IX. SANCTIFICATION

12. We believe that the souls of justified persons must be purified and cleansed from all inbred sin or the corruption of the natural human heart, which cleansing we term Sanctification or being made holy as truly, sanctification is that act of God, subsequent to forgiveness, by which believers are made free from original sin, or depravity, and brought in to a state of entire devotement to God, and the holy obedience of love made perfect. This is not a suppression or counteraction of inbred sin as to make it inoperative, but its destruction or eradication so that the believer not only has a right to heaven but is so conformed to God's nature that he will enjoy heaven forever (I Thess. 3:13; 5:23; Rom. 6:6, 18, 22).

13. We believe also that sanctification is provided through the shed blood of Jesus (Heb. 10:10; 13:12; I Pet. 1:2; I John 1:9) and is wrought instantaneously by the believer's faith in the blood, preceded by entire consecration (Rom. 12:1) and to this work of grace the Holy Spirit bears witness (Rom. 6:6; Gal. 2:20; II Cor. 1:22; Heb. 10:14-15).

14. We further believe that this experience is wrought by the baptism with the Holy Ghost, and is that essential "holiness without which no man shall see the Lord" (Heb. 12:14); and that it is a two-fold act of cleansing the heart from sin and filling the believer with the indwelling presence of the Holy Ghost, empowering him for life and service (Acts 2:1-4; John 7:39; 14:16; 17, 26; 16:13, 14; Acts 15:8, 9).

X. WITNESS OF THE SPIRIT

15. The witness of the Spirit is that inward impression wrought in the soul, whereby the Spirit of God immediately and directly assures our spirit that Bible conditions are met for salvation, and the work of grace is complete in the soul (Rom. 15:16). Therefore the Spirit bears witness to both the justification of the sinner and the sanctification of the believer (I John 5:10; Heb. 10:14-15).

XI. THE SECOND COMING OF CHRIST

16. We believe that the Lord Jesus Christ will come again and that his personal return will be "in like manner" as he ascended (Acts 1:11; Phil. 3:20; I Thess. 4:14-18).

FOOTNOTE: It is to be understood that a dissenting understanding on the subject of the second coming of Christ shall not be held to break or hinder either church fellowship or membership.

XII. RESURRECTION, JUDGMENT, AND DESTINY

17. We believe in the resurrection of the dead, "They that have done good, unto the resurrection of life; and they that have done evil, unto the resurrection of damnation" (I Cor. 15:52; John 5:28, 29; Phil. 3:21). We believe also in the future judgment in which every man shall appear before God to be judged according to his deeds in this life (II Cor. 5:10; Heb. 9:27). We believe that glorious and everlasting life is assured to all who savingly believe in, and obediently follow Jesus Christ our Lord; and that the finally impenitent shall suffer eternally in Hell (Matt. 25:41; II Peter 3:7; Jude 15).

ARTICLES OF FAITH (WESLEYAN TABERNACLE ASSOCIATION)

ARTICLE I

There is one God over all, the same yesterday, today and forever; the Creator of all things, and in Whom all things consist.

ARTICLE II

There is one Saviour, Jesus Christ, the only begotten Son of God, Who is the Supreme head of the Church, which He redeemed unto God by His own blood.

ARTICLE III

There is one Holy Spirit, the third person in the Trinity, Who is now the representative of the God-head on earth, Who came from the Father and the Son, to convict the world of sin, of righteousness and of judgment.

God the Father, God the Son and God the Holy Spirit are three persons, united and inseparable, of one substance and eternal.

ARTICLE IV. THE HOLY SCRIPTURES

We emphatically affirm our unwavering faith in the Holy Scriptures of the Old and New Testaments, as divinely and supernaturally inspired, infalibly true as originally given and our only divinely authorized rule of faith and practice.

ARTICLE V. THE PLAN OF REDEMPTION

True repentance toward God and faith in the shed blood of our Lord Jesus Christ bring the forgiveness of all our sins and the experience of the New Birth, whereby we become children of God.

The unconditional abandonment of all we are and have to God forever and unwavering faith in the promise of the Father, bring the Baptism with the Holy Spirit by Whom we are sanctified wholly. This baptism is always subsequent to regeneration. It is an instantaneous experience received by faith, cleansing the heart of the recipient from all sin and endowing him with power for service.

Regeneration and sanctification thus wrought by God's free grace are witnessed to by the Holy Spirit.

ARTICLE VI

We believe in the resurrection of the body, the judgment of all mankind, the everlasting punishment of the wicked and the eternal happiness of the righteous.

RECOMMENDATIONS

DIVINE HEALING

We urge our people to embrace the Bible doctrine of Divine Healing and to offer the prayer of faith for the healing of the sick, according to James 5:14-16; Acts 4:10, 14; and Luke 9:2, 10:9.

THE ORDINANCES

(A) BAPTISM. Recognizing the fact that water baptism is an outward sign of an inward work wrought in the heart by the Holy Spirit, we recommend that this ordinance be observed by the members of this Association.

(B) THE LORD'S SUPPER. Believing the sacrament of the Lord's Supper represents our redemption through Christ, we recommend that this ordinance be reverently observed.

THE RETURN OF OUR LORD

We believe that the Holy Scriptures teach the personal and premillennial return of the Lord, and that we are commanded to be ready and daily watching for His glorious appearing. We therefore recommend that our preachers proclaim this truth from time to time.

Notes: *The brevity of the statement of the Wesleyan Tabernacle Association, with significant items placed under the heading of "recommendations," reflects the looseness of its congregations' affiliation with the association.*

* * *

Black Holiness

ARTICLES OF FAITH [CHURCH OF CHRIST (HOLINESS)]

I. GOD

We believe in one God, and that He only is God, and that as God, He is Triune, being revealed as Father, Son and Holy Spirit.

II. THE SON OF GOD

We believe that the Son of God is the Second Person of The Holy Trinity, and as The Son of God, He became incarnate by the Holy Spirit, and being born of The Virgin Mary, united with Himself the divinely begotten Son of Man, called Jesus, thus uniting in one person, God and man.

III. THE HOLY SPIRIT

We believe that the Holy Spirit is the Third Person of the Godhead, and is ever present, and active in and with the Church of Christ, convicting, and regenerating those who believe and sanctifying believers, and guiding into all truth as it is in Jesus.

IV. THE HOLY BIBLE

We believe that the Holy Bible is composed of sixty-six books, commonly known as the Old and New Testaments, and that they are the revealed words of God written by Holy men as they were moved by The Holy Ghost.

V. ORIGINAL SIN

We believe that original sin is that corruption of the nature of all offsprings of Adam, by which we all are separated from original righteousness; and that in the Scriptures it is described as "the carnal mind," "the flesh," "sin that dwelleth in me," and such like. It continues to exist until eradicated or destroyed by The Holy Ghost, through the blood of Christ, I John 1: 6-10; Rom. 7; Heb. 9: 11-14; 10: 29; 13: 12.

VI. ATONEMENT

We believe that the atonement made by Jesus Christ through the shedding of His blood for the remission of sins, is for the whole human race; and that whosoever repents and believes on the Lord Jesus Christ is justified and regenerated and saved from the dominion of sin. Rom. 3: 22-26; 5:9, Heb. 2:9.

VII. REPENTANCE

We believe that a repentance is a sincere change of the mind, involving a sense of personal guilt of sin, and a turning away from the same. And that the pentinent heart is graciously helped by the Spirit of God. Acts 2: 38; 26: 18; 3: 19.

VIII. JUSTIFICATION

We believe that justification is God's word done for us, by which full pardon is granted to all who believe and receive Jesus Christ as Savior and Lord. Rom. 3: 24; Acts 10: 43.

IX. REGENERATION

We believe that regeneration is the new birth, that is, God's work done in us, by which the believer is given a Spiritual life, and rectifying the attitude of the will toward God and Holy things. John 3: 6; Titus 3: 5.

X. SANCTIFICATION

We believe that sanctification is that act of Divine grace whereby we are made holy. In justification, the guilt of sin is removed; in sanctification, the inclination to sin is removed. Sanctification must be definitely experienced to fit us to see the Lord. I Thes. 5: 23; Heb. 10: 14; John 17: 17; Heb. 12: 1-14.

XI. RESURRECTION

We believe that Christ truly rose from the dead, and ascended into heaven, and is now sitting at the right hand of God The Father making intercession for us. I Cor. 15: 14-20.

XII. THE SECOND COMING

We believe that The Lord Jesus Christ will return to judge the quick and the dead; and that we who are alive at His coming shall not precede them that are asleep in Christ Jesus. I Thes. 4: 13-18.

XIII. BAPTISM

We believe that baptism is commanded of Our Lord and that it belongs to the believer of the Gospel, "not infants who cannot believe," and that the Bible way of administering it is by immersion. Matt. 28: 19-20; Mark 16: 14-16; Rom. 6: 1-7.

XIV. THE LORD'S SUPPER

We believe that The Lord's Supper is a New Testament Ordinance, and that it was instituted when our Lord celebrated His last Passover with His disciples, and that it consists of bread and wine, and that as often as we take it we show forth the Lord's death till He comes again. Matt. 26: 26-29; Mark 14: 22-25; Luke 22: 19-20; I Cor. 5: 11: 23-24.

XV. THE GIFT OF THE HOLY GHOST

(a) We believe that every true believer is heir to the gift of the Holy Ghost. Gal. 4: 6-7.

(b) We believe that He is the gift of God in Christ Jesus to the Children of God, sanctifying, quickening, guiding into all truth, and giving power to obey and witness God's Word. John 14: 16-26; Acts 1:8.

(c) We believe that the receiving of The Holy Ghost is subsequent to conversion. Acts 8: 14-16; 19: 1-4.

(d) We believe that a backslider must be reclaimed before he or she can receive the Holy Ghost.

(e) We believe that The Holy Ghost baptized the whole church on the day of Pentecost because of the Jewish nation, and the whole Church in Cornelius' house because of the gentile nation; and that always thereafter, He is referred to as a gift, Acts 2: 38-39; a receiving, Acts 19: 1-2, a filling, Eph. 5: 18; an annointing, John 2-27; II Cor. 1: 21. He is never again referred to as a baptism for there is but one baptism. Eph. 4: 1-5.

XVI. FOOTWASHING

We believe in foot washing as an act of obedience in following the example given by our Lord Jesus Christ.

XVII. SPIRITUAL GIFTS

We believe that spiritual gifts are set forth in the 12th, 13th, and 14th chapters of First Corinthians.

1. That no one gift is the specific sign or evidence of the Holy Spirit's presence, but faith (Heb. 11: 1) and Love (I Cor. 13; John 13: 35) are the evidences; not even power alone is the evidence for that may be as Satan.

2. That these gifts, though they may be of use to edification, may be counterfeited and are not to be trusted as evidence. II Thes. 2: 7-12; II Tim. 3: 8.

3. That there are three essential evidences of true religion. Faith, Hope, and Love. I Cor. 13: 13.

4. That the Bible endorses speaking in tongues, or a gift of tongues, but that no one really speaks in tongues unless he speaks a language understood by men, as in Acts 2.

5. That though one speak with tongues, it is no evidence of the Holy Ghost at all, but merely a sign.

XVIII. DIVINE HEALING

1. We do not condemn physicians and medicines because the Bible does not. Prov. 17: 22; Ezek. 47: 12; Col. 4: 44; Matt. 9:12.

2. We believe and teach Divine Healing according to the Scriptures. Isa. 8: 20.

3. We believe that it is a gift set in the Church and that the prayer of faith will save the sick and The Lord will raise them up. James 5: 15.

Notes: *The holiness movement, which drew much of its strength from the South, very quickly segregated along racial lines. Although the racial question determined the outward life of these groups, it is not reflected in their statements of doctrine, which follow similar patterns.*

The Church of Christ (Holiness) is the oldest of the predominantly black holiness bodies. Its statement of faith was derived from that of the Church of the Nazarene. The statement was also adopted by the Associated Churches of Christ (Holiness).

DOCTRINAL ELEMENTS OF THE CHURCH, GENERALLY [CHURCH OF GOD (SANCTIFIED CHURCH)]

The doctrinal elements of the Original Church of God or Sanctified Church consists of: Hearing, Repentance, Faith, Confession, Baptism.

On the merits of the sinner putting these elements into actions or, other words, obeying from the heart this form of doctrine he is then JUSTIFIED by the blood and he is a Regenerated child; and he is received into fellowship with God through Jesus Christ. He is made a partaker of His divine life and an heir to the Holy Spirit. The Holy Spirit imparts entire Sanctification to or in the believer. "Not by works of righteousness which we have done, but according to his mercy he saved us, by the washing of REGENERATION, and renewing of the HOLY GHOST; which he shed on us abundantly through Jesus Christ our Lord and Saviour; that being justified by his grace, we should be made heirs according to the hope of eternal life." Titus 3:5-7.

This is called by some, the Second Blessing or a Second Work of Grace, or Entire Sanctification. It is so called because man, in his unregenerated state, is a two fold sinner. A sinner by nature, also a sinner by practice. When he believes on the Lord Jesus Christ, the atoning blood of the cross cleanses him from all sin. And the stain of guilt washed away leaving him with a clean heart or a clear conscience. "For if the blood of bulls and of goats, and the ashes of an heifer sprinkling the unclean, sanctifieth to the purifying of the flesh; How much more shall the blood of Christ, who through the eternal Spirit offered himself without spot to God, purge your conscience from dead works to serve the living God? Heb. 9;13-14.

In this it will clearly be seen, that the believer is clean when he is converted to Christ, because the New life from God to us through Christ makes us new Creatures. That act places us in a New State which is a Justified State, clean. But this converted one must be filled with the Holy Ghost. To be clean is one thing, and to be filled with the Holy Ghost is another. The following scriptures will surely convince anyone who has any knowledge or respect for what the Bible teaches. Luke 24:49-The Holy Ghost was given to the disciples after they were believers. It was promised to those who believed on Christ through John the Baptist's preaching. Matt. 3:11-12.

READ CAREFULLY

Luke 3:16-17	Acts 1:8-9
John 1:33	Eph 1:13
Rom. 5:1-5	Acts 19:1-6
Acts 8:14	Acts 1:5
Mark 1:8	I. Cor 6:9
Rom. 15:16	

The scriptures referred to will show that all of the primitive disciples or christians received the Holy Ghost as a second blessing after they were regenerated. The doctrine of Holiness gets its foundation on regeneration of the sinner. This places him in a Justified state. The person then receiving the proper teaching, has right to believe that the same God who has the power to regenerate him through Christ, has the power to fill him with the Holy Ghost, which is Sanctification.

Because Sanctification is the work of the Holy Spirit in the believer subsequent to Regeneration, or Born again. "But we are bound to give thanks to God for you brethren beloved of the Lord, because God hath from the beginning chosen you to salvation through sanctification of the Spirit and belief of the truth." 2 Thes. 2:13.

When the doctrine ceased to be preached the results were, carnal ministers, carnal Churches and worldly profess christians. The doctrine of Holiness, coupled with a holy life is the only remedy. Heb. 12:14; I Pet. 1:1-4.

ARTICLE 26. MARRIAGE AND DIVORCE

Is it lawful for a Christian to put away their husbands or wives and marry while the other lives?

The law on the "second marriage" was clearly set forth by Christ, the law giver of the New Testament. Hear His words: "The Pharisees also came unto him, tempting him, and saying unto him, Is it lawful for a man to put away his wife for every cause? And he answered and said unto them, Have ye not read, that he which made them at the beginning made them male and female, And said, for this cause shall a man leave father and mother, and shall cleave to his wife; and they two shall be one flesh. Wherefore they are no more twain, but one flesh. What therefore God hath joined together, let not man put asunder. They say unto him, Why did Moses then command to give a writing of divorcement, to and to put her away? He saith unto them, Moses because of the hardness of your hearts suffered you to put away your wives: but from the beginning it was not so. And I say unto you, Whosoever shall put away his wife, except it be for fornication, and shall marry another, committeth adultery; and whose marrieth her which is put away doth commit adultery. Matt. 19:3. Mark 10:2-12; Luke 16:18; Rom. 7:1-4; I Cor. 7:10-15. These references should serve to convince us that Christ, the Law Giver of the New Testament Church makes only one exception. Matt. 5:32; Matt. 19:9.

ARTICLE 27

Should a Holy man marry people to the Second Husband or wife if he knows that their husband or wife is living?

We have no direct scriptures forbidding it. But if it is wrong for them to marry, it surely would be wrong for a saved Minister to encourage it. I Tim. 5:21-22.

ARTICLE 28. PAYING TITHES

There is no special command given in the New Testament to pay tithes and there is none directly against it. If any one makes a vow to that effect, God would hold them responsible if they deferred to pay. Tithes were paid under the old Covenant because it was a law to that effect. There must be something about it that merited God's approval because He encouraged it before the law was given. Gen. 14:18; Gen. 28:18-22.

God renewed the command to Israel through Malachi 3:8-12; Matt. 23:23. In this you can see that it had Christ's attention. Yet He gave no special command to pay them. The saints paid a slight tribute to paying tithes under the law, but only to show that the libidical priesthood which was made so by the law, changed when Christ came. Therefore the law that supported it was changed. If you will read carefully the seventh chapter of Hebrews, you will see that Paul labored to show the converted Jews that they were not under the same compulsory law to pay tithes as did the fathers under the law, verse 19. For the law made nothing perfect, but the bringing in of a better hope did; by which we draw nigh to God. Heb. 7:19.

* * *

Glenn Griffith Movement

ARTICLES OF RELIGION (BIBLE MISSIONARY CHURCH)

ARTICLES OF RELIGION (1955)

I. THE TRIUNE GOD

1. We believe in one eternally existent, infinite God, Sovereign of the universe; that He only is God, creative and administrative, holy in nature, attributes, and purpose; that He, as God, is Triune in essential being, revealed as Father, Son, and Holy Ghost. (I John 5:7; John 1:1; Matt. 3:16-17; John 14:16-17, 26)

II. GOD THE FATHER

2. The Father is the supreme Person in the Godhead, to Whom the Son and the Holy Ghost, though of equal essence, are subordinate in office. The Father sent the Son into the world; He also sends the Holy Ghost. To the Father the Son reconciles the penitent sinner; and to the Father pertains the worship of every believer.

ARTICLES OF RELIGION (CURRENT)

I. GOD THE FATHER

1. We believe there is but one living and true God; everlasting, of infinite power, wisdom and goodness; the Maker and Preserver of all things, visible and invisible; that in unity of the Godhead there are three persons, of one substance, power and eternity—the Father, the Son and the Holy Ghost.

II. GOD THE SON

2. We believe in Jesus Christ, the only begotten Son of God, the Second Person of the Triune God-head; that He was eternally one with the Father, that He was conceived by the Holy Ghost, was born of the Virgin Mary and became incarnate, so that two whole and perfect natures, that is to say, the Godhead and manhood, are thus united in one person, very God and very man, the God-man.

We believe that Jesus Christ died for our sins, and not only for actual sins, but also for original sin, that He might reconcile us to God. He arose from the dead and took again His body, together with all things appertaining to the perfection of man's nature, wherewith He ascended into heaven and is there

engaged in intercession for us (Luke 1:27-35; John 1:14; John 3:16; Acts 4:12; Rom. 5:10; Heb. 7:25).

III. GOD THE HOLY GHOST

3. We believe in the Holy Ghost, the Third Person of the Triune Godhead; that He proceeds from the Father and the Son as the true and eternal God, of one substance, majesty and glory with the Father and Son. (Matt. 28:19; Acts 5:32; Rom. 8:9-11). He is ever present and efficiently active in and with the Church of Christ, convincing the world of sin, regenerating those who repent and believe, sanctifying believers, and guiding into all truth as it is in Jesus (John 16:18; John 3:5-9; Acts 15:8-9; John 16:13).

IV. THE HOLY SCRIPTURES

4. We believe that the sixty-six canonical books of the Old and New Testaments were given by divine inspiration (2 Tim. 3:16), and are the Word of God. We believe the Holy Scriptures inerrantly reveal the will of God concerning all things necessary to our salvation, so that whatever is not contained therein nor may be proved thereby, is not to be enjoined as an article of faith (2 Pet. 1:20-21).

V. ORIGINAL SIN, OR DEPRAVITY

5. We believe that original sin, or depravity, is that corruption of the nature of all the offspring of Adam by reason of which every one is very far gone from original righteousness or the pure state of our first parents at the time of their creation, is averse to God, without spiritual life, and inclined to evil, and that continually (Gen. 6:5; Rom. 3:12; 5:12-18; 1 Cor. 15:22). In the Scriptures, it is spoken of as the carnal mind, the old man and the flesh (Rom. 6:6; Rom. 7:7; Rom. 8:5-8). We further believe that original sin continues to exist after regeneration, though suppressed, until crucified (eradicated) and destroyed by the baptism with the Holy Ghost (Acts 15:8-9; 1 John 3:8).

VI. THE ATONEMENT

6. We believe that Jesus Christ, by His suffering (Acts 3:18), by the shedding of His own blood (Rom. 5:8-10; Heb. 9:12), and by His meritorious death on the cross (Eph. 2:13-16), made full atonement (Rom. 5:11) for all sin, and that this atonement is the only ground for salvation (Acts 4:12; Eph. 1-7), it being sufficient for every individual of Adam's race (John 3:16; 1 John 2:2). The atonement is graciously efficacious for the salvation of the irresponsible, the righteous who have become irresponsible (Rom. 4:5) and children in innocency (Mark 10:14), but is efficacious for the salvation of those who reach the age of responsibility only when they repent and believe (Luke 24:47; Acts 16:30-31; 17:30).

VII. FREE WILL

7. We believe that man was created with ability to choose between right and wrong and thus was made morally responsible. The condition of man since the fall is such that he cannot prepare himself by his own natural strength and works, to faith and calling upon

God. But the grace of God through Jesus Christ is freely bestowed upon all men, enabling all who will to turn from sin to righteousness, believe on Jesus Christ for pardon and cleansing from sin and follow good works pleasing and acceptable in His sight. "Whosoever will, let him take of the water of life freely" (Rev. 22:17; John 4:14, 15).

8. We further believe that man, though in the possession of the experience of regeneration and entire sanctification, may fall from grace and apostatize, and unless he repents of his sin, be hopelessly and eternally lost.

VIII. FAITH

9. We believe that living faith is the gift of God, and without it, it is impossible to please God (Heb. 11:6). Faith becomes effective as it is exercised by man, with the aid of the Spirit, which aid is assured when the heart has met the divine condition (Heb. 5:9).

IX. REPENTANCE

10. We believe that genuine repentance toward God consists in a knowledge of, a godly sorrow for, and a voluntary confession and forsaking of sin. This is brought about by the knowledge of the goodness and severity of God, through the medium of the truth and the convincing power of the Holy Spirit. It is demanded of all who have by act or purpose become sinners against God. The Spirit of God gives to all who will repent, the gracious help of penitence of heart and hope of mercy, that they may believe unto pardon and spiritual life (Matt. 3:2; Rom. 3:23; 2 Cor. 7:10; John 16:7-11; Luke 13:5).

X. JUSTIFICATION, REGENERATION AND ADOPTION

11. We believe that justification is that gracious and judicial act of God, by which He grants full pardon of all guilt and complete release from the penalty of sins committed, and acceptance as righteous to all who believe on Jesus Christ and receive Him as Lord and Saviour (Rom. 3:23-25; Rom. 5:1).

12. We believe that regeneration, or the new birth, is that gracious work of God whereby the moral nature of the repentant believer is spiritually quickened and given a distinctly spiritual life, capable of faith, love, and obedience (2 Cor. 5:17; 1 Pet. 1:23).

13. We believe that adoption is that gracious act of God by which the justified and regenerated believer is constituted a son of God.

14. We believe that justification, regeneration and adoption are simultaneous in the experience of seekers after God and are obtained upon the condition of faith in the merits of the shed blood of Jesus Christ, preceded by repentance; and that to this work and state of grace the Holy Spirit bears witness.

XI. ENTIRE SANCTIFICATION

15. We believe that entire sanctification is that act of God, subsequent to regeneration, by which believers

are made free from original sin, or depravity, and brought into a state of entire devotement to God and the holy obedience of love made perfect.

16. It is wrought by the baptism with the Holy Ghost and comprehends in one experience the cleansing of the heart from sin and the abiding, indwelling presence of the Holy Ghost, empowering the believer for life and service.

17. Entire Sanctification is provided through the blood of Jesus; is wrought instantaneously by faith, preceded by entire consecration; and to this work and state of grace the Holy Spirit bears witness (Rom. 12:1; Rom. 6:11, 13, 22; Rom. 6:6; Gal. 2:20; Rom. 15:16; Heb. 13:12-13; Heb. 10:14-15).

18. This experience is also known by various terms representing its different phases, such as "Christian Perfection," "Perfect Love," "Heart Purity," "The Baptism with the Holy Ghost," "The Fullness of the Blessing," and "Christian Holiness."

XII. THE WITNESS OF THE SPIRIT

19. The Witness of the Spirit is that inward impression wrought on the soul, whereby the Spirit of God immediately and directly assures our spirit that Bible conditions are met for salvation and the work of grace is complete in the soul (Rom. 8:16). Therefore, the Spirit bears witness to both the salvation of the sinner and the sanctification of the believer (1 John 5:10; Heb. 10:14-15).

XIII. GROWTH IN GRACE

20. We believe that growth in grace is possible and necessary to maintain a right relationship with God, both before and after sanctification (Eph. 4:15-16; 2 Peter 3:18).

XIV. THE SECOND COMING OF CHRIST

21. We believe that the Lord Jesus Christ will come again. We believe that His coming will be literal and bodily and that we who are alive at His coming shall not precede them that are asleep in Christ Jesus; but that, if we are abiding in Him, we shall be caught up with the risen saints to meet the Lord in the air, so that we shall ever be with the Lord. We believe that the coming of Christ will be premillennial and that we should distinguish between His coming for His saints (1 Thess. 4:4-18) and with His saints (Jude 1:14). The latter will not occur until after the manifestation of the Antichrist and the Great Tribulation (Rev. 19:20; 2 Thess. 2:7-11). The one hope of the church is the premillennial coming of Jesus (Acts 15:13-17; Titus 2:13).

XV. RESURRECTION, JUDGMENT AND DESTINY

22. We believe in the resurrection of the dead, that the bodies both of the just and of the unjust shall be raised to live and unite with their spirits. "They that have done good, unto the resurrection of life; and they that have done evil, unto the resurrection of damnation" (John 5:29) (1 Cor. 15:52; 2 Cor. 5:10; 1 Thess. 4:15-16; Phil. 3:21).

We believe in future judgment in which every man shall appear before God to be judged according to his deeds in this life.

We believe that glorious and everlasting life is assured to all who savingly believe in and obediently follow Jesus Christ our Lord; and that the finally impenitent shall suffer eternally in hell (John 6:38; Matt. 6:20; Matt. 5:29; Matt. 10:28; Matt. 23:33; Matt. 25:41; Luke 16:23).

XVI. BAPTISM

23. We believe that Christian Baptism is a sacrament signifying acceptance of the benefits of the atonement of Jesus Christ. It is to be administered to believers as declarative of their faith in Jesus Christ as their Saviour, and full purpose of obedience in holiness and righteousness.

Baptism may be administered by sprinkling, pouring or immersion, according to the choice of the applicant.

XVII. THE LORD'S SUPPER

24. We believe that the Memorial and Communion Supper instituted by our Lord and Saviour Jesus Christ is essentially a New Testament sacrament, declarative of His sacrificial death, through the merits of which believers have life and salvation and promise of all spiritual blessings in Christ. It is distinctively for those who are prepared for reverent appreciation of its significance and by it they show forth the Lord's death till He comes again. Being the Communion feast, only those who have faith in Christ and love for the saints should be called to participate therein (Luke 22:19-20; 1 Cor. 11:23-29; Matt. 26:26-29).

XVIII. THE CHRISTIAN SABBATH

25. We recognize the first day of the week as being the Christian Sabbath under the present dispensation. It was the custom of the New Testament churches to meet for worship on the first day of the week. It was also selected and held sacred because the Lord Himself was resurrected on that day and He further emphasized it by pouring out the Holy Spirit on the day of Pentecost (1 Cor. 16:2; Matt. 28:1; Mark 16:2; Luke 24:1; John 20:1-19).

XIX. DIVINE HEALING

26. We believe in the Bible doctrine of divine healing and urge our people to seek to offer the prayer of faith for healing of the sick. Providential means and agencies, when deemed necessary, should not be refused (James 5:16; Matt. 10:8; Luke 9:2).

XX. THE CHURCH

27. The invisible church of God is composed of all spiritually regenerated persons whose names are written in heaven.

Notes: *The most conservative and strict wing of the holiness movement, the Glenn Griffith Movement emerged in the 1950s as a reaction to what its leaders considered a loss of holiness standards among the older holiness churches. The issues of contention were not doctrinal, but behavioral;*

therefore, the movement's doctrinal statements closely follow those of the parent bodies.

The Bible Missionary Church was organized by former members of the Church of the Nazarene. At the time of its formation, it accepted the articles of religion of the Nazarenes, with two changes. The first article on the Trinity was slightly rewritten, scriptural references were appended, and a second article on God the Father was added.

More recently, the Bible Missionary Church completely rewrote its Articles of Religion. The first article is taken from the Twenty-five Articles of Religion common to Methodism.

*   *   *

CREEDAL STATEMENTS (CHURCH OF THE BIBLE COVENANT)

1. THE HOLY TRINITY. We believe there is but one living and true God, everlasting, of infinite power, wisdom, and goodness; the Maker and Preserver of all things, visible and invisible. And in unity of this God-head there are three persons of one substance, power, and eternity—the Father, the Son (the Word), and the Holy Spirit. The Father is specially related to God's work in creation; the Son by incarnation is specially related to God's work in redemption; and the Holy Spirit by His indwelling is specially related to God's work in sanctification.

5. JESUS CHRIST. We believe the only begotten Son of God was conceived by the Holy Spirit, born of the Virgin Mary, suffered under Pontius Pilate, was crucified, dead and buried—to be a sacrifice, not only for original sin, but also for the actual sins of men, and to reconcile us to God. In resurrection He came forth from the dead, took again His body, together with all things appertaining to the perfection of man's nature, wherewith He ascended into heaven and is there engaged in intercession for us.

10. THE HOLY SPIRIT. We believe the Holy Spirit, proceeding from the Father and the Son, is of one substance, majesty and glory with the Father and the Son, very and eternal God. He is ever present and efficiently active in and with the Church of Christ, convincing the world of sin, righteousness and judgment, regenerating those who repent and believe, sanctifying belivers and guiding into all truth.

15. THE HOLY SCRIPTURES. We believe in the plenary inspiration of the Holy Scriptures, by which we mean the sixty-six books of the Old and New Testaments to be given by divine inspiration. These Scriptures we hold to be the infallible written Word of God, superior to all human authority, containing all things necessary to our salvation, so that whatever is not contained therein is not to be considered an article of faith.

20. ORIGINAL SIN. We believe original sin is the corruption of the nature of every man and is naturally engendered of the offspring of Adam, whereby man is wholly gone from original righ-

teousness, and of his own nature inclined to evil and that continually. We believe that original sin continues to exist in the life of the regenerate until eradicated by the baptism with the Holy Spirit.

25. THE ATONEMENT—GROUND OF SALVATION. We believe that Jesus Christ, by the shedding of His own blood, and by His meritorious death on the Cross, made a full atonement for all human sin, and that this atonement is the only ground of salvation, and that it is sufficient for every individual. The atonement is graciously efficacious for the salvation of the irresponsible and those not having reached the age of accountability, but is efficacious for the salvation of all others only when they repent and believe. Wherefore, to expect salvation on the ground of good works, or by the suffering the pains our sins deserve, either in the present or future state, is derogatory of Christ's sacrifice for us, and is a dangerous deceit.

30. FREE WILL. We believe the condition of man after the fall of Adam is such that he cannot turn and prepare himself, by his own natural strength and work, to faith and calling upon God. But being created in God-likeness we believe all have been granted the ability to choose between right and wrong, and that they are made morally responsible. Thus, grace is freely bestowed upon all men, enabling them to turn from sin to righteousness, believe on Jesus Christ, for pardon and cleansing from sin, and follow good works pleasing and acceptable in His sight. Despite this, man after receiving the experience of regeneration and entire sanctification, is free to elect the way of sin again and may thus apostatize and be eternally lost except he repent of his sin and be restored to Divine favor.

35. REPENTANCE. We believe that genuine repentance toward God consists in a knowledge of, a sorrow for, and a voluntary confession and forsaking of sin. This is brought about by the knowledge of both the goodness and severity of God, through the medium of the truth and the convincing and convicting power of the Holy Spirit. It is required of all who have by act or purpose become sinners before God. The Spirit of God gives to all who repent, the gracious help of penitence of heart and hope of mercy, that they may believe unto pardon and spiritual life.

40. JUSTIFICATION, REGENERATION AND ADOPTION. We believe that *justification* is that gracious and judicial act of God, by which He grants full pardon of all guilt and complete release from the penalty of sins committed, and acceptance as righteous, to all who believe on Jesus Christ and receive Him as Lord and Saviour. We believe *regeneration* is that work of the Holy Spirit by which the pardoned sinner enters spiritual life. This work is received through faith in Jesus Christ, whereby the regenerate are delivered from the power of sin which reigns over

all the unregenerate, so that they love God and through grace serve Him with the will and affections of the heart. We believe that *adoption* is that gracious act of God whereby the justified and regenerated believer is made a son of God, receiving even the Spirit of adoption whereby he cries, Abba Father.

We further believe that justification, regeneration and adoption are simultaneous in the experience of seekers after God and are obtained upon the condition of faith in the merits of the shed blood of Jesus Christ, preceded by repentance; and that to this work and state of grace the Holy Spirit bears witness.

45. ENTIRE SANCTIFICATION. We believe entire sanctification to be that work of the Holy Spirit by which the child of God is cleansed from all inbred sin through faith in Jesus Christ. It is subsequent to regeneration, and is wrought when the believer presents himself a living sacrifice, holy and acceptable unto God, and is thus enabled through grace to love God with all the heart and to walk in His holy commandments blameless. Entire sanctification is provided by the blood of Jesus, is wrought instantaneously by faith, is preceded by entire consecration and is attested to by the direct witness of the Spirit as well as by the fruit of the Spirit. It is wrought by the baptism with the Holy Spirit and comprehends in one experience the cleansing of the heart from sin and the abiding indwelling presence of the Holy Spirit empowering the believer for life and service. We believe that this experience admits of expansion both in this life and the next, but that it is, by the Scriptures, the end of the commandment.

50. THE SECOND COMING OF CHRIST. We believe in the second coming of Christ and that this precious truth and good hope is an inspiration to holy living and godly effort. We believe the Scriptures to teach the coming of Christ in bodily return to the earth and that He will cause the fulfillment of all prophecies made concerning His final and complete triumph over all evil. Faith in the imminence of Christ's return is a rational and inspiring hope to the people of God. We further believe that those who are abiding in Him when He so comes will be caught up with the risen saints to meet the Lord in the air, so that they shall ever be with the Lord.

55. RESURRECTION, JUDGMENT AND DESTINY. We believe in the resurrection of the dead, both of the just and the unjust. We further believe that God is the Judge of all mankind and that His administration of judgment will culminate the final meeting of mankind before His throne of great majesty and power where records will be examined and final awards and punishments administered. In this light, everlasting life is assured to all who savingly believe in, and obediently follow, Jesus Christ our Lord, and the finally impenitent shall suffer eternally in hell.

60. THE SACRAMENTS. We believe the sacraments ordained by Christ are not only tokens of Christian profession, but they are certain signs of grace and

God's good will toward us, by which He works in us the strengthening of our faith in Him. There are two sacraments, namely, Baptism and the Lord's Supper. *Baptism* is not only a sign of profession and mark of difference whereby Christians are distinguished from others who are not so walking, but it is a sign of regeneration or new birth. The *Lord's Supper* is not only a sign of love and a memorial feast, but it is a sacrament of our redemption by Christ's death, and a token of His coming again; insomuch to such as rightly, worthily and with faith receive the same, it is made a medium through which God communicates blessing and strength to the heart.

65. DIVINE HEALING. We believe in the Bible doctrine of divine healing and urge our people to seek to offer the prayer of faith for the healing of the sick. Providential means and agencies when deemed necessary are not to be refused.

70. RELATIVE DUTIES. We believe those two great commandments which require us to love the Lord our God with all the heart and our neighbors as ourselves, contain the sum of the Divine law as it is revealed in the Scriptures. They are the measure and perfect rule of human duty and are for the ordering and directing of families and nations, and all other social bodies. By them we are required to acknowledge God as our only Supreme Ruler and all men as created by Him, equal in all natural rights. Wherefore, all men are bound so to order all their individual and social and political acts as to render to God entire and absolute obedience, and to secure to all men the enjoyment of every natural right as well as to promote the greatest happiness of each in the possession and exercise of such rights.

CONDENSED STATEMENT OF BELIEF

75. Following is a summary of our doctrinal position:

a. We believe that the Bible, both Old and New Testaments, is the inspired Word of God, and that it is the final authority governing the faith and practice of His people.

b. We believe in the Triune God; that is, the existence of one God manifested in three persons: Father, Son and Holy Spirit.

c. We believe that Jesus Christ was verily conceived of the virgin, and that He is the God-Man. We believe that He alone is mediator between God and man.

d. We believe in the personality of the third person of the Trinity, and that He is presently engaged in the great work of making Christ known to human hearts.

e. We believe that man was created in the image and likeness of God and that, through his disobedience, he sinned and brought upon himself spiritual death.

f. We believe in the vicarious death of Jesus Christ and that His shed blood is the meritorious means of our redemption.

g. We believe our salvation rests upon our attitude toward God's Son, and that repentance and contrition are necessary to the appropriation of saving faith.

h. We believe that entire sanctification is a second, definite work of grace wrought in the heart of the believer by the Holy Spirit when conditions for such a work are properly met.

i. We believe in the second coming of Jesus Christ and His subsequent reign upon the earth.

j. We believe in the resurrection of Jesus Christ from the dead and the resurrection of the just and unjust. We believe in the eternal happiness of the just and the everlasting punishment of the unjust.

Notes: *The Church of the Bible Covenant has printed two statements in its* Manual: *a longer set of articles of faith and a condensed statement of belief. The longer statement is derived in large part from that of the Church of the Nazarene, but has been extensively edited. Also, a final article on relative duties, taken from the Wesleyan Methodists, has been added.*

* * *

SUMMARY STATEMENT OF BELIEF (NATIONAL ASSOCIATION OF HOLINESS CHURCHES)

God the Father, God the Son, and God the Holy Spirit are three persons, united and inseparable, of one substance, and eternal.

The Holy Scriptures are divinely inspired and are infallibly true as originally given. They constitute our only divinely authorized rule of faith and practice.

Man in his natural state is sinful apart from saving grace. Repentance is the attitude toward sin which stems from conviction and godly sorrow, involving abandonment of the practice of sin, suitable confession to God and men, and restitution of all that is due to others, according to one's ability.

Justification is a legal act on the part of God whereby sins are forgiven through faith in the Lord Jesus Christ on the part of guilty sinners.

Regeneration is the quickening to spiritual life by the Holy Ghost through faith in the Lord Jesus Christ.

Entire sanctification is the complete purification of the nature from inherited sin and the complete renewal of the nature in Holiness, whereby the Child of God is enabled to love God with all his soul, mind, and strength, and to serve Him in righteousness and true Holiness. This experience is attended by the infilling of the Holy Spirit. This gracious work of God is wrought instantaneously in answer to faith.

There is one true Church which is composed only of those who have savingly believed in the Lord Jesus Christ.

The second coming of Christ is personal and visible.

The Scriptures affirm the resurrection of the body, both of the just and the unjust, the judgment of all mankind, the

everlasting punishment of the wicked, and the eternal
happiness of the righteous.

*   *   *

DOCTRINE (WESLEYAN TABERNACLE ASSOCIATION OF CHURCHES)

ARTICLE I. GOD

We believe in one eternal, infinite God, Sovereign of the
universe; that He only is God, creative and administrative,
holy in nature, attributes, and purpose; that He, as God, is
triune in essential being, revealed as Father, Son, and Holy
Ghost. (Matt. 3:16-17; John 1:1; John 14:16, 17, 26; I John
5:7)

A. FATHER. The Father is the supreme person in the
Godhead, to whom the Son and the Holy Ghost,
though of equal essence, are subordinate in office.
The Father sent the Son into the world. He also
sends the Holy Ghost. To the Father the Son
reconciles the penitent sinner, and to the Father
belongs the worship of every believer.

B. SON. We believe in Jesus Christ, the only begotten
Son of God, the second person of the triune
Godhead; that He is eternally one with the Father;
was born of the Virgin Mary and became incarnate,
so that two whole perfect natures, that is to say the
Godhead and manhood, are thus united in one
person, very God and very man, the Godman.

We believe that Jesus Christ died for our sins and not
only for committed sins but also for original sin that
He might reconcile us to God. He truly arose from
the dead and took again his body, together with all
things appertaining to the perfection of man's nature,
wherewith He ascended into Heaven and is there
engaged in intercession for us. (Luke 1:27-35; John 1:
14; John 3:16; Acts 4:12; Rom. 5:10; Heb. 7:25.)

C. HOLY GHOST. We believe in the Holy Ghost, the
third person of the triune Godhead, that He proceeds
from the Father and the Son as the true and eternal
God, of one substance, majesty and glory with the
Father and Son. (Matt. 28:19; Acts 5:3-4; Rom. 8:9-
11.) He is ever present and efficiently active in and
with the church of Christ, convincing the world of
sin, regenerating those who repent and believe,
sanctifying believers, and guiding into all truth as it
is in Jesus. (John 3:5-9; John 16:8, 13; Acts 15:8-9.)

ARTICLE II. BIBLE

We believe that the sixty-six canonical books of the Old
and New Testaments are the Holy Scriptures, were given
by divine inspiration and are the invincible Word of God.
We believe that it unerringly reveals the will of God
concerning us in all things necessary to our salvation, so
that whatever is not contained therein nor may be proved
thereby, is not to be enjoined as an article of faith. We
definitely take our stand against the Revised Standard

Version as not being acceptable. (II Tim. 3:15-17; II Peter
1:20-21.)

ARTICLE III. SIN

A. ORIGINAL SIN. We believe that original sin, or
depravity, is the corruption of the nature of all the
offspring of Adam, and that man is born a fallen and
depraved creature, far removed from the righteousness and pure state of our first parents at the
time of creation. We believe that this sin, spoken of
in the Bible as the carnal mind, the old man and the
flesh is averse to God, is without spiritual life, and
though it be suppressed, is continually inclined to
evil and war against God, even after regeneration.
We believe that only by complete surrender and
consecration on the part of the believer can the Holy
Ghost eradicate and destroy this sin nature. (Gen.
6:5; Acts 15:8-9; Rom. 3:12, 5:12-18; I Cor. 15:22; I
John 3:8.)

B. COMMITTED SINS. We believe that sin is the
willful transgression of the known law of God, and
that such sin condemns a soul to eternal punishment
unless pardoned by God through repentance, confession, restitution, and believing in Jesus Christ as his
personal Savior. This includes all men "For all have
sinned and come short of the glory of God," Rom.
3:23. (Prov. 28:13; John 6:47; Acts 16:31; Rom. 6:23;
I John 1:9; I John 3:4.)

ARTICLE IV. GOD'S PLAN OF REDEMPTION

"For God so loved the world, that he gave His only
begotten Son, that whosoever believeth in Him should not
perish, but have everlasting life." (John 3:16.)

A. ATONEMENT. We believe that Jesus Christ, by His
suffering, by the shedding of His own blood, and by
His meritorious death on the cross, made full
atonement for all sin.

This atonement is the only source of salvation and is
sufficient for every individual of Adam's race. The
atonement is graciously efficacious for the salvation
of the irresponsible from birth, for the righteous who
have become irresponsible and for children in innocency, but is efficacious for the salvation of those
who reach the age of responsibility, only when they
repent and believe. (Mark 10:14; Luke 24:47; John
3:3, 3:16; Acts 3:18, 4:12, 16:30, 31, 17:30; Rom.
4:15, 5:8, 11; Eph. 2:13-16; Heb. 9:12.)

B. FREE WILL. We believe that man was created with
ability to choose between right and wrong and thus
was made morally responsible. The condition of man
since the fall is such that he cannot prepare himself,
by his own natural strength and works, to faith and
calling upon God. But the grace of God through
Jesus Christ is freely bestowed upon all men,
enabling all who will, to turn from sin to righteousness, believe on Jesus Christ for pardon and
cleansing from sin, and follow good works, pleasing
and acceptable in His sight. "And whosoever will, let
him take the water of life freely." Rev. 22:17. (John
4:14-15.)

We also believe that man through the transgression of God's law by using his free will to choose wrong, will fall from that state of regeneration and entire sanctification and be eternally lost, unless he repents of his sin.

C. FAITH. We believe that living faith is the gift of God and without faith it is impossible to please God. Faith becomes effective as it is exercised by man, with the aid of the Spirit. This aid is assured when the heart has met the divine condition. (Eph. 2:8; Heb. 11:6; Heb. 5:9.)

D. REPENTANCE. We believe that genuine repentance toward God consists in a knowledge of, sorrow for, and voluntary confession and forsaking of sin. This is brought about by the knowledge of the goodness and severity of God, through the medium of the truth and the convincing power of the Holy Spirit. Repentance is demanded of all who have by act or purpose become sinners against God. The Spirit of God gives to all who will repent, the gracious help of penitence of heart and hope of mercy, that they may believe unto pardon and spiritual life. (Matt. 3:2; Luke 13:5; John 16:7-11; Rom. 3:23; II Cor. 7:10.)

E. JUSTIFICATION. We believe that justification is the gracious and judicial act of God, by which He grants full pardon of sins committed and acceptance as righteous, to all who repent, believe on Jesus Christ and receive Him as Lord and Savior. (Romans 3:23-25; Romans 5:1.)

We believe that regeneration, or the new birth, is that gracious work of God whereby the moral nature of the repentant believer is spiritually quickened and given a distinct spiritual life, capable of faith, love and obedience. (II Cor. 5:17; I Peter 1:23.)

We believe that adoption is that gracious act of God by which the justified and regenerated believer is constituted a son of God.

We believe that justification, regeneration, and adoption are simultaneous in the experience of seekers after God and are obtained upon the conditions of repentance and faith in the merits of the shed blood of Jesus Christ. To this work and state of grace the Holy Spirit bears witness.

F. SANCTIFICATION. We believe that entire sanctification is that act of God, subsequent to regeneration, by which a believer is made free from original sin or depravity and brought into a state of entire devotement to God and the holy obedience of love made perfect.

It is wrought by the baptism with the Holy Ghost, and includes in one experience the cleansing of the heart from sin and the abiding, indwelling presence of the Holy Ghost, empowering the believer for life and service.

Entire Sanctification is provided by the blood of Jesus, is wrought instantaneously by faith, preceded by entire consecration, and to this work and state of grace the Holy Spirit bears witness. (Rom. 6:6; Rom.

6:11, 13, 22; Rom. 12:1; Rom. 15:16; Gal. 2:20; Heb. 10:14-15; Heb. 13:12-13.)

This experience is also known by various terms representing its different phases such as "Christian Perfection," "Perfect Love," "Heart Purity," "The Baptism with the Holy Ghost," "The fullness of the Blessing," and "Holiness of Heart."

G. WITNESS OF THE SPIRIT. The witness of the Spirit is that inward impression wrought on the soul whereby the Spirit of God immediately and directly assures our spirits that Bible conditions are met for salvation, and the work of grace is complete in the soul. In this way the Spirit bears witness to both the salvation of the sinner and the sanctification of the believer. (Heb. 10:14-15; I John 5:10.)

H. GROWTH IN GRACE. We believe that growth in grace is possible and necessary to maintain a right relationship with God, both before and after sanctification, and that only he that endureth to the end shall be saved.

ARTICLE V. ETERNAL DESTINY

We believe that man is born an eternal living soul, who will exist forever from birth throughout the endless ages of eternity. The short span appearing on the horizon of eternity is called time, the period of probation which God has allotted man to make his choice and preparation of where he will spend eternity. Either death or the return of Jesus will end this period, and the destiny of the soul will have been fixed. Then only the judgment and eternal life or eternal death remain.

A. SECOND COMING. We believe that the Lord Jesus Christ shall bodily come to earth again. This second coming will be premillennial and shall be distinguished between His coming for His saints and with His saints. The latter will occur after the great Tribulation, while the former will occur before the great Tribulation and is the "blessed hope" of the saints.

We believe at this time the righteous dead shall be resurrected and their glorified bodies shall be united with their spirits. The just who are alive shall be caught up with the risen saints to meet the Lord in the air and taken to the Marriage Supper of the Lamb, where they shall receive their rewards and will reign with Christ forever. The unjust shall be left behind on earth to endure the agonies of the great Tribulation, and at the end of the millennium, the unjust dead shall be resurrected. (Phil. 3:21; I Thess. 4:14-18; Jude 1:14; Rev. 19:20.)

B. JUDGMENT. We believe that following the Tribulation and Millennium comes the great and final Judgment Day of God in which every member of Adam's race shall appear before God to give an account and to be judged according to his deeds done in the body. (Dan. 12:2; Matt. 25:31-41; Rev. 20:12-13.)

C. HELL. We believe that after the Judgment, the impenitent sinner is banished forever from the presence of God and cast into a place of eternal punishment and outerdarkness prepared for the devil and his angels, which is the Lake of Fire, called Hell. Here the damned and doomed shall die an eternal death of suffering, torment and endless agony forevermore. (Matt. 10:28; Matt. 25:41-46; Mark 9:44-48; Luke 16:23; John 8:21.)

D. HEAVEN. We believe, and humbly thank God that, through His mercies, the Christian has the glorious hope of eternal life with Christ, our Savior and Redeemer, in a place of everlasting joy, contentment and bliss, called Heaven. This place of eternal peace is being prepared by Jesus for those who have been washed in Jesus's blood and cleansed from all sin. (Matt. 25:34; Luke 23:39-43.)

ARTICLE VI. STATEMENTS OF RELIGIOUS FAITH

A. BAPTISM. We believe that the sacrament of Baptism is an outward sign which signifies the inward acceptance of the benefits of the Atonement of Jesus. It is to be administered to each believer as a testimony of his faith in Jesus as his personal Savior and showing intention to obey in following the paths of righteousness. Baptism may be administered by sprinkling or pouring, but preferably by immersion. (Matt. 28:19; Acts 2:38; Acts 8:36-38; I Peter 3:21.)

B. THE LORD'S SUPPER. We believe that the Memorial and Communion Supper instituted by our Lord and Savior Jesus Christ is essentially a New Testament sacrament, declarative of His sacrificial death. Through the merits of His death believers have life and salvation and promise of all spiritual blessings in Christ. It is distinctively for those who are prepared for reverent appreciation of its significance. By it they show forth the Lord's death till he come again. Being the Communion Feast, only those who have faith in Christ and love for the saints should be called

to participate. (Matt. 26:26-29; Luke 22:19-20; I Cor. 11:23-29; Matt. 26:26-29.)

C. THE CHRISTIAN SABBATH. We recognize the first day of the week as being the Christian Sabbath under the present dispensation. It was the custom of the New Testament churches to meet for worship on the first day of the week. It was selected and held sacred because the Lord Himself was resurrected on that day and He further emphasized it by pouring out the Holy Spirit on the day of Pentecost. (Matt. 28:1; Mark 16:2; Luke 24:1; John 20:1-19; Acts 20:7; I Cor. 16:2; Rev. 1:10.)

D. DIVINE HEALING. We believe in the Bible doctrine of divine healing for the body through Jesus, the Great Physician, Who is touched by our infirmities and by His stripes are the sick healed. It is the privilege of every child of God to call upon the elders to anoint him with oil in the name of the Lord, and pray the prayer of faith for healing. We realize that there is no particular virtue in the human agency but through faith in Jesus is the work done. (Isa. 53:5; John 9:1-34; James 5:14-16.)

E. THE CHURCH. We believe that God's church is composed of all spiritually regenerated persons who have separated themselves from the world, have a living faith in Christ as their personal Savior, and have their names written in the Lamb's Book of Life in Heaven. (Luke 10:20; Acts 2:46-47; II Cor. 6:17-18; Phil. 4:3-4; Rev. 3:5, 13:8.)

Notes: *The Wesleyan Tabernacle Association of Churches was formed by former members of the Bible Missionary Church. The association's doctrinal statement was derived from the original articles of religion of that church, which were in turn derived from those of the Church of the Nazarene. The articles have, however, been extensively edited to include an article on God's Plan of Redemption, a statement opposing the Revised Standard Version of the Bible, and an expanded presentation of eschatological beliefs.*

Creed/Organization Name and Keyword Index

Creed names are indicated by italic type, while organizations and religious traditions appear in regular type. Page numbers are preceded by their volume numbers (roman numerals); boldface references indicate entries found in this volume.

B

C

E

T

Y

Z